THOMAS
HARDY

THOMAS HARDY
A Biography

MICHAEL
MILLGATE

RANDOM HOUSE
NEW YORK

FIRST AMERICAN EDITION

Grateful acknowledgment is made to the following for permission to
reprint previously published material:

Macmillan Publishing Co., Inc.: Brief selections from "Concerning Agnes,"
"He Resolves to Say No More," "The Musing Maiden" and "Standing
by the Mantelpiece." Copyright 1928 by Florence E. Hardy and
Sydney E. Cockerell, renewed 1956 by Lloyds Bank Ltd. Brief selections
from "the Month's Calendar," "Coming Up Oxford Street: Evening,"
"A Hurried Meeting," "Shortening Days at the Homestead," "Singing
Lovers," and "To C.F.H." Copyright 1925 by Macmillan Publishing Co.,
Inc., renewed 1953 by Lloyds Bank Ltd. All selections reprinted by
permission of Macmillan Publishing Co., Inc.

Library of Congress Cataloging in Publication Data

Millgate, Michael.
Thomas Hardy, a biography.

Includes index.
1. Hardy, Thomas, 1840–1928—Biography.
2. Authors, English—19th century—Biography.
I. Title.
PR4753.M54   1982   823'.8   81-15873
ISBN 0-394-48802-4   AACR2

To
R. L. P.

CONTENTS

LIST OF
ILLUSTRATIONS

PLATES

ILLUSTRATIONS IN THE TEXT

SOURCES

Illustrations are reproduced with the kind permission of the owners: Mr Frederick B. Adams, 36, 54; Miss Gertrude S. Antell, 11; Mr John Antell, 5; the Henry W. and Albert A. Berg Collection, The New York Public Library, Astor, Lenox and Tilden Foundations, 21, 22, 38; Mrs Gertrude Bugler, 24; Special Collections, University of California Library, Riverside, 46, 50; the Syndics of Cambridge University Library, 29, 53; W. & R. Chambers Ltd., 18; the Dorset County Library, 4, 6, 10, 39; the Trustees of the Thomas Hardy Memorial Collection in the Dorset County Museum, Dorchester, 2, 7, 15, 19, 20, 25, 26, 27, 28, 30, 34, 37, 45, 48, 49, and Hardy's own map of Wessex; Eton College, School Library, 8; Hoffman Papers, Miami University of Ohio, 9; Mr David Holmes, 44; Mr T. W. Jesty, 42; Mr Henry Lock, 3, 41; Mrs Elfrida Manning, 33; the Morris L. Parrish Collection, Princeton University Library, 35; Mr Richard L. Purdy, 12, 13, 14, 40, 47, 52; The Tate Gallery, London, 43; the Robert H. Taylor Collection, Princeton, New Jersey, 51; the Humanities Research Center, University of Texas at Austin, 23. Copyright illustrations reproduced with permission: Aerofilms Ltd., 17; Pitkin Pictorials Ltd., 1 (photograph Percy Butler).

GENERAL ACKNOWLEDGEMENTS

In writing this biography of Hardy, I have inevitably drawn at many points upon my work as co-editor of the Clarendon Press edition of *The Collected Letters of Thomas Hardy*. My indebtedness to the many institutional and individual owners who have helped me as editor and as biographer by allowing me to see and use Hardy letters and other materials is recorded elsewhere in this volume (see p. 579), but I should like to make particular acknowledgement here of permissions granted by the following: Mrs Celia Barclay, for the materials written and collected by the late Nathaniel Sparks; Professor Quentin Bell, for unpublished letters by Sir Leslie Stephen; Mr Alan Clodd, for the diaries of Edward Clodd; Miss Jennifer Gosse, for unpublished letters and reminiscences by Sir Edmund Gosse; Mrs Ann Hoffman Perry, for the materials written and collected by the late Harold Hoffman; the Countess Zamoyska, for the diary of Wynne Albert Bankes; the Master and Fellows of Magdalene College, Cambridge, for the diaries of A. C. Benson; Macmillan, London and Basingstoke, and the Macmillan Publishing Co., Inc., for *The Complete Poems of Thomas Hardy*, edited by James Gibson; the Trustees of the Hardy Estate and Macmillan, London and Basingstoke, for Florence Emily Hardy, *The Early Life of Thomas Hardy* and *The Later Years of Thomas Hardy*; and, above all, the Trustees of the

Estate of the late Miss E. A. Dugdale, for unpublished materials by Thomas Hardy, Emma Hardy, and Florence Emily Hardy.

At various stages of my work I have had the advantage of the relief from teaching duties afforded by the award of a Killam Senior Research Scholarship and a John Simon Guggenheim Memorial Fellowship; the University of Toronto also awarded me a Connaught Senior Fellowship in the Humanities in order to complete this biography and accelerate the editing of Hardy's letters. These opportunities for uninterrupted writing and research were of immense importance to me, and I am delighted to have this occasion to express my appreciation of them. The Social Sciences and Humanities Research Council of Canada, by its generous support of the Hardy letters edition, has also made a valuable indirect contribution.

During the preparation and writing of this book many people have helped me in many different ways—by supplying documents, information, or advice, by directing me to sources of which I had been unaware, by consenting to be interviewed, by allowing me to go over their houses—and I should like to put on record my gratitude to them all, including those whose names I may for the moment have overlooked and those who have already passed beyond the reach of such acknowledgement. Among those from whom I have received help of these and other kinds are Mrs Kathleen Alden, Academician M. P. Alekseev, Miss Gertrude S. Antell, Mr Norman Atkins, Professor Henry Auster, Professor John Baird, Mr Gordon Barclay, Professor David Baron, Miss Nancy Bastow, Wing Commander A. R. G. Bax, Mr A. S. Bell, Mrs Anne Olivier Bell, Professor Quentin Bell, Dr Robin Biswas, Professor Naomi Black, Professor Caesar Blake, Mrs Claire Blunden, Miss Mary A. Blyth, Professor Kristin Brady, Mrs Joan Brocklebank, Mr Herbert Cahoon, Professor James Cameron, Professor Richard Cary, Mr T. R. Cary, Mr Anthony Chambers, Dr Maureen Clarke, Dr J. Fraser Cocks III, Mrs Nancy Coffin, Miss H. M. Coles, Professor William Coles, Professor Pierre Coustillas, Mr Gregory Stevens Cox, Mrs Monica Dance, Mr Lovat Dickson, Mrs Ellen Dollery, Mr Arnold Duffield, Mr Frank Duffield, Miss Ellen S. Dunlap, Professor Leon Edel, Dr Grant A. Farrow, Mr Gerald M. Fitzgerald, Mr E. M. Forster, Professor Denton Fox, Mr Charles Gale, Miss Pamela Ganly, Mr Richard Garnett, Dr Marjorie Garson, Professor Henry Gifford, Mr Robert Gittings, Professor Ian Gregor, Dr Theodore Grieder, Dr Juliet Grindle, Professor Phyllis Grosskurth, Mrs Viola Hall,

Mr David Hamer, Mrs Mary Hart, Mrs Alice Harvey, Mr Nicholas Hillyard, Miss Vanessa Hinton, Mrs Elsie Honeywell, Professor Samuel Hynes, Professor J. R. deJ. Jackson, Mr Hedley James, Mr John Jenkins, Mr Denys Kay-Robinson, Mr E. G. H. Kempson, Mr W. M. King, Miss Cherry Klein, Professor Dale Kramer, Mr Karl Krauss, Professor Martin Kreiswirth, Professor J. T. Laird, Mrs Sally Leach, Mr Henry Lock, Dr April London, Mr Desmond MacCarthy, Mrs Michael MacCarthy, Miss Lesley Mann, Professor Paul Mattheisen, Professor James B. Meriwether, Mr Reginald S. Miller, Professor Sylvère Monod, Sir Owen Morshead, the Revd G. R. K. Moule, Mr H. C. C. Moule, Dr A. N. L. Munby, Mrs Christine Nickell, Professor A. Nikoljukin, Mr C. J. Norris, Professor Harold Oliver, Professor Harold Orel, Miss May O'Rourke, Mr Timothy O'Sullivan, Mr Ivon Owen, Dr Lisa Paddock, Professor Norman Page, Mr David Pam, Mr Charles P. C. Pettit, Dr F. B. Pinion, Professor Thomas Pinney, Dr J. S. Pippard, Professor Noel Polk, Mr E. W. Powers, Mlle Christine Pouget, Mr F. Rampton, Mrs Monica Ring, Dr Marguerite Roberts, Professor J. M. Robson, Professor S. P. Rosenbaum, Mr George Rylands, Mr and Mrs J. P. Skilling, Mrs Ethel Skinner, Mrs Jacqueline Simms, Dr Jeremy Steele, Professor Anthony Stephenson, Miss Barbara Sturgis, Mrs Lilian Swindall, Mrs Lola L. Szladits, Dr Richard H. Taylor, Mr Francis Warre-Cornish, Dr Douglas Wertheimer, Mr Stephen G. Wildman, Miss Irene Cooper Willis, Mr Ian Willison, Professor Gordon Wilson, Mr Murray Winer, Professor Judith Wittenberg, and Dr Janet Wright.

I am particularly grateful to those—among them Mrs June Boose, Mrs Gertrude Bugler, Dr Fran Chalfont, Mr Alan Clodd, Mrs Jane Cooper, Mr James Stevens Cox, Dr Simon Gatrell, Dr James Gibson, Mr Desmond Hawkins, Mr Montague Harvey, Mr Charles Lock, Mr David Masson, Mr Michael Meredith, Mr David Newsome, Miss Pamela Richardson, Mrs Anna Winchcombe, and Miss Marjorie Wynne—who have gone to great trouble to make information and materials available. Professors Michael Collie and Robert C. Schweik have been unfailing in their support and encouragement of my work, Mr John Antell, Mrs Celia Barclay, Professor Lennart Björk, Professor W. J. Keith, Mr Michael Rabiger, and the Revd J. M. C. Yates have been most generous in sharing ideas and information with me, and it is impossible for me to speak too highly of the kindness and active assistance I have received from Mr and Mrs Frederick B. Adams, Dr and Mrs C. J. P. Beatty, Mr David Holmes, Mr Malcolm Tomkins, and especially Mr Roger Peers, the indefatigable Curator of the Dorset County Museum, and Mr Henry Reed, who in conversations over several years has allowed me to draw upon his own rich insight into Hardy's life and work.

The typescript of this book—admirably prepared by Mrs Freda Gough—received meticulous readings from Miss Catharine Carver, Mr Albert Erskine (who first suggested that I work on Hardy), Mr Richard L. Purdy, Mr Michael Rabiger, and Mr Henry Reed, and I have profited greatly from their criticisms and suggestions. Mr and Mrs William Jesty of Max Gate commented on sections of the book, and I am also deeply grateful to them for their hospitality and friendship and for the many investigations into local records so generously and tirelessly undertaken on my behalf. Finally, and most importantly, I want to acknowledge my profound indebtedness, both personal and professional, to Richard Purdy, whose knowledge, scholarship, and magnificent Hardy collection have been made freely available to me, and to my wife, Jane Millgate, whose wisdom, patience, and critical intelligence have, as always, done so much to sustain and shape my work.

M. M.

Toronto
February, 1981

THOMAS
HARDY

I

HARDYS AND HANDS

FEW English writers have been so self-consciously 'modern' in their ideas as Thomas Hardy; fewer still have shared his intense, apparently paradoxical, preoccupation with the personal, local, and national past. Born of humble parents in an out of the way corner of the English countryside, nothing in his immediate ancestry offered the remotest hint that he would live to become the most famous man of letters of his day. In his work he was to register with extraordinary sensitivity and precision the historic changes which swept over England, and especially over his native Dorset, during the course of the nineteenth century. In his personal life he retained to the very last a wry fascination, compounded of an artist's vanity and a child's sense of wonder, with those quirks of heredity, of human affection, of social history, and of the class system which had combined, or collided, in the conception and birth of a man who could come from rural obscurity and yet live to achieve recognition as both a major novelist and a major poet.

In the historical distance, beyond reach of certainty, it was possible to discern, or to project, the outlines of family connections of a rather more distinguished kind. Among the several works of genealogy in Hardy's library at the time of his death was an anonymous account of the ancient le Hardy family of Jersey, in the Channel Islands, and he liked to think that it was from a late-fifteenth-century Clement le Hardy and his son John that 'the Dorset Hardys' were all derived, including the Thomas Hardye of Frampton who endowed the Dorchester Grammar School in 1579 and the Thomas Masterman Hardy of Portisham who was Nelson's flag-captain at Trafalgar. Various landowning Hardys figure in the pages of John Hutchins's *The History and Antiquities of the County of Dorset,* originally compiled in the eighteenth century, and Hardy's markings in his own much-prized copy clearly show that he was well aware of those families and of the possible links between them and his own 'branch', the Hardys of Owermoigne, Bockhampton, and other places in or near the valley of the river Frome.[1]* Such links, however vague, were important to Hardy in that they fed his sense of belonging to a family that had come down in the world. To have a family crest but not to use it was intricately pleasurable in itself; it also validated the scornful presentation of family pretensions in a novel like *Tess of the d'Urbervilles.* Complaining in his early seventies that there were still people in Dorchester who thought themselves too grand to speak to him, Hardy exclaimed: 'Ours was also a county family if they only knew!'[2]

But the name Hardy is by no means uncommon in Dorset, and it is often encountered in Dorset records and on Dorset headstones. Hardy underlined in his copy of Hutchins a reference to a Thomas Hardy of Wareham who had died in 1723 at the age of one hundred and four; a Thomas Hardy, shoemaker, was admitted as a Freeman of Dorchester in 1755; the burial of James Hardy, 'The Blind Singing Man', was recorded at Wimborne Minster in 1814; and there was a Henry Hardy, post boy, at Blandford Forum in the last of the coaching days. There is scarcely a parish in southern Dorset whose registers will fail to yield one or more pockets of Hardys, and in drawing up a family tree—rather portentously entitled 'The Hardy Pedigree'—towards the end of his life (see below, p. 524) Hardy wisely chose to advance only a generalized claim to be descended from the le Hardys and the families memorialized by Hutchins.

Gently suggesting that 'the less people know of a writer's antecedents (till he is dead) the better', Hardy was nevertheless willing to tell Charles Kegan Paul in 1881 that 'From time immemorial —I can speak from certain knowledge of four generations—my

---

* Superscript numbers in the text refer to the References, p. 582.

direct ancestors have all been master-masons, with a set of journeymen masons under them: though they have never risen above this
level, they have *never* sunk below it—i.e. they have never been
journeymen themselves.'³ If there is exaggeration here it is of the
mildest kind. Although Hardy's paternal forebears may not always have been employers, they were certainly masons and, as
such, self-employed and independent—much like Michael Henchard at the beginning of *The Mayor of Casterbridge*. And the
acknowledged uncertainty about the remoter reaches of the ancestral line allows for a family tradition that a John Hardy, his
mason's tools in a flask basket over his shoulder, simply appeared
(like Henchard again) one day in the late eighteenth century from
nobody knew where.⁴

That particular John Hardy lived from 1755 to 1821. He
appears in the 'pedigree' as John Hardy of Puddletown—to use
the modern name of the village, five miles north-east of Dorchester,
that was earlier, and less decorously, known as Piddletown—and
can be plausibly identified as the son of a John Hardy of Owermoigne and his wife, Elizabeth Swire, who were married in 1746.*
In 1777 John Hardy of Puddletown was married at Woodsford, in
the Frome valley, to Jane Knight of that parish, several of whose
relatives her great-grandson took the trouble to track down in the
Stinsford church registers nearly a hundred and fifty years later.
And in December 1799 Thomas Hardy, the eldest child of that
marriage, was himself married, in Puddletown, to Mary Head,
the orphaned daughter of James and Mary Head of the Berkshire
village of Fawley. Seven months later, in July 1800, Mary gave
birth to a daughter in Puddletown; some time in the following
year, 1801, the couple first went to live in the cottage John Hardy
had built for them a few miles away in the parish of Stinsford.⁶

Although only three miles from Dorchester, the county town
of Dorset, the cottage stood—solitary, deep among trees—at the
end of a narrow lane and on the very edge of what was then open
heathland, stretching almost uninterrupted across south Dorset
and into Hampshire. The area immediately adjacent to the cottage
remains uncultivated even today, though thick in many places
with interloping rhododendrons and encroached upon by the dark

* Elizabeth Swire was presumably that 'pure Irish' great-great-grandmother
to whom Hardy once laid claim in a letter to Lady Gregory, and her husband
the sea-going ancestor whose telescope descended to Hardy's father, and
ultimately to his brother Henry—who is said to have used it to spy on court-
ing couples on the heath.⁵

The Family of Thomas Hardy, Sen.

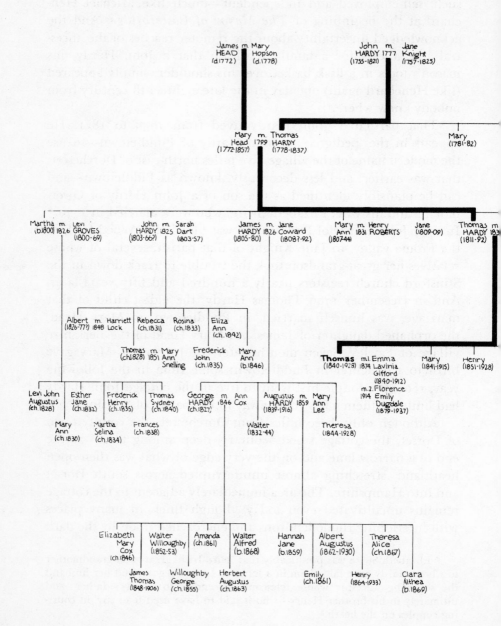

James m Mary
HEAD Hopson
(d.1772) (d.1778)

John m. Jane
HARDY 1777 Knight
(1755-1821) (1757-1825)

Mary m. Thomas
Head 1799 HARDY
(1772-1857) (1778-1837)

Mary
(1781-82)

Martha m. Levi
(b.1800) 1826 GROVES
(1800-69)

John m. Sarah
HARDY 1825 Dart
(1803-66?) (1803-57)

James m. Jane
HARDY 1826 Coward
(1805-80) (1808?-92)

Mary m. Henry
Ann 1831 ROBERTS
(1807-44)

Jane
(1809-09)

Thomas m
HARDY 183
(1811-92)

Albert m. Harriett
(1826-77?) 1848 Lock

Rebecca
(ch.1831)

Rosina
(ch.1833)

Eliza
Ann
(ch.1842)

Thomas m Mary
(ch.1828) 1851 Ann
Snelling

Frederick
John
(ch.1835)

Mary
Ann
(b.1846)

Thomas m1. Emma
(1840-1928) 1874 Lavinia
Gifford
(1840-1912)
m.2. Florence
1914 Emily
Dugdale
(1879-1937)

Mary
(1841-1915)

Henry
(1851-1928)

Levi John
Augustus
(ch.1828)

Esther
Jane
(ch.1832)

Frederick
Henry
(ch.1835)

Thomas
Sydney
(ch.1840)

George m Ann
HARDY 1846 Cox
(ch.1827)

Augustus m. Mary
HARDY 1859 Ann
(1839-1916) Lee

Mary
Ann
(ch.1830)

Martha
Selina
(ch.1834)

Frances
(ch.1838)

Walter
(1832-44)

Theresa
(1844-1928)

Elizabeth
Mary
Cox
(ch.1846)

Walter
Willoughby
(1852-53)

Amanda
(ch.1861)

Walter
Alfred
(b.1868)

Hannah
Jane
(b.1859)

Albert
Augustus
(1862-1930)

Theresa
Alice
(ch.1867)

James
Thomas
(1848-1906)

Willoughby
George
(ch.1855)

Herbert
Augustus
(ch.1863)

Emily
(ch.1861)

Henry
(1864-1933)

Clara
Althea
(b.1869)

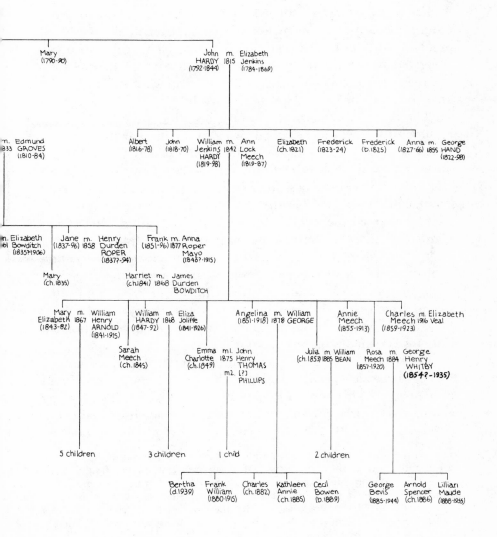

Mary
(1790-90)

John m. Elizabeth
HARDY 1815 Jenkins
(1792-1844) (1784-1869)

m. Edmund
833 GROVES
(1810-84)

Albert
(1816-78)

John
(1818-70)

William m. Ann
Jenkins 1842 Lock
HARDY Meech
(1819-98) (1819-87)

Elizabeth
(ch.1821)

Frederick
(1823-24)

Frederick
(b.1825)

Anna m. George
(1827-66) 1855 HAND
(1822-98)

m. Elizabeth
61 Bowditch
(1835?-1906)

Jane m. Henry
(1837-96) 1858 Durden
ROPER
(1837?-94)

Frank m. Anna
(1851-96) 1877 Roper
Mayo
(1846?-1915)

Mary
(ch.1835)

Harriet m. James
(ch.1841) 1868 Durden
BOWDITCH

Mary m. William
Elizabeth 1867 Henry
(1843-82) ARNOLD
(1841-1915)

William m. Eliza
HARDY 1868 Joliffe
(1847-92) (1841-1926)

Angelina m. William
(1851-1918) 1878 GEORGE

Annie
Meech
(1855-1913)

Charles m. Elizabeth
Meech 1916 Veal
(1859-1923)

Sarah
Meech
(ch.1845)

Emma m1. John
Charlotte 1875 Henry
(ch.1849) THOMAS
m2. [?]
PHILLIPS

Julia m William
(ch.1853) 1885 BEAN

Rosa m. George
Meech 1884 Henry
(1857-1920) WHITBY
(1854?-1935)

5 children

3 children

1 child

2 children

Bertha
(d.1939)

Frank
William
(1880-1915)

Charles
(ch.1882)

Kathleen
Annie
(ch.1885)

Cecil
Bowen
(b.1889)

George
Bevis
(1885-1944)

Arnold
Spencer
(ch.1886)

Lillian
Maude
(1888-1955)

plantations of the Forestry Commission. In this isolated and commercially unpromising spot—which only later acquired the name of Higher Bockhampton—Hardy's grandfather set himself up in business as a mason and bricklayer, the trade he had learned from his father and which he passed on in turn to his three sons, John (born 1803), James (born 1805), and Thomas (born 1811).* Its lonely situation just a few miles from the sea made the cottage an ideal staging post for the smuggling which was then an active business along the Dorset coast, and Hardy's grandfather allowed it to be used for that purpose from 1801 to 1805 or thereabouts, when his wife put a stop to it: 'He sometimes', Hardy once noted, 'had as many as eighty "tubs" in a dark closet . . . each tub containing 4 gallons. The spirits often smelt all over the house, being proof, & had to be lowered for drinking. The tubs, or little elongated barrels, were of thin staves with wooden hoops: I remember one of them which had been turned into a bucket by knocking out one head, & putting a handle.'[7]

The Hardys did a good deal of the building work for Kingston Maurward house, the principal property in the parish, but they were also tenants of the estate, and in both capacities found themselves in a position inferior to that of another Thomas Hardy, no relation, who held the position of estate steward and the status of gentleman. When in 1832 the death of an old woman automatically terminated the 'lifehold' lease of the cottage in which John Hardy, eldest of the Hardy sons, was living, a new lease was drawn upon the lives of the steward's own son and daughters.[8]† Effectively expelled from Bockhampton by this apparent exercise of social privilege, John Hardy moved with his growing family (he was to have seven children in all) to the Dorchester suburb of Fordington, where he seems gradually to have become isolated from his Bockhampton relatives.

In October 1835 a new lease on the cottage of Thomas and Mary Hardy was executed upon the lives of Thomas himself and of his two younger sons. Two years later the father died, leaving an estate consisting of the leasehold of the cottage itself, valued at £180, together with £60 in cash and a further £61 in uncollected

* Of the four Hardy daughters, Martha departed for Upwey, a village near Weymouth, as the wife of a butcher, Mary married a shopman, Jane died in infancy, and the second Jane, born in the year of Waterloo, also moved to Upwey as the wife of Martha's brother-in-law, a thatcher.

† Hardy would have heard as a child the story of how the steward, who had lost an arm, fell into the river Frome the following year and was unable to save himself from drowning.[9]

debts. After funeral and other expenses had been met the youngest son, Thomas, was allowed a substantial portion of the residue
in recognition of wages left unpaid over the past eight years:
these were reckoned at 14 shillings a week, less what he was
deemed to have received in the form of his keep, clothes, and
pocket money. (The other son, James, as a married man with
children, had been receiving his wages on a regular basis.)[10] Hardy
always insisted upon the lack of commercial ambition shown by
his father and grandfather, and the casualness of the financial
arrangements between them lends support to such a view. So,
too, does their failure, over a period of several years, to collect
the payments due to them from the Kingston Maurward estate,
although it must in any case have been difficult to bring pressure
to bear on their own landlord.[11] For several years after their
father's death the two brothers, James and Thomas, ran the business together under their mother's name, but by the late 1840s
they had decided to divide the 'goodwill' and go their separate
ways. One account has it that the division took the form of physical combat, out on the heath, but the determining factor seems
rather to have been Mary Hardy's partiality for her youngest son
—and, on his part, an assumption of responsibility for his mother
in her old age. Her will, dated 24 January 1841 (sixteen years
before her death), leaves all her property 'to my Son, Thomas
Hardy, for his kindness and affection towards me'.[12]

In December 1839, some thirteen months before the date of his
mother's will, Thomas Hardy had married Jemima Hand (born
1813), daughter of George Hand and his wife Elizabeth, or Betty,
Swetman. George Hand was the eldest of the nine children of a
Puddletown couple, William and Betty (Symonds) Hand, whose
ancestors had come, respectively, from Affpuddle, on the edge of
the heath, and from Puddletown itself. His wife, however, came
from Melbury Osmond, in north-western Dorset, where the Swet-
mans had been small landowners—or, as Hardy was fond of saying, 'yeomen'[13]—for generations,* farming land subsequently

* Anecdotes of Swetman ancestors had been preserved from the time of
the Monmouth rebellion—when Hardy believed the family to have been
'ruined'[14]—and were to be drawn upon, years later, in Hardy's short story
'The Duke's Reappearance'. 'Townsend', the house in which they lived, and
in which Betty Swetman was born in 1778, has survived, though altered, to
the present day.

The Family of Jemima Hand

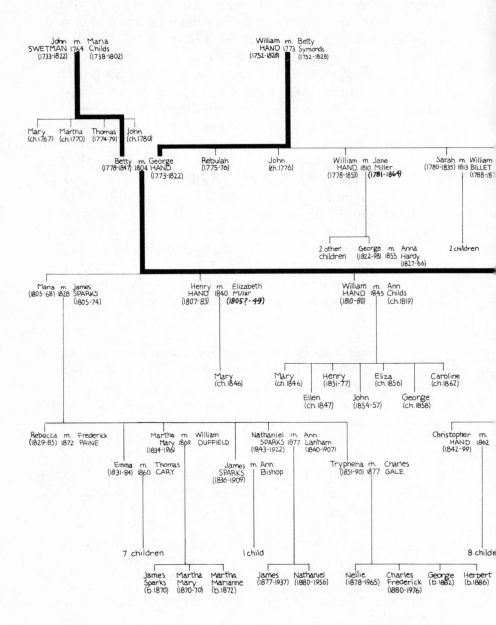

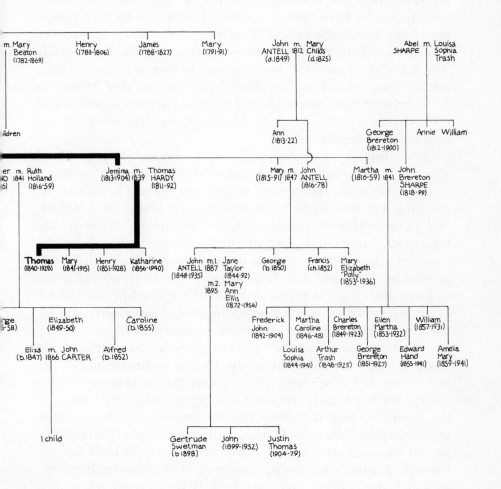

m. Mary Beaton (1782-1869) — Henry (1783-1806) — James (1788-1827) — Mary (1791-91) — John ANTELL (d.1849) m. 1812 Mary Childs (d.1825) — Abel SHARPE m. Louisa Sophia Trash

...ildren

Ann (1813-22) — George Brereton (1812-1900) — Annie — William

...er m. Ruth ...1841 Holland (1816-59) — Jemima m. Thomas (1813-1904) 1839 HARDY (1811-92) — Mary m. John (1815-91) 1847 ANTELL (1816-78) — Martha m. John (1816-59) 1841 Brereton SHARPE (1818-99)

Thomas (1840-1928) — Mary (1841-1915) — Henry (1851-1928) — Katharine (1856-1940) — John m.1 ANTELL 1887 (1848-1935) / Jane Taylor (1844-92) m.2 1895 Mary Ann Ellis (1872-1956) — George (b.1850) — Francis (ch.1852) — Mary Elizabeth "Polly" (1853-1936)

...rge (...-58) — Elizabeth (1849-50) — Caroline (b.1855) — Frederick John (1842-1904) — Martha Caroline (1846-48) — Charles Brereton (1849-1923) — Ellen Martha (1853-1932) — William (1857-1931)

Eliza (b.1847) m. John 1866 CARTER — Alfred (b.1852) — Louisa Sophia (1844-1941) — Arthur Trash (1848-1925) — George Brereton (1851-1927) — Edward Hand (1855-1941) — Amelia Mary (1859-1941)

1 child — Gertrude Swetman (b.1898) — John (1899-1952) — Justin Thomas (1904-79)

absorbed into the Melbury House estates of the Earls of Ilchester. The land had been theirs, Hardy once told a friend, at a time 'when the Ilchesters were at plow'. Betty Swetman's mother, Maria, came from another long-established Melbury family, the Childses, who in Hardy's own generation were mostly professional people, active in medicine and publishing.[15]

Some mystery attaches to the marriage of George Hand and Betty Swetman on 27 December 1804 and to the birth of Betty's first child, Maria, just eight days later. The 'pedigree's' description of that marriage as 'clandestine' hardly squares with the fact that it was performed in Melbury Osmond itself after the banns had been called in the normal fashion. Conceivably Hardy confused the Hand-Swetman marriage with that of Betty's parents, which does appear to have been a runaway match. Or he may simply have been repeating a phrase his mother had used, for it certainly appears that Betty's father, John Swetman, so disapproved of his daughter's pregnancy and her marriage to a man of lower social and economic status that he refused to have anything further to do with her.[16] John Swetman may also have known something of those darker aspects of George Hand's personality which all too soon revealed themselves.

Described in some documents as a 'servant', George Hand seems to have worked, when he worked at all, chiefly as a gardener, or as a shepherd. His meagre wages were largely consumed in drinking, a propensity for which his sons were also to be notorious, and Jemima Hardy's recollections of her violent, drunken, unregenerate father—who died of consumption, sitting up by the fire—contributed major strands in the creation of such characters as Michael Henchard and Jude Fawley. George Hand was given to fierce anti-religious prejudices, further inflamed by resentment of his wife's claims of social and educational superiority. He refused to have his children christened in church, and on the very day in 1822 when their father was buried—even, according to one account, while his coffin sat in the church awaiting burial—the two youngest children were 'received into the congregation', after having been 'privately' baptized several years earlier.[17] Some of the older children, including Jemima herself, had also received private baptism after this fashion, although formal registration of the act followed after a briefer interval and within their father's lifetime. Jemima's harrowing memories of these secret baptisms, in which the children were involved as in a conspiracy against

their father, stimulated many years later her son's imagination of
the midnight baptism scene in *Tess of the d'Urbervilles*, while
Betty Hand's insistence on having her husband buried alongside
the woman who had been his mistress was the source of the poem
'Her Late Husband'.[18]

Widowed, disinherited, with a large family of young children,
Betty Hand was eventually obliged to seek poor relief—to 'go on
the parish'—and a letter she wrote to her daughter Mary in
January 1842 is eloquent of her resentment at her poverty and of
her unyielding sense of personal injustice:

> it is a true saying that poverty seperates chiefest friends—and
> I should not have been poor if right had took its place—you
> wished me to let you know what beef I had att Christmas it was
> a small bit of lean cut of the leg or shene—it would have been
> quite dear att. 3d. Chrises [i.e., her son Christopher's] was worth
> 20. of it because his was good.[19]

Because of the family poverty Jemima, the fifth of the Hand children,* was forced out into the world at an early age. She went
into service under the patronage of the 3rd Earl of Ilchester,
working for his uncle, the Revd Charles Redlynch Fox-Strangways,
when he was rector of Maiden Newton in central Dorset, and
apparently accompanying his family when they went up to London
for the 'season'.[20] When the Revd Mr Fox-Strangways died in
November 1836, her now developed skills as a cook took her to
Stinsford and another Strangways household, that of the vicar of
Stinsford, the Revd Edward Murray,† brother-in-law of Lord
Ilchester, the patron of the living.

Murray, a keen musician himself, had long been an active

---

* Maria, the eldest, was for some reason brought up in relative affluence
by her paternal grandparents in Puddletown, where, on Christmas Day 1828,
she married a local cabinet-maker named James Sparks. Of the three Hand
brothers, William seems to have remained in Melbury Osmond while Henry
(sometimes spelled Henery) and Christopher moved to Puddletown as building tradesmen. Mary married John Antell, the Puddletown shoemaker, in
1847 while Martha, the youngest, moved away from the family, first to
Hertfordshire and then to Canada, as the wife of John Brereton Sharpe.

† Murray did not live at the vicarage but, more grandly, at nearby Stinsford House, owned by the Strangways family since the sixteenth century and
the home until her death in 1827 of Lady Susannah Fox-Strangways, in
whose runaway marriage to William O'Brien, the actor, Hardy was later to
take a romantic interest.[21]

supporter of the Stinsford choir, the little group of singers and instrumentalists which provided the music for the church services in the manner so affectionately recreated in the pages of *Under the Greenwood Tree*. Hardy's grandfather had become the leading spirit of this choir in the early years of the century, not long after his arrival in the parish. His own instrument was the bass viol, a predecessor of the modern cello, and by the early 1830s he was regularly assisted each Sunday by the violins of his sons James and Thomas and his neighbour James Dart.[22] From time to time the elder Hardy played at Puddletown and other nearby churches, and the extravagant account of his local reputation (as assigned to Clym's late father) in the fifth chapter of *The Return of the Native* is given some countenance by Lady Dorothy Nevill's childhood memories of the 'most doleful and melancholy impression' made upon her by the regular Puddletown choir of trombone, 'cracked fiddle', and 'ancient flute'.[23]

The younger Thomas Hardy was no less passionately devoted to music, but it increasingly interfered with his business, so that relief was mingled with regret when the Stinsford choir was disbanded in the early 1840s. Weakened in 1837 by the death of the elder Hardy and the replacement of Murray by a new vicar who did not share his musical enthusiasms, the final demise of the choir was signalled by the decision of the Stinsford churchwardens in 1843 that any future payments to choir members should be made by public subscription and not from the regular parish revenues.[24] Excluded from the church, the surviving members of the choir continued to perform on secular occasions, such as village weddings and christenings, while the custom of Christmas carolling from house to house was kept up for a good many years thereafter.

Edward Murray's musical association with the Hardys—who often practised at Stinsford House under his supervision—seems to have provided the context for Jemima Hand's first meeting with her future husband. Hardy's poem 'A Church Romance' clearly has some validity as an image of an early—according to Jemima, the earliest—stage of their courtship:

> She turned in the high pew, until her sight
> Swept the west gallery, and caught its row
> Of music-men with viol, book, and bow
> Against the sinking sad tower-window light.

She turned again; and in her pride's despite
One strenuous viol's inspirer seemed to throw
A message from his string to her below,
Which said: 'I claim thee as my own forthright!'[25]

Family tradition, characteristically emphasizing earthier aspects of
the affair, has the young mason catching sight of the young servant
woman while working on a near-by building and promptly seduc-
ing her under the bushes by the river Frome—near the spot,
presumably, from which Stinsford Church was photographed for
the frontispiece to the Wessex edition of *Under the Greenwood
Tree*. The first meeting, whatever its precise nature, must have
taken place not later than 1837, for Jemima met her future husband's father and could vividly recall in old age the spectacle of
'the three Hardys' arriving at church on a Sunday morning, wearing 'top hats, stick-up shirt-collars, dark blue coats with great
collars and gilt buttons, deep cuffs and black silk "stocks" or
neckerchiefs'.[26] It was not until late in 1839, however, that she
found herself pregnant. The marriage which was then arranged—
rather against the inclinations, so it is said, of both the contracting
parties—took place at Melbury Osmond on 22 December 1839,
with Jemima's younger sister Mary and her brother-in-law James
Sparks as the two witnesses. Hardy's story 'Interlopers at the Knap'
is partly based upon his father's journey to Melbury Osmond on
the eve of the wedding. Family tradition concurs in the insistence
upon the bridegroom's hesitancy and in the anecdote about
climbing a signpost in order to read it in the dark, but also holds
that James Sparks had been assigned the responsibility of getting
his man to the church, that the two of them walked together from
Puddletown, arriving somewhat tipsily in the early hours of the
wedding morning, and that the whole party then sat up drinking
until the time came for the actual ceremony.[27]

Jemima set up house in the cottage at Higher Bockhampton,
sharing it with her widowed mother-in-law,* and it was there on
2 June 1840, less than five and a half months after the marriage,
that her first child was born—at eight in the morning, as that
child himself, with his customary precision, later recorded.[29] On

---

* The possibility of some initial disharmony is raised by the curious
story, originating with Hardy himself, that his mother planned shortly after
marriage to leave her husband at home and go off again to London to be 'a
club-house cook'.[28]

5 July, at Stinsford Church, the baby was christened Thomas after his father and grandfather, although he was to declare many years later that he would have preferred to be called Christopher, after the Childses and other members of his mother's family: there were 'so many Thomas Hardys', the family showing no more inventiveness in the choosing of names than 'Dandie Dinmont in the christening of his dogs'.[30]

The account in *Early Life**** of Jemima's difficult delivery and of Hardy's being cast aside as dead, only to be rescued by the watchful optimism of the midwife, was inserted at a late stage, probably without Hardy's specific authorization. Apocryphal or not, the story serves to dramatize his early feebleness and the doubts that were for some time entertained as to his survival. Hardy always gratefully remembered Elizabeth Downton, the neighbour who cared for him at his (perhaps premature) birth and in infancy, and retained into extreme old age a vivid sense of his early experiences of sickness and weakness.[31] The poem 'In Tenebris. III' pictures him sitting in the chimney-corner of the cottage, 'the smallest and feeblest of folk there, / Weak from my baptism of pain'. And he even recalled his parents saying in his hearing, thinking him asleep, that they did not expect to rear him. There is a story that Hardy was for some time after his birth no better than a 'vegetable', so lacking in motion or discernible intelligence as to convince Jemima that she had borne an idiot, and Thomas and Jemima perhaps took little interest in, or feared to make any great emotional commitment to, a weakly child whom they had not wanted and who was unlikely to live.[32]

'I hope the little girl will not be so tiresome as Tomey,' wrote Betty Hand shortly after the birth of Hardy's sister Mary: 'pretty little fellow I love him so well to[o]—how happy I should be to see them'.[33] Evidently there had been problems in 'Tomey's' rearing, and some parental impatience at his unresponsiveness. It perhaps needed the arrival of the healthier and more naturally active Mary in December 1841 to animate the family circle and centre it more persistently and attentively on both the children: a doll's tea service and a tiny china house were among Hardy's earliest toys.[34] A degree of initial passivity would square well enough

---

* Properly *The Early Life of Thomas Hardy 1840–1891* (London, 1928), the first of two biographical volumes published under the name of Florence Emily Hardy, Hardy's second wife, but in fact largely ghost-written by Hardy himself; the second, *The Later Years of Thomas Hardy 1891–1928*, appeared in 1930. See below, pp. 516–19, for the history of their composition.

with the early anecdote of Hardy's being found asleep in his crib with a snake curled up beside him and with his later habits of quiet observation and physical withdrawal, but any quasi-catatonic phase, if it existed at all, can scarcely have been of long duration: if the claim that Hardy could read almost before he could walk is rendered less impressive by the suspicion that he may have been a late walker, there still remains his mother's assertion—and indeed his own—that he could read by the age of three.[35]

No more than hints can be gathered of the precise nature of Hardy's deeply affectionate relationship with his sister Mary, who was close to him in age and remained far closer to him in interests, enthusiasms, and sympathies than either Henry, born when Hardy was ten, or Katharine, born when he was sixteen. Mary cared about music, literature, and drawing—she later displayed a modest talent for portrait-painting—and Hardy depended heavily upon her both in childhood and in early manhood, when she remained until the time of his marriage his 'chief confidante'. Like him, she was private and introspective, and shy to a degree which made her eventual career as a schoolteacher something of a perpetual burden.[36] She seems also to have been sexually timid—perhaps inevitably so, given her temperament and her apparent lack of any particular charm of face or manner*—and may have contributed something to the creation of Sue Bridehead. After her death in 1915 Hardy wrote several poems to her memory, but these offer only a generalized reflection of his lasting devotion to 'the country girl', as she is called in one of the titles, only occasional glimpses of the child who climbed with him the apple trees in the garden at Bockhampton, 'her foot near mine on the bending limb, / Laughing, her young brown hand awave'.[38] Their early intimacy, however, is beyond question, intensified as it was by their isolation from other children† and by the cramped conditions of life in the cottage itself—it is likely that they shared a bedroom, and perhaps a bed, in infancy and even beyond, and that their grandmother slept in the same room as well.

The widowed Mary Hardy—'granny', as Hardy called her—

---

* The sons of Stephen Toghill Harding, a local farmer, are said to have found Mary attractive, however.[37]

† Although there were other children in Higher Bockhampton, including those of his uncle James, Hardy seems not to have spent much time with them—perhaps because of family conflicts, perhaps because Jemima thought he was not strong enough to look after himself or sought, snobbishly, to keep him from mixing with those she considered socially inferior.

lived on in the Bockhampton cottage until her death in 1857. Of her orphaned and desperately unhappy childhood she would say little, nor can anything much better than guesses now be made as to the causes of that unhappiness or the sequence of events that brought her from Berkshire to Dorset at the end of the eighteenth century.* She was certainly, however, an important daily presence during Hardy's early years, the source of many of the stories and songs with which he grew up. Her memories of a Dorset threatened by Napoleonic invasion—when her husband had mustered as a private with the Puddletown Volunteer Light Infantry—were later drawn upon in *The Trumpet-Major,* and it was she, as the early poem 'Domicilium' makes clear, who brought alive for the boy the extraordinary isolation of their home as she had first known it: 'Heathcroppers / Lived on the hills, and were our only friends; / So wild it was when first we settled here'. She seems to have been the model for Mrs Martin, Swithin St. Cleeve's grandmother in *Two on a Tower,* who is described as 'quietly re-enacting in her brain certain of the long chain of episodes, pathetic, tragical, and humorous, which had constituted the parish history for the last sixty years'.[40] In the poem 'One We Knew' it is Hardy and Mary who sit at their grandmother's knee as (like Scott's Elspeth Mucklebackit) she gazes into the fire and talks—'not as one who remembers, / But rather as one who sees'—of a past that was to be re-evoked, years later, in several of Hardy's novels and poems:

> She showed us the spot where the maypole was yearly planted,
>> And where the bandsmen stood
> While breeched and kerchiefed partners whirled, and panted
>> To choose each other for good.
>
> She told of that far-back day when they learnt astounded
>> Of the death of the King of France:
> Of the Terror; and then of Bonaparte's unbounded
>> Ambition and arrogance.

---

* It is possible, though by no means certain, that she was the Mary Head who gave birth to an illegitimate daughter in Reading in 1796; if so, she would have been only thirteen or fourteen years old. She cannot, however, have been the Mary Head charged at Newbury Quarter Sessions in April 1797 with the theft of a copper kettle: that Mary Head died in 1816 in the very parish in which the alleged theft had occurred and (unlike Hardy's grandmother) was exactly of the age cited in the Calendar of Prisoners for the April 1797 Quarter Sessions.[39]

Of how his threats woke warlike preparations
    Along the southern strand,
And how each night brought tremors and trepidations
    Lest morning should see him land.

She said she had often heard the gibbet creaking
    As it swayed in the lightning flash,
Had caught from the neighbouring town a small child's shrieking
    At the cart-tail under the lash. . . .[41]

Hardy's other grandmother, Betty Hand, had moved from Melbury Osmond to Puddletown just a few years before her death. Hardy was not quite seven when she died, but he remembered her in later years and she was evidently the singer of the songs associated with 'G. Melbury' (i.e., 'Granny [from] Melbury') in his annotated copy of John Hullah's *The Song Book,* among them 'Black-Eyed Susan', 'Poor Tom Bowling', and 'Shepherds, I Have Lost My Love'.[42]

Important as these and other family presences were to the young Hardy, they loomed less large than the sharply contrasted figures of his parents—Jemima hard-driving, her husband easy-going to the point of indolence.* Hardy's affection for his father emerges movingly from the description in *Early Life* of his fondness for going alone to the woods or the heath to gaze at the landscape through his telescope or simply to lie in the summer sun 'with the grasshoppers leaping over him'. The elder Hardy was, by his son's account, a man

who in his prime could be, and was, called handsome. To the courtesy of his manners there was much testimony among the local county-ladies with whom he came in contact as a builder. . . .
He was about five feet nine in height, of good figure, with dark Vandyke-brown hair, and a beard which he wore cut back all round in the custom of his date; with teeth that were white and regular to nearly the last years of his life, and blue eyes that never faded grey; a quick step and a habit of bearing his head a little to one side as he walked. He carried no stick or umbrella till past middle-life, and was all together an open-air liver, and a great

* Hardy perhaps exaggerated his father's lack of practicality. The family business survived and eventually prospered, and Kate Hardy once told of her father paying the fine of one of his workmen in order to keep him out of jail and subsequently adding a corresponding amount to the bill for the job then in progress—which happened to be on the estate of the sentencing magistrate.[43]

walker always. He was good, too, when young, at hornpipes and jigs, and other folk-dances, performing them with all the old movements of leg-crossing and hop, to the delight of his children, till warned by his wife that this fast-perishing style might tend to teach them what it was not quite necessary they should be familiar with, the more genteel 'country-dance' having superseded the former.[44]

Many women other than the 'local county-ladies' are said to have found the elder Hardy's manners charming and his person attractive. As a young man he had a reputation as a womanizer and an occupation which provided ample opportunities for sexual adventure. When a job took him beyond convenient walking distance from Higher Bockhampton he would often lodge in the vicinity during the working week: in 1911 a farmer at Owermoigne—the 'original' of the village in which Hardy's 'The Distracted Young Preacher' is set—was able to point out the cottage in which 'Mr Hardy's father used to lodge as a young man, when he was engaged in the building of Galton Farmhouse near by. I've often heard my mother speak of him. She knew him well, and a very charming fellow he must have been. He was living at Bockhampton then, and used to go home for weekends.'[45]

Such excursions were presumably terminated, or severely curtailed, following his marriage. Jemima's was the dominant personality—Hardy almost invariably refers to the Bockhampton cottage as his mother's rather than as his father's house—and she was to play much the more decisive role in her children's lives. Like her mother and her sisters, she was short, with a head a little too large for her body and a Roman nose and strong chin that approached each other, Punch- or nutcracker-like, in old age. Her son's recollections of her stress that she had 'wonderful vitality', remaining slim and active, with a 'buoyant' walk, at least into her late sixties.[46] He spoke, too, of her natural cheerfulness and sense of humour, but the humour could also be sardonically expressive of that harsher, more abrasive side of her personality which seems first to have developed following the dangerous miscarriage she suffered some time during the period 1843–6. According to family tradition she was stricken with 'brain fever', remained close to death for several weeks, and emerged from the illness a changed woman, harder, sterner, altogether more assertive in her relationships with her husband and children.[47] Her sister, the still unmarried Mary Hand, moved into the cottage as nurse to her sister and housekeeper to the family, and Hardy once mentioned (apro-

pos of the controversy over the Deceased Wife's Sister legislation)
his mother's distress at her husband's refusal to promise to marry
Mary for the children's sake if she herself should die.[48]*

As Hardy himself acknowledged, Mrs Yeobright in *The Return of the Native* was closely based upon Jemima as she was in
early middle age—a woman 'who, possessing two distinct moods
in close contiguity, a gentle and an angry, flew from one to the
other without the least warning'. Although she seems always to
have commanded the unquestioning devotion of her children,
Jemima could be cold in her manner, intolerant in her views,
and tyrannical in her governance. She had inherited in full measure the ancient pessimism of the rural poor, their perpetual
imagination of disaster, and she kept it alive with a diet of sensational tales: when in 1849 she puzzled her son by declaring of
the murderer James Rush that 'the governess hanged him' she
was probably drawing her information not from newspapers but
from the broadside ballad of that year direfully entitled 'The
Sorrowful Lamentation and Last Funeral of J. B. Rush'.[50] The
devil played an active role in Jemima's morality and fate stood
waiting with hand uplifted to knock down all human aspirations
—the counterpart of Sue's conception, in *Jude the Obscure,* of
the 'something external to us which says, "You shan't!" '[51] But her
fatalism co-existed with a fierce determination to move her family
forward in the world, to prevent it at all costs from slipping back
into the kind of destitution she had known as a child. She sought
to weld it together with an intense clannishness which went far
beyond the countryman's instinctive localism and distrust of outsiders, teaching her children to be above all things loyal to each
other and to their parents, to defend the family's reputation and
their own, to seek always to be well spoken of and present an
impeccable front to outsiders. She wanted them never to marry
but to live together in pairs, a son with a daughter, and thus
maintain throughout life the unity and interdependence of their
childhood.[52] In her terror of poverty she preached solidarity in
financial matters, instilling the principle that money amassed by
any member of the family should be kept within the family, and

* The situation is echoed at the end of *Tess of the d'Urbervilles* when
Tess urges Angel to marry 'Liza-Lu after her own death, adding, 'People
marry sister-laws continually about Marlott'. Since Jemima did not die, she
referred sardonically to the experience as a 'wasted' illness, a phrase her son
was to take up when writing about a serious illness of his own some thirty-five
years later (see below, p. 215).[49]

urged her husband to a commercial aggressiveness that went right against the grain of his whole personality. She also kept her children unyieldingly to the marks she had set for them, not only putting a stop to their learning dance steps no longer deemed 'genteel' but sometimes forcing them to go to school even when they were unwell.[53]

Jemima's ambitions for her eldest son—and for herself through her son—strikingly resemble Mrs Morel's for Paul in *Sons and Lovers,* and the other kinds of tension so powerfully dramatized in Lawrence's novel had their milder counterparts within the Hardy household. A glimpse of the psychological battles being fought, within himself as well as between his parents, can be caught from Hardy's childhood memory—echoed in the poem 'Childhood Among the Ferns' and in a famous passage in *Jude the Obscure*—of lying on his back in the sun, gazing up through the interstices of a straw hat, and deciding that he did not want to grow up to become a man and take on adult responsibilities. Unmistakable here is the implicit identification with his father's passivity and the corresponding resistance to his mother's drive, her constant planning and projecting on his behalf. Understandably enough, Jemima showed distress when her son told her of his conclusions, and she never let him forget the incident in the years of his literary success.[54] Nor is it surprising that Hardy should once have declared that if he had lost his mother in early childhood his 'whole life would have been different'. In the poem 'In Tenebris. III' he recalls his childhood dependence upon her as 'matchless in might and with measureless scope endued'. In *The Return of the Native* Clym Yeobright's overt conflict with his mother occurs within the context of a love so sure as to need no expression: he is 'a part of her', their conversations are 'as if carried on between the right and left hands of the same body'.[55]

Hardy was undoubtedly strengthened in certain respects by the absolute security of such a relationship, and it was his mother's strong-willed impulsion alone which enabled him to resist, for good or ill, his father's infinitely attractive example, defy his own native instincts, and break away from the traditional patterns of families grounded, generations deep, in the almost inert conservatism of the Dorset countryside—although it was no doubt his physical weakness as a child which first called into question the otherwise automatic assumption that he would become a mason like his father. But Hardy was at the same time damaged, like Clym Yeobright, by so extreme an emotional dependence upon his mother, by his early and perhaps inevitable surrender to her all-encompassing influence and direction. The tenacity of that maternal hold was to hamper him at all stages of his first marriage, and it was the primary cause, along with his early ill health, of that prolonged immaturity which left him, in his own estimation, 'a child till he was sixteen, a youth till he was five-and-twenty, and a young man till he was nearly fifty'.[56]

2

BOCKHAMPTON

Bᴄ 1840, when Hardy was born, there were seven or eight cottages scattered along 'Cherry Lane' at Higher Bockhampton, with some fifty people crowded into them. Hardy's uncle James and his family, for example, occupied one half of the cottage next nearest to the heath, William Keates (the 'tranter' of *Under the Greenwood Tree*) and his family the other half. The hamlet's earlier nickname of 'Veterans' Alley' derived from the military men who had retired to live along its single street, and although Hardy himself would have known only one of these, a Lieutenant Thomas Drane who had fought at Trafalgar, his father told him anecdotes of an army officer, Captain Meggs, who had lived in the 'house by the well'—presumably the one subsequently inhabited by John Cox, the relieving officer and registrar, of which Hardy sketched a ground plan many years later, annotating it: 'Mr C's house— / (near the well.) / now pulled down— / Ground plan / Adopted as Eustacia's house'.[1]

The Hardys' own cottage—'standing alone, mud walls and thatched', as it was described in an insurance policy of 1829, which put a value of £100 on all the furniture, linen, wearing apparel, and 'liquors in private use therein'[2]—was no more substantial than most of those near by, but it was occupied by a single family and boasted extensive outbuildings and 1¾ acres of attached land. There seems originally to have been only one room on each of the two floors, the lower with a large open fireplace at one end, the upper divided up by curtains into separate sleeping areas. At some later date—probably following the birth of a third child in 1851—Hardy's father decided to add new rooms at the south end: the slightly lower roof line of the extension is clearly visible still, although possibly it existed from the first, as a barn and store-room, and was simply taken into the main building later on. The front door was moved further to the south, to keep it more or less central, and it was probably at this same time that the original ground-floor room was divided into two, partitions built between the bedrooms, and the staircase reversed—destroying those effects of sunset upon its red-painted walls in which Hardy had so delighted as a child.[3] Thus improved and enlarged, the building had some claims to be called a 'house'—even though its very picturesqueness has doomed it to remain a 'cottage'.

The outbuildings were used chiefly for the family business, which continued over the years to survive and even to expand in a modest way. In the 1851 census Thomas Hardy was described as a 'bricklayer' (he had been called a 'mason' in 1841) employing only two men. By 1861 the number of his employees had risen to six, and by 1871 to eight men and a boy; in a directory of 1880 he is described as a 'builder'. Later on, after his younger son had taken over the business, it seems to have prospered still further: during the 1890s the work done for the Kingston Maurward estate alone amounted in some years to well over £1,000.[4] During the early stages of his marriage, however, Hardy's father was still in business on a very small scale, and his prized independence left him dangerously exposed to fluctuations in the wholly agricultural economy of the limited area within which he could operate. His family often found itself in difficulties—even, at times, in 'bitter poverty'—and great sacrifices are said to have been made for the children's sake.[5]

Hardy's parents could nevertheless think of themselves, and with some justice, as being a cut above most of their neighbours. In the village society of that period, not yet seriously disturbed by rural depression or migration to the towns, much weight was attached to the narrowest gradations of class and status. There was a sharp and sometimes cruel division between those who worked for themselves and those who worked for others, and it was precisely on the mobility of individuals across that line, in either an upward or a downward direction, that so much of the action of the Wessex novels was later to turn. As Hardy himself put it in 1927:

> Down to the middle of the last century, country villagers were divided into two distinct castes, one being the artisans, traders, 'liviers' (owners of freeholds), and the manor-house upper servants; the other the 'work-folk', i.e. farm labourers (these were never called by the latter name by themselves and other country people till about 70 years ago). The two castes rarely intermarried, and did not go to each other's house-gatherings save exceptionally.[6]

Though the elder Thomas Hardy, like his wife, had relatives who clearly belonged to the second and lower of the two castes, his own position as a master mason, an employer of men (however few), and the lifehold tenant of a substantial cottage, with its adjoining land and outbuildings, put his immediate family firmly into the superior rank. Such discriminations mattered at the time —they have not, in England, ceased to matter even now—and it was a desire for accuracy rather than a sense of snobbery which led Hardy to insist, in his later years, upon distinctions which had to do not only with his own background but also with the fates of such fictional characters as Stephen Smith, Gabriel Oak, Michael Henchard, and Giles Winterborne.

There were perceptible speech differences, too, at a time when the Dorset dialect was still a distinctive linguistic form, although Hardy's observation that the dialect was 'not spoken in his mother's house, but only when necessary to the cottagers, & by his father to his workmen', rather slides over the fact that both his parents spoke with strong local accents—so much so that their father's speech became, for Hardy and his elder sister, a shared source of affectionate humour, and their mother's, in her old age, an occasion of amusement to outsiders. When Hardy told a friend in 1888 that he had heard the Dorset 'Ich' (for 'I') just the previous Sunday,[7] it was almost certainly from his father's or his mother's lips. The reality of such class and speech distinctions is vividly evoked in the pages of *Under the Greenwood Tree,* where there is a marked difference in the ways in which the Dewys conduct themselves towards their social equals (such as Mr Penny and Uncle James) and towards those inferiors to whom, as loyal members of the choir, they are benevolently extending their hospitality. Mrs Dewy's aspersions upon the coarseness of her husband's speech and manners surely recall, within a humorous context,

remarks made by Jemima to her own husband in all sharpness—
only to have them deflected by a good-humoured imperturbability
quite as impregnable as Mr Dewy's, if distinctly less boisterous
in tone.

The size of the Hardys' garden made it possible for them to be
in large measure self-supporting. Though a mason by trade
Thomas Hardy was a countryman by birth and a smallholder by
necessity, and it was not for nothing that his son sometimes referred to their cottage as 'the homestead'. He dug in his garden
and filled it with vegetables—successive beds of carrots, onions,
parsnips, broad beans, peas, and potatoes. In the autumn he
gathered in the apples from the garden trees ready for the arrival
of the cider-maker, with his 'mill, and tubs, and vat, and press'.[8]
He fattened a pig for slaughtering and salting down each autumn;
he kept a hive or two of bees and, at least when times were good, a
horse to carry building materials and tools. Jemima, for her part,
was obliged to add to her maternal responsibilities the roles of
cook, housekeeper, nurse, sempstress, and family economist; she
helped with the garden and probably kept hens, selling the eggs
that were surplus to her own family's needs; she also earned a
little extra by glove embroidery, one of several local cottage in-
dustries which died out as the century drew on.

Even when the money began to come more easily the Hardys
continued to occupy the Bockhampton cottage—the father dying
there in 1892, the mother in 1904—and to lead simple rural lives
on a pattern that had changed little in several hundred years.
When Jemima Hardy sent her younger daughter, Katharine, to a
music teacher in 1873, she paid the bill partly in honey; when, in
early December 1878, that same daughter was preparing to return
home from college for the last time, her father wrote:

> Dear Katie—We should wrote to you before But We Have been
> expecting to Heard from you About your School How it was
> settled. We are going on much as usale it is very Cold Hear. . . .
> We are going to kill the Pig about next thursday so you will be
> Home to Help make the blackpudding with Mother Monday &
> just in time for the White Meat.[9]

Beyond the Hardys' garden lay, in one direction, Thorncombe
Wood, in another, Snail's Creep, the path leading down to the
main London road. To the east it was all heath, a wild and sometimes frightening territory, almost unmarked by human habita-
tion or activity and hence uniquely available for imaginative

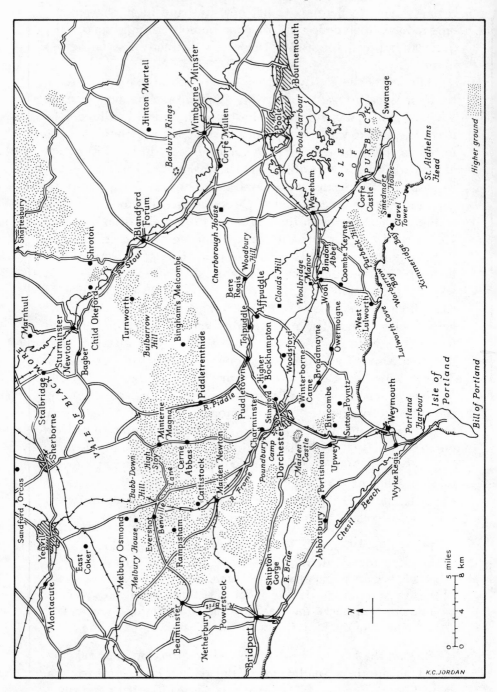

THOMAS
HARDY'S
DORSET

K.C. JORDAN

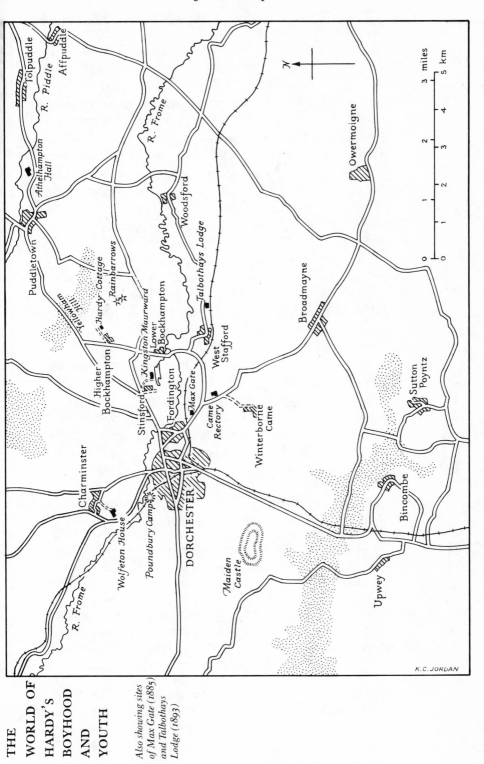

THE
WORLD OF
HARDY'S
BOYHOOD
AND
YOUTH

*Also showing sites
of Max Gate (1885)
and Talbothays
Lodge (1893)*

K.C. JORDAN

colonization. Below the heath lay the lush landscape of the Frome valley, best seen from the ancient burial mound known as Rain-barrow, on which, in Napoleonic times, a beacon fire was kept ready to be lit in the event of an invasion. Still further afield but visited from time to time were the county and market town of Dorchester and the several villages and hamlets which were home to various uncles, aunts, and cousins, among them Puddletown, Portland, Upwey, and Melbury Osmond.

Like any nineteenth-century countryman, Hardy learned from childhood to know his own district with an intimacy which is today hard for most people to imagine. Travelling everywhere on foot—or at best on a wagon drawn by a slow-paced horse—he became familiar with the occupants of every cottage, the name of every field and every gate, the profile of every tree, the depth and temperament of every pond and stream. He knew, too, the his-tories of all these, their associations with old crimes or follies or family quarrels, and whatever of legend or folklore might attach to them. So the Hardy children heard at an early age that Rushy Pond on the heath had been dug by fairy shovels, that a drowned traveller had given his name to Heedless William's Pond, and that no one was ever present to see the first flowing of a 'winterbourne' after its summer dryness. The brief entries in the diary kept, years afterwards, by Hardy's younger sister Kate are full of local place-names and local gossip.[10] Hardy himself saw England as a land 'scored with prints of perished hands' and wrote in *The Wood-landers* of the conditions necessary to give meaning to life in an isolated place:

> They are old association—an almost exhaustive biographical or historical acquaintance with every object, animate or inanimate, within the observer's horizon. He must know all about those in-visible ones of the days gone by, whose feet have traversed the fields which look so grey from his windows; recall whose creaking plough has turned those sods from time to time; whose hands planted the trees that form a crest to the opposite hill; whose horses and hounds have torn through that underwood; what birds affect that particular brake; what bygone domestic dramas of love, jealousy, revenge, or disappointment have been enacted in the cottages, the mansion, the street or on the green.[11]

Through the tale-telling and gossip of his elders Hardy ab-sorbed just such knowledge of the past and current history of the parish. Through his own childhood games and rambles he attained the kind of absolute topographical familiarity which lies behind the reference, in *Jude the Obscure,* to Phillotson's walking unhesitatingly across country in darkness 'as a man goes on, night or day, in a district over which he has played as a boy'.[12] He knew, too, what birds affected which brakes, and possessed an extraordinary sensitivity to the sights, the smells, and especially the sounds of the countryside at every hour of the day or night: 'To dwellers in a wood', runs the opening sentence of *Under the Greenwood Tree,* 'almost every species of tree has its voice as well as its feature.' In his notebooks he developed early and retained late the naturalist's habit of specifying the precise time and circumstances of his observations: a drawing of a crane-fly is annotated ' "Granfer Longlegs" / Outside my bedroom window / 7.30 a.m. 10 Sep: 1913'.[13] In other respects, however, the whole experience of his childhood gave him attitudes quite distinct from those of a naturalist.* He was interested in nature not so much as a spectacle but as an environment. He knew things by their country names rather than by their technical designations, but that did not mean he knew them less well. As he told William Archer: 'The town-bred boy will often appreciate nature more than the country boy, but he does not know it in the same sense. He will rush to pick a flower which the country boy does not seem to notice. But it is part of the country boy's life. It grows in his soul—he does not want it in his buttonhole.'[15]

The Dorset countryside with which Hardy began to become familiar in his childhood was in many respects a pleasanter and more prosperous place than most contemporary accounts would suggest. A guidebook of 1856 describes Dorset as 'a bleak country of chalk downs and sandy heaths, thinly peopled, and below the average of the English counties in fertility'—though possessing 'a certain charm in its very wildness and the forlorn aspect of its villages'.[16] Topographically speaking, this is only to account for the second and third of the three divisions of Dorset, *Felix, Petraea,* and *Deserta,* which nineteenth-century writers were fond of invoking, and to omit such 'happy' vales as those of Blackmoor

---

* This point is discussed in the last chapter of my *Thomas Hardy: His Career as a Novelist.* The practice of recording the circumstances of sketches and observations Hardy probably learned from Aaron Penley's *A System of Water-Colour Painting*; he owned a copy of the 16th edition (London, 1857) and put a pencil line against the relevant passage on p. 36.[14]

and Frome. It is indicative enough, however, of the county's contemporary reputation as a poor, backward, and somewhat uncouth corner of the kingdom. Ten years before Hardy's birth the countryside had erupted in riots, rick-burnings, and machine-breakings, and while such outbreaks touched only the fringes of the Dorchester area, his father recalled, among the numerous retributive executions which followed, the hanging on little more than suspicion of a youth so light through hunger that weights were attached to his feet to ensure that strangulation would occur.[17] In 1834 the six 'martyrs' from Tolpuddle, just a few miles across the heath from Bockhampton, were sentenced to transportation for their attempts to organize a primitive trade union.

In the mid-1840s the vicar of Durweston, Lord Sidney Godolphin Osborne ('S.G.O.'), conducted in the columns of *The Times* a vigorous campaign to draw attention to the economic hardships and insanitary living conditions of the Dorsetshire labourer. Corroborative articles by a *Times* special correspondent cited examples of men with large families who earned a mere seven shillings a week and were frequently forced, from sheer inability to purchase other food, to take much of their wages in the form of 'grist', poor quality wheat for which they were liable to be overcharged. In some areas it was the custom to make the labourer an allowance of grist, and sometimes of fuel, on top of his wages, but such relative generosity still left him in a position of total dependence. Because farmers and landowners sought to discourage that rapid expansion of the rural population—and consequent increase in poor-relief payments—which became evident in the late eighteenth century, they lost interest in either building or repairing cottages and would often pull them down as leases fell in. Villages thus became places of filth and disease, with farmyard drainage running into the streets or beneath the earth floors of the ruinous cottages in which whole families, of both sexes and all ages, were sometimes forced to sleep in a single bedroom.

Twenty and more years later investigators for a Parliamentary Commission found conditions and wages somewhat improved but received ample evidence—including submissions from 'S.G.O.' himself and from such other Dorset notables as the Revd Henry Moule, the Revd William Barnes, and the Revd Charles Kegan Paul—that the labourer was always on the edge of pauperism, that women were often employed (like Hardy's Tess Durbeyfield) on threshing machines and at such heavy tasks as swede-hacking, and that boys typically went into regular employment at the age of nine or ten. From Stinsford, as from many other districts, came reports of men being hired only on the understanding that all the family—wife and children—would come to work at the farmer's need and call. 'Wages are so low', wrote Kegan Paul in 1868,

> that a man with children above eight years old is glad of the few shillings which may be earned by them, and the employers of labour insist on these boys being sent into the fields, even if the parents would willingly make an effort to keep them at school. The farmer finds it pays him well to get two boys who, under a man, will do a man's work, but whose combined work costs less than an able-bodied man's wages.[18]

In Higher Bockhampton itself, mostly inhabited in his childhood by tradesmen's families of much the same class as his own, Hardy was relatively isolated from such realities, but he could not remain unaware of their implications for the 'work-folk' at near-by farms. Asked by Rider Haggard in 1902 about the lot of the Dorset agricultural labourers, he replied that 'down to 1850 or 1855 their condition was in general one of great hardship', citing as an admittedly extreme case his childhood memory of 'a sheep-keeping boy who to my horror shortly afterwards died of want—the contents of his stomach at the autopsy being raw turnip only. His father's wages were six shillings a week, with about two pounds at harvest, a cottage rent free, and an allowance of thorn faggots from the hedges as fuel.' Hardy also knew the squalid semi-rural, semi-urban slums of Fordington, on the outskirts of Dorchester, which were a breeding ground for the cholera, and he was to remember all his life the terrible final epidemic of 1854 when Henry Moule, as vicar of Fordington, ignored personal danger to visit the sick, organize the boiling or burning of the clothes and linen of those who had died, and direct various other attempts to prevent the spread of infection.[19]

'Vice ran freely in and out certain of the doors of the neighbourhood,' wrote Hardy in *The Mayor of Casterbridge* of a Fordington street whose 'original', the pointedly named Cuckold Row, had been the address of his uncle John in the early 1840s.[20] But he also knew that the villages and hamlets and isolated cottages of the Dorset countryside were too often the scenes not just of sexual licence but of sexual brutality. Ignorance, the daily hardships of rural life, and the anxious strain of living always at

a level of minimal survival were inevitably productive of drunk-
enness and hence of violence. Market days and hiring fairs easily
degenerated into the kind of rowdyism which occurs during and
after the Chaseborough dance in Chapter 10 of *Tess of the
d'Urbervilles*. The communal dances at Lower Bockhampton,
less than a mile away from the smaller and newer hamlet of
Higher Bockhampton, were said to be 'very lively' affairs, and
there was domestic violence even within the circle of Hardy's own
relatives. Writing to her daughter Mary in 1842, Betty Hand
expressed the wish that her son Christopher would stop drinking
and striking his pregnant wife: 'I am afraid there will be something wrong in the child—as he throws her in such ways sometimes—still he is very kind to her in all respects beside.' Hardy's
grandmother had experienced just such treatment from her own
husband, and when Mary, in turn, encountered similar difficulties
after her marriage to John Antell, her sisters Maria Sparks and
Jemima Hardy are said to have come not just morally but physically to her aid.[21]

In later years Hardy could articulate more clearly what as a
child he had observed but only half understood, and on 24
February 1888 he jotted down a remarkable reminiscence of life
on the Kingston Maurward estate during the late 1840s:

> A farm of Labourers, as they appeared to me when a child in
> Martin's time; in *pink & yellow Valentine hues:*—
>   Susan Sq——, & Newnt (e.g. leaning & singing at harvest-
> supper) their simple husbands: Newnt's lovers; Ben B's wife, &
> her lover, & her hypocrisy; T. Fuller—the schoolmaster, far above
> his position in education, but a drunkard; also wife—the
> lech——'s boy T. M....s. Also Walt, Betsy, & Eliza. The school
> kept by latter, & their chars, sensuous, lewd, & careless, as visible
> even to me at that time—all incarnadined by passion & youth—
> obscuring the wrinkles, creases, & cracks of life as then lived.

It is worth setting against this a note for a possible poem: 'Cf
Theocritus & the life at Bockn when I was a boy—in the wheat-
field, at the well, cidermaking, wheat weeding, &c.'[22] The conflict
revealed by such a juxtaposition is one which troubled Hardy
all his life. Though he had so richly celebrated the old culture of
Bockhampton in *Under the Greenwood Tree,* he acknowledged
in a later preface to the novel that 'the realities out of which it
was spun were material for another kind of study . . . than is

found in the chapters here penned so lightly, even so farcically and flippantly at times'.[23] The old rural England of ballads, folk dances, the organic community, and the oral tradition had a vitality, an integrity, above all a continuity, which the changes occurring in Hardy's own lifetime had very largely destroyed; his own childhood had been generally happy, and even the pastoral poets had allowed for the presence of Silenus. On the other hand, Hardy could not but acknowledge that the changing times had also brought with them many social and economic and even ethical improvements, and that there had been much that was less than idyllic about the early Victorian world in which he had grown up.

Because he could always call up so clearly the dark as well as the more cheerful aspects of his early experience, Hardy in his mature years was rarely tempted to indulge in indiscriminate nostalgia for the past. He was always deeply conscious, however, of the process of change itself and of the many relics, good and bad, of earlier days and ways which were constantly being swept away—including those which had disappeared before he could have known them: the church choir, the smugglers' kegs, the gibbets such as his grandmother recalled with terror from her Berkshire childhood, the public whippings his parents had witnessed in Yeovil and in Dorchester itself. As a child he had himself seen maypoles, mummers, tinder boxes, men in the stocks, and the coaches which—despite the coming of the railway to Dorchester in 1847—continued for some years to depart daily from the Antelope and King's Arms hotels.[24] Hardy, in fact, was born just in time to catch a last glimpse of that English rural life which, especially in so conservative a county, had existed largely undisturbed from medieval times until the onset of the new forces —population expansion, urbanization, railways, cheap printing, cheap food imports, enclosures, agricultural mechanization and depression, pressures and opportunities for migration and emigration—which so swiftly and so radically impinged upon it in the middle of the nineteenth century.

Life at Bockhampton in Hardy's childhood—like that invoked in *Under the Greenwood Tree* and *Far from the Madding Crowd*— was still paced by the procession of the seasons, the generations, and the agricultural and ecclesiastical calendars. Its markers were lambing time, hay-making, and harvest; the first cuckoo, the longest day, the last swallow; Easter, Whitsun, and Christmas; births, marriages, and deaths. Hardy once declared that his boyhood was not only solitary but 'singularly uneventful'; he might more accurately have said that its crowding events were at once recurrent and repetitious, formalized in accordance with time-honoured customs. There were Christmas parties at Mr Cox's house by the well—'The House of Hospitalities' of the poem, where they 'broached the Christmas barrel, / . . . sang the Christmas carol, / And called in friends'[25]—and dances and 'wedding-randies' at other houses in the neighbourhood. In March 1846 Hardy's cousin George Hardy was married to Anne Cox, also of Higher Bockhampton, and on 14 November 1847 it was from the Hardys' own cottage that Jemima's sister, Mary Hand, was married to John Antell. The 1840s also saw a number of family funerals, including those of Hardy's grandmother Hand in 1847 and of twelve-year-old Walter Hardy, another of his Bockhampton cousins, in 1844.

Because the great annual festivals and seasonal evolutions were so regular and predictable in their coming, they were looked forward to long in advance, and Hardy's second wife once said that many of his pleasures to the end of his life were those 'of anticipation'—for example, the coming of spring. Her remark on another occasion that her husband was very superstitious, 'as was natural', serves as a reminder that a world so traditional was inevitably credulous, that the 'fetishistic' attitude of a Mrs Durbeyfield, with 'her fast-perishing lumber of superstitions, folk-lore, dialect, and orally transmitted ballads', was familiar to Hardy from his own childhood, that the witches and weather prophets and 'planet-rulers' had not yet entirely disappeared,[26] that he received at first hand those tales of images burned in slow fires, of blood 'turned' by touching the corpse of a hanged man, and of miller-moths emerging from the mouths of the dying, which he drew upon in *The Return of the Native*, 'The Withered Arm', and 'A Few Crusted Characters'.

These early, pre-school years of Hardy's were far and away the most significant for his later career as a novelist and poet. He was surrounded by gifted narrators—by the rapt grandmother of 'One We Knew', by a mother who was an inexhaustible source of stories, sayings, and country lore, by a father who could give a 'vivid and captivating' description of an apparently uneventful walk[27]—and by other elders, outside the family, who delighted in recounting their memories and in telling the tales and singing the songs they had themselves inherited from their parents and grandparents. Hardy was—to an extraordinary degree—a child of the oral tradition, and perhaps, in England, that tradition's last and greatest product. He came, too, from a culture in which singing and music-making were natural forms of expression, and from a family in which music was a major preoccupation. Although he never saw the Stinsford choir occupying its old place in the church gallery—which was itself removed during the 1840s—there was no lack of music in his own home. He displayed from an early age an ecstatic musical sensitivity, so that the sounds of his father's violin of an evening could move him to dance and weep simultaneously, and in the poem 'Song to an Old Burden' memories of his father's playing are mingled with those of his mother's singing. At the age of four he was given a toy concertina; not long afterwards he was introduced to the violin; a little later still he went with his father to local dances and other festivities and even performed himself from time to time with an energy that sorted oddly with the delicacy of his appearance.[28]

Hardy always treasured his father's violin and the old music books which had been laboriously written out by hand for the use of the Stinsford choir. He also preserved some of the books of dance tunes and their steps as performed on more secular occasions, and entered into his copy of Hullah's *The Song Book* the names of people whom he particularly associated with this song or that. From time to time he took the trouble to write out the words of ballads, chiefly from Stinsford and Melbury Osmond, which his mother or some other relative had remembered, or which he himself had heard sung at parties, harvest suppers, and the like. Most of them tell, conventionally enough, of love disappointed or betrayed. Others turn, like those in *Tess of the d'Urbervilles*, upon sexual innuendo.* In the novel much of Tess's confusion as to her place in the world and in the universe derives from the 'gap of two hundred years' between what she was taught at school

---

* Among the latter was the little comic 'opera'—as Hardy himself called it when he wrote it out for performance—of 'O Jan, O Jan, O Jan', which he remembered being sung at home when he was about four years old. Years later he found a version called 'The Keys of Canterbury' in a book of folksongs sent him by a friend, and wrote back: 'The ending, containing the lover's last proposal, which wins her, is much tamer than ours was. Like so many of these old songs & dialogues it had a rather broad double-entendre in it, quite Shakespearean, at which the men used to laugh, some of the women smirk, others stiffen, & wh. others wd paraphrase for domestic performance.' It was only in after years, he added, that he realized why his father always smiled when he heard it.[29]

and what she was told by her mother.[30] It might be said of Hardy himself that much of his best work emerged directly from the juxtaposition of deeply traditional attitudes and intensely localized country lore with an early emotional susceptibility to the music and rituals of the Church of England and a subsequent intellectual acceptance of some of the more radical and sceptical trends in late nineteenth-century thought. Remarkably, these influences did not supersede each other but coexisted, so that Hardy could say in 1901 that although he had been unable to find any evidence whatsoever for the existence of the supernatural he would cheerfully have given ten years of his life to see 'an authentic, indubitable spectre': 'I should think [he added] I am cut out by nature for a ghost-seer. My nerves vibrate very readily; people say I am almost morbidly imaginative; my will to believe is perfect. If ever ghost wanted to manifest himself, I am the very man he should apply to. But no—the spirits don't seem to see it!'[31]

Hardy's introduction to the Church came early, as a natural consequence of his parents' regular attendance and especially of his father's participation, until so recently, in the performances of the Stinsford choir. The family sympathies were strongly High Church, and the services had for Hardy a dramatic appeal which was soon reflected in his dressing himself in a tablecloth at home in order to play the parson and read the morning service from the altitude of a chair.[32] In Stinsford Church itself he was fascinated by the skull which formed part of the Grey family monument in the north aisle, where the Hardys habitually sat; the inscription on the monument (containing in its third line the name Angel, used in *Tess of the d'Urbervilles*) he learned so thoroughly that he could repeat it word for word even in old age.[33]

No doubt influenced by family resentment over the fate of the choir, Hardy disliked the Stinsford vicar, the Revd Arthur Shirley, but he attended confirmation classes in the vicarage and later shared with Shirley's sons in the teaching of the Sunday School. Though the old choir had gone—to be replaced by a barrel organ turned by Hardy's uncle James, one of the former players—the church was still a place of music and colour, of satisfying rituals and magnificent language. Whatever his personal feelings about Shirley, Hardy could not but recognize that the vicar and even the curate occupied, both in church and outside it, positions of dignity and prestige. The church thus answered to Hardy's immediate emotional and aesthetic needs and offered, at the same time, a possible—though difficult—direction for the social ambitions already being instilled into him by his mother. 'As a child', reports *Later Years,* 'to be a parson had been his dream.'[34]

Once it became clear that her eldest son was destined to survive into adulthood Jemima took an intense interest in his upbringing. She saw that he had books, and she indulged his fiddling expeditions with his father as a way of his learning and practising music. Just how much she herself directly contributed to his education is far from certain. Her mother had the reputation of a literate and knowledgeable woman, a great reader of novels, and she could certainly write letters with vigour and fluency, if not with impeccable grammatical precision. Jemima is said, like her mother, to have 'read omnivorously',[35]* but she seems not to have had any facility with a pen. She certainly put her name (rather than an illiterate's cross) in the church register on the occasion of her own marriage and as a witness to her sister's marriage, but no letters written by her have survived, and just as her mother was sending messages to her by way of her sister in 1842 so her eldest son was writing and receiving letters on her behalf in 1859. Even the inscription—'Thomas Hardy / the gift of his Mother'—in her remarkable early present of Dryden's translation of *The Works of Vergil* is in the recipient's hand and not her own. The combination of good reading ability with poor—because unpractised— writing ability was common enough among people of Jemima's class and time, but this legacy of her poverty-stricken childhood contrasts sadly with her obvious strengths of intelligence and character and lends an additional poignancy to the image of her as sighing sadly over a piano she could not play.[37]

Hardy once said that his childhood hobby had been 'the collecting of books', but his library during the first ten years or so of his life must have been scanty indeed. He recalled weeping as a boy over the romances of Bulwer-Lytton, purchased because they were available in cheap editions, confessed more than once to an

---

* In a passage published anonymously but obviously originating with Hardy himself, she is described as having been 'catholic in her taste for books, enjoying the philosophy of Johnson's "Rasselas" in turn with the frivolities of Combe's "Doctor Syntax." She preferred "Marmion" to any of Scott's prose works, of the latter liking "Kenilworth" the best. Byron, of course, she admired, influenced possibly by his vogue in her youth. It was "Vanity Fair" which she seemed to rate above all other novels by deceased writers.' The plausibility of these statements is not enhanced by the fact that several of the judgements coincide with Hardy's own. On the other hand, Jemima's doctor asserted that her favourite book was Dante's *Commedia*.[36]

early passion for the Scottish poet William Julius Mickle, and at the age of ten was frightened by a picture of Apollyon in a copy of *The Pilgrim's Progress*.[38] Jemima is said to have caused a family quarrel by making off with Betty Hand's books following the latter's death in 1847; if so, few if any of them have survived, and it is impossible to tell just what volumes Hardy can in fact have had access to—other than the *Cries of London*, the little book of words and pictures which he is said to have read before he was three, and *The Rites and Worship of the Jews*, the gift in 1847 of his godfather A. King—who seems otherwise to have left no trace.[39]* An early signature ('Master Hardy') appears, however, in Thomas Dilworth's *A New Guide to the English Tongue*, which carries a firm pencil line alongside the following passage: 'It is a commendable thing for a boy to apply his mind to the study of good letters; they will be always useful to him; they will procure him the favour and love of good men, which those that are wise value more than riches and pleasure.'[41]

Jemima's attempts to keep her son supplied with examples of 'good letters' did not lack ambition: in addition to Dryden's *Vergil* she gave him *Rasselas* and a little volume containing translations of Bernardin de Saint-Pierre's *Paul and Virginia* and *The Exiles of Siberia*. Though *Paul and Virginia* is certainly a work of impeccable morality, Jemima was perhaps unaware of its quietist message, its preaching of a virtuous obscurity, when she put it into the hands of a son already dangerously sympathetic to the genial unambitiousness of his father. A marker still draws attention to the following passage:

> 'My son! talents are still more rare than birth or riches, and are, undoubtedly, an inestimable good, of which nothing can deprive us, and which everywhere conciliate public esteem. But they cost

---

* Copies of Gifford's *History of the Wars Occasioned by the French Revolution* and of a translation of Salomon Gessner's *The Death of Abel* (inscribed by his grandmother, Mary Hardy, in 1800) must also have been in the Bockhampton cottage. Hardy's lifelong habit of annotating Bibles and prayerbooks seems to have begun to develop when he was nine years old, and there survives from an even earlier date a publication of the Religious Tract Society, *Companion to the Bible, Intended for Bible Classes, Families, and Young Persons in General*, given to him by his maternal grandmother. There is also a copy of *The Psalter, or Psalms of David*, published in 1843, which contains what seems to be some of Hardy's earliest surviving writing. Hardy's first dated signatures appear in Francis Walkingame's *The Tutor's Assistant; Being a Compendium of Arithmetic* ('Thomas Hardys / Book / 1849') and John M. Moffatt's *The Boy's Book of Science* ('Thomas Hardy / Dec 24th 1849').[40]

dear; they are generally allied to exquisite sensibility, which renders their possessor miserable. But you tell me that you would serve mankind. He who, from the soil which he cultivates, draws forth one additional sheaf of corn, serves mankind more than he who presents them with a book.'[42]

There was a dame school in Lower Bockhampton in Hardy's childhood, kept by Elizabeth Plowman—presumably to be identified with the deplorable 'Eliza' of Hardy's Kingston Maurward memories (see above, p. 34)—but it is not certain that Hardy ever attended it. In any case, it was only with the establishment of a National (i.e., Church of England) School in the parish in 1848 that Hardy first entered a formal classroom, arriving on opening day still wearing a frock and looking 'fresh, / Pink, tiny, crisp-curled'. The same poem, 'He Revisits His First School', pictures him sitting at a desk as 'in Walkingame he / Conned the grand Rule-of-Three / With the bent of a bee', and he seems in fact to have progressed well in arithmetic and geography under the direction of the two teachers, Thomas Fuller and his wife[43]—the same 'T. Fuller' whom Hardy later recalled as 'far above his position in education, but a drunkard'.

It was at this first school that Hardy suffered the earliest of those experiences of love, the slighting of the loved one, and subsequent guilt which were to recur throughout his life. He was much attracted to one of his schoolfellows, a girl from Higher Bockhampton called Fanny Hurden, later immortalized in 'Voices from Things Growing in a Churchyard' as 'poor Fanny Hurd' who once 'flit-fluttered like a bird'. One winter day, in a moment of childish play or anger, he pushed her back against the schoolroom stove, burning her hands. It was an action, he told Walter de la Mare some seventy years later, for which he could never forgive himself, especially since her early death (in 1861, at the age of twenty) had prevented him from making any kind of restitution.[44]

In starting school Hardy encountered for the first time a sizeable group of his own contemporaries and became exposed to their habits, values, and attitudes. He also learned something of their capacity for persecution when they persisted in chanting at him:

> Thomas a-Didymus had a black beard;
> Kissed all the maidens & made 'em afeard.[45]

It is possible that the chanting began as a response to the little episode with Fanny Hurden, or to the lady-killing propensities of his father. Otherwise the point of the rhyme—in so far as it had any beyond the mere association of names—presumably lay in some ironic allusion to Hardy's still rather weakly appearance and to his shyness and instinctive reserve: the observation in *Early Life* about his dislike of being touched by his schoolfellows —or, in adult life, by other men—is no less significant for its having been inserted, at the suggestion of Sir James Barrie, after Hardy's death.[46]

The fact that Hardy, until the age of eight, had been surrounded by an almost exclusively adult—and largely feminine—world was to be of the utmost significance for his future development. Hardy spoke of Mary as almost his only childhood companion,[47] but even she must often have been absent—attending the dame school, playing with the friends she had made there, or occupied in household tasks of one kind or another. The attitude of uninvolved spectatorship which so often characterizes the narrative voice in his novels is in part a reflection of his early situation as a sickly, solitary boy—often at home because of his weakness, his lack of friends, and his mother's protectiveness—and the constantly repeated experience of sitting by, silent and unnoticed, while his parents and their relatives and friends sang, played, joked, and talked together, singing the old songs, telling the old stories of the local past, trotting out the scraps of inherited wisdom and credulity, drawing upon the resources of their colourful and vigorous local speech, with its long-learned fatalisms and self-protective humour. The note so often caught in the pages of the Wessex novels and tales is unmistakably audible, for example, in Jemima's canny view of baptism—that it could do no harm, and she wouldn't want her children to blame her in another life for failing in some duty in this one.[48] During the composition of *Far from the Madding Crowd*, Hardy was to tell Leslie Stephen how advantageous it was to be actually among the people described at the time of describing them,[49] and that novel, like *Under the Greenwood Tree*, owes a particularly direct and substantial debt to the early years of passive but observant listening—to his parents first of all, but also to those who visited the cottage and were themselves visited in their turn.

The loneliness of the cottage was, indeed, partly counteracted by its being something of a social centre for immediate neighbours and for the former players and singers of the old Stinsford choir. It was, too, only a modest walk (for those days) across the heath from Puddletown and the several Puddletown households to which the Hardys were related. Throughout his life Hardy remained acutely aware of his position within an extended family which included cousins, second cousins, and even more distant connections on both his father's and mother's sides, and he always kept in touch, either directly or through his sisters, with the families he had known and visited during his childhood. There was some coolness between his father and his two brothers, and Hardy seems never to have been particularly intimate with his uncle John's children in Fordington or even his uncle James's smaller family in Higher Bockhampton itself. On the other hand, there was a close connection with some of the Puddletown Hardys, including Elizabeth, widow of his great-uncle John (his grandfather's younger brother), and some of her children, especially the third son, Walter Jenkins Hardy, also a mason, and his wife, Ann. The nine children of Walter and Ann Hardy were born over roughly the same period as the four children of Thomas and Jemima, and Hardy seems to have had a particular affection for Angelina and Charles and, later still, for Angelina's son Frank George (see below, p. 504).

Also at Puddletown were various members of Jemima's family, including two or three of her brothers and, until her death in 1847, her mother, the former Betty Swetman. Jemima depended a good deal for advice and practical assistance on her sister, Maria Sparks, and since Maria was the eldest of the family and the first to have children of her own—since, too, she was in many ways the most solidly established—she provided the family with a natural focus. From his earliest years Hardy was familiar with his uncle and aunt Sparks, with his Sparks cousins—especially Martha, who was slightly older than himself, and James, who was somewhat younger—and with their 'cheerful house', as Mary Hardy later recalled it, 'with the sparkling river in front, and in the near distance the old Church tower with the clock & rambling chimes, around which so many of our people are sleeping'.[50]

In December 1846 Jemima's younger sister Mary had written to her mother* from Hitchin, Hertfordshire, where she was stay-

---

* Since she so often acted as family correspondent, and since her son was later to establish a local reputation as a poet, Mary Hand was presumably the aunt of Hardy's 'who wrote verses all her life and was wonderfully quick at off-hand rhyming'.[51]

ing with Martha, the youngest and prettiest of the Hand sisters, the wife since May 1841 of John Brereton Sharpe. A man of some education, Sharpe had apparently served for a time in the army and then returned to his native county of Hertfordshire and gone (like his father) into farming, first at Hitchin and later at Hatfield. He was employed as an agricultural bailiff by the Marquess of Salisbury, for whom he wrote, in 1848, a report on possible improvements to farming methods on the Hatfield House estate.[52] Martha's health was never strong, and Mary Hand's visit in 1846 had been timed to coincide with the birth of her sister's third child in November. That child died less than two years later, just four days before the fourth was born, and when Martha again became pregnant in 1849 Jemima Hardy undertook to stay with her as nurse and housekeeper until the crisis should be over. The baby was expected in December and Jemima set off for Hatfield well ahead of time, taking her own nine-year-old son with her— 'for protection', as she put it.[53]

To Hardy the journey was memorable, not just because it was his first absence from home but also because it involved a combination of old and new modes of travel—to London by the railway which had reached Dorchester in 1847, and on to Hatfield by coach. Once there he was enchanted by his 'handsome aunt', who later served as the model for Bathsheba Everdene in *Far from the Madding Crowd*.[54] John Sharpe, for his part, seems to have been in some degree the 'original' of Sergeant Troy. His educated manner, good looks, and romantic military past made him an altogether more stylish figure than any of the men in Hardy's own family, while the lively letter he wrote to Martha's family soon after the marriage and the gift of story-telling he retained into old age are both suggestive of Troy's verbal facility. Unfortunately, Sharpe also had something of Troy's restlessness and improvidence. He left his position on the Hatfield estate in the spring of 1851 and, unable to find permanent employment in England, emigrated to Canada that July with his wife and five children, the youngest just a month old.[55] Wretchedly short of money—dependent even for the cost of the passage on the generosity of Lord Salisbury and of the family with whom his sister was employed as a governess—he set off at short notice with a promise of temporary employment on an estate near Guelph, Ontario, and only the vaguest prospects of eventually obtaining a farm of his own. Within a few years, however, he had found a different and perhaps more appropriate outlet for his talents: when Martha Sharpe died giving birth to her tenth child on 28 August 1859, the local newspaper gave her address as South Dumfries, Ontario, and her husband's occupation as 'School Teacher'.[56]

Hardy stayed long enough at Hatfield in the late autumn of 1849 to be sent, as a day boy, to the school—'somewhat on the Squeers model'—kept in Fore Street, Hatfield, by a Congregationalist minister named Thomas Ray.[57]* Martha's child was not born until just before Christmas and it was probably well into the new year before Jemima and her son returned home. Hardy caught glimpses of various London landmarks as they passed through the city, and once claimed to have made a tour of the streets described in *Old St. Paul's* by Harrison Ainsworth, one of his favourite authors at that period. It seems doubtful that he would have had time or opportunity for such an expedition, but he certainly retained the horrific impression made upon him by the sights and sounds of Smithfield meat market, which was close to the coaching inn, the Cross-Keys, Clerkenwell, at which he and his mother stayed the night—and which he later discovered to have had associations with Shelley and Mary Godwin. Before going to bed Jemima searched every corner of the room for a possible intruder; for all her great spirit and energy, she was capable of timidity, and had perhaps not been altogether joking when she spoke of taking her son with her 'for protection'.[59] It was a timidity, a sense of personal vulnerability, which communicated itself to her son. As a child he felt nervous when alone on the heath at night,[60] hurrying home without stopping when frightened by the picture of Apollyon,† and in later years there was to be an extraordinary discrepancy between the public boldness of his literary persona and the defensive reticence of his private self.

Because the visit to her sister had already been impending in the early autumn of 1849, Jemima had apparently not thought it worthwhile to send Hardy back to the Bockhampton school to begin classes he would not be able to finish, especially since he would soon be physically strong enough to undertake the daily walk—three miles in each direction—to one of the Dorchester

* The school, now a private house, still stands, although the Sharpes's cottage on the other side of Fore Street has long since disappeared, apparently to allow for an extension of the churchyard.[58]

† See above, p. 40. So Jude, out after dark, 'started homewards at a run, trying not to think of giants, Herne the Hunter, Apollyon lying in wait for Christian, or of the captain with the bleeding hole in his forehead and the corpses round him that remutinied every night on board the bewitched ship'.[61]

schools.[62] She must also have been fearful of the current cholera epidemic, which killed a Stinsford boy of Hardy's age in October of that year. It was, in fact, the following September before Hardy was sent to the Dorchester British School, an elementary school established by the British and Foreign Bible Society and conducted therefore on the same monitorial system as the National Schools—such as that at Bockhampton—but with a Nonconformist rather than Anglican bias in all religious matters.

The immediate consequence of the decision to send Hardy to the British School was a quarrel between Jemima and Julia Augusta Martin, wife of Francis Pitney Brouncker Martin, who had purchased the Kingston Maurward estate in 1844; the quarrel led in its turn to Hardy's father losing the estate business.[63] Mrs Martin, who had paid for the building of the Bockhampton school, was angered by what she saw as a desertion both of the school itself and of the Church of England precepts it sought to instil. But more than principle was at stake. She had known the Hardys, as people who lived on the estate and occasionally did work for it, ever since her arrival at Kingston Maurward, and, lacking children of her own, she 'had grown passionately fond of Tommy almost from his infancy—he is said to have been an attractive little fellow at this time—whom she had been accustomed to take into her lap and kiss until he was quite a big child'. Hardy, unusually small and delicate, could even at the age of eight scarcely have been called a big child, and Mrs Martin's caresses evidently continued into his first school days. She encouraged him to draw and sing for her, and many years later she was to remind him that she had 'taught you yr letters',[64] by which she evidently meant not that she had taught him to read but that she had, in effect, taught him to write. His progress in that direction had languished under his parents' inexpert tuition, and even in the *Early Life* it is acknowledged, with characteristic indirection, that his handwriting was 'indifferent' at the time he first started school.[65] Hardy flourished under Mrs Martin's supervision, and it is tempting to assign to this period the surviving copy book pages on which he wrote out, several times over, a brief but suggestive series of sententiae:

> Passion is a bad counsellor.
> Quit vicious habits.
> Encourage diligence.
> Forget not past favours.[66]

Hardy did not forget, then or ever, the woman who had over-whelmed him not only by her fond and flattering encouragement but also by a cultivation and elegance, a voluptuousness of dress and person, that were altogether new to his experience. Whether or not Jemima's carrying off her son to Hatfield was an episode in her campaign of avoidance of Mrs Martin, she seems when on her home ground to have gone so far as to stop attending Stinsford Church—probably taking the children to Fordington instead—and it was in the hope of seeing Mrs Martin after a long interval that Hardy went in the early autumn of 1850 to a harvest supper held in an old barn on the Kingston Maurward estate. Attended chiefly by local girls and soldiers from the Dorchester barracks—'Red shapes amid the corn'—the occasion lingered romantically in his memory for many reasons: because the young woman who brought him was so busy dancing and flirting that she failed to take him home until the early morning hours, because she and the other girls, sitting and leaning together 'in their light gowns', joined in singing 'The Outlandish Knight' and other old ballads they had 'learnt from never a book',[67]* and because Mrs Martin did eventually appear and speak briefly, and coquettishly, to him: 'O Tommy, how is this? I thought you had deserted me!'[69]

The interruption of their friendship was deeply painful—as the poem 'In Her Precincts', specifically associated with Kingston Maurward, appears to attest†—and the feeling, 'almost that of a lover', with which he had responded to her attentions was to linger with him for many years. As a young man in London some twelve years later he attempted to re-establish the relationship on something like its old footing, only to fall back when confronted by the brutal fact that Mrs Martin now looked all of her more than fifty years—a visual trauma that he was to recreate imagina-tively at the end of *Two on a Tower* and in poems such as 'Amabel' and 'The Revisitation'. Another dozen years on, a letter from her was still capable of reviving 'throbs of tender feeling in him' and memories of 'the thrilling "frou-frou" of her four grey silk flounces when she used to bend over him, and when they

* It was no doubt for these same girls that Hardy acted as an amanuensis when their military sweethearts had departed—an experience which con-tributed many years later to the conception of the story 'On the Western Circuit'.[68]

† Florence Hardy, however, once suggested that 'In Her Precincts' re-flected Hardy's temporary infatuation with Emily Gertrude Fellowes, the daughter of Martin's successor as owner of Kingston Maurward.[70] See also below, p. 149.

brushed against the font as she entered church on Sunday'.[71] No less remarkably, Hardy's rereading of that letter when he was himself in his seventies was enough to stimulate speculation of a quite wildly romantic kind: 'Thus though their eyes never met again after his call on her in London, nor their lips from the time when she had held him in her arms, who can say that both occurrences might not have been in the order of things, if he had developed their reacquaintance earlier, now that she was in her widowhood, with nothing to hinder her mind from rolling back upon her past.'[72] Like so many of Hardy's attachments, the relationship loomed larger in his imagination than elsewhere, but there seems little doubt that much of the autobiographical intensity which went into his first novel, *The Poor Man and the Lady,* derived from his feeling for Mrs Martin and his sense that they had been separated by hostile forces which had nothing to do with their own emotions but everything to do with conventional attitudes towards age, religion, and class.

3

DORCHESTER

I T WAS at Michaelmas 1850 that Hardy first presented himself at the British School kept by Isaac Glandfield Last in Greyhound Yard, Dorchester. Because of his early physical weakness and slow development, and of his late begun and already interrupted schooling, he was a year or two older than most of the other boys —although he looked much younger. Fellow pupils remembered him as a small, serious, clever, rather solitary child with a large head, who customarily carried a satchel full of books and was always ready to help slower students with their lessons.[1] According to one story he went for his lunch each day to Rebecca and Amelia Sparks, the unmarried sisters of his uncle by marriage James Sparks. They lived in Dorchester, working at home as shoebinders, and are said to have not especially appreciated Hardy's enthusiasm for conjuring tricks—such as tossing buttered bread to the ceiling and making it stick there or throwing the contents of the sugar bowl into the air and catching them in his cupped hands as they descended.[2]

As the evocation of mid-century Dorchester in *The Mayor of Casterbridge* so strikingly indicates, the town had scarcely begun to overflow its original Roman fortifications, and yet its smallness did not prevent it from being, in certain respects, intensely urban. It was the county town, the centre of local government, and it was a garrison town, made colourful by the constant presence of the red-coated and splendidly accoutred soldiery of those days. The county court met there, and the Dorset Assizes, presided over by visiting judges who were attended with pageantry and (especially in a town which had seen Judge Jeffreys at work after the Monmouth rebellion) with the awe due to men invested with power over life and death. It had banks and solicitors, markets and hiring fairs, and served as the commercial centre for the whole of southern Dorset. A sharper awareness of local and, indeed, national affairs was one of the most immediate, and most important, consequences of Hardy's transfer to his new school, and the patterns of his future fiction were in part established by the daily experience of walking to and fro between Bockhampton and Dorchester, between a 'world of shepherds and ploughmen', still in touch with the customs and beliefs of past centuries, and 'a county-town of assizes and aldermen, which had advanced to railways and telegraphs and daily London papers'.[3]

During his earliest years Hardy had been made vaguely aware of major events and outbursts of popular feeling through their impact upon his parents, and in later years he vividly recalled the agitation at the time of the Corn Law repeal in 1846, the passage of the Prince Consort through Dorchester in the summer of 1849, and the 'lurid' scenes of 5 November 1850 when the annual Guy Fawkes celebrations turned into ugly anti-popery demonstrations and effigies of the Pope and Cardinal Wiseman were burned in Maumbury Rings, the old Roman amphitheatre.[4] He now became more sensitive to the subtler but often larger implications of events such as the Great Exhibition of 1851, made accessible to country people by the new excursion trains, and, a little later on, the increased military activity of the Crimean War. He also shared eagerly in the excitement provided by successive Parliamentary elections and—since the Hardys seem always to have been staunchly Liberal—he was proud to have had a hand on the rope of the carriage in which the Liberal candidate was drawn around the town after winning one of the Dorchester seats in July 1852.[5]

Hardy's cousin Tryphena, the youngest child of James and Maria Sparks, was born at Puddletown in March 1851, and his own mother gave birth to her third child and second son, Henry, in August of that same year—about four weeks after John and

Martha Sharpe and their children, also Hardy's cousins, had made what must have been recognized as their irrevocable departure for Canada. Hardy's chief preoccupations during these years were, however, his school work and the occasional expeditions with his father to play 'Haste to the Wedding', 'The New-Rigged Ship', and other country dances at village functions.[6] His mother, who had forbidden him to gamble after he had unexpectedly won a hen by throwing dice at a local raffle, also warned him not to accept payment for his services as a fiddler; but in September 1853 he risked her disapproval and collected a sum sufficient to purchase *The Boy's Own Book: A Complete Encyclopaedia of all the Diversions, Athletic, Scientific, and Recreative, of Boyhood and Youth,* previously seen and lusted after in the window of a Dorchester bookshop.[7] Hardy was eager, then as always, for the kind of miscellaneous information the book offered, but its emphasis upon normal boyish activities and skills perhaps had a special appeal at a time when he still felt weak and immature alongside most of his school fellows. Nearly seventy years later, after his friend Edmund Gosse had spoken in a letter of spending some months in Weymouth in 1853, Hardy replied:

Curiously enough I remember my father driving to Weymouth on business one day about that very year (there was no railway further than Dorchester then) & taking me with him as a treat; so that you may certainly have 'brushed up against a boy called T.H.' in the streets there—though not a 'big' boy, for I was small & delicate, & had scarcely started off growing & reaching the robust condition into which I plunged between then & my 21st year.[8]

It was in 1853 that Isaac Last left the British School to establish an independent 'commercial academy' for older and more advanced pupils. For Hardy, who went with Last to the new school, the years between 1853 and 1856 were a period of rapid intellectual development—and of physical development too, as the daily exercise of walking six and more miles gradually built up his strength. Last, according to one account, was a harsh disciplinarian who would 'frequently chase a boy round the room lashing him with his cane until he was white in the face'.[9] But it is the lot of schoolmasters to be caricatured, and Hardy, at least, made good progress under Last's direction. He began, at his mother's instigation, to take Latin as an additional subject—his copy of

An Introduction to the Latin Tongue was purchased in 1852, but he added a second date, September 1853, when he first began to use it regularly.[10]* In 1854 Hardy bought the *Breviarum Historiae Romanae* of Eutropius, and at about the same period he set out in his copy of the *King Edward VIth Latin Grammar* a scheme for learning genders, in which the masculine nouns were coloured red, the feminine white, and the neuter blue, while those of 'Epicene Gender' were distinguished by red diagonal stripes. Another purchase of 1854, Cassell's *Manual of the French Language,* evidently marks the beginning of French lessons from a teacher at the Ladies' School, conducted at South Grove Cottage, Dorchester, by the Misses Charlotte and Jemima Harvey, which his sister Mary now attended.[12] In March of that same year he began at Last's a notebook headed 'Miscellaneous Questions', in which he worked out in a meticulous copperplate hand a series of mathematical problems related to bricklaying, carpentry, plumbing, and other building trades. In December another notebook, 'Conic Sections and Their Solids', was started, and although the problems were now more theoretical they were still framed in down-to-earth terms:

> Two porters agreed to drink off a pot of strong beer at two pulls or a draught each; now the first having given it a black eye as it is called or drunk till the surface of the liquor just touched the opposite edge of the bottom, gave the remaining part to the other; what was the difference of their shares, supposing the pot was the frustum of a cone whose top diameter was 3.7, bottom diameter 4.23 and perpendicular depth 5.7 inches?[13]

Isaac Last evidently believed that education should not be too remote from the world of his students' experience, and his competence in technical as well as in academic subjects† was no doubt an important factor in determining Hardy's parents to leave their son in his care rather than send him either to Hardye's Grammar School or to the 'Classical and Mathematical School' over which

---

* The survival of Last's receipt for the five shilling supplementary charge made for 'Instructing Thomas Hardy in Latin till Xmas 1853' is indicative of the symbolic importance it had for Jemima Hardy, ambitious as she always was for her son's educational and social advancement.[11]

† Last's son, William Isaac Last, was director of the Science Museum at South Kensington from 1904 until his death in 1911; a grandson, Hugh Macilwain Last, became a distinguished Roman historian and principal of Brasenose College, Oxford.

the Revd William Barnes, the philologist and dialect poet, had been presiding for a good many years. Last, for his part, was sufficiently satisfied with Hardy's progress to present him, at Christmas 1854, with a volume entitled *Scenes & Adventures at Home and Abroad* as a prize for diligence and good behaviour—a choice which suggests that the master thought of his pupil not as an excessively bookish boy but as having the interests and activities normal to his years; as such it belongs with his contemporary reading of Harrison Ainsworth, Dumas *père*, James Grant's *The Scottish Cavalier*, and Shakespeare's tragedies 'for the plots only'. In 1855 Hardy made further progress in mathematics and French, and Last thought his Latin good enough to justify another prize, Theodore Beza's *Novum Testamentum*, at midsummer. During the ensuing summer Hardy continued to receive instruction from Last, and there survives an exercise book containing specimen commercial letters, receipts, and so forth, written out in copperplate and bearing Hardy's signatures and various dates between April and September 1855. That Christmas he put his name in the first two volumes of *The Popular Educator*, originally published by 'that genius in home-education, John Cassell'; he obtained the third volume five months later, on Whit Monday, 12 May 1856.[14]

At midsummer of 1856, shortly after his sixteenth birthday, Hardy's schooldays came to an end. By this time he had bought (from the Dorchester stationers' shop kept by the widowed Rebecca Treves, whose son Frederick was to become a famous surgeon), the leather writing case which he still owned at the time of his death.[15] He had also ventured upon his first literary exercises. On 19 December 1855 he had copied out Charles Swain's poem 'The Old Cottage Clock' on the inside of the door of the grandfather's clock which the family owned, and then added his own signature—probably out of comic bravado rather than in a deliberate attempt to deceive.[16] Not long after, according to *Early Life*, he got into print by tricking a Dorchester paper into publishing 'an anonymous skit . . . on the disappearance of the Alms-House clock, . . . the paragraph being in the form of a plaintive letter from the ghost of the clock'.[17]* The skit itself has never

* The possibility—though it is no more than that—of his having attempted at an even earlier date to get a letter published in the *Dorset County Chronicle* is suggested by an item in that newspaper's 'Our Correspondent. Notices' column for 19 October 1854: 'The letter of *Thomas H——* is legible enough in one sense, but quite unintelligible in another. The words are

been confidently identified, and Hardy's recollection of it may
have been at fault, but one possible candidate is a paragraph in
the *Dorset County Chronicle* of 17 January 1856. Appearing in
the column of Dorchester news, it made particular reference to
the clock which still hangs in South Street outside the former
almshouse known as Napper's Mite:

> THE TOWN CLOCKS.—We wish to draw the attention of the proper
> authorities to the irregularity of the various public time-pieces
> in this our good town of Dorchester. . . . The Trinity Clock
> scorns the society of its neighbour St. Peter's, and obstinately re-
> fuses to keep company with it; while the South-street Clock has
> an infinite contempt for both, and keeps on its own course; but
> whether it determines the hour of the day by the sun, or by
> railway time, or by a system of its own, it is impossible to tell.
> Now, in the midst of such perversity, what can the public do? . . .
> We hope that this remonstrance will be listened to in the proper
> quarter, so that for the future there will be "no more complaining
> in our streets" of the eccentric behaviour of our Town Clocks.

There is no speaking ghost here, but the paragraph is certainly
humorous, perhaps mischievous, in intent, and bears a sufficient
resemblance to a regular news item to have tricked a hasty or un-
wary editor into printing it. If it is indeed Hardy's it scarcely
constitutes a distinguished inception of his literary career. On the
other hand, its ironies, though ponderous, are not contemptible,
and it would not be the only instance in his career of his seeking
publication under a disguise.

On 11 July 1856, shortly after leaving school, Hardy was articled
for three years to John Hicks, a Dorchester architect, to receive
instruction 'in architectural drawing and surveying'—Jemima
Hardy characteristically persuading Hicks to knock down the
standard premium of £100, payable in mid-term, for £40 cash.[19]
She no doubt saw the step as a logical one for a boy with a sound
technical education, some connections in the building trade, and
a capacity for social and economic advancement. Hardy allowed

---

excessively large, but the meaning so small as to be wholly imperceptible.'
There is no reason to suppose that Hardy had any hand in the humorous
pieces 'Mishaps of Cupid and Hymen' and 'Ejaculations', both signed 'T.H.',
which appeared in the same newspaper early in 1857.[18]

himself to be carried along by his mother's energetic scheming. He knew that Last had given him an unusually good grounding for a boy of his time, place, and class. But he also knew that his imperfect knowledge of Latin and almost total ignorance of Greek left him ill-prepared for that university admission which was essential to the advancement of his private 'dream', and that his future progress towards an adequate level of classical education must depend upon his own energy and perseverance. That process of self-education was to prove slow and painful, the hope of being admitted to study for the ministry was not fulfilled, and Hardy never quite lost the sense of inferiority and resentment stemming from the incompleteness of his schooling—especially as symbolized by the lack of a university degree—and from his bitter memories of the long hours of sterile private labour he had wearily invested and the social barriers he had had to confront. He never forgot, in particular, the humiliation of sitting in Stinsford Church at his mother's side in that early summer of 1856 while the Revd Mr Shirley preached against the presumption shown by one of Hardy's class in seeking to rise, through architecture, into the ranks of professional men.[20]

In other respects the move to Hicks's office on the ground floor of 39 South Street—next door to William Barnes's school and almost opposite the almshouse clock—was a happy one. Of the two pupils already in the office, one, Herbert Fippard, was about to leave, while the other, Henry Bastow, nearer to Hardy in age and temperament, was to remain and become one of his earliest and closest friends. Hicks himself, who had come to Dorchester from Bristol a few years earlier, was a genial, well-educated man in his early forties, quite prepared to be indulgent towards his pupils' pursuit of self-improvement even during business hours. The office seems, indeed, to have been altogether an informal place, likely to be invaded at any time by the children of Hicks's brother, the vicar of Piddletrenthide, one of whom Hardy was to remember as 'inconveniently smart sometimes at riddles &c'.[21]

Of Hardy's specifically architectural studies at this period few relics remain, although he was sufficiently proud of some tracings 'from Paley's Mouldings' to preserve them in a specially made folder.[22] Hicks, himself a clergyman's son, was primarily an ecclesiastical architect, a specialist in the rebuilding and 'restoration' of Gothic churches, and this became, perforce, Hardy's own speciality. One of his first assignments was to draw—or perhaps only copy—a ground plan of St. Peter's, Dorchester, scheduled for further minor 'improvements' in addition to those just completed under Hicks's direction; these alterations involved the relocation of the church's Easter Sepulchre, and Hardy was given the job of delineating and numbering the stones of the Sepulchre so that it could be exactly reconstructed. Other Dorset churches with which Hicks was concerned as builder or, more often, restorer during these years included Athelhampton, Coombe Keynes, Powerstock, Rampisham, Shipton Gorge, and St. Mary's, Bridport, and some of the reports of Hicks's work which appeared in the *Dorset County Chronicle* are said to have been drafted by Hardy himself for the newspaper's 'grateful reporter'.[23]

While he was an articled pupil Hardy naturally performed only the relatively mechanical tasks appropriate to his position— chiefly making surveys and measurements of churches that were to be restored. He would work alone, or in the company of a fellow pupil, and in the opening paragraph of *A Laodicean* the description of the architect hero measuring and drawing a church tower is clearly based upon Hardy's own memories of such pleasant and peaceful expeditions into the Dorset countryside. Because he proved to be an excellent draughtsman, Hardy also spent a great deal of time in the office copying or tracing existing plans; a little later on he would have been employed in 'improving' plans, both of churches and of secular buildings, which Hicks had sketched out.

In those days of enthusiastic 'medievalism' and religious re-vivalism there was much demand for the kind of restoration work in which Hicks was so largely engaged, but as the century wore on there came a growing realization, chiefly articulated by the Society for the Protection of Ancient Buildings, of the destruc-tion involved. As Hardy himself acknowledged years later in 'Memories of Church Restoration'—a kind of public confession of the part he had himself unwittingly played—it was clearly necessary to maintain the fabric of old churches so that they could continue to be used for their original purpose, but disaster too often attended the zealous attempts of incumbents, parishioners, architects, and builders to regularize what for centuries had been irregular, give consistency to what was stylistically various, mod-ernize in the interests of efficiency what was quaint and incon-venient. What Hardy came most to deplore was the interruption of ancient continuities: 'Life, after all, is more than art, and that which appealed to us in the (maybe) clumsy outlines of some

structure which had been looked at and entered by a dozen generations of ancestors outweighs the more subtle recognition, if any,
of architectural qualities.'[24]

Hardy's account of himself as having remained a child until he
was sixteen suggests that his leaving school and beginning his
articles coincided with an equally significant stage in his emotional development. A surviving photograph of this date shows
him to be solemnly and quite self-consciously engaged in asserting
and even exaggerating his age—the hair is arranged with some
care, a shadow of moustache is just visible on the upper lip—and
his aspirations towards gentility: there is a loosely tied cravat
under the slightly wayward collar, and a smart hat, almost of
sombrero proportions, clutched under the right arm. He has, in
fact, the look of a youth pretending to be a young man rather
than of a child aspiring to be a youth, and Hardy's retrospective
catalogue of his ages evidently reflected an inner lack of maturity
and confidence—a shyness and hesitancy that his outward appearance was specifically designed to conceal, especially from the as-
sessing eyes of young women.

All his life Hardy was to be highly susceptible to the attraction
of women only briefly glimpsed or slightly known—*The Well-
Beloved*, fantasy though it may be, speaks with remarkable directness to its author's condition—and there were, not surprisingly,
several such episodes during the years when he was growing up,
his head already crammed with the romantic conceptions and
aspirations accumulated during his lonely but literate childhood.
In addition to his extraordinarily charged feelings towards the
much older Mrs Martin, he had a more readily understandable
admiration for the handsomest of the village girls who were just
a few years older than himself—among them Unity Sargent, whom
he once thought of as a possible model for a 'Wessex Faustina',
and Elizabeth Bishop, a gamekeeper's daughter from Lower Bockhampton, later poetically addressed as 'Lizbie Browne'.[25] When
Hardy was working at Hicks's he did not fail to take notice of
William Barnes's daughter, Lucy, just two or three years older
than himself, as she went in and out of the house next door. As
he recalled in the obituary he wrote of her in 1902:

At that time of her life she was of sweet disposition, but provokingly shy, with plenty of brown hair, a tripping walk, a face

pretty rather than handsome, and extremely piquant to a casual observer, having a nose tip-tilted to that slight Tennysonian degree which is indispensable to a contour of such character. . . . Her appear⁀nce, gracefulness, and marked gentleness, made her a typical 'Lu⌄y', from whom the numerous Lucys in the novels of that date seemed to be drawn.[26]

To roughly this same period belonged his infatuation with a girl who once smiled at him from horseback and his longer-lasting devotion to Louisa Harding, a year younger than himself, the daughter of Stephen Toghill Harding of Stinsford Farm.[27]

The Hardings, people of some substance, considered themselves much superior to the Hardys, and Stephen Harding had been one of the churchwardens at the time of the dissolution of the old choir. But the apparent failure of Hardy's relationship with Louisa to progress even to the point of speech, let alone vows, must be attributed as much to shyness as to barriers of class. In the poem 'The Passer-by' Louisa Harding is imagined as recalling her youthful admirer:

> He used to pass, well-trimmed and brushed,
>   My window every day,
> And when I smiled on him he blushed,
> That youth, quite as a girl might; aye,
>   In the shyest way.[28]

Hardy's affections were deeply, if naïvely, engaged.* When Louisa was sent to boarding school in locally fashionable Weymouth (the Budmouth of the Wessex novels) Hardy is said to have travelled there on Sundays in the hope of catching a glimpse of her in church, and it is possible that she was the occasion, as late as 21 August 1859, of his hearing read at Evensong in St. John's Church, Weymouth, that lesson for the Ninth Sunday after Trinity which always moved him so profoundly: 'and after the fire a still small voice' (I Kings 19:12). Hardy's attention eventually shifted elsewhere; Louisa remained in the neighbourhood, unmarried. They never met in later years, but when, in September 1913, she died and was buried in Stinsford churchyard, Hardy wrote not only the poem 'Louie', associating her death with that

---

* According to *Early Life,* no words beyond 'a murmured "Good evening"' ever passed between Hardy and Louisa Harding. That account was, however, inserted into the typescript after Hardy's death, apparently at the instigation of Sir James Barrie.[29]

of his first wife less than a year previously, but also 'To Louisa in the Lane', a moving expression of regret for a moment and an opportunity lost. During later visits to Stinsford in old age he would often visit her unmarked grave and lament her family's failure to erect a stone to her memory.[30]

Hardy's shyness made his Puddletown cousins especially important to him. Simply because they *were* his cousins, Hardy could approach the older Sparks sisters with an ease and informality impossible to him in his contacts with strangers. But Rebecca, who worked at home as a sempstress, was eleven years Hardy's senior and possessed, unlike Mrs Martin, none of the glamour derived from superior wealth and rank, while Emma, the second sister, went early into service away from home and in 1860 was married, at Hemington in Somerset, to Thomas Cary, with whom she subsequently emigrated to Australia. Hardy's feelings for Martha, the third sister, six years older than himself, seem for a time to have been sufficiently serious to rouse both mothers to active opposition, ostensibly on the grounds that the two were cousins but essentially because each thought her child could make a better marriage. Martha was the handsomest of the Sparks sisters —Rebecca once referred to her as 'the flower of our flock'[31]—and her experience as a lady's maid in London and, briefly, in Paris, brought her both the skill and the means to dress smartly. There is a story of Hardy flirting outrageously with Martha during a rehearsal for a mummer's play in Puddletown;* he certainly saw something of her in London during the early 1860s, and when she emigrated to Australia after her marriage in 1870 to William Duffield, the butler in the London household in which she was then working, she took with her at least one volume affectionately inscribed 'to dear Patty' in Hardy's hand.[33] With James and Nathaniel, the two Sparks sons, Hardy seems always to have been on good terms, while Tryphena, the youngest child, born in 1851, he as yet knew only as a small girl just beginning school.

Although Hardy's home life during these important years seems to have been a constant source of stability and assurance, there was no diminution of the fundamental opposition between his

---

* Nathaniel Sparks, Jun., the source of this story, speaks of Hardy's flirting with the 'eldest' of the Sparks daughters, but it is clear from his subsequent description of her (e.g., as having recently returned from the Continent) that it is Martha, not Rebecca, who is intended.[32]

parents. It was Jemima who confronted Mrs Martin, who stirred her husband to find sources of business other than the Kingston Maurward estate, who insisted that her son should study Latin, who bargained with his teachers and employers for cheaper terms. Meanwhile her husband's very passivity not only constituted his own best defence but allowed her the fullest scope of action and initiative. Conflict was thereby contained and prevented from becoming deep-seated hostility, even during the period when the cottage was at its most crowded following the birth of Katharine, the fourth child, on 2 September 1856. Since Jemima was already in her forties—since, too, the presence of a doctor at Katharine's birth rather than just a midwife suggests that a difficult delivery was anticipated[34]—it is not surprising that she should have had no more children, even though her family was small by comparison with those of her sisters and of most countrywomen of that period. Hardy, now sixteen, and Mary, nearly fifteen, were almost of a different generation from this youngest member of the family, and there was always to be a sharp division in personality and interests as well as in age between Hardy and Mary on the one hand and Henry and Kate (as she was called) on the other. Hardy and Mary were private, anxious, and intellectual, absorbed in themselves, in each other, and in their personal hopes and ambitions. Henry and Kate seemed to have had altogether less of their mother in them, more of their father; astute and intelligent, they were none the less easygoing and self-indulgent, giving little thought to the future or to anything beyond their immediate pleasure and comfort. But the ties of affection and kinship were strong and constantly renewed. Firmly instructed by their mother on the necessity for family solidarity, the Hardy children remained devoted to their parents and to each other, and the images of the life of Higher Bockhampton that find their way into Hardy's work are almost without exception positive and warm.

By the late 1850s Hardy was old enough to take a more active part in the festivals and observances of the local community. His father and his Uncle James were much in demand as musicians at cottage weddings, christenings, and dances, and Hardy would sometimes go with them, playing second violin to his father's first, while James Hardy played the cello.[35] The christening of Katharine Hardy on 26 October 1856 was no doubt celebrated with all due conviviality—even though the rite itself was necessarily performed by the choir's old enemy the Revd Arthur Shirley—and two months later the Hardy musicians played for their neighbour

William Keates, whose daughter Sarah was married on Christmas Day (then a favourite date for Dorset weddings) to Thomas Russell, a gardener from Charminster.*

There were also more sombre occasions, among them the death and funeral, in January 1857, of Mary Hardy, the last and by far the closest of his grandparents.† Less than two years later came news from Canada of the death of Martha Sharpe. Little had been heard from the Sharpes since their departure, and Hardy apparently received no reply to the letter he wrote, on his mother's behalf, in January 1858. As Martha's brother-in-law observed, 'My brother was always a very bad correspondent except when quite forced to write & poor Martha with her numerous duties & weak health—no doubt found much to lead her to put aside writing.' It now became clear that the family was still almost destitute, and George Brereton Sharpe acknowledged in his letter the £3 Jemima had sent to help alleviate their distress.[38] That she evidently found difficulty in raising even so modest a sum is a reminder of the heavy expenses with which the Hardys themselves were burdened. The family business was in a fairly healthy state, but the costs of private schooling and professional training for both Hardy and Mary (destined to become a schoolteacher) had to be reckoned in terms not just of fees, books, and lodging but also of the loss to the family exchequer of the income that young people of their age would normally be expected to bring home.

Throughout this period Hardy continued to walk back and forth between the rural isolation of Higher Bockhampton and the comparative bustle of Dorchester—although by the early 1860s he seems to have been staying in town during the week and returning home only at the weekends.[39] Dorchester, as the social as well as political and commercial centre of its region, could boast con-

---

* It was evidently this occasion which Hardy had particularly in mind when writing both the Christmas party and the wedding episodes of *Under the Greenwood Tree*, although he drew also upon memories of other parties and other weddings, including that of William Keates's elder son and Ann West, also of Higher Bockhampton, on 2 February 1855. The latter event was always associated in Hardy's mind with a natural phenomenon of unusual beauty: some twenty years later, inscribing into a notebook a reference to the Canadian 'silver frost', he added: '(precisely as when Ann West was md)'.[36]

† Although Mary Hardy died at Bockhampton, of causes 'unknown', it was Maria Sparks from Puddletown who registered the death and claimed to have been present when it occurred.[37]

certs, lectures, and public performances of all kinds, and Hardy took advantage of such opportunities at least to the extent of indulging that life-long love of circuses* which so curiously co-existed with his passionate hatred of cruelty to animals. Cooke's Circus was a particular favourite of his youth, and he saw that 'celebrated equestrian troupe' when it came to Dorchester in July 1856 with a programme featuring 'The battle of the Alma, and other scenes of the late war, . . . together with the various equestrian feats and exercises peculiar to such establishments'.[41] The occasion, evidently one of Hardy's sources for the description of Sergeant Troy's performance in the closing chapters of *Far from the Madding Crowd,* provides a useful reminder that Dorchester as well as Bockhampton was capable of contributing to his as yet unconscious store of usable novelistic material.

Less than two weeks earlier, on 30 June, Dorchester had merged its annual commemoration of Queen Victoria's corona-tion with a somewhat belated celebration of the Peace which had concluded the Crimean War. On the ancient earthwork called Poundbury, just outside the town, a programme of sports was offered, including 'donkey races, foot races, climbing greasy poles for legs of mutton, &c, jumping in sacks, and many other games of like character'. Later there were wheelbarrow races and a highly popular competition for clambering across the river on a greasy pole, with a pig for a prize. Meanwhile tea was served on tables laid out in the West Walks and, as night fell, banners, flags, and Chinese lanterns suspended from the trees in the South Walks created a 'most enchanting' effect: 'the sombre shade of the trees above, the soft subdued light from the lanterns, and the crowds of gaily dressed people beneath, all smiling and happy, combined to make a most fairy-like scene'.[42] The scenes thus enthusiastically recorded by the reporter for the local paper were vividly recalled by Hardy himself when writing Chapter 16 of *The Mayor of Casterbridge*—though he may have gone back to the contemporary account to check some of the details.†

In the summer of 1856 occurred, after a sensational trial, the first of the two public hangings in Dorchester that Hardy wit-

---

* Just a few days short of his eighty-sixth birthday Hardy was capable of declaring that 'Lord' George Sanger's autobiography, *Seventy Years a Show-man,* was the best book he had read in a year.[40]

† It is possible that he also witnessed, and later re-created for the novel, the scene at the King's Arms Hotel that November when the retiring Mayor observed the custom of entertaining the Town Council and many of his friends at what the *Southern Times* called a *'recherché* repast'.[43]

nessed and, understandably enough, remembered to the end of his life. On 9 August 1856, when Martha Browne was executed at Dorchester prison for the murder of her husband, Hardy stood close to the gallows, among the watching crowd of three or four thousand; as his account of the occasion nearly seventy years later reveals, his reaction had a strong sexual component, focused not on the execution itself but on its immediate aftermath: 'I remember what a fine figure she showed against the sky as she hung in the misty rain, & how the tight black silk gown set off her shape as she wheeled half-round & back.' As it came on to rain, Hardy recalled on another occasion, 'I saw—they had put a cloth over the face—how, as the cloth got wet, *her features came through it*. That was extraordinary.'[44] The other execution, that of James Seale, almost exactly two years later, Hardy witnessed only at long distance, through the family telescope, from the heath near his home. Even so, the experience was profoundly disturbing: 'He seemed alone on the heath with the hanged man, and crept homeward wishing he had not been so curious.'[45]

The execution of Seale took place at eight o'clock in the morning. By that time, if *Early Life* is to be believed, Hardy would have been up reading for three or even four hours before setting off for Dorchester and Hicks's office: at a period when candles supplied the only illumination it was necessary to keep a countryman's hours and take advantage of all the available daylight. He had now added the study of Greek to his continuing study of Latin: the signature in his copy of the *Iliad* is dated 1858, and he seems to have worked persistently through it until some time in 1860, later ascribing to Jude Fawley precisely his own familiarity with certain passages of Homer as recorded in the volume itself.[46]

Hardy's determination to pursue his self-education in this new direction had been largely stimulated by the enthusiasm for the classics evinced both by Henry Bastow and by Hicks himself. But Bastow was interested in the Greek New Testament rather than in Homer. Brought up at Bridport in a Baptist family, he was baptized on his admission to the Dorchester Baptist congregation in September 1858 and became immediately zealous for the conversion of his fellow pupil to his own belief in personal salvation and adult baptism. He was a year older than Hardy and his senior in Hicks's office, and tended to cast himself in the role of an elder brother. He gave Hardy a photograph of himself, inscribing it 'for Tom Hardy.—from *HRB* with *love*', presented him with a Bible, and wrote out for him the words of Charlotte Elliott's hymn, 'Just as I Am', with its refrain 'O Lamb of God, I come'.[47] The two young men were, indeed, devoted to each other. They had animated religious discussions both in and out of office hours —often meeting in a field on the Kingston Maurward estate about half-way between Dorchester and Higher Bockhampton—and Hardy's hitherto unreflective Anglicanism was severely tested by the argumentative resources brought to bear by Bastow and his allies Alfred and William Perkins, sons of the local Baptist minister and (though no older than Hardy himself) students at Aberdeen University. Somewhat dismayed by the absence of New Testament authority for infant baptism, still more dismayed by his opponents' familiarity with the Greek New Testament, Hardy responded as best he could by laborious perusal of the Griesbach text, purchased for the purpose in February 1860.[48]

What Hardy chiefly retained from the whole experience was a lasting respect for the example of 'plain living and high thinking' set by the Perkins household and especially by the father, the Revd Frederick Perkins, on whom Mr Woodwell, the Baptist minister of *A Laodicean,* is affectionately based. But he also long remembered and brooded over the occasion when Bastow and the younger Perkinses had persuaded him to attend a Baptist prayer meeting, only to strand him there, alone and embarrassed, while they were seduced by the secular attractions of a circus parade. A note of the middle 1860s on the discovery that one may blame oneself unnecessarily for actions or feelings which prove in fact to be morally superior to those of others ('that what we blamed is not blameable but great') cites as one instance 'going to the P. meeting that eveng & not finding the Perkins's there having been blaming self for wish to stay away'.[49]

Bastow left Hicks's office soon after the expiration of his articles, going first to London and thence to Hobart, Tasmania, where he set up on his own as an architect and surveyor. If it was indeed true, as Bastow claimed, that Hardy 'once professed to love a crucified saviour', such evangelical fervour did not long survive his friend's departure. 'Dont you dear Brother', wrote Bastow on 17 February 1861, soon after his arrival in Tasmania, 'forget our little meetings together at our place of assignation— and oh do let Jesus have the very best of all your time & thoughts.' As it became apparent from the perfunctoriness of Hardy's replies that his interests and enthusiasms were shifting elsewhere, Bastow's exhortations grew still more urgent: 'Dear old Tom dont you let your eye get off Jesus.—I did hear a whisper that *you* had begun

to think that *works may do something* in the way of salvation—
but dear fellow if you think so—dont oh dont for a moment let
it prevent your leaning for <u>all your</u> salvation on "Him".'[50] Hardy
eventually let the correspondence drop—even though he kept the
letters themselves to the end of his life—and continued in those
habits of regular churchgoing which Bastow and the Perkins
brothers had never quite managed to interrupt.* It is clear from
his marked copies of the Bible, *The Book of Common Prayer*,
and Keble's *The Christian Year* that throughout 1860 and especially 1861 he was reading his Bible regularly, attending church
frequently, and generally conducting himself as a 'churchy' young
man who might conceivably—should circumstances prove favourable—offer himself one day as a candidate for the ministry. Nor
is this surprising in view of the extent to which he was, during
this whole period, exposed to a variety of influences from the
remarkable Moule family.

The Revd Henry Moule, the vicar of Fordington St. George from
1829 until his death in 1880, was a strong Evangelical who became a national figure through his writings on a wide range of
theological, social, and horticultural topics, and his courageous
efforts, both parochial and political, at the time of the 1854 cholera
outbreak. He was also an inventor of some ingenuity and won
considerable fame, as may well be imagined, by his introduction
of the earth-closet. Of his seven sons who survived infancy most
had effective and even distinguished academic or ecclesiastical
careers. It is not clear just how the Hardys' connection with the
Moules began—whether through Hicks or William Barnes, as a
consequence of the family building business or even of Jemima's
service in the household of the vicar of Stinsford†—but so far as
Hardy himself was concerned it had a good deal to do with the
interest in water-colour sketching which he shared with Henry
Joseph Moule, the eldest of the 'seven brethren', subsequently
Curator of the Dorset County Museum.

Although Hardy is said to have made water-colour drawings

---

* Some special moment of spiritual decision or crisis does seem, however,
to have prompted Hardy's note alongside Ephesians 5: 8–24 in the Bible
given to him by Bastow: 'Wednesday night, April 17th/ 61, ¼ to 11.'[51]

† Jemima had certainly known the Revd Henry Moule for many years,
if only in his formal ministerial capacity; in her old age she recalled hearing
him preach in Dorchester barracks in the early 1830s.[52]

of animals for Mrs Martin at the age of nine or ten, the earliest such sketch which seems to have survived belongs to March 1856. It is indeed of an animal, 'Juno the I Half lop doe, six months old', but the preponderance among the early sketches is of architectural or topographical subjects: a view 'From Black Heath Corner', annotated 'Thos Hardy's first attempt at sketching from nature', is not dated, but the Old Manor House on the Kingston Maurward estate was drawn in May 1859 and Athelhampton Hall in August of the same year.[53]* After Henry Joseph Moule's death in 1904 Hardy wrote: 'His figure emerges from the obscurity of forgotten and half-forgotten things somewhere between 1856 and 1860, when I recall him as he stood beside me while I was attempting a sketch from nature in water colours. He must have been about thirty, and had already become an adept in out-door painting. As I was but a youth, and by no means practised in that art, he criticized my performance freely.' Hardy goes on to suggest that this may not have been a first encounter, since their fathers had had much discussion 'about a field which my father owned but had no use for, which the vicar had a mind to take for experiments in his well-known hobby of spade husbandry. Every year the question was renewed, and the field looked at, heads shaken, and the matter again shelved.'[55] If the shelving was characteristic of Hardy's father, the enthusiasm of the vicar, the readiness of Henry J. Moule to offer criticism and advice was to prove no less typical of the Moule family in general.

By the late 1850s Hardy had become friendly not only with the eldest of the brothers but also with the second, George, who December 1857; with the fifth, Charles, just launched on a successful academic career at Cambridge; and with the youngest, gave him a copy of the *Epitome of Alison's History of Europe* in Handley, later to become Bishop of Durham, who was exactly the same age as Mary Hardy.[56] Of far greater emotional and intellectual importance than these relationships—it seems safe to say, than any other male relationship throughout his life—was that with the fourth of the Moule brothers, Horatio Mosley, usually known as Horace. They were on close terms at least as early as 1857—when Horace gave Hardy a copy of Jabez Hogg's *Elements of Experimental and Natural Philosophy* ('T. Hardy / from his friend Horace')—and saw much of each other during the late

* A pencil drawing of an up-ended cart in a somewhat dilapidated farmyard is signed 'T. Hardy / 1854'.[54]

1850s and early 1860s, a period when Horace was 'much at home', largely as a result of his failure to complete a degree either at Oxford, to which he had first gone in 1851, or at Cambridge, to which he had transferred in 1854.[57]

The reasons for these difficulties are far from clear. Conceivably he ran into trouble, as many others had done, with the mathematical component of the Cambridge Tripos,* but this possibility squares neither with his Oxford difficulties nor with his tutoring in mathematics at a later date. Handley Moule remembered him as a much-loved brother, an excellent classical scholar, and a gifted teacher: 'Wonderful was his subtle faculty for imparting, along with all due care for grammatical precision, a living interest in the subject-matter, and for shedding an indefinable glamour of the ideal over all we read.'[58] Hardy always emphasized Horace Moule's devotion to music and the promise he had shown of becoming 'a distinguished English poet'.[59] At home in Fordington, Moule helped with the teaching of the group of paying pupils which his father had for some years gathered at the vicarage. He was chosen as the president of the 'Fordington Times Society', composed of the Moule brothers, their friends, and their father's pupils, which held weekly meetings on literary topics between April 1856 and December 1859: several of his pieces appear in *Tempora Mutantur*, a collection of prose and verse by members of the society which appeared in 1859. At the same time he was contributing reviews and occasional essays to national periodicals —a poem by his brother Charles portrays him as 'snatching rest, / Ere his review to "Fraser" goes'[60]—and completing work on his long dissertation, *Christian Oratory; An Inquiry into its History during the First Five Centuries,* which won the Hulsean Prize at Cambridge in 1858, and on *The Roman Republic; Being a Review of Some of the Salient Points in its History, Designed for the Use of Examination Candidates,* published by Bradbury and Evans in 1860.

Horace Moule's impact upon Hardy was immense. He was handsome, charming, cultivated, scholarly, thoroughly at home in the glamorous worlds of the ancient universities and of literary London. Although only eight years Hardy's senior, he was already an accomplished musician, a publishing poet and critic, and an

---

* Mathematics remained a compulsory element in the Previous Examination (taken in the student's second year) even after the separation of the Classical Tripos from the Mathematical Tripos in 1854.

independent thinker. He not only helped Hardy with his Greek but introduced him to new books and ideas—to Walter Bagehot's *Estimates of Some Englishmen and Scotchmen* of 1858, for example, and the controversial *Essays and Reviews* of 1860.[61] Although Moule seems never to have abandoned at least a formal allegiance to the Church, his attitude towards a work such as *Essays and Reviews* would certainly have been more open, more 'liberal', than that of his father and his clerical brothers—who were later to serve as models for Angel Clare's father and brothers in *Tess of the d'Urbervilles*. Moule's *Christian Oratory* carried an affectionate dedication to his father when it appeared in book form in 1859, but relations between them were sometimes strained. Indeed, the episode in Chapter 18 of *Tess* in which Angel Clare is rebuked by his horrified father for ordering a theologically offensive book from a local bookseller was based on just such a confrontation between Horace Moule and his father—the two volumes of the condemned work, Gideon Algernon Mantell's *The Wonders of Geology*, being passed on from Moule to Hardy in April 1858.[62]

In Horace Moule, Hardy recognized for the first time a model of what he himself most deeply wished to become, and his contact with the Moule brothers and with the life of Fordington vicarage both exacerbated his sense of inferiority and incited his ambition for self-improvement. He was deeply impressed by the kind of ideas and feelings reflected in the lecture on 'Oxford and the Middle Class Examinations' which Horace Moule gave in Dorchester Town Hall before the local Working Men's Mutual Improvement Society on 15 November 1858. Before explaining how recent changes at Oxford would make its advantages available to a wider middle-class public Moule sought to evoke the history of Oxford and the achievements of such Oxford men 'as Sir Robert Peel, Dr. Arnold, Professor Newman, and Mr. Gladstone'. So, in Hardy's *Jude the Obscure,* Jude Fawley hears the ghostly voices of great Christminster men—among them Peel, Newman, and Dr Arnold's son—as he walks among the colleges the night of his arrival. Moule's peroration, too, was evocative of just that kind of aspiration which moved Jude—and Hardy himself—to labour in solitude at Latin and Greek and to cherish for many years the hope of eventually going to university: 'The lecture was brought to a close by a recapitulation of some of the advantages arising from the study of a foreign literature, particularly that of a remote and ancient people, like the Greeks of the classical period. In enlarging upon this point Mr. Moule warmed into an eloquence which carried his audience away with him, and he sat down amid loud applause.'[63]

Unfortunately Hardy was to encounter all too soon the darker side of Moule's personality. Early in 1860 Moule went to live in the Cathedral Close at Salisbury—in lodgings kept by a former dancing master and Master of Ceremonies at the Salisbury balls— with two pupils whom he had undertaken to coach in Greek, Latin, and mathematics preparatory to their sitting Oxford and Cambridge entrance examinations. One of these pupils, Wynne Albert Bankes (of the Bankes family of Corfe Castle and Kingston Lacy), recorded in his diary that it quickly became apparent that Moule was 'a Dypsomaniac—and that he was suffering from D.T.', a condition which had its origin in his 'taking opium when reviewing books for Macmillan of Cambridge* at which he worked for 48 or 72 hours at a stretch'. Moule eventually recovered, and Bankes, whose previous naval experience had given him a good deal of worldly experience, agreed to continue with the otherwise satisfactory tutorial arrangement if Moule would neither have drink in the house nor go out of the house alone. The little group moved on 22 April to Lynton, in Devon, spent a few days in Oxford (where the second pupil took and failed his examination), and then proceeded to Saint-Germain-en-Laye for the summer. On Saturday, 28 July, Bankes went into Paris; Moule was to meet him there in time for church the following morning. On the Tuesday, when Moule still had not appeared, Bankes went back to Saint-Germain and discovered that he 'had ordered a bottle of claret on Saturday, that he had cut his whiskers off & had disappeared'. Bankes made daily visits to the Paris morgue and Horace's brothers Henry and Charles came to France to help in the search; on the following Sunday, 5 August, they heard by telegram that the truant had arrived safely back in England.[64]

Hardy visited Salisbury in 1860, catching (like Jude Fawley) his first glimpse of the cathedral 'through a driving mist that nearly hid the top of the spire'.[65] If, as seems most likely, he was accompanying his sister Mary on her admission to the Salisbury Training College on 3 April 1860,† he would have seen Moule in the course of recovery from the first of the two collapses recorded by Bankes. Hardy was certainly at Fordington Church for

---

* The Macmillan publishing house had its headquarters in Cambridge until 1863.

† She should have gone in January, like the other students in her year, but had perhaps been delayed by illness.[66]

Evensong on 5 August, the day on which Moule resurfaced after the second episode, and while he may have gone partly to hear that 'still small voice' lesson for the Ninth Sunday after Trinity, his choice of Fordington must have been made in the hope of hearing some news and perhaps as a gesture of sympathy to Horace's father —was it on this occasion, one wonders, that the latter preached on the text 'All the days of my appointed time will I wait, till my change come'?[67] By 1860, therefore, Hardy was already thoroughly familiar with Moule's alcoholism, and the survival of their friendship says much for that extraordinary charm which Moule in his happier moments seems to have exercised over all who encountered him.

In the aftermath of his French escapade, however, Moule seems to have made an extraordinary effort to restore stability to his life. In February 1861 he lectured on temperance at East Fordington, urging total abstinence upon those who lacked the self-discipline to drink in moderation; in January 1862 he gave the first performance on the new organ at West Fordington Church; two years later he went with his father to a missionary meeting at West Stafford.[68] There was nothing hypocritical about Moule's participation in such activities. His desperate search for approval from his austere father was at the heart of his difficulties, and his share in the moral earnestness characteristic of the Moule family served only to intensify the agonies of guilt and self-contempt which succeeded each episode of failure. What cannot be so precisely pinned down is the part played in his personal tragedy by that ambiguous sexuality which seems to have constituted the obverse, so to speak, of his gifts as a teacher and his devotion to the boys and young men who were his pupils.[69]

Hardy was very much aware at this period of the dazzling presence of one of those pupils, a brilliant young contemporary named Hooper Tolbort. Tolbort lived with his mother and his stepfather, a Dorchester ironmonger, and was apprenticed to a local chemist, but his talent and prodigious appetite for languages were so effectively encouraged both by his former schoolmaster, William Barnes, and by Horace Moule that he took first place, nationally, in the Oxford Middle Class (or Local) Examinations of 1859 and, three years later, in the competitive examinations for entry into the Indian Civil Service.[70] Hardy later incorporated several aspects of Tolbort's career in the presentation of Oswald Winwood, hero of a story called 'Destiny and a Blue Cloak', published in 1874 but probably written earlier. Winwood, product of an 'obscure little academy', looks forward to a successful future in India: ' "Thanks to Macaulay, of honored memory, I have as good a chance as the best of them!" he said, with ardor. "What a great thing competitive examination is; it will put good men in good places, and make inferior men move lower down; all bureaucratic jobbery will be swept away." '[71] The optimistic note of the mid-nineteenth-century success ethic and, more specifically, of Horace Moule's speech to the Dorchester working men can clearly be heard, although it is perhaps characteristic of Hardy that in the story the passage should be humorously undercut by Winwood's inability to explain what he means by the word 'bureaucratic'.

The wryness in Hardy's story may have sprung from the recollection of having himself seemed to Moule the less promising of his two protégés—slower intellectually, less gifted linguistically, not so well prepared academically, with less time to spend on his studies and smaller financial resources to fall back upon: 'the easy circumstances' of young Tolbort's situation, Hardy later recalled, 'left him much spare time, which he devoted entirely to study'. At the time when Moule was urging Tolbort on to spectacular examination successes he was counselling Hardy to concentrate on his architectural career rather than persist with the study of Greek plays. Though always loyal to Moule's memory, Hardy seems rather to have resented this advice, and that resentment may have contributed not only to Hardy's judgement that Tolbort's 'genius, as far as it showed itself, was receptive rather than productive',[72] but also to the patronizing attitudes displayed by Henry Knight towards his protégé Stephen Smith in *A Pair of Blue Eyes* and to that sense of promise denied which provides so much of the emotional impetus of *Jude the Obscure*.

In the meantime he remained very much in the shadow of Tolbort's brilliance. He is said to have written a number of poems in 1858 and 1859,* together with critical essays on Lamb and Tennyson, but not to have attempted to publish them; in his hesitancy and lack of self-confidence he perhaps did not show

* The surviving verses entitled 'Domicilium' perhaps belong with this group: the self-conscious Latin title suggests these years, and the marked Wordsworthian flavour may have derived from Horace Moule, who a few years later opened a debate at Marlborough College on the motion 'that Wordsworth, as a poet of thought and reflection, is superior to Tennyson'.[73]

them to anyone: even so close a friend as Bastow had no notion, as he later wrote, that Hardy 'considered the pen as one of the weapons of [his] *struggle for life*'.[74]

Hardy's articles with Hicks should have ended in 1859 but were extended for a further year 'in consideration of his immaturity', apparently an acknowledgement not of incompetence on his part but of a sense, shared by his employer and his parents alike, that he was still 'young' for his years and not quite ready to seek regular employment. When his fourth year was up, in the summer of 1860, Hicks kept him on as a paid assistant at the rate of fifteen shillings a week.[75] He was now for the first time earning money of his own, and could claim seniority over two more recent arrivals in the office. Business both ecclesiastical and secular was flourishing—there still survives a front elevation of some houses 'Designed by T. Hardy 1861'—but a sketch of Glastonbury Abbey dated March 1861, like a drawing of Stinsford Church done some time in the same year, suggests that Hardy, with his employer, was still primarily interested in churches. Hardy's drawing of the font at the little church of Coombe Keynes, restored by Hicks in 1860–1,[76] is a reminder of the way in which his early architectural experience gave him an ever broader and deeper familiarity with his native county, in this instance with the neighbourhood of Wool and Bindon Abbey, much drawn upon in *Tess of the d'Urbervilles*.

Hardy's departure for London in April 1862 seems in certain respects to have been a rather hurried affair, undertaken in response to some immediate pressure or distress. On 8 February 1862, a Saturday, he was in Trinity Church, Dorchester, writing the date in his prayerbook against the last verse of the Tate and Brady version of Psalm 43, one of the psalms for the day:

> Why then cast down, my soul? and why
> So much oppress'd with anxious care?
> On God, thy God, for aid rely,
> Who will thy ruin'd state repair.[77]

A flurry of notations in Bible, prayerbook, and *Christian Year* during the early months of 1862 may signify no more than a simple recording of date and place, an appreciation of a particular text, or the point reached in a programme of systematic reading through the New Testament or, less often, the Old. Some, on the other hand, have a directly personal reference, and the appearance among them of the initials 'M.' and 'M.W.' lends some support to the story that early in 1862 his proposal of marriage was rejected by Mary Waight, a young woman seven years his senior who was an assistant in one of the more genteel of the Dorchester shops.[78]

But if the actual timing of his departure was influenced by considerations of an emotional nature, the decision to go to London was in itself a perfectly rational step for a young man in his situation. Lacking the capital and social position—and perhaps the self-confidence—that might have enabled him to go into independent architectural practice, the obvious course, especially at that period of spectacular urban expansion, was to seek employment in London. Bastow had already advised him to that effect,[79] and the moment now seemed reasonably propitious. He was approaching his twenty-second birthday. He had completed his articles and gained experience as an architect's clerk—as his occupation is recorded in the 1861 Census. His father was in a bigger way of business than formerly and, while Henry and Kate were still at school, Mary had overcome a period of illness and was now out in the world, qualifying herself as a teacher at the Salisbury Training College: indeed the local newspaper had just announced that she had received 'a first-class certificate at the recent inspector's examination'.[80] It was clearly incumbent upon him to take another step along the path his mother had marked out for him, and architecture remained his only visible means of employment and advancement, whatever dreams he might retain —in the face of so many practical obstacles—of becoming a clergyman or even a clergyman-poet.

4

LONDON

T HE twenty-one-year-old Thomas Hardy who took the train
from Dorchester to London on Thursday, 17 April 1862, was
not an especially prepossessing young man.[1] His moustache had
grown in size and dignity, his hair was swept across the top of his
head in a slightly crested wave, and the face that looks, faintly
smiling, out of photographs taken in 1861 has aspirations towards
the kind of conventional Victorian handsomeness exemplified,
and somewhat caricatured, in the figure of Alec d'Urberville. But
Hardy was, at five foot six inches, noticeably below the average
in height, and while he was altogether healthier and stronger than
he had been in childhood he remained lightly built and distinctly
lacking in presence. Wide reading and exposure to the influence
and example of the Moule brothers had taught him much that
he could otherwise never have learned in Bockhampton or even
in Dorchester, but he was sadly lacking in worldly experience and
social assurance, and unmistakably countrified in his manners and
his speech—matters of some importance at a time when (as Hardy
himself later recalled) Londoners took a supercilious view of rural
newcomers and it was 'the aim of every provincial, from the squire
to the rustic, to get rid of his local articulation at the earliest
moment'.[2]

Hardy cannot have seemed especially likely to succeed or even to survive in London, and since he appears to have made no prior arrangements for employment or even for accommodation—since, too, he departed with a return railway ticket in his pocket—it is scarcely surprising that Hicks, for one, confidently expected him to return home defeated within a few weeks.[3] In fact, Hardy established himself in the city with quite remarkable rapidity and ease. He found lodgings at 3 Clarence Place, Kilburn,* on the east side of the Edgware Road just north of the junction with Quex Road. The area was still largely one of fields and farms, in the process of becoming absorbed into the vast urban mass to the south, and the Kilburn Gate from which he took the omnibus 'for London' each day was an actual turnpike gate until 1868. Hardy quickly located the parish church, St. Mary's, found it 'rather to my taste', and became a regular worshipper there throughout the remainder of 1862.[4] His immediate professional future was determined with similar promptness. Of the two letters of introduction he carried, the one to Benjamin Ferrey (the designer of Dorchester Town Hall) proved of little value, but the other, written by Hicks, led almost immediately to his employment by Arthur Blomfield, who happened to be in need of 'a young Gothic draughtsman who could restore and design churches and rectory-houses'.[5]

Blomfield, the son of a former Bishop of London, was already, in his early thirties, a successful architect with a large ecclesiastical practice. His office was at 9 St. Martin's Place, just off Trafalgar Square, where Hardy soon became 'as familiar with St Martin's bells as one so near could well be, and with the clock face—or rather the half of it visible from our windows'.[6] Hardy found his new employer extremely congenial, while Blomfield, for his part, was sufficiently impressed with his new draughtsman to propose him, as early as October 1862, for membership of the Architectural Association (motto: 'Design with Beauty. Build in Truth'); Hardy's formal election along with that of John Lee, another of Blomfield's assistants, followed in November.[7] Clearly, Hicks had given his pupil a good grounding. Clearly, too, Hardy was extremely fortunate in his early London contacts and arrangements.†

* Several families appear to have lived in this building and it is not clear with whom Hardy actually lodged. The shop at street level was occupied by Thomas Edwards, a master shoemaker. A young architect's clerk named Charles Muncey was living near by and it was perhaps through his agency that Hardy found his way there.

† John Norton, to whom Hicks's letter of introduction was addressed, had been a vice-president of the Royal Institute of British Architects, the senior professional association; Blomfield himself was president of the Architectural

He could manage comfortably, though not lavishly, on the salary of £110 a year he now received from Blomfield, especially since he shared his Clarence Place rooms with another young architect named Shaw. The two got on well together, despite the fact that Shaw's background was both socially and financially superior to Hardy's own. A visible sign of this difference was the set of silver cutlery with which Shaw's parents had equipped him. The young men's landlady resented the responsibility of these expensive items and showed her disapproval by noisily rattling them in her basket as she carried them upstairs after dinner each evening—a performance Hardy later alluded to as 'the procession of the plate'.[8] It was Shaw, naturally enough, to whom Hardy turned for the loan of a dress coat in which he could attend the Architectural Association Conversazione on 31 October at which his name was to be proposed for membership. Though impressed by the presence of numerous ladies 'in full dress', Hardy in his subsequent letter to his sister Mary referred rather scathingly to the proceedings themselves ('After lots of speechifying by learned professors, there was music &c, and coffee—this last rather in small quantities'),[9] and he seems to have taken little further part in the social side of the Association's activities.

In February 1863 Blomfield moved his office the short distance to 8 Adelphi Terrace, the fine Adam Brothers block which stood on part of the site now occupied by Shell-Mex House. 'The new office is a capital place,' Hardy told his sister. 'It is on the first floor and on a terrace that overlooks the river. We can see from our window right across the Thames, and on a clear day every bridge is visible. Everybody says that we have a beautiful place.'[10] From the window nearest him and from the balcony outside he was able to watch the building of the Thames Embankment and the Charing Cross railway bridge; on his way to work each day he saw the station itself going up on ground previously occupied by the old Hungerford Market. At that period of unprecedented urban expansion both the physical and the social faces of London

Association for 1861–2. J. A. Bunker, seconder of Hardy's nomination to the A.A., and Walter Paris, a pupil of Benjamin Ferrey's with whom he became friendly, were on the Committee of the A.A. in 1862–3; while Paris and G. T. Molecey, Hardy's other friend in Ferrey's office, were joint secretaries of the Class of Design at the A.A. in 1863–4—during the second presidency of Professor T. Roger Smith, later to be Hardy's employer.

were undergoing rapid and permanent change, and Hardy was later to treasure the glimpses he had caught of men, customs, manners, entertainments, and ways of life that were soon to vanish forever: 'It was quite Dickens's London in those days.'[11]

He heard Dickens himself lecture in the spring of 1863; in September 1864 he went along the Strand to the London School of Phrenology to have his head read by the proprietor, 'Dr' C. Donovan; soon after his first arrival he heard Palmerston speak; on 27 October 1865 he went with John Lee and with Blomfield's colleague Clement Heaton, the glass painter, to attend Palmerston's funeral in Westminster Abbey. In his letter to Mary the next day he was fully sensitive to the historical dimensions of Palmerston's career—to the fact that he had 'been connected with the govt off and on for the last 60 years, & that he was contemporaneous with Pitt, Fox, Sheridan, Burke &c. I mean to say his life overlapped theirs so to speak'. Hardy danced at Willis's Rooms in St. James's—the former Almack's—almost, it would seem, for the sake of being able to say that he had done so (as in the poem 'Reminiscences of a Dancing Man'), but he was otherwise too unsure of himself, and too impecunious, to venture far or often into the dubious world of the saloons and cider cellars, of 'gallant resorts' such as the Cremorne and the Argyle: with characteristic ambiguity he recorded of these latter that 'he did not dance there much himself, if at all'.[12]

Apart from visits to theatres and occasionally to restaurants— including Bertolini's, off Leicester Square, with Paris and Molecey, his friends from Benjamin Ferrey's office—Hardy seems, in fact, to have kept to a fairly strict routine of work and study during his first London years and deliberately shunned the more garish aspects of the city's night life, with its teeming crowds, its casual violence, and its open and even aggressive prostitution. But he walked regularly through Soho and across the Seven Dials, along the Strand and past the Adelphi arches, and could not remain unaware of the extraordinary juxtapositions of splendour and squalor, of optimism and despair, which London then offered. Nor was he immune to the excitement caused by the scandals of the day, by the annual holidays and sporting occasions, or by such events as the public execution of five pirates at Newgate in February 1864. His worst experience of London crowds was on 10 March 1863 when he went out to see the illuminations following the wedding of the Prince of Wales and the Princess of Denmark and was caught in a dense mass in Piccadilly, 'where my waistcoat buttons were torn off and my ribs bent in before I could get into a doorway'.[13]

During his first six or seven months in London Hardy spent much of his free time at the International Exhibition at South Kensington, the successor to the Great Exhibition of 1851 and the predecessor of the Victoria and Albert Museum. Though his own interest was chiefly in the displays of materials and artefacts related to architecture and in the rich collection of English paintings (European artists were more thinly represented), the popular appeal of the exhibition was far wider and more various. One evening in the early summer he 'found' his cousin Martha Sparks, then working in London as a lady's maid, and took her to the Exhibition. Visitors from Dorset—including his sister Mary—had also to be taken there, and at least one visit was made in the company of Horace Moule, whose poem, 'Ave Caesar', inspired by one of the paintings in the Exhibition, Gérôme's *Roman Gladiators,* Hardy was to recall to public attention sixty years later.[14]

On 7 August Moule had descended upon him in a state of high excitement at the news of Hooper Tolbort's spectacular success in the Indian Civil Service competitive examinations for 1862.[15] Moule—whether out of curiosity, genuine religious inclination, or self-conscious rebellion against his background it seems impossible to say—was on his way to attend the service held each seventh of August in the Jesuit Chapel in Farm Street to celebrate the anniversary of the Society's restoration. Hardy went with him to what proved to be an impressive occasion and then on by cab— a vehicle to which Hardy was evidently unaccustomed—to Covent Garden and supper at the Hummums Hotel, named for its Turkish baths and known as a favourite haunt of young bachelors.[16] Of particular importance for Hardy's intellectual development at the time was the renewal of his friendship with Hooper Tolbort himself, who had come to London in the autumn of 1861 to facilitate his further linguistic studies: 'In 1862 I frequently met him there', wrote Hardy later, adding that he was usually to be found, either at his rooms or at the Marylebone Library and Scientific Institution, 'scribbling translations into and from dead and living languages'.[17]

Just before the International Exhibition closed at the end of October 1862, Thomas Hardy, Sen., came to town for a few days and was given into the care, while Hardy himself was at work, of a 'Miss A.'—evidently a family friend or connection of his father's generation.[18]* Hardy was an enthusiastic opera-goer at this period —in after years the music of *Il Trovatore* always carried him back to his first year in London when he was 'strong and vigorous and enjoyed life immensely'— and he took both his father and Miss A. to see Wallace's *Lurline* at Covent Garden; nothing, however, as he reported to Mary, 'would satisfy Father unless he went to see the Thames Tunnel'. In the same letter Hardy made gentle fun of their father's broad Dorset accent and indulged in a little verbal humour for his sister's amusement: 'I wish you wd tell me how u.r. when u. write. I have a "cowdid by head" so I have stayed in all day to be all right to morrow.'[20] The Hardys were reunited at Bockhampton that Christmas—Mary enjoying a brief respite between the conclusion of her training at Salisbury and the commencement of her first teaching appointment in a Berkshire village—and there was talk of Shaw coming too. The latter had already met Hardy's father at Clarence Place in October; even so, it is worth noting that Hardy, while registering that his friend would be considered 'a great gun' in the world of Stinsford, evinced no social qualms about introducing him—as he had already introduced Bastow and the Moules—into the intimacy of his family circle.[21]

Hardy's submission of prize-winning entries for two architectural competitions in the spring of 1863 should have marked a high point in his professional aspirations, but neither success was unqualified. At a General Meeting of the Royal Institute of British Architects on 18 May he was presented by the president, T. L. Donaldson, with the Institute's Silver Medal for his essay 'On the Application of Colored Bricks and Terra Cotta to Modern Architecture', based largely on researches he had made in the Reading

* She was almost certainly Eliza Amey, the unmarried aunt of the orphaned Eliza Amey of Dorchester, a classmate of Mary Hardy's at Salisbury. The 'H.A.' mentioned in two of Hardy's letters to Mary during the 1860s was said by Kate Hardy (interviewed by Harold Hoffman shortly before her death) to have been a friend of their mother's with the first name of Henrietta. She can perhaps be identified, therefore, with the Henrietta Adams who was one of the witnesses of a marriage at Stinsford Church in 1852 and seems to have been in service at Stinsford House—where Jemima Hardy had once worked. A June 1866 note of Hardy's, partly in shorthand, reads: 'In a novel,—Make H. (Antell) an orphan, brought up with a large family.' No feasible H. Antell has been traced, however, and it is possible that the 'H.' here stood for 'Hero' and that the 'Antell' (if I have indeed read the shorthand correctly) was John Antell, the Puddletown shoemaker.[19]

Room at South Kensington. The judges, not disarmed by the somewhat self-deprecating motto ('Tentavi, quid in eo genere possem') under which the essay had been submitted, had earlier announced that since the author had 'scarcely gone sufficiently into the subject proposed' and had seriously skimped 'that portion referring to moulded and shaped bricks', he would not be given the additional cash prize of ten pounds—which was reserved as a prize for an essay on the same subject the following year. Since the portion Hardy was accused of skimping had not been part of the topic as originally announced but had been added in a subsequent announcement, he wrote to the RIBA to explain that he had been unaware of the change and to ask that he be allowed to enlarge his essay and thus qualify for the prize in its entirety; his request was, however, refused on the grounds that he could resubmit for the cash prize in a year's time.[22] Although the RIBA position was not unreasonable, Hardy resented the way in which the announcement of the prize had significantly diminished its honorific as well as its financial value. A few years later that resentment surfaced in an episode in his first novel, *The Poor Man and the Lady,* in which a company publicly retracted an award it had already made. Although Hardy carefully preserved his Silver Medal, the essay itself has disappeared, and it is tempting to give credence to the story that shortly after the prize had been awarded Hardy went to the Institute library, asked for the essay, and simply walked off with it.[23]

On 19 February 1863, before he had learned the result of the RIBA competition, Hardy reported to Mary that he was 'now very busy getting up a design for a Country Mansion for which a small prize is offered—£3 the best & £2 the second best'.[24] The competition* was open to members of the Architectural Association—the plan of the imaginary site having been 'laid on the table' at the Association's meeting in 12 December 1862. Hardy again won the first prize and presumably borrowed Shaw's dress coat once more in order to make a proper appearance at the Conversazione of 17 April 1863 at which the prizes were presented—Hardy's coming in the form of William Nesfield's *Specimens of Mediaeval Architecture* and Norman Shaw's *Architectural Sketches from the Continent.*[25] Professor T. Roger Smith and the other judges of the competition made no public criticism of Hardy's entry, but it

---

* It bore the name of William Tite, its instigator and donor, but should not be confused with the prestigious Sir William Tite Prize of later date.

The Hardy cottage, Higher Bockhampton

Jemima Hardy, photographed by W. Pouncy of Dorchester, 1876

Thomas Hardy senior, photographed in Bath, 1877

Kate Hardy, as a young woman

Believed to be Mary Hardy, as a young woman

Horace Moule

Thomas Hardy, photographed by
W. Pouncy of Dorchester, *c.* 1856

Horace Moule *(centre, in front of window)* with his mother and some of his
father's pupils, Fordington vicarage, *c.* 1860

Louisa Harding

Tryphena Sparks

became embarrassingly clear that the number of competitors had been extremely small—perhaps no more than the two prize-winners themselves.*

On 12 May 1863 Hardy began, in a notebook headed 'Schools of Painting', succinct summaries of factual information about major painters and their works from the Renaissance onwards. The notebook is obviously relevant to his frequent statement that about this time he considered the possibility of training himself to become an art critic, and other notes on paintings survive from the same period: in his copy of the *Golden Treasury,* for example, the line 'The bloom of young Desire and purple light of Love' from Gray's 'The Progress of Poesy' is annotated 'mem: S.K. Museum. Etty. 1863', evidently a reference to William Etty's *Cupid and Psyche* in the Sheepshanks Collection.[27] But the notebook also bore upon his ambitions as an architect: he was thinking of sitting the Voluntary Architectural Examinations of the RIBA, and may have embarked upon the study of art history (one of the components of the examination) in one of the summer classes provided by the Architectural Association for the assistance of prospective candidates. 'You never told me a word about the voluntary examination,' wrote Bastow late in 1863. 'Surely you are the very fellow who would go in for it . . . and get it too.'[28]

Although Hardy does not seem to have sat the actual examination, he had by no means resigned himself to the prospect, as Bastow put it, of writing 'A.A. for Architects assistant' all his life. His work for Blomfield had turned out to be generally—and disappointingly—of a routine kind. Although he had been taken on as an assistant architect, he spent most of his time in preparing the working drawings necessary for the realization of the designs more broadly outlined by Blomfield himself. Even when annotations in Hardy's hand appear on surviving plans, as in the case of All Saints, Windsor, built by Blomfield in 1862–4,[29] it remains probable that he was not directly responsible for the actual design work, except for certain details here and there.† Blomfield, as his

---

* Again, the design is not known to have survived, although ground plans of large houses sketched in Hardy's architectural notebook may bear some relation to it. A plan of some labourers' cottages in the same section of the notebook suggests that he may at least have contemplated a submission to another Architectural Association competition, 'for the most approved Designs for Cottages for the Labouring Classes'.[26]

† It is proper to add that in the judgement of Dr C. J. P. Beatty, the leading authority on Hardy's architectural career, Hardy's participation in this and other projects of Blomfield's was of a more active and creative kind.

own nephew later recalled, was too busy and successful to give much attention to the instruction and supervision of his pupils and assistants, or even to the continuing development of his own architectural style.[30] For Hardy, however, this at least meant that he was kept in constant employment and had frequent opportunities to get out of the office and visit some of the many sites where building was going on.

Hardy also much appreciated his employer's wry humour—when one of the pupils rubbed clean a portion of the Adam fireplace at Adelphi Terrace as a broad hint to the charwoman, Blomfield made him wash it all himself—and the unfailing geniality that made the office such an easygoing place, known then and later for its boisterous good fellowship and its practical jokes, some of them played upon what Blomfield's young men regarded as the unnecessarily solemn and dangerously radical members of the Reform League, whose headquarters were on the ground floor of 8 Adelphi Terrace. Hardy shared Blomfield's love of music and joined as best his rather weak voice would allow in the glees and catches with which the office often resounded; the 'choir' lacked an alto, however, and Blomfield would tell Hardy that if ever he met an alto in the Strand he should 'ask him to come in and join us'.[31] Precisely because his own labours were generally of a mechanical kind, Hardy was able to allow his mind to dwell on nonarchitectural matters even during working hours, and he struck one of his juniors at that time as being quieter than most of his colleagues, 'very regular' in his attendance, gentle in speech and movement, 'rather dreamy' in manner, and much given to talking about literature and the writers of the day.[32]

In November 1863 Hardy went to Windsor with Blomfield to be present at the laying of the memorial stone of All Saints by the Crown Princess of Germany—the Princess's embarrassed uncertainty as to what to do with the mortar-laden trowel subsequently providing him with material for a brief scene in *The Poor Man and the Lady*. Other expeditions outside London appear to have been nonprofessional, including a visit to Dover in September 1862 and another to Brighton—where he sketched the crowds on the beach—on Good Friday of 1863.[33] One weekend in late April 1863 he paid a short visit to his sister Mary, who was now teaching in the little National School at Denchworth, about fifteen miles from Oxford. In addition to her regular duties Mary had been obliged, much against her will, to undertake the role of church organist, although her previous experience had been confined to the piano and harmonium. Burdened with new responsibilities, isolated from the accustomed society and reassurances of her home, Mary felt lonely and starved of affection and begged that Kate be allowed to join her. Jemima eventually yielded, and in 1863, when she was still only six, Kate was sent to Denchworth to live with Mary and get her early schooling—the beginning of an arrangement which lasted, with only occasional interruptions, for the rest of their lives. Jemima's willingness to part with her youngest child at such a tender age suggests (not for the first time) a certain lack of maternal warmth; on the other hand, it is indicative of the closeness of the Hardy children, despite their differences in age and temperament, that Kate should have looked back on this time as one of particular happiness.[34]

On a subsequent visit to Denchworth, in 1864, Hardy went over to the village at Fawley, just south of Wantage, where his maternal grandmother had been born, as Mary Head, in 1772. Mary Hardy had already been there and reported to her brother that the inhabitants, 'among the most original & hearty set [that] could ever be', seemed 'quite cut off from the rest of us'; she could find no Heads living there, but was told of two farmers of that name, brothers, from the nearby hamlet of Chaddleworth, one of whom had married but remained childless while the other had disappeared the day after his wedding and returned many years later as an old man.[35] Hardy evidently found out more about the Heads of Chaddleworth—from the parish registers if not from personal contact—and made, in Fawley itself, the acquaintance of those who could tell him more of the history of his grandmother's people and thus lay, all unconsciously, some of the foundations of *Jude the Obscure*.

Early in 1863 Hardy for some reason made a temporary move from 3 Clarence Place to 9 Clarence Place, occupied by a plumber named Isaac Bounford. Four months later he took lodgings at 16 Westbourne Park Villas, a street of solid and comfortable semi-detached houses running parallel to the Great Western Railway line just west of the Paddington terminus. Hardy's room was on the second floor at the rear of the house, looking out over the gardens and stables to the backs of the houses on the north side of Westbourne Park Road and the spire which at that time crowned the tower of St. Stephen's Church.* Although the West-bourne Park area was 'better' and more convenient than Clarence Place, these were clearly not its only advantages from Hardy's point of view. On at least two occasions during his residence at Kilburn he had walked the mile and more to the south-west to attend service at St. Stephen's. It is possible that Martha Sparks or one of her brothers was living in the vicinity: both Nathaniel and James seem to have been living in London at this period.[36] It is certain that at 2 (later renumbered 40) Orsett Terrace, just a few minutes' walk from 16 Westbourne Park Villas, a young woman named Eliza Bright Nicholls was employed as a lady's maid in the family of Charles Richard Hoare, barrister-at-law, the son of the Ven. Charles James Hoare, Archdeacon of Surrey.[37]

Eliza Nicholls was the most important figure in Hardy's early emotional life—they seem to have been more or less formally engaged from about 1863 until 1867—and a focus for some of the many indecisions of his London years. Born in Sussex, Eliza had lived for many years in the coast-guard cottages at Kimmeridge Bay, on the South Dorset coast, where her Cornish-born father, George Nicholls, served as a coast-guard until the late 1850s. A serious operation then forced his retirement to his wife's birth-place, the Sussex village of Findon, and the management of the Running Horse inn (now Nepcote House).[38] It is not impossible that Hardy met Eliza while her family was still at Kimmeridge, but their emotional involvement seems to date from Hardy's London period. 'I suppose you have scarcely been and gone and lost your heart yet, young man,—have you?' Henry Bastow had written from Tasmania in May 1861 '—you must let me know when it has come to that and tell me who is the fair damsel—though I still am of opinion that you are not of a highly inflam-mable nature—.'[39] Even allowing for Bastow's imperfect insight into his character, it seems safe to assume that Hardy had not deeply committed himself at the time of Bastow's departure, and by then Eliza Nicholls, who was only a year younger than Hardy, was already in service in London—as the personal attendant of Charles Richard Hoare's wife, Emma, the daughter of Lieutenant-Colonel John Mansel of Smedmore House, situated within a mile or so of Kimmeridge Bay.

---

* The spire, visible in a sketch drawn by Hardy in 1866, was damaged during the Second World War and taken down shortly afterwards.

Eliza and her father were to become major sources for Hardy's interest in the South Dorset coast and in its lively smuggling past. More immediately, his relationship with her was the principal source of the 'She, to Him' sequence and the several other sonnets related to it. Although the drawing by Hardy printed opposite 'She, to Him. I' in *Wessex Poems* is somewhat dark and indistinct, it shows a male and a female figure walking or standing hand in hand on a path leading towards a building identifiable as Clavel Tower, which still stands on the cliff-top at the eastern side of Kimmeridge Bay, immediately above the coast-guard cottages in which Eliza Nicholls once lived. Hardy naturally associated the spot with her and may well have visited it in her company on 3 September 1863, the date which appears on his sketches of Gad Cliff and Worbarrow Bay, not far along the coast from Kimmeridge.[40] If the visit to Brighton on Good Friday of 1863 had in fact been an incident in a longer visit to Eliza and her parents at Findon, then it is possible that by the late summer of 1863 an understanding between them had become firmly established, warranting Eliza's introduction to Bockhampton and to Hardy's own parents. Eliza's departure from London for Godstone, Surrey, at about this time in order to nurse Archdeacon Hoare during his last illness may have been a factor in bringing matters to a head. The 'She, to Him' sonnets are dated 1866 by Hardy and reflect in their tone and subject matter the decline rather than the climax of his relationship with Eliza Nicholls—a relationship which seems always to have been somewhat one-sided, with the commitment greater and deeper on her part than on his, but whose mere existence, as a settled and reasonably satisfactory arrangement, perhaps gave Hardy a confidence he had hitherto lacked, while Eliza's religious earnestness and interest in books served to re-awaken enthusiasms and ambitions that had become temporarily overlain by the practical business of establishing himself in London and in his profession.

It was at 16 Westbourne Park Villas, at all events, that Hardy's literary career can be properly said to have begun. In that summer of 1863 he was already reading a great deal of Shakespeare, in the ten-volume edition purchased soon after his arrival in the new lodgings; he also worked his way through much of Samuel Neil's *The Art of Reasoning: A Popular Exposition of the Principles of Logic, Inductive and Deductive, with an Introductory Outline of the History of Logic,* and addressed himself to the study of models of argumentative prose. On Horace Moule's recommendation he purchased J. R. M'Culloch's *Principles of Political Economy,* only to be further instructed by his friend, in a letter of 2 July 1863, that he should not read M'Culloch or *The Times* or any such examples for their style but only for their content: 'you must in the end write *your own* style,' Moule insisted, 'unless you wd be a mere imitator. It always appears to me that a man whose mind is full of a subject, or who can before writing make his mind full of it, has only to pay that attention to method and arrangement which is obvious to any mind of vigorous tone, in order to write well.'[41] In the autumn of that year Hardy began the study of short-hand—the date 1 October 1863 appears in one of several primers, embodying different systems, he purchased at about this time—and by Christmas he was able to report to Mary that he could do forty words a minute.[42]

These latter preparations were all directed towards the possibility of undertaking some sort of literary journalism. In February 1864, when Moule wrote to advise Hardy on the use of the subjunctive in English, he also raised the possibility of his becoming the London correspondent of a country newspaper: 'You know the sort of berth I mean—that of a man who sends down a column of condensed London news & talk.' The piece Hardy had just sent him, he added, a 'chatty description of the Law Courts & their denizens', was 'just in the style that wd go down'.[43] Hardy was by now ready to try almost anything in his search for some kind, any kind, of journalistic work. In that period of proliferating quarterlies, monthlies, and weeklies—some political, some literary, some humorous, some highly miscellaneous—it seemed reasonable to hope that he might find a niche somewhere. Moule, after all, had published articles, reviews, and poems in *Fraser's,* the *Saturday Review,* the *Quarterly Review,* and elsewhere, and Hardy also had before him the example—no less seductive for being cast in fictional terms—of those busy literary men of Thackeray's, George Warrington and Arthur Pendennis. At this stage he was still too unsure of himself, too countrified and inexperienced, to imagine that he might one day make a living as a writer. His hopes were still fixed upon that persistently cherished dream of entering the Church, and he had it in mind to follow the example of his aunt Martha's brother-in-law, George Brereton Sharpe, who had abandoned his first profession of medicine, gone through Cambridge and become a curate in Wales. Hardy had as yet no capital, however, and no source of income other than that architectural career which was still necessarily occupying the bulk of his time, and literary journalism seemed a feasible and appealing way of financing himself during the many years he would need to devote to his university studies.

Hardy was at home in Dorset for the Christmas festivities of 1864, spending the evening of Boxing Day in Puddletown with his cousin Nathaniel Sparks.[44] On New Year's Day Horace Moule presented him with the copy of *The Thoughts of the Emperor M. Aurelius Antoninus* that he was to keep at his bedside until he died, inscribed with the quotation from within the volume that was to become one of his principal watchwords, 'This is the chief thing: Be not perturbed: for all things are according to the nature of the universal.'[45] Whether Moule intended the inscription to bear directly upon Hardy's personal situation or upon the anxieties he had expressed for Moule himself in his erratic course, it is hard to guess, but 1865 was in any case a year in which some of Hardy's central uncertainties about his life and career began to move towards resolution. In December 1864 he had submitted to the Edinburgh-based *Chambers's Journal* a prose sketch, 'How I Built Myself a House', originally written for the amusement of his colleagues in Blomfield's office as a satirical comment upon the current building boom and the architect–client relationship. The acceptance and publication of the sketch, in March 1865, Hardy once spoke of as having 'determined' his career, no doubt because the sale of the copyright brought him his first literary earnings, of £3.15.0.[46] No less significant, however, was his deliberately setting himself up as a poet in that same year.

He bought several volumes of poetry—writing 'T.H. 1865' against the title of 'Winter' in Thomson's *Seasons*—and copies of Nuttall's *Standard Pronouncing Dictionary* and Walker's *Rhyming Dictionary*. He also began a notebook, headed 'Studies, Specimens &c', which provides a wonderfully detailed insight into the nature of his early literary enthusiasms and the methodicalness with which he set about the business of making himself a poet. The chief sources of the many quotations and word lists in the early part of the notebook include the Old Testament, *The Golden Treasury*, Spenser, Shakespeare, Burns, Byron, Wordsworth (*The Excursion*), Scott (chiefly *The Lord of the Isles* and *Marmion*), Shelley (*Laon and Cythna*), Tennyson (*In Memoriam*), Jean Ingelow, William Barnes, and especially Swinburne, to whose

Poems and Ballads, published in 1866, Hardy responded with something like rapture, reading the volume while walking along crowded London streets at imminent risk (so he told Swinburne thirty years later) of being knocked down.[47] Hardy makes brief technical observations upon some of these, as upon a number of prose passages dating mostly from the late 1860s.

In the same notebook are lists of citations, headed 'Dic' (for 'Dictionary' or 'Diction'), in which various usages of the same word are exemplified. The following comes from a paragraph devoted to words beginning with the letter *c*: 'to *carry high*: *carry* me *away*: *carry back* to: *carry* me *down to* future years: *carry forth*: [her eyes *carried f.* the tale of her heart]: to *carry on*: days may *carry out* the dream: . . .' It was perhaps an idea suggested by Horace Moule's typically abortive experience as collector of entries for letter *H* of the *New English Dictionary*.[48] Other paragraphs bear the sub-heading 'Inv.', presumably for 'Inventions', and list word coinages on particular patterns, as in: 'a clouding—: an icing—: a grounding: a toning—: a shaping—: a curing—: a nerving—: a leafing: . . .' Especially remarkable are the long word lists headed 'Con' or 'Concoc' (apparently for 'Concoctions'), in which Hardy worked through a passage from the Old Testament or *The Book of Common Prayer,* picking up particular words and using them in modified grammatical forms and totally different contexts, evidently with the objective of developing and exercising a literary vocabulary of his own, generating new expressive phrases from the impulsion of great models from the past, or even of evolving the outline of a possible poem. Years later Hardy was to tell his second wife that the best way to find a starting point for a piece of writing was to go to some work by a major writer— Carlyle, for instance—and read at random until one came across an image or idea that stimulated one's own inventiveness.[49]

At the back of 'Studies, Specimens &c' is a page on which Hardy seems to be trying out phrases entirely of his own making, deliberately inventing new epithets or fresh uses for old ones—as in '*clanging* thunder, humble bee: *pealing* waves *whooping* storm: *clicking* twigs: *flapping* of leaves: *creaking* of trunks, & *wrenching* of branches: . . .' Although the setting down of these particular images probably dates from 1868 rather than from 1865, they simply represent a later stage in the process of self-education and self-development to which the whole notebook is dedicated. Hardy's comments upon Shakespeare, Byron, Swinburne, and the rest are not incidental critical observations but personal memoranda, directive reminders of the ways in which particular literary effects might best be achieved, a distinctive poetic voice projected. An early note, probably dating from about this same period, is eloquent of his conception of working through imitation to originality: 'Lyrical Meth Find a situn from expce. Turn to Lycs for a form of expressn that has been used for a quite difft situn. Use it (Same sitn from experience may be sung in sevl forms.)'[50]

Hardy was meanwhile filling his pocket-books with notes and occasional drawings of things observed from day to day—street scenes, skyscapes, human encounters seen or heard—and especially with ideas and outlines of potential stories or poems. One such note begins:

?[1863–7]

July 18. *Poem* (ballad metre) [good]
    rough outline—
1. "I sat me down in a foreign town,
    And looked across the way: { sitting
      At a window there was a lady { fair
    Far] fairer than the day.   { leaning
      [Rhyme only 2nd & 4th lines]
2. "Twelve blessed days she won my gaze
    Twelve days She looked at me", &c

Then follows a prose summary of a story about a man and a woman who fall in love by correspondence without ever meeting. The man sees the woman by chance, but she eludes him until, at last, she writes that she will marry him secretly if he will trust her sufficiently to meet him at the church at an agreed hour. Just as the marriage is about to take place it becomes apparent that she is dumb: 'He jumps from her in horror—She falls—He goes away —thinks of her—returns—dead.' The note concludes with another draft stanza:

    "Six times I named a trysting place,
      Six times replièd she:
    "Perhaps I prize thy love likewise
      But to meet—it cannot be!"
[This ballad was never finished][51]

The three pocket-book pages on which the original entry was made were torn out many years later and inserted in a notebook headed 'Poetical Matter' in which Hardy systematically gathered together fragments from the past which might still prove useable as material for new poems. The words and dates within square brackets were evidently added at this second stage, and the combination of these later notations with the original prose outline and verse fragments provides an excellent example of Hardy's working methods, of what he meant when he spoke of a poem as being 'from an old draft',[52] and of the way in which, early and late, his perpetual fascination with the possibilities of narrative found its natural expression in verse at least as often as in prose.

In the margin of Henry Reed's *Introduction to English Literature,* purchased in 1865, Hardy drew a line against the words: 'It is a bewildering thing to stand in the presence of a vast concourse of books—in the midst of them, but feeble, or uncertain, or helpless in the using of them. . . . It is mournful to think that the multitudinous oracles should be dumb to us.'[53] He was now poetically active, and had received from the editor of *Chambers's* the message that he was capable of writing what magazines were interested in printing; even so, he had lost none of his old sense of the need for further self-education if he was to be successful in a literary or indeed in any career. In October 1865 he enrolled in a French extension class at King's College, London—a short walk from Adelphi Terrace—and worked his way, under the guidance of Léonce Stièvenard, through substantial portions of both Stièvenard's own *Lectures françaises* and the *Half Hours of French Translation* compiled by Alphonse Mariette, the Professor of French at King's. Sixty years later Hardy spoke warmly of Stièvenard and clearly remembered the old room and its desks, but added, 'I did not do much in class, I fear'—an impression which his heavily annotated copies of the two textbooks do not entirely confirm.[54]

There is little surviving evidence of Hardy's early thinking on the great contemporary issues of science and religion, of social and political change. He used to say that he was among the earliest readers of *On the Origin of Species,* first published in 1859, but it is possible to document for these years only his reading of such thinkers as Fourier, Comte, Newman, and Mill. In 1863 he drew a series of elaborate 'Diagrams shewing Human Passion, Mind, & Character', based in all essentials upon the ideas of Fourier. In the summer of 1865 he was reading John Stuart Mill—no doubt moved to do so by the impressive glimpse he had caught of Mill himself as he stood on the hustings in Covent Garden on the occasion of his nomination as a Parliamentary candidate for Westminster—and Newman's *Apologia,* on which he made quite extensive notes.[55] Horace Moule, who had urged him to read Newman, also passed on his copy of the 1865 translation of Auguste Comte's *A General View of Positivism.* Some of the numerous marginal markings appear to be Moule's, but others are certainly Hardy's and show that he was particularly familiar with the chapters on 'The Intellectual Character of Positivism' and 'The Influence of Positivism on Women'. His outlook at this period seems, in fact, to have been of a quite strenuously idealistic and altruistic cast: in his copy of M'Culloch a reference in purely economic terms to the human urge 'to improve our condition' has been expanded in the margin to include the words 'either socially, morally or intellectually, & that of others'.[56]

Hardy, in 1865, had not yet abandoned his clerical 'dream' nor consciously discarded his religious beliefs. It seems entirely possible, in fact, that he never did experience a 'loss of faith' of the classic Victorian kind. His attraction to the Church seems always to have depended not so much upon intellectual conviction as upon the emotional appeal of its rituals and, later, upon its perceived possibilities as an avenue of social and especially educational advancement. Though not insincere—because never consciously examined—his early adherence to Anglican principles was largely automatic, taken for granted upon the basis of family and local example. His fundamental beliefs, meanwhile, appear to have differed little from the instinctive, inherited fatalism of a Tess Durbeyfield—or of a Jemima Hardy—and, as sophisticated by exposure to Marcus Aurelius, they found little difficulty in accommodating themselves to the prevailing pessimism of the post-Darwinian intellectual world into which he emerged in early manhood. The erosion of Hardy's religious convictions was thus a gradual process rather than the consequence of a single moment of crisis, and he was never to lose entirely his imaginative adherence to the Church, his love of its music and its services, and his belief in its civilizing and socializing functions. From the early summer of 1864 onwards a decline in his church attendance and private Scripture reading can be traced with some precision from the decreasing frequency of dated annotations in his Bible and prayer book, although as late as the summer of 1865 he is said to have been still practising 'orthodoxy'* with a view to preparing

---

* A note in his prayerbook, however, shows that the Westminster Abbey communion cited on page 66 of *Early Life* was actually taken not in July 1865 but in July 1863.

himself for Cambridge and the eventual prospect of 'combining poetry and the Church' by means of 'a curacy in a country village'.[57]

It seems necessary to ascribe to this period, when he was being pulled in so many directions by conflicting needs, ambitions, and emotions, some of those moods of terrible depression to which Hardy occasionally referred in laters years: 'As to despondency', he told a friend in 1887, 'I have known the very depths of it— you would be quite shocked if I were to tell you how many weeks & months in byegone years I have gone to bed wishing never to see daylight again.' He was lonely in London, confined and wearied by the long hours of private reading which he added to his daily labours, and after Eliza's departure he had no one upon whose reassurance and good advice he could constantly depend: Horace Moule, always elusive, was in any case scarcely the man to go to in search of personal guidance. Thrown back constantly upon his own judgement and resources, Hardy could not always muster sufficient confidence in his own powers and prospects to be able to withstand the pressures that seemed to push him inexorably towards safe and conventional courses of action. As the narrator of *Two on a Tower* authoritatively observes: 'Only those persons who are by nature affected with that ready esteem for others' positions which induces an undervaluing of their own, fully experience the deep smart of such convictions against self— the wish for annihilation that is engendered in the moment of despair, at feeling that at length we, our best and firmest friend, cease to believe in our cause.'[58]

At the same time, there is no indication that Hardy was in any way skimping or even resenting the tasks assigned by Blomfield. Describing many years later the little literary lectures he had given to the other people in the office—always exalting the merits and reputations of poets far above those of mere novelists such as Dickens—he explained that architecture did not tax the brain as writing did:[59] indeed, the dating of poems from 8 Adelphi Terrace as well as from 16 Westbourne Park Villas suggests that one of his central conflicts found at least temporary resolution in the opportunities he had not only to talk about literature while he was at the office but to do some writing there as well.

Hardy's ascription of a specific date and place to the composition of a particular poem has always to be treated with some caution, but many of the surviving poems were indeed first written in 1865 and 1866, though often in a form considerably cruder than that in which they were eventually published thirty and more years later. Such early poems as 'Amabel' and 'Her Confession' are essentially self-conscious exercises in conventional modes, although this is not necessarily to say that they had no basis in Hardy's own experience—'Amabel', for instance, may reflect the disastrous re-encounter with the much aged Julia Augusta Martin shortly after his first arrival in London:

> I marked her ruined hues,
> Her custom-straitened views,
> And asked, 'Can there indwell
> My Amabel?'

Other poems (at least in the revised form in which they have come down to us) speak already with a voice that is unmistakably Hardy's, among them the heavily alliterative 'Postponement', the densely narrative 'Her Dilemma', the bitter 'Discouragement', with its allusion to the dependence of 'A whole life's circumstance on hap of birth', and those no less resentful verses which take 'Hap' as their title:

> —Crass Casualty obstructs the sun and rain,
> And dicing Time for gladness casts a moan. . . .
> These purblind Doomsters had as readily strown
> Blisses about my pilgrimage as pain.

Even in poems such as these[60] it is difficult to distinguish literary from personal impulse, although there seems little doubt that 'A Confession to a Friend in Trouble' was directly prompted by Hardy's anxieties about Horace Moule. In quite another vein— and more indicative of the attitudes and talents which were to produce *The Poor Man and the Lady*—are such comic and satirical pieces as 'The Fire at Tranter Sweatley's', 'The Ruined Maid', 'The Two Men', and 'Dream of the City Shopwoman'. The poems about women—poems of love, of loss, of 'revulsion'—range so widely in mood and argument as to offer little clue as to the state of Hardy's emotions at this period, except in so far as they fit into an over-all pattern of ambivalence and lack of confidence, of rapid alternations between romantic enthusiasm and sullen self-reproach.

The comments about women ascribed in *Early Life* to the spring of 1865 show the same kind of restless uncertainty, while a note made on his twenty-fifth birthday ('Walked about by moon-light in the evening. Wondered what woman, if any, I should be thinking about in five years' time') suggests that there had already been a marked deterioration in his relationship with Eliza Bright Nicholls. They had seen very little of each other during the past two years, while Eliza was at Godstone and Hardy still in London, and at Archdeacon Hoare's death in January 1865 Eliza had apparently not returned to Orsett Place but had gone to live with her parents at Findon. Hardy could, and did, visit her in Findon, and during the Whitsun weekend of 1866 he sketched the little village church—the church 'near the Downs', as it is called in his architectural notebook, where the erased word 'Findon' is still faintly discernible.[61] The speaker in 'The Musing Maiden', dated October 1866, may well be Eliza Nicholls, standing on 'the hog-backed down',* watching ships pass along the coast, imagining that her lover in London will eventually see them too from his window 'near the quay', but wondering whether he continues to think of her:

> 'I go to meet the moon at night;
> To mark the moon was our delight;
> Up there our eyesights touch at will
> If such he practise still.'[63]

A somewhat similar note is struck at the end of 'Her Confession' and it seems, indeed, safe to infer from the evidence of the 'She, to Him' and obviously related sonnets—fragments, Hardy once said, of a much longer sequence—that by the end of 1866 the relationship was foundering upon his growing indifference. The poem 'Her Reproach' suggests a rejection of love for the sake of literary ambition, but 'She, to Him. IV' speaks of a transfer of affections—and in bitter tones which evidently reflect Eliza Nicholls's distress at discovering Hardy's preference for her younger, prettier, and livelier sister, Mary Jane, whom he had met during his Findon visits:

> This love puts all humanity from me;
> I can but maledict her, pray her dead,
> For giving love and getting love of thee—
> Feeding a heart that else mine own had fed![64]

---

* A note of Hardy's gives this as the popular name for Creech Down, behind Kimmeridge Bay;[62] on the other hand Hardy could have had the Sussex coast near Findon in mind.

. . .

Throughout 1866 Hardy was in a restless mood, full of hopes and ideas but despairing of their realization. A contemporary note— 'The defects of a class are more perceptible to the class immediately below it than to itself'—suggests that he may already have been planning a novel along the lines of *The Poor Man and the Lady,* which he was to recommend to Alexander Macmillan in just such terms. But to conceive of a work on a grand scale was not to solve the problems encountered in attempting to write it, as a note attributed to 19 June 1866 sufficiently reveals: 'A widely appreciative mind often fails to achieve a great work from pure far-sightedness. The very clearness with which he discerns remote possibilities is, from its nature, scarcely ever co-existent with the minute & microscopic vision required to trace out the narrow path which leads to them.' Hardy apparently took a short holiday, beginning on Saturday, 2 June, his twenty-sixth birthday, but a retrospective visit to Hatfield the following week only oppressed him with an awareness of time's passage: 'Pied rabbits in the Park, descendants of those I knew. The once children are quite old inhabitants.' On 22 June, sitting in his room at Westbourne Park Villas, he made a sketch of the view from the window in the direction of St. Stephen's Church, and noted on it not only the date but also the time, '½ past 8 in evening'.[65] The view itself is chiefly of architectural interest, but the open books in the foreground provide a more accurate register of the direction his thoughts were now taking.

It was this year, and probably this summer, which saw the final collapse of his long-cherished, essentially quietist, ambition of a country curacy. He asked Horace Moule to send him a copy of the Students' Guide to Cambridge and forced himself to face the discomforting realities of his situation. His financial resources were far from adequate, despite his later assertions that his father would have lent him whatever additional funds he needed, and he may well have been a good deal less well prepared for university entrance—especially in Greek—than he had been pretending to himself for the past several years.[66] And even if these difficulties could somehow be overcome, no less than seven years would have to elapse before he finally received a degree. As he explained to Mary: 'I find on adding up expenses and taking into consideration the time I should have to wait, that my notion is too far fetched to be worth entertaining any longer.' It seemed absurd, he added, 'to live on now with such a remote object in view'—a judgement promptly echoed in the four lines of 'A Young Man's Epigram on Existence', written that same year:

> A senseless school, where we must give
> Our lives that we may learn to live!
> A dolt is he who memorizes
> Lessons that leave no time for prizes.[67]

The decision, though painful, brought in its train a sense of relief and even of release. Hardy's instinctive impulse was towards the life of the mind and the world of books, and if it had first taken the shape of a desire to enter the Church, that was largely because the Church had provided him with his earliest awareness of the beauty and excitement of language allied to music, his first overwhelming sense of the magic and sanctity of the word. Nor, on a more practical level, could he forget the hours he had spent in the Revd Arthur Shirley's study, receiving confirmation lessons from a man whom he disliked, and whose intelligence he probably despised, but who compelled respect by virtue both of his social position and his superior education. By 1866 Hardy's views had greatly changed; he no longer accepted many of the Church's doctrinal positions,* and he was thus obliged to realize that—like the Halborough brothers in his own short story 'A Tragedy of Two Ambitions'—he had been clinging to the prospect of a clerical career for essentially selfish and non-religious reasons. Hardy's ambitions encompassed, first, the university education preparatory to such a career and, secondly, the ultimate prospect of comfortably combining a dutiful performance of his clerical functions with the pursuit of literature and, above all, the writing —conceivably, but not necessarily, the publishing—of poetry. His social and financial aspirations were far less urgent than those of the Halboroughs', or even those entertained by his mother on his behalf, and there is no reason to question the assertion in *Early Life* that Hardy, 'caring for life as an emotion rather than for life as a science of climbing',[68] was singularly unambitious at this and indeed all periods.

The abandonment of Cambridge and the Church threw into

---

* Religious differences perhaps played a part in the breakdown of his relationship with Eliza Nicholls: she seems always to have been deeply devout and may have contributed something to the religiosity of Sue Bridehead in the closing chapters of *Jude the Obscure*.

sharp relief the possibility, hitherto only dimly glimpsed, of pursuing a literary career for its own sake. But that meant giving up architecture, and it was easier to forswear long-term hopes than present realities. Although he was bored and unfulfilled by his architectural work, and had small prospect of advancement, the profession had already brought him a status and security far beyond anything that could reasonably have been predicted for him in his Bockhampton childhood. Architecture was often tedious and time-consuming in itself, but it had not eroded his psychic and creative energies, and might therefore be preferable, as a source of income, to a life of drudgery as a professional writer. In any case he had not yet demonstrated—despite the publication of 'How I Built Myself a House'—the capacity to earn even the barest of livings from writing alone. Already in the middle 1860s he was pondering a decision he would not finally make until the early 1870s. His observation to the effect that one might blame oneself for actions that proved in fact to be worthy of praise, primarily based upon the experience of turning up alone at the Baptist prayer meeting after having felt guilty at wanting to stay away, was further supported by a second, more enigmatic, instance: 'Also cutting Arche if successf.'[69] Success in architecture would render the desired renunciation of it harder to justify to his family —who had so long planned and sacrificed for just such a consummation—and even, economically, to himself. On the other hand it would somehow lend a kind of purity to the gesture and forestall any suggestion that he had simply failed in the upward struggle.

Hardy's last year with Blomfield, from the summer of 1866 onwards, was a 'buoyant time' in his creative life, a period when the intoxication of Swinburne's verse merged with a growing sense of his own capacities as a poet.[70] None of his poems were published, the rejections he had already received from editors having quickly discouraged him from further attempts—a characteristic demonstration of lack of self-confidence which he later represented to himself as an avoidance of vulgar haste.* But his imagination and enthusiasm had been somehow liberated by the final rejection of all thoughts of a clerical career and the consequent polarization of his architectural and literary options, so that

---

* The number of submissions to editors at this period must have been small indeed, since no specific references to them have been found either among Hardy's own papers or elsewhere.

he could subsequently recall the period as one of extraordinary excitement, in which more prudential aspirations and considerations were progressively swept aside: 'A sense of the truth of poetry, of its supreme place in literature, had awakened itself in me. At the risk of ruining all my worldly prospects I dabbled in it. . . . All was of the nature of being led by a mood, without foresight, or regard to whither it led.'[71]

His enthusiasm for architecture meanwhile dwindled further during the autumn of 1866 as a consequence of his frequent attendance at the St. Pancras cemetery to prevent irregularities during the removal of graves in the path of the new railway line. Although the episode is treated humorously in *Early Life*—which reports that Blomfield's greeting to Hardy in later years was always, 'Do you remember how we found the man with two heads at St. Pancras?'—and wryly in the poem 'The Two Men', it was a macabre experience, scarcely enhanced by the public outcry over what one contemporary headline called the 'Horrible Desecration of the Dead at St. Pancras'—a protest intensified by an erroneous rumour that the bones of William Godwin and Mary Wollstonecraft were among those swept into anonymity.[72]

Hardy knew much depression and darkness during these London years, deplored many aspects of the city's teeming life, and was eventually driven back to Dorset by the effects upon his own health of its fog, smoke, and dirt, its 'rayless grime'. 'From Her in the Country', one of the sonnets dated from Westbourne Park Villas in 1866, turns upon a contrast between countryside and 'crass clanging town'[73] of which Hardy must have been very much aware. But he was always to speak with pride of his knowledge of London, and to the very end of his period with Blomfield he continued to take such advantage as his time and means allowed of those opportunities which London uniquely offered. Because he was working in the centre of London every day, he probably paid little attention to events taking place in the neighbourhood of his Paddington lodgings. But the newly built Westbourne Hall in near-by Westbourne Grove was a popular place for lectures and concerts, and it is tempting—in view of the episode in the fifth chapter of Part Second of *Jude*—to think that Hardy might have gone there in March 1866 to hear the Revd John Straight speak on 'Jerusalem and Its Environs'. It certainly seems possible that he heard—and remembered when he was writing *The Hand of*

Ethelberta, whose heroine becomes a professional teller of stories
—one or both of the offerings of the locally celebrated woman
lecturer Miss Julia Corke, 'The Life and Times of Lady Jane
Grey' and 'The Life and Times of Marie Antoinette'. His experience of hearing William Harrison after his serious illness may
have occurred at a Westbourne Hall concert of December 1865,
although he could also have heard him—like the other singers
mentioned in *Early Life*—on numerous occasions during the
middle 1860s.[74]

The opera was an enthusiasm he shared with Horace Moule—
one of Moule's few surviving letters to him refers to Patti and
Tietjens[75]—but most of his theatre-going was undertaken alone or
with office colleagues. W. O. Milne, who arrived at Blomfield's in
1866, later recalled that Hardy was fond of music and of the
theatre, and that they 'used occasionally to indulge in a pit, at
Drury Lane especially when a Shakespeare play was on, I remember especially going with him once to see old Phelps in "King
John", & we used afterwards to go in for a modest fish supper at
one or other of the old places there used to be round about the
Strand'.[76] Hardy particularly admired Samuel Phelps's Falstaff,
and he could have seen him in that role as early as March 1864.
He saw Phelps in *Othello* in 1865 and recalled fifty years later the
'knocking scene' in Phelps's *Macbeth,* adding that he was 'impressionable' at that time and read Shakespeare 'more closely from
23 to 26 than I have ever done since'. There were fewer opportunities for him to have seen Helen Faucit, whom he also recalled
from those years, but she appeared with Phelps in *Cymbeline* and
Macbeth and played Rosalind in *As You Like it* in November
1866—although if Hardy saw that latter performance he must
have been less impressed by it than by Mrs Scott-Siddons's, the
occasion of the poem 'To an Impersonator of Rosalind' the following April.[77]

Throughout his life Hardy was to be simultaneously attracted
by the excitement of the theatre and repelled by its artifice—as
the unfinished poem 'At a Victorian Rehearsal' rather crudely
suggests.* He was also to absorb, and adapt to his own artistic
purposes, many of the techniques and conventions of both the
serious and the popular theatre. At the end of 1866 and the beginning of 1867 he is said to have contemplated a scheme for

* Despite its title (itself a revision from 'The Rehearsal') this has been
speculatively identified[78] as a late poem, suggested by a rehearsal of J. M.
Barrie's play *Mary Rose.*

obtaining stage experience as a preparation for the writing of blank-verse plays, and he did go so far—though surely for more frivolous reasons—as to take, apparently for just one night, a walking-on part in Gilbert à Beckett's pantomime *Ali-Baba and the Forty Thieves; or, Harlequin and the Genii of the Arabian Nights!,* which opened at Covent Garden on 26 December 1866 and ran for several weeks thereafter. As a 'nondescript' Hardy took some now unimaginable part in the 'Oxford and Cambridge Boat Race', a scene which on the first night had drawn applause from the audience and praise from the critic of *The Times* as 'one of the best exhibitions of its kind that has been witnessed for some time'.[79]

Hardy had spent the Christmas holiday of 1866 at home at Bockhampton, giving Mary a copy of *The Golden Treasury* and Kate, now ten years old, Wood's *Illustrated Natural History.*[80] The new year brought on a series of personal crises, chief among them the end of his engagement, if such it was, with Eliza Nicholls. Hardy's infatuation with Jane Nicholls had rendered impossible the continuation of his former relationship with her sister. He went to Findon one last time, and had the final interview with Eliza which is recorded in 'Neutral Tones', the poem's overwhelming sense of personal immediacy deriving from the extraordinary imagist precision with which Hardy recreated its setting—almost certainly the now dried-up pond surrounded by old lime kilns on the ridge overlooking Tolmare Farm, just west of Findon. The note is not now (as it had been in 'She, to Him. IV') one of ordinary sexual betrayal—only the moralizing last stanza alludes to deceit—but rather of sheer deprivation, of a relationship drained of all vitality, colour, and meaning:

> Your eyes on me were as eyes that rove
> Over tedious riddles of years ago;
> And some words played between us to and fro
> On which lost the more by our love.[81]

Eliza herself was comfortless. She never married; almost fifty years later, after the death of Hardy's first wife, she called upon him in the remote hope that her hour had at last arrived.* Nor could Hardy find much compensation in his new infatuation: though Jane Nicholls may have taken some satisfaction in a mischievous

---

* She was perhaps the woman in 'Known Had I' whom the speaker regrets having left 'lonely / With wringing doubt, to cow / Old hope'.[82]

flirtation with her sister's fiancé, she evidently did not think of him as a serious marriage prospect and soon bestowed her affections elsewhere.

The experience left Hardy emotionally exhausted, intensifying the physical weakness which forced him to leave Blomfield and London and return to Dorset in July 1867. Too much reading, too little sleep and exercise, the general insalubrity of the city and especially of the tidal sewer that was the Thames—all these factors contributed to a serious deterioration in Hardy's health, until he scarcely had strength in the mornings 'to hold the pencil and square'. Family tradition adds that he was not getting regular meals in London and that his doctor prescribed a daily bottle of milk stout.[83] Just what his feelings about architecture were at this stage it is impossible to say: there is no indication that he seriously contemplated abandoning his career in the near future, and yet the poem 'Heiress and Architect', dated from Adelphi Terrace in 1867, is so hostile to both sides of the grim debate that Blomfield can scarcely have relished the dedication. Meanwhile Hardy's work at the office was suffering, and a request from John Hicks, back in Dorchester, for an assistant to help with church-restoration work was welcomed as providing a happy opportunity for at least a temporary change of scene, atmosphere, and working rhythm.[84]

5

THE POOR MAN AND THE LADY

I N SOCIAL and economic terms Hardy was little further forward
when he returned from London in the summer of 1867 than
when he first went there in the spring of 1862, and he had to
face the scorn of friends and neighbours who interpreted his retreat to Bockhampton as a clear sign that he had been defeated in
his attempt to make his way in the larger world.[1] He had, of
course, developed intellectually, accumulated experiences and
memories, and learned how much his writing mattered to him,
but he had neither made substantial progress in the architectural
profession nor gained an alternative foothold in journalism. Architecture as a career was by no means unattractive in itself: shortly
before his death he was to say that his life might have been happier
if he had lived it, like Hicks, as an architect in a small country
town.[2] But the independent position Hicks enjoyed, as an architect in private practice, seemed wholly beyond the reach of the
young Hardy of the 1860s. Not only did he lack the friends, money,
and education necessary to set up in practice for himself, he had
none of the assertiveness, poise, and personal charm that might
supplement professional skill and win him a partnership by ability
alone. When he was first in London he was still being propelled
by the social ambitions instilled in him by his mother, still trying
to make a mark for himself by sheer hard work and (like Hooper

Tolbort) by success in open competitions. But by the mid-1860s it had come home to him that he was doomed, as an architect, to a Tom Pinch-like future, always improving and finishing other men's projects. That sense of utter dejection which overwhelmed him every so often during his last years with Blomfield was the natural consequence of such a realization, and of the related perception that by following the route of ambition and class mobility opened up by his mother's payment of his articling fees, he had in a sense sold his birthright—abandoned forever the freedom and independence enjoyed by his father within the narrow but local (hence beloved) limits of his life as a jobbing builder.

In returning to Dorset as, in effect, a jobbing architect, Hardy was none the less paralleling in a curious way the life he might have led had he followed in his father's (and grandfather's, and great-grandfather's) steps as a master mason. He was working for Hicks again, but on a basis of mutual convenience, so that he had time for his writing and for renewing his intimacy with his native countryside. A Tuesday in September, for example, found him sketching in the hills just north of Minterne, where his sister had taken over the local school—seizing the first available opportunity to return to Dorset if not, as yet, to the immediate vicinity of her home.[3] It was a situation with which he seems, for the time being, to have been perfectly content. Although Blomfield was willing to keep his job open for him, Hardy evidently did not contemplate any early return to London: a brief visit in October to collect his belongings served only to confirm his original departure.[4] After his recent illnesses and disappointments he was ideally receptive to the restorative influences of Dorset in general and of Bockhampton in particular, and soon recovered health and spirits. He now had time to pause and take stock of himself, to weigh his dwindling options—for even his renewed attraction to his father's personality and way of life cannot seriously have deluded him (like Clym Yeobright) into imagining that he could somehow return to what he might have been, and what his far sturdier and more extrovert brother Henry was in the process of becoming.

But it was one thing to take stock, quite another to take action. Architecture offered safety, modest comfort, and (even without going into private practice) that lower-middle-class status his mother had originally projected for him. Literature offered no economic assurance whatsoever, and yet it was unquestionably the goal towards which his whole being was instinctively directed. Unquestionably, but not yet irresistibly. It is perfectly conceivable that Hardy's uncertainty about his gifts, in combination with his mother's persuasions and his own sense of economic realities, could at this point have drawn him decisively away from literature and into a permanent architectural career—perhaps, like Henry Bastow in Australia, into some position under local government.* He probably escaped that fate, indeed, only by his very failure to act, his willingness to let matters drift until the situation somehow clarified itself.

This is not to suggest that Hardy was totally dependent and insecure. His apparent deference to the opinions of others was rather a process of allowing them to become the mouthpieces through which his alternative choices could become articulated. Just as in later years he was to make some of his most passionate statements in response to the criticisms of hostile reviewers, so in the years when his life had not yet taken its final shape he seems to have been best able to define and refine his own ideas in response—which often meant in opposition—to the advice he received from those around him. While never venturing upon sudden and unexpected moves, never severing his connections with his home and his personal past, Hardy was entirely capable of whittling down his position by a kind of slow friction until it had shaped itself into a single unmistakable point, and then of adopting the direction thus indicated with a dogged and implacable absoluteness. Though a man of radical thought, Hardy was never a man of radical action. He could, and did, wedge himself into positions of stubborn opposition to his family's wishes, but it is almost impossible to imagine him, in the late 1860s, cutting adrift from his family and his background and opting for, say, emigration or a reckless plunge into Grub Street—even though these and other possibilities may well have passed through his mind. He was always ready to respond to the opportunities that chance threw in at a time, awaiting an occasion for the future to reveal itself, so that his crucial life-decisions took on the character of gradual and accept them as a form of fate; but he always proceeded one step his way, and sometimes (as in his first marriage) too prone to

* Bastow left Tasmania in 1866 upon his appointment as a draughtsman in the Water Supply Department of the state of Victoria. He held a series of other civil service positions, culminating in 1885 with that of Senior Architect in the Department of Public Works, until government retrenchments forced him into early retirement in 1894. He spent his last years as a fruit grower in Harcourt, Victoria, where he was a leading member of the local group of Plymouth Brethren until his death in 1920. Bastow wrote to Hardy in 1907 and his son Arthur visited Max Gate not long afterwards.[5]

almost instinctive shifts in direction rather than of calculated actions, intellectually conceived and deliberately undertaken.

If patterns of this kind can be traced in the slow and painful development of Hardy's professional career, they are no less clearly present in the history of his emotional life. His relationship with Eliza Nicholls was allowed to drag on far beyond the span of its inherent vitality, and once he was back in Dorset in 1867 he seems to have slipped, naturally and quite unreflectingly, into an enjoyment of the available companionship of his cousin Tryphena Sparks, now a pupil-teacher in the Puddletown elementary school.ᶜ

Tryphena at the age of sixteen was pretty, lively, and intelligent. She had a strong sense of fun, as surviving letters show, and exhibited both energy and determination in her subsequent career as schoolteacher and headmistress. The absence of her name from the pages of *Early Life*—in which so few of Hardy's family are mentioned—has in recent years been highlighted (rather than made good) by suggestions that she had a passionate love affair with Hardy during the summer of 1867 and bore him an illegitimate son in 1868, but did not marry him because they were in fact not cousins but uncle and niece. For none of these speculations is there any evidence capable of withstanding scholarly or even common-sensical scrutiny.[7] It has, of course, long been known —largely on the basis of Hardy's own reference to a 'cousin'—that Tryphena Sparks was the subject of 'Thoughts of Phena: At News of her Death', first published in *Wessex Poems* as 'Thoughts of Ph—a':

> Not a line of her writing have I,
> Not a thread of her hair,
> No mark of her late time as dame in her dwelling, whereby
> I may picture her there;
> And in vain do I urge my unsight
> To conceive my lost prize
> At her close, whom I knew when her dreams were upbrimming
> with light,
> And with laughter her eyes.[8]

That Hardy chose to publish this poem as early as 1898 is evidence in itself that his affectionate memories of his dead cousin were unclouded by guilt or self-reproach—except in so far as the unhappiness of his own marriage had given him cause to regret past failures to claim Tryphena or Louisa Harding or either of the

Nicholls sisters or any of the other young women whom his idealizing memory transformed into 'lost prizes'.

For most of the period between the summer of 1867 and the
summer of 1869 Hardy was at Bockhampton, Tryphena at Puddletown, and he is said to have undertaken to teach her French.
Family tradition tells of some form of understanding or even engagement between them, the second Mrs Hardy spoke of Hardy
having given his first wife a ring originally intended for a local
girl, and Nathaniel Sparks, Tryphena's nephew, ascribed to his
father the story that 'Thomas Hardy first wanted to marry Martha!
then he tried to marry Tryphena, but grandmother [i.e., Tryphena's mother, Maria Sparks] put a spoke in his wheel on the
ground of its being against the laws of the church'.[9] Though some
of this evidence seems questionable—Maria Sparks died on 2
November 1868, and the marriage of first cousins was not in fact
forbidden by the Church of England 'Table of Kindred and
Affinity'—it is likely enough that Hardy and Tryphena walked
out together and that some members of the family, among them
the still unmarried Martha Sparks, were not greatly pleased.

Hardy was attracted by Tryphena's good looks and youthful
optimism, by the way 'her dreams were upbrimming with light, /
And with laughter her eyes', but she cannot have seemed—least
of all to Jemima's jealous eyes—an especially good match for an
up-and-coming young professional man. Tryphena, while perfectly
content to be escorted and mildly courted by her grown-up cousin,
with his London experience and literary pretensions, was at the
age of sixteen and seventeen less interested in marriage than in the
prospect—exciting enough for a girl of her background—of a
college education and eventual economic independence as a schoolteacher. The two were often alone together, and it would not be
extraordinary if they made love. But there was certainly no child,
probably no formal engagement, and perhaps not even a dramatic
parting but simply a gradual erosion of intimacy, an eventual
relapse into the friendly and cousinly terms of the past.

In January 1870 Tryphena went off to London for a two-year
course at the Stockwell Normal College of the British and Foreign
Bible Society. In January 1872, immediately following the completion of her training, she was appointed headmistress of a girls'
elementary school in Plymouth. A year later she was joined there
by her eldest sister, Rebecca, whose own marriage with Frederick
Paine, a Puddletown saddler, had quickly failed and who had
turned naturally enough to her prosperous and still unmarried

sister as someone with whom she could make a home.* By 1875 Tryphena was being courted by Charles Gale, owner of a public house in Topsham, near Exeter, and in December 1877 the two were married. Hardy could have met Tryphena in London in 1870–2 and kept in touch with her after she went to Plymouth, but there is no evidence that the attachment was prolonged even so far as Hardy's first meeting with Emma Lavinia Gifford in March 1870. Indeed, in the poem 'The Wind's Prophecy', the lover about to be supplanted by the Emma figure has 'ebon loops of hair', more suggestive (as her photograph shows) of Jane Nicholls than of Tryphena Sparks, whose hair is said to have been a dark chestnut.[11]

At the time of her mother's illness and death Tryphena apparently stayed with her (and Hardy's) aunt, Mary Antell, wife of John Antell, the Puddletown shoemaker, of whom Hardy saw a good deal during the late 1860s. A few years later he would introduce into *Far from the Madding Crowd* the figure of the old maltster, based in part upon John Antell's father, also called John, who had come from Cerne Abbas to Puddletown as a maltster early in the century. And in *Under the Greenwood Tree* he presented through the figure of Mr Penny the image of the shoemaker and his shop as the natural centre for village life and gossip. But while John Antell shared Mr Penny's professional pride, he is painted by family tradition as a man of very different stamp, active in local affairs and—denied the formal education for which he longed —a prodigy of self-education, achieving some competence in Latin, Greek, and even Hebrew. He was also knowledgeable about the natural life of the countryside, especially that of the near-by heath, and was clearly of a type not uncommon at that period—a man of the working class who found no adequate outlet for his native abilities in the social conditions then prevailing, and whose frustrated energies erupted in bitterness, alcoholism, and violence. To what extent Antell was a radical in politics, after the tradition of village shoemakers, it is now impossible to say.† But as he grew

* Rebecca and her husband are said to have parted as they came out of church after the wedding; according to Tryphena's son Charles Gale, however, the marriage broke down over a period of two or three months.[10]

† Not too much can be inferred from his appearance as one of the many signatories of *An Address from the County of Dorset on the Elementary Education Bill,* printed in Dorchester in 1870, which pleads against any impairment of the principle of perfect liberty of religious teaching in existing schools.

older and lost business to the new shoe factories, there was a corresponding increase in his bitterness and self-destructive drinking, until Hardy could describe the 'almost brutal—at least fierce' aspect of one of the Turberville profiles in Wool Manor House as being 'like J.A. when drunk at Noah's Ark', a Dorchester public house.[12] When Antell was dying of a wasting disease—presumably cancer, or 'lumbar abscess', as his death certificate called it—he was himself responsible for the posing of a remarkable photograph in which his emaciated figure leans upon a chair which bears, on a carefully lettered placard, the accusatory words 'SIC PLACET', addressed presumably to God, Fate, or even the President of the Immortals.

In the late 1860s John Antell was only in his forties and had not yet reached the more desperate stages of his illness and alcoholism, or of his hostility towards the order of the universe. But as Hardy sat in the workroom at the back of the shop in High Street, Puddletown, he listened to many tirades on the fundamental injustice of man's fate, and it is quite clear that John Antell's deeply divided and tragically driven personality was central, many years later, to the whole conception of *Jude the Obscure*.[13] It may also have contributed something, more immediately, to the pervasive class hostility of Hardy's first novel, *The Poor Man and the Lady*.

Hardy continued to write verse following his return to Dorset in the summer of 1867, and later recalled that it was only after he had left London that he learned to avoid the 'jewelled line' in poetry, as being 'effeminate', and first read Wordsworth's preface to the *Lyrical Ballads*. 'The Widow Betrothed' was conceived, if not taken further, in 1867, both 'Retty's Phases' and 'Gallant's Song' were drafted in 1868, and in June of that same year Hardy 'recorded at some length the outline of a narrative poem on the Battle of the Nile', an indication both of continuing poetic ambition and of an early interest in Napoleonic material and themes.[14] But it was to the writing of the first draft of *The Poor Man and the Lady* that he chiefly devoted himself during the last five months of 1867, drawing freely upon ideas and even episodes which had been formulated earlier: most of the poems referred to in the first sub-title he set down—'A Story with No Plot: Containing some original verses'—had probably been written at Westbourne Park Villas.[15]

Although the novel was never published, and no portion of the manuscript survives, it is possible to reconstruct from various sources the broad outlines of its episodic, if not quite plotless, narrative.* Will Strong, a young architect of peasant background, falls in love with the daughter of the squire on whose estate his parents work. The two become betrothed, despite the lady's distress at the poor man's political radicalism, but are eventually separated by the opposition of the squire, who arranges for his daughter to marry the son of a local landowner. On the eve of that wedding the lovers meet and reaffirm their vows, but their own secret marriage is followed immediately by the lady's sudden death in her father's house. Hardy's first draft, completed early in 1868, still left some of his narrative difficulties unresolved. His hero had to suffer temporary blindness at one point and his heroine was required to die with complete suddenness, without previous warning, and while still in full possession of her faculties. In search of expert advice upon these medical matters, Hardy wrote to his aunt Martha's clerical brother-in-law, George Brereton Sharpe, who had formerly practised as a physician and surgeon in Hertfordshire. Sharpe agreed that 'continued study late at night of small print or Greek characters' might well produce loss of sight, especially if the light were poor, and he recommended 'Hemorrage of the lungs' as the best way of disposing of the heroine in the manner Hardy had specified. 'I hope', he went on, 'you are not building much on expectation of certain profit from your work. As that is the lot of but few. I do not say it may not be yours.'[17]

The process of writing out a fair copy of *The Poor Man and the Lady* thus involved expansion as well as revision, and it not surprisingly occupied all of Hardy's spare time between mid-January and early June of 1868. On 25 July the completed manuscript was sent off to Alexander Macmillan on the recommendation of Horace Moule, whose connections with the Macmillan firm dated back to his Cambridge days. In his accompanying letter Hardy acknowledged that his main concern was to attack the manners of the upper classes, but insisted that the novelty and subtlety of the book lay in its use of the point of view of 'a com-

---

* Shortly after Hardy's death, Edmund Gosse published in the *Sunday Times* a summary of the plot of *The Poor Man* as Hardy had once narrated it to him. Gosse's account has generally been regarded with some suspicion, but it was first written as a kind of diary record of a date on which he and Hardy were certainly together,[16] and the details it offers, whatever their origin, do not significantly conflict with what can be inferred from other sources.

parative outsider' and in the indirection of the satire: whereas
upper-class readers might throw down in disgust a book which
was openly hostile, 'the very same feelings inserted edgewise so
to say; half-concealed beneath ambiguous expressions, or at any
rate written as if they were not the chief aims of the book (even
though they may be)—become the most attractive remarks of all.'[18]

Alexander Macmillan can hardly have been much moved by so
tenuous an argument, but he was sufficiently impressed by *The
Poor Man* itself to write, on 10 August, a reply so long and detailed that it represents the clearest surviving indication of what
the novel was like. Although he praised Hardy's presentation of
'country life among working men' Macmillan felt that the portraits
of upper-class Londoners were too hostile to be convincing:

> The utter heartlessness of *all* the conversation you give in draw-
> ingrooms and ballrooms about the working-classes, has *some*
> ground of truth I fear, and might justly be scourged as you aim
> at doing, but your chastisement would fall harmless from its very
> excess. Will's speech to the working men is full of wisdom—
> (though by the way would he have told his own story in public,
> being as you describe him a man of substantially good taste?—)
> and you there yourself give grounds for condemning very much
> that is in other parts of the book. Indeed nothing could justify
> such a wholesale blackening of a class but large & intimate
> knowledge of it. Thackeray makes them not greatly better in
> many respects, but he gave many redeeming traits & characters,
> besides he did it all in a light chaffing way that gave no offence—
> and I fear did little good, and he soothed them by describing the
> lower class which he knew nothing of & did not care to know, as
> equally bad when he touched them at all. He meant fair, you
> *'mean mischief.'*

The story as a whole struck Macmillan as extravagant and
implausible—was it 'within the range of likelihood', he asked,
'that *any* gentleman would pursue his wife at midnight & *strike*
her?'—but he praised the characterization and style and spoke of
one particular scene in Rotten Row as 'full of real power & insight'. 'You see,' he added, 'I am writing to you as to a writer
who seems to me of, at least potentially, considerable mark, of
power & purpose. If this is your first book I think you ought to
go on. May I ask if it is? and—you are not a lady so perhaps you
will forgive the question—are you young?'[19]

Accompanying the letter was another remarkable document,

the report by an unidentified reader—in fact, John Morley—to whom Macmillan had sent the manuscript:

> A very curious and original performance: the opening pictures of the Christmas Eve in the tranter's house are really of good quality; much of the writing is strong and fresh. But there crops up in parts a certain rawness of absurdity that is very displeasing, and makes it read like some clever lad's dream: the thing hangs too loosely together. There is real feeling in the writing, though now and then it is commonplace in form as all feeling turning on the insolence and folly of the rich in face of the poor is apt to sound: . . . If the man is young, there is stuff and promise in him: but he must study form and composition, in such writers as Balzac and Thackeray, who would I think come as natural masters to him.[20]

Although the prevailing tone of the novel is sufficiently suggested by these references to Balzac and especially to Thackeray, it would appear from the inclusion of such an obvious set-piece as 'Will's speech to the working men'—which perhaps owed something to George Eliot's 'Address to working-men, by Felix Holt', first published in the January 1868 number of *Blackwood's*—that the assault on upper-class attitudes and privileges was sometimes pressed home in specifically political terms. *Early Life* speaks of the 'tendency' of the work as 'socialistic, not to say revolutionary', but with what justification it is now impossible to say: the several sections of the manuscript eventually adapted for use in other works—including the Rotten Row scene in Chapter 14 of *A Pair of Blue Eyes* and the 'pictures of the Christmas Eve in the tranter's house' in *Under the Greenwood Tree*—do not include those mentioned by the readers of the manuscript as having been most overtly hostile. That these episodes were none the less central to Hardy's vision rather than merely peripheral is affirmed by their re-emergence at the very end of his career as a novelist, when Jude's public narrative of his own life sounds a clear echo of Will's autobiographical speech to the working men, and the dealings of the atheistical Sue in Christian images look back to the music-hall dancer in *The Poor Man and the Lady* who became 'the kept mistress of an architect' and assisted him in his work by designing 'pulpits, altars, reredoses, texts, holy vessels, crucifixes, and other ecclesiastical furniture'.[21]

Several characters and episodes from *The Poor Man* were absorbed, with only slight modification, into 'An Indiscretion in the

Life of an Heiress', the novella which Hardy put together in 1878 from those portions of the *Poor Man* manuscript which still remained unused. The architect, Will Strong, became Egbert Mayne the schoolmaster, but 'main' is nearly synonymous with 'strong', as both are with 'hardy', and Hardy's second wife once said that the young schoolmaster in 'Indiscretion' was unmistakably based upon the author himself.[22] Whether Tollamore, as the name of the main scene of the action, was new in 'Indiscretion' cannot now be known, but it seems in any case to have come from Tolmare valley and farm, just outside Findon, thus providing one among several indications that Hardy drew in *The Poor Man* upon various aspects of his relationship with Eliza Nicholls.

In the opening paragraph of his letter to Hardy of 10 August 1868, Alexander Macmillan spoke of some 'fatal drawbacks' likely to impede the novel's success, but his tone was generally encouraging ('if this is your first book I think you ought to go on') and he ended by saying that he was seeking the advice of someone more directly familiar with the upper classes as to possible modifications which might render the manuscript acceptable. Hardy apparently wrote an immediate reply, and then awaited further developments, devoting himself meanwhile to his occasional architectural duties and to his other customary activities of walking, sketching, writing, and, of course, reading—including volumes of Thackeray and Macaulay, Horace Walpole's Letters, some Shakespeare plays, and portions of the *Aeneid*.[23]* He was also able to enjoy the company of his sister Mary, at home for her summer holidays, and a record has survived of an outing they made together:

> Aug. 26. 1868. To Weymouth with Mary. Found it was Wth Races. To Lulworth by steamboat. A woman on the paddle-box steps: all laughter: then part illness & the remainder laughter. M. & I alighted at Lulth Cove: she did not, but went back to Weyth with the steamer. Saw her for the last time standing on deck as the boat moved off. White feather in hat, brown dress, Dorset dialect, Classic features, short upper lip. A woman I wd have married offhand, with probably disastrous results.

* *Early Life* also mentions Whitman at this point, suggesting that Hardy may have been among the earliest readers of the first English selection of his poems, edited in 1868 by William Michael Rossetti.

The significance of this as yet another instance of Hardy's romantic (or adolescent) readiness to fall immediately, if temporarily, in love with women glimpsed in the street, in railway carriages, on the tops of omnibuses, or indeed in any public place, is implicitly acknowledged in the suggestion for a poem which was added to the note at a later date: 'Combine her with the girl from Keinton Mandeville, &c, as "Women seen".'[24]*

When, after a month, Hardy had heard nothing further from Macmillan, he sent off on 10 September 1868 a letter eloquent of his professional and emotional vulnerability at this period, his desperate and almost despairing need to find and secure some sort of foothold in the literary world after so many years of laborious aspiration:

> Dear Sir,
>   I have become anxious to hear from you again. As the days go on, & you do not write, & my production begins to assume that small & unimportant shape everything one does assumes as the time & mood in which one did it recedes from the present I almost feel that I don't care what happens to the book, so long as something happens. The earlier fancy, that *Hamlet* without Hamlet would never do turns to a belief that it would be better than closing the house.
>   I wonder if your friend meant the building up of a story, & not English composition, when he said I must study composition. Since my letter, I have been hunting up matter for another tale, which would consist entirely of rural scenes & humble life; but I have not courage enough to go on with it till something comes of the first.
>   Faithfully yours
>   Thomas Hardy.
> Would you mind suggesting the sort of story you think I could do best, or any literary work I should do well to go upon?[26]

The initial consequences of this appeal were the return of the manuscript and an attempt on Hardy's part to remove or dilute some of the passages to which objection had been made. Early that December—evidently following a resubmission of the manuscript in November—he went up to London for an interview with Macmillan, and while the latter declined to publish the novel he did

---

* No poem along quite these lines seems ever to have been written, although one named after 'The Maid of Keinton Mandeville' was first published in *Late Lyrics and Earlier* (1922).[25] See below, p. 193.

not declare it unpublishable. Indeed, he supplied a letter of introduction to another publisher, Frederick Chapman, and it was at
the offices of Chapman & Hall that Hardy left the manuscript
before returning to Bockhampton a few days later.[27]

Restless, deeply uncertain about the future, anxious at not having heard from Chapman & Hall, Hardy went once more to
London on 17 January 1869. In his prayerbook he wrote the date
and the words 'Leaving for London' against one of the Psalms
for the day, number 86,[28] which begins: 'Bow down thine ear,
O Lord, and hear me: for I am poor, and in misery'. He saw
Macmillan again and met Morley for the first time. Both suggested
kinds of magazine work which might produce a little income, but
Hardy could always earn extra money from architecture and his
real need now was for 'a clear call to him which course in life to
take—the course he loved, and which was his natural instinct,
that of letters, or the course all practical wisdom dictated, that of
architecture'.[29]

That call would still not be heard for a few years yet. On 8
February 1869, Chapman & Hall reported that their reader,
though confident that Hardy would do good work in future, had
advised against acceptance of the present manuscript, chiefly on
the grounds 'that you have not got an interesting story to work
upon and thus some of your episodic scenes are fatally injured'.[30]
Because Hardy was still in London—'studying pictures' and 'reading desultorily'—he was able to call in person at Frederick Chapman's office, where he was distressed to find the aged Thomas
Carlyle being attended to by a clerk rather than by the proprietor
himself. Chapman offered to publish the book if Hardy would
put up £20 as a guarantee against loss; Hardy agreed, and went
back to Dorset in a more cheerful frame of mind—less anxious than
he might otherwise have been that the unexpected death of John
Hicks on 12 February would deprive him of his most convenient
source of occasional employment.[31] At the end of February, however, he received, instead of the expected proofs, an invitation,
when he was next in London, to meet 'Mr Chapman & the gentleman who read your manuscript'. The latter turned out to be
George Meredith—'a handsome man with hair and beard not at
all grey, and wearing a frock coat buttoned at the waist and loose
above'. Meredith, his tone 'trenchant, turning kind', said that
publication of The Poor Man and the Lady in its present form
would doom it to a hostile reception, and recommended either a
drastic reduction of its satirical element, or its abandonment al-

together in favour of an entirely new work with a stronger plot and an artistic rather than a social purpose: 'Don't nail your colours to the mast just yet.'[32]

Hardy returned with his manuscript to Bockhampton, where he jotted down later that same spring a note reflective of a dilemma he was never quite to resolve: 'One of those evenings in the country which make the townsman feel "I will stay here till I die—I would, that is, if it were not for that thousand pounds I want to make, & that friend I want to envy me".'[33] Meredith's advice had impressed him, but he was reluctant to abandon the results of so much labour and decided to seek at least one more opinion on *The Poor Man*. On 15 April, therefore, he sent it off to the firm of Smith, Elder, expressing the hope that they would, whether they liked the story or not, 'make some remark' upon it. Their rejection came back within two weeks. In June Hardy tried yet another publisher, Tinsley Brothers, who kept the manuscript for three months before communicating—apparently through Horace Moule—an offer to print it in return for a guarantee which Hardy said was beyond his means but which, remembering Chapman & Hall's terms, he may simply have thought excessive. In September 1869 the manuscript returned finally into its author's reluctant hands, subsequently to be plundered for material which could be used, virtually ready-made, in the composition of other, more readily publishable works. It was a severe setback, and Hardy, who always believed *The Poor Man and the Lady* to have been the most original work, for its time, that he had ever written, never forgot the bitterness of its several rejections and ultimate dismemberment.[34]

When requesting the return of his manuscript from Tinsley Brothers on 14 September 1869, Hardy specified that it be sent 'by *railway,* addressed "to be left at Weymouth Station till calld for" '.[35] In April 1869 he had been asked by G. R. Crickmay, a prosperous Weymouth architect, to assist with some unfinished church-restoration work his firm had taken over following the death of John Hicks. Since Hardy was already familiar with the designs in question, he was willing enough to spend a few weeks working on them in Dorchester at the old South Street office. At the end of May much remained to be done, and—influenced no doubt by the third rejection of his novel—Hardy accepted Crickmay's offer of three months' regular employment in Weymouth itself. His main task was to be the direction of the rebuilding (apart from its west tower) of Turnworth Church, west of Bland-ford Forum—a major undertaking in which he was, perhaps for the first time in his architectural career, given an almost free hand (the stone capitals of the nave, for example, were carved to his designs). Feeling 'much lightness of heart at having shelved further thought about himself for at least three months', Hardy moved into Weymouth lodgings and proceeded to enjoy the pleasures of a seaside summer.[36]

Weymouth—subsequently the 'Budmouth' of Hardy's fictional Wessex—was then a fashionable resort, made newly accessible by the railway but looking back nostalgically towards those glamorous years at the beginning of the century when the patronage of George III and his court had made it a kind of summer capital of the nation during some of the worst crises of the Napoleonic period. It had a naval establishment and a prosperous harbour—the port for regular steamship services to Cherbourg and Jersey—and it was still a garrison town: during the 1869 season the band of the 51st Regiment played in the ornamental gardens every Thursday afternoon, occasionally including in its programme the Strauss 'Morgenblätter' waltz which Hardy associated with Wey-mouth in the poem 'At a Seaside Town in 1869'. That same sum-mer there were plays at the Theatre Royal and musical perform-ances—including a production of Gounod's *Faust* by Mr Henry Manley's English Opera Company—at the Royal Hotel Assembly Rooms, and sedan chairs could still be rented at the rate of six-pence per two hundred yards.

Hardy seems—on the evidence of 'At a Seaside Town in 1869' —to have taken less advantage of these amenities than of the simpler ones afforded by 'The boats, the sands, the esplanade, / The laughing crowd': he went swimming in the mornings and rowing in the evenings, and enjoyed the colour and gaiety of the holiday crowds, including the experience of 'Light-hearted, loud / Greetings from some not ill-endowed'. Later in the year, in com-pany with another architectural assistant who had recently come to work for Crickmay, he attended a quadrille class, evidently not at all dismayed to discover that it constituted in reality 'a gay gathering for dances and love-making by adepts of both sexes'.[37] He also spent a good deal of time on the near-by 'Isle' of Portland —where two of his cousins, sons of James Hardy of Bockhampton, were working as prison warders—and showed the still intact manuscript of *The Poor Man and the Lady* to a friend named Harry Patten, then an insurance agent at Fortuneswell, later the manager of the local branch of the Dorsetshire Bank.* His own lodgings were at 3 Wooperton Street, part of a short terrace in a narrow street near the inner harbour—warranted respectable by the presence in the adjoining houses of the town surveyor and the superintendent of police[39]—and here he kept working away at his poetic exercises and writing down the outlines of possible stories and poems. A note of 15 June 1869 reads: '*Good tragic ballad. A woman who has been seduced finds that the man has married. She kills him. Finds then that his wife is her sister (whom he has also seduced?).*'[40] At the same address he wrote, during the autumn of 1869, the greater part of *Desperate Remedies*. He probably began work on the novel in late September, after Tinsley Brothers had shown at least some interest in *The Poor Man and the Lady,* but it was only towards the end of the year, when his arrangement with Crickmay came to an end, that he was able to give it his full attention.

Determined to produce something that publishers would accept, Hardy now acted all too literally upon the advice he had received from George Meredith and made of *Desperate Remedies* a heavily plotted and deliberately sensational work involving murder, abduction, impersonation, illegitimacy, and a good deal of fairly explicit sexuality. While he seems to have taken Wilkie Collins's *Basil* as a model for several narrative aspects of the book,[41] he also had *The Woman in White* very much in mind as an example of the way a novel could successfully combine the revelation of mysteries, especially those involving crime, with effects of melodramatic horror, especially those derived from the situations of physically or psychologically threatened heroines. As Hardy himself acknowledged in a later preface, the methods adopted in writing the book were 'too exclusively those in which mystery, entanglement, surprise, and moral obliquity are depended on for exciting interest',[42] yet it was by no means a shoddy performance. The character of Cytherea is arresting in its very passivity, and Hardy's sound instinct as a novelist reveals itself in

---

* Hardy seems to have become friendly with Patten through the family of Elizabeth Cozens, widow of the former miller at Lewell in the Frome valley, just a mile or so from Lower Bockhampton. The three Cozens daughters, Dorcas, Annie, and Eliza, ran a school in Portland, and Hardy attended Dorcas's wedding in 1878, when she was thirty-three.[38]

the way she is kept firmly at the centre of the sensation-novel plot: were it not for the appeal of her innocence and helplessness the rather modest apparatus of tension and terror would collapse.

In his desire to finish *Desperate Remedies* as quickly and efficiently as possible Hardy initiated the melancholy process of 'cannibalizing' the manuscript of *The Poor Man and the Lady*. The second Mrs Hardy once spoke of the extent to which *Desperate Remedies* had been drawn from *The Poor Man*,[43] and much other evidence—including the similarities between Knapwater House and the Tollamore House of 'Indiscretion' (see above, p. 112) and the use of the same calendar (for 1864) in the two works—points in the same direction. Indeed, the occurrence in *Desperate Remedies* of passages almost identical with sections of 'Indiscretion' makes it perfectly clear that Hardy had the *Poor Man* manuscript open beside him as he wrote, and that several episodes in the new work were transposed, more or less directly, from the one which had now been abandoned: the power of landlords over their tenants provides a plot element in both works, and those social barriers between the lovers which in *Desperate Remedies* seem somewhat contrived are evidently survivals from the divisions established in *The Poor Man*—the scene in which Edward and Cytherea clasp hands across the stream may well have been an almost unmodified borrowing.

Nor did Hardy disdain the convenience of incorporating such characters and scenes as were most readily to hand. Edward Springrove, though said to be based on a new architectural assistant at Crickmay's, seems autobiographical in his 'very humble origin', his love of books, his knowledge of Shakespeare 'to the very dregs of the foot-notes', and his claim to be 'a poet himself in a small way': indeed, it is by no means impossible that the 'new assistant' was Hardy himself.[44] Weymouth figures largely in the novel under the name Creston (changed to Budmouth in later editions) and an excursion steamer visits parts of the Dorset coast where Hardy himself had recently been with Mary, and where George Nicholls had once served as a coast-guard. Nicholls's daughter Eliza claimed to have been the model for the heroine of Hardy's first novel—by which she presumably meant *Desperate Remedies*—and in the book's single most moving moment, Cytherea's protest to her unresponsive brother against the personal cost extorted by a woman's acceptance of her 'duty to society',[45] she perhaps recognized an echo of her own voice as earlier transposed into the second of the 'She, to Him' sonnets:

Perhaps, long hence, when I have passed away,
Some other's feature, accent, thought like mine,
Will carry you back to what I used to say,
And bring some memory of your love's decline.

Then you may pause awhile and think, 'Poor jade!'
And yield a sigh to me—as ample due,
Not as the tittle of a debt unpaid
To one who could resign her all to you—

And thus reflecting, you will never see
That your thin thought, in two small words conveyed,
Was no such fleeting phantom-thought to me,
But the Whole Life wherein my part was played;
And you amid its fitful masquerade
A Thought—as I in your life seem to be![46]

Though 'prosed' in *Desperate Remedies,* this was presumably one
of the 'original verses' incorporated into the first version of *The
Poor Man and the Lady,* and if that novel, as Hardy later claimed,
showed an extraordinarily accurate knowledge of women,[47] it was
a knowledge that must have been largely derived from Eliza
Nicholls and especially from the letters she wrote during their
long separations. At the beginning of the serial version of *The
Well-Beloved* the central character is engaged in burning some
letters preserved from his youth, many of whose sentiments, 'he
was ashamed to think, he had availed himself of in some attempts
at lyric verse, as having in them that living fire which no lucubra-
tion can reach':[48] the allusion was almost certainly to those letters
of Eliza's which had lent such authenticity to the 'She, to Him'
sonnets and thus to the presentation of the heroines of *The Poor
Man* and *Desperate Remedies.*

Of the several Hardy poems specifically associated with Weymouth during those months of late 1869 when *Desperate Remedies*
was being written, a few—for example, 'Her Father' and 'The
Dawn after the Dance'—probably reflect nothing more than the
casual flirtations of the dancing class. In 'Singing Lovers', however, it is apparently a bereft Hardy who rows the boat on Weymouth Bay while the two lovers sit happily in the stern, and the
sour allusion in this poem to the beloved ('she of a bygone vow')
who has 'gone away,— / Whither, I shunned to say!' is taken up
in other verses of the period. In 'At Waking', for instance, the
speaker suddenly perceives that his beloved is 'but a sample / Of

earth's poor average kind, / Lit up by no ample / Enrichments of mien or mind'. It is this unidealizing vision which controls the poem, and the rejection it implies is only confirmed by the final stanza's overstrenuous and obviously doomed attempt to shake it off:

> Off: it is not true;
> For it cannot be
> That the prize I drew
> Is a blank to me![49]

Because of the occurrence of 'prize' both here and in the one poem ('Thoughts of Phena') which can confidently be associated with Tryphena Sparks, 'At Waking' has been read as in some sense documenting the breakdown of that relationship. But the word is common enough in Hardy's work and the poem probably refers— as both 'Her Initials', also of 1869, and the slightly later 'The Wind's Prophecy' appear to do—to the final renunciation of a vainly cherished loyalty to Jane Nicholls.* It was a renunciation made necessary by her marriage on 29 July 1869 and made bitter by her choice of a man (Harry Beach) who, as a widower with an established position as an inspector of waterworks, must have been her senior by a good many years.[50]

---

* Hardy was also emotionally involved with a young woman named Cassie Pole at about this time, however (see below, p. 149), and his cousin Martha Sparks was married to William Duffield in November 1869. In the drawing which accompanies 'Her Initials' in *Wessex Poems* the initials, though imperfectly decipherable, seem to be either 'T.S.' or 'P.S.' If these are not simply a disguise, they could refer to Tryphena Sparks or, more probably, to Patty (Martha) Sparks, Hardy having perhaps been struck by the correspondence between her initials and those of Shelley, almost certainly the 'high singer' of the poem.

6

ST. JULIOT

Hardy stayed on in Weymouth into the early weeks of 1870, but the town's social life became increasingly distracting and at the beginning of February he withdrew once again to 'the seclusion of his mother's house' in order to work more quietly, and more cheaply, on his manuscript. He had apparently finished supervising the restoration of Turnworth Church (reopened in April 1870), and most of the work on the other churches which Crickmay had taken over at Hicks's death, including West Lulworth and Hinton Martel, was also well advanced. There was, however, one Hicks restoration outside of Dorset which Crickmay had not yet taken in hand, and it was on 11 February 1870 that he wrote to ask Hardy if he would go to Cornwall and 'take a plan and particulars' of the dilapidated church in the tiny hamlet of St. Juliot. Hardy delayed his journey until he was ready, on 5 March, to send off to Alexander Macmillan the nearly completed manuscript of *Desperate Remedies*. Two days later he set off from Bockhampton in the small hours of the morning ('starlight lit my lonesomeness') and reached St. Juliot that same evening.[1]

At the door of the rectory he was greeted not by the rector himself, the Revd Caddell Holder, who was in bed with gout, nor by the rector's wife, who was nursing her husband, but by a 'young lady in brown' who proved to be Miss Emma Lavinia

Gifford, the rector's sister-in-law. Miss Gifford felt, as she later recorded, 'a curious uneasy embarrassment at receiving anyone, especially so necessary a person as the Architect. I was immediately arrested by his familiar appearance, as if I had seen him in a dream —his slightly different accent, his soft voice; also I noticed a blue paper sticking out of his pocket.'[2]

Emma Gifford's nervousness sprang from much anticipatory speculation 'as to what the Architect would be like'. Tiny and remote, St. Juliot offered little in the way of society beyond the occasional visiting clergyman or school inspector, and any visitor was welcome—'even the dentist from Camelford who called regularly & actually dined with us at our mid-day dinner, Mr. Holder having much employment for him'.[3] Following the death of his first wife in 1867, when he was sixty-four, Holder had married Helen Catherine Gifford, daughter of John Attersoll Gifford of Bodmin,[4] formerly a solicitor in Plymouth, and a niece of Canon Edwin Hamilton Gifford, later Archdeacon of London. When the second Mrs Holder, thirty-five years her husband's junior, moved into the rectory in the autumn of 1868 her younger sister, Emma Lavinia, came with her—chiefly, it would seem, as a way of escaping from the pressures of life at home with an embittered and often drunken father.* The situation at the rectory, however, was itself far from idyllic. The rector, though generally tolerant and humorous in his outlook upon life, was subject to frequent illnesses, while Helen Holder's loyalty to her husband did not change the fact that she had married a man so much older than herself in order to escape the alternative fate of a life as a governess or companion. She was often at odds with her sister, and perhaps resentful of Emma's freedom from domestic responsibilities, but ready enough to co-operate in any campaign to find her a husband. Before Hardy's appearance upon the scene a local farmer—probably John Jose, son of the widowed Cordelia Jose of Pennycrocker —had been 'nearly secured' for Emma, but his active pretensions

* J. A. Gifford appears in the Law Lists for 1845 and 1850 as a solicitor practising in Plymouth. He does not appear in the 1855 List, but it is not clear whether (as his daughter Emma states) he deliberately gave up a profession he disliked in order to live 'a life of quiet cultivated leisure' on his mother's income, or (as the second Mrs Hardy once alleged) was struck off the List for some offence. Emma herself acknowledged that her father was given to bouts of heavy drinking—'never a wedding, removal, or death occurred in the family but he broke out again'—and a friend wrote sympathetically in 1872 of the 'many sorrows & trials' Emma and her sister had had to endure.[5]

to her hand were no doubt exaggerated for Hardy's benefit, like those of the young churchwarden who 'scanned / Her and me' and lit the candles with a 'vanquished air', and of the dying William Henry Serjeant of St. Clether, the apparent 'original' of 'The Face at the Casement'.[6]

There can be little doubt that Hardy's engagement and eventual marriage to Emma Gifford were in some measure the calculated outcome of a conspiracy—if only of discretion—involving the entire rectory household. But if he was 'caught' by Emma, it is no less true that he was in the early stages of their courtship entirely captivated by her: he did indeed return from Lyonnesse with 'magic' in his eyes. Although Emma was born on 24 November 1840, less than six months after Hardy himself, he probably believed her to be younger. At the 1871 Census her age was entered as only twenty-five when it was in fact thirty, and it is hard to think that she would have told so gross an official lie if she had not been anxious to sustain a deception of every day. At twenty-nine, when Hardy first met her, Emma wore her spectacular and as yet unfaded corn-coloured hair in long ringlets down either side of her face—giving her, as a friend wrote, 'the look of the old pictures in Hampton Court Palace'—and she made a striking figure as she rode dashingly about the countryside in her 'soft deep dark coloured brown habit, longer than to [her] heels'. Writing after Emma's death to the then rector of St. Juliot, Hardy suggested that some of the old parishioners might yet 'recall her golden curls & rosy colour as she rode about, for she was very attractive at that time'.[7]

There was talk of literature during those first days together in March 1870, Emma having discovered that the blue paper protruding from Hardy's pocket was not a plan but a poem. There was also music in the evenings (as recalled in the poem 'A Duettist to Her Pianoforte'), and Emma behaved with a bewitching mixture of freedom—as they ran down to the edge of Beeny Cliff together—and of coyness—as she 'provokingly' read while walking along at Hardy's side.[8] Hardy, bookish and reticent, was overwhelmed by her sheer physical and nervous energy and by the kind of fey charm—naïve yet by no means unselfconscious—later attributed to Elfride Swancourt in *A Pair of Blue Eyes*. Emma, for her part, was far from overwhelmed by Hardy's personal attractions. He seems to have been somewhat the shorter of the two, and her initial impression was of a man with a 'yellowish' beard, 'a rather shabby great coat', and 'quite a business appearance', who looked 'much older than he was'. Some indication of the terms in which Emma, a little later on, announced their engagement to a friend can be gained from the latter's reply. Congratulating Emma on her engagement and thanking her for her 'sweet photo: & letter full of romantic ideas', Margaret Hawes comments: 'They say that a poetical mind keeps one young, & I am sure you do not look more than 18.' Apropos of the 'fortunate' Mr Hardy, she recounts a discussion with a friend in which they 'both agreed that we did not like handsome *men!* but decided that clever, well read ones were more to our taste—your ideas are the same I find'. Emma painted an alarmingly similar portrait of her future husband in 'The Maid on the Shore', an unpublished novella-length story set in and around Tintagel and perhaps begun at St. Juliot, although not finished until some time later (the surviving typescript was not made until 1910). The heroine of the story, Rosabelle Carlenthen, jilted by her cousin, transfers her affections to his best friend, Alfred During (i.e., Hardy): 'Mr. During's insignificant face and figure and quiet thoughtful manner had an interest for her more matured mind that no merely dashing handsome man like her cousin and some she had been in contact with lately at Truro could have for her again.'[9]

Emma's isolated geographical and social situation obliged her to make the best of the unprepossessing lover who had happened to come her way. For Hardy, ironically enough, Emma's appeal was sharply enhanced by the lonely beauty of the setting in which he first encountered her:

> I found her out there
> On a slope few see,
> That falls westwardly
> To the salt-edged air,
> Where the ocean breaks
> On the purple strand,
> And the hurricane shakes
> The solid land.[10]

St. Juliot Church, though in ruinous condition, was ancient and picturesque, with a pair of fine stone crosses in the churchyard. Even its name, pronounced 'Juliet', was charming, despite the local use of the pronunciation 'jilt'. The rectory, a solid double-gabled stone house tucked into the hillside on the site of an old quarry, was of fairly recent construction, but it had an extensive and ambitious garden and looked out over the valley through which the little Valency River tumbled down to the sea at Boscastle, two miles to the west. To the south-west, beyond Boscastle, stood the majestic ruins of Tintagel Castle, immemorially associated with Arthurian legend. To the north-west, not much more than a mile away, were Pentargan Bay and the stark cliffs running northwards from Beeny to Cambeak.

As Emma, 'with bright hair flapping free', rode on her brown mare across this romantic landscape she created a vision which seized Hardy's imagination at the time and returned to him with overwhelming force when, after her death, he wrote the 'Poems of 1912–13':

> Time touches her not,
> But she still rides gaily
> In his rapt thought
> On that shagged and shaly
> Atlantic spot,
> And as when first eyed
> Draws rein and sings to the swing of the tide.[11]

The moments from the visit to which Hardy returned most obsessively in later years were those of the first meeting on Monday, 7 March—the date to which, after Emma's death, his desk calendar was always set—and of the parting at dawn on Friday, 11 March, when Emma rose early to call the two servants and see Hardy safely on his way. It was then, so the poem 'At the Word "Farewell"' suggests, that the two first kissed and spoke specifically of love:

> Even then the scale might have been turned
>   Against love by a feather,
> —But crimson one cheek of hers burned
>   When we came in together.[12]

In the midst of this emotional turbulence Hardy found time to survey and measure St. Juliot Church, and soon after his return to Dorset he moved back into lodgings in Weymouth in order to complete the detailed drawings, which were approved and signed by Crickmay on 2 May 1870.[13] Hardy later claimed to have done no more than assist in the restoration, and the decision to pull down the whole of the existing tower, north aisle, and north transept had indeed been made as early as 1866, long before he

became involved.* Deeply as he regretted in later years the ruthlessness of the St. Juliot restoration—including the destruction of
the original rood screen and handsomely carved pew ends—Hardy
could plead in partial extenuation that the condition of the original structure was so bad that it was something of an achievement
to have preserved even the old south aisle, which forms the nave
of the church as it now stands.

On 4 April 1870, shortly after Hardy's return from St. Juliot,
Alexander Macmillan rejected *Desperate Remedies,* declaring
that while it had 'very decided qualities, & very considerable
power' it was 'of far too sensational an order for us to think of
publishing'. The judgement echoed the report by John Morley,
who had objected to the extravagance of much of the novel, and
especially to 'the disgusting and absurd outrage which is the key
to its mystery', but felt none the less that 'the book shows *power*—
at present of a violent and undisciplined kind'.[15] Immediately the
manuscript returned to his hands Hardy sent it off again, this
time to William Tinsley, who had been willing, at a price, to
publish *The Poor Man and the Lady.* On 3 May Tinsley forwarded the reader's report and pointed out that there seemed to
be 'rather strong reasons why the book should not be published
without some alteration'. Two days later, in response to a suggestion of Hardy's, he stated that he would be willing to undertake
publication of a revised manuscript on payment of £75 by the
author in advance of printing. To this Hardy, however reluctantly,
agreed.[16]

Once he had finished the St. Juliot drawings Hardy again left
Weymouth for Bockhampton. In mid-May he went on to London,
where he took lodgings at 23 Montpelier Street, a three-storey
terrace house about half-way between Montpelier Square and the
Brompton Road. On the Wednesday following his arrival in
London Hardy was at the Royal Academy, admiring the work
of Gérôme; on the Sunday he attended service at St. Mary's,
Bryanston Square. Later he worked briefly for Blomfield and, for
a rather longer period, for Raphael Brandon, co-author of *An*

* 'This ancient Parish Church', ran the original restoration appeal of
June 1866, 'has for many years been in a ruinous condition. The Tower
threatens to fall; and the roof, floor, and a large portion of the walls of the
nave, are too dilapidated for any partial repairs, and render the interior
unhealthy to the congregation, and unfit for the celebration of Divine
Service; with the exception of the walls of the South aisle and Porch, an
entire rebuilding will be necessary.'[14]

Analysis of Gothick Architecture, a book which he had studied
in earlier years. Hardy much admired Brandon's steadfast adherence to English Gothic despite the current fashion—exemplified by Blomfield—for French Gothic, and was sufficiently struck
by his office at 17 Clement's Inn to use it as a model for Henry
Knight's 'Bede's Inn' chambers in *A Pair of Blue Eyes.*[17]

Horace Moule, whose career was in some respects to be reflected in Knight's, was in London that same summer of 1870. In
September 1865 Moule had obtained a post as assistant master at
Marlborough College—no doubt through the influence of his
younger brother Charles, who had taught there from 1858 to 1864
—and for more than three years he played an active part in
school life, speaking at debates, arranging for William Barnes and
other visitors to address the boys, and helping with the school
magazine. A surviving letter of his to the Bursar, dating from 1867,
complains rather fussily about 'the way the maid-servants have of
singing and calling loudly to each other in the passages during
their work'.* Then, in December 1868, Moule had left the school,
apparently without previous notice: the first issue of the school
magazine in 1869 simply states that 'All Marlburians were sorry
to hear of the unexpected retirement of H. M. Moule, Esq., from
the Common Room. His services to the *Marlburian* have been
very valuable.' No reason is given for his sudden departure, and a
letter to the Bursar the following May deals so straightforwardly
with the settlement of a small account and the examination successes of former students as to give no grounds for assuming that
he had left under a visible cloud.[18] In view of his previous and
subsequent history, however, it seems reasonable to speculate that
he had experienced, during the Christmas vacation of 1868,
another of his alcoholic breakdowns.† The May 1869 letter to the

---

* A similar fussiness appears in Moule's notice of George Eliot's *Adam
Bede* in the *Saturday Review*, 26 February 1859, which raises fastidious objections to the way in which the stages of Hetty's pregnancy had been 'indicated
with a punctual sequence that makes the account of her misfortunes read
like the rough notes of a man-midwife's conversation with a bride. This is
intolerable.'

† It is possible that he had been accused of some homosexual involvement: there is certainly a story of his being deeply grieved by the early
death of a boy on whom he had 'lavished' his affections. On the other hand,
Wynne Albert Bankes speaks in his diary of encountering Moule unexpectedly
during a visit to Marlborough some years after the Paris episode; although
Moule met Bankes 'as if nothing had happened', he may well have felt that
his past had caught up with him and made his position at the school no
longer tenable.[19]

Bursar was written from Dorchester, but by the time Hardy saw him in London in 1870 Moule seems to have been working as a coach for the Indian Civil Service competitive examinations in which Hooper Tolbort, now in India, had been so successful.[20]

Hardy told Moule of Miss Gifford and wrote the poem 'Ditty (E.L.G.)' about 'the spot / That no spot on earth excels, / —Where she dwells!'. A regular correspondence with Emma had been maintained since the previous March, and a note of Hardy's attributed to 25 April 1870 ('Nine-tenths of the letters in which people speak unreservedly of their inmost feelings are written after ten at night')[21] suggests that he—or perhaps she—had written in passionate terms. Throughout this courtship, indeed, repeated separations bridged by correspondence did much to sustain the high pitch of Hardy's feelings. The need and opportunity to re-create again and again the image of the absent beloved and to reassert his own romantic qualifications led Hardy to project to Emma, and to himself, hopes and promises that reality could not in the nature of things fulfil.

On 8 August 1870 he returned to St. Juliot and found Emma waiting for him in 'summer blue', the 'original air-blue gown' of later recollection. Hardy stayed in Cornwall for three ecstatic weeks. He and Emma explored the local countryside together, visited Tintagel Castle—where they nearly got locked in for the night—and went down to Boscastle and across to Beeny Cliff on sketching expeditions. On Sundays they attended the services held in the schoolroom at St. Juliot—Emma, as usual, playing the harmonium for the hymn-singing—and on the first Sunday, 14 August, they went also to nearby Lesnewth Church for evening service, Hardy recalling years afterwards the sight of the church-warden—evidently the 'vanquished' one of the poem—lighting the candles for the evening hymn.[22] As the poem 'Quid Hic Agis?' indicates, he also long remembered his exchange of smiles with Emma as they 'heard read out / During August drought' those words from I Kings 19:12—part of the lesson for the Ninth Sunday after Trinity—which had already so established themselves in his imagination: 'and after the fire a still small voice'. It is, of course, precisely the lesson which Knight is given to read in church in *A Pair of Blue Eyes*.[23]

The Franco-Prussian War had broken out in mid-July 1870, and on 18 August, the day of the battle of Gravelotte, Hardy observed, from the end of the rectory garden, the profoundly un-dramatic scene which was to inspire many years later the poem

'In Time of "The Breaking of Nations" '. The notes made on this occasion were scribbled in pencil on the endpapers of Lackmann's *Specimens of German Prose . . . with a literal and interlineal translation,* from which Hardy, perhaps disturbed by the course of European events, was endeavouring to learn some German: 'Sc. rusty harrow—behind that rooks—behind them, 2 men hoeing mangel, with bowed backs, behind that a heap of couch smoking, behind these horse & cart doing nothing in field—then the ground rising to plantn.'[24] Some time that same day Emma, in gay mood, sketched her lover as he sat on a fence with a makeshift flag in his hand. The following day Hardy drew Emma as, sleeves pulled up and ringlets falling forward, she groped in the water for a tumbler which had fallen between the rocks of the waterfall by which they had picnicked in the Valency valley. A tiny sketch by Emma showing a tomb-like slab beneath a tree carries Hardy's annotation 'Our Stone' and evidently records a spot in the extensive rectory garden where they were accustomed to sit in a shared privacy which neither Mrs Holder nor her husband would have been anxious to disturb. Occasionally it rained —one day on Beeny they remained sketching until the shower passed—but one of Hardy's notebooks records a more sympathetic and (that summer) more typical day of serene sunshine and stillness: 'The smoke from a chimney droops over the roof like the feather in a girl's hat. Clouds, dazzling white, retain their shape by the half-hour, motionless, & so far below the blue that one can almost see round them.'[25]

The exceptional dryness of the summer of 1870 provides a basis for associating with it the poem entitled 'The Place on the Map': 'Weeks and weeks we had loved beneath that blazing blue, / Which had lost the art of raining, as her eyes to-day had too.' The place itself—'a jutting height' with 'a margin of blue sea'[26]—is immediately suggestive of Beeny, but because the subject of the poem appears to be the harsh interruption of an idyllic love relationship by the woman's discovery of her pregnancy, it has not generally been associated with the childless Hardy and Emma. But it is not impossible that Emma, desperate at twenty-nine to catch and hold the man who had so fortuitously intruded upon the isolation of St. Juliot, had permitted sexual intimacy and then announced a real, imagined, or pretended pregnancy— 'the thing we found we had to face before the next year's prime' —only to confess, once Hardy had publicly committed himself to marriage, that, like Arabella in *Jude the Obscure,* she had been mistaken. Such a reading is at least consistent with the sexual excitement which pervades the Cornish poems and with the sexual, if somewhat childish, provocativeness of Emma's appearance and behaviour as they emerge both from those poems and from *Early Life*. Emma's mild adventurousness in intellectual matters—Hardy once said she had been an agnostic at the time of their first meeting[27]—may have been accompanied by some degree of sexual freedom, and Hardy's later sense of having been personally cheated in marriage was perhaps founded upon an exasperating parallelism between Emma's sexual advances and retreats and her gradual shift from religious doubt to Evangelical orthodoxy and even a form of religious mania. Hardy's second wife believed, on the basis of what her husband had told her, that he was trapped into marriage by the scheming of Mrs Holder,[28] and even if nothing precisely corresponding to 'The Place on the Map' occurred, there is no doubt that Emma was very anxious to marry, that her sister and brother-in-law conspired to render circumstances propitious, and that when Hardy returned to Bockhampton at the end of August 1870 he considered himself betrothed.

That autumn, according to the account in *Early Life,* Hardy revised the manuscript of *Desperate Remedies* and then sent it to Emma Gifford to be written out again in fair copy, turning his own attention meanwhile to the completion of the 'three or four remaining chapters'[29]—although Tinsley's letters nowhere indicate that the original manuscript was incomplete, and it seems improbable that a novel of sensation and criminal detection would have been submitted without a fully worked out dénouement. The nonsurvival of the manuscript—said to have been destroyed by Hardy himself when he was moving lodgings and found it would not go into his portmanteau—makes it impossible to guess just how extensively it was revised at this stage. Hardy did remove the 'violation of a young lady [Miss Aldclyffe] at an evening party' which Morley had castigated as 'a disgusting and absurd outrage', but he retained, to the fascination of post-Freudian critics, the scene 'between Miss Aldclyffe and her new maid in bed' which Morley had found 'highly extravagant'.[30]

No longer in regular employment, Hardy now reformulated in economic terms his earlier dictum about the irreconcilability of high conceptions and practical necessities: 'It is, in a worldly sense, a matter for regret that a child who has to win a living

should be born of a noble nature. Social greatness requires little-
ness to inflate & float it, & a high soul may bring a man to the
workhouse.' That same month of October 1870 Emma wrote of
their love as 'This dream of my life—no, not dream, for what is
actually going on around me seems a dream rather'. Hardy had
evidently been disappointingly undemonstrative in word or deed,
for she added: 'I take him (the reserved man) as I do the Bible;
find out what I can, compare one text with another, & believe
the rest in a lump of simple faith'. These extracts perhaps cast
some doubt on Emma's agnosticism; together with one other
fragment, similarly transcribed by Hardy into one of his notebooks, they represent all that now survives of a correspondence
which Hardy, in his old age, claimed to have been comparable to
the love letters of Robert and Elizabeth Browning.[31]

On 28 October, immediately after receiving the letter just
quoted, Hardy wrote Emma's initials in his Bible against verse
2 and part of verse 3 in the fourth chapter of the Song of Solomon:
'Thy teeth are like a flock of sheep that are even shorn, which
came up from the washings; whereof everyone bear twins, and
none is barren among them. Thy lips are like a thread of scarlet,
and thy speech is comely.' But other notations hint at difficulties
and forebodings, originating in self-doubt or in family disapproval
of the professional and emotional courses he was now following.
The date 22 September 1870, for example, appears in his Bible
against Proverbs 14:22: 'Do they not err that devise evil? but
mercy and truth shall be to them that devise good.' That his
mother's influence, now that he was again in her daily presence,
asserted itself more strongly than it had done during those mag-
ical weeks of the summer is clear from the profoundly revealing
note of 30 October 1870—'Mother's notion, & also mine: That a
figure stands in our van with an arm uplifted, to knock us back
from any pleasant prospect we indulge in as probable'—while his
dominant mood of mingled determination, apprehension, and
resignation finds a precise reflection in a passage from *Hamlet*
which he marked on 15 December: 'Thou wouldst not think how
ill all's here about my heart: but it is no matter!' A marking on
16 November of Revelation 10:11—'And he said unto me, Thou
must prophesy again before many peoples, and nations, and
tongues, and kings'—may be indicative of a resolution to proceed
with a literary career, but it is also apparent that Hardy, during
these latter months of 1870, was again reading systematically
through much of the New Testament.[32]

It seems safe to assume that many of the markings and annotations in Hardy's editions and translations of classical authors—among them Aeschylus, Euripides, Horace, and Lucretius—also belong to this period, although it is impossible to assign them to specific dates. But there is again little direct evidence of his exposure, let alone his response, to the current intellectual ferment. In one of his Milton volumes, alongside the paragraph beginning at line 167 of Book Three of *Paradise Lost,* Hardy has written: 'The difficulty of reconciling Freewill and Omnipotce very apparent here.'[33] The comment is again undated, but it is apparent that in the late 1860s and early 1870s Hardy was himself attempting to reconcile a whole series of radically opposed philosophies and creeds, his very lack of a formal and traditional education no doubt making the transition from belief to unbelief a good deal smoother for him than for many of his more sophisticated contemporaries. Long experience of having to find his own intellectual way had made him an habitual eclectic, and he thus found little difficulty in ranging ideas newly derived from Darwin and Huxley alongside the necessitarian views already instilled in him by both the peasant fatalism of his upbringing and the tragic patterns of the Greek dramatists. He spoke again and again in later years of his essentially emotional and non-intellectual approach to life and of his lack of any systematic philosophy, and in his early adult years his most persistent search seems to have been for philosophical formulations which answered to his own perceptions of the world, to his instinctive sense of the way things were. What mattered emotionally, in terms of human experience, was the fact of individual unfreedom; identification of the inscrutable controlling 'Omnipotence' was, by comparison, a matter of perhaps fascinating but ultimately irresolvable intellectual debate.

Hardy resubmitted the manuscript of *Desperate Remedies* in early December 1870. Shortly before Christmas he received, at Bockhampton, Tinsley's firm offer to publish the novel on the terms already agreed, his reader having reported that, as now revised, it would probably sell—though it might still be wise not to insist quite so specifically that Mrs Manston's *'substitute'* was Manston's *'mistress'.* In response to a request for clarification of the terms, Tinsley explained that Hardy would not, as he had assumed, receive back his £75 once the proceeds equalled the expenditures, but that publisher and author would divide between them any *surplus* of income over expenditure. Hardy seems to have felt that the terms had been changed for the worse, but while Tinsley may indeed have been guilty of allowing an inexperienced author to persist in a misapprehension, the final balance sheet, which includes only actual printing and advertising costs and not Tinsley's office expenses, shows plainly enough that the arrangement Hardy had in mind would not, on a printing of 500 copies, have been a worthwhile undertaking from a publisher's standpoint. Though still resentful of what he considered Tinsley's sharp practice, Hardy paid over the money in cash*— and in person—in January 1871, when he was again in London. The proofs reached him back in Bockhampton shortly afterwards and *Desperate Remedies: A Novel* was published, anonymously, on 25 March 1871.[34]

The first review, in the *Athenaeum* of 1 April, was remarkably positive: it found the unknown author guilty of 'occasional coarseness' but concluded that if he would 'purge himself' of this fault 'we see no reason why he should not write novels only a little, if at all, inferior to the best of the present generation'. In the context of such encouragement it was galling for Hardy to have to report his occupation in the Census, taken on 2 April, as 'architect's clerk', precisely the way he had been categorized in the 1861 return. For all his efforts in the ten intervening years he had made very little upward progress, and the three volumes of *Desperate Remedies* stood alone as tangible evidence of what he was, against all odds, capable of achieving. The novel was praised again in the *Morning Post* of 13 April, but the 22 April number of the *Spectator* contained a review whose opening paragraphs seemed so savage and contemptuous that Hardy had scarcely the emotional resilience to withstand their impact:

> This is an absolutely anonymous story; no falling back on previous works which might give a clue to the authorship, and no assumption of a *nom de plume* which might, at some future time, disgrace the family name, and still more, the Christian name of a repentant and remorseful novelist,—and very right too. By all means let him bury the secret in the profoundest depths of his own heart, out of reach, if possible, of his own consciousness. The law is hardly just which prevents Tinsley Brothers from concealing their participation also.

* It was in the form of Bank of England £10 notes. Where Hardy obtained so considerable a sum is not quite clear: he perhaps drew upon savings originally intended to help support him at university.

The remainder of the review, as Hardy came eventually to recognize, spoke positively of his handling of the rustic characters and his power to arouse in his readers his own 'sensitiveness to scenic and atmospheric effects', but as he first read it, sitting on a stile at the edge of the Kingston Maurward ewe-leaze, he wished himself dead—showing at this early moment, when his identity was as yet unknown, that extreme vulnerability to hostile criticism which was to recur again and again, even in the days of his greatest success and fame.[35]

At the end of March 1871, a few days after the publication of *Desperate Remedies,* Hardy had resumed work for Crickmay in Weymouth and taken lodgings again at 3 Wooperton Street, although he still spent most weekends at Bockhampton.[36]* A long entry in the architectural notebook taken from a published account of the new St. Thomas's Hospital in London probably relates to work Crickmay was doing on two Weymouth hospitals at this time, and Hardy seems also to have been involved with the restoration of Stoke Wake Church, with extensions to schools in and near Weymouth, and with alterations to Slape House, Netherbury.[38] It was probably a professional errand which took him to Upwey, just north of Weymouth, on the morning of 17 April 1871—although he did have relatives in the village, his aunts Martha and Jane Groves and their families. He had kept up the habit, first adopted in London during the 1860s, of carrying with him everywhere little lined pocket-books in which observations, ideas, plots, even pencil sketches, could be entered on the spot, so to speak, and although such notebooks were later systematically destroyed (see below, p. 518n.) an occasional detached page, often partly erased, survives to give some indication of what his working habits were. On this occasion he recorded a visual phenomenon ('A range of hills endways—the near end brilliant in a green dress softening away to blue at the other') and then—probably, though not necessarily, on the same day—went on to jot down the outline of a story about a village girl who became a school mistress.[39]

The advantages of architecture, as Hardy now engaged in it,

* On Sunday, 7 May 1871, he recorded a characteristic comment of his mother's about a man and a woman involved in an incident she had witnessed: 'They were mother & son I supposed, or perhaps man & wife, for they marry in such queer ways nowadays that there's no telling which. Anyhow, there was a partnership of some kind between them.'[37]

were that it allowed ample opportunity for outdoor observation and exercise and could be taken up or left off almost at will. But although this was a sufficiently pleasant mode of existence, it was neither the complete literary life he had long envisaged nor an adequate economic resource for a man contemplating marriage to a young lady with a horse of her own and—as the daughter of a solicitor, the sister-in-law of a rector, and the niece of a Canon —considerable pretensions to gentility. He saw Emma Gifford again when he went down to Cornwall in late May, just before his thirty-first birthday, and it was while on his return journey at the beginning of June that he found, on Exeter station, copies of *Desperate Remedies* being remaindered for the derisory price of 2*s*.6*d*. for the three volumes. Nor would he have been much comforted by the knowledge that Mudie's were asking 6*d*. more for the book. Horace Moule—whom Hardy had apparently not told in advance of the publication of the novel—attempted to salvage the situation with a laudatory notice in the *Saturday Review*. Moule's review did not appear until 30 September, however, and although Tinsley agreed to Hardy's suggestion that an extract from it be used in future advertisements, he feared that it had come too late to affect the sales: 'when once a book has been offered cheap it is almost impossible to get the Librarians to buy it in again.'[40]

During the late spring and early summer of 1871, spent partly at Weymouth, subsequently at Bockhampton,[41] Hardy brought to completion a manuscript on which he had done a certain amount of work even before the writing of *Desperate Remedies*. The new novel, *Under the Greenwood Tree,* seems to have derived partly from the early scenes of *The Poor Man and the Lady* and partly from the tale 'entirely of rural scenes & humble life' he had mentioned to Macmillan in September 1868. Many years later, in response to an interviewer's questions as to how he had 'drifted into literature', Hardy replied:

I suppose the impressions which all unconsciously I had been gathering of rural life during my youth in Dorsetshire recurred to me, and the theme—in fiction—seemed to have absolute freshness. So in my leisure—which was considerable—I began to write "Under the Greenwood Tree" but after writing it about half, laid it aside to write "Desperate Remedies." This novel was a success soon after its publication, but under my contract with the publisher I made nothing out of it. However, it encouraged me to go on with "Under the Greenwood Tree." I finished it as I began it, which I now regret, because much more could have been made of the story.[42]

In speaking of 'the story' Hardy can scarcely have been referring to the minimal plot line of *Under the Greenwood Tree*. The unusual beauty of the novel depends very largely upon its lack of 'story', and its sub-title, *A Rural Painting of the Dutch School*, not only reflects a conscious attempt to apply to literature something of what Hardy had learned in his artistic studies but points to a 'composed' quality in the book as a whole. Carefully confined and framed in terms of both time and space, it is presented as a kind of woodland pastoral in which the momentary flurry of the foreground is at once diminished (in its individuality) and magnified (in its representativeness) by being set against the immemorial customs of the community and the inevitable onward movement of the seasons. The characters, though sufficiently individualized for the purposes of narrative, are players of time-honoured roles, as in a ballad or mumming play, inheritors for their brief moment of joys and sorrows common to all mankind. What Hardy learned, as a novelist, to 'regret' was the way in which his parents', and especially his mother's, longevity had effectively prevented him from returning, with a matured technique and a sharpened and more sombre vision, to that intimate childhood world from which *Under the Greenwood Tree* had drawn so much of its surface detail. Eight years after his mother's death, when he had long abandoned fiction, he spoke of the basic 'realities' of *Under the Greenwood Tree* as potential material for a book of quite a different kind: 'But circumstances', he went on, 'would have rendered any aim at a deeper, more essential, more transcendent handling unadvisable at the date of writing.'[43] Like many another beginning novelist, Hardy in his earliest fiction— *The Poor Man and the Lady* and the episodes in other novels adapted from it—drew heavily upon immediately autobiographical resources. But he treated them humorously for the most part, as a kind of protective device, and if he sometimes seems condescending towards the characters of *Under the Greenwood Tree*, that is in part the consequence of self-conscious distancing—although it would not be surprising, given the date of the novel's composition, if confusion about his own class situation should surface as tonal uncertainty in a novel dealing so closely with his own background.

Much of the detail of the Mellstock Choir's activities, in and out of church, must have been reconstructed from the old music books and from the recollections of his parents and their neighbours—such as James Dart, who had played in the actual Stinsford choir in Hardy's grandfather's time. But the early descriptions of the cottage and of Grandfather James in his mason's clothes come directly from Hardy's own memory, while Mrs Dewy's way of grilling rashers of bacon before an open fire was one he associated with his mother to the very end of his life—on his deathbed he asked for a rasher to be cooked for him before his bedroom fire for just that reason. The topography of the novel conforms almost exactly to that of Stinsford parish, and while it may be true that the book contains no family portraits as such, there is little doubt that not only tricks of phrase associated with Hardy's parents but also some of their quirks of personality are reflected in the placidly antagonistic domestic dialogues between Tranter Dewy and his wife:

'You've no cause to complain, Reuben, of such a close-coming flock,' said Mrs. Dewy; 'for ours was a straggling lot enough, God knows!'

'I d'know it, I d'know it,' said the tranter. 'You be a well-enough woman, Ann.'

Mrs. Dewy put her mouth in the form of a smile and put it back again without smiling.[44]

Offering *Under the Greenwood Tree* to Macmillan on 7 August 1871, Hardy explained that the reviewers' praise of the 'rustic characters & scenery' of *Desperate Remedies* had prompted him to attempt a story entirely of rural life in which the characters would be drawn 'humorously, without caricature'. But the basic debt to *The Poor Man and the Lady* is made explicit by his reference in the same letter to a scene of which the 'accessories' might be recognized 'as appearing originally in a tale submitted originally a long time ago (which never saw the light)'. Ten days later, in response to an enquiry from Macmillan, Hardy supplied copies of the reviews of *Desperate Remedies,* claiming that, though so contradictory, they seemed to indicate not only that he should not 'dabble in plot again at present' but that 'upon the whole a pastoral story would be the *safest* venture'—a conclusion which perhaps accorded less with the evidence than with the circumstance of his happening to have a pastoral story at hand.[45] Malcolm

Macmillan, in mid-September, hinted at probable acceptance but regretted that the firm was not yet ready to make a final decision. Meanwhile he forwarded a copy of John Morley's report, which was full of praise for the novel's 'extremely careful, natural and delicate' workmanship, but advised the author to study George Sand's rural tales, to restrain his tendencies towards excessive realism, and to 'shut his ears to the fooleries of critics, as his letter to you proves he does not do'. Although Hardy was never to prove capable of adopting that last piece of sensible advice, he did obtain, and read, translations of three George Sand novels two or three years later.[46]

No further word came from Macmillan and on 14 October 1871—when he was again in Cornwall*—Hardy wrote to draw attention to the *Saturday Review* notice of *Desperate Remedies* and request news of *Under the Greenwood Tree*. A reply then came from Alexander Macmillan, on whom publishing decisions finally depended, to the effect that the tale, though charming, was rather slight and too short to be printed in the standard three-volume form. He concluded: 'We could not venture on it now, as our hands are full of Christmas books; besides it is hardly a good time for "Under the Greenwood Tree". But if you should not arrange otherwise before the spring I should like to have the opportunity of deciding as to whether we could do it for an early summer or spring book. I return the MS.'[48] If not ambiguous this was certainly temporizing, and Hardy and Emma, still together at St. Juliot, perhaps took it as a final rejection: in any case, they could have had little expectation of Hardy's making much money out of such pastoral idylls. Determined to take full stock of his situation, Hardy wrote at once to Tinsley to ask about the sales of *Desperate Remedies* and, more obliquely, to sound out his interest either in *Under the Greenwood Tree*—represented as 'a little rural story' as yet unfinished—or in *A Pair of Blue Eyes,* not given any title but spoken of as a work, still in its early stages, 'the essence of which is plot, *without crime*—but on the plan of D.R.' Tinsley's reply avoided direct reference to either of these alternatives, confining itself to a warning that Hardy was unlikely to retrieve the whole of his investment in *Desperate Remedies* and to a few words of general encouragement: 'I think the

---

* It was during this visit that Hardy, at Crickmay's request, had the rood screen of St. Juliot Church taken out to be measured and examined prior to restoration—and thus gave the builder the opportunity to make the well-meaning but ill-judged gesture of supplying a brand-new screen in its place.[47]

"Saturday Review" notice of *"Desperate Remedies"* should induce you to write another three volume novel. At all events if
you do I quite think I shall be glad to take it of you without
any risk to you.'[49]

This was as unsatisfactory in its own way as Alexander Macmillan's letter had been, and Hardy was deeply puzzled as to how
best to proceed. The manuscript of *Under the Greenwood Tree*
must evidently be put aside, with or without the hope of a more
positive response from Macmillan in the spring. As for the three-
volume novel, there was doubt about the solidity of Tinsley's
interest and even about Hardy's capacity to satisfy the requirements of the critics and the reading public. He did not respond
to Tinsley's gesture, perhaps because the new book was as yet
hardly begun, and his mood was not lightened by the necessity of
leaving Cornwall once more at the very end of October—perhaps
the occasion, reflected in the poem 'Love the Monopolist', when
he was hurt by Emma's turning 'round quite / To greet friends
gaily'[50] before the train had carried him out of sight. Attentive as
he had been to the often bewildering advice of readers and reviewers, no publisher had yet proved willing to accept his work .
without a subsidy, while architecture, though valuable as a stand-
by, continued to demand time and energy which might otherwise
be devoted to literature. There was always, too, the sense of social
underprivilege which had provided much of the impetus for *The
Poor Man and the Lady*: as recently as August 1871 he had underlined in his Bible the words 'having men's persons in admiration
because of advantage' from the 16th verse of the General Epistle
of Jude.[51]

7

FAR FROM THE MADDING CROWD

Though strongly encouraged by Emma to continue with his writing, Hardy saw no immediate alternative to that architectural career in which he was—in one sense fortunately, in another ironically—becoming steadily more experienced, proficient, and sought after. The beginning of 1872 found him in lodgings at 1 West Parade, Weymouth, still working for Crickmay, but just before Easter he went once more to London, this time to the Bedford Street offices of T. Roger Smith, who had been one of the judges for the Tite competition in 1863 and now needed assistance in preparing submissions to a London School Board competition for the design of new schools.[1] Hardy took lodgings at 4 Celbridge Place,* in a terraced block (now part of Porchester Road) about a hundred yards from 16 Westbourne Park Villas, and was still enough of a churchgoer to attend service at St. George's, Notting Hill, on Good Friday, at St. Paul's Cathedral on Easter Day, and at St. George's, Hanover Square, the next Sunday, 7 April.[2]

Busy as he was with his work, discouraged as he felt about his

---

* His landlord, a Cornishman named James Williams, had a tailor's shop at street level and lived with his wife and four children on the upper floors. In recent years the shop has been occupied by the Porchester Hairdressing Salon.

literary prospects, Hardy remained keenly interested in the fate of *Desperate Remedies*. Writing to Tinsley on 3 January 1872 he declared, perhaps with more bravado than truth, that he had 'rather delayed the completion' of his new manuscript 'till the result of the other is clear'. Tinsley, after a little delay, sent the account for the novel and then, in March, a cheque for £59.12.7 —representing a smaller loss on the original £75 than Hardy had come to anticipate. Knowing that Hardy was again in London, Tinsley invited him to call at his Catherine Street office, 'as I should like to know what you are going to do about your next book. I hardly think you should be disheartened because the first book has not done well, but this you know best about.'³ According to *Early Life*, Tinsley accosted Hardy in the Strand one day and demanded in a broad cockney accent* that he deliver up his new manuscript, whose whereabouts Hardy could not quite recollect. The actual sequence of events appears to have flowed fairly naturally from Hardy's making, in late March, the visit Tinsley had suggested in his letter: on 8 April he sent Tinsley the manuscript of *Under the Greenwood Tree*; by 15 April Tinsley had read it; and on 22 April, after discussing with Hardy the book's likely prospects, he made an offer of £30 for the copyright.⁵

That same day, probably as he sat in Tinsley's office, Hardy signed away the copyright for the sum Tinsley had offered.⁶ It was an act which caused him much inconvenience and annoyance in later years, but at the moment, lacking both experience and self-confidence, he was glad to get anything at all for a story he had despaired of seeing in print—except, perhaps, at his own expense. The transaction gave a renewed sense of reality to his literary ambitions and provided some reassurance at a time when, in addition to all his other personal and professional doubts, he was sufficiently worried about his eyesight to get from Horace Moule the name and address of William Bowman, one of the leading ophthalmic surgeons of the day.⁷ The problem proved not to be serious, however, and there is no indication of any further eye trouble at that time or for many years thereafter. By early May 1872 he was correcting the proofs of *Under the Greenwood Tree*, and in early June the two-volume first edition was published, to be greeted shortly afterwards by enthusiastic re-

* George Moore, in *Confessions of a Young Man,* describes Tinsley as a 'worthy man' who 'conducted his business as he dressed himself, sloppily; a dear kind soul, quite witless and quite *h*-less.'⁴

views in the *Athenaeum* and the *Pall Mall Gazette*. Horace Moule's anonymous notice in the *Saturday Review* was long and appreciative, but it was again much delayed and Hardy may have felt some annoyance—in view of Moule's background and of his own—at being taken to task, as he had been in the earlier reviews, for allowing the country characters 'to express themselves in the language of the author's manner of thought, rather than in their own'.[8]

By the time Moule's review made its belated appearance, on 28 September, Hardy's career had already taken some crucial turns. In early July—shortly after Hardy had seen a disturbing image of his own possible fate in the figure of the 'city-clerk' who saw 'no escape to the very verge of his days / From the rut of Oxford Street into open ways'—Tinsley wrote to say that he needed a serial to begin in the September number of *Tinsleys' Magazine* and would be glad to consider 'any portion of the new story' that might be ready. Hardy protested that his manuscript needed 'a great deal of re-consideration'—which probably meant that it was as yet unwritten—but was unable to resist either the opportunity of serialization or the £200 which went with it. Somewhat wiser now than he had been in the previous April, he did not dispose of the copyright of *A Pair of Blue Eyes* but only of the right to the serialization and the three-volume first edition.[9]*
At the end of July, when the school competition entries were submitted, Hardy made his departure from Smith's office. By 7 August 1872 he had supplied copy for the first instalment of his serial—due to appear on 15 August!—and was on his way by sea to Cornwall once more.[11]

Before he left London Hardy directed that the proofs of that first instalment should be forwarded, not to St. Juliot, but to Kirland House, near Bodmin,[12] the home of Emma's parents and their dependent eldest son, Richard Ireland Gifford, Jun. On the strength of Tinsley's commission and the promised £200 he evidently felt in a position to make a formal request for Emma's hand. But John Gifford greeted his prospective son-in-law with open contempt: he is said to have referred to him in a later letter

---

* The story of his promptly going out to purchase Walter Arthur Copinger's *The Law of Copyright in Works of Literature and Art* is rather spoiled by the fact that the signature in his library copy is dated 1873.[10]

as a 'low-born churl who has presumed to marry into *my* family', and Hardy once glossed as 'Slander, or something of that sort' a reference (in the poem, 'I Rose and Went to Rou'tor Town') to the 'evil' done at Rou'tor Town, identifiable as Bodmin, not far from Rough Tor.[13] Not surprisingly, Hardy did not stay long at Kirland House. By late August he was addressing letters from St. Juliot rectory again, and he seems also to have spent some time at St. Benet's Abbey, near Lanivet, the home of Captain Charles Sergeant and his wife, friends of Emma's. To this period belongs the foreboding moment, recorded in the poem 'Near Lanivet, 1872', when, pausing to rest on the St. Austell to Bodmin road one evening, Emma stretched out her arms against the arms of a signpost and 'Her white-clothed form at this dim-lit cease of day / Made her look as one crucified'.[14]

In the opening instalment of *A Pair of Blue Eyes,* written in London, Hardy had already drawn upon his Cornish adventure for the first meeting of Elfride Swancourt and the young architect Stephen Smith and for Elfride's distractingly provocative behaviour while Stephen tries to give his attention to the drawing and measuring of the church he has come to restore: 'Has the reader ever seen a winsome girl in a pulpit?' asks the narrator, with ponderous indirection. 'Perhaps not. The writer knows somebody who has, and who can never forget that sight.'[15] In the ensuing months the unfamiliar pressures of writing against a deadline forced Hardy to rely heavily on recent experiences, available scenery, and the active co-operation of Emma in suggesting usable incidents and details. Emma's phrases about 'the reserved man' appear almost word-for-word in one of the later chapters, although it is not clear whether Hardy was drawing extensively upon her letters (as he had upon Eliza's in *Desperate Remedies*) or simply using passages already transcribed into his notebooks. The second instalment (Chapters 6 to 8) of the serial, written in Cornwall in Emma's company and partly recopied in her hand, introduces the lost earring, the game of chess, and other courtship episodes derived from the shared experiences—or the joint imaginative resources—of the two lovers, and when Elfride expresses astonishment at Stephen's inability to ride a horse she is clearly echoing what Emma must have said or at least thought of Hardy, registering it among other accumulating indications that he was not quite a 'gentleman'. It is in this same instalment that Stephen, remarkably enough, is given a family background even humbler than

Hardy's own—a 'journeyman mason' for a father, a 'dairymaid' for a mother.[16]* Whether these details reflect a deliberate, even defiant, honesty on Hardy's part in the wake of his reception by Emma's father, or simply his adaptation of existing material from the highly class-conscious *Poor Man* manuscript, it is impossible to tell. In any case, Emma's loyal copying out of part of the scene dealing with Stephen's parentage constituted a symbolic declaration that she not only intended to marry her architect but would have done so had their difference of class been even greater than it actually was.

Despite the high incidence of details drawn from his courtship of Emma, Hardy later insisted that the plot of the novel had been 'thought of and written down' long before he had ever visited Cornwall, and since much of the novel (most notably the Rotten Row scene) evidently derives from *The Poor Man and the Lady*, it is likely enough that the story was first conceived of as having a different heroine and a different setting—possibly Eliza Bright Nicholls and that area of south-east Dorset, including the heights of Gad Cliff and Worbarrow Bay, with which she was always associated in Hardy's mind.[18]† The chapters focused on Stephen's parents and on his own situation mid-way between two distinct social groups living side by side and even interdependently—as the Hardys and the Martins had lived on the Kingston Maurward estate—must have been derived more or less directly from the *Poor Man* manuscript; it is, indeed, possible to perceive an extraordinary degree of underlying continuity among the basic social patterns, and hence the basic dramatic premises, of *Desperate Remedies, Under the Greenwood Tree,* and *A Pair of Blue Eyes,* all three ultimately dependent in one way or another upon

---

* In the Wessex Edition of 1912 Stephen's father became a 'working master-mason', while of his mother it was now said that 'Her people had been well-to-do yeomen for centuries, but she was only a dairy-woman'.[17]

† Surviving sections of the manuscript of *A Pair of Blue Eyes* show that he was at one time working with the same 1864-7 calendar and time scheme he had employed in *Desperate Remedies* and, earlier still, in *The Poor Man and the Lady.* Dorset and Somerset place-names—Benvill Lane and Binegar Fair—also appear in early versions of the story, and it was not until he revised the novel for the Wessex Edition in 1912 that Hardy finally changed a reference to 'poor deaf Grammer Cates' which had hitherto asserted the essential identity of the world of Stephen Smith's parents not only with the world of *Under the Greenwood Tree,* in which Grammer Caytes (later Kaytes) also appears, but also with the world of Hardy's Bockhampton childhood, where the elderly Rachel Keates (recorded as 'deaf' in the 1851 Census) was an immediate neighbour.[19]

John Antell, shoemaker, of Puddletown

Thomas Hardy, c.1862: the photograph, taken
in London, which he gave to Eliza Nicholls

Eliza Nicholls

Ch. near the Downs. From the hill
1860

Hardy's sketch of Findon Church,
from his architectural notebook

Jane Nicholls

Hardy's illustration for 'She, to Him. I'   From *Wessex Poems* (1898)

Kimmeridge Bay, Dorset, showing Clavel Tower on the headland and the
former coast-guard cottages to its right

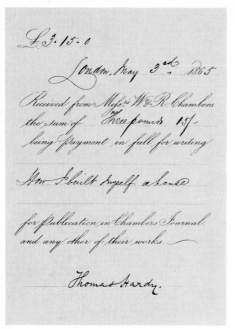

Hardy's receipt for his first
literary earnings

Hardy's sketch of the view from his
room at 16 Westbourne Park Villas

Turnworth Church, Dorset, restored by Hardy in 1869

The Poor Man and the Lady. Though Hardy adapted the materials from his quarry with considerable skill, it seems necessary to conclude that the parents of Dick Dewy, Edward Springrove, and Stephen Smith had common antecedents in the parents of Will Strong, and that they in turn were composite portraits for which Hardy's own parents served as the principal models. So, in *A Pair of Blue Eyes,* Stephen's mother retaliates with all the vigour of Jemima when detected in a logical inconsistency:

> 'Yes, there, there! That's you; that's my own flesh and blood. I'll warrant that you'll pick holes in everything your mother says if you can, Stephen. You are just like your father for that; take anybody's part but mine. Whilst I am speaking and talking and trying and slaving away for your good, you are waiting to catch me out in that way. So you are in [Elfride's] class, but 'tis what *her* people would *call* marrying out of her class. Don't be so quarrelsome, Stephen!'
>
> Stephen preserved a discreet silence, in which he was imitated by his father, and for several minutes nothing was heard but the ticking of the green-faced case-clock against the wall.[20]

The directness of Hardy's borrowing from his home background is no less remarkable—no less naïve—than his use of episodes from his courtship of Emma. It is almost as though he were deliberately juxtaposing within the world of the novel the two sharply separated halves of his own life. He seems, meanwhile, to have made little determined effort to bring Emma face to face with his family, and his passivity, his readiness to let matters take their own course, is said to have aroused Emma to the extraordinary—and predictably disastrous—expedient of making an unheralded visit to Bockhampton to plead, or proclaim, her case for recognition and acceptance.[21] Jemima, like Stephen Smith's mother, felt threatened by Emma's social pretensions and what they might imply for her own future relations with her son, and nothing in Emma's appearance or manner was conducive, then or ever, to dispelling the Bockhampton prejudice against her as an interloper who had neither youth, wealth, domestic virtues, nor even a Dorset background, to recommend her. Emma, for her part, may well have been shocked to discover just how 'countrified' the Hardys really were, and if the visit was indeed made it was not repeated before her marriage, or even for some time afterwards.

In mid-August 1872, while Hardy was still in Cornwall, Roger

Smith wrote to say that since one of the school designs had been successful in the competition he would be glad to take Hardy on again for a time. Smith's letter prompted debate at St. Juliot about the entire direction of Hardy's future career—especially since the design in question seems to have been largely his own work—and evidently constituted that crucial moment when he 'stood at the parting of the ways' and asked himself whether he would 'rather lose money & opportunities by writing than gain them by not writing'. After putting that same 'test' question to someone else years later, Hardy went on: 'If you can honestly say yes, I think you are called by nature to do it.'[22] His own answer in 1872 was strongly affirmative, but he could no doubt have returned just such a reply at any point during the past several years and the crucial step might even now have been missed or delayed if Emma had not been physically present at the necessary moment and if the immediate decision had not been in itself of a simple undramatic kind—a mere matter of saying no to Smith's offer. Given the understanding which already existed between them, the definitive resolution to abandon architecture as a profession could not in any case have been made without Emma's support, grounded though that support necessarily was in automatic loyalty and inexperienced romanticism rather than in any clear perception of economic realities.

The days passed pleasantly away meanwhile, with excursions to Beeny and Tintagel and as far away as Brent Tor, near Tavistock, and Hardy allowed himself to get behindhand with the second instalment of *A Pair of Blue Eyes*.[23] On 8 September, the final Sunday of his visit, he went with Emma to afternoon service in the now renovated and reopened church at St. Juliot and read both of the lessons—Jeremiah 36 and Romans 9. He made appropriate annotations in his Bible and prayerbook,[24] and the occasion obviously had deep significance for him, perhaps because he knew that the reading of the lesson was a class prerogative and felt that the invitation in some sense constituted a ratification of his status, not simply as Emma's betrothed, but as a professional man.

He was back at Celbridge Place by 11 September, but by the end of the month he had withdrawn once more to the seclusion of Bockhampton. In early October Tinsley announced that he would be sending an additional £10 as half the proceeds from the sale of the continental reprint rights of *Under the Greenwood Tree,* and added that he was longing to read the next instalment of *A Pair of Blue Eyes,* 'for I *shall lose my reputation* as a judge of good fiction if you dont do great things'.[25] That same autumn Leslie Stephen, editor of the *Cornhill Magazine,* came to much the same conclusion about Hardy's future, but exclusively on the basis of a reading of *Under the Greenwood Tree.* 'I hear from Mr Moule',* he wrote to Hardy on 30 November 1872, 'that I may address you as the author of "Under the Greenwood Tree".' Although that novel had too little incident and plot for magazine purposes, Stephen went on, it was admirably written, and had induced him to request, for the *Cornhill,* the offer of any new novel Hardy might now have in progress: 'if any agreement could be made between us I have no doubt it would be satisfactory in a pecuniary point of view.' This was an extraordinary moment for a hitherto unknown writer, in that the *Cornhill,* first edited by Thackeray, stood in the very forefront of contemporary magazines in terms both of circulation and prestige. Delighted at so positive an approach from so distinguished a quarter, Hardy replied that he was busy with *A Pair of Blue Eyes*—of which Stephen apparently knew nothing—but would subsequently be turning his attention to a pastoral tale he had in mind, to be called *Far from the Madding Crowd.* Stephen wrote back to say that he was sorry at the delay but would be patient: 'I like your proposed title,' he added.[27]

Before hearing from Stephen, Hardy had arranged another visit to St. Juliot. In a letter of 29 November Caddell Holder thanked him for the plan he had drawn of a projected railway line which would pass through St. Juliot and said that they were 'all' hoping to see him on 18 December for as long as he cared to stay. 'The young lady,' he added, somewhat coyly, 'Miss Gifford, whom you mention is still here & sends her regards &c &c &c &c'. Whether or not Hardy did in fact spend Christmas in Cornwall is not quite clear—*Early Life* speaks of his staying at Bockhampton until the end of the year—but he was certainly there on 7 January 1873 when he drew up, for Holder's signature, a final statement of the donations and expenses connected with the restoration of

* This seems simply to have meant that Stephen had asked Moule, as the latest reviewer of *Under the Greenwood Tree,* if he could identify the author. Frederick Greenwood subsequently claimed to have been the first to draw the book to Stephen's attention.[26]

St. Juliot Church.[28]* By mid-January 1873 Hardy was back in Bockhampton, where he was to remain for the next several months. With *Far from the Madding Crowd* already in his mind, he would scarcely have missed the opportunity of attending the annual hiring fair held in Dorchester on 14 February (Old Candlemas Day) and hearing Joseph Arch, the leader of the National Agricultural Labourers' Union, denounce from a wagon on Fordington Green the inadequacy of agricultural wages and the iniquity of the hiring system itself.[30] On 12 March he sent off the final chapters of *A Pair of Blue Eyes*; these were not to appear in *Tinsleys' Magazine* until the July number (published in mid-June), but their earlier submission was made necessary by the standard practice of publishing the book version of a new novel shortly ahead of completion of the serial.[31]

Early in April Leslie Stephen renewed his enquiry about a story for the *Cornhill* and looked forward to an early meeting in London. Hardy, meanwhile, still lingered at Bockhampton, awaiting the book proofs of *A Pair of Blue Eyes* and enduring the scoldings of his mother, who feared that her son's new social standing would be endangered by his embarking upon so dubious a career as novel-writing. She also seems to have objected to his use of specifically local and family material, and to have received from him the assurance that the books would circulate only in London and not penetrate into Dorset itself.[32] One of his friends, Charles Walter Moule, also worried over Hardy's change of direction and wrote him a letter of heavy-handed advice upon the desirability of regular employment for men engaged in literary pursuits. Moule evidently felt, as his brother Horace had done earlier, that Hardy lacked the talent or, perhaps, the energy—the physical and psychical resilience—to earn a living by writing alone. He may also have found it hard to reconcile the idea of Hardy as author with what he knew of his background, and the postscript to his letter

---

* The patron of the living, the Right Revd Richard Rawle, Bishop of Trinidad, had contributed just over £900, by far the greater part of the cost, but prominent in the list (not in Hardy's hand) of the smaller contributors are Holder himself, with £55.19.6, Mrs Holder with £5, and Crickmay, the architect, with the same amount. Emma's mother had collected over £6 in Bodmin; Hardy and Emma gave ten shillings each, the latter adding another eight shillings and tenpence 'by sale of sketches'; one of Emma's brothers, Walter, and her friend Margaret Hawes sent five shillings apiece. The absence from the list of any of Hardy's relatives or friends tends to reinforce the impression that he was maintaining a strict separation between the Cornish and Dorset aspects of his life.[29]

certainly indicates an awareness of the difficult class transition in which Hardy seemed to be caught: 'I trust I address you rightly on the envelope. I conjectured that you wd prefer the absence of the "Esqre" at Upper Bockhampton.'[33]

Hardy's own sense of the complexity of that transition emerges poignantly from a letter written early in 1874 to Geneviève Smith, the accomplished and much-travelled wife of the rector of West Stafford, in which he alludes admiringly to her 'varied knowledge & experiences, which are of that precise kind that has a peculiar charm for all engaged in such pursuits as mine', and speaks of his 'having been denied by circumstances until very lately the society of educated womankind, which teaches men what cannot be acquired from books, and is indeed the only antidote to that bearishness which one gets into who lives much alone'.[34] Something of the strength of Emma's initial appeal can be detected in these remarks, but the edginess of the letter as a whole seems chiefly a response to his having been waited upon at table the previous evening by James Pole, the butler at Stafford House, whom the Smiths were accustomed to 'borrow' on formal occasions. Pole—later described by one of the Smith daughters as 'an intensely old-fashioned butler . . . very servile and grovelling in his manner'—had all the class-consciousness of his calling, and no doubt objected to being asked to wait upon the son of a local artisan. But what was genuinely embarrassing about the situation at the Smiths' dinner table was Pole's angry belief that Hardy had recently 'jilted' his daughter Catherine (Cassie) Pole, a lady's maid at Kingston Maurward House.[35]

The precise nature and duration of Hardy's involvement with the pretty if somewhat insipid Cassie Pole remain obscure, but he seems to have courted her some time in the late 1860s and early 1870s, when she was in her early twenties, and she (rather than Eliza or Jane Nicholls) may have been the local girl for whom he is said to have originally intended the ring he eventually gave to Emma Gifford. Since Cassie accompanied her mistress, Emily Fellowes, when she went to London to be married in April 1872, the likelihood is that Hardy had broken rather abruptly with her soon after meeting Emma—or, at any rate, after engaging himself to marry Emma. Cassie died in London in 1894, the wife of a prosperous publican in Shepherd's Market, and it has been persuasively argued that her death was the occasion of Hardy's poem 'At Mayfair Lodgings'.[36] Hardy's relationship with her may already, by 1873, have contributed something to the original conception of *A Pair of Blue Eyes,* and the painful evening at West Stafford rectory certainly became, a few years later, one of the sources for the basic situation of *The Hand of Ethelberta,* in which a butler finds himself waiting upon his own daughter.

The three-volume first edition of *A Pair of Blue Eyes* was published by Tinsley Brothers in late May of 1873. Hardy had made a number of revisions between the serial and the book, most of them to the opening pages, where he had excised seven paragraphs in which Elfride was introduced as reading a three-volume novel and sighing over the death of its hero.[37] Whatever his specific reasons for these changes, Hardy's concern for his text must have stemmed in part from his awareness that the new novel, unlike its two predecessors, would not be published anonymously but would appear over his own name. It was all the more satisfactory that the reviews should have been so generally favourable. Even John Hutton, who had identified himself in a letter as the author of the offensive *Spectator* review of *Desperate Remedies,* now proved to be a warm admirer of *A Pair of Blue Eyes,* writing, again for the *Spectator,* a review which recalled previous strictures but went on to make handsome amends for them by praise of this new and 'really powerful' story. Yet Hutton did criticize *A Pair of Blue Eyes,* both for its sentimental title and for the bleakness of its ending, and while Hardy's letters to Hutton seem not to have survived, it is possible to infer from the other side of the correspondence the terms in which he defended himself: 'I agree with you', wrote Hutton on 3 July 1873, 'as to the *truth* of [Elfride's] death: but there are two views of a novel—as a work of art & as what that work is produced for—the advantage and re-creation of the public.'[38] Loosely constructed and imperfectly organized as *A Pair of Blue Eyes* might be, it already displayed— as indeed the close of *Under the Greenwood Tree* had done—that refusal of the comfortable and conventional resolution which was to be so characteristic of Hardy's mature work.

Another early reader of the novel was Horace Moule, who showed himself to be still capable of mingling warm enthusiasm with cold condescension.* 'You understand the *woman* infinitely better than the *lady*—' he wrote in May 1873, '& how gloriously you have idealized here & there, as far as I have got. Yr slips of

---

* Mr Henry Reed, noting Moule's apparent failure to introduce Hardy into the London literary society he evidently frequented, has suggested to me that an initial sense of class superiority on Moule's part may subsequently have been reinforced by a growing envy of the younger man's creativity.

taste, every now and then, I ought to say pointblank at once, are
Tinsleyan.' Moule signed himself 'Yrs ever & most affectionately',
and exclaimed: 'By & bye—only let me be indefinite as to time—
I long to meet you again & must & will meet. Besides, I have
properties of yours.' Hardy returned to Celbridge Place in June,
accompanied by his brother Henry, now twenty-two years old. He
met Moule on 15 June, spent the next few days showing Henry
around London, and on the 20th travelled to Cambridge to stay
with Moule at Queens' College. The following 'never-to-be-for-
gotten morning' they climbed together to the roof of King's
College Chapel and saw Ely Cathedral 'gleaming in the distant
sunlight'.[39]

That same day Hardy travelled back to London and on to
Bath, where Emma was staying with her friend Miss Anne
d'Arville, an elderly lady whom Hardy had previously met at St.
Juliot—and remembered, absurdly enough, for her possession of
a canary which fell fainting to the bottom of its cage at the sight
of a cat or even a picture of one. Hardy took lodgings in Great
Stanhope Street and the next ten days were spent with Emma in
exploring Bath, Bristol, and the neighbouring countryside, even
as far afield as Tintern Abbey.[40] The appearance of John Hutton's
review of _A Pair of Blue Eyes_ on 28 June—though somewhat
offset by the supercilious tone of the notice in the _Athenaeum_ on
the same day—was an encouraging indication to the two lovers
of the progress Hardy was making in the world of letters. There
had also been some recent correspondence with the New York
publisher, Henry Holt, who was producing editions of _Under the
Greenwood Tree_ and _A Pair of Blue Eyes_,[41] and, above all, the
active interest shown by Leslie Stephen in the projected _Far from
the Madding Crowd._

When writing to Stephen late in 1872 Hardy had apparently
specified of his pastoral tale no more than that it would have as
its chief characters 'a young woman-farmer, a shepherd, and a
sergeant of cavalry'. The fact, however, that at some point during
the summer of 1872 he had abandoned _A Winning Tongue Had
He_ as a title for _A Pair of Blue Eyes_ suggests that by that time he
had already foreseen the way in which the M. G. Lewis song, 'The
Banks of Allan Water', might be used as an element in both the
plot and the prefigurative structure of the novel he had as yet
only projected.[42] Heavily as he was to draw on familiar scenes and

people—including his aunt and uncle Sharpe—in working out the narrative in detail, the basic 'idea' of the new book was essentially literary, hallowed by long usage, bolstered by allusive possibilities, dependent upon the formal traditions of pastoral verse and the narrative patterns, both romantic and moralistic, of the traditional ballad. At the same time, the broad melodramatic sweep of the novel, its density of incident, and its dependence upon well-established character types—the Diana Vernon-ish heroine, the dashing soldier villain, the modest but stalwart hero, ultimately successful both in love and in upward social mobility—are strongly suggestive of the Victorian theatre and popular novel, and it seems fair to say that the strength, and success, of *Far from the Madding Crowd* depended very largely upon its assimilation of nineteenth-century interests and situations within a recognizably 'pastoral' framework. Gabriel Oak is thus a traditional shepherd, playing a flute with 'Arcadian sweetness', and at the same time an exceptionally competent Victorian workman, shown in action in a series of closely observed agricultural scenes—although one such scene, involving a technical description of the causes and effects of sheep rot, was left out of the text as published, perhaps because it threatened to strain the limits of the assimilable.[43]

A Pair of Blue Eyes had in certain respects 'risked' more than *Far from the Madding Crowd* in so far as it had explored with some psychological sensitivity a figure such as the nervously feminine Elfride, a forerunner of Sue Bridehead, or the coldly intellectual and sexually ambiguous Henry Knight. But it had suffered from its too hasty conception and composition, from Hardy's consciousness of the need to meet his obligations as a writer of serials, and from his attempt to resolve some of those practical problems by carrying one stage further the cannibalization of the *Poor Man* manuscript. *Far from the Madding Crowd* marks such an astonishing advance in Hardy's achievement and self-confidence not just because he rose to the opportunity and challenge with which Leslie Stephen had presented him, but also because he for the first time left *The Poor Man and the Lady* firmly behind him—even though class and economic differences still play an important role in the completed novel, and Gabriel Oak, whose surname constitutes yet another approximation to Hardy, was in the manuscript first called Strong.

It was to the writing of the new story that Hardy turned his full attention when, on 2 July 1873, he returned from Bath to Bockhampton—where 'nightingales sang in the garden' and he still had 'the stimulus and sympathy of his mother's companionship'. He also had the not inconsiderable benefit of his mother's care and cooking, and could indulge in the luxury of working at his manuscript until she called him to a meal—at which summons he would run up to the top of the little hill behind the cottage before coming in to the table. Hardy especially treasured the association between Bockhampton and *Far from the Madding Crowd*, and on the day in 1918 when the manuscript of the novel was sold at auction on behalf of the Red Cross, he went to sit in the garden there and look up 'at the window of the little room in which it was written'.[44] From the first he made no secret of having drawn upon his native countryside and its inhabitants for many of his scenes and characters. Writing to Stephen in 1874 of his desire to stay in Bockhampton until the novel was finished, he explained that his home was 'within a walk of the district in which the incidents are supposed to occur'—the village of Puddletown is clearly intended—and that he found it 'a great advantage to be actually among the people described at the time of describing them'.[45] It is not surprising, therefore, that Joseph Poorgrass's song in the novel, 'I Sow'd the Seeds of Love', was associated in Hardy's mind with the Whitings, once the keepers of the beacon on Rainbarrow, or that on Sunday, 21 September 1873, he walked over the heath to Woodbury Hill Fair, on which his fictional Greenhill Fair was to be based.[46]

On the evening of that same day—though the news did not reach Bockhampton until two or three days later—Horace Moule committed suicide in his Cambridge rooms. Few details are available of Moule's career during the late 1860s and early 1870s. He seems to have lived mostly in London, supporting himself somewhat tenuously by examination coaching, journalism, and literary work of various kinds: an undated letter (ascribed by Hardy to 1870) speaks of his having two articles in the *Echo* (a London evening newspaper) for that day, and signed articles by him appeared in *Fraser's* and *Macmillan's* magazines in the latter half of 1871.[47] Economic pressures led to his acceptance, in July 1872, of a position under the Local Government Board (with which his father had some influence as the result of his work in the cause of better sanitation) as an assistant Poor Law inspector for the East Anglian district. He found it convenient to take rooms in his college to be closer to his work, and it was there that Hardy had visited him the previous June. They had parted 'cheerfully', and it was only in retrospect that Hardy read a superstitious significance into the fact that the previous evening, as Moule stood talking by the mantelpiece, he had pointed unconsciously at a candle whose wax was 'shaping to a shroud'.[48]

The reasons for his cutting his throat in those same rooms three months later were explored in a Coroner's inquest, which heard evidence from Charles Moule, who had been caring for his brother at the time of his death, and from Horace's doctor. The picture that emerged was of a recurrent cycle of depression, recourse to 'stimulants', and resultant incapacity for work—followed by fear of losing employment and hence a return of depression.[49] Moule had never succeeded in conquering the alcoholism his pupil Albert Bankes had observed thirteen years earlier. In the more recent past he had every now and then slipped off into the East Anglian countryside and stayed drunk for days at a time, until his brother Frederick, then vicar of Yaxley, near Peterborough, would find him and bring him back to the vicarage to recover. On at least one such occasion he had spoken of suicide and secreted a razor beneath his pillow.[50] Since Charles Moule also declared himself to be familiar with such threats there is perhaps little point in speculating about the immediate 'causes' of Horace's death. He had been for many years an alcoholic, perhaps an opium addict, certainly a potential suicide. He had recently taken on a job which was both demanding and deeply depressing, involving as it did constant visits to workhouses, among whose unhappy occupants he must often have seen examples of what he himself dreaded to become. Coincidentally or otherwise, he had returned from a tour of workhouses just two days before his death.

The sources of Horace Moule's tragedy lie deeper than those purely academic difficulties specified in a final paragraph added, no doubt at the instigation of the Moule family, to the report of the inquest published in a London newspaper: 'He was reputed one of the best classics of his time in the university, and was expected to head the classical tripos, but he failed in his mathematical examination, and according to the usage of the university at that period was prevented from competing in classics, and this preyed upon his mind ever afterwards.'[51] Hardy's second wife believed, on the basis of what her husband had told her, that Horace Moule had had an affair with a 'Mixen Lane' girl of doubtful reputation who became pregnant and was shipped off to Australia, where her son—of whom Moule might or might not have been the father—was later hanged.[52] True or false—and it must be at least partly true despite the suspiciously Hardyan conclusion—this lurid tale would appear to belong to the late 1850s or early 1860s when Moule was living at Fordington, although the 1873 date assigned to the apparently relevant poem 'She at His Funeral' leaves open the possibility that the girl, in her 'gown of garish dye', could have been present as a distant observer of the burial of her 'sweetheart'. More immediately connected with Moule's suicide is the story of his engagement to a governess, 'highly cultivated' and of 'sterling character', whom his sister-in-law, Frederick Moule's wife, thought a 'splendid person', perhaps capable of solving Horace's difficulties. But the governess broke off the engagement, probably because of Horace's drinking —the reason cited in another version of the same story, which speaks of the fiancée as a 'lady of title'.[53]*

Hardy was deeply shocked by the death of one who had, in many respects, been closer to him than anyone would ever be again. No other man, certainly, would ever subscribe a letter to him, 'Yrs ever and most affectionately'. The easy assurance of Moule's letters to Hardy reflected in part that position of patronage which flowed naturally enough from superior age, education, and class, and which (so *A Pair of Blue Eyes* would suggest) Hardy in 1873 was just beginning to resent. That there was real affection between them there can be no doubt. Within a day or two of learning of Moule's death Hardy marked, in his copy of *The Golden Treasury*, Shakespeare's sonnet 32, which concludes with the poet's exhortation to the friend who will survive him:

> O then vouchsafe me but this loving thought—
> 'Had my friend's muse grown with this growing age,
> A dearer birth than this his love had brought,
> To march in ranks of better equipage:
> But since he died, and poets better prove,
> Theirs for their style I'll read, his for his love.

Almost fifty years later Hardy was to say of Moule that he 'had early showed every promise of becoming a distinguished English

* As Horace Moule's great-niece once suggested, the confusion between the two versions could readily be explained if the governess had worked for a titled family. Possibly relevant is the indication that Moule was at one time employed in the household of Sir Henry Taylor, the dramatist, as a tutor for one of his sons. Moule's review of Taylor's works in *Fraser's Magazine* for March 1869 may offer some indication of the date of his connection with the family; his fiancée was perhaps employed as a governess for the poetically named Taylor daughters, Eleanor, Ida, and Una.[54]

poet. But the fates said otherwise.' When he again visited Queens' College in 1880 Hardy wrote '(Cambridge H.M.M.)' against the famous stanza of *In Memoriam,* 'Another name was on the door'. Also to be associated with Moule are Hardy's markings alongside the lines 'And on the depths of death there swims / The reflex of a human face' and against the stanza:

> O last regret, Regret can die!
> No—mixt with all this mystic frame
> Her deep relations are the same,
> But with long use her tears are dry.[55]

Such a lifelong devotion to Moule's memory seems explicable only in terms of a complete surrender to his personal charm. In most readings of Hardy's enigmatic poem 'Standing by the Mantelpiece', subtitled 'H.M.M., 1873', Moule is imagined as addressing the woman who has broken off their engagement, and the lines can indeed be so construed. But the poem seems to make more sense, and to give more point to the candle-wax image, when read in homosexual terms, with Moule speaking directly to Hardy himself. Their relationship must, in any case, have had a sexual component, however unrealized on Hardy's part. For him it had no doubt seemed, and been, the kind of verbally expressive male friendship characteristic of the period, similar to, though more intense than, the one he had enjoyed with Bastow. Hardy, lacking Moule's educational advantages, probably knew little or nothing of homosexuality—the evidence of *Desperate Remedies* certainly suggests ignorance of lesbianism—and if Moule, in June 1873, did make a direct sexual approach it is no wonder that Hardy bore himself angrily and (as the poem puts it) 'as if surprised',[56] that he subsequently responded so powerfully to Moule's death, or that he withheld 'Standing by the Mantelpiece' from publication until his last and, as it proved, posthumous volume.

Moule was buried in Fordington churchyard—a religious burial having been made possible by the inquest verdict of 'Temporary Insanity'—on 26 September 1873, and it was perhaps fortunate for Hardy's state of mind that he was under pressure from Leslie Stephen to produce by the end of the month a completed first instalment of *Far from the Madding Crowd.* Precisely on 30 September the pages of manuscript were sent off—probably corresponding, at least in outline, to the first ten chapters of the novel as published, though Hardy may not yet have assigned major roles to Boldwood or Fanny Robin.[57] A week later Stephen wrote to express his satisfaction with such of the novel as he had seen and to raise the possibility that serialization might begin as early as January or February. As the autumn and the manuscript progressed, more letters passed between Hardy and Stephen, then between Hardy and Smith, Elder—publishers of the *Cornhill* and, when the time came, of *Far from the Madding Crowd* in volume form—and by the end of November it had been agreed that the first part of the twelve-part serial would appear in the January 1874 *Cornhill,* and that Hardy would receive a total payment of £400.[58]

Hardy had remained at Bockhampton during the autumn, assisting his father for the last time with the annual rituals of cider-pressing—'a work whose sweet smell and oozings in the crisp autumn air can never be forgotten by those who have had a hand in it'. He was to recall such scenes, and his father's unassertive personality, when he came to write *The Woodlanders* and create the character of Giles Winterborne. As he continued to work on *Far from the Madding Crowd* he jotted down ideas for possible stories, notes on conversations with local people—among them James Dart, once a member of the old Stinsford choir—and observations of natural phenomena, including a storm in early November which no doubt provided some of the details of the storm in which Gabriel Oak saves Bathsheba's ricks.[59]

On 8 December Hardy went to London for a few days, staying once again at Celbridge Place, and took the opportunity of calling for the first time upon Leslie Stephen at his South Kensington home:

> He welcomed me with one hand, holding back the barking 'Troy' with the other. The dog's name I, of course, had never heard till then, and I said, 'That is the name of my wicked soldier-hero.' He answered caustically: 'I don't think my Troy will feel hurt at the coincidence, if yours doesn't.' I rejoined, 'There is also another coincidence. Another Leslie Stephen lives near here, I find.' 'Yes,' he said, 'he's the spurious one.'

The success of that first meeting led to an invitation to lunch for the following day, when Mrs Stephen and her sister, Annie Thackeray, wore shawls against the cold and the conversation

round the fire was largely of their father, William Makepeace
Thackeray. Hardy's own account of the occasion splendidly preserves Stephen's characteristic blend of geniality and moroseness,
which was perhaps made the more endearing to his guest by its
resemblance to Jemima's rapid alternations of mood:

> We also talked of Carlyle, whom Stephen had visited on the
> previous day; and he illustrated by enactment the remarkable
> way in which the philosopher lit his pipe. Somehow we launched
> upon the subject of David and Saul. . . . I spoke to the effect that
> the Bible account would take a deal of beating, and that I won-
> dered why the clergy did not argue the necessity of plenary in-
> spiration from the marvellous artistic cunning with which so
> many Bible personages, like those of Saul and David, were
> developed, though in a comparatively unliterary age. Stephen,
> who had been silent, then said, 'Yes. But they never do the
> obvious thing'; presently adding in a dry grim tone, 'If you wish
> to get an idea of Saul and David you should study them as pre-
> sented by Voltaire in his drama.' Those who know that work will
> appreciate Stephen's mood.[60]

Christmas was spent with Emma, and Hardy's return journey,
on 31 December, was made memorable by his purchase, in Plymouth, of a copy of the *Cornhill* containing the first instalment of
his novel.[61] Although there is no evidence to suggest that the
visit to Cornwall was other than happy,* there is little doubt that
as his marriage became more feasible in economic terms Hardy
became increasingly uncertain as to its wisdom. He certainly remained susceptible to the attractions of other women, and felt
(in his own Dorset phrase) 'quite romantical' about two women
in particular. One of these—though he later claimed the feeling
to have been 'more on her side than his'—was Annie Thackeray,
whom Leslie Stephen once described as 'the most affectionate and
sympathetic woman I ever knew'. Although she was four years
older than Hardy and distinctly plain—'as delightful as she is
homely', according to one account, 'and that is saying a good
deal'—he was impressed by her parentage and her own authorship of several popular novels, and charmed, as were so many
others, by the gaiety, vivacity, and warmth which characterized

---

* Except in so far as Emma seems already to have begun that quarrel with
her sister which drove her from St. Juliot by the end of 1873.[62]

her tumultuous flood of often quite inconsequential conversation.[63]* Edmund Gosse, who also first encountered her about this time, observed that 'when her mind and her tongue had parted company she was capable of uttering strange oracles'.[65]

Much as Hardy enjoyed Miss Thackeray's company, she did not represent a serious threat to his engagement with Emma. But his feelings for Helen Paterson, the illustrator of *Far from the Madding Crowd,* were of a different order, though he can have seen her on only a very few occasions. When they first met in the spring of 1874 Miss Paterson was a handsome young woman of twenty-five, a professional artist who had already been on the staff of the *Graphic* for three years. Immediately attracted, Hardy exploited their *Cornhill* association as a basis for further meetings and correspondence. He supplied sketches of Dorset farm implements that she might make her illustrations more authentic, and it was no doubt at his instigation that Miss Thackeray wrote from Southwell Gardens to invite Miss Paterson to dine with Hardy and herself at the Pall Mall Café: they could meet at the restaurant itself, she suggested, or 'if you liked better to come *here* & go with us we wd take gt care of you'. Miss Paterson, however, married the fifty-year-old William Allingham, the poet and editor, that same summer, and Hardy was left with his memories—imaginatively inflated as they doubtless were—of the 'charming young lady' whom he described to Gosse in 1906 as 'the best illustrator' he had ever had and the woman he should have married 'but for a stupid blunder of God Almighty'. In the poem, 'The Opportunity (For H.P.)', however, the error is seen as quintessentially human:

> Had we mused a little space
> At that critical date in the Maytime,
> One life had been ours, one place,
> Perhaps, till our long cold claytime.
>
> —This is a bitter thing
> For thee, O man: what ails it?
> The tide of chance may bring
> Its offer; but nought avails it![66]

* Writing to Hardy many years later, Lady Ritchie, as she became, thanked him for recalling 'the junketting of my youth'; many years later still, Siegfried Sassoon, after reading her published letters and journals, exclaimed: 'Why didnt T.H. marry *her*? . . . *She'd* have made Max Gate *hum!*'[64]

. . .

By the time Hardy met Helen Paterson the writing of *Far from the Madding Crowd* was well advanced. Earlier in 1874 he had feared that he would run behind the printer—largely because serialization had begun earlier than anticipated—and remained at Bockhampton, working steadily at his manuscript, from the beginning of January until some time in April.[67] He was sustained in his labours by the good reception that the first instalment had generally received—the *Spectator* declaring that if the story was not by George Eliot, 'then there is a new light among novelists'—and by the shrewd advice and warm encouragement of Leslie Stephen. On the manuscript itself Stephen's only intervention seems to have been the correction of 'parabolic curve' to 'hyperbolic curve' in the third paragraph of Chapter 15, but a series of letters guided Hardy, gently but firmly, to the necessary tightening up of scenes which had been allowed to become unduly prolix and unfocused. Like so many magazine editors of the Victorian period, Stephen was fearful of giving offence to his subscribers on sexual and religious grounds, and on 12 March he confessed to having deleted 'a line or two in the last batch of proofs from an excessive prudery of wh. I am ashamed; but one is forced to be absurdly particular'. A month later, he expressed anxiety about the explicitness with which the causes of Fanny Robin's death had been specified, and wondered whether there was any need for Bathsheba to find the dead baby in the coffin. Acknowledging that the omission 'certainly rather injures the story' and 'might be restored on republication', he nevertheless continued: 'But I am rather necessarily anxious to be on the safe side; and should somehow be glad to omit the baby.' Since there were sound aesthetic grounds for omitting the baby—whose cheeks and hands had, in the manuscript, reminded Bathsheba of 'the soft convexity of mushrooms on a dewy morning'—Stephen's invocation of the *Cornhill's* readers can be read, at least in this instance, as a considerate way of advocating a critical judgement of his own.[68]

Hardy had already made clear his readiness to compromise: 'The truth is that I am willing, and indeed anxious, to give up any points which may be desirable in a story when read as a whole, for the sake of others which shall please those who read it in numbers. Perhaps I may have higher aims some day, and be a great stickler for the proper artistic balance of the completed work, but for the present circumstances lead me to wish merely to be con-

sidered a good hand at a serial.'[69] Although Hardy had not lost
sight of those exalted literary aspirations which had first led him
to the writing of poetry, he was perfectly willing to accept the
limitations within which, as a novelist beginning his career in the
1870s, he must necessarily work. At a moment when he was still
struggling to get ahead of the printer, it was enough for him to be
recognized—in purely professional terms—as 'a good hand at a
serial', one who met his deadlines with instalments which contained the required number of words and an appropriate density
of sufficiently dramatic episodes. Once his identity as the author
of *Far from the Madding Crowd* had been revealed in the *Spectator* of 7 February 1874, he soon began to receive approaches
from editors and publishers. He cheerfully contracted with the
New York Times for a short story, but a misunderstanding over
the American book publication of *Far from the Madding Crowd*
itself brought him sharply face to face with some of the more
tiresome aspects of professional authorship: 'The sharp practice
in literature which apparently exists in America perfectly aston-
ishes me,' he exclaimed in a letter to Smith, Elder.[70]

During his brief visit to London in late April and early May
1874 Hardy saw Leslie Stephen and Annie Thackeray on a number of occasions, and was introduced not only to Helen Paterson
but also to George Smith, founder of the *Cornhill,* and to Mrs
Procter, the widow of the poet who wrote under the pseudonym
of 'Barry Cornwall'. Hardy was now beginning to move in literary
circles of some elevation—Mrs Procter, in particular, knew and
had known an enormous range of writers, artists, and public
figures—and while Emma Gifford was presumably unaware of
Hardy's interest, actually or potentially romantic, in Annie
Thackeray and Helen Paterson, she was not insensitive to his
increasing absorption in his career: 'My work', she wrote in July,
'unlike your work of writing, does not occupy my true mind
much.' She added: 'Your novel seems sometimes like a child all
your own & none of me.'[71] On the other hand, Hardy's greatly
improved literary and hence economic prospects had now eroded
the last reasons—on Hardy's part, perhaps, the last excuses—for
postponing marriage, and in late May he obtained a passport for
himself and his wife, 'travelling on the Continent'.[72]

It was in the middle of July 1874 that the writing of *Far from
the Madding Crowd* was finally completed and Hardy's last extended stay at his birthplace came to an end. Although some notes
of March 1874 about a mail-coach guard who used to live at Higher

Bockhampton are practically all that survive from these last months at home, it is likely that Hardy made many more, in a deliberate attempt to amass specifically local material for future literary use.[73] It was in the manuscript of *Far from the Madding Crowd*, after all, that he first gave the name Wessex to his fictional region, and there are other indications within the early pages of that manuscript of his becoming progressively aware of the implications and possibilities inherent in the use of a regional or pastoral strategy: the word 'Pastoral', indeed, is introduced into the title of the fifth chapter.[74] Although he was always to keep in close touch with his family, Hardy's departure from Bockhampton, and the world of his rural subject matter, for London, and the world of his publishers, his critics, and his essentially urban audience, represented a sharp break with both the place and the manner of his upbringing. Marriage to Emma was soon to render that break irreversible, and the composition of *Far from the Madding Crowd* can be seen in retrospect as marking the end of the earliest, happiest, and in certain respects most generously creative period in his career—the period especially of the idyllic perfection of *Under the Greenwood Tree* and the exuberant richness of *Far from the Madding Crowd*, both intimately connected with Higher Bockhampton, its people, and its way of life.

8

SURBITON
TO SWANAGE

Hardy now returned once more to 4 Celbridge Place. In late July 1874 he went to theatres, made some final revisions to the manuscript of *Far from the Madding Crowd,* and saw a good deal of Leslie Stephen. In August Miss Paterson became Mrs Allingham, and Hardy corrected proofs for the autumn numbers of the *Cornhill:* 'I will speak about the November proof tomorrow,' wrote Stephen on 25 August. 'I saw nothing to alter, unless that it seemed to me in one or two cases that your rustics—specially Oak—speak rather too good English towards the end.'[1] By this time Emma was in London, and at the beginning of September—in the midst of finishing off 'Destiny and a Blue Cloak', the story he had promised to the *New York Times*—Hardy made the arrangements for the wedding to be conducted by her uncle, Dr Edwin Hamilton Gifford, then headmaster of King Edward's School, Birmingham.[2]

'The day we were married', Emma later recalled, 'was a perfect September day—the 17th, 1874—not brilliant sunshine, but wearing a soft, sunny luminousness; just as it should be.' This was to make the best of otherwise unpropitious circumstances. St. Peter's, the parish church for near-by Chippenham Road, where Emma had been staying, was barely four years old, and its lack of history and associations or even of any particular architectural distinction made it a bleak setting for the marriage between a romantic not-so-young lady from St. Juliot and the author of *Far from the Madding Crowd*. Family hostility on both sides evidently ruled out St. Juliot and Stinsford as possible locations for the wedding and limited the attendance at the St. Peter's ceremony to Hardy and Emma, Dr Gifford, and the two obligatory witnesses, Walter Gifford, Emma's brother, and Sarah Williams, the daughter of Hardy's Celbridge Place landlady.[3] In the register Hardy's profession is firmly entered as 'Author', that of his father as 'Builder', but those differences of class which were to be a source of such friction in later years are already fully apparent in the report, prepared by Hardy himself, which appeared in the 'Marriages' column of the *Dorset County Chronicle* on 24 September:

HARDY–GIFFORD. Sept. 17, at St. Peter's Church, Paddington, by the Rev. E.H. Gifford, D.D., hon. canon of Worcester, uncle of the bride, Thomas Hardy, of Celbridge-place, Westbourne Park, London, son of Mr. T. Hardy, of Bockhampton, to Emma Lavinia, younger daughter of J. A. Gifford, Esq., of Kirland, Cornwall.

Quite apart from the prominence given to the name and dignities of the bride's uncle, the entry is eloquent in terms both of Hardy's identification of himself as a Londoner and of the contrast between *Mr* T. Hardy and J. A. Gifford, *Esq.*

Hardy and Emma spent the first night of their marriage in Brighton, at D. Morton's Family and Commercial Hotel, not far from the railway terminus. The next day (Friday, 18 September 1874) Hardy wrote to his brother Henry to 'tell you all at home that the wedding took place yesterday, & that we are got as far as this on our way to Normandy & Paris'. He added a note of thanks for Henry's good wishes and explained that he was 'going to Paris for materials for my next story', almost as if the honeymoon were unimportant in itself and merely the occasion for the completion of a necessary piece of business. The Brighton weather that weekend was far from kind, but Emma was fascinated by the aquarium —'Seals eyes flash extraordinarily as they flownder over in the water,' she wrote in her little pocket diary—and the pier and the Pavilion offered concerts and other amusements. On the Sunday they went twice to church; on Monday Hardy went for a swim, though the sea was rough. It was still rough when they took the boat to France that evening. After an uncomfortable crossing to Dieppe they went straight on to Rouen and to the Hotel d'Albion,

Emma recording how they went up to their bedroom after the
table d'hôte dinner—itself delightedly itemized—and found that
the bed had been turned back and their 'night dresses' laid out
upon it.[4]

Armed with an English-language guide-book, they spent the
next day visiting the cathedral and other local sights which were
later to figure, if only briefly, in the pages of *The Hand of Ethelberta*. To that extent the trip did furnish materials for the next
story—even if subsequent abridgement of the plot complications
made it unnecessary for the heroine to go on to Paris, the principal
destination of the Hardys. They arrived there in the evening of
Thursday, 24 September—'Place de la Concorde first seen by
moonlight,' Emma recorded—and put up at the Hotel St. Peters-
bourg, not far from the Opéra. Hardy had prepared for his first
foreign expedition, and especially for this portion of it, by pur-
chasing a copy of Murray's *Handbook for Visitors to Paris* and
inserting newspaper cuttings about hotels and notes of the correct
tips to offer waiters, cab men, and door-openers in theatres. He
now took it with him each day as a guide to the Paris sights, en-
hancing its usefulness by indicating—as any architect might—the
direction of North on the plans of the Louvre and adding a very
occasional comment of his own. A note of 26 September on the
Escalier de Marbre at Versailles—that it was 'of every colour—
marble walls & all'—was later echoed in the description of Lord
Mountclere's mansion in *The Hand of Ethelberta*. They visited
the Petit Trianon that same day and stopped at a café on their
walk back to the railway station to drink *vin ordinaire*, 'like French
people', as Emma put it. Among the other sights duly visited were
Notre-Dame, the Invalides, the Morgue—Emma finding the three
bodies on view to be '*Not offensive* but repulsive'—and the Père
Lachaise cemetery, where they paid their romantic respects at the
tomb of Héloïse and Abélard and picked an ivy leaf from the
grave of Balzac.[5]

Emma was fascinated with France, recording details not only
of food, dress, and furnishings—including those of their bedroom
at the hotel—but also of customs ('Les Latrines Publique most
strange for English eyes & notions') and what struck her as racial
characteristics ('Very small babies in Paris'). At the same time she
was deeply suspicious of priests—whose age, she decided, could
be told by 'their harshness & closeness of expression'—and uneasy
at her own reception in a country where people showed their
curiosity more directly and frankly than in England:

Wherever I go, whoever I pass—at whatever time day-time or by night—the people gaze at *me* as much or more than I at them & their beautiful city—so full of strange things, places—shops—people dress—ways—

Query—Am I a strange-looking persons—or merely picturesque in this hat—

Women sometimes laugh a short laugh as they pass Men stare, some stand, some look back or turn, look over their shoulders—look curiously inquisitively—some tenderly [Emma first wrote 'admiringly'] without my being mistaken—they do in a French manner

As it is remarkable I note it—

Children gape too—

Emma, with her long bright hair and her tendency to overdress, was indeed a striking figure, and some of the interested men no doubt believed her to be actively inviting their attention. Though her diary reveals a sensibility sharply perceptive of special qualities of light, colour, and movement, and capable at times of defining them in a vivid phrase, it is also eloquent of that inconsequentiality and trusting childishness which she was to display throughout her life. Entirely characteristic was the little farewell to Paris which she jotted down—from a sense of touristic obligation or from a need to compete or communicate with her literary, note-taking husband—while waiting at the Gare St-Lazare on 30 September for the train back to Rouen:

> Adieu to Paris.
> Charmante ville [Emma first wrote 'citie']
> Adieu to the Boulevards.
> To the gay shops—
> To the *'gens'* sitting in the streets
> To the vivants enfants
> To the white caps of the femmes
> To the river & its boats
> To the clear atmosphere & brilliant colourings[6]

Given Emma's failure to respond physically to her husband, and the diminished enthusiasm for the marriage he had himself demonstrated over the past several months, it is difficult even to guess at the kind of personal and sexual relationship the couple managed to establish during their honeymoon. Her undiminished girlishness (she was now nearing thirty-four) scarcely seems pro-

pitious—nor, for that matter, does the fact that Hardy had a cold.
The mood of Emma's diary is one of happy excitement, but she
speaks almost exclusively of impersonal matters. Hardy, for his
part, left no comment whatever, or none that has survived: if the
poem 'Honeymoon Time at an Inn' has any bearing upon his
own experience it can only be in a very distant and generalized
way.

They returned to London after another bad Channel crossing, began house-hunting the following day, and eventually found rooms
to rent on the outskirts of Surbiton. In the afternoon of 6 October
they arrived at St. David's Villa, Hook Road, to find Emma's
father already in the garden, playing with a young relative and a
large dog.[7] How Mr Gifford came to be there—especially since
he had not been at the wedding—Emma does not record, nor does
she give any indication of the reasons, which may have been largely
financial, why she and her husband had chosen to live in so remote
a suburb.* Hook Road was in the Hardy's time still chiefly an
area of fields, with a small group of houses—almost certainly including St. David's Villa itself†—clustered just south of the junction with Ditton Road. But the location, however pleasant in
itself, was distinctly inconvenient. A visit to town meant a walk
of ten or fifteen minutes to Surbiton station, the twenty- to thirty-
minute train ride itself, and often an awkward journey from
Waterloo, the London terminus, to one's eventual destination.
The Hardys knew from the start that they would not be able to
stay long in their first home, and almost the only glimpse of the
five and a half months they spent at St. David's Villa is provided
by the poem, 'A Light Snow-Fall after Frost', whose location Hardy
specifically identified as 'Near Surbiton'. Conceivably the companion poem in *Human Shows,* the better-known 'Snow in the
Suburbs', belongs to the same period, and it was certainly during
the course of a walk from Surbiton that Hardy, on 19 December
1874, saw snow on some graves at Long Ditton and entered in his

* Hardy seems to have been friendly, however, with Francis Tycho Vincent
Honeywell, formerly of Weymouth, who had set up as a teacher of music at
Surbiton Park Terrace and later became a piano manufacturer.[8]

† It was apparently a newly built house, occupied (and doubtless named)
by a William David Hughes immediately prior to the Hardys' arrival; if it
still survives, it must have undergone a change of name—perhaps several
such changes.[9]

notebook the characteristic comment: 'A superfluous piece of cynicism in Nature.'[10]

Yet it was while he was living at Surbiton that Hardy first became famous. *Far from the Madding Crowd* was published in two volumes on 23 November 1874 but he and Emma were for a time quite unaware of the stir which the novel was making, except that when they went up to Waterloo on the train they often noticed 'ladies carrying about copies of it with Mudie's label on the covers'. In early September, however, while the serial parts were still appearing, Mrs Procter had written: 'I can hardly make you understand, how one wants the next Number. It is perhaps a taste of Purgatory to wait for the drop of cold water.'[11] And in November, Hardy received a letter from the novelist Katharine S. Macquoid on the subject of Bathsheba. His reply sounds, gently as yet, a note that was to become very familiar over the years: 'I myself, I must confess, have no great liking for the perfect woman of fiction, but this may be for purely artistic reasons.' The imperfections of his own heroines, he explained, were not intended as a 'satire on the sex' but were 'merely portrayed in the regular course of an art which depends rather on picturesqueness than perfect symmetry for its effects.'[12]

Meanwhile the reviews had begun to appear—many more of them than had greeted any of Hardy's previous works. His combination of descriptive specificity with melodramatic extravagance worried some of the critics, and there were complaints about abrupt variations in style and treatment and the implausibility of some of the wise and witty speeches assigned to agricultural labourers. But most of the reviews were positive in tone, and all of them took the book seriously—even Henry James's condescending notice of the American edition. Richard H. Hutton, in the *Spectator*, defined the special appeal of *Far from the Madding Crowd* as a regional novel grounded in intimate knowledge of a functioning community: 'The details of the farming and the sheep-keeping, of the labouring, the feasting, and the mourning, are painted with all the vividness of a powerful imagination, painting from the stores of a sharply-outlined memory. . . . A book like this is, in relation to many of the scenes it describes, the nearest equivalent to actual experience which a great many of us are ever likely to boast of.' Hutton was one of those made uneasy by the philosophical rustics, but John Hutton wrote to assure Hardy that his brother knew too little of the rural poor 'to estimate correctly their intimacy with & constant use of Bible language nor their quaint good humoured cynicism'.[13]

In December 1874 Leslie Stephen showed his own satisfaction with Hardy's work by asking if he could have a new story ready for the *Cornhill* for the following April. Hardy begged for a little more time, and a July starting date was eventually agreed upon.[14] In mid-January George Smith offered Hardy the opportunity—of which he actively availed himself—to make corrections for incorporation in a second printing of *Far from the Madding Crowd,* the first having been almost completely sold out. Hardy could now think of Smith, Elder as 'his' publishers, and he entertained the hope that his previous work might reappear over his own name and with the more distinguished imprint. But Smith advised against any immediate reprinting of *Desperate Remedies,* and when Tinsley was asked to name a price for the copyright of *Under the Greenwood Tree* he demanded £300, precisely ten times what he had paid for it. Although remaining sheets of the novel and the stereotype plates were to be thrown in, the amount was still, as George Smith exclaimed, 'preposterous'. Hardy declined to pay, and never, in fact, regained control of this one copyright, which subsequently passed from Tinsley to Chatto & Windus.[15]

In mid-January 1875 Hardy submitted 'a rough draft of the first part' of *The Hand of Ethelberta,* as his new novel was to be called. On 27 February, grown impatient for a decision, he wrote to Smith, Elder, observing that

> as a matter of common prudence it would be better if I had some definite ground to go upon in replying to communications which reach me on the same subject. I also find a difficulty in applying myself thoroughly to the story whilst there is any uncertainty about it, which leads me to believe that it would be greatly to the advantage of the tale if we could get this cause of distraction cleared out of the way; and I have thought that you would probably take the same view of the matter on my mentioning it to you.

Although George Smith was nervous at having seen so little of the story, he had sufficient faith in it, or in Hardy, to offer, on 9 March, £700 for English serial and volume publication. Also in March Hardy settled with the *New York Times* for serialization in the

THOMAS HARDY: A Biography • 170

United States at the rate of £50 for each *Cornhill* instalment, to be supplied in the form of advance proof sheets—thus assuring himself of another £550, making a total for the novel of £1,250 even before arrangements had been made for such things as American and continental editions.[16]

As if in confirmation of his new standing in the literary world Hardy received that same year invitations to write for a number of other journals, including the *Glasgow News, Good Words,* and the *Examiner,* and a striking compliment from Coventry Patmore, whom he had not then met: 'I trust that you will not think I am taking too great a liberty in writing to tell you with what extraordinary pleasure and admiration I have read your novels, especially that called "A Pair of blue Eyes." I regretted at almost every page that such almost [un]equalled beauty and power should not have assured themselves the immortality which would have been impressed upon them by the form of verse.'[17] Although the letter gave Hardy pleasure he was disturbed by the implication that he might, as a writer, be on the wrong track. He was already worried about his lack of interest in manners—as a novelist such as Jane Austen or Henry James would understand the term—and hence about his capacity to sustain reasonable levels not only of productivity but of popularity. The self-doubting was characteristic, even constitutional, and matters were not helped by Annie Thackeray's breezy assertion that 'a novelist must necessarily like society!'[18]

Although Hardy was not—and could not afford to be—deflected from the career in prose fiction on which he had now so successfully embarked, he was still thinking about poetry, writing it occasionally, making notes for future poems and volumes, even proposing to an unreceptive Leslie Stephen the publication of a series of 'tragic poems'—evidently to be identified with the Napoleonic ballads, 'forming altogether an Iliad of Europe from 1789 to 1815', mentioned in a note of May 1875.[19] And while some of the tentative volume titles in the following list, of 3 April 1873, may have been added when Hardy copied it out at a later date, it remains a remarkable testimony to the early development and subsequent persistence of his poetic interests and objectives:

Titles—The Look of Life/Lives	Poems imaginative & incidental
Mindsights & other verses	Poems in Sundry shapes
Souls of men	Souls shewn in verse
Minutes of years	Poems probably final

Winter flowers & other verses	Winter words said in Verse.
Seemings said in verse	Wintry Things thought in Verse with other poems.
A Wintry Voice/in Various Metres Speaks in Verse[20]	

Hardy sought to profit as a prose writer from his experience as a poet. Reflecting early in 1875 upon the desirability of cultivating an appearance of slight stylistic casualness, he invoked Herrick's 'sweet disorder in the dress' and concluded that it was simply a matter of 'carrying into prose the knowledge I have acquired in poetry—that inexact rhymes and rhythms now and then are far more pleasing than correct ones'. Ezra Pound's famous remark about Hardy's verse as the 'harvest' of the novels might well be inverted, and Leslie Stephen, looking back from an end-of-the-century perspective upon the first appearance of *Far from the Madding Crowd,* was to recall his admiration of 'the poetry that was diffused through the prose'.[21]

Hardy could now afford to live closer to the centre of things, and on 22 March 1875 he and Emma moved from Surbiton to 18 Newton Road, Westbourne Grove,* within a few streets of Hardy's former lodgings at Westbourne Park Villas and Celbridge Place. The day after their arrival, Hardy received a note from Leslie Stephen, asking him to call that evening. He found Stephen in his library, a 'tall thin figure wrapt in a heath-coloured dressing-gown', and there witnessed his signature to a deed of renunciation of holy orders under the provisions of the Clerical Disabilities Act of 1870.† Hardy later recalled Stephen's saying, 'grimly', that 'he thought it as well to cut himself adrift of a calling for which, to say the least, he had always been utterly unfit', but made only a tantalizing allusion to their subsequent conversation as having

* A modern local government building (the Paddington and Kensington Chest Clinic) now stands on the site.
† It is not clear why Stephen took this action, which had little or no practical significance, at this particular moment, but Professor S. P. Rosenbaum has suggested that he might have postponed it, for reasons of delicacy, until after the death of his mother a few weeks previously. The deed itself mentions only the resignation, in 1862, of his Trinity Hall tutorship.

turned 'upon theologies decayed and defunct, the origin of things, the constitution of matter, the unreality of time and kindred subjects'.[22] It is an index of Stephen's respect for Hardy's integrity and intelligence that he should have chosen him as sole witness to a document so personal and so symbolic, and the incident suggests that Stephen's influence on Hardy—acknowledged by the latter as stronger than that of any other contemporary—was exerted as much through his personality and conversation as through his writings: Hardy later told Virginia Woolf that her father had had a 'peculiar attractiveness for me, & I used to suffer gladly his grim & severe criticisms of my contributions & his long silences, for the sake of sitting with him'. It was remarkably fortunate for Hardy that Stephen not only admired his work but liked him personally and found him good intellectual company. For Stephen was, as philosopher, polemicist, and editor, near the centre of the great contemporary controversies of thought and belief, and it was through association with Stephen that Hardy learned to feel more at ease with precisely such topics as 'theologies decayed and defunct, the origin of things, the constitution of matter, the unreality of time'. Hardy's sonnet, 'The Schreckhorn', sub-titled 'With thoughts of Leslie Stephen', is finely evocative—as Virginia Woolf herself acknowledged—of Stephen's 'spare and desolate figure' and of the 'quaint glooms, keen lights, and rugged trim' of his personality, and it is pleasant to learn that Stephen, on the day of his death in 1904, asked to be given a new poem of Hardy's to read, probably 'A Trampwoman's Tragedy'.[23]

Thanks largely to Stephen, Hardy could now think of himself as an established novelist. But his background and early experience had given him little conception of what it meant to be a professional writer, and he therefore greeted the success which so suddenly and astonishingly overtook him with a very fearful joy, a tentative grasp, as if unsure of its reality or permanence. He was, in purely practical and economic terms, right to do so. He had indeed raised himself by his own exertions and talents out of the class into which he was born, and he had recently confirmed his new status by marrying a daughter of the middle class. But he had forgotten nothing of what he had learned in childhood about the reversibility of class transitions, his married status exposed him more nakedly than ever to that cruel trickery of fate which he seems to have accepted as the norm of all human experience, and abandonment of his original career as an architect left the maintenance of his achieved position wholly dependent upon an infinite continuation of his literary exertions—concretely, upon his capacity to attract invitations from the editors of magazines.

At the time when he was still struggling for recognition Hardy had shown himself to be almost pathetically open to advice from those more experienced than himself—asking Alexander Macmillan to suggest 'the sort of story you think I could do best', writing *Desperate Remedies* in obedience to what he took to be George Meredith's prescription, and telling Leslie Stephen that he wanted chiefly to prove himself as a 'good hand at a serial'. He now remained, at the moment of success, extraordinarily sensitive to the strictures of reviewers, as if they represented some body of independent authority vaguely to be identified with the world of literature, and when they mingled with their general praise of *Far from the Madding Crowd* a few complaints about the exaggerated presentation of rustic characters and an occasional implication that he was rewriting *Adam Bede* he seized nervously upon such negative comments and allowed them to determine his thinking about the immediate future. He became anxious to assert his independence of other writers and resist categorization as an exclusively rural or regional author—the restricting fate which had befallen William Barnes—and sought to achieve both these goals by demonstrating an ability to perform effectively in a variety of modes and settings. Instead of building upon the success of *Far from the Madding Crowd,* therefore, and especially upon its rich exploitation of the 'given' material of childhood, Hardy set off, with what seems in retrospect an almost perverse determination, upon an entirely different tack—possibly setting aside in the process an already formulated scenario for what eventually became *The Woodlanders*.[24]

The Hand of Ethelberta certainly begins in Wessex—the region is invoked by name in its opening sentence—and several of its scenes occur there. But it is essentially a social comedy of London life, turning satirically upon inversions of normal master–servant relationships, and deriving much of its point from the basic 'idea' of viewing fashionable life from the vantage-point of the domestics, upstairs from downstairs. Ethelberta, the daughter of a butler, has aspirations as a poet and makes a successful career for herself as a professional teller of tales, performing at fashionable parties and even (like the Julia Corke whom Hardy had heard of and perhaps seen in the 1860s) on the public stage. She is motivated primarily by a desire to provide her own family— her parents and her nine brothers and sisters—with financial security, and eventually achieves that ambition by becoming the wife of a wealthy viscount. The marriage is, however, loveless and childless, Lord Montclere himself thoroughly disreputable, and Ethelberta in the end somewhat ambiguously presented, as being neither wholly happy nor wholly admirable in her success, or even in her self-sacrifice. Hardy's handling of upper-class characters and episodes is less disastrous than might have been anticipated, but the comic aspects of the novel seem in general much too contrived, its social values are dubious, and the entire narrative never quite frees itself from a sense of strain, of having been elaborately 'got up'. It seems, indeed, to have been written without any intense creative engagement, and it certainly lacks that dense texture of personal experience which toughens all of Hardy's major fiction.

It is, of course, possible to argue that many aspects of Hardy's own situation are reflected in Ethelberta's—that some of his closest relatives, including Martha Sparks and Jemima herself, had been servants, and that in presenting a character who used 'storytelling' as a way of moving upward from such a background he must in some sense have been writing an allegory of his own career. But Hardy had already shown himself in *A Pair of Blue Eyes* to be capable of extraordinary innocence in dealing with autobiographical material, and he seems to have been less interested in the new novel as an exposition of his personal situation than as a generalized fable of the dangers of upward mobility. Any awareness of the story's implications for himself was effectively disguised and deflected by his thoroughgoing adoption of a solidly middle-class narrative persona, his mastery of a tone of unyielding comic detachment. It is for this reason that Ethelberta emerges so ambiguously, and that the sheer unattractiveness of most of the upper-class characters is balanced by the shadowiness of most of the lower-class characters: Hardy may have been returning, as it were surreptitiously, to the material of *The Poor Man and the Lady,* and perhaps even to something of its manner, but he stopped well short of reviving its 'socialistic' fervour. If, therefore, Hardy saw in Ethelberta's career any reflection or prefiguration of his own, it can only have been in the same coolly ironic terms. The figure closest to Hardy in the novel, after all, is the one who bears the Christian name he would himself have preferred, the pallid Christopher Julian, and it is clearly no accident that Christopher makes in his career as a musician just the kind of modest progress Hardy had made as an architect, and settles happily at the end of the novel for a quiet marriage and a steady income. It is almost as if Hardy, in the aftermath of his first triumph, were already pondering, as he was to do at the very end of his life, whether he would not after all have been happier as an architect in a small country town. He may also have begun to ask himself about the wisdom of his marriage as set off against that 'family affection between close blood-relations' which Christopher describes at one point in the novel as being the 'only feeling which has any dignity or permanence or worth'.[25]

Stephen responded favourably to the successive sections of the novel as Hardy forwarded them. He worried in May about the propriety of Ethelberta's referring to herself and her verse as 'amorous', and in August took mild fright at 'the suggestion of the very close embrace in the London churchyard'. His most substantial intervention, however, seems to have been a recommendation, prompted by the arrival of the proofs of the first instalment, that Hardy's sub-title, 'A Comedy in Chapters', be omitted from the serial version—on the grounds that it led readers to expect 'something of the farce description', the funniness of the 'professional joker'. Hardy immediately agreed:

> My meaning was simply, as you know, that the story would concern the follies of life rather than the passions, & be told in something of a comedy form, all the people having weaknesses at which the superior lookers-on smile, instead of being ideal characters. I should certainly deplore being thought to have set up in the large joke line—the genteelest of genteel comedy being as far as ever I should think it safe to go at any time.[26]

Before he finished the novel Hardy was in fact to risk something very close to farce in the presentation of the various would-be foilers of the marriage between Ethelberta and Lord Mountclere and the subsequent mock-Gothic hide-and-seek at Enkworth Court, and Stephen's dissatisfaction with these developments was to be reflected in his coolness towards the possibility of publishing anything else of Hardy's in the pages of the *Cornhill*.

In March 1875 Hardy, as a professional writer, saw fit to join the recently established Copyright Association, and on 10 May he waited upon the Prime Minister, Disraeli, as one of a deputation of authors seeking an improvement in domestic and international copyright laws.[27] The following day he had engaged himself to travel to Oxford, watch the college boat races, and respond, with

Austin Dobson, to the toast of 'Literature' at the Second Annual Shotover Dinner. There is perhaps a hint here of a student prank, especially since the invitation had come from Francis Griffin Stokes, an undergraduate of Merton College, and since the contents of *The Shotover Papers, or, Echoes of Oxford,* published in thirteen numbers between February 1874 and February 1875, are largely of a satirical cast. But a programme of the dinner has survived, the *Oxford Undergraduate's Journal* of 13 May refers to the 'Shotover Staff' as having entertained 'several distinguished Metropolitan and Oxford Literati' at the Mitre, and it seems necessary to assume that Hardy's visit to Oxford did indeed take place—and to suspect that he may have encountered, in such company, a certain amount of social condescension.[28]

By the time the first instalment of *The Hand of Ethelberta,* handsomely illustrated by George Du Maurier, appeared in the July 1875 *Cornhill,* the Hardys had decided to move on again from Newton Road, perhaps because they found city living unduly expensive, probably because London was not, then or ever, a place which Hardy found conducive to continuous and intensive literary labour. They began looking for a house in Dorset, and *Early Life* lists places where they made inquiries or answered advertisements: Child-Okeford, Shaftesbury, Blandford, Wimborne.[29] Strikingly, none of these is within easy reach of Dorchester or Bockhampton. Strong as the pull of Dorset always was, Hardy was not yet ready to confront Dorchester itself in his new guise as a member of the professional middle class. Nor was he yet prepared to put himself, or his wife, squarely within his mother's orbit. Jemima herself was entirely aware of the situation, if not perhaps of all that lay behind it. When Emma wrote in mid-July of 1875 to suggest that she might meet Hardy and herself at Bournemouth, Jemima got Kate to send back a message that was not overtly hostile but certainly reflected—in its fidelity to her characteristic half-humorous, half-hectoring manner—her strong disapproval of their deliberate avoidance of 'home':

My dear Emma,
 Mother is much obliged to you for your kind invitation but she is so very busy just now that she cannot possibly come. She would like to have come as she says she wants to see you again.
 Mother says you are not to get into the sea or go boating at

Bth [i.e., Bournemouth] because she is afraid you will both be drowned or come to some untimely end. You would be much safer she says on *Rainbarrows* or Cowstairs—

Yrs affectly
K Hardy.[30]

When Hardy and Emma arrived at Bournemouth they had an angry quarrel—for reasons doubtless connected with Kate's letter, with the bad weather, and with Hardy's dislike of Bournemouth itself, the 'Sandbourne' of *Tess of the d'Urbervilles*. On St. Swithin's Day, 15 July—if the evidence of the poem 'We Sat at the Window', dated 'Bournemouth, 1875', is to be accepted—they sat and stared at the rain in a mood of mutual hostility:

> We were irked by the scene, by our own selves; yes,
> For I did not know, nor did she infer
> How much there was to read and guess
> By her in me, and to see and crown
>   By me in her.
> Wasted were two souls in their prime,
> And great was the waste, that July time
> When the rain came down.

The nature of the scene is made more explicit in the manuscript of the poem, where the first line of this second and final stanza reads: 'We were irked by the scene, by each other; yes.'[31]

Later that same day they left Bournemouth and went by steamer the short distance to Swanage, a small port and seaside resort on the 'Isle' of Purbeck. There they found rooms at West End Cottage, a two-storeyed semi-detached house which still stands high on the hillside above the town, looking out over the bay towards the sea and the cliffs of the Foreland—a setting and outlook ascribed in *The Hand of Ethelberta* to the lodgings taken by Ethelberta upon her first arrival at 'Knollsea', 'a seaside village lying snug within two headlands as between a finger and thumb'. The Hardys' landlord, Captain Joseph Masters, master mariner and lodging-house keeper, also makes an appearance in the novel as Captain Flower, who spoke in a 'rich voice, developed by shouting in high winds during twenty years' experience in the coasting trade', and yet 'slipped about the house as lightly as a girl' while assisting his wife in the preparation of dinner.[32]

The completion of *The Hand of Ethelberta* was Hardy's chief occupation in Swanage during the closing months of 1875. The

obligation to send advance proofs to the *New York Times* made
it necessary for him to keep further ahead of the printer than he
had done with *A Pair of Blue Eyes* or even *Far from the Madding
Crowd,* but he seems to have maintained his schedule without
particular difficulty, even though Stephen was still suggesting
minor improvements and issuing such admonitions as 'Remember
the country parson's daughters. *I* have always to remember
them!'[33] Although serialization was not due to conclude until
May 1876 the manuscript was finished in January and the proofs
of the final chapters sent off to New York by the middle of March.
But there were only eleven instalments instead of the twelve
originally planned—to attempt a twelfth number, Hardy told
Smith, Elder in January, 'would be to run the risk of making the
latter part dull by undue extension'[34]—and portions even of this
shortened text seem diffuse, eked-out, and heavily dependent upon
immediately accessible or recently 'researched' topographical details from Swanage, Corfe Castle, and Rouen.

Life went on quietly enough at West End Cottage while the
novel was in progress. Captain Masters was a constant source of
nautical and smuggling anecdotes, the harbour offered regattas
and boat trips,* and there were plenty of local sights to visit and
sketch. Hardy's sisters Mary and Kate came to Swanage for a fortnight's visit in early September, and several sketches by Mary of
scenes in and near Swanage were made during joint expeditions
with her brother and his wife, including a trip round the Isle of
Wight in the steamer *Heather Bell.* The visit ended on the 13th,
when they all set off early by carrier's cart for a breakfast picnic
at Corfe Castle, and then separated, Mary and Kate going on to
Wareham (thence to Dorchester), Hardy and Emma returning to
Swanage.[36] Emma's diary, which records without comment the
visit of Mary and Kate, also contains what appear to be notes
related to the composition of her story, 'The Maid on the Shore'.
That she was engaged in some kind of writing, or thought of
herself as very actively assisting her husband, is indicated by a
remark in Miss D'Arville's letter to her of 26 December 1875:
'You are I dare say both very busy with your new work, which I
hope to read when published.' If Emma's participation was at all
substantial in any novel of Hardy's other than *A Pair of Blue*

* Hardy's copy of E. D. Burrowes's *Swanage and Its Immediate Neighbourhood* contains some almost illegible notes apparently scribbled by Emma
while being tossed up and down in a small boat.[35]

Eyes and *A Laodicean* (see below, p. 216) it must have been *The Hand of Ethelberta;* unfortunately, the manuscript did not survive, and Hardy destroyed the fragment of it which unexpectedly turned up in 1918.[37]

It was while he was living at Swanage that Hardy first had one of his poems published. In September 1875 Richard Gowing, editor of the *Gentleman's Magazine,* wrote to ask for 'a short sketch, or brief story, or an article on some literary, art or social subject for my next January number—a mere chip from your workshop'. Hardy offered a poem, 'The Fire at Tranter Sweatley's', apparently written while he was with Blomfield in the 1860s; Gowing accepted the offer, and the poem appeared that November in a text which had suffered mild bowdlerization at the hands of either a cautious editor or an apprehensive author. Henry Holt—with whom, despite the misunderstandings over the American publication of *Far from the Madding Crowd,* Hardy had maintained a cordial connection—arranged for simultaneous publication of the ballad in America,[38] and a copy was sent off to amuse R. D. Blackmore,[39] whom Hardy had met earlier in the year and addressed in terms of mingled admiration and fellowship.* It seemed 'almost absurd', he said, that he had not read *Lorna Doone* before writing *Far from the Madding Crowd*: 'Little phases of nature which I thought nobody had noticed but myself were continually turning up in your book—for instance, the marking of a heap of sand into little pits by the droppings from trees was a fact I should unhesitatingly have declared unknown to any other novelist till now. A kindred sentiment between us in so many things is, I suppose, partly because we both spring from the West of England.' Blackmore's response was very much in kind, and spoke of Hardy's generosity in praising 'one who works in your own field, at any rate to some extent'.[41] But it was perhaps Hardy's firm establishment of himself as the superior practitioner in that same regional field which prevented this friendship, so propitiously begun, from flourishing in the years between 1875 and Blackmore's death in 1900.

---

* Blackmore, however, had found *Far from the Madding Crowd* to be '*in parts* revolting', and it is likely that even the bowdlerized version of 'The Fire at Tranter Sweatley's' was not greatly to his taste.[40]

9

STURMINSTER NEWTON

Aᶠᵗᵉʳ the conclusion of the *Cornhill* serialization of *The Hand of Ethelberta* Leslie Stephen sought to steer Hardy back to the course he had seemed to be charting with *Far from the Madding Crowd*. Urging him not to allow his own 'perfectly fresh & original vein' to be cramped by excessive respect for critical canons, Stephen recommended instead the reading of 'the great writers, Shakespeare, Goethe, Scott &c &c, who give ideas & dont prescribe rules', and above all of George Sand, 'whose country stories seem to me perfect & have a certain affinity to your's.'[1] Hardy, as it turned out, was never again to have the benefit of Stephen's editorial guidance, but his relations with the publishing house of Smith, Elder continued for some time longer. On 5 March 1876 he had suggested to George Smith the possibility of issuing cheap editions of *A Pair of Blue Eyes* and *Far from the Madding Crowd* during the approaching summer, explaining: 'I do not wish to attempt any more original writing of any length for a few months, until I can learn the best line to take for the future; & the interval would be a convenient one for reading over & amending any previous book.'[2] Smith, Elder gave a cautious response to this suggestion, which Hardy repeated that July, but no one-volume editions were forthcoming from them until the following year.

Hardy's desire for additional exposure and income received more immediate gratification from some negotiations with Freiherr (later Baron) von Tauchnitz, who paid £40 for the continental rights to *The Hand of Ethelberta* in May 1876 and subsequently added most of Hardy's other novels to his series. It was also in 1876 that Hardy was approached by a prospective translator of *Far from the Madding Crowd* into German—a matter over which, as his publishers informed him, he really had very little control—and that he read the long and warmly appreciative article on his work published in the *Revue des deux mondes* for November 1875 under the title 'Le roman pastoral en Angleterre'. Hardy's letter to the author, Léon Boucher, was presumably in English, for while he had an adequate reading knowledge of French, and was generally precise in his quotations, he had little occasion to write or speak it. Boucher's reply thanked Hardy (in English) for a kind and flattering letter but was pessimistic about the prospects for any French translation of *Far from the Madding Crowd,* especially since the translation of *The Mill on the Floss* had sold so poorly.[3]

The irritating association of Hardy's work with George Eliot's was kept alive in the summer of 1876 by the appearance of *Daniel Deronda* and the comment in the *Westminster Review* that it was fortunate that *The Hand of Ethelberta* had been published first, 'or else ill-natured critics would have declared that his principal character was only a copy'. To such a criticism, had it in fact been made, Hardy might justifiably have pointed out that George Eliot had, in that same novel, borrowed from *Far from the Madding Crowd* the designation 'Wessex' for certain southwestern portions of contemporary England.[4] He could also have cited, in support of his own prior claim to that regional concept, the remarkable article entitled 'The Wessex Labourer' which appeared in the 15 July 1876 number of the *Examiner*. Charles Kegan Paul, the anonymous author, was loud in his praise of Hardy's intimate knowledge and exact representation of the Dorset countryside, the Dorset peasantry, and the special quality of the region's still isolated way of life: 'Time in Dorset has stood still; advancing civilisation has given the labourer only lucifer-matches and the penny post, and the clowns in *Hamlet* are no anachronism if placed in a west country village of our own day.' The article, which made frequent and familiar use of 'Wessex' as of a term already in general circulation, played its part in determining Hardy's return to the Dorset countryside for the material of his next novel, and it is little wonder that he kept a copy by him and drew upon it, twenty years later, in writing a Preface to a new edition of *Far from the Madding Crowd*.[5]

The Hardys meanwhile resumed their wanderings, still keeping on the far side of an invisible arc centred upon Higher Bockhampton. In early March of 1876 they left Swanage for Yeovil, Somerset, taking lodgings at 7 St. Peter Street.[6]* Here Hardy corrected the final proofs of the first edition of *The Hand of Ethelberta*, which was published in two volumes by Smith, Elder on 3 April and generally well received by the reviewers—the *Spectator*, for instance, excusing the implausibility of much of its action on the grounds that it could be viewed 'as a humorous fable illustrating the vices and weakness of the upper ten thousand, rather than as a picture of the most characteristic figures in the intellectual society of modern London'. In mid-May of 1876 Hardy and Emma spent a fortnight in London, staying in lodgings at 61 Margaret Street, near Oxford Circus, and viewing the pictures at the French Gallery in company with William Black, the novelist. They then left, on 29 May, for Harwich, the night crossing to Rotterdam, and their second continental holiday.[8]

In Rotterdam they had two nights at the New Bath Hotel— Emma copying into her diary the menu of the table d'hôte dinner —before setting off on 2 June, Hardy's thirty-sixth birthday, for a tour of the Rhine valley. At the Hotel de Hollande, on the river bank at Cologne, Emma recorded that her husband was angry 'about the brandy flask', and while she may simply have lost a valued object it is possible that Hardy, always a near-abstainer, disapproved of her having brought with her what he saw as a symbol either of hypochondria or of that weakness for strong liquors which had already wrought such havoc in both their families. They moved south by steamer to Coblenz—Emma trying to define the precise colour of the river as 'a soft whitish green— not blue but brown-white-green'—and thence, on 6 June, to Mainz and another Hotel de Hollande, described by Emma as a 'very high class, rich hotel'.[9]

The weather was hot, and by the time they reached Heidelberg Emma was becoming exhausted. The evening of their arrival they climbed the tower of the Königstuhl. Because of the mist, Hardy observed, the landscape was invisible, but the Rhine itself 'glared like a riband of blood, as if it serpentined through the atmosphere

* It was in a row of small terrace houses which has recently been pulled down to make way for a car park.[7]

above the earth's surface'. Emma was in less poetic mood: *'wished
I had not,'* she wrote of the climb to the tower. 'Intensely hot,
immensely tired, a mist spread everywhere saw nothing—great
fatigue next day.' They moved on, despite her weariness, to
Karlsruhe and Baden Baden, and then to Strasbourg, where, on
10 June, she felt weak and ill, with an ulcerated throat and a sensation 'as if I were either recovering from or going to have a
fever'. Emma's distress was obvious, and Hardy now made no
objection to her drinking brandy. He did not, however, change
their travel plans and they went on from Strasbourg to Metz and
thence by slow train to Brussels, a journey of eight and a half
hours.[10]

The first day in Brussels was entirely given over to a visit to
the field of Waterloo, and on the morrow Emma recorded that
she was still greatly fatigued and that her husband was 'cross about
it'. The next day things were little better: 'Tom is gone to see the
picture gallery which was closed yesterday—so I have missed it
altogether. Quite worn out with the day at Waterloo—.'[11] No
doubt Hardy was tired too, but anxious to see as much as he could
and reluctant to disturb arrangements—including reservations at
a number of good hotels—which had been carefully made in advance. But there is at least a hint here that, within two years of
their marriage, he was finding Emma something less than the ideal
companion, intellectually free and physically active, he had originally believed her to be—and responding to the discovery with
irritation rather than with sympathy.

The visit to the Waterloo battlefield was, for Hardy at least, a
major objective of the entire holiday. He had been fascinated
since childhood with the period of the Napoleonic Wars, during
which his own corner of England had enjoyed a brief moment of
national significance and his namesake, Admiral Hardy, had become famous through his association with Nelson. On 18 June
1875, the sixtieth anniversary of Waterloo, Hardy had gone with
Emma to Chelsea Hospital to seek out the few pensioners who
were still alive to tell of the experiences of that day. Now, on
the endpapers of his Baedeker for Holland and Belgium, he drew
a 'Plan of Hougoumont—Sketched on the spot by T.H.', and in
Brussels itself he attempted to find the house at which the
Duchess of Richmond's ball had been held the night before the
battle—an historical puzzle which continued to tease him in later
years. Since the Hardys' itinerary was so arranged as to bring them
back to England, by way of Antwerp, on the eve of another Water-

loo Day—no doubt another reason for Hardy's reluctance to change his plans—he was able to go once again to Chelsea and talk with some of the survivors 'in the private parlour of "The Turk's Head" over glasses of grog'.[12] He was, in short, already firmly in the grip of that grand Napoleonic obsession which was to culminate some thirty years later in the publication of *The Dynasts*.

As one of the last entries in her diary of the continental trip Emma had written: 'Going back to England where we have no home & no chosen county.'[13] In less than two years they had moved from Surbiton to Westbourne Grove to Swanage to Yeovil, quite apart from house-hunting expeditions and foreign travels, and Emma at least was weary of such gipsying. The 'search for a little dwelling' begun in Yeovil was now resumed in greater earnest, and on 3 July they moved from Yeovil to Sturminster Newton, a little north Dorset town situated, once again, just outside the fifteen-mile radius of the *cordon sanitaire* they seem to have placed around Higher Bockhampton.[14] Here they rented Riverside (or Rivercliff) Villa, their first real home, semi-detached, bay-windowed, and—like almost all the houses they occupied during their married life—essentially a Victorian villa, solid, 'comfortable', and of quite recent construction. They seem, indeed, to have been the first occupants of Riverside Villa, and it was Hardy who planted in the garden which extended without a division in front of the two houses* a pair of 'monkey-puzzle' trees (Chile pines)—perhaps in memory or emulation of those growing in the rectory garden at St. Juliot. Though unremarkable

* In view of the erroneous tradition which has grown up in recent years, it is necessary to insist that the Hardys lived in the more northerly of the two houses—the one further from the present recreation ground. When the Hardy Players visited Sturminster Newton in June 1921 they were entertained by William Ponting and his wife, occupants of the more northerly house; they were also photographed in front of that house. Hardy was present, with his wife, and indicated that *The Return of the Native* had been written in the first-floor front room, overlooking the river; a photograph of the same house carries on the back a note in Hardy's hand, 'House in which "The Return of the Native" was written—1877. "Riverside" Sturminster Newton. Dorset.' In 1936 the house was again pointed out by Mrs Hardy as the one in which Hardy and Emma had lived. It is clear from Kelly's directories and the electoral rolls that the Pontings had lived since the 1880s in the house they were occupying in 1921 and that Robert Hallett, the occupier of the other house in Hardy's time, had continued to occupy it for many years after the Pontings arrived next door.[15]

in itself, the house had—and has now, despite the recent loss of so many elm trees—a splendid situation on a bluff overlooking the river Stour and its water-meadows. The scene is captured in the poem 'Overlooking the River Stour' and in one of Hardy's note-book entries, made shortly after their arrival: 'Rowed on the Stour in the evening, the sun setting up the river. Just afterwards a faint exhalation visible on surface of water as we stirred it with the oars. A fishy smell from the numerous eels and other fish beneath. Mowers salute us. Rowed among the water-lilies to gather them. Their long ropy stems.'[16]

That the Sturminster Newton period was for Hardy and Emma their 'happiest time' need not be doubted. Hardy's comment was made retrospectively, and the poem 'A Two-Years' Idyll' acknowl-edges the power of nostalgia to transform what at the time of its happening had seemed ordinary enough. Yet the poem also insists that the 'idyll' was real:

> Yes, such it was;
> Just those two seasons unsought,
> Sweeping like summertide wind on our ways;
> Moving, as straws,
> Hearts quick as ours in those days;
> Going like wind, too, and rated as nought
> Save as the prelude to plays
> Soon to come—larger, life-fraught:
> Yes, such it was.[17]

That quickness of heart affected not only their own relationship but also their attitude towards the people amongst whom they were now living.

Sturminster, a market town of some 1,500 inhabitants, was a focal point for the eastern part of the Vale of Blackmoor, the 'Valley of the Little Dairies' of *Tess of the d'Urbervilles*. William Barnes had been born near by at the very beginning of the cen-tury and had written much of his poetry about the Vale and its way of life, but Hardy himself had previously known at first hand only the Vale of Blackmoor's southern fringes around Melbury Osmond and High Stoy. Now, however, both he and Emma entered into the life of Sturminster as though they intended to make it their permanent home. They were soon friendly with various members and generations of the Young family, the owners of Riverside Villa, and especially with Robert Young—'Rabin Hill', the Dorset dialect poet—who was a storehouse of local anecdotes and traditions, and by the autumn of 1876 they were on calling and dining terms with several of the leading Sturminster families. Emma, in particular, was to maintain for many years her friendship with Mrs Dashwood, the wife of Henry Charles Dashwood, a local solicitor.[18]

The notebook entries Hardy preserved from this period testify to an active, energetic, and outgoing appetite for whatever was lively, local, and curious—from the 'beheading' of a woman in a twopenny sideshow at Shroton Fair to the springtime singing of thrushes and blackbirds, 'with such modulation that you seem to see their little tongues curl inside their bills in their emphasis'. At Blandford Forum, another market town not far distant: 'Night on the bridge at the bottom of the town. Light shines from a window across the stream; the surface of the stream seen moving on, the little ripples showing. Occasionally an insect of night touched the water just in the spot of light, & was, unknown to himself, as visible as in day.' Another note records a charming remark of Emma's, made in late autumn: 'A gentle day, when something seems gone from the garden, & you cannot tell what.'[19]

During the closing months of 1876 some attempt was made to bring the Hardy and Gifford families closer together. Two of Emma's brothers came to Sturminster in late October for a brief visit, and that December Hardy took Emma to spend Christmas with his parents. Surviving studio portraits of Jemima and of Thomas Hardy, Sen., show them just as they were at this period, still vigorous in middle age. Jemima's hair seems not to have turned grey; Thomas, broader and handsomer than his elder son, looks the solid, moderately prosperous tradesman he had by this time become. Hardy's father that Christmas told stories of his childhood, when the hobby-horse had not yet died out, and was evidently very much his kindly self.[20] But Jemima's mood can scarcely have been so genial. She and Emma never liked or trusted each other, and in later years a mutual antagonism flourished on the basis of real or imagined slights—Jemima, for example, is said to have created a permanent grievance out of Emma's having once served her tea in a cracked cup.[21] Too much, however, has been made, in this and other contexts, of Emma's snobbery. The refusal of trust and liking seems originally to have been Jemima's —believing, no doubt, that her son had married a foolish woman unlikely either to help his career, bear his children, or honour his parents—and Emma's pride of family essentially a retaliatory resource.

In returning to Sturminster at the end of the Bockhampton visit Hardy was also returning to work on his new novel, set not in the Vale of Blackmoor where he was now living but in the immediate neighbourhood of his parents' cottage, the spot where he had been born and brought up. It seems on the face of it surprising that Hardy should decide to write about Bockhampton and the heath and yet deliberately persist in living elsewhere, but he was now beginning to realize (in contradistinction to what he had felt at the time of writing *Far from the Madding Crowd*) that because distance enforced a more active and absolute dependence upon memory it could actually enhance the imaginative recovery of past scenes and emotions. It is perhaps scarcely less remarkable that he should, while living at Sturminster, entirely have foregone the opportunity of using as a setting a landscape that had already been poetically colonized, claimed as it were for literature, in the Dorset poems of William Barnes. A note of 1876 shows that Hardy was vividly aware of the local association with Barnes—'At Bagber —(where Barnes lived): pool: appletrees: remains of garden, &c— all is there except the house'—and he certainly valued his friendship with Barnes himself—then still living, a venerable and venerated figure, on the outskirts of Dorchester. It was in 1876 that he received a copy of *Poems of Rural Life in Common English* inscribed 'With the Author's kind regards and good wishes for his writings'.[22] Hardy probably owned the dialect poems already; even so, Barnes's choice of volume points suggestively towards Hardy's own firm rejection of dialect and hence towards a probable reason for his not writing about the Vale of Blackmoor —except, later on, as one of a whole sequence of Dorset settings in *Tess of the d'Urbervilles*. Still unsure of his own position in the literary world, Hardy was anxious, as a Dorset writer, to escape any sense of being under Barnes's shadow, and no less anxious, as a novelist craving a wide audience, to avoid the eccentricity and obscurity inevitably associated with dialect forms.

Just how far the writing of *The Return of the Native* had progressed by the beginning of 1877 is not quite clear, but on 5 February Hardy told George Smith that he had sent Leslie Stephen the manuscript 'as far as written'. Stephen did not reject the novel outright but made some temporizing reply, and Hardy, in his anxiety to get into print again, felt himself free in the meantime to seek publication elsewhere. On 13 February he wrote to inquire about a possible opening in *Blackwood's Magazine* for a 'story dealing with remote country life, somewhat of the nature of "Far from the Madding Crowd"'. In view of Hardy's earlier dealings with Stephen and Smith it seems odd that he should tell John Blackwood, in that same letter, that he had 'not yet written enough to be worth sending', but the difficulty appears to have been that he had not yet had his manuscript returned. On 1 March he wrote to Smith, Elder: 'Will you be good enough to return to me the manuscript of the new story, as soon as you conveniently can: I cannot well get on for want of it, as I have no exact copy.'[23]

On 12 April he wrote again to Blackwood to say that he had just forwarded the first fifteen chapters, an estimated one-third of the novel's total length, and to insist that 'should there accidentally occur any word or reflection not in harmony with the general tone of the magazine, you would be quite at liberty to strike it out if you chose. I always mention this to my editors, as it simplifies matters.' Blackwood, however, declined the novel, objecting that the opening chapters were far too static,[24] and in May Hardy sent it back again to Stephen, only to receive a firm rejection about the middle of the following month. Though Stephen liked the opening, Hardy later recalled, 'he feared that the relations between Eustacia, Wildeve, and Thomasin might develop into something "dangerous" for a family magazine, and he refused to have anything to do with it unless he could see the whole. This I never sent him; and the matter fell through.'[25] After another unsuccessful approach, to the editor of *Temple Bar*, Hardy eventually found a home for the serial version in *Belgravia*, edited for Chatto & Windus by Miss Braddon. *Belgravia* was a far less prestigious journal than the *Cornhill*, and Mrs Proctor, for one, was to be astonished to find a serial by 'the divine Hardy' in its pages: 'I suppose Hardy could not stand Leslie Stephen,' she concluded; 'I could not.'[26]

The payment from *Belgravia* amounted to no more than £20 for each monthly part, making a total of £240 for the whole novel.[27] Although that sum did not include publication in volume form, it none the less compared poorly with the £700 received for the English serial and volume rights of *The Hand of Ethelberta*. Book publication—subsequently arranged with Smith, Elder, despite the break with Stephen and the *Cornhill*—and American serialization brought in additional amounts, but Hardy found himself depending rather more than he had anticipated upon such supplementary sources of income as the new one-volume editions of *A Pair of Blue Eyes, Far from the Madding Crowd,* and *The Hand of Ethelberta* which appeared in 1877. In March 1877 he wrote to Anthony Trollope for advice as to the most profitable way of disposing of the rights to novels,[28] a question which had much exercised him ever since that too hasty sale of *Under the Greenwood Tree*—of which Tinsley had recently brought out a new one-volume illustrated edition. It was another stage in the process of turning himself into an efficient literary agent, a shrewd though never grasping manager of his professional affairs, fully aware of all the possibilities open to a writer of fiction in that particular period. Later in the year he sold to Tauchnitz the continental rights to *Far from the Madding Crowd* and published a children's story, 'The Thieves Who Couldn't Help Sneezing', in an annual called *Father Christmas.*

By the end of 1877 *The Return of the Native* was all but complete. Copy for the first two instalments was sent off on 28 August; by early November three more instalments were ready and Hardy was already turning part of his attention to the kind of historical and regional material he was to draw upon in *The Trumpet-Major.* In September 1877 he wrote to a local antiquary, the Revd Charles Bingham of Binghams Melcombe—the 'original' of Parson Tringham in *Tess of the d'Urbervilles*—to ask where he could find files of local newspapers for the early years of the century or, indeed, 'any county records, notes, or memoranda relating to that time'.[29] He had also begun by this time his exploration of Hutchins's *History and Antiquities of the County of Dorset,* a resource of the first importance for Hardy's gradual evolution of Wessex as a total imaginative world with a solid, complex, comprehensively realized existence in space and time.

Several notes from Hutchins appear in the early pages of a notebook which Hardy, with Emma's active assistance, began keeping in the spring of 1876. He had of course kept working notebooks for many years, but this new one was in the nature of a commonplace book, recording information and ideas, new or strikingly expressed, encountered during his reading of books, newspapers (chiefly *The Times* and the *Daily News*), and magazines (especially the *Saturday Review, Spectator,* and *Fortnightly*). The notebook was in frequent use at Sturminster Newton and was drawn upon several times during the composition of *The Return of the Native,* and the fact that Emma wrote out the original batch of notes and continued to add others from time to time—

it was she who copied a long series of sayings by the Jesuit
Balthasar Gracian from the *Fortnightly Review* of March 1877[30]—
is suggestive of the extent to which the Hardys, during these early
years of their marriage, saw themselves as a 'team', sharing the
same interests and activities, working together in the common
project which was Hardy's career.

But Sturminster Newton itself supplied Hardy with material of a
more substantial kind. The episode in *Jude the Obscure,* for instance, in which Father Time arrives by train without warning,
his ticket in his hat, the key of his box on a string round his neck,
probably owes a good deal to the interest aroused in Sturminster
by the little girl who arrived at the railway station on 3 January
1877 in care of the guard and carrying a parcel addressed to a local
resident, who denied all knowledge of the child. It later transpired
that the girl's mother, Christine Rideout, had worked as a bar-
maid while living with the child's father, a publican; after being
deserted by another man who had bigamously married her, she
sent the child, unannounced, to her own parents, apparently so
that she herself might make a new unencumbered start.[31]*
    In describing the Club-day walking and dancing at the be-
ginning of *Tess of the d'Urbervilles* Hardy certainly drew upon
what he had seen of such events in the Vale of Blackmoor. The
anniversary festival of the Sturminster branch of the Dorset
County Friendly Society on Whit Monday, 21 May 1877, included
a procession with a band, a church service, and a dinner; in the
evening the festivities moved to a near-by field, 'where dancing
and athletic sports were enjoyed'. Hardy's visit to Marnhull, the
'Marlott' of *Tess of the d'Urbervilles,* on 30 May was probably
made in order to witness similar celebrations there, and he specifically recorded his presence at the festivities held at Sturminster
on 28 June, the fortieth anniversary of Queen Victoria's coronation. There were sports, and dancing on the green, and Hardy
observed that 'The pretty girls, just before a dance, stand in inviting positions on the grass. As the couples in each figure pass
near where their immediate friends loiter, each girl-partner gives
a laughing glance at such friends, and whirls on.'[33]
    The proximity of this note to the account of the Hardys' trou-

* Hardy could also have had in mind the story, later that same year, of
the nine-year-old Blandford boy with a mania for railway travel, although
he was specifically unlike Father Time in not having a ticket.[32]

bles, that same night, with their servant Jane has additional importance for the genesis of *Tess of the d'Urbervilles*. Although Jane had probably not been with them long—she was presumably the successor to Georgiana, whose dismissal the previous November is noted in Emma's diary—it is clear from their concern for her welfare that they did indeed, as Hardy says in his note, like her very much. When she ran off in the early hours of the morning after having been caught in the act of bringing a man into the house at night, Hardy went to inform her parents, finding them 'poorer than I expected (for they are said to be an old county family)'. A few days later Hardy and Emma seem to have looked for the girl at Stalbridge, where she was rumoured to have gone to join her lover, and on 13 August they learned that she was expecting a baby.[34]

It seems reasonably safe to identify the Hardys' Jane with Jane Phillips, whose two-day-old son Tom was buried at Sturminster by the Revd S. Keddle on 3 December 1877.* The same bastard child had been privately baptized before its death—presumably by its mother, as the Hand children had been by their mother— and it is tempting to imagine as lying behind the bare parish records a sequence of events approximating to the brief life and pathetic death of Tess's child, Sorrow, in Hardy's novel. A Jenny Phillips is named in Hardy's copy of John Hullah's *The Song Book* as the singer of several of Hardy's favourite songs, including 'When the Rosebud of Summer' and 'My Man Thomas', and in view of the reference to 'an old county family' it is worth noting that Hutchins gives the pedigree of the Phelips family of Corfe Mullen (a village near Wimborne with which Hardy later became familiar) and records the existence of a family vault there and the decline into cottages of the former mansion of the Phelipses.[36]

One or two of Hardy's poems associated with this period appear to contain references to Jane Phillips. The speaker in 'Overlooking the River Stour' regrets that in gazing out at the natural world he had failed to notice the more significant human events occurring, behind his back, within the house itself; and although this has generally been read as an allusion to Hardy's own marriage, the first stanza's mention of 'the wet June's last beam' seems to relate it specifically—since the Hardys spent only one June in Sturminster—to the moment of their troubles with their servant at the very end of June 1877. What Hardy evidently recognized

* The death—caused by 'Debility from Birth'—actually occurred on 28 November 1877. None of the official records gives the name of the father.[35]

in the fate of a Jane Phillips—and dramatized in the story of Tess Durbeyfield—was the sheer power of sexuality and the gross injustice of a social system which thrust upon the woman the burden of sexual responsibility and guilt. But he also came to see her as a tragic instance of the emotional ferment that could lie beneath the apparent placidity of familiar domestic appearances, and as a warning of the precariousness of that modest everyday happiness which may never even be recognized until it has been irrecoverably lost. Whoever is imagined as uttering the message of 'The Musical Box'*—' "O make the most of what is nigh!" '—its bearing is chiefly upon the subsequent course of the Hardys' marriage, the fading of 'the fair colour of the time'. The final stanza of 'A Two-Years' Idyll' makes the point quite explicitly:

> What seems it now?
> Lost: such beginning was all;
> Nothing came after: romance straight forsook
> Quickly somehow
> Life when we sped from our nook,
> Primed for new scenes with designs smart and tall. . . .
> —A preface without any book,
> A trumpet uplipped, but no call;
> That seems it now.

The book that remained unwritten—like the first stanza's 'plays / Soon to come—larger, life-fraught'—surely included children among its *dramatis personae*. A wealth of sad and perhaps bitter implication lies behind Hardy's comment on the news that their former servant was expecting a child: 'Yet never a sign of one is there for us.'[38] Although they had not long been married, the Hardys were not especially young in years; at thirty-six, nearing thirty-seven, Emma was already at an age at which child-bearing might be difficult and dangerous, and as each year of the late 1870s slipped by the likelihood of her ever having children grew steadily more remote.

In late October 1877 Hardy made a brief trip to Bath to meet his father, who had gone there in search of a cure for his rheumatism —the consequence of his never bothering to take off wet clothes

---

* In the manuscript of this companion poem to 'Overlooking the River Stour' the singular pronouns of stanzas 2 to 6 are all plural, suggesting that it was perhaps Jane Phillips who, in stanza 4, waited 'white-muslined' in the porch for Hardy and Emma to return from their walk, and that she, not

when he came home from work. Hardy found lodgings for his father, took him to the theatre, saw him safely to the baths the next day, and then returned to Sturminster.[39] Christmas that year seems to have passed without a family gathering at Higher Bockhampton: the evening of 22 December, at any rate, Hardy spent with his friend Dr John Comyns Leach, the local surgeon and Coroner, who had to conduct an inquest into the death of a boy at a village a few miles from Sturminster. Holding a candle to provide light for the autopsy, Hardy observed that two cuts, one vertical and the other horizontal, had been used to open up the body.[40]

By the beginning of 1878 the Hardys had decided to leave Riverside Villa and move closer to London. Professional reasons were apparently uppermost in Hardy's mind, but Emma had come to believe that the air from the river was unhealthy and to fret at their living, as one of her brothers had scornfully remarked, in a place so isolated that 'a strange bird on the lawn was an event'. Emma now felt buried in Sturminster and was ambitious for her husband, as a successful author, to cut more of a figure in the literary world, believing that in London she, too, as the successful author's wife, would have a more satisfying role to play. She had already caused Hardy some embarrassment by exaggerating to one of their neighbours—probably Mrs Dashwood—the extent to which she helped her husband in the actual writing of his novels.[41]

Ironically enough, the Hardys left Sturminster just as they were becoming locally known and established: at least two Dorset newspapers recorded their presence, on 5 March 1878, at the Sturminster Literary Institute concert at which a Miss Marsh, from the Somerset village of Keinton Mandeville, sang Sir Henry Bishop's 'Should he upbraid' with a skill and charm which prompted Hardy, years later, to make her performance the basis of his poem 'The Maid of Keinton Mandeville'.[42] Within two weeks of the concert they had packed up their furniture—most of it purchased new at the time of their moving into Riverside Villa twenty months earlier—spent a final night at the Dashwoods', and left for the house in the London suburb of Tooting on which they had taken a three-year lease during an expedition to London the previous month.[43] It was not to prove a fortunate move in personal or even in professional terms.

Emma, was the 'spirit' who, in the second stanza, sang to the tune of the musical box the unheeded words, 'O value what the nonce outpours— / This best of life—that shines about / Your welcoming!'[37]

THE RETURN
OF THE NATIVE

O N 22 March 1878 the Hardys moved into 1 Arundel Terrace,
Trinity Road, Tooting—sometimes called 'The Larches'—
the end house of a three-storeyed red-brick Victorian terrace.
Wandsworth Common and Wandsworth Common Station were
only a few minutes' walk away, but the house was not otherwise
notable for charm or convenience. Writing rather apologetically
to Kegan Paul on 21 June, Hardy explained that 'for such utter
rustics as ourselves Tooting seemed town enough to begin with'.
Emma meanwhile sent Mrs Dashwood a harrowing account of the
problems of furnishing a house considerably bigger than Riverside Villa.[1]

At Tooting, during the first half of 1878, both the scope and
pace of Hardy's literary work began to increase. There were the
Napoleonic ballads, the corrections to the Tauchnitz edition of
Far from the Madding Crowd, a new short story ('The Impulsive
Lady of Croome Castle'), and the reworking of what remained of
the manuscript of *The Poor Man and the Lady* into the novella-
length story called 'An Indiscretion in the Life of an Heiress',
published that July in the *New Quarterly Magazine.*[2] Meanwhile
the serial proofs of *The Return of the Native*—running in *Belgravia* from January to December 1878—had to be corrected and
a duplicate set sent across the Atlantic to *Harper's New Monthly*

Magazine; the illustrator, Arthur Hopkins (younger brother of Gerard Manley Hopkins), also needed guidance as to the way Eustacia should look and what the mummers would have worn and carried.[3] Because he expected only a relatively small financial reward from *The Return of the Native,* Hardy was prepared to pursue other forms of literary remuneration, and he reconciled himself to the London move, undertaken primarily at Emma's insistence, by the prospect of being able to put himself in the way of more business—and perhaps more friendly reviews—by making the acquaintance of publishers, editors, and agents, and mixing freely and clubably with the literary world in general.

In the spring of 1878 the editor of a Boston journal asked Hardy to supply some notes for a biographical article—itself an encouraging index of his growing reputation—and received in return a manuscript which, though written out in Emma's hand, was clearly Hardy's own work, embodying the professional self-image he wished to project at that particular period. It spoke in particular of his 'higher education' as having been taken in hand by 'an able classical scholar & Fellow of Queen's College, Cambridge' and described how, after winning two architectural prizes, 'he formed the idea of becoming an art-critic & undertook special studies for the purpose, but his early taste for romantic literature having revived, he sent a short attempt in fiction to one of the London Magazines: it was accepted at once; & fiction thence forward became his hobby. But he did not altogether neglect art & visited several of the great collections of paintings in Continental Capitals from time to time.'[4] Like so many of Hardy's later statements of a public nature, the article was not so much inaccurate as misleading. Its exaggeration of the formality and extent of his education and his artistic studies seems very much of a piece with the ponderous displays of literary and artistic information in the early fiction and with the somewhat laborious autodidacticism which appears in the notebooks. More significant, perhaps, is the deliberate creation of an impression of a literary gentleman of wide interests, a countryman by birth, a Londoner by adoption, for whom architecture had been a perfectly natural first career and who had arrived effortlessly at novel-writing in the course of rediscovering an 'early taste for romantic literature'.

The dispatch of this document on 9 May 1878 needs to be correlated with Hardy's election that June to membership of the Savile Club, the principal literary club of the day, and with the whole process by which he 'fell into line as a London man again'.

From Tooting he was able to visit galleries and theatres, call on publishers such as George Smith of Smith, Elder, and give dinners at the Savile to editors such as William Minto of the *Examiner*; he could also take Emma to visit the Alexander Macmillans, who lived quite close by, encountering there such figures as T. H. Huxley and John Morley. Now and again these occasions provided him with 'material'—when writing *A Laodicean*, for example, he was able to draw upon his memories of a sudden downpour of rain during one of Mrs Macmillan's garden parties—but his relative inexperience of the London literary world, in combination with his necessary professionalism, tended to expose him to some of that world's most characteristic dangers. London valued facility, energy, panache—the dependable productivity of a Walter Besant, the infinitely adaptable talent of an Edmund Gosse—and in none of these did Hardy's genius reside. London tempted him with journalistic opportunities, invited him to be trivial, exacerbated his vulnerability to contemporary opinion, undermined him with sheer occupation—an excess of gossip, shop-talk, dining out, and 'keeping-up'. The founding of the Rabelais Club by Besant in 1879 is treated in *Early Life* as an event of major importance—though a certain wryness enters into the account of the inaugural meeting[5]—and Hardy put some effort, at least in the 1870s and '80s, into maintaining cordial relations with a whole series of second- and third-rate metropolitan littérateurs. This was, however, precisely the literary life towards which he had aspired —so impossibly, as it then seemed—in the '60s, the contemporary counterpart of those earlier worlds so beguilingly evoked in the pages of Thackeray's *Pendennis* and the conversations of Horace Moule. And the friendship of such a man as Besant—founder of the Incorporated Society of Authors and indefatigable defender of authors' rights—at least served to keep him informed about current publishing practices and the best ways of maintaining a tight and profitable control over his own productions.

Ironically enough, one of the immediate advantages of Hardy's new location was that he could work in the Reading Room of the British Museum on the background of his native region during the Napoleonic period and so supplement and document the long-familiar family anecdotes of his own grandparents' experiences during the period of threatened invasion. By the spring of 1878 the scheme of *The Trumpet-Major* had taken definite form, although little if any of the actual writing had yet been done, and the visits to the British Museum began in late May.[6] Although the serial of *The Return of the Native* had now run two-thirds of its course, there were still proofs to correct, illustrations to supervise—his disappointment with Hopkins's first presentation of Eustacia being quite dispelled by her appearance in the August number—and various business details to settle: it was only in September that arrangements were made with Smith, Elder for publication of *The Return of the Native* in volume form, the payment to be £200 for an edition of 1,000 copies.[7]

Although parallel serialization had been proceeding in *Harper's New Monthly Magazine,* rights in the American first edition were again secured by Henry Holt, who had been the first to publish a Hardy novel *(Under the Greenwood Tree)* in the United States and had since brought out all the other novels in his one-volume Leisure Hour series. Holt had a settled working arrangement with Hardy, paying him a straight royalty of ten per cent of the retail price and undertaking on his behalf such commissions as the disposal of the American rights of 'An Indiscretion', and after Harper & Brothers had negotiated their independent agreement with Hardy for *The Return of the Native* Holt persuaded Joseph W. Harper, Jr., that 'trade courtesy required him to turn the book-right over to me, who had introduced Hardy here'—the argument he had earlier used to obtain *Far from the Madding Crowd.* Hardy grew increasingly uneasy in his relationship with Holt, suspecting that he could get better terms elsewhere, and in a letter to Harper & Brothers of 24 June 1878 he made it clear that he would like to do more business with them: 'If at any time you should wish to make a proposal for including novels of mine in your series, it will be treated in confidence. I am not sufficiently acquainted with the usage of American publishers to know if an English author is held to be justified there, as in England, in arranging with whomsoever he chooses for the publication of any particular book or books, irrespective of those that have preceded it.' Meanwhile negotiations with Tauchnitz for a continental edition of *The Return of the Native*[8] completed one more stage in that sequence with which Hardy was now becoming thoroughly familiar: English serial, American serial, English first edition, American first edition, continental edition, cheap one-volume edition.

Much of the remembered happiness of the Sturminster Newton period had its source in the generous and confident flow of Hardy's creative energies as he worked on the manuscript of *The Return of the Native*. He had striven more deliberately than ever before to make the book an unmistakable work of art, not just another run-of-the-mill serial, and hence to prove himself not merely a good serial hand but (to use another phrase from that same February 1874 letter to Stephen) 'a great stickler for the proper artistic balance of the completed work'. In particular, he had sought to enhance the novel's claims to be regarded as a serious work of literature by manipulating his story of a primitive and isolated Wessex community so as to sustain unity of place, approximate unity of time, and parallel the foreground action with classical and biblical allusions and structural echoes of the patterns of Greek and Elizabethan tragedy.[9] But while the critical reception of the work as published in three volumes by Smith, Elder on 4 November 1878 was indeed characterized by general respect for Hardy as an artist, it displayed a disappointment no less general in *The Return of the Native* as a manifestation of that art. Several reviewers found it cold, intellectual, and unnecessarily depressing, others criticized the theatricality of the scene-painting, and there was a widespread feeling that while the dialogue of the rustic characters was often striking and amusing it was rarely like life: 'The language of his peasants may be Elizabethan, but it can hardly be Victorian.'[10]

The *Athenaeum* review, the source of that smart formulation, was one of the most hostile responses the book received, and one of the earliest. Hardy, venturing for the first time to answer one of his critics in print, wrote a letter which ranged so far beyond the specific point made by the reviewer as to suggest that he was seizing the opportunity to issue a long-contemplated manifesto on issues that were fundamental to his entire position as a regional novelist:

An author may be said to fairly convey the spirit of intelligent peasant talk if he retains the idiom, compass, and characteristic expressions, although he may not encumber the page with obsolete pronunciations of the purely English words, and with mispronunciations of those derived from Latin and Greek. In the printing of standard speech hardly any phonetic principle at all is observed; and if a writer attempts to exhibit on paper the precise accents of a rustic speaker he disturbs the proper balance of a true representation by unduly insisting upon the grotesque element; thus directing attention to a point of inferior interest, and diverting it from the speaker's meaning, which is by far the

chief concern where the aim is to depict the men and their na-
tures rather than their dialect forms.

A note made two days before the letter was published is highly
suggestive of Hardy's anxiety over the novel's reception—and of
the way in which a particular distress could rapidly expand in his
mind to quite overwhelming proportions: 'Woke before it was
light. Felt that I had not enough staying power to hold my own
in the world.'[11]

The critics were not deflected by Hardy's intervention. One
of the last to pass judgement, on 8 February 1879, was the
Spectator reviewer (almost certainly Richard Holt Hutton), who
repeated and amplified reservations about the speech of the
peasants expressed by earlier critics and developed a sustained
criticism of the author's 'gloomy fatalism', his having 'found
Schopenhauer far superior to all the prophets and all the seers'.
Although the burden of these remarks was to be taken up by a
great many critics in succeeding years and generations, Hardy's
notebooks show no indication of any familiarity with Schopenhauer's writings at this date. Since his German, unlike his French,
seems always to have remained quite minimal, *The World as Will
and Idea* would in any case have become directly accessible to
him only on the publication of an English translation in 1883.
Edmund Gosse told an inquiring scholar in 1909 that Hardy did
'not admit any influence from Schopenhauer on his work'. He
went on: 'The ideas which have animated Mr Hardy's books were
already present in his mind and conversation, and were the result
of temperament and observation, rather than of "influence".'[12]

Gosse might have added that such ideas were also rooted in
both general and particular aspects of Hardy's personal background—a background he had implicitly acknowledged in the
first edition of *The Return of the Native* by persuading Smith,
Elder to print his own sketch map of 'the supposed scene' as a
frontispiece.[13] For while that map had been deliberately dis-
oriented, so that what should be its North-South axis actually
appears as East-West, it clearly showed—to anyone familiar with
the countryside around Dorchester—that the place whose unity
Hardy had sought so earnestly to preserve was the tract of heathland immediately adjacent to Higher Bockhampton, with the
position of the fictional Bloom's End roughly approximating to
the position of the house in which he himself had been born and
his parents still lived.

Because the personal connection was so direct and obvious, it seems almost inconceivable that Hardy would consciously have allowed the narrative to fall into autobiographical patterns. Yet the story is that of an idealistic and gifted young man who abandons the professional goals set for him by his ambitious and strong-minded mother, becomes distracted from both practical and idealistic ambitions by his infatuation with a free-spirited woman unexpectedly encountered in a wild and lonely place, and subsequently endures—having largely provoked—the social and perhaps sexual frustrations of his disappointed wife and the bitter hostility which springs up between his wife and his mother. Hardy liked to think of Clement, as Clym Yeobright was christened, as a name traditional in his own family; he based Mrs Yeobright, Clym's mother, on his own mother; he gave Clym's dead father his own father's and grandfather's love of music and church choirs; and he probably had his sister Mary in mind when creating the patient, unprotesting Thomasin, whose very name echoes Hardy's own and who in the manuscript was once cast as Clym's sister rather than his cousin.[14] If Emma perceived any of these analogies, one wonders what she can have made of her own presumable role as the beautiful but sexually restless and foolishly romantic Eustacia Vye, the direct though unwitting cause of Mrs Yeobright's death and the active seeker (so the text suggests) of her own.

Emma, however, had already survived the experience of seeing substantial elements of her personality and behaviour merged into the characterization of Elfride Swancourt, and she was by this time familiar with the transformational processes of her husband's imagination—which is not to say that she had any real grasp of those processes themselves, or of the way they might feed into his personal life as well as upon it. Many aspects of *A Pair of Blue Eyes, Under the Greenwood Tree,* and even *Far from the Madding Crowd* are clearly autobiographical, and the later evidence of *The Woodlanders, Tess of the d'Urbervilles,* and *Jude* urges the conclusion that Hardy's best work tends to have strong and specific roots in his own background and experience—that, indeed, the existence of such roots was essential to the fullest and freest flow of his creative impulse, their absence a major source of the relative failure of works such as *The Trumpet-Major* and *Two on a Tower* in which he attempted to make the results of deliberate research do duty for a missing core of personal experience. Hardy's settings, as all Wessex pilgrims know, are famous for what might be called their flexible fidelity to actuality: scenes and buildings recognizably 'real' are adapted, developed, shifted, arranged in new topographical relationships, in order to meet the overriding demands of the fiction, the work of art itself. So it often seems to be with characterization and even with individual incidents and passages of dialogue. Hardy's plots may be invented or borrowed, but much of his richest narrative material is re-worked more or less directly from the life. If he never tells a wholly autobiographical story, the texture of his work is never-theless thick with remembered experience and observation, and with family and local traditions possessed so absolutely by the imagination as to be indistinguishable from memory itself. Though deeply autobiographical, therefore—and in ways which cannot have been wholly unconscious—*The Return of the Native* is hardly a *roman à clef*. The significance of the sketch map is not (despite a teasing allusion, deleted from *Early Life,* to the map in *Treasure Island*)[15] as a guide to buried biographical treasure but rather as an indication that Hardy had not yet developed those habits of defensive secretiveness which have so often been charged against him.

Of all the 'autobiographical' elements in *The Return of the Native,* the one that in the end remains the most fascinating derives from Hardy's use of his narrative not to recreate his own past experiences but rather to explore in hypothetical terms a road he had not taken—and, in so doing, to see more plainly, and perhaps justify to himself, the course he had in fact chosen to follow. Clym's decision to reject his profession and return to the heath was quite distinct from the direction of Hardy's life since he had finally given up architecture, and while he had perhaps made some of Clym's mistakes (notably in marrying Emma/ Eustacia) he had not taken the false step of trying to go home again. Hardy had consistently resisted the temptation, and the parental pressure, to meld Emma with the world of Bockhampton, recognizing with a clear-sightedness not available to the blinded Clym—nor, indeed to his own later self—that such an arrange-ment would never work. The fact that he had taken the Tooting house, in its turn, on only a temporary basis suggests that a solution to his central dilemma had not yet revealed itself, and that he was in some sense using the writing of his novel not as an act of self-analysis but, more simply, as a way of 'laying out' his situation and problems, of projecting what might have followed —what might still follow—as a consequence of his playing in a radically different fashion the hand dealt him by fate. Like *The Hand of Ethelberta* before it, *The Return of the Native* took on for Hardy himself something of the significance of a private fable or cautionary tale.

In early September 1878, shortly before he first mentioned the sketch map to Smith, Elder, Hardy visited Dorset for ten days and made a series of excursions that asserted, in small and un-dramatic ways, his new position as an acknowledged man of letters and a member of the professional middle class. He called as a literary equal on William Barnes at Came rectory. He visited Kingston Lacy 'to see the pictures'. When he and Charles W. Moule made a similar expedition to Forde Abbey they arrived outside the normal visiting hours but were invited in and shown round by the owner himself.[16] There was not the slightest sug-gestion, however, of his drifting out of touch with his own family. He stayed at Bockhampton as usual, and on returning to London wrote to ask his brother to get their mother to make up her mind to come to London for a visit 'while the fine weather lasts'. With a curious but characteristic affinity for the actual, he sent with the letter—indeed, wrapped within it—a chip of wood he had himself taken from the wreck of the *Princess Alice,* which had sunk in the Thames with heavy loss of life just ten days earlier.[17]

The experience of moving in his old world armed with his new status perhaps gave Hardy the confidence to assert, through the sketch map, his own intimate connection with the scenes he had portrayed. Although he was not anxious to publicize his back-ground, he clearly regarded it with neither shame nor embarrass-ment: it was at this period that Charles Kegan Paul referred to him in print as 'sprung of a race of labouring men' and that he simply wrote back to say that his forebears had in fact been independent master masons.[18] Kegan Paul was, however, a privi-leged friend, one who possessed a special understanding and appreciation of Hardy's work as a result of the twelve years he had himself spent as vicar of the Dorsetshire village of Stur-minster Marshall and of his sympathy, during those years, with the aspirations of Joseph Arch and his National Agricultural Labourers' Union. Now a London reviewer and publisher, Kegan Paul 'took up' the Hardys following their arrival at Tooting, inviting them to parties and considerably expanding their London acquaintance. Jane Panton, one of the daughters of W. P. Frith, the painter of *Derby Day* and other crowded Victorian canvases, recalled her first meeting with Hardy—'a short, frail-looking man'

—in the Kegan Pauls' drawing room during the 1870s, and this was perhaps the beginning of Hardy's friendship with Frith himself and with other members of his family.[19]

Hardy, now as always, was very actively interested in painting, both for its own sake and as the source of materials and perhaps even of techniques relevant to his own work. Many of the references to art in *The Return of the Native* belong with that somewhat obtrusive classical apparatus by which he sought to elevate the novel above the common run of contemporary fiction. But he was to tell the Pre-Raphaelite sculptor Thomas Woolner just a year or two later that *The Return of the Native* 'embodied' his views on 'the art of the future', and it is clear both that he thought of the novel form as a potential vehicle for the expression of ideas, and that those ideas were as often formulated in aesthetic as in social or moral terms. In the letter to Woolner he specifically drew attention to the opening sentences of Book Third:

> In Clym Yeobright's face could be dimly seen the typical countenance of the future. Should there be a classic period to art hereafter, its Pheidias may produce such faces. The view of life as a thing to be put up with, replacing that zest for existence which was so intense in early civilizations, must ultimately enter so thoroughly into the constitution of the advanced races that its facial expression will become accepted as a new artistic departure. People already feel that a man who lives without disturbing a curve of feature, or setting a mark of mental concern anywhere upon himself, is too far removed from modern perceptiveness to be a modern type.[20]

Although he is ostensibly writing about art, Hardy's emphasis is clearly upon what he calls—in dull monosyllables as expressive as those of Pope's famous alexandrine—the 'view of life as a thing to be put up with', and the passage falls into place as an element in the over-all presentation of Clym Yeobright as a naïvely idealistic, anxiously cerebrating, and ultimately defeated intellectual. Clym has often been called Arnoldian, but Hardy's reference to the 'ethical systems' Clym has picked up in Paris seems to point rather to Comte, and hence to a deliberate undercutting of those broadly Positivist values—service to others, compromise, and 'loving-kindness'—which had been specifically celebrated in *Far from the Madding Crowd*.[21] Certainly the intellectual content of the later novel is denser, more purposeful, and decidedly more

pessimistic. Although he wrote it during the Sturminster Newton
period subsequently remembered as one of particular happiness,
Hardy's intellectual travels during the 1870s had led him to
project in *The Return of the Native* a mood far darker than that
of any of his previous works, and not simply because of the novel's
self-conscious aspirations to tragic status.

A mild melancholy pervades the few notes which have survived
from the closing months of 1878, and the winter of 1878–9 was
evidently a period of increasing tension within the Hardys'
marriage—perhaps because of its continuing childlessness, perhaps because of disagreements over the wisdom of the move to
London or the particular choice of 1 Arundel Terrace as their
new home: 'they seemed to begin to feel', says *Early Life,* 'that
"there had past away a glory from the earth." ' The poem 'A
January Night (1879)', with its central lines 'There is some hid
dread afoot / That we cannot trace', chimes both with this feeling
of having lost 'The glory and the freshness of a dream' and with
the statement, also in *Early Life,* that it was at Tooting, a little
later on, 'that their troubles began'.[22] That the relationship was
not yet seriously disturbed, however, is suggested by a note of
19 January 1879—headed 'Shines' and entered into the 'Poetical
Matter' notebook as potential material for a poem—which preserves with extraordinary and, it seems fair to say, affectionate
precision a peaceful moment from the Hardys' domestic life at
Tooting:

> In the study firelight a red glow is on the polished sides & arch
> of the grate: firebrick back red hot: the polish of fireirons shines;
> underside of mantel reddened: also a shine on the leg of the
> table, & the ashes under the grate, lit from above like a torrid
> clime. Faint daylight of a lilac colour almost powerless in the
> room. Candle behind a screen is reflected in the glass of the win-
> dow, falling whitely on book, & on E's face & hand, a large shade
> of her head being on wall & ceiling. Light shines through the
> loose hair about her temples, & reaches the skin as sunlight
> through a brake.[23]

Hardy's father had written at the New Year to say that Jemima
was ill, and at the beginning of February 1879 Hardy left Emma
at Tooting and took the train to Dorchester, where he was met
by his brother Henry and driven out to Bockhampton in a wagon-

ette pulled by 'Bob', the horse kept for the family business. Although the weather was unusually cold, Hardy took advantage of the opportunity to visit Weymouth, Portland, and Sutton Poyntz, places which would figure in *The Trumpet-Major,* on which he was now actively engaged. He also took a wry amusement in learning the fate of some church fittings torn out by John Wellspring, the builder who had done restoration work at Coombe Keynes and elsewhere during his own time with Hicks: 'chickens roost under the gilt-lettered Lord's Prayer and Creed, and the cock crows and flaps his wings against the Ten Commandments.' Because his mother was ill, he talked much with his father about old times: one such tale, about a parson's son who became a miller, may have contributed something, several years later, to the presentation of Angel Clare in *Tess of the d'Urbervilles.*[24]

When Hardy sounded out the prospects for serialization of *The Trumpet-Major* in the pages of the *Cornhill,* Leslie Stephen replied that he would be interested in seeing the story when it was further advanced, adding that his own preference was for novels like *Vanity Fair* in which the historical characters were kept in the background and a figure such as George III, though felt to be 'just round the corner', was not seen 'in full front'.[25] Although Captain Hardy appears briefly in *The Trumpet-Major* and George III himself—perhaps to tease Leslie Stephen—is once seen 'in full front', this was essentially the method Hardy followed. But precisely because his characters were unknown to history and of relatively humble rank, it was essential that their lives be seen as suspended within a network of large and intricate historical events, and it was in search of additional sustaining details that Hardy, in the late spring and early summer of 1879, renewed from time to time his British Museum researches into studies and memoirs of the Napoleonic period and especially into contemporary newspapers and drawings.

The Trumpet-Major proved, like its immediate predecessor, somewhat difficult to place. In May 1879 Hardy seems to have sent a portion of the manuscript to Macmillan, presumably in the hope of serialization in *Macmillan's Magazine.* In early June he approached John Blackwood with the offer of 'a cheerful story, without views or opinions' which was 'intended to wind up happily'. By the end of that same month negotiations with William Isbister, the publisher of *Good Words,* were sufficiently well advanced for the editor, the Revd Dr Donald Macleod, to define for Hardy the kind of material he was seeking: 'We are anxious that all our stories should be in harmony with the spirit of the Magazine—free at once from *Goody-goodyism*—and from any-thing—direct or indirect—which a healthy *Parson* like myself would not care to read to his bairns at the fireside.' Given the 'cheerful' nature of his story, Hardy could accept these otherwise ominous terms with a reasonable degree of complacency. In the event, he was obliged to make a number of minor changes to ac-commodate Dr Macleod's ministerial susceptibilities but, as he recalled many years later, it was easy enough to restore the original readings when the novel appeared in book form.[26]

By the summer of 1879 work on the manuscript was well advanced—no doubt stimulated by a glimpse, on 12 July, of Prince Napoleon, whose profile struck Hardy as 'altogether ex-traordinarily remindful of Boney'—and in August he found time to go down to Dorset again to see his now convalescent mother. Kate had recently completed her training as a teacher at the same Salisbury college Mary had attended years before, and both sisters were at home for the summer holidays. Hardy walked over to Puddletown on at least one occasion and talked with his cousin James Sparks about their common great-great-great-grandfather, who had lived in Puddletown in the seventeenth century and built the cottage which had remained in the family ever since. He would also have visited his aunt Mary Antell, whose husband the shoemaker had died the previous December, and seen the little death-bed sketch of John Antell drawn by his son—whom Hardy was later to advise on the design of a headstone for John Antell's grave. *The Trumpet-Major* was not forgotten, however. When Emma came down to Dorset a week or so after her husband they soon moved to Weymouth, as the obvious centre for visits to places associated with the novel, and this time Hardy's mother came over from Bockhampton, despite the wet and exceptionally windy weather, to join in several of their excursions.[27]

Hardy seems to have begun writing *The Trumpet-Major,* as he had *Far from the Madding Crowd,* with a relatively simple plot line, a broad sense of how the story might go, and then allowed the situations initially established to develop their own momentum. As the writing proceeded he pointed up the class differences between the characters, especially between the poten-tial marriage partners, saw further comic possibilities in Festus Derriman and his uncle, and added new twists to the central plot. By early September 1879 the first fourteen chapters were already in proof and Hardy was putting the finishing touches to the manuscript of the next seven. A few weeks later he supplied the illustrator, John Collier, with sketches of military and domestic details, and one at least of the published illustrations, that of the miller's kitchen in the February 1881 instalment, was closely based on Hardy's own drawings. He did some last-minute research in the British Museum on 25 November and had probably completed the entire manuscript by the time serialization began that December in the January 1880 number of *Good Words*.[28]

The Trumpet-Major did not absorb all of Hardy's literary energies during 1879. His friendship with Charles Kegan Paul had developed into a kind of working partnership useful and profitable to both, and it was during Kegan Paul's editorship that the *New Quarterly Magazine* published two of Hardy's earliest and finest short stories: in April 1879, 'The Distracted Young Preacher' —based largely on the smuggling stories he had heard from George Nicholls and Captain Masters and from people still living in the Lulworth district in which the story was set—and in April 1880, 'Fellow-Townsmen', set in the Bridport area. At Kegan Paul's request Hardy also wrote for the *New Quarterly* an anonymous review of William Barnes's *Poems of Rural Life in the Dorset Dialect*, entirely positive in its emphases yet recognizing Barnes's avoidance of 'the strong passions which move mankind, great and small', and stressing that his scenes and characters derived not from Dorset generally but specifically from the Vale of Blackmoor, 'a limited district . . . having marked characteristics of its own'.[29]

Since the Barnes volume was published by Kegan Paul's firm, Hardy's first and only experience as a reviewer involved an element of log-rolling. Kegan Paul in any case made a generous return by publishing in the same issue of the *New Quarterly* a long and generally admiring essay by Mrs Sutherland Orr on 'Mr. Hardy's Novels', the first extended survey of its kind. Kegan Paul's own high estimate of Hardy's work appeared in the *British Quarterly Review* of April 1881—to be supplemented in May 1883 by an article on 'The Rustic of George Eliot and Thomas Hardy' in the first number of *Merry England*—and there can be little doubt that he was, after Leslie Stephen, the literary figure who did most to assist Hardy and advance his reputation at this still early period when his work had not yet (as Kegan Paul himself put it) 'taken hold on the great popular mind, sometimes slow to discover when a new genius has arisen in the intellectual sky'.[30]

Hardy's popular reputation had, in fact, reached an early peak with *Far from the Madding Crowd* and then fallen back somewhat. But he had remained steadily productive and established himself more firmly amongst his fellow professionals: Walter Besant, in inviting Hardy to join the Rabelais Club, had praised *The Return of the Native* as 'the most original the most virile and most humorous of all modern novels'.[31] Wider recognition resulted in a considerable expansion of Hardy's London acquaintance throughout 1879 and the first half of 1880. It was while he was living at Tooting that he seems first to have met George Greenhill, teacher of mathematics at the Royal Artillery College, Woolwich, on whom he was to rely, directly or indirectly, for much of the scientific and technical information invoked in *A Laodicean* and *Two on a Tower*. In June 1879 he saw something of the proceedings of an International Literary Congress being held in London and spent a weekend with his friend R. Bosworth Smith (son of the rector of West Stafford), who was then a housemaster at Harrow. On 10 March 1880 he went with Mrs Procter to lunch with the Poet Laureate and his family and was charmed by Tennyson's geniality and his praise of *A Pair of Blue Eyes*. Browning was often at Mrs Procter's when the Hardys called there during the late winter and spring of 1880, and Hardy persuaded their hostess to make a list of all the celebrities she had known, going back almost to the beginning of the century. High among her current favourites was Henry James, and Hardy—who had already learned to dislike James as a man, much as he always admired him as an artist—recorded with mingled amusement, scepticism, and distaste her assertion that James had made her an offer of marriage.[32]

Hardy was reading James's *Roderick Hudson* at about this time, as well as some of his critical works, including the essay on Balzac in *French Poets and Novelists* and the English Men of Letters volume on Hawthorne. Doubtful perhaps about his own expedition into the past in *The Trumpet-Major,* Hardy extracted from James's Hawthorne study the famous sentence in 'The Custom-House' in which Hawthorne expresses regret at having chosen an historical theme instead of attempting to diffuse thought and imagination 'through the opaque substance of to-day', thus making it 'a bright transparency'.[33] Stimulated by meeting Mat-

Left Locket miniature of
Emma Lavinia Gifford, *c.* 1870

Below St. Juliot rectory,
c. 1870; Helen Holder *(seated)*,
Emma Gifford, and the Revd
Caddell Holder

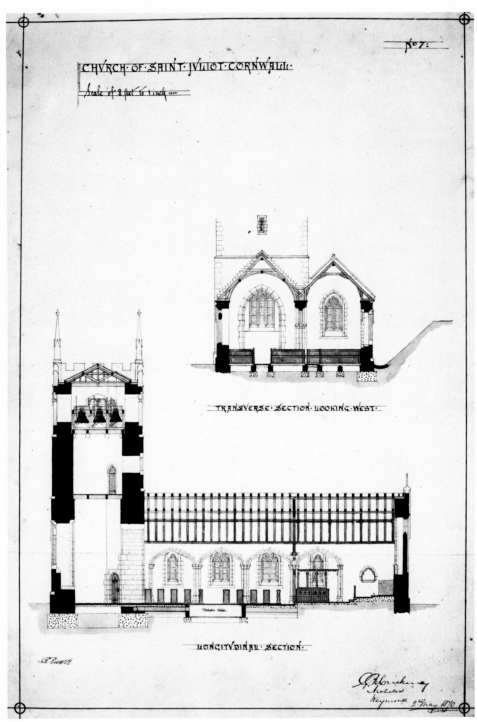

One of Hardy's drawings for the restoration of St. Juliot Church, 1870

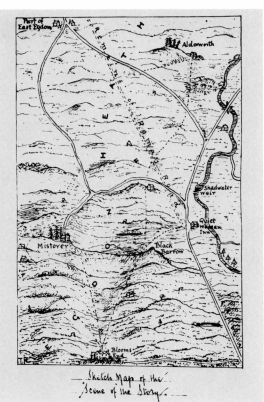

Above 'Riverside', Sturminster Newton; the Hardys lived (1875–7) in the nearer of the two semi-detached houses.

Left Hardy's sketch map of the setting of *The Return of the Native*

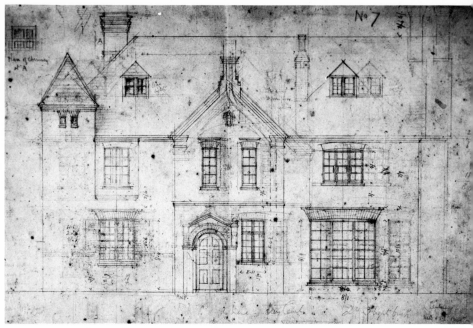

Hardy's architectural drawing of the south elevation of Max Gate

Max Gate when first built

thew Arnold at a London dinner in February 1880, Hardy read several of his essays during this same period. A passage from 'Pagan and Mediaeval Religious Sentiment' on the relationship between 'the modern spirit' and 'the imaginative reason' is partly quoted, partly summarized, in Hardy's notebook,[34] and was to be central to his next novel, *A Laodicean,* sub-titled *A Story of To-day.*

He began work on *A Laodicean* some time in the first half of 1880, having proposed it to Harper & Brothers in response to their handsome offer of £100 for each of thirteen instalments of a serial to inaugurate the new European edition of *Harper's New Monthly Magazine.* Asked to find a first-class illustrator for the story, Hardy wrote at once to Helen Allingham, romantically remembered (as Helen Paterson) from the days of the *Far from the Madding Crowd* serial, only to receive by return of post the disappointing information that she had entirely given up book illustration. He then approached three or four other artists more or less simultaneously before finally coming to terms with George Du Maurier, with whom he had already worked during the serialization of *The Hand of Ethelberta.*[35]

J. Henry Harper, one of the partners in Harper & Brothers, came over from New York in July, followed later that same month by R. R. Bowker, whose primary responsibility was to oversee the launching of Harper's European edition. Within a few days Bowker had called at Tooting and been

> received in a pretty parlor by Mrs. Thomas Hardy, with her Kensington-stitch work, and her pet cat; she is an agreeable youngish English lady, immensely interested in her husband's work, and we were at once good friends. Hardy presently came down, a quiet-mannered, pleasant, modest, little man, with sandyish short beard, entirely unaffected and direct. . . . Told me he had the greatest difficulty in remembering the people and incidents of his own stories so that Mrs. Hardy had to keep on the look-out for him. . . . I came home, having made two pleasant friends, I think.

In view of the difficulties that were to attend the completion of *A Laodicean* it was fortunate that Hardy and Bowker should have got on so well from the first. Bowker learned to respect Hardy's professionalism, even in trying conditions, and to think of him as 'a thoroughly good fellow, quietly companionable',[36] while Hardy, for his part, seems to have found Bowker's American straightforwardness entirely congenial.

It was also in July 1880 that Hardy contracted with Smith, Elder for the publication of *The Trumpet-Major* in volumes. Serialization was continuing in *Good Words,* but Hardy had corrected all the remaining proofs and felt free, at the end of July, to take Emma on another brief continental excursion. They went on this occasion no further afield than north-western France, first to Amiens, to see the cathedral, and thence, on 1 August, to Etretat, where Hardy's love of swimming induced him to stay too long in the chilly waters of the Channel and hence contributed, or so he believed, to his long illness of the following autumn. At the hotel in Le Havre, their next stopping place, they were overcome by just the kind of nervous terror which Jemima had displayed in the London hotel room during Hardy's childhood and spent much of the night setting up barricades of furniture against a wholly imaginary threat of intrusion. They stayed at Trouville and Honfleur before moving on, finally, to Lisieux and Caen— towns which Hardy had perhaps already envisaged as stages in Paula Power's pursuit of Somerset in the closing chapters of *A Laodicean.* It is on the beach of that 'romantic watering-place' Etretat, however, that the pursuit ends—the reversal of the Hardys' own itinerary being no doubt deliberate—and Du Maurier later responded to Hardy's expressed admiration for the illustration of that scene by presenting him with the original drawing.[37]

Back in England by mid-August 1880, Hardy applied himself to *A Laodicean* and was able to send off the first instalment well before the end of the month. During these same busy weeks of late August and early September he also completed his final revisions for the forthcoming first edition of *The Trumpet-Major.* The changes were, for the most part, very minor, involving the restoration of most (though by no means all) of the oaths and other offensive details which had been omitted from the *Good Words* version at Dr Macleod's behest. But Hardy also deleted the dates which had occurred at various points in the serial— perhaps because he felt, quite correctly, that the time scheme had got rather out of hand—and at the very end of the book he effected a profound change of mood by explicitly forecasting the trumpet-major's death: John, who in the serial had simply departed 'to blow his trumpet over the bloody battle-fields of Spain', now, in the first edition, went off 'to blow his trumpet till silenced for ever upon one of the bloody battle-fields of Spain'.[38] It was entirely characteristic of Hardy to thus twist the knife at the conclusion of a book that was scarcely less of a pastoral idyll than

Under the Greenwood Tree and, in so doing, to compound the crime of which he was accused by Leslie Stephen, that of allowing the heroine to marry the wrong man. (When Hardy objected that they mostly did, Stephen retorted: 'Not in magazines.')[39] The novel has generally been regarded as slight, but Hardy took seriously both his historical researches and his use of material that had come to him through oral tradition, and was unusually attentive to the appearance of the first edition, sending Smith, Elder a copy of the Chandos Classics edition of Butler's *Hudibras* to show the kind of red he wanted for the binding and supplying in his own hand the design for the cover, with its twin vignettes of camp and mill connected by a winding path.[40]

ILLNESS

Hᴀʀᴅʏ went down to Dorset for a few days in mid-September 1880. The talk at his parents' home dwelt largely upon the past disposition of family property, and part of his visit was given over to exploring with his brother Henry the possibility of finding a plot of land in or near Dorchester on which to build a house. This radical shift of direction on Hardy's part was accompanied by, and dependent upon, a corresponding shift in the balance of power as between Emma and Jemima. Hardy had thus far preserved the peace by keeping them apart, but the policy had severe practical drawbacks. Throughout their six years of still childless marriage he and Emma had moved constantly from one place to another, driven in part by economic considerations and by his own perception of his needs as a literary professional but also by Emma's whims and fancies, her always vague and always disappointed ambitions for a richer social life. The first disagreements between them had occurred, and Hardy was simply no longer prepared to fight on his wife's side as staunchly as he had done during their first years together: 'We faced but chancewise after that,' as Hardy wrote in his poem 'The Rift'.[1] He had long seen residence in Dorset as meeting many of his requirements as a novelist of rural and, more especially, 'Wessex' life, but what now persuaded him to reverse the apparent thrust of *The Return of the Native* was his reawakened sense of family responsibility. The death of his uncle James at Higher Bockhampton in March 1880 had reminded Hardy that his own parents were now in their late sixties, and that his father suffered acutely from rheumatism. It was true that Henry was well able to run the family business and that Mary was now headmistress of the Bell Street National School in Dorchester itself, but Kate's departure for a teaching career had left their mother without regular assistance in the house. And he himself, at the age of forty, wanted a more settled existence in a home of his own. So the decision to build in Dorchester was debated and confirmed—no doubt at a family conclave from which Emma was absent—and Jemima's victory constituted for Emma a corresponding defeat, one which she never forgave and from which she never fully recovered.

The clannishness of the Hardys was intense—as both Hardy's wives discovered to their cost. Hardy's marriage had disrupted his mother's plans for her children to live permanently together in pairs (see above, p. 21), and it was largely for that reason that it had been so bitterly opposed—and would have been opposed even if he had chosen someone other than Emma. But he still felt—perhaps felt all the more deeply and guiltily—that it was incumbent upon him as the eldest child, as the most prosperous member of the family, as (quite simply) a Hardy, to assume a direct responsibility for the welfare of his parents and, especially, of his two unmarried sisters. It was a responsibility which he was to discharge consistently, generously, even excessively, for the rest of his life.

At the time when the idea of building in Dorchester was first mooted family relationships seem to have been superficially smooth. Kate, in particular, always far more outgoing than her older sister, had formed a cheerful friendship with Emma that was grounded in the latter's kindness to her while she was attending the training college at Salisbury. Although never in trouble at college, Kate was desperately unhappy there, fretting rebelliously against the stern discipline and the requirement that the students perform domestic duties, and she came to rely for comfort on the letters Emma wrote her from Sturminster Newton and Tooting. In a letter of 1881, written from her first school in the little village of Sandford Orcas (not far from Sherborne) she tells Emma to 'write soon and then Ill answer you again like you used when I was at Salisbury'. In a later letter to Emma she reported a conversation with a girl from the college which had suggested that the students there were now 'having rather better times than we used to have', but she added, with an unconscious glance forward to *Jude the Obscure*: 'I dont mind if Tom Publishes how badly we were used.' The letter ends, 'Give him my love and the same to you', and is signed 'Yrs very affectly Katie'.[2] Other letters from Kate to Emma in the late 1870s and early 1880s display the same warmth and openness; there are also letters, less open perhaps but not notably less warm, from Mary to Emma; and it was while the Hardys were at Tooting that Emma—in a remarkable gesture of *rapprochement*—offered to employ as a servant one of Hardy's Hand cousins from Melbury Osmond.*

The dangerous and prolonged illness which Hardy suffered during the autumn and winter of 1880–1 no doubt contributed further to the suspension of family differences. In mid-October 1880 Hardy and Emma spent a week in Cambridge. They were entertained by three of Horace Moule's brothers, and Hardy's mind was full of poignant and perhaps painful memories of Horace himself: even his fascination with the shapes made by the dripping candle wax in King's College Chapel must have been stirred by recollections of the 'shroud' formed by Moule's candle during their last evening together.[4] Hardy felt unwell soon after his arrival at Cambridge, but it was not until he returned to Tooting on 23 October that he acknowledged that something was seriously wrong. The next day his condition had further deteriorated, and a doctor, hastily summoned from near by, diagnosed an internal haemorrhage and urged an immediate operation. A terrified Hardy and alarmed Emma then appealed to their nearest friends, the Alexander Macmillans, who sent their own doctor. He confirmed the diagnosis and emphasized its gravity but gave it as his opinion that an operation might be avoided if Hardy could be kept in bed, his feet raised above the level of his head, for an extended period.[5]

The pain was at first intense and Hardy felt sure that he was

* In a letter of 10 January 1881 Mary Hand (eldest child of Jemima's brother William) accepted the offer of work but protested that there was no need to pay her fare from Dorchester to London: 'I feel I owe you a great deal for your kind consideration when my poor Father died.' Four weeks later, however, she was still vague about the date of her arrival, and the whole arrangement may well have fallen through.[3]

going to die—an experience reflected in the poem 'A Wasted Illness':

> Through vaults of pain,
> Enribbed and wrought with groins of ghastliness,
> I passed, and garish spectres moved my brain
> To dire distress.
>
> And hammerings,
> And quakes, and shoots, and stifling hotness, blent
> With webby waxing things and waning things
> As on I went.
>
> 'Where lies the end
> To this foul way?' I asked with weakening breath.
> Thereon ahead I saw a door extend—
> The door to Death.

Contemplating the experience in retrospect, Hardy (like his mother before him) found matter for regret in the reflection that recovery meant only that the same terrible route must some day 'be ranged again / To reach that door'. It was, however, to be almost another fifty years before the door was finally reached, and during that long interim he seems to have suffered no other serious illness but only a series of milder recurrences of the 'same bladder inflammation' which had brought him low on this one traumatic occasion. The nature and source of that inflammation are not easy to determine. A bladder or even a kidney stone would seem to provide a possible explanation, and it is true that more than six months later, when Hardy was at last able to get up and go out again, he had a consultation with Sir Henry Thompson, the distinguished surgeon, famous especially for his success in removing stones from the bladder.[6]* But a patient suffering from the stone might normally be expected (in the absence of an operation) to die or to recover with some rapidity, and the extraordinary length of Hardy's illness and convalescence suggests either that such a diagnosis is incorrect or that there were complicating factors—such as typhoid fever, perhaps, contracted in France during the previous summer. Gosse, who visited Hardy during his illness, remembered him as suffering from jaundice. It seems in any case entirely likely that the treatment prescribed—consisting chiefly

---

* Kegan Paul had recommended this consultation in order that Hardy might get 'quite free from the fear you had of some worse mischief'.[7]

of total inactivity in an inclined position and a very restricted diet —was itself extremely debilitating and a major reason for the delayed recovery.[8]

At the time when Hardy's illness overwhelmed him he had already sent off to the printer the first thirteen chapters of *A Laodicean,* equivalent to the first three instalments and a little over, and was probably well advanced with the manuscript for the next few chapters, enough to make up the fourth instalment. But there were still nine instalments left of the thirteen for which he had contracted. Ill as he was, Hardy felt that he had no option, economically and professionally, but to persevere—should it prove humanly possible to do so—and Emma's devoted assistance as nurse, housekeeper, and amanuensis eventually enabled him to finish the novel and meet his obligations. But it was, as he said later, 'an awful job'. Harper & Brothers' original hope that they would have the entire manuscript in their hands by December or January was now absolutely unrealizable, but Hardy staved off any early crisis by putting the finishing touches to the fourth instalment and dispatching it to Bowker more or less on schedule. That was done, heroically, in early November, although he was in great pain and unable to receive visitors, not only then but throughout the remainder of the month.[9]

The letters sent to Bowker at this time give no hint of the real seriousness of the illness, and Hardy seems to have felt that such concealment was a necessary precaution against possible impairment of that reputation for professional efficiency which he had been so carefully cultivating. At a time, therefore, when Hardy himself was fearing that the illness might prove his last, his friends and colleagues were being told that he was suffering from the consequences of a severe cold, and Bowker, in particular, was being assured that the indisposition 'does not affect my writing—indeed it gives me more leisure for the same'. When such close friends as Charles Kegan Paul and George Smith began writing to Emma to find out how Hardy really was, a fuller explanation was required. On 19 November she told Smith that Hardy's illness had 'not been altogether so severe as has been supposed', although 'a temporary weakness resulting from the very low diet ordered' had prevented him from writing himself. The illness, she added, 'has been a sudden local inflammation that seems to have resulted from a cold, & it will keep him from going out for some time, as he is mostly obliged to preserve a reclining position, but his work has hitherto been but little hindered, and we are assured that his rate of recovery is extremely rapid for the nature of the complaint.' The qualifications and half-truths here are very Hardyan, and the letter—like much of the manuscript of *A Laodicean*—was doubtless dictated.[10]

The members of Hardy's own family seem similarly to have been put off with half-truths, partly no doubt because he wanted to save them from ineffectual anxieties, partly because he dreaded the tensions that might be consequent upon their arrival at his bedside. By early 1881, however, when the worst was safely over, the true situation could be more fully revealed. A letter from Mary, dated 28 January 1881, gives some sense of the relations then existing between Emma and her in-laws as well as of the separate and very different lives Hardy's parents and siblings were living at a time when they had not yet succeeded in reconciling the demands of social mobility with those of family cohesiveness:

> My dear Emma,
>
> I was very glad to hear from you but the iron has again entered into my Soul respecting Toms illness. I am glad you told me just how he was & I hope he is again recovering. Perhaps the headache was simply due to keeping the head lower than usual. If I have a lower pillow than usual my head aches the next morning. I am glad to find from your letter that our enemies 'winter and rough weather' only affect you in a modified degree. Poor Katie was reduced, a few days ago, to a few onions jam and potatoes—a little coal and no candle. She wishes, poor little Soul to hear from one of you. It is I know as dull and comfortless as the grave at Sandford [Orcas]. All the schools have been closed but we hope to begin again on Monday. I don't think there has been such a winter since Granny went to Church walking on the hedges. . . . I have heard nothing of them from home during the sharp weather except the Dorchester news which has been that the Bockhampton folk had to live wholly on potatoes. No bakers could get there I know: but don't be alarmed. Henry is young and strong and they killed a pig quite recently, but I suppose they don't wish to risk Bob's legs if they can avoid it. . . . I should very much like to come and see you again. All this dull weather Katie has been quite lonely & so have I. I wish we could have been with you—if you would have liked us.
>
> Yrs affectly
> M. Hardy.[11]

Hardy was able to take mild satisfaction during that distressing winter from the generally positive reception of *The Trumpet-*

Major, published in three volumes just two or three days after he had taken to his bed. Although some reviewers thought the final volume showed signs of hasty writing and found a certain lack of 'finish' throughout, there was in general a clear and appreciative awareness of what he was setting out to do and of how nearly he was succeeding. The *Pall Mall Gazette,* in particular, put matters squarely:

> Mr. Hardy's tales are genuine pastorals, having indeed the form of prose to suit an age which is pre-eminently the age of the novel, but full of a poetry of their own. When we say genuine pastorals, we are thinking not of the exquisitely wrought unrealities of Virgil and of Pope, but of Theocritus, who, dweller in a city though he was, had always the true feeling of country life, and of whom, both when he is serious and in his humoristic touches, Mr. Hardy often reminds us.[12]

But the novel with which Hardy was now struggling was of quite a different character—not especially urban, perhaps, but quite self-consciously modern in setting as well as in spirit, and certainly not in the least pastoral. He had thus denied himself the option, when faced with the necessity of completing the novel under adverse conditions, of falling back upon the kind of local and traditional materials which he had used with so much confidence and success not only in *The Trumpet-Major* but in such earlier novels as *Under the Greenwood Tree, Far from the Madding Crowd,* and even *The Return of the Native.* On the other hand, the chapters already in type before the onset of his illness had created an architect hero, George Somerset, and placed him in situations not unassociated with episodes in Hardy's own past: the debate over paedobaptism, for instance, derived directly from those arguments of twenty years earlier with Bastow and the Perkinses. By spinning out the architectural 'business', therefore, by introducing a series of more or less melodramatic plot developments, and by exploiting the notes he had taken during his French and German travels, Hardy was able to stay the course and fulfil his contract to the satisfaction of Harper & Brothers—if not, perhaps, to their unqualified delight. Hardy had somehow managed to correct the proofs in his own hand throughout his illness, and as time went on he became less and less dependent on dictation, writing the final sections of the manuscript in his own hand—the last pages of all on 1 May 1881.[13]

At that date—more than six months after the beginning of

his illness—Hardy had still not been out of doors alone. He was confined to his bedroom until well into March—'rather a dreary place to invite friends to', he told Bowker in mid-February—and as late as 6 April 1881 he told George Greenhill:

> I am getting on pretty fairly, but don't go out yet—passing my days over the fire, with my feet on the mantelpiece, & a pen in my hand, which does not write as often as it should. . . . I am doing the 12th number of my story, & the nearness of the end prevents my attaining to it quickly—the consciousness that it can be done at any time causing dilatoriness. I should probably have gone out by this time if it had not been for the East wind. But patience is necessary.[14]

Greenhill was one of several London friends whom Hardy learned to appreciate more thoroughly during his illness. Others included his loyal Tooting neighbours, the Alexander Macmillans, and Edmund Gosse, then energetically establishing his own semi-scholarly, semi-journalistic career. Charles Kegan Paul, too, had made himself useful by supplying information about doctors and tracking down items of information which Hardy needed, or thought he might need, for his novel: 'Louis says that the Telegraphic Instrument with the letters arranged in a circle is known as "Wheatstone's A.B.C. Machine",' he wrote on 7 February.[15]

During these weary months Hardy found himself with all too much time and occasion to reflect upon his work and career, and upon life and art in general. Some of his more aphoristically formulated conclusions found their way, like so much else, into the pages of the novel itself. Other observations are so densely argued and so similar to views expressed by Hardy throughout the rest of his life as to suggest that he used this period of personal danger and enforced inactivity as an occasion to think out, once and for all, his own position in relation to some of the central questions that had presented themselves to him as a man and as an artist. A note on Positivism,* prompted by the death of George Eliot in December 1880, seems to take Hardy a long way in the direction of adherence to an optimistic 'Religion of

---

* In April 1881 Hardy and Emma were invited to attend a presentation ceremony—the Positivist equivalent of baptism—at the Positivist headquarters at Newton Hall. Because the letter was addressed to Emma, it has been interpreted as indicating that she was herself actively engaged with Positivist ideas, but the child in question was the daughter of Hardy's Dorchester friend Benjamin Fossett Lock and it seems clear that etiquette alone had impelled Mrs Lock to write to Mrs Hardy rather than to Hardy himself.[16]

Humanity': 'If Comte had introduced Christ among the worthies in his calendar it would have made Positivism tolerable to thousands who, from position, family connection, or early education, now decry what in their heart of hearts they hold to contain the germs of a true system.' A few months later, however, he elaborated the view of the radical imperfection of the universe—its inability to accommodate the human emotions and, as a later note puts it, 'supply the materials for happiness to higher existence'— that was to permeate his later thought, provide the groundnote of the late novels and the basic philosophical structure of *The Dynasts,* and gain him that label of 'pessimist' which he so much resented but was never able to shake off:

> *May 9.* . . . Law has produced in man a child who cannot but constantly reproach its parent for doing much and yet not all, and constantly say to such parent that it would have been better never to have begun doing than to have *over*done so indecisively; that is, than to have created so far beyond all apparent first intention (on the emotional side), without mending matters by a second intention and execution, to eliminate the evils of the blunder of overdoing. The emotions have no place in a world of defect, and it is a cruel injustice that they should have developed in it.
>
> If the Law itself had consciousness, how the aspect of its creatures would terrify it, fill it with remorse![17]

The lack of congruence between the positions adopted on these two occasions did not disturb Hardy himself. George Somerset, the hero of *A Laodicean,* adopts a deliberate eclecticism in matters pertaining to architecture, and Hardy seems to have been constantly drawn towards a 'Laodiceanism' of his own—a reluctance to adopt absolute or even firm positions, a willingness to see virtue in all sides of a question, an insistence upon the provisionality of his opinions and the need to register them rather as a series of tentative impressions than as the systematic formulations of a philosopher. Since the emotions were for Hardy at least as powerful and persuasive as the intellect—hence, perhaps, his attraction to Arnold's concept of 'the imaginative reason'—it becomes necessary to take such disclaimers seriously, and to respond sympathetically, without bemusement or outrage, to those juxtapositions of apparently antithetical statements which occur with some frequency both within published works and in the sequence of his surviving notes and reflections.[18]

. . .

Hardy's illness had seemed to provide a harsh confirmation of
earlier indications, dating back to the '60s, that he could not hope
to live in London and remain healthy. It also confirmed him in
the opinion, whatever Emma might argue to the contrary, that
the move from Sturminster Newton, or at least from Dorset, had
been a mistake even in purely professional terms—that, as *Early
Life* puts it, 'residence in or near a city tended to force mechanical
and ordinary productions from his pen, concerning ordinary
society-life and habits'. As soon as he was fit to travel, he and
Emma went house-hunting once again. The plan for a permanent
move to Dorchester was set aside for the time being—presumably
because no suitable land had yet become available—and on 25
June 1881 they moved into 'Lanherne', The Avenue, Wimborne.*
Writing to his cousin John Antell a few days later, Hardy explained that they had 'come down here for the air, which is
considered necessary to my complete restoration'.[19]

Wimborne is indeed described in Victorian guidebooks as a
clean and airy town. Though small, it was considerably bigger
and busier than Sturminster Newton. It was a focal point for the
economy of the area, and its ancient Minster made it something
of an ecclesiastical and musical centre as well. Little was left, even
at that time, of the medieval town, but there were handsome
eighteenth-century streets leading off from The Square and some
substantial houses on the higher ground to the north. The Avenue,
however, was in a lower-lying area towards the railway station
and the river; its houses were newly built and the lime trees which
justified its name had as yet made little growth—as Hardy later
recalled:

> They are great trees, no doubt, by now
>   That were so thin in bough—
>   That row of limes—
> When we housed there; I'm loth to reckon when;
>   The world has turned so many times,
>   So many, since then![20]†

* The house, numbered 12, is still called 'Lanherne'; the spelling 'Llan-
herne' seems to occur only in *Early Life*.
† It is sad to have to record that although the limes did indeed grow to be
'great trees', their boughs touching across the road, they were later cut down
to ease the passage of vehicles.[21]

'Lanherne' itself, like the house at Sturminster, was a typical Victorian villa—'modern', in Hardy's and Emma's terms, comfortable, modestly substantial. It was detached, unlike most of the other houses on the street, and made attractive by its conservatory and large garden, full of old-fashioned flowers and fruit trees and bushes of many kinds. Since Hardy had no use for the stables and carriage house at the bottom of the garden he made them available to a young Scotsman who was studying farming in the area and lodging near by, the younger brother of Sir George Douglas, a Scottish landowner and gentleman of letters who had already published an admiring sonnet addressed 'To the Author of "Far from the Madding Crowd" ' and beginning, 'Yours is the empire of an Arcady / More precious than the dreamland of the Greek'. A first meeting with Douglas that autumn, when he came to visit his brother, subsequently developed into one of Hardy's most enduring friendships.[22]

The Hardys spent two years in Wimborne, taking some part in its social life but making no attempt to establish themselves as they had done at Sturminster, even though their presence at the ball given by Lord and Lady Wimborne in late December 1881 would certainly have assured them of a secure place in the society constituted by the local gentry and professional middle class.[23] The local Shakespeare Reading Society, which met in private houses, each member taking a part assigned beforehand, attracted Hardy for a time, but he was by now too much the sophisticated Londoner to find anything other than amusement in these amateur occasions: 'The General reads with gingerly caution, telling me privately that he blurted out one of Shakespeare's improprieties last time before he was aware, and is in fear and trembling lest he may do it again.' He soon dropped out, after gaining for himself the reputation of a poor performer who put no expression into his reading.[24] Henry Tindal Atkinson, the closest of Hardy's few Wimborne friends, was on the contrary much admired for his Shakespearian renditions, playing Shylock in a public reading of the trial scene from *The Merchant of Venice* in May 1883. Although Atkinson had been since 1880 a county court judge on the Dorset, Hampshire, South Somerset and Salisbury circuit, Hardy liked to refer to him by his title of Serjeant-at-Law, an ancient legal rank which had become obsolete shortly after his appointment to it in 1864. He was urbane, witty, outgoing, a great reciter of poems—from Macaulay's 'Henry of Navarre' to Hood's 'Faithless Nellie Gray'—and, to the Hardys, a 'genial neighbour' who 'took care that they should not mope if dinners and his and his daughter's music could prevent it'.[25]

Clearly, the Hardys did mope: Wimborne, situated on one of the main railway lines between London and Dorchester, had seemed to offer a workable compromise between the two locations, but it proved in practice to have neither the glamour of the one nor the associations of the other, and they seem to have intended from the beginning to move away from the town and on to Dorchester itself as soon as their lease allowed. This sense of impermanence served, however, to increase rather than discourage Hardy's desire to familiarize himself with the entire area. He had known much of southern and central Dorset from childhood, largely as a result of the extensive network of family connections, and greatly expanded that knowledge during his years with Hicks and Crickmay; more recently he had spent several months at Swanage, in the south-eastern corner of the county, and the best part of two years at Sturminster Newton, in the north; he had now—deliberately or otherwise—given himself the opportunity of exploring eastern Dorset. He made excursions into the surrounding countryside, alone or in the company of his friend Walter Fletcher, architect, land agent, and county surveyor: in February 1883 they walked together to Corfe Mullen, where the tombs of Jenny Phillips's ancestors, the Phelipses, could—and can—be seen. Within a month of their arrival in the town he and Emma hired a wagonette from a local inn and spent a day visiting Badbury Rings, a large Iron Age fort a few miles to the north-west—although the eight pages of notes Hardy made that day dealt not with the fort itself but with the reminiscences of their driver, who had been a postilion in the old coaching days, and with his gossip about the past and present inhabitants of Kingston Lacy and Charborough Park, the two great houses they passed on their journey.[26]

Also of the Badbury Rings party was Hardy's younger sister Kate, who was still lonely at her school at Sandford Orcas and had been delighted to be given a day off for the outing. 'I shall eat such a lot', she warned in advance of her arrival, 'and talk a great deal so I shall be rather troublesome. Come to meet me mind and make a fuss about my coming. I hope you've got some cake.' A letter written after her return begins 'My dearest dears' and describes how fearful she had been of missing her connection during the cross-country train journey from Wimborne back to Sherborne. In another warm and affectionate letter to Emma that

September she sends thanks for a cape—presumably a birthday present—and announces that she is 'going home tomorrow night as Mary thinks I had better go and see father'. She adds, 'I dont know when I have felt so anxious about any thing—never I know. The examinations are nothing compared to it.' It is not, however, clear whether Kate's anxieties relate to an anticipated visit to the school by Her Majesty's Inspectors or to her father's nervous participation, as singer and violinist, in a village concert got up by the Misses Evangeline and Blanche Smith, daughters of the rector of West Stafford.[27]

Another visitor to Lanherne that first autumn was Henry Joseph Moule, the eldest of Horace's brothers. Moule, fifteen years Hardy's senior, had known him as a youth—and taken a kindly interest in his early exercises in water-colour—but they had lost touch during the intervening years, most of which Moule had spent working as a land agent in Scotland. On the occasion of Moule's first visit they talked 'till the small hours' and discussed ways in which Hardy's literary talents might be combined with those artistic skills which Moule had diligently cultivated over the years. In a subsequent letter Moule took up the suggestion, first made by Emma, of 'a book on Dorset written by you with landscape and architectural illustrations by me', and while Hardy turned down the idea—on the grounds that it would not pay—the friendship was not again interrupted but became, despite the difference in their ages, closer and warmer than it had ever been.[28] From 1883 onwards, when Hardy had moved to Dorchester and Moule become Curator of the Dorset County Museum, they had ample opportunity to share their different but often overlapping interests in local history, topography, and folklore.

Although Hardy had a number of reasons for not wishing to write a book on Dorset—which would, among other things, have under-cut the autonomy of that fictional world of Wessex with which his name was already so closely associated—those economic considerations cited to Moule were no doubt the most decisive. Sir George Douglas was to recall the Hardy he first met in Wimborne as 'a robuster figure than any I ever saw again, robuster and less over-weighted by care. His talk, too, was light and cheerful—mainly about literature.'[29] But that is perhaps no more than to say that Hardy was delighted to entertain a visitor capable of

leavening the lump of Wimborne. He was in fact anxiously aware
of the weakness of *A Laodicean,* still shaken by the physical and
emotional debilitation of his illness, and urgently in need of reassurance as to his professional standing as a writer of imaginative
literature—which meant, immediately, fiction, although notes
made during the period of the illness show that poetry was never
far from his thoughts, nor even the grandiose scheme that eventually became *The Dynasts.*[30] After a damp and uncomfortable
Scottish tour with Emma in late August and early September—
taking in Edinburgh, Roslin, Stirling, and the Trossachs and, on
the return journey, Windermere and Chester—Hardy settled
down at Lanherne to make the final corrections to *A Laodicean*
before its appearance in three-volume form. The serial version,
meanwhile, was continuing into the January 1882 number of
Harper's, and it was not until mid-October 1881 that he could
write to Bowker: 'I have examined the revises of Parts 12 & 13, &
find nothing further to correct: so that my task, I believe, is done
for the magazine in that matter.'[31]

Almost simultaneously he received from Thomas Bailey Aldrich, editor of the *Atlantic Monthly,* a request for a serial for the
following year, and responded promptly with the outline of a
new novel.[32] It was to be called *Two on a Tower* and to centre
on the conflict between a young astronomer's scientific enthusiasm
and his love for an older woman of superior wealth and rank.*
Current interest in the Transit of Venus—due to recur in December 1882—had suggested the astronomical theme, while the
conception of the hero was inspired in part by the early-seven-
teenth-century astronomer, Jeremiah Horrocks, who—young,
poor, and equipped with very crude instruments—had made remarkable observations of the Transit of Venus and many other
phenomena before dying in his early twenties. The idea of making
observations from a tower built for quite other purposes on a
private estate seems to have come from Charborough Park, seen
during the expedition to Badbury Rings. Surprisingly, perhaps,
the book's specifically scientific emphasis—its attempt 'to set the
emotional history of two infinitesimal lives against the stupendous

* This central theme seems to have been suggested in part by a passage
in *The Mill on the Floss*: speculating as to whether all astronomers must
necessarily hate women, Maggie Tulliver concludes, 'I suppose it's all astronomers: because, you know, they live up in high towers, and if the women
came there, they might talk and hinder them from looking at the stars.'[33]

background of the stellar universe'[34]—rendered it, in some respects, even more aggressively 'modern' than *A Laodicean* of so recent and such troubled history.

Towards the end of 1881 Hardy began preparations for the writing of *Two on a Tower*. He obtained expert information about lenses and the making of telescopes and applied for permission to visit the Royal Observatory at Greenwich in order to 'ascertain if a hollow memorial pillar, with a staircase inside, can be adapted for the purpose of a small observatory'.[35] Meanwhile, the first edition of *A Laodicean* was published at the beginning of December and received for the most part lukewarm reviews—always respectful, never wholly dismissive, and in general considerably more favourable than might have been anticipated. Hardy's attention was, in any case, distracted from them, and from work on *Two on a Tower*, by the distressing controversy which followed the first performance of *The Squire*, by Arthur Wing Pinero, at the St. James's Theatre, London, on 29 December 1881. The 'squire' of the title was a woman farmer, and it was immediately apparent that Pinero's conception owed a good deal to *Far from the Madding Crowd*. More troubling still was the fact that a stage version of that novel, entitled *The Mistress of the Farm: A Pastoral Drama,* had been prepared by Hardy himself in collaboration with J. Comyns Carr, the dramatist and critic, and submitted to John Hare and William Hunter Kendal, the managers of the St. James's Theatre, about a year previously. Hare and Kendal provisionally accepted the play and even (so Hardy claimed) put it into rehearsal before finally deciding against it in November 1880. Some time later Kendal's wife, Madge Kendal, the actress, retailed the plot to Pinero, apparently without identifying its source, and *The Squire* was the result.[36]

Hardy knew nothing of Pinero's play until he saw it reviewed in the *Daily News* the morning after the first performance. Puzzled, angry, and more than a little insecure, Hardy rushed to the defence of his professional interests, seeking advice from Tindal Atkinson and composing a letter of protest which duly appeared in *The Times* and the *Daily News* on 2 January 1882 along with a letter from Comyns Carr citing various corroborative details. The *Daily News* also published a reply from Pinero, admitting that he had read the novel but insisting that his inspiration had come from quite independent sources and his 'motive, characterisation, and dialogue' were wholly different from Hardy's: 'I merely put my horse's head to the open country and take the same hedges and ditches with him.' Pinero's letter was ill-advised, wrote William Black to Hardy that same day: 'We no longer live in an Age of Faith.'[37]

As the arguments rumbled on—the *Theatre* had a 'symposium' on the subject in its February number, *Punch* printed an anti-*Squire* cartoon as late as 8 April—the whole affair became increasingly distasteful to Hardy, not just because it had thrown up some uncomfortably plausible counter-charges of plagiarism against sections of *The Trumpet-Major* and *A Laodicean** but because it made the entire business of authorship seem as abrasively and sordidly competitive as any other walk of life. A note made on 10 February 1882 spoke poignantly to many features of his past, present, and future career: 'I find that a certain defect in my nature hinders my working abreast with others of the same trade. Architecture was distasteful to me as soon as it became a shoulder to shoulder struggle—literature is likewise—& my only way of keeping up a zest for it is by not mixing with other workers of the same craft.'[39]

But while Hardy was hoping that the entire episode would quickly be forgotten, Comyns Carr had seen that there was advantage to be taken of the controversy. He made a thorough revision of *The Mistress of the Farm*—cutting out the first act, writing a new final act, patching together large segments of the printed text with pages of fresh manuscript—got a company together, and opened the play, as *Far from the Madding Crowd*, at the Prince of Wales Theatre, Liverpool, on 27 February 1882.[40] Hardy had little part in all this but was sufficiently encouraged by the enthusiastic reception of the play, and by the realization that he would have no other opportunity of seeing Marion Terry in the part of Bathsheba, to travel north for the last Liverpool performance on 11 March. At the party given after the final curtain he made what was to become his standard speech on occasions when the necessity for speaking at all could not in the end be

---

* The *Academy* of 18 February 1882 reprinted from two American journals parallel passages designed to show that Hardy had plagiarized A. B. Longstreet's *Georgia Scenes* in Chapter 23 of *The Trumpet-Major* and a *Quarterly Review* article by 'Nimrod' (Charles Apperley) in Chapter 5 of *A Laodicean*. Hardy seems indeed to have been guilty of drawing in these two instances upon notebook material copied earlier from published sources —although his source for the passage in *The Trumpet-Major* was in fact Gifford's *History of the Wars Occasioned by the French Revolution* (see above, p. 40n.), both Gifford and Longstreet having apparently drawn upon a common source.[38]

avoided: 'I have written many speeches for other people, but when I have to make one for myself I'm utterly nonplussed.'[41]

Hardy's life-long fascination with the theatre—despite distrust of its artifice and contempt for the contemporary fashion for elaborate staging—was much indulged during the 1870s and early '80s, and it is little wonder that he was impatient with the Shakespearians of Wimborne. He had already met Irving, Toole, and other leading actors as a natural consequence of his immersion, while at Tooting, in that London world of clubs and convivial societies—the Savile, the Rabelais, and the rest—in which practitioners of literature, journalism, the theatre, and (in those days) the fine arts were continually being brought together. He wrote to Irving to get seats for *Romeo and Juliet* for Emma and himself on their way home from Liverpool. He invited Bowker to lunch with the Comyns Carrs and Marion Terry (who didn't turn up).[42] He entered into negotiations for a possible French production of *Far from the Madding Crowd,* though he had no hand in the disastrous New York adaptation, and in April he attended rehearsals for the London production, which ran for just over ten weeks.[43]* Hardy was present at the successful opening night at the Globe Theatre on 29 April and seems to have responded to the applause by making a brief appearance: 'I should so much like to see Tom on the stage,' wrote Kate to Emma. 'I daresay he looked very nice.'[45]

Hardy had another professional annoyance to put up with in the summer of 1882 when there appeared over his name in a magazine called *London Society* a poem entitled 'Two Roses', the work, as it turned out, of another Thomas Hardy, whom Hardy had known and lent money to during his days with Blomfield. Offended not only by the appropriation of his name but also by the badness of the verses to which it had been attached, Hardy wrote to W. Moy Thomas, as secretary of the Copyright Association, to ask what rights he had to the exclusive literary use of his own name when he happened to share it with someone else. It seemed, as he complained to Thomas, that he was 'doomed to squabbles this year!'[46]

---

* Mrs Bernard Beere now had the part of Bathsheba, while Oak was again played by Ellen Terry's husband, Charles Kelly—of whose frequent inebriation on stage W. S. Gilbert is said to have remarked, during a performance of *Far from the Madding Crowd:* 'No one admires Charles Kelly's acting more than I do, but I always feel it more or less indelicate to overhear what he says.'[44]

Nor was this to be the last. As he worked on *Two on a Tower* at Wimborne throughout the summer—sending off the final portion of the manuscript to Aldrich in mid-September—Hardy was creating future trouble for himself by allowing the story to drift towards topics and situations of doubtful propriety. Perhaps because the novel was to be relatively short, perhaps because it was being written for an American rather than for a British magazine, and in part, no doubt, because he had not quite recovered from all the after-effects of his illness, Hardy did not give *Two on a Tower* his full creative attention. He allowed his work to be interrupted by short expeditions to Dorchester (where he was still seeking a plot of building land) and to places in the vicinity of Wimborne itself, by a tour in September to Salisbury, Axminster, and various towns in west Dorset—the part he now knew least well—and by a trip of several weeks to Paris during October and early November. This time he and Emma did not stay in a hotel but took a small apartment in the rue des Beaux Arts, did much of their own housekeeping, and spent their days in a pleasantly desultory fashion, shopping, dining out, seeing sights, buying books, visiting galleries and theatres—though they caught bad colds, as usual, 'owing to the uncertain weather'.[47] As Hardy later confessed to Gosse, the planning of *Two on a Tower* had been careful enough but 'the actual writing was lamentably hurried—having been produced month by month, & the MS dispatched to America, where it was printed without my seeing the proofs. It would have been rewritten for the book form if I had not played truant & gone off to Paris.'[48]

The novel was published by Sampson Low, in three volumes, in late October 1882. Some of the reviewers were prepared to be impressed and even moved by the 'astronomical' aspects of the book, and especially by the conversations between Swithin St. Cleeve and Viviette Constantine on the tower, but few felt that these elements had been sufficiently integrated into the central story. Almost all expressed some degree of distress at the narrative twists by which Viviette, finding herself pregnant by the absent Swithin, entraps into marriage—and hence into substitute parenthood—the somewhat pompous Bishop of Melchester. Kegan Paul, himself a former Anglican clergyman, told Hardy it was 'a marvellously comic touch' that the victim should be a bishop, but public comment was generally in line with the *Saturday Review*'s condemnation of the episode as 'extremely repulsive'.[49] The advertisement which Hardy himself drew up for insertion in various journals at the beginning of December did little to improve matters, in that it drew attention to precisely those aspects of the novel which had provoked hostility: 'Being the story of the unforeseen relations into which a lady and a youth many years her junior were drawn by studying the stars together; of her desperate situation through generosity to him; and of the reckless *coup d'audace* by which she effected her deliverance.'[50] In mid-January 1883 the reviewer in the *St. James's Gazette* argued that the bishop's fate not only shocked the reader, as it was evidently intended to do, but insulted the Church. Hardy's defence, printed in the *Gazette* on 19 January, once again seems less than persuasive:

> Purely artistic conditions necessitated an episcopal position for the character alluded to, as will be apparent to those readers who are at all experienced in the story-telling trade. Indeed, that no *arrière-pensée* of the sort suggested had existence should be sufficiently clear to everybody from the circumstance that one of the most honourable characters in the book, and the hero's friend, is a clergyman, and that the heroine's most tender qualities are woven in with her religious feelings.[51]

It is impossible not to side with Hardy in the various Grundyan difficulties he encountered during his career. It is not always easy to sympathize so wholeheartedly with the tactics by which he sought to exculpate himself. His response in this particular instance does not begin to meet the real objections of his critics, and he later displayed even greater evasiveness when he countered charges of immorality brought against *Two on a Tower* by arguing that there was 'hardly a single caress in the book outside legal matrimony, or what was intended so to be'.[52] There *is*, after all, a difference—on which, indeed, much of the action of the novel turns—between the fact of matrimony and the intention, and in any case the phrase 'hardly a single caress' scarcely does justice to the circumstance that the one caress to which the moralists objected occurred precisely at the moment when the marriage between the hero and heroine was known to be invalid—and was sufficiently prolonged to result in the child who was so promptly fathered upon the unsuspecting bishop. Hardy appears at his least attractive at such moments, and while his comments are always organized around a kernel of literal truth, he cannot be acquitted of disingenuousness. It is of course true that he felt himself impugned and threatened as a professional by unfavourable criticism, and that he lacked for many years the social assurance and economic stability that might have enabled him to take a bolder or more self-consistent stand—or even to have remained confidently silent. But he never learned to follow John Morley's shrewd advice about ignoring the 'fooleries of critics', and the editor of the *Atlantic Monthly* was not the last to have grounds for complaining—as Aldrich is said to have done—that Hardy had promised him a family story but supplied instead a story in the family way.[53]

Sending his friend Edmund Gosse a copy of *Two on a Tower* on 4 December 1882, Hardy expressed confidence that he at least would 'perceive, if nobody else does, what I have aimed at—to make science, not the mere padding of a romance, but the actual vehicle of romance'. Gosse first wrote merely to acknowledge the gift and to say how much the American novelist, William Dean Howells, on a recent visit to London, had regretted not being able to meet Hardy, 'the man in all England whom he most wanted to see'. But once he had actually read the novel, Gosse expressed great admiration for it—though hinting that he would have liked a little more 'Dorset conversation'—and even greater admiration for Hardy's achievement as a whole:

> Your books are very important to me. I look upon you as without approach the best English novelist living. Sometimes I think you will be the last of the school which Fielding began. Nothing in your style or manner offends me, although I admit that you are a little Alexandrian sometimes. . . . But you still preserve the great manner, the originality and audacity, the real breath of imaginative inspiration. I watch you as if you were the Dodo. When English fiction loses you, it will lose everything.[54]

Gosse's deliberate cultivation of his great, his aristocratic, and even his potentially useful contemporaries has often been commented upon. It was an essential ingredient in his career and one of the bases of his eventual influence and success. But if Gosse was eager to please he was also able to please. He had charm, humour, a ready tongue, and a facile and indefatigable pen. If he became the recipient of some of the best letters of Henry James, Robert Louis Stevenson, and many others, that was largely because he was himself so lively and entertaining a correspondent. The devotion with which he pursued his game often became indistinguishable from friendship itself, and, in the end, not notably more self-serving than many of the relationships dignified by that name. In later years Hardy was to learn to distrust Gosse, for his trouble-making, his deliberate indiscretions, his gossip's inability to resist the pleasures of malice, but for much of the 1880s and 1890s Gosse was to provide him with his nearest approach to an intimate literary friendship. Hardy doubtless registered the touch of extravagance in Gosse's letter, but its warmth and directness provided just the kind of reassurance he needed at that particular moment. His illness and its professional consequences still weighed upon him; some 'warm epithets', as he said later, had been employed during the attacks on *Two on a Tower*; there had been news in late November of the death of Emma's brother-in-law, the Revd Caddell Holder; and life at Wimborne was proving increasingly irksome.[55]

12

RETURN TO DORCHESTER

'WE propose to leave Wimborne for good about March,' Hardy reported to Gosse in December 1882: 'the house we are in lies rather too near the Stour level for health.'[1] Emma's suspicion of the air from the Stour in its higher reaches, at Sturminster Newton, had been one of the reasons for their leaving Riverside Villa, and, as on that occasion, the official explanation did duty for a multitude of others not so readily expressible to outsiders. Hardy was as ready as Emma to be hypochondriacal about dampness and bad air—one of his most frequent recommendations of Dorchester houses in later years was that they were built 'on the chalk'—but she was also dissatisfied, as she had been at Sturminster, with the smallness and dulness of the town, its failure to answer to those exaggerated notions of social and literary eminence she was again projecting both on her husband's behalf and on her own.* Mrs Dashwood, writing to Emma from

* A tiny glimpse of the Hardys at Wimborne seems worth recording. When it was learned that they were leaving, the daughter of a local farmer was sent by her mother to make enquiries about hiring their cook. At 'Lanherne' she found Emma lying on a sofa with her hair hanging in plaits on either side of her face, evidently offended by her caller's youthfulness: 'Well, your mother can try her anyway,' she said shortly, and the interview ended. The cook herself, a young woman with a broad Dorset accent, later described

Sturminster about this time, asks about Hardy's work but continues, with perhaps a touch of irony: 'I hope your stories will emerge one after the other and pleasantly astonish the literary world, they have been concocting in your brain long enough and should now see the light.'[3]

Although the Hardys did not get away from Wimborne in April 1883, they did do so at the expiry of the second year of their lease at midsummer—much to Hardy's 'exhilaration', as he told Gosse at the time.[4] But if the Wimborne experience had not been fortunate in itself, it had provided an opportunity for him to get the 'feel' of Dorset again and to begin that reconsideration of his whole career—past, present, and future—which was eventually to bear fruit in *The Mayor of Casterbridge* and the other major achievements of the next several years. Some notes from the summer of 1882 suggest that Hardy had realized, before he had finished writing *Two on a Tower* and long before it was published and reviewed, that he had somehow lost his way in his last two novels and that it was necessary for him to attempt to return to the material which he best knew and understood and to the narrative modes which had won him his earlier successes and established for his readers a sense of his individuality. A comment in May 1882 about the 'slow meditative lives of people who live in habitual solitude' finds an echo that August in a more specifically literary formulation: 'An ample theme: the intense interests, passions, and strategy that throb through the commonest lives.' A note made on 3 June, the day after his forty-second birthday, evolved a theoretical justification for trusting more absolutely to his own deepest instincts as an observer and recorder of the human and natural world: 'As, in looking at a carpet, by following one colour a certain pattern is suggested, by following another colour, another; so in life the seer should watch that pattern among general things which his idiosyncrasy moves him to observe, and describe that alone. This is, quite accurately, a going to Nature; yet the result is no mere photograph, but purely the product of the writer's own mind.'[5]

The Wimborne period also saw the surfacing of some of the social and humanitarian concerns that would be central to Hardy's

---

to her new employers how Hardy would spend much time in the kitchen, smiling at the servants and encouraging them to talk, and then disappear into his study (the room behind the conservatory) and write for the rest of the day, ignoring even mealtimes.[2]

subsequent life and work. His interest in recording and, whenever possible, preserving oral and physical survivals from the local past found expression in his membership in the Dorset Natural History and Antiquarian Field Club and his co-operation with the Society for the Protection of Ancient Buildings in its attempts to prevent both the destruction of old buildings and the mutilation of churches by the kind of 'restoration' in which he had himself participated while working for Hicks and Crickmay. He offered, in particular, to keep a watchful eye on work being done on Wimborne Minster, and his poem, 'Copying Architecture in an Old Minster', though perhaps not written at Wimborne, certainly relates to his experiences at that time—as, in a rather different way, does the broad comedy of jumbled tombstones ('Here's not a modest maiden elf / But dreads the final Trumpet, / Lest half of her should rise herself, / And half some sturdy strumpet!') of 'The Levelled Churchyard'.[6]

By this time, too, the iron had begun to enter into his soul (to use one of his and Mary's favourite phrases) in respect of the sufferings of animals, and there is praise for Emma—to be repeated on many subsequent occasions—for her 'admirable courage' in protesting, on the spot and in defiance of the disapproval of others, against the abuse of horses and other creatures by being beaten, inadequately cared for, or given tasks too great for their strength. Hardy himself was particularly oppressed by the mass slaughter of gamebirds on local estates: Lord Wimborne's guests, a few weeks before the ball which the Hardys attended in December 1881, killed in one day 1,418 pheasants, 35 hares, 48 rabbits, and 2 partridges.[7] Early in January 1882, after a conversation with a gamekeeper he had met, Hardy made a note in which his anger visibly rises to the point at which it begins to evolve from the keeper's words the outlines of what was to become one of the most powerful episodes in *Tess of the d'Urbervilles*:

> [T]ells me that one day this season they shot—(3 guns) 700 pheasants in one day—a *battue*—driving the birds into one corner of the plantation. When they get there they will not run across the ground—rise on the wing—then are shot wholesale. They pick up all that have fallen—night comes on—the *wounded* birds that have hidden or risen into some thick tree fall, & lie on the ground in their agony—next day the keepers come & look for them. (They found 150, on the above occasion, next day)—Can see the night scene—moon—fluttering & gasping birds as the hours go on—the place being now deserted of humankind.[8]

In the novel, of course, Tess suffers along with the birds—their fate in some sense imaging hers—and it was also during the Wimborne period that a deeper, or at least a more directly expressed, concern for the rural working class began to appear in Hardy's writings. Although relatively little space is given to the rural characters in *Two on a Tower,* they are handled sympathetically and allowed to be more specific about their economic hardships than their predecessors in earlier Hardy novels. In the essay on 'The Dorsetshire Labourer', written at the invitation of *Longman's Magazine* during the early months of 1883, Hardy had an opportunity to explore the topic much more fully. He accepted that opportunity, however, with some gingerliness. Although he personally supported the Liberals in their undertaking to give agricultural workers the vote—or so it would appear from his sending copies of the published essay to Gladstone and John Morley—he was anxious, then as always, to avoid the appearance of adopting or advocating any particular political viewpoint. For this same reason he evaded, later in 1883, an invitation to write an article dealing specifically with the political aspects of the agricultural labourers' situation,[9] and even when working to the much broader specifications indicated by *Longman's* he chose to present several separate facets of the subject rather than to argue a case or offer an over-all assessment.

Although Hardy has often been discussed as if he were primarily a chronicler of agricultural decline, the evidence of 'The Dorsetshire Labourer' suggests that he viewed the depressed state of agriculture in the early 1880s as less than disastrous. Dorset, because of its emphasis on livestock farming, was in any case much less severely affected than other parts of the country by the consequences of cheap cereal imports from North America, and it is now generally accepted that the 'great depression' in agriculture during the late nineteenth and early twentieth centuries was, as a whole, less severe than used to be believed.[10] The essay, then, does not dwell upon the general state of agriculture, and while it sharply evokes the exploitation and virtual serfdom to which the labourer had been exposed in the past it presents his current situation—enhanced by improved wages and a 'pastoral environment'—as reasonably satisfactory. On the other hand, it devotes a good deal of space to some of the less fortunate effects of that increased mobility which is seen as both the source and the consequence of the labourer's exercise of greater economic power. It laments above all the loss of the old intimacy between man and the land, sustained over many generations, the disappearance of that 'interesting and better-informed' class of rural tradesmen and craftsmen which had contributed so much to the old self-sufficient village community, and the erosion of that oral tradition which—though the essay itself does not say so—had played so important a part in Hardy's own upbringing and been so richly drawn upon in his fiction.[11]

Hardy was too much of a progressive to believe that the social consequences of this historical process were entirely bad, and too much of a realist to imagine that the process could somehow be reversed. But such recognitions only endorsed the conclusions he had already reached about his strengths and needs as a writer and the necessity of an early return to the country of his youth—since reclaimed as the country of his imagination—before the old ways of thinking, speaking, and acting had entirely vanished, before all the witnesses of the days before his own childhood had finally passed away. The essentially negative impulses which were driving the Hardys away from Wimborne thus served to reinforce the many positive reasons Hardy himself had earlier discovered for a permanent removal to Dorchester, and perhaps did something to reconcile Emma to such a step.

Hardy's Wimborne writings of late 1882 and early 1883 had included the short stories 'The Romantic Adventures of a Milkmaid' and 'The Three Strangers', and in the summer of 1883 he completed for an American magazine the children's story 'Our Exploits at West Poley', which was to remain unpublished for almost ten years. When 'The Dorsetshire Labourer' and the various revisions of *Two on a Tower* (for the second printing of the first edition, the Tauchnitz edition, and the first one-volume edition) are added, the list testifies to Hardy's revived energy and to that 'versatility of his genius' which was praised, along with much else, by Havelock Ellis in a long and discriminating survey in the *Westminster Review* of April 1883.[12] But there is equally a hint of uncertainty in the very miscellaneity of Hardy's production. 'The Romantic Adventures of a Milkmaid'—hastily composed, as Hardy acknowledged, and with occasional sections of the manuscript written out in Emma's hand[13]—is a loosely constructed exercise in fantasy-romance which derives its modest charm from the juxtaposition of authentic rural description with a vaguely 'Gothic' element embodied in the mysterious figure of Baron von

Xanten. 'The Three Strangers', on the other hand, is a tightly organized story in which the very considerable narrative excitement depends directly upon the integration of the plot with the precisely relevant circumstances of period, setting, and characterization. If 'Romantic Adventures' represents, in the completeness of its surrender to nonrealism, the culmination of the phase of Hardy's career most substantially represented by *A Laodicean* and *Two on a Tower*, the future of that career was to be in the direction marked out by 'The Three Strangers', later collected as the first in a volume of *Wessex Tales*.

In the poem 'He Abjures Love', specifically dated 1883, what seems to be abjured is not love as a personal emotion but rather that 'conception of love as the one business of life' which Havelock Ellis had identified as one of the earliest and most persistent characteristics of Hardy's work. The poem, in this sense, signals a prospective change in both theme and technique, a shift away from love as a dominating motive and from romance as a method:

> No more will now rate I
> The common rare,
> The midnight drizzle dew,
> The gray hour golden,
> The wind a yearning cry,
> The faulty fair,
> Things dreamt, of comelier hue
> Than things beholden! . . .

The implications, however, of such a renunciation, whether personal or professional, are acknowledged in all their bleakness:

> But—after love what comes?
> A scene that lours,
> A few sad vacant hours,
> And then, the Curtain.[14]

The stoicism for which the poem has often been praised is here scarcely distinguishable from disillusion, life-weariness, and it is interesting to set alongside these lines the conservative message— 'the sufficiently apparent moral', as Hardy himself phrased it—of 'Our Exploits at West Poley'. If the youthful narrator of that story is occasionally reminiscent of the young Thomas Hardy, there is more than a hint of the mature Hardy in the odd figure of the Man who has Failed, whose wisdom is said to derive from his having 'failed, not from want of sense, but from want of energy' (that lack of which Hardy so often complained), and whose final advice (to his younger self?) is strongly against meddlesome interference in the established patterns of nature and society: 'Quiet perseverence in clearly defined courses is, as a rule, better than the erratic exploits that may do much harm.'[15] As he contemplated his return to Dorchester, Hardy was perhaps already speculating whether it might not have been better if he had never left—and never embarked upon some, at least, of his erratic professional, emotional, and geographical exploits of the past several years.

Hardy and Emma anticipated the end of their 'Lanherne' lease by spending a good deal of time in London during the late spring of 1883, 'seeing pictures, plays, and friends'. They lunched with Browning and Rhoda Broughton at Lord Houghton's and called upon Mrs Procter — Browning, who was again present, irritating Hardy by his habit, during a conversation, of glancing around the room in search of bigger social game. For Hardy, there was a Rabelais Club dinner in honour of Henry Irving and a private dinner at which Gosse at last succeeded in bringing him together with William Dean Howells in the company of such older ac- quaintances as Austin Dobson, William Black, George Du Maurier, and the sculptors Thomas Woolner and Hamo Thornycroft.[16] Hardy's perception of his need not to mix with other workers in the same craft clearly did not demand an absolute seclusion from London and its overlapping social and artistic worlds. Nor was Dorchester to be regarded as a place of impregnable retirement: Gosse himself—in so many respects a quintessential representative of the London literary scene—was, on 21 July 1883, one of the first visitors to the house in the county town to which the Hardys had moved at the end of June.

Shire-Hall Place, as it was called, was formerly the headmaster's house of the Dorset County School and stood on the west side of Shire-hall Lane (now Glyde Path Road) immediately adjoining the grounds of Colliton House—on part of the site now occupied by the Dorset County Council's health clinic. A long, narrow building, it extended along the back of several houses on the north side of High West Street, and the only access to it from Shire-Hall Lane was through an archway and up a passage. In a letter to Thornycroft, Gosse referred to it as 'a rambling house . . . of which a townsman said, "He have but one window and she do look into Gaol Lane." It is indeed a kind of mole, for the entrance is almost invisible and its burrow extends to the back of everything.' Writing to his wife he described it as 'a most queer rambling old house, such as would rejoice your heart, built on ever so many levels at ever so many periods'.[17]

Hardy had met Gosse at the station, walked him to the house, and there introduced him to Emma, whom Gosse somewhat unkindly described in that same letter home as a middle-aged and less handsome version of the notoriously garrulous Mrs William Bell Scott. 'She means', he added, 'to be very kind.' Henry J. Moule joined them at high tea, and in the evening the three men walked together around the town and into the fringes of that countryside to which—like the fictional Casterbridge in the novel Hardy was soon to begin writing—it was so sharply juxtaposed. Dorchester, Gosse told his wife,

> is extremely bright & pretty; there are two barracks just outside it, one cavalry, one infantry, so that the narrow streets are full of colour & animation, & being a country town, the farmers and labourers were crowding in to their Saturday night's shopping, so it looked in the dusk like a bright foreign town. Mr Moule left us presently, but Hardy & I continued to walk in & out of the town, and round the old walls, which now are walks avenued with chestnuts, until 10.30, by the light of the moon.[18]

The next day, a Sunday, Hardy took Gosse to visit William Barnes at his church and rectory of Winterborne-Came, just outside Dorchester in the direction of Wareham. Gosse had already corresponded with Barnes and reviewed one of his volumes in favourable terms, but Hardy, setting up the arrangement in advance, knew the old poet well enough to insinuate a touch of supplementary flattery: Gosse, he said, was not only one of Barnes's 'sincerest admirers' but had declared himself ready to 'come to Dorset any day or hour for the pleasure of seeing you'. Barnes, for his part, responded with a characteristic touch of theatricality, performing his pastoral duties with an obtrusive punctiliousness and delivering a standard sermon that was in no way dressed up for the benefit of his literary visitors. After the service Barnes stayed on at the church to hear a choir practice before walking back to the rectory with his guests—to whom he persisted in talking about antiquarian and philological subjects rather than about his poetry, the topic on which Gosse had hoped to draw him out.[19]

Within just a week or two of this visit Hardy found himself attending the death-bed of Barnes's most brilliant pupil, Thomas William Hooper Tolbort, at the house of John Pouncy, the Dorchester photographer. Tolbort, now forty-one years old, had risen after his spectacular examination successes to the rank of Deputy Commissioner in the Bengal Civil Service and published transliterations into 'the Roman character', as one of the title-pages puts it, of a Persian translation of *Robinson Crusoe* and an Urdu translation of the *Arabian Nights*. He had, however, contracted consumption in the early 1880s and been forced to leave India, spending part of the summer of 1882 in Dorchester and the succeeding winter in Algiers. Hardy's obituary of him in the *Dorset County Chronicle* for 16 August 1883 brings the story to its sad conclusion:

> To Dorchester he again returned about three weeks ago, shattered in health, but still full of plans for the future. A sudden accession of his dreadful cough broke down his fragile frame completely, and in five days after his arrival he was dead. Even on the last day that sanguine mood which so often prevails in those who are the victims of this malady permitted him to entertain only a slight suspicion that his death-warrant had come; and there is on this account intense pathos in the words which now lie before me—the last he ever wrote—directions jotted down in pencil (for he could not speak) in a hand remarkably firm and flowing for one in his dying condition. The words are: 'I daresay I shall get over this all right, but in case anything should happen to me before my book is printed I would ask you to get it published for me. . . . The papers are all on the table in the next room—a big heap of them. . . .'[20]

Tolbort's manuscript, entitled 'The Portuguese in India', proved unpublishable—his 'sanguine mood' having no doubt enabled him to exaggerate its degree of completeness—but the cruelly premature termination of his career moved Hardy deeply and became merged in his mind with his memories of Horace Moule, who had helped and encouraged Tolbort and whose own bright promise had ended in wholly unanticipated disaster. Moule is specifically mentioned in Hardy's obituary of Tolbort, and the two doomed careers evidently contributed, at some level, to Hardy's conception of the rise and fall of Michael Henchard, the central figure of *The Mayor of Casterbridge*.

The juxtaposition of the names of William Barnes, Horace Moule, and Hooper Tolbort is indicative of the degree to which Hardy, in these early months of his return to Dorchester, found himself driven, willingly and unwillingly, back upon his past—especially upon his memories of the times, twenty and thirty years back, when he was a schoolboy in Dorchester and then an apprentice architect, condemned by the vicar of Stinsford as an overambitious upstart. At the same time, he and Emma were quietly establishing themselves in the town in a manner appropriate to his new middle-class status, seeking a comfortable niche for themselves within the local social life. Hardy's reputation as a writer counted for something even here: if it did not bring him honour in his own country it at least meant that people knew who he was. Mary Sheridan, wife of the grandson of Richard Brinsley Sheridan and daughter of the American historian John Lothrop Motley, was an early friend. That autumn Evangeline and Alice Smith came with their father and brother (Bosworth Smith) to call 'on Mr. Hardy the Author in the nice house'. The Hardys were also on friendly terms with their solicitor, Arthur Henry Lock, whose son later recalled going to a party given by the Hardys at Shire-Hall Place for Emma's young nephew and niece, Gordon and Lilian Gifford, the children of her brother Walter, who were staying with them at the time.[21]

It was while he was living at Shire-Hall Place that Hardy was first 'taken up' by members of the aristocracy. An introduction to Lady Portsmouth in June 1884 was followed in March 1885 by an invitation to visit her and her husband (the 5th Earl) at Eggesford House, their country seat in Devon. Since Emma was forced by illness to remain in Dorchester, Hardy went alone and was quite overwhelmed by the welcome he received not only from Lady Portsmouth herself but from her family of young daughters —who were, as he reported to Emma, 'very attentive, & interested in what I tell them'. Hardy was supposed to be carrying on with his writing during the visit, and the library was put at his exclusive disposal, but the company and the local countryside proved too attractive and he spent most of his time driving, walking, and talking with Lord Portsmouth ('a farmer-like man with a broad Devon accent') and more especially with his womenfolk.[22]

The pattern of Hardy's subsequent relationship to the world of rich, titled, and handsome women can already be perceived in this first visit to the Portsmouths—if, indeed, it was not already perceptible in his responsiveness, years before, to Julia Augusta Martin and Geneviève Smith. He was always to be aware of the expensiveness and extravagance of that world, the artificiality of the elegance which made its inhabitants so alluring: 'But these women!' he exclaimed after a London social gathering early in 1890. 'If put into rough wrappers in a turnip-field, where would their beauty be?'[23] Neither that awareness, however, nor his profound sympathy with the victimized women of the lower classes—with those, like Tess, who actually worked in turnip fields—prevented him from enjoying the social and intellectual companionship of upper-class women nor from responding to their physical attractions. Hardy's emotional susceptibility was as naïve and adolescent as it had ever been, and he was readily charmed by physical and social graces which had been quite unknown to his early experience and which even since his marriage had scarcely become things of every day. It is also possible to perceive in the circumstances of the Eggesford visit—in Emma's absence, in Hardy's delight at finding himself the centre of interest for an 'extraordinarily sympathetic group of women', and in his somewhat insensitive expression of that delight in his letter home— ominous signs of those difficulties within his own marriage which were to cause such grief only a few years later. Emma's first reaction, however, was one of satisfaction at the social elevation which the Portsmouths' invitation seemed to imply. She wrote to tell Archdeacon Gifford the good news and received in reply an expression of hope that Hardy would find his friendship with Lady Portsmouth 'of permanent advantage to him'.[24]

Meanwhile Hardy did not remain without recognition in Dorchester itself. Within a year of his return he had received public acknowledgement of his new status in the form of an appointment as a local magistrate. He qualified as a Justice of the Peace for the Borough of Dorchester in April 1884, swore the necessary oaths in August, and took his seat upon the bench early in September. Although his attendance was always erratic he took his sometimes painful duties with all due seriousness, bought himself a copy of Samuel Stone's *The Justices' Manual,* and—no less characteristically—introduced into *The Mayor of Casterbridge* the scene in which the old furmity-woman turns the tables upon Henchard as he presides over the Borough Petty Sessions.[25] Hardy's specifically literary credentials had led even earlier to his being invited to meet Oscar Wilde, following his talk on 'The House Beautiful' under the auspices of the Dorchester Lecture Society on 27 September 1883. A few weeks later Hardy was prevailed upon to invite Bret Harte down to give a lecture for the Society, throwing in, all hospitably, the offer of a bed, 'if plain accommodation will suffice'.[26] He soon drew back, however, from activities that were merely shadows or off-shoots of his London milieu, preferring to devote himself to organizations and interests of a specifically local character. Already a member of the Dorset Natural History and Antiquarian Field Club, when the Dorset County Museum re-opened in its new (that is to say, its present) premises on 1 January 1884 he immediately became a frequent visitor. The presence of Henry J. Moule as Curator made him feel especially comfortable at the Museum, and within a few years he allowed himself to be elected to its Council—although it is impossible to tell whether or not he approved of the identification of himself in the Council's minutes as 'Mr Thomas Hardy junr', a formula which was, in Dorchester, so plainly indicative of his social as well as of his biological origins.[27]

Even before the reopening of the Museum Hardy seems to have found himself at cross-purposes with Edward Cunnington, a local antiquary of what Hardy evidently took to be rather rapacious habits: Henry J. Moule, writing on the last day of 1883, reports that he has told Mr Cunnington about some arrow points Hardy had found on the heath, 'carefully concealing name of person & *places*. He was much moved.' Cunnington made a number of significant archaeological 'finds' near Dorchester in the early 1880s—including, according to a recent authority, 'an amber cup, allegedly complete till Cunnington trod on it'—and his excavation of a Romano-Celtic temple at the eastern end of the great Iron Age hill fort known as Maiden Castle was made— almost libellously, one would think—the subject of Hardy's story 'A Tryst at an Ancient Earthwork', published in the *Detroit Post* in March 1885 but not printed in England until December 1893.[28]

Cunnington was the 'local Schliemann' half-ironically referred to by Hardy in a paper he read at a Dorchester meeting of the Field Club on 13 May 1884. (Remarkable in itself in view of Hardy's later distaste for such public performances, the paper was mysteriously omitted from the Club's published *Proceedings* for a full six years—possibly because of animosity towards Hardy on the part of Cunnington or one of his friends.) It dealt with the discovery of skeletons, urns, and other Romano-British relics during the digging of the foundations of the house which Hardy was having built for himself to the south-east of Dorchester, just off the Wareham Road and about a mile from the town centre.[29] His search for a plot of building land, begun before his removal from Tooting to Wimborne, ended at last when he managed to obtain one from the Duchy of Cornwall, far and away the largest landowner in the area.

The one-and-a-half-acre site, in the possession of the Duchy since the fourteenth century, was at first leased to Hardy, but when he had finished his house and paid the agreed—and, for those days, very considerable—purchase price of £450 (£300 an acre) a conveyance of the freehold was executed in September 1886. If the negotiations were not already well in hand by the time the Hardys moved to Shire-Hall Place, they must have been entered into very shortly afterwards: an undated letter of Kate's, evidently written while her brother and sister-in-law were still at Wimborne, concludes, '*Success to the building scheme! ! !*', and an estimate for the installation of a lifting pump for the well is dated 31 August 1883. Work on the preparation of the site began on 26 November that year, and New Year's Eve found Hardy planting some of the hundreds of trees, chiefly Austrian pine, which were needed to provide a windbreak for the house in its high and exposed position, looking out across the great sweep of Fordington Field, but which, when fully grown, were to have the effect of shutting the house in and the world out.[30]

He was living meanwhile in the centre of town, within three minutes' walk of the new Museum and its handsome reading room, well stocked with works on the history, natural history, geology, and archaeology of the locality, and regularly supplied with the latest issues of the leading newspapers and magazines.* Remote as Dorchester might seem from the perspective of a Londoner, Hardy

---

* Some journals were retained for binding—*Notes and Queries,* for example, and the major quarterlies—but others were auctioned off to members on a yearly basis; in 1886 these included *Punch,* the *Graphic,* the *Illustrated London News,* the *Spectator,* the *Saturday Review, Chambers's Journal, Harper's Monthly,* the *English Illustrated Magazine,* the *Fortnightly Review,* the *Nineteenth Century,* and the *Musical Times.*[31]

was never cut off from regular access to the main organs of intellectual communication—the London papers, morning and afternoon, would of course reach him on the day of publication—and it is clear from his literary notebooks and the markings in surviving books from his library that he read his way, during the late 1870s and early 1880s, through numerous works by Arnold, Carlyle, Comte, Macaulay, Mill, Stephen, and Spencer*—to mention only the names which most often recur—and through books and articles on a wide range of historical, philosophical, and literary topics. Arnold's influence was especially strong, and new works of his were seized upon as they appeared—the 'Wordsworth' essay in 1879, for example, and 'Numbers; or the Majority and the Remnant', one of the American discourses, shortly before a second encounter with Arnold in person at a dinner in June 1884. Although he found Arnold's idealism somewhat remote and rarefied and his specifically religious arguments tiresomely 'hair-splitting', Hardy was deeply sympathetic to his ethical approach and found in his analyses of such phenomena as the 'modern spirit' formulations which gave eloquent expression to some of his own deepest, most instinctive feelings about the contemporary world and especially about those great social and intellectual currents in which he was himself so ineluctably caught up. Arnoldian ideas are clearly apparent—which is by no means to say unambiguously endorsed—in novels as diverse as *The Return of the Native, A Laodicean,* and *Jude the Obscure,* and there is a real sense in which Hardy's later career, from *Tess* and *Jude* to *The Dynasts* and the reflective poems, constitutes a conscientious exercise in 'the noble & profound application of ideas to life'.[33]

The darker, more sceptical strain in Hardy's thinking continued to be fed meanwhile by some of his reading in general works on philosophy—including Caro's *Le Pessimisme au XIXe siècle* and G. H. Lewes's *The History of Philosophy*—and in periodical articles on such figures as Schopenhauer and von Hartmann, neither of whom, it would appear, he had yet confronted directly.[34] Even in later years, however, Hardy consistently resisted such labels as pessimist and determinist, and in the mid-1880s he was still much influenced by Positivism. His friendship

---

* In 1893 Hardy referred to Spencer's *First Principles* as 'a book which acts, or used to act, upon me as a sort of patent expander when I had been particularly narrowed down by the events of life. Whether the theories are true or false, their effect upon the imagination is unquestionable, and I think beneficial.'[32]

with Frederic Harrison, the leader of the English Positivists, dates from this period, and it was in 1885 that, in writing to John Morley on the political issue of Church disestablishment, he expressed what seems in retrospect an excessively optimistic hope for ethical regeneration through gradual modification of the existing Church of England structure and organization:

> I have sometimes had a dream that the church, instead of being disendowed, could be made to modulate by degrees (say as the present incumbents die out) into an undogmatic, non-theological establishment for the promotion of that virtuous living on which all honest men are agreed—leaving to voluntary bodies the organization of whatever societies they may think best for teaching their various forms of doctrinal religion.[35]

Unbeliever though he was, Hardy retained to the end of his life not merely a personal attachment to the Anglican traditions with which he had grown up but a strong sense of the social—what might now be called the socializing—value of such traditions and of the rituals and observances in which they were outwardly embodied.

Hardy had returned to Dorchester precisely in order to be in closer touch with all the traditions and customs and values of his family and his region. His journey from London by way of Wimborne was not a frantic flight from the city—to which, indeed, he remained a constant visitor—but an orderly falling back upon his oldest, deepest, and surest creative resources. Bockhampton was now within daily reach, an hour's walk away along those same roads and paths he had travelled daily as a boy and youth. Notes made in late 1883 and early 1884 are full of memories gathered from elderly people in the neighbourhood. There is also a personal reminiscence, immediately before Christmas, of the group of trees at Bockhampton which he had known in his childhood as 'The Birds' Bedroom', and a description, again dating from December, of what he calls a 'Still life scene': 'Pond by T. Lock's. Pond wrinkled, a cow having just come out: the slow waves *bend* the inverted reflections of the other cows without breaking them. The rich reds & duns are as full coloured in the reflection as in the reality.'[36] The meticulousness of the perception is familiar—Hardy's verbal equivalent of Constable's cloud studies—but its sharpness seems enhanced by a pervasive sense of context: these cows, that is to say, emerge more vividly and portentously as a simple consequence of their being local, regionally typical, and hence immemorial—hence again, peculiarly available to the Hardyan imagination.

This reinvigorated interest in regional material—not just for its own familiar sake but as embodying accessible particularizations of general themes and universal phenomena—reveals itself most strikingly in the pages of a notebook headed 'Facts, from Newspapers, Histories, Biographies, & other Chronicles—(mainly Local)' and begun in late 1882.[37] Its chief purpose was to record material which might prove usable in the writing of future stories or poems —a note on the first page, on the fallen fortunes of ancient families, is directly relevant to *Tess*—and it was with the notebook beside him and *The Mayor of Casterbridge* specifically in mind that Hardy sat down, in or about March 1884, to read his way systematically through the files of the local newspaper, the *Dorset County Chronicle,* for the period beginning January 1826.

As he read, he jotted down items which caught his attention either by their oddity, their incorporation of some ironic narrative twist, or their illumination of the social life of the period—particularly, though by no means necessarily, the life of Dorset itself. Several such items—among them the report of a wife-selling in Somerset—were soon to be drawn upon for narrative and descriptive elements in *The Mayor of Casterbridge,* and the entire exercise was part of a preconceived intention on Hardy's part to establish the fictional Casterbridge as a densely and concretely realized image of a busy market town, and to base that image firmly upon whatever research, imagination, and personal memory could recover of the historical Dorchester of the second quarter of the nineteenth century—an approximate terminal point being provided by the implicit allusion, in Chapter 37 of the novel, to Prince Albert's passage through Dorchester in July 1849.[38] The solidity of the presentation of Casterbridge was intimately related to its role as the social, economic, and geographical centre of an entire Wessex world, hitherto evolved in somewhat piecemeal fashion, now for the first time perceived and projected as distinct, integrated, and autonomous. Although such an imaginative leap seems, in retrospect, inevitable, professional shrewdness probably played as large a part as sheer creative vision in bringing Hardy to the point at which he could clearly see what might and should be done with the world he had thus far only half made.

After the marvellous and in a sense almost accidental success of *Under the Greenwood Tree* and *Far from the Madding Crowd*—novels which he had written quite unselfconsciously out of direct experience, delicately reworking the remembered and the traditional—Hardy had listened too attentively to the complaints of the reviewers about the exaggerated presentation of his rustic characters and his excessive indebtedness to George Eliot. Anxious to assert both his competence and his independence, he had quite deliberately set out to do something different in each succeeding novel. Even *The Return of the Native,* though drawing upon deeply personal material, was distorted by Hardy's ambitions for it as at once a work of art and a statement about art. It was only with *The Mayor of Casterbridge* that he regained, through what was now an entirely conscious choice of story, setting, and treatment, those levels of achievement at which he had so much more spontaneously arrived in the finest of his early works.

The structural and imaginative grasp of the new novel depended largely upon two central elements which, while not *determined* by Hardy's professional sense, were certainly conditioned by it. The first of these was the emphasis, to a much greater extent than in *The Return of the Native,* upon the presentation of a confined and closely knit community seen, as in *Far from the Madding Crowd,* in all phases of its economic and social life. The second was the placing of that community at the centre of a fully developed conception of Wessex. Hardy had learned that his popularity depended largely upon his comic rustics, and he had managed to squeeze a few of them into almost every book. But he also knew that they only really 'worked' as elements within a larger fiction when presented as part of a community to which they naturally and inevitably belonged. As for the larger world of Wessex, Hardy was now shrewd enough to recognize the benefits that might flow from the exploitation of a regional setting—as in the Scottish novels of Sir Walter Scott and, nearer home, in R. D. Blackmore's *Lorna Doone*—and from the linking of novels one with another within some kind of narrative or geographical framework—as Balzac had done, or Trollope in the Barchester series. 'Could you, whenever advertising my books,' wrote Hardy to one of his publishers, 'use the words "Wessex Novels" at the head of the list? . . . I find that the name *Wessex,* wh. I was the first to use in fiction, is getting to be taken up everywhere: & it would be a pity for us to lose the right to it for want of asserting it.'[39]

The assertion, or reassertion, of Wessex in the pages of *The*

HARDY'S OWN MAP
OF HIS
FICTIONAL WESSEX

E X P L A N A T I O N

*

Italics, small & capital = Fictitious Names
Upright old text   = Real names

*

It is to be understood that this is an
imaginative Wessex only, & that the places
described under the names here given
are not portraits of any real places,
but visionary places which may
approximate to the real places
more or less.

Mayor of Casterbridge may indeed have sprung from a mixture of motives, but it was to provide the foundation for the greater assurance and more consistent strength of Hardy's later novels. Years later he made large claims for the historical authenticity of his work: 'At the dates represented in the various narrations things were like that in Wessex: the inhabitants lived in certain ways, engaged in certain occupations, kept alive certain customs, just as they are shown doing in these pages.' Had he not taken the trouble to discover and verify such details, he went on, 'nobody would have discovered such errors to the end of Time. Yet I have instituted inquiries to correct tricks of memory, and striven against temptations to exaggerate, in order to preserve for my own satisfaction a fairly true record of a vanishing life.'[40] As Hardy came to recognize, such a pursuit went beyond the demands of novelistic need or duty: a far less scrupulous application of surface detail would doubtless have evoked for the mass of urban readers a sufficiently specific image of the rural world in which he wished the lives of his characters to be set. But, as the phrase 'for my own satisfaction' suggests, the self-imposed demand for accuracy accorded with his own deeply personal need to preserve the local past, to keep it alive in memory if not in fact. No less important, it enhanced his literary self-confidence—as if it were somehow 'truer' to present scenes, objects, and ways of life as they actually had been—and was inseparable from that fundamental puritanism which obliged him in his best and most characteristic work to tell the truth about the lives of his characters, to follow them, faithfully and unflinchingly, to whatever fates their personalities and circumstances seemed to lead or compel them.

Both impulses—to recreate the local past and project the truths of human experience—are powerfully present in *The Mayor of Casterbridge*. In terms of topography, of history, of social and economic realities, it is easy to recognize everywhere in the presentation of the fictional town the lineaments of the actual town in which it was being written—the composition of the novel and the construction of the new house proceeding side by side as the twin, obviously interrelated, preoccupations of the Shire-Hall Place period. In terms of characterization and story, it is immediately clear that the mild-mannered and evasively fantastic romances of the years since *The Return of the Native* have been firmly superseded. The sub-title of the first edition, *The Life and Death of a Man of Character,* sounds more strongly than ever before the note of overt moral fable and directly reflects the 'wheel of fate' pattern of Michael Henchard's rise and fall. In almost Bunyanesque fashion, Hardy establishes Henchard in all his particularity of time, place, and class, and then surrounds him with patterns of classical, biblical, and Shakespearian imagery which demand that he be viewed as an heroic figure within complexly tragic terms of reference, susceptible to analogies with Oedipus, Samuel, and Lear. Though Henchard's compulsions are primitive and often obscure, he emerges as a figure on the grand scale of a Heathcliff or Captain Ahab.

As such he is perhaps Hardy's most remarkable exercise in characterization, the richly and sympathetically imagined embodiment of those qualities of ambition, authority, vigour, violence, and sexual aggressiveness which Hardy knew to be most lacking in himself—though he had a 'source' for at least some of them in his maternal grandfather George Hand. It was perhaps psychically necessary for Hardy that so virile a figure should suffer so catastrophic a fall, yet admiration for Henchard remains the dominant note: for all his faults and self-destructive follies he is clearly a far greater man than those (such as Farfrae) who surround and follow him, and he takes on a new and humaner greatness at the time of his worst and final defeat. Given the extent to which Casterbridge was deliberately modelled upon early Victorian Dorchester and the social and economic structures of the novel made so specifically those of the world Hardy had known as a child, there seems every reason to see Henchard as in some degree the representative of those traditional rural beliefs, attitudes, and values which Hardy saw crumbling all around him —doomed, like Henchard, because incapable of withstanding the onset of new ways of thinking and doing, yet leaving behind them a sense of tragic loss at the disappearance of an ancient, deep-rooted, peculiarly English quality of life that could never be replaced or revived.

As the embodiment of those irrecoverable values, Henchard had necessarily to remain without descendants. At the same time, the agony of Henchard's realization that he does not have a daughter, followed though it is by his discovery of a capacity to love Elizabeth-Jane for her own sake, had implications for Hardy's own childlessness—which he must by now have accepted as permanent. But it seems no less significant that it should be not Henchard himself but the modest and womanly Elizabeth-Jane who represents the novel's nearest approach to the distinctively Hardyan voice and point of view—not just because she is endowed with much of the inconspicuous ubiquity characteristic of Hardy's authorial narrators, but because she alone steadily learns and grows in the course of the narrative and achieves through quiet suffering a kind of disillusioned yet compassionate understanding that the reader comes to recognize and accept as wisdom.* At the very end of the book, therefore, Hardy is able to permit himself the full and passionate negativity of Henchard's last testament ('that no man remember me') and then contain and qualify it in terms of Elizabeth-Jane's cautiously positive appraisal of life's possibilities, her belief in the feasibility of making 'limited opportunities endurable' by means of 'the cunning enlargement, by a species of microscopic treatment, of those minute forms of satisfaction that offer themselves to everybody not in positive pain; which, thus handled, have much of the same inspiriting effect upon life as wider interests cursorily embraced'.[41]

Such words offered cold comfort to the contemporary reader at the end of a novel which had in any case offended against conventional expectations by focusing upon a central figure already middle-aged and upon a heroine who neither expects nor receives much from her life. They may, however, have contained a private domestic message, either for Emma or for Hardy himself, and they certainly constituted an admirable summary of both the aspirations and the essential methods of that consciously regional artist whom Hardy had become during his progress from the beginning of work on the manuscript of The Mayor of Casterbridge early in 1884 to its completion in mid-April 1885. The writing of the novel had been much interrupted—by excursions to London and to Eggesford House, by a trip with Henry to the Channel Islands in late August of 1884, above all by the need to supervise the building of the new house.[42] There was now a considerable interval of time available for reconsideration of the manuscript before the commencement of serialization in the January 1886 number of the Graphic, but Hardy made no gesture towards revising the novel at this stage—partly because he was already committed to the writing of another serial, for Macmillan's Magazine, but chiefly because his house was at last nearing completion.

* The note is close at times to that of Cytherea in Desperate Remedies, and if Elizabeth-Jane was in some sense based, like Cytherea, upon Eliza Nicholls, it seems ungracious of Hardy to have linked her name with that of her treacherous sister. On the other hand, he may have thought of Elizabeth-Jane as incorporating the best qualities of each.

In the long run, of course, that meant release from the burdens and anxieties of supervision, but in the short run it meant decorating, furnishing, the hiring of servants, the creation of a garden out of what had hitherto been pasture, the re-establishment of all his domestic and working arrangements upon an entirely new footing. It also meant claiming a new social position and living the kind of life that went with it, and on this score Hardy seems still to have been unsure of himself, and perhaps of Emma. His professional and creative reasons for returning to Dorchester were of course to find their justification in the stories and poems he wrote there. His personal reasons, in so far as they related to his parents, needed no justification beyond that easy access to the Bockhampton cottage of which he was loyally to avail himself as long as there were Hardys there to visit. But he began to doubt the wisdom of the building scheme before it was even accomplished: when Lady Portsmouth urged him to abandon 'benighted Dorset' and move to Devonshire he observed that 'Em would go willingly, as it is her native county; but alas, my house at Dorchester is nearly finished'.[43]

13

MAX GATE

O N 29 June 1885 Hardy and Emma made the shortest but most important—and certainly most permanent—of all their removals, from Shire-Hall Place to Max Gate. In Hardy's early drawings for the house the name appears as 'Mack's Gate',[1] in obvious reference to the toll gate of that name* which stood (until quite recent years) on the opposite side of the Wareham Road, but it soon underwent its subtle Latinization and aggrandisement: just once, in a letter to Gosse, Hardy permitted himself the humourous indulgence of calling it 'Porta Maxima'.[3] The site itself was an open field, its situation fairly isolated—though close to the road and within sound of the railway and the whistle of the Eddison steam-plough works[4]†—and its elevation sufficient to expose it to the full rigour of the winds from almost every direction. To the south and south-west, however, it commanded magnificent views across to Came Wood and the monument to

---

* Henry Mack, retired toll-gate keeper, and his wife, both aged eighty, were still living in Fordington in 1851.[2]

† In the early years of the twentieth century Hardy was also to suffer annoyance—and become involved in controversy with the Borough Council —as a consequence of odours emanating from the sewage works which had been constructed in the Frome valley, some five hundred yards from the back of the house.[5]

Admiral Hardy and the downs which, from their reverse slopes, overlooked Weymouth and the sea. From the upper windows of the new house it was possible (as in the poem 'Looking Across') to look northward over the Frome valley to Stinsford Church and churchyard, Kingston Maurward House, and the heath and woodlands surrounding the Bockhampton cottage itself.

That Max Gate had taken some twenty months to complete was to some extent the consequence of its being built solidly at a time when building techniques (e.g., the drying time of mortar) were much slower than they have since become, but Hardy brought some of the delays upon himself by giving the job—naturally enough—to his father and brother. The number of men employed on the job at one time was never very large—it seems significant that Hardy was one of only two people present when the Romano-British skeletons were dug up—and the reference in *Early Life* to Hardy's 'constantly overlooking operations' hints at a multitude of family consultations, debates, and even arguments, on the pattern of those described in 'How I Built Myself a House'. Hardy was no doubt insistent upon a meticulous adherence to the drawings he had himself made for the house he was himself to inhabit, and his father is said to have declared, when it was all over, that he would never again undertake to build such a house for the £1,000 his son had paid him.[6] The figure sounds a little high, however, and he may simply have meant, and said, that not *even* for a thousand pounds would he again go through the experience of building such a house. In any case, Thomas Hardy, Sen., was now in his mid-seventies and largely incapacitated by rheumatism, so that the main burden of the work and responsibility must in fact have fallen upon Henry.

An early sketch plan shows the house on a north-west–south-east axis, with the main entrance facing north-east, but it was in fact built west–east, with the entrance porch facing almost due south. As Hardy originally designed and constructed it, Max Gate was by no means on a large scale—quite appropriately referred to as a 'villa' in one of the letters he received from the Duchy of Cornwall.[7] On the ground floor there was a generous central hall with a dining room to the left and a somewhat larger drawing room to the right; at the rear, a kitchen and scullery. The first floor consisted of two bedrooms, a water-closet, a box room, and a study—at first, at the time of *The Woodlanders*, the room over the drawing room, but later, at the time of *Tess*, the smaller room at the north-west corner of the house. (The third and final study, with its large eastward-facing window, was built during one of several subsequent extensions to the original structure.) Servants —whose number was to vary over the years between two and four—were provided with accommodation in the attic and, to the side and back of the house, there was a small carriage house and stabling for two horses—although it would appear that the Hardys never in fact kept horses of their own.* Architecturally, the house had one or two unusual features, including a square turret at the west end of the front (the one at the east end was another late addition) and an arrangement by which a glass partition between the well of the servants' staircase and the main staircase allowed the latter to receive light from outside. It also had some particularly attractive aspects, including the Portland stone window-sills and oak window-frames and the unusually large south-facing windows on the ground floor, with their solid wooden shutters which could be closed for warmth by folding out (in the living room) or sliding upwards (in the dining room).

The garden was also very deliberately laid out and planted, although it was to be a good many years before the former field lost the last of its rawness and took on a thoroughly domesticated appearance: even in 1895 a visitor could speak of it as 'still only growing into comeliness'.[8] A brick wall almost six feet high was built around the southern and eastern sides of the property, where it abutted on public thoroughfares, and within the wall were two thickly planted rows of trees, just far enough apart to allow for a pathway in between. The area to the east and south-east of the house was mostly occupied by a lawn, later divided into two separate lawns. At the edge of the lawn closest to the house, the preferred spot for taking tea outside in the summer, stood (and stands) the so-called 'Druid Stone', a monolithic slab turned up during the digging of the foundations. The ground to the north and north-east became a kitchen garden, an orchard, and a place to hang the laundry; beyond it was a field which, in the 1920s, the second Mrs Hardy purchased as a run for her chickens. The remaining area to the south was taken up by the oval driveway to and from the front door and by the thick shrubbery which was encouraged to grow both in the centre of the oval and in the extreme south-west corner of the garden, where the pathetic little stones of the pets' cemetery can still be seen. Although the ex-

* They seem to have hired horses and vehicles from local livery stables as required.

tensive planting of Austrian pines was undertaken for climatic protection and, secondarily, for privacy, Hardy deliberately sought to include within the one and a half acres of his property a wide variety of characteristic English trees and shrubs. He began with a list of possibilities, written out long before by his uncle, John Antell,* among them yew, double-blossom elder, and apple on quince stock, and the garden still contains examples not only of the familiar trees of the Dorset countryside but also of walnut, holly, wych elm, and spindle. The surviving fruit trees are similarly various, and one or two of them may even be of Bockhampton ancestry.

It is customary to condemn Max Gate as being ugly and uncomfortable, deficient alike in aesthetic qualities and domestic arrangements. In 1912 Arthur Christopher Benson found it 'a structure at once mean & pretentious, with no grace of design or detail, & with two hideous low flanking turrets with pointed roofs of blue slate'. George Gissing, however, called it 'a very nice house' after staying there for a weekend in 1895,[10] and it is clear that the impressions formed by various visitors depended very largely upon their particular architectural and social preconceptions. So many of those who made slighting comments were actually sneering at Hardy himself as an *arriviste*. Others were simply accustomed to living in a far more elegant style in far older and grander houses—or, like Benson, within the gracious precincts of Cambridge and Oxford colleges. It is, indeed, hard to defend on any architectural principles the turrets of Max Gate or some of its older decorative features, except in so far as they can be said to embody distant and even playful allusions to such architectural styles as the Gothic, the neo-classical, and even (in those offending turrets) the Saxon. Essentially, Hardy seems to have designed the house from the inside outwards, first deciding upon the number, function, and size of the rooms and then contriving to fit those requirements within a reasonably coherent over-all structure, at whatever cost in terms of external symmetry. The failure of the various elements of the front elevation to balance one with another is a direct consequence of Hardy's concern to give each win-

---

* Since the list is scribbled on the opened-out inside of an envelope addressed to Hardy and postmarked 1868,[9] its existence may indicate that the building of a house had long been in Hardy's mind. In 1868, however, he could have sought his uncle's assistance either in advising an architectural client or in supplying authentic details to some aspect of *The Poor Man and the Lady*.

dow precisely the size, shape, and location demanded by the function of the room to which it belonged and by the arc of the sun
at different periods of the year.* The south-facing window of the
living room is low, so that those inside can look out; the corresponding window of the dining room is high, to prevent those
outside from looking in; both are large, in order to catch as much
of the sunshine as possible. Although Max Gate became a dark
house as a consequence of the unchecked growth of the surrounding trees, Hardy originally designed it to be—what it has now
again become—a house full of light.

The complaints made by Florence Hardy during the 1920s
about the antiquated lighting, heating, cooking, and plumbing
arrangements at Max Gate[12] have similarly tended to obscure the
fact that in the early 1880s the house represented a high standard
of middle-class comfort and convenience. One of the reasons it
took so long to build was that it had to be provided with its own
entirely independent systems for water, drainage, and sewage, and
because of its high and isolated position it long remained beyond
the reach of municipal services—it is not connected to a main
drainage system even now. There had to be a well and a pump and
a cess pit, oil lamps (which are in fact capable of providing a
steady light of considerable brilliance), and stoves and fires capable of burning coal or peat—the latter a local product, from the
near-by heaths. The servants—those, at least, of the 1920s—resented the time and labour involved in pumping water up into
the roof tank every morning, but the well and the pump were
both inside the house and the existence of the tank made possible
running cold water in the kitchen and a flushing w.c. on the first
floor within a few paces of each of the bedrooms. There was,
indeed, no bathroom† at Max Gate until after Hardy's second
marriage, and the servants were obliged to carry up jugs of hot
water for morning ablutions in the bedrooms and for the hip
baths which Hardy and Emma presumably took—like most
English people of their time, and indeed well into our own time—
at weekly intervals, and in front of a fire. But few houses had
bathrooms in the days before gas geysers and running hot water.

* See the note on 'Aspect' in Hardy's architectural notebook.[11]

† Since there has been some confusion about the Max Gate plumbing it
seems worth emphasizing that while the upstairs room containing the water-
closet (i.e., flushing toilet) existed from the first, the room containing the
bath and wash basin (but no w.c.) was created in 1920 by reducing the size of
the west bedroom. A hot-water system was also installed in 1920.

The complaints of the 1920s were justifiable in terms of the standards of that decade, but they arose from Hardy's failure or refusal, as a man in his middle eighties, to respond to improved technology and changed social expectations. They have little bearing upon the comfortable and well-equipped house which he built for himself in his middle forties.

The very red-brick solidity of Hardy's house was disturbing to the visitors who came down from London in the expectation of finding him snugly ensconced in some old manor house or thatched cottage, and many of his metropolitan friends were less at ease with the raw modernity and puzzling class assumptions of Max Gate than they would have been with the conventionally picturesque simplicities of Bockhampton. But Emma had all the ideas of what she thought of as her station, and Hardy, too, was sufficiently a product of his period to want to take advantage of the modern comforts and conveniences his income made accessible: his devotion to the past by no means excluded a belief in the virtues of scientific and technological progress. Max Gate, even so, was a modest house, providing neither more nor less than the accommodation they needed—if Hardy was to have a study to himself, and if they were to have a spare bedroom for occasional guests. Hardy had not set himself up as a landowning 'gentleman', but as precisely what he now was, a man of the professional middle class, the social equal of the doctor, the solicitor, or, for that matter, the architect in private practice. An early journalistic visitor to Max Gate commented more than once on the lack of ostentation inside the house, observing of the entrance hall that 'The appointments here, as elsewhere, are distinguished by a simplicity truly in keeping with the character of the novelist', and of Hardy's study that it was 'solidly furnished, without a single article in it that is not required for use, our author's indifference to *things,* as such, showing strongly here'.[13]

That same anonymous visitor put on record the earliest verbal portrait of Hardy himself, describing him as he rose from his 'writing-table' as

a somewhat fair-complexioned man, a trifle below the middle height, of slight build, with a pleasant thoughtful face, exceptionally broad at the temples, and fringed by a beard trimmed after the Elizabethan manner; a man readily sociable and genial, but one whose mien conveys the impression that the world in his eyes has rather more of the tragedy than the comedy about it, and that he is disposed to rate life, and what it can give, at no very extravagant value.

Apart from the beard—apparently grown as a self-consciously 'artistic' gesture during the period of his first literary endeavours and shaved off round about 1890, when his reputation could no longer be questioned—this is already very much the image of Hardy which his later fame was to make so familiar. The phrase 'a trifle below the middle height' is accompanied in *Early Life* by the gloss, 'he was actually 5 ft 6½ ins.',[14] but even this figure is in excess of the '5 ft 6¼, in shoes' he specified on a subsequent occasion (see below, p. 438). He was, in fact, distinctly 'below the middle height', and that dislike of being touched mentioned in *Early Life* probably had more than a little to do with his resentment of and resistance to those arm-around-the-shoulder gestures of familiarity and implicit condescension to which short men are peculiarly exposed.

If the Hardy of later years is already clearly recognizable in the new owner of Max Gate, it is no less true that the basic patterns of life and work adopted at this time remained little changed thereafter. The study was always for Hardy the heart of the house. Though its location shifted, it was always upstairs, as far as possible removed from household activities and callers at the front door, and always impregnable, except by rare invitation to especially favoured visitors. It was there that Hardy, to the very end of his life, spent the greater part of almost every day. 'When he has a story in hand', that early interviewer reported, 'he begins writing immediately after breakfast, and remains indoors until he has finished for the day, even a very little time spent in the open air before beginning proving fatal to any work till after nightfall.'[15]* His personal habits were as abstemious as they had always been—as, in childhood, they had had to be. He told an inquirer in

* In July 1884 Hardy responded as follows to a series of questions about his working habits put to him by an American medical journalist:

> Mr Thomas Hardy begs to state in reply to Dr Hugo Erichsen's circular that (1) he prefers night for working, but finds daytime advisable as a rule; that (2) he follows no plan as to outline; that (3) he uses no stimulant unless tea can be considered as such; that (4) his habit is to remove boots or slippers as a preliminary to work; that (5) he has no definite hours for writing; that (6) he only occasionally works against his will.[16]

1882 that he had never smoked, and at the Dorset County Museum he consistently voted to exclude smokers from the reading room for a certain part of each day. He also reported in 1882 that he very rarely drank, 'having never found alcohol helpful to novel-writing in any degree';[17] he seems none the less to have had a liking for cider (if he can be identified with the speaker of the poem 'Great Things'), and in later years he developed a belief in both champagne and St. Raphael's wine as occasional tonics.

The badness of the cooking at Max Gate—on which almost all visitors were in agreement—would tend to suggest that Hardy was indifferent to what he ate. Jemima, however, was evidently a good cook, and Hardy's tastes seem, in fact, to have been definite but simple, his preferences always for those things (such as cider, kettle-broth, and grilled bacon) associated with, and capable of reviving, the memories of childhood. The mealtime distress experienced by sophisticated visitors to Max Gate derived in part from their unfamiliarity with a somewhat countrified cuisine and, all too often, from their snobbish readiness to condemn a style of living that was, like the house itself, less gracious than their own. But Emma was a poor manager, distressing at least one visitor by the way she 'scolded her servants noisily for being late with lunch',[18] and the household was in constant disarray. The parlourmaids were for ever getting married, the cooks leaving for other, doubtless more appreciative, situations, and it was by no means unknown for a parlourmaid to be promoted to a culinary role almost overnight, with entirely predictable consequences.

The garden which surrounded the house on three sides became increasingly Emma's province, although it was Hardy who supervised its maintenance, paid the gardener, and refused to allow the trees to be cut back for fear of 'wounding' them. Hardy's habits of daily exercise took him beyond the garden and into the local lanes and paths, accompanied for the first few years by a black retriever bitch called Moss. But he was not an ambitious walker, and seems in general to have spent far less time outdoors than either his birth, his vocation, or his choice of domicile might have suggested. People meeting him for the first time often remarked upon the paleness of his complexion and his failure to look like a countryman, and it was not until he was released from the sheer hard labour of novel-writing and took, almost simultaneously, to cycling that he can be said to have led an especially active life.

Higher Bockhampton is no more than an hour's walk from Max Gate, however, and Hardy early formed the habit of visiting

his parents there every Sunday—although for some years Thomas
and Jemima were also occasional visitors to Max Gate.* Henry
Hardy was often at his brother's house to carry out repairs or, a
little later on, additional building work; he seems also to have
sought Hardy's architectural advice from time to time. Mary and
Kate were both now teaching at the National School in Bell Lane,
Dorchester, and in the late 1880s Hardy bought them a small
terrace house in Wollaston Road in which they could live together
close to their work. When Hardy and Emma went away for a holiday, or for their annual visits to London, Max Gate would sometimes be left in the care of one or both of the sisters or even of
other relations—on at least one occasion the caretakers were
Hardy's cousin Mary (Polly) Antell and her mother, Jemima's
sister, the widow of John Antell the shoemaker.

Hardy's own life at Max Gate was intensely private, centred
primarily upon his work and secondarily upon the maintenance
of family ties and the observance of family pieties—often, no
doubt, at the expense of those marital obligations he had contracted, in despite of family opposition, in 1874. It was a life
characterized by daily habits of hard work and plain living—
disciplines early learned from his mother and subsequently admired in such men as the Revd Frederick Perkins. Warned (so he
said) by the example of Sir Walter Scott, Hardy was determined
not to ruin himself by house-building, and he once declared that
the only way for a writer to cope with success was not to allow it
to change his mode of living.[20] Max Gate might be considerably
larger and more pretentious than the Bockhampton cottage, but
for Hardy himself, shut up in his study and emerging only for
meals and exercise, the routines and rewards of each day cannot
have seemed astonishingly different.

Built into the pattern of life at Max Gate, however, was the
annual visit to London during those months of spring and early
summer when the 'season' was in full swing, and from their first
arrival in Dorchester to Emma's death in 1912 there were few
years in which the Hardys did not rent a house, a flat, or (at the
very least) 'rooms' in London for all or part of the April–July

* During the winter of 1890–1, when she was seventy-seven years old,
Jemima walked alone from Bockhampton to Max Gate along icy roads. Asked
why she had set out in such conditions, she retorted, 'To enjoy the beauties
of Nature of course: why shouldn't I?'[19]

period. Hardy's apparent weakness for London 'Society' has often been criticized as sheer snobbery and social climbing, and it is certainly true that his engagements in London during the 1880s and 1890s occupy a disproportionate amount of space in the two volumes of the official 'Life'. It is also true that in old age he developed a concern for social appearances which seems from a late-twentieth-century perspective to have been excessive. But that concern did not necessarily seem extraordinary to his own contemporaries—especially to fellow members of that south-of-England professional middle class to which he by then belonged—and it is only necessary to keep in mind the rigid and unforgiving nature of the English class system as it existed in Hardy's day to begin to wonder if he ought not rather to be congratulated upon his remarkable success in maintaining such an effective and, on the whole, painless division between his social life, which was to a large extent professionally oriented, and that family life on which, at the deepest emotional and creative levels, he so much depended.

By the time he began to build Max Gate, Hardy saw clearly what he had only dimly and intermittently perceived during the 1870s—that his career as a writer was founded upon his capacity to mediate between essentially rural material and a predominantly urban audience, rather as his childhood and youth had involved a daily experience of seeing 'rustic and borough doings in a juxtaposition peculiarly close'. In his essay on 'The Profitable Reading of Fiction', first published in 1888, he acknowledged that an unfamiliar setting was one of the simplest and most basic sources of reading pleasure: 'The town man finds what he seeks in novels of the country, . . .'[21] While such a recognition ratified, as it had largely motivated, his decision to settle in his native countryside, it simultaneously confirmed his early and continuing assumption that it was necessary to his career that he maintain his London connections, keep in touch with that 'town man' who represented his chief audience, and move with some regularity in those literary circles on the fringes of 'Society' where professionals and amateurs (including titled amateurs such as Lord Houghton and Lord Lytton) met on friendly terms, and where publishers, editors, and reviewers—past, present, and potential—were also to be encountered. It thus became perfectly natural for him not only to spend substantial periods of time in London each year but also to accept invitations to more exclusive circles as his growing reputation brought such opportunities his way. Since the upper echelons of

Victorian social life were open to men of distinction in many different fields of endeavour, Hardy found himself in a world that was by no means anti-intellectual, and the respectful welcome he there received gave him a sense not so much of 'arrival'—since he never thought of himself as anything other than an occasional visitor—as of recognition. That he was there at all was an acknowledgement of his status as a successful author, and the active interest of men and women of rank, importance, intelligence, and beauty provided a flattering reassurance to set off against the cheerful incomprehension of most of his own family, the envious disbelief of many of his neighbours, and the multiplying disappointments of his marriage.

Aside from one or two elaborately polite letters to such figures as Frederick Locker and Lord Lytton,[22] there is little indication that Hardy was sycophantic in his relationships with his elegant acquaintances, and he certainly discovered that their world could be as productive as any other of tedium and disillusionment. His friendship with Lady Portsmouth led in the spring of 1885 to invitations from her sister-in-law, Lady Carnarvon, and hence to encounters with Lord Carnarvon's leading colleagues in the Conservative Party, among them Lord Salisbury himself, shortly to become Prime Minister for the first time. Although the poor opinion which Hardy formed of some of these figures was not unaffected by his own Liberal sympathies, it led him to formulate some important general observations about the relationship between individuals and historical events:

> History is rather a stream than a tree. There is nothing organic in its shape, nothing systematic in its development. It flows on like a thunderstorm-rill by a road side; now a straw turns it this way, now a tiny barrier of sand that. The offhand decision of some commonplace mind high in office at a critical moment influences the course of events for a hundred years. Consider the evenings at Lord Carnarvon's, and the intensely average conversation on politics held there by average men who two or three weeks later were members of the Cabinet. A row of shopkeepers in Oxford Street taken just as they came would conduct the affairs of the nation as ably as these.[23]

Such comments make it clear that Hardy was from the first capable of being sharply critical of those representatives of rank, wealth, and power whom he encountered during his visits to London in the last fifteen years of the century. They also indicate the healthy survival, just below the surface, of that strong note of social criticism which had been so largely suppressed in the years since *The Poor Man and the Lady,* and the steady development—fostered by his philosophical reading—of that larger scepticism about the pattern and purpose of human events which was to find its fullest expression in *The Dynasts.*

There was, as always, a price to be paid. When he moved in circles socially superior to his own, Hardy—like most other people in similar situations—found it convenient to adopt a certain degree of protective coloration. He learned to dress smartly when occasion demanded; he bought books on genealogy and on social etiquette; he took up billiards, a favourite country-house diversion of the period; he allowed himself to refer to Max Gate as merely a country cottage to which he retreated when he had to get some work done. But that *was,* after all, one of the primary functions of Max Gate, and if the deprecating terms of the description were partly intended to discourage people from visiting and disturbing him in Dorchester, that too was largely a matter of professional necessity.

This alternation between London and Dorchester constituted the basic pattern of Hardy's life during the remainder of the 1880s, throughout the 1890s, and into the early years of the twentieth century. He was always ready to entertain particular friends (such as Gosse and Douglas) at Max Gate or to invite people down for special reasons. When the American painter John Alexander wanted to undertake a portrait of him in September 1886, he replied: 'I could run up to Town for a day, if you are unable to leave; but what I suggest is that you come here & do it. This place is only a cottage in the country which I use for writing in, but we could make you comfortable for a couple of nights. . . .'[24] But he generally preferred to see people in London for the simple reason that his annual visits there were part of the total economy of his life, a period specifically given over to social engagements and obligations, to the maintenance of friendships and professional contacts, and, no doubt, to the pacification of Emma. In seeking to discourage, or at any rate to control, any overlapping of his London world and his Dorset world—especially the world of his own family—he can scarcely have been motivated by mere snobbishness or social vanity: the trained English ear and eye for nuances of speech and behaviour gave Hardy's London acquaintances a sufficiently shrewd idea of his background and upbringing, although few of them can have realized just how humble and isolated his childhood had been. It was simply that he felt his family affairs were his own business and no one else's: as he had told Kegan Paul in 1881, 'I have an opinion that the less people know of a writer's antecedents (till he is dead) the better.'[25]

He wanted above all to protect his family from exposure to the curiosity of outsiders—a concern which took on fresh urgency once Wessex became established in the popular imagination as a visitable place—and, at the same time, to conceal the autobiographical elements in his work. His profound sense of regret at the disappearance of the stable village community led him to cherish his parents not only for what they were to him but for what they represented in themselves, as people uniquely of their time and place, and he sought to preserve for and through them as much as possible of that old way of life in which they had grown up—the way which he had himself known as a child and subsequently drifted away from as a result of pressures which had seemed irresistible at the time but whose consequences in terms of personal happiness and satisfaction he was already beginning to question.

On 31 December 1885 Hardy recorded that he felt sadder than he had done on many previous New Year's eves: 'Whether building this house at Max Gate was a wise expenditure of energy is one doubt, which, if resolved in the negative, is depressing enough. And there are others.' The others are not specified, but Hardy was certainly anxious about the reception of *The Mayor of Casterbridge*, not only because it was so identifiably set in Dorchester itself but also because it represented a deliberate effort to recover the literary ground he felt he had lost over the last several years. He had never found an opportunity—he had perhaps not felt the need—to revise the novel since he had finished writing it in April 1885. Now, as the first of the weekly instalments appeared in the 2 January 1886 issue of the *Graphic*, he told himself: 'I fear it will not be so good as I meant, but after all, it is not improbabilities of incident but improbabilities of character that matter. . . .'[26]

Some of the incidents in the serial version were, however, quite strikingly improbable—partly because of the difficulties consequent upon the attempt to shelter magazine readers from the knowledge that Lucetta had been Henchard's mistress—and Hardy did undertake an extensive revision of the entire text ahead of the novel's reappearance in book form in May 1886. Later in

the year he confessed to William Dean Howells that he had failed
to realize on paper the story 'as it existed in my mind', adding: 'I
ought to have improved it much—for the greater part was finished
in 1884—a year & half nearly before publication. But I could not
get thoroughly into it after the interval.' Most modern critics have
felt that Hardy, in revising the *Mayor*, made it into perhaps the
most shapely of all his novels, tightly organized and structurally
eloquent. The contemporary reviewers, however, were not especially enthusiastic. They praised the portrait of Henchard, indeed,
as 'almost magnificent in its fullness of expression', but found
Elizabeth-Jane 'rather more than a trifle dull' and the book as a
whole pervaded by a pessimism which seemed both extraneous
and excessive in relation to the situation as given: 'we might',
observed the *Pall Mall Gazette*, 'have been spared the concluding
Enoch-Ardenism.'[27]*

Conclusion of the serialization of *The Mayor of Casterbridge*
on 15 May 1886 and publication of the two-volume first edition
by Smith, Elder on 10 May coincided almost exactly with the
appearance of the first instalment of *The Woodlanders* in the
May 1886 issue of *Macmillan's Magazine*. Hardy had been working on both books at different times during the preceding six or
seven months, and in mid-November 1885, when he was still calling the newer novel *Fitzpiers at Hintock*, he recorded that he had
gone back to his 'original plot' for it—presumably the one he had
had in mind as long ago as the mid-1870s when he 'put aside a
woodland story' in favour of *The Hand of Ethelberta*—and was
working from ten-thirty in the morning until twelve at night 'to
get my mind made up on the details'.[29]

The frequent appearance of Emma's hand in the manuscript
of *The Woodlanders* makes it plain that she was still actively
assisting her husband in his work—although neither this nor any
other surviving manuscript provides evidence of her participating
in the actual process of literary creation.[30] But she was increasingly
out of sympathy with the directions his mind was now taking,
and their domestic difficulties had been intensified rather than
reduced by the move to their new home. It is customary to blame
these difficulties upon Emma's extravagant sense of class superiority—the source of Grace Melbury's failure to recognize the true

* Praise from an unexpected quarter came while the serial was still in
progress: the *Church of England Temperance Chronicle*, impressed by Henchard's vow of abstinence, awarded the *Graphic* 'a vote of thanks for giving
our movement this friendly lift'.[28]

worth of Giles Winterborne—and she certainly had more than her share of vanity and silliness. On the other hand it was extraordinarily difficult for her to cope with her tough-minded and harsh-tongued mother-in-law, whose grip on her son had never significantly relaxed, and with the stubborn family solidarity displayed by all the Hardys, and not least by Hardy himself. Emma's belonging to the 'poor gentry', a class the Hardys affected to despise, was one of the sources of the deep-seated prejudice against her which always prevailed at the Bockhampton cottage. Kate, in her cheerful way, bridged the gap for a time, but the others never quite lost their initial resentment of the marriage—nor was Max Gate ever left in doubt as to how Bockhampton felt. Such tensions had proved sufficiently manageable while the two households were many miles apart, and especially during the first years of marriage when Emma was making a brave effort to 'belong', but the move to Dorchester boxed everyone in and made possible—perhaps inevitable—that unhappy situation for which, as the second Mrs Hardy once observed, no one was wholly to blame but everyone was a little to blame.[31]

The difficulties in the marriage even at the time of the move to Max Gate were sharply perceived—perhaps more sharply and unkindly than the circumstances then justified—by Fanny Stevenson, who called at the new house with her husband, Robert Louis Stevenson, in late August 1885. Describing the visit in a letter to Sidney Colvin, she wrote: 'Also we saw [Hardy's] wife—but here one naturally drops a veil. What very strange marriages literary men seem to make.'[32] To a woman friend she was more forthcoming:

[Hardy] is small, *very* pale, and scholarly looking, and at first sight most painfully shy. He has a very strange face, quite triangular, with a nose that bends down very suddenly at the point.* His wife, he is lately married, is *very* plain, quite underbred, and most tedious. . . . There was something so modest, gentle, and appealing about the creature that one remembers him as a quite pathetic figure. They had just built a new house, which he recoiled from, preferring the freedom of rooms in an attic, and a 'loose foot,' as the hoosiers say.[34]

* Sir Sydney Cockerell described Hardy's nose as distinctly crooked, having 'a very marked turn to the left, or to the right from the spectator's point of view', and believed that the peculiarity, apparently the result of a childhood accident, was of some psychological importance.[33]

Stevenson, in his usual poor health, was living in Bournemouth at this period and had passed through Dorchester on his way to Dartmoor in search of restorative air. In Exeter, however, he broke down completely and was forced to return to Bournemouth without ever reaching his destination. There was some correspondence between Emma and Fanny during the winter months, and in June 1886 Stevenson himself wrote to praise *The Mayor of Casterbridge* and ask if he might dramatize it; a few days later the two men dined together with Sidney Colvin in his apartment at the British Museum, where he was Keeper of Prints and Drawings. They seem never to have met again, although Gosse was to report to Hardy a year later that Stevenson, about to leave for Colorado, had carefully included a copy of *The Woodlanders* in his luggage.[35]

It had been a simple matter for Hardy to accept Colvin's dinner invitation, since he and Emma spent the weeks between early May and late July 1886 in a series of Bloomsbury lodgings, chosen specifically for their proximity to the British Museum Reading Room:

> Reading in the British Museum [he wrote in May 1886]. Have been thinking over the dictum of Hegel—that the real is the rational and the rational the real—that real pain is compatible with formal pleasure—that the idea is all, etc., but it doesn't help much. These venerable philosophers seem to start wrong; they cannot get away from a prepossession that the world must somehow have been made to be a comfortable place for man. If I remember, it was Comte who said that metaphysics was a mere sorry attempt to reconcile theology and physics.[36]

Hardy was himself being made uncomfortable by the intense political activity which surrounded Gladstone's introduction of the first Irish Home Rule bill: he was in the House of Commons on 13 May, and probably on other days as well. His long-standing Liberalism had been shaken by his perception of Home Rule as posing an irreconcilable conflict between what was humanly desirable and what was politically feasible, and by his feeling that it was therefore specious of either party to claim that it had right as well as reason on its side. The general direction of his thought, indeed, was becoming increasingly pessimistic and disenchanted, and he evidently shared some of the fears which Matthew Arnold and others had recently expressed about the dangers of democracy. A year or so later he was to insist that he belonged neither to the right nor to the left but might best be called 'an Intrinsicalist':

> I am against privilege derived from accident of any kind, and am therefore equally opposed to aristocratic privilege and democratic privilege. (By the latter I mean the arrogant assumption that the only labour is hand-labour—a worse arrogance than that of the aristocrat,—the taxing of the worthy to help those masses of the population who will not help themselves when they might, etc.) Opportunity should be equal for all, but those who will not avail themselves of it should be cared for merely—not be a burden to, nor the rulers over, those who do avail themselves thereof.[37]

Although Hardy never shifted his political allegiance, his opposition to Gladstone's Irish initiatives made it easier for him to accept the fact that most of his London acquaintance was strongly Conservative. One of the newest, and certainly the closest, of his Conservative friends in the spring of 1886 was Mary Jeune, the wife of Francis Henry Jeune, a prominent lawyer and divorce court judge who was to be knighted in 1891 and created Baron St. Helier just before his death in 1905. Mrs Jeune, whose first husband had been one of the Stanleys of Alderley, took an active interest in politics and social causes—she became an alderman of the London County Council after her second husband's death—and was in the process of establishing herself as one of the leading hostesses of the day. Her friendship was to be of great importance to Hardy, not just because he met so many people under her aegis but because he reached such terms of happy intimacy with the members of her family, and particularly with Dorothy and Madeleine Stanley, her children by her first husband. They called him 'Uncle Tom', confided in him, went with him to the theatre, and displayed an unselfconscious warmth and openness which he found entirely captivating—and which was sustained, especially by Dorothy Allhusen (as she became), to the time of his death. The fact that Francis Jeune happened to be a brother-in-law of Emma's uncle, the Archdeacon, seems to have had little or no bearing upon either the making or the keeping of Hardy's friendships with the various members of the Jeune and Stanley families. Sadly enough, none of them could 'stand' Emma—'We all hated her,' Dorothy Allhusen once declared—and the Archdeacon himself seems to have shared their dislike.[38]

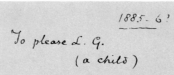

1885- 6?

To please L. G.

(a child)

Diogenes rolling in hot sand

Diogenes embracing statues covered with snow.

Diogenes telling Alexander to stand out of the sunshine.

Socrates suspended in a basket to help contemplation.

Plato teaching in the avenues of the Academy.

Aristotle delivering his lectures in the shady walks of the Lyceum – Peripatetics.

Jupiter coming to Danae in a shower of gold.

Perseus looking at the sleeping Gorgon Medusa, through the mirror, to avoid being turned into stone.

Scenes from classical history, drawn by Hardy for the amusement
of his wife's niece, Lilian Gifford

Emma Hardy *(facing camera)*, Nellie Gosse, and Hardy,
photographed on Weymouth pier by Edmund Gosse, 1890

Hardy and his dog, Moss, in the garden of Max Gate,
photographed by Edmund Gosse, 1890

Above, left Florence
Henniker, photographed by
Chancellor of Dublin
From the frontispiece to her
book, *Outlines* (1894)

Above, right Agnes Grove
From the frontispiece to her
book, *The Social Fetich* (1907)

Below, right Hamo and
Agatha Thornycroft

Hardy also renewed and expanded his circle of literary acquaintances. Henry James was again encountered at a Rabelais Club dinner on 6 June 1886, but neither at this period nor later did the two men develop a relationship of any warmth. The same Rabelais dinner was the occasion of Hardy's meeting Meredith again—apparently for the first time since they had discussed *The Poor Man and the Lady* in 1869—and during the course of the summer he also met Walter Pater, 'whose manner is that of one carrying weighty ideas without spilling them', Oliver Wendell Holmes, 'a very bright, pleasant, juvenile old man', indefatigably enjoying his English celebrity, and George Gissing, who seems to have approached Hardy as a relative neophyte addressing an acknowledged master—and with expectations of sympathetic rapport which the event was not entirely to justify.[39]

Writing to Gissing on 1 July 1886, Hardy expressed the fear that the other's 'keen eye for good work' would be disappointed by *The Woodlanders,* then a quarter of the way through its *Macmillan's* serialization: 'It would have made a beautiful story if I could have carried out my idea of it: but somehow I come so far short of my intention that I fear it will be quite otherwise— unless I pick up towards the end.' Both the note of self-deprecation and the particular terms in which it is sounded are familiar enough in Hardy's comments on his work, but he does seem to have experienced real difficulty in writing *The Woodlanders,* and especially in completing it to schedule. This was partly because he had started work on the novel late and then broken off to make the final revisions to *The Mayor of Casterbridge*; partly because each instalment had to be completed in time for advance proofs to be sent across the Atlantic for simultaneous publication in *Harper's Bazar*; but also because he had not yet finally learned the impracticability, for him, of attempting serious work in London: 'I have some writing to do whilst in town', he told Stevenson on 7 June, '& *can't* touch it: it is becoming quite a nightmare.'[40]

He also found himself increasingly at odds with Mowbray Morris, the editor of *Macmillan's.* Frederick Macmillan, complimenting Hardy in late March 1886 on the first instalment of *The Woodlanders,* had remarked upon 'one or two little things' which Morris had marked in the proofs but insisted that 'these are merely suggestions and . . . we have no desire to "Edit" your work in any impertinent way'. In September, however, when the serial was well under way, Morris himself wrote to warn Hardy against overstepping the bounds of propriety in handling the affair between

Suke Damson and Fitzpiers. The readers of the magazine, he explained, were 'pious Scottish souls who take offence wondrous easily', and it would therefore be well if the 'human frailty' could be 'construed mild' and Suke not brought to 'too open shame'.[41] Hardy had already accepted, or even initiated, the deletion of the crucial last sentence of Chapter 20 ('It was daybreak before Fitzpiers and Suke Damson re-entered Little Hintock'),[42] and he now observed due discretion in treating both Fitzpiers's relationship with Suke and his later relationship with Mrs Charmond. He subsequently insisted, however, that the 'hinted' ending of the story—'that the heroine is doomed to an unhappy life with an inconstant husband'—would have been made much stronger and clearer if current conventions had permitted. Though Hardy suffered little practical inconvenience as a result of such pressures, he was deeply troubled as an artist, and in an essay written a few years later he described at some length the circumstances in which a novelist might find himself forced to 'do despite to his best imaginative instincts by arranging a *dénouement* which he knows to be indescribably unreal and meretricious, but dear to the Grundyist and subscriber'.[43]

In late July of 1886 Hardy returned with Emma to Dorchester in order to be able to work more continuously and effectively on *The Woodlanders*. Three weeks later, however, he sent an invitation to Gosse, whose house he had visited several times during the course of the spring and early summer and who was by now the most nearly intimate of his London friends. 'Can you come now?' Hardy wrote: 'Our life here is lonely & cottage-like, as you know, but I think you would be interested in going to one or two curious places in the neighbourhood recently opened up by the railway.' Making it clear that the invitation was to Gosse alone, he explained: 'Next year we hope to have a regulation spare-bedroom for married couples: at present we have only a bachelor's room— my wife particularly wishes you to mention this to Mrs Gosse—to whom she sends her love.' Gosse arrived at the end of August, and the Misses Eva and Alice Smith, calling at Max Gate on the 31st, enjoyed 'an old-fashioned cold supper tea with Mr Henry Moule who told ghost-stories and Mr Gosse, a poet and critic'.[44]

One of the places Hardy wanted Gosse to see was Bridport, but their visit there was fraught with disaster. Hardy referred apologetically in a subsequent letter to 'that terrible kettle at the

Bridport pot-house', and ten years later, in dedicating to Hardy his volume of essays entitled *Critical Kit-Kats,* Gosse amusingly recalled how they had missed the train back from Bridport after being elaborately misdirected by a local inhabitant. While they waited between trains at Maiden Newton on their outward journey Gosse took the opportunity to send home a description of the visit to William Barnes which he and Hardy had made the previous day:

> Mr Barnes . . . is dying no less picturesquely than he has lived. He has a bed made up in his study, with the books on all the walls, except the one at his back which is hung with a dark green tapestry. He lies in his white bed, for he is now bedridden, in a scarlet dressing-gown, with a dark red soft biretta on his head, his long grey beard falling on his breast, & his white hair scattered on the pillow. He looks like a dying Pope. He was very cordial in welcoming us, & wld not let us go. But he is greatly altered, his memory fails him, & he says the same thing over and over.[45]

When the old poet died on 7 October 1886, Hardy described him in an *Athenaeum* obituary as 'probably the most interesting link between present and past forms of rural life that England possessed'—a man from remote 'pastoral recesses' whose 'great retentiveness and powers of observation' had made him 'a complete repertory of forgotten manners, words, and sentiments'. But while Hardy could write with great sympathy of this aspect of Barnes's career—he might almost have been writing his own obituary of more than forty years later—he felt obliged to enter some reservations about the other man's achievement as a poet. He saw Barnes as a gifted lyricist and a deliberate craftsman, but found something evasive in his use of the dialect and especially in the restrictiveness of his subject matter: 'he entirely leaves alone ambition, pride, despair, defiance, and other of the grander passions which move mankind great and small. His rustics are, as a rule, happy people, and very seldom feel the sting of the rest of modern mankind—the disproportion between the desire for serenity and the power of obtaining it.'[46] Although Hardy served on the committee which commissioned the statue by Roscoe Mullins that stands outside St. Peter's Church in the centre of Dorchester, his most substantial acts of piety were the selection of Barnes's verse he edited for the Clarendon Press in 1907 and his own poem, 'The

Last Signal', which records how, as he walked across the fields to Barnes's funeral, a flash of sunlight reflected from the coffin seemed 'a farewell . . . signalled on his grave-way, / As with a wave of his hand'.[47]

The imagined gesture and responsive poem perhaps constituted for Hardy an exchange not just of farewells but of salutes, an acknowledgement of his own succession to the headship of Wessex letters. It may in retrospect seem extravagant to think of Hardy's genius as capable of being rebuked by Barnes's, and yet Hardy was always conscious of Barnes as the true reviver of the name Wessex for the region they shared and as possessing a special claim to be regarded as that region's authentic voice. In seeking to make the life and values of Wessex accessible to an urban audience Hardy—like any interpreter, ambassador, or spy— always ran the risk of falsifying the original in the interests of comprehensibility, and while Barnes's exclusion of the darker aspects of the regional world might be deemed responsible for far more serious distortions, there none the less remained something splendidly uncompromising and 'pure' about his persistence in the use of the local dialect in his verse and his celebration of that dialect in his specifically philological writings. In returning to Dorchester and building Max Gate, Hardy was seeking to re-establish himself geographically in the countryside that Barnes had never left. In witnessing the burial of Barnes he was experiencing for the first time the sense of full and unchallenged proprietorship over the fictional world he had himself created.

Relocation in Wessex did not, for Hardy, mean reabsorption into the regional consciousness. The red brick of Max Gate—in such contrast to the mellow thatched charm of Barnes's rectory of Came, just a little further along the Wareham Road—was precisely indicative of the refusal of the returning native to revert to the assumptions of his own past. Simple as his tastes and even his personal habits remained, profoundly sympathetic as he was to the fundamental truths (in a Wordsworthian sense) of his earliest experience, Hardy had learned through years of deliberate self-education and of London living that there were other, more sophisticated, and in some respects better ways of thinking and acting—more humane ways, for example, of treating animals, and broader views of the nature of the universe. He was able as an artist to articulate the thoughts and feelings of country people precisely because he could look back upon his own early self from the vantage point provided by a much altered set of attitudes and beliefs.

The people of Dorchester were right to be suspicious of what lay behind these high boundary walls of Max Gate. Though neither house nor owner could properly be described as suburban, both were in important respects semi-urban. Barnes at Came had been a prophet almost exclusively within and to his own country. Hardy was an interpreter of that regional world to the urban world that had grown from it (by historical processes comparable to those later charted in Lawrence's *The Rainbow*) but no longer knew it. Max Gate was a well-defended outpost from which he sent back to his fellow members of the dominant metropolitan culture eloquent reminders of those ancestral values which they might modify at need but could lose sight of only at their peril. It provided an efficient work place and a pleasant and healthy daily environment, and it bore a sufficient resemblance to a miniature country estate to keep him actively aware of the seasonal round of household and horticultural tasks and hence perpetually reminded of those rural and regional realities from which so much of the material of his novels and poems was always to be drawn.

14

THE WOODLANDERS

ALTHOUGH *The Woodlanders* drew heavily on his own family background, and especially on what his mother had told him of her Melbury Osmond childhood, Hardy made no attempt to visit that area of north-west Dorset while the novel was in progress. As in the intensely personal *The Return of the Native*, he wrote at a deliberate distance from the scenes being recreated in fictional terms, chiefly in order to preserve the freshness and vitality of the emotionally charged impressions already fixed upon his imagination. He was accustomed to speak of Wessex as a 'partly real, partly dream-country',[1] and though his immediate reference was to matters of topography the formulation had genetic implications as well. While he could draw upon his notebooks, or upon deliberate research into books, newspapers, and local records, for descriptions of buildings, dress, and décor, for impressions of weather and landscape—the physical and natural aspects of his fiction—his characters and their motivations and actions were the products of a more purely imaginative endeavour. Indeed, the distinction between the minor fiction and the major falls precisely at the line of demarcation between, on the one hand, characters and patterns of action which seem to have been deliberately invented and contrived and, on the other, those which—as Bowker put it in a splendid phrase possibly borrowed from Hardy himself—'walk[ed] out from the chambers of memory through the gates of the imagination'.[2] Hardy's childhood experiences and traumas, like those of any artist, profoundly affected his works in ways of which he remained entirely unconscious. But he was also consciously dependent upon that childhood—on memories of things heard as well as of things seen and done—as a basic creative resource, and learned to tap it through exercising the disciplines of personal isolation and physical distance, both of which enhanced the likelihood that the figures emerging from 'the chambers of memory' would be creatively transformed by their passage through 'the gates of the imagination'. Bowker's reference to such figures as 'walking', as self-propelled, stresses the passivity of the artist throughout the process and coincides with Hardy's own insistence upon the extent to which his characters shaped their own destinies; and it is tempting to speculate how far the curious voyeuristic and theatrical devices of his fiction —the repeated concern with specific angles of vision or with what a putative observer 'would have' seen—may derive from his own habits of watching his people gradually develop and take on quasi-independent lives of their own. He told his second wife that once the characters began to take hold of a story and carry it forward he knew that all would be well.[3]

Hardy did not of course feel precluded from revisiting the scenes of a story once the manuscript had been completed, and it was during such a visit to Melbury Osmond that he made a drawing of 'Townsend', the house in which his grandmother Betty Swetman had lived with her parents. On the back of that drawing, almost obliterated by subsequent erasures, is a sketch plan of the house and orchard and the just-visible annotation: ' "Townsend" where G. Melbury & her father were born'.[4] Hardy's 'G.' stands, here as elsewhere, for 'Granny' rather than for 'Grace', but it seems possible that he in some sense identified Grace Melbury with his own grandmother, that he saw both of them as unhappily caught between conflicting class backgrounds and family loyalties, and that Betty Swetman's disastrous marriage to George Hand found an oblique reflection in the difficulties of Grace's relationship with her husband, Edred Fitzpiers.

Hardy said many years later that he liked *The Woodlanders*, as a story, more than any of his other novels, and that preference may have been related to its drawing so richly upon memories of his mother's talk while avoiding those aspects of his personal relationship with her which had played so large and painful a part in *The Return of the Native*. His imagination was challenged by the restrictedness and seclusion of the woodland setting itself, and by the opportunity to celebrate in the figure of Giles Winterborne the qualities he had learned to admire in his own father —although the latter's characteristic weaknesses of dilatoriness and unassertiveness also form part of the total portrait. The description of Giles at the cider press, surrounded by 'that atmosphere of cider which . . . has such an indescribable fascination for those who have been born and bred among the orchards', is strikingly similar to the account in *Early Life* of Hardy's assisting in his father's cider-making for the last time in the autumn preceding his marriage, and there are indications throughout *The Woodlanders* of nostalgic yearnings towards those simpler days and ways which were always identified with Bockhampton in his imagination.[5]

During the evening of 4 February 1887—at 8.20 p.m. precisely—the manuscript of *The Woodlanders* was at last completed: 'Thought I should feel glad', Hardy wrote, 'but I do not particularly,—though relieved.' He spent the remainder of February revising the serial text of the novel in readiness for its appearance in three-volume form, made a brief visit to London to be present at a conference on copyright organized by the Incorporated Society of Authors, and then—on 15 March, publication day for *The Woodlanders*—set off from London with Emma on a long-contemplated visit to Italy.[6]

The early stages of their journey were unpropitious. They encountered heavy snowfalls all the way across France, and when they stopped at Dijon for dinner Hardy was dyspeptic and consequently 'very vexed'. On the train from Aix to Turin the conductor carried off their tickets for some mysterious reason and when he was slow to reappear (Emma noted in her diary) 'We recriminated, & grew more & more uneasy about them.' They spent a night in Turin and two nights in Genoa, where a visit to the Palazzo Doria helped to counteract the rather depressing first impression of the city ('not as the Beauty but the Dowd') which Hardy later recorded in the poem 'Genoa and the Mediterranean'. That afternoon Hardy went out exploring by himself while Emma made friends with a Japanese child and some kittens, although she later complained that Italian cats were all short-haired, unlike the long-haired beauties of France.[7]

The next day they travelled southward to Florence, seeing Leghorn and the landscape of the poem 'Shelley's Skylark' only from the train window but breaking their journey at Pisa long enough to visit the Cathedral and the Baptistry and climb up the Leaning Tower. At Florence they were met by William Barnes's daughter Lucy Baxter and her husband and taken by carriage to the Villa Trollope, at the northernmost corner of the Piazza dell' Indipendenza. At this time a pension run by a Scottish couple, the house had previously belonged to the Trollope family, and Anthony Trollope himself had written *Doctor Thorne* there just thirty years before. There followed several days of regulation sightseeing, sometimes in the company of Mrs Baxter and her sister, usually by themselves: the Medici tombs, the Uffizi, the Pitti Palace,* and so on. By the Wednesday evening, Emma recorded, 'Tom is quite wearied out & in his bed'; the next morning, though they both felt exhausted, they went to the Duomo. As they drove back to the pension, Emma, with her usual sensitivity to such matters, noticed that the horse was very weak, but she was disconcerted by the driver's responding to her rebuke not with the 'offensive reply' of a London cabman but with expressions of gratitude for her interest in the animal's well-being.

At the end of the week they took the train to Rome. After two miserable nights at a hotel on the Piazza Barberini ('hard bed, noisy square, & b–gs, noise of fountain as well as traffic') they moved to pleasanter quarters at the Hotel Allemagne in the Via Condotti, just below the Spanish Steps. Since Hardy's interest in classical rather than in Christian Rome conveniently coincided with Emma's distrust of Catholicism (the churches seemed to her to be *'full of trash'*)[9] they were drawn back repeatedly to the area of the Forum—despite Emma's breaking her umbrella on their first visit while repelling the attentions of a persistent little shoeblack and courageously intervening on another occasion to drive off the three thieves who had attacked her husband and stolen a picture he had just bought. One day they drove out to the Protestant Cemetery on a pilgrimage to the graves of Shelley and Keats, both pre-eminent in Hardy's poetic pantheon. Sending Gosse two violets from Keats's grave later that same day, Hardy reported

* At the Pitti Hardy jotted down in his Baedeker for Northern Italy brief notes on several works, including a bust of Napoleon by Canova ('the morose exprn preserved') and a Canova Venus ('pressing robe to bosom'), and observed of Titian's Magdalene that the artist had been interested only in painting a handsome woman.[8]

that he was so overpowered by the prevailing sense of decay in the ancient parts of the city that he felt it 'like a nightmare in my sleep'. There was furious building activity in contemporary Rome, he added, 'but how any community can go on building in the face of the "Vanitas vanitatum" reiterated by the ruins is quite marvellous.' He made entries in his notebook to this same effect— perhaps with some recollection of the portrayal of Rome in Hawthorne's *The Marble Faun,* which he had read some years before —and drew upon them when writing 'Rome: Building a New Street in the Ancient Quarter', one of the four poems about the city which he worked up at a later date. On Friday, 1 April, they visited the Catacombs—Hardy registering, as he had elsewhere in Rome, the 'cynical humour' of the monks who acted as guides— and the Appian Way, which he described to his mother that evening (on a postcard written in a large, round, almost painfully clear hand) in exclusively Christian terms: 'We went to-day along the Appian Way towards the Three Taverns, the road by which St Paul came to Rome, as described in the last Chapter of Acts.'[10]

On 3 April, after staying in Rome a day longer than they had intended, they returned to Florence and the Villa Trollope. Emma had a cold and felt 'very feverish' in the train but was well enough the next day to call on Mrs Baxter and visit the monastery of San Marco—where she thought the cells quite large and comfortable and decided that Savonarola looked like George Eliot. Fra Angelico, however, seems not to have impressed her: she confided to her diary the following day that 'old frescoes are horrid entre nous'. The remainder of the week was once again filled with sightseeing and social expeditions—including a call on Violet Paget ('Vernon Lee') and her disabled half-brother Eugene Lee-Hamilton and a trip to Fiesole with Mrs Baxter which nearly ended in disaster when the horse of their omnibus suddenly bolted—and by the final day the Hardys not surprisingly felt 'utterly prostrate', confining their activities to shopping and a farewell call upon the Baxters.[11]

Arriving in Venice on Wednesday, 13 April, Hardy was seriously displeased at finding that their room at the Hotel Angleterre (on the Riva degli Schiavoni) did not face on to the Grand Canal. They had met some congenial Americans on the train and did much of their early sightseeing in their company, although the cold, wet weather discouraged lengthy expeditions and Emma had to spend one day resting in her room ('my knee being jointless'). On the Sunday, Hardy, armed with letters of introduction, called on two leaders of the Anglo-American community in the city, Mrs Bronson and Mrs Curtis—known to literary history for their friendships with Browning and Henry James—and their attentions combined with warmer weather to enliven the Hardys' last few Venetian days. Hardy, who had had Shelley and Keats and Browning in mind throughout his Italian travels, was now especially concerned to identify places associated with Byron and later regretted that he had made no attempt to find local inhabitants who might have remembered Byron's presence in the city some seventy years earlier.[12]

They left Venice on Friday, 22 April, for Milan. Here Hardy's imagination was chiefly seized by Napoleonic associations, and on the Saturday he visited the Bridge of Lodi in the company of a young Scotsman, on his way back from India, whom they had met in the train. Emma meanwhile went out to buy presents to take home, including a tie for her brother-in-law, Henry Hardy. The next day, boarding the Paris train in Lucerne, there was a quarrel over seats between Hardy and a man with three restless children whom they had previously encountered on the train from Milan. That Hardy's defeat in the exchange was due largely to lack of support from Emma is made clear by her own account of subsequent events: 'Changed at Basle—gentleman apologised for not getting out for me—& seemed really sorry—no doubt out of gratitude for my taking his part, & pitying his trying situation with the children.' When they arrived in Paris early Tuesday morning Emma was ill with diarrhoea and unrested: there had been another man in the carriage and she felt it would have been 'odd' in his presence to stretch herself out on the seats as she liked to do when she and Hardy were alone. She was well enough, however, to drive and walk about Paris that day, and to travel back to London on the Wednesday, 27 April.[13]

When Hardy got back to England he found that *The Woodlanders* had already attracted a number of enthusiastic reviews. Its over-all reception, indeed, was to prove altogether more favourable, and more thoughtful, than that of its predecessor. *The Times* compared Hardy to Millet and praised his capacity to harmonize the poetry and the penury of rural life. Gosse, writing in the *Saturday Review,* spoke warmly of the book's 'richness and humanity', but made a number of criticisms—one of them, to the effect that Giles was 'a little too consciously treated as the incarnation of a phase of village civilization', rather ungraciously derived from a private remark of Hardy's. Some reviewers found the moral tone distasteful: one blamed Hardy for surrendering to the influence of 'the French novel', and even Coventry Patmore, incited by Gosse to review the book for the St. James's Gazette, followed lavish praise of Hardy's previous work with severe reservations about the repulsiveness of Fitzpiers and Mrs Charmond and the implausibility of an ending which depended—as he, like many readers then and since, assumed—upon the permanent reformation of the deplorable Fitzpiers.[14] Obviously Mowbray Morris was not unique in his sensitivity, but neither was Hardy wrong to fear that he had compromised his novel's conclusion and final effect.

All of the reviews were respectful, however, none entirely negative, and before the end of May it was clear that *The Woodlanders* was Hardy's greatest critical success since *Far from the Madding Crowd*—with which, indeed, it was rather acutely compared by a reviewer in the *Dublin Evening Mail*.[15] Much encouraged, Hardy ventured to send presentation copies of the first edition to Sir Frederick Leighton, the president of the Royal Academy, to Lord Lytton, who responded with a letter of extravagant praise, and to his old hero, Swinburne, whom he had never yet met.[16] He was also able to respond with full professional confidence, as well as considerable economic satisfaction, to an offer of one thousand guineas from Tillotson & Son's Newspaper Fiction Bureau* for exclusive serial rights to his next full-length novel, although it was well for his peace of mind when he signed the contract on 29 June 1887[18] that he could not foresee the vicissitudes through which the book would pass before it was finally published, as *Tess of the d'Urbervilles,* four and a half years later.

Hardy's gesture in sending his book to Sir Frederick Leighton is indicative of his active interest in painting and sculpture at this period. Shortly before completing *The Woodlanders* he noted: 'I don't want to see landscapes, *i.e.*, scenic paintings of them, because I don't want to see the original realities—as optical effects, that is. I want to see the deeper reality underlying the scenic, the expression of what are sometimes called abstract imaginings.' He added: 'The "simply natural" is interesting no longer. The much decried,

---

* Based in Bolton, Lancashire, Tillotson's was a syndicated fiction business which purchased the serial rights to novels and stories and then distributed them, in proof or stereotyped form, to magazines and, more frequently, provincial newspapers both in England and abroad.[17]

mad, late-Turner rendering is now necessary to create my interest.' Other notebook entries—including quotations from Mill, Spencer, and Ruskin—show that Hardy was currently much exercised over the whole question of the nature of reality and the relationship between the ideal and the real, and such ruminations had a direct relevance to some of the technical effects he was striving towards in his fiction, his desire somehow to make visible 'the true realities of life, hitherto called abstractions'. It was characteristic of Hardy's visualizing imagination that he should so often use analogies from painting to help define the essentially literary problems he was trying to confront, and when, two years later, he saw some Turner water-colours at the Royal Academy he tried to draw a generalized lesson from what he regarded as Turner's attempt to concoct a 'pictorial drug' capable of producing in the eye of the viewer an effect approximating to that of the unreproducible actuality: 'Hence, one may say, Art is the secret of how to produce by a false thing the effect of a true. . . .'[19]

The profusion of artistic references and visual effects in Hardy's novels and poems has often been remarked, and at one level these are simply an aspect of that intricate interaction between narrative literature and narrative painting which prevailed throughout the Victorian period. It seems impossible to determine, for example, the precise degrees of reminiscence and coincidence involved in the relationships between *Under the Greenwood Tree* and Thomas Webster's painting called *The Village Choir,* between Angel's transportation of the milkmaids through the flooded lane and Mulready's *Crossing the Ford,* or between the abandoned title, 'Too Late, Beloved!' (see below, p. 295), and William Lindsay Windus's *Too Late*—itself a visualization of Tennyson's poem 'Come not, when I am dead'.[20] If the headings given to the successive 'phases' of *Tess of the d'Urbervilles* are readily imaginable as the titles of Victorian paintings (e.g., 'Maiden No More', 'The Consequence', 'The Woman Pays'), that is perhaps only to say that Hardy, like so many contemporary painters, was working deliberately in terms of moral fable, incorporating within the individual artefact a moral or social statement which, though not always explicit, would none the less be perfectly legible.

But Hardy's artistic interests went far beyond the nineteenth century and the function of paintings as didactic tableaux. He was extraordinarily sensitive to colours (he records covering up a letter lying on a red velvet tablecloth so that it would not 'hit my eyes so hard') and deeply absorbed in fundamental questions of artistic technique both for their own sake and as sources of practical or theoretical analogies with his own problems as novelist and poet: 'My art', he declared in 1886, 'is to intensify the expression of things, as is done by Crivelli, Bellini, etc., so that the heart and inner meaning is made vividly visible.'[21] He kept up an active acquaintance with several of the most prominent sculptors, painters, and illustrators of his day, and his visits to London found much of their importance, and justification, in the opportunity they provided for maintaining such connections, visiting galleries, exhibitions, and museums, and, in general, keeping up with the artistic world almost as actively as with the literary and social worlds. He became particularly friendly with Gosse's friend Hamo Thornycroft and with Gosse's brother-in-law, Laurence Alma-Tadema, and was on terms of some intimacy with Alfred Parsons (who stayed at Max Gate while preparing the illustrations for 'The First Countess of Wessex') and with several members of the family of William Powell Frith, as well as with Frith himself. It was in 1887, following the publication of *The Woodlanders,* that Frith made his own gesture of friendship by referring publicly to Hardy as unsurpassed among living English writers for 'absolute truth to nature and a far sight into the depths of the human heart, . . . He is now his own rival, whom I sincerely hope he will live to throw into shade.'[22]

The Hardys had returned from Italy in time for Hardy to attend his first Royal Academy dinner on 30 April 1887. They subsequently found lodgings in Kensington, at 5 Campden Hill Road, and stayed on in London until late July and the end of a 'season' made especially colourful by the celebrations associated with Queen Victoria's Golden Jubilee. The time passed 'gaily enough'. Mrs Procter was still going strong, and Browning still in regular attendance. At a Savile Club dinner Hardy found himself in distinguished political company—including the then Chancellor of the Exchequer, George Goschen, and a future Prime Minister, A. J. Balfour—and at a Royal Academy soirée he once more encountered Matthew Arnold.[23] Mrs Jeune was also present on that occasion, and Hardy's friendship with her continued to prosper. His most frequent hostess, however, seems still to have been Lady Carnarvon, and while he had mixed feelings about the entertainment she offered—he noted of one occasion that it was the 'dullest and stupidest of all her parties this season'—he evidently took pleasure in sustaining his friendship with her, with the Portsmouths, and especially with the Portsmouth daughters, who were almost always present. Even that dullest of parties was redeemed by his first meeting with Lady Catherine Milnes-Gaskell, 'the prettiest of all Lady Portsmouth's daughters. Round luminous enquiring eyes.'[24]

Since some of the notes Hardy made at this period were later drawn upon for the 'society' chapters of his late novel, *The Well-Beloved,* it is conceivable that he attended such social functions partly in that spirit of professional obligation, of 'resignation' to novel-writing 'as a trade', in which—according to *Early Life*—he put in occasional appearances at the law courts. Such references, however, seem less reflective of his views at the time than of his concern, in old age, to assert the superior importance of his verse. Though he doubtless found his note-taking onerous, and sometimes engaged in it 'mechanically', the practice had become indispensable to his creative method as a novelist, while the sheer accumulation of so many images, scenes, incidents, and narrative ideas was to prove, in later years, a primary source of his extraordinarily prolonged fecundity as a poet. Note-taking was, of course, a common Victorian activity—an offshoot of the new respect for the methodology of science—and yet Hardy's persistence in the habit seems to betray some degree of continuing insecurity about his educational background and his capacity to hold his own in the exclusive circles in which he now found himself—his 'right', in short, to be where he was. There certainly seems to be more than a hint of self-doubt, perhaps not unmixed with amazed self-congratulation, in the note dated 2 June 1887: 'The forty-seventh birthday of Thomas the Unworthy.'[25]

When, however, Hardy returned to Max Gate at the very end of July he was in unusually high spirits. Responding to a letter from Gosse in late August he recalled the almost suicidally depressive states which had overwhelmed him in the past but now seldom recurred:

One day I was saying to myself "Why art thou so heavy, O my soul, & why art thou so disquieted within me?" I could not help answering "Because you eat that pastry after a long walk, & would not profit by experience". The stomach is no doubt a main cause, if there is no mental reason: but I totally disagree with those who insist upon blaming the stomach always. In my worst times years ago my digestion was as sound as a labourer's.

In a note made on New Year's Eve he concluded that the year 1887 had been on the whole friendly to him, bringing new experiences and new acquaintances and enabling him, with the successful publication of *The Woodlanders,* 'to hold my own in fiction, whatever that may be worth'.[26]

During that autumn and winter Hardy was chiefly engaged in the writing of short stories. Though he had written stories since the very beginning of his career—'How I Built Myself a House', his first published work, falls marginally within that category—he had done so only occasionally, as a kind of diversification and to supplement his income as a novelist. As long ago as November 1880, however, Leslie Stephen had suggested that he might write a series of 'prose-idyls of country life—short sketches of Hodge & his ways'[27] and give them enough continuity to make their eventual collection into one or more volumes an attractive publishing proposition. Hardy now realized that he had already published several stories of good quality—including 'The Distracted Young Preacher', 'Fellow-Townsmen', 'The Three Strangers', and 'Interlopers at the Knap'—which had at least their Wessex settings in common and, arguably, certain similarities of period, subject matter, treatment, and theme. Once, therefore, he had disposed of 'Alicia's Diary', a cumbersome story dependent in many of its details upon his recent Italian travels, Hardy settled down to write, with far greater care and imaginative investment, one of the finest of his shorter narratives, 'The Withered Arm', using material drawn not only from familiar Wessex settings, including Casterbridge itself, but also from the kind of half-legendary tales he had heard from the lips of his mother and grandmother—both of whom are invoked in notes surviving from September 1887.[28] When the story was completed he submitted it first to *Longman's Magazine,* which had printed 'The Three Strangers' a few years earlier, only to be told that it was much too grim and unrelieved for a magazine read mostly by girls. Hardy promptly sent it off again, this time to *Blackwood's,* with the comment that the main incidents were essentially true and that he had himself known the two women concerned. *Blackwood's* accepted the story, and it appeared—with a last-minute change in the manner of Farmer Lodge's death, from suicide to natural causes—in the January 1888 number.[29]*

* Leslie Stephen characteristically criticized the story on the grounds that the withering was neither scientifically explained nor specifically called hallucinatory.[30]

Having received £24 from *Blackwood's* for his new story, Hardy now put it together with those four previous stories he thought particularly well of and offered the collection, as *Wessex Tales*, to Frederick Macmillan. He subsequently accepted Macmillan's suggestion that it be published in two volumes at the same royalty of one-sixth the retail price as had earlier been agreed for the one-volume edition of *The Woodlanders*.[31] It was only since the Macmillan firm had become his publishers that Hardy had begun receiving royalties instead of cash payments for book publication of his works. The new arrangements reflected general changes taking place in the relationship between authors and publishers, partly as a result of the activities of the Incorporated Society of Authors under the indefatigable leadership of Walter Besant, but they also indicated—as did Macmillan's eagerness to sign him up for colonial editions*—the growing strength of Hardy's own negotiating position. Within a few years he was to have a falling out with Macmillan over the interpretation and application of the agreements between them, but the shift to a royalty system, and hence to his gaining a continuing financial interest in his literary properties, was eventually to make for a great improvement in his financial situation, and especially in the stability and, indeed, enhancement of that situation over long periods of time. The sense that things were, on the whole, going well for him is reflected not only in that genial retrospective assessment of the year 1887 but also in a note made early in 1888: 'Be rather curious than anxious about your own career; for whatever result may accrue to its intellectual or social value, it will make little difference to your personal well-being. A naturalist's interest in the hatching of a queer egg or germ is the utmost introspective consideration you should allow yourself.'[32]

Hardy spent the winter writing at Max Gate, in accordance with what had become and was to remain his standard practice. By early March 1888, however, he was in London, staying—as, again, he almost always did—at a temperance hotel, although he moved into lodgings when Emma joined him in late April. In London he frequented the Savile Club, and the Reading Room of the British Museum ('Souls are gliding about here in a sort of dream

* Hardy received a single cash payment of £50 for a colonial edition of *Wessex Tales*, the same amount he had accepted for such editions of *The Mayor of Casterbridge* and *The Woodlanders*.

—screened somewhat by their bodies, but imaginable behind them'), visited Mary Jeune, Lady Catherine Milnes-Gaskell, and Edmund Gosse, and attended a musical afternoon given by the Alma-Tademas.[33] On 4 May *Wessex Tales* was published, and on the 28th the Hardys left for another holiday in Paris, remaining there for almost four weeks and amusing themselves in a variety of unstrenuous ways. They visited picture galleries and the royal tombs at Saint-Denis, went shopping together, and attended the annual running of the Grand Prix at the Longchamps race-course. Combining simple curiosity with a vague sense of professional obligation, Hardy visited the Archives Nationales in the Hôtel de Soubise ('much more interesting than I had expected'), inspected an exhibition of manuscripts and drawings by Victor Hugo, and even sat through a few cases of a minor nature in one of the law courts.[34]

Back in London in late June 1888 they took lodgings at 5 Upper Phillimore Place, part of a series of late-eighteenth-century terraces which then stood on the north side of Kensington High Street, just east of Holland House: it was Walter Pater, living near by, who recalled for them that George III had called the terraces the 'dish-clouts' because of the carved swags of drapery with which they were ornamented. The Hardys' bedroom faced on to Kensington High Street and they were liable to be disturbed in the early hours of the morning by the noise of the market wagons making their way in from the country to Covent Garden, each with 'its weighty pyramid of vegetables'—an experience irritating at the time but later to be laid under contribution in the story 'The Son's Veto'. Though Hardy suffered his usual heavy cold (*Early Life* calls it 'a rheumatic attack') as a consequence of his holiday, he was soon tasting the standard pleasures of the 'season', visiting the theatre—most notably Ada Rehan's performance as Katharina in Augustin Daly's production of *The Taming of the Shrew*—and enjoying the company of such friends as Lady Portsmouth and Mrs Ritchie, whom he had not met since she was Miss Thackeray.[35]

Hardy had intended to remain in London until the end of July, but he left rather hurriedly on the 16th—perhaps because he had received the news that part of the drawing-room ceiling at Max Gate had fallen down.[36] Once he was back in Dorchester, he set about writing the two stories, 'A Tragedy of Two Ambitions' and 'The First Countess of Wessex', he had promised to magazines. It was late September 1888 before he could turn his full attention to the manuscript that became *Tess of the d'Urber-villes:* a note of 30 September 1888 mentions for the first time the fictional names he had given to the vales of Blackmoor and Frome, 'The Valley of the Little Dairies' and 'The Valley of the Great Dairies', and that last phrase may have been used as an early working title for the manuscript as a whole. At the time of the original agreement with Tillotson's, Hardy had undertaken to deliver four instalments of the serial by 30 June 1889 and 'the remainder by Weekly Instalments, until completed'.[37] The date for delivery of the initial batch of material was later put back to September 1889, so that Hardy, beginning work in September 1888, was giving himself just twelve months to get the job done.

15

THE WRITING
OF *TESS*

THE whole period since the spring of 1887 had been for Hardy one of great imaginative activity, prompted by the completion and public success of *The Woodlanders,* by a sense of ever-increasing power and confidence, and by the deliberately renewed exposure to his richest sources of creative impulse—the recollections and associations of his childhood, the personal and traditional memories of his elders, the scenes and buildings most intimately connected with local and family history. In August 1887 he made the visit to Melbury Osmond he had chosen to deny himself during the writing of *The Woodlanders;* in September he was walking in the Frome valley, the setting of 'The Withered Arm' and of 'The Waiting Supper', another story written and published at this time. His recollections of the 'farm of Labourers, as they appeared to me when a child in Martin's time' (see above, p. 34) were written down in late February 1888, and a few days later he was reminding himself of the reigning 'village beauties' of his youth.[1] The very experience of planning and writing a number of short stories had given him the need and opportunity to make additional explorations, both temporal and spatial, of the Wessex landscape and thus confirmed more strongly than ever his sense of the region as an integrated whole,

related indeed to the map of south-western England but fundamentally his own unique and separate fictional world.

One day in that early autumn of 1888 he took a train to Evershot station and walked a short distance northward to visit what
remained of Woolcombe, an estate (so he had learned from
Hutchins) once in the possession of one of those branches of 'the
Dorset Hardys' to which he fancied himself to be related. The
pilgrimage was part of a deliberate process of thinking himself
into the social as well as the emotional texture of his new story,
of invoking that sense of historical time and visitable place which
provided the essential underpinning for his most ambitious imaginative enterprises. On this occasion he found ample evidence of
the 'decline and fall of the Hardys', recalled a childhood encounter
with a remnant of the Woolcombe Hardys walking 'beside a horse
and common spring trap', and concluded with the satisfactorily
melancholy reflection: 'So we go down, down, down.'[2] It was a
mood appropriately fed by the discovery, at Evershot station, of
some mistletoe that had been there 'ever since last Christmas
(given by a lass?), of a yellow saffron parchment colour'—evidently the 'source' of the mistletoe which Tess finds hanging
meaninglessly over the marital bed after she has made her disastrous confession to Angel Clare.[3] Hardy was now in the country
of *The Woodlanders* and of 'The First Countess of Wessex'—the
story he had recently based upon an episode in the past history of
the Ilchester family of Melbury House—and before returning to
Dorchester that day he walked on to the top of Bubb-Down Hill,
whence he could look out over the Vale of Blackmoor, associated
in his mind with William Barnes, Riverside Villa, and Jenny
Phillips—and now with the heroine of his as yet unwritten novel.

Thirty and more years later Hardy was to recognize in a young
local actress named Gertrude Bugler a striking physical resemblance to Tess Durbeyfield as she had so long existed in his mind,
and he once confessed that the association was made more poignant by the fact that it was Mrs Bugler's mother, Augusta Way,
seen working as a milkmaid on the Kingston Maurward estate,
who had first suggested the figure of Tess to his imagination.[4]
Augusta, who was eighteen in 1888, shared with her sisters in the
milking and other chores of the dairy run by their father, Thomas
Way, on much the same basis as that of Dairyman Crick in *Tess
of the d'Urbervilles*. These circumstances, together with the fact
that the Way family lived in part of the old Kingston Maurward

manor house, close by the barn in which Hardy as a child had attended the harvest supper and heard the old ballads so memorably sung, undoubtedly helped to establish the idea of Tess the milkmaid in Hardy's mind, but once it was so established other images and associations began to accrete to it, above all those relating to Jenny Phillips of Sturminster Newton (see above, p. 191). Not only does Jenny Phillips's situation conform more closely to the narrative details of the novel than that of any other known 'original', but Hardy's memories of her singing make her by far the likeliest possessor of that voice which is described in the novel as unforgettable by those who once heard it. What other elements went into the novel it is impossible to tell. The early experiences of Mary Head no doubt made their contribution, though her grandson seems chiefly to have associated her with *Jude the Obscure,* and the scene of the midnight baptism owed something not only to Jenny Phillips but to Jemima's memories of her mother's private performance of the baptisms her father had forbidden: Hardy more than once told correspondents that the episode was factual and that he could take them to the bedroom where it had occurred. It has been said that Kate Hardy 'was' Tess,[5] but specific evidence for such an identification is lacking,* and when Hardy remarked that he would have called the novel *Tess of the Hardys* if it had not seemed 'too personal'[7] he seems to have been chiefly referring to his own family's experience of having come down in the world—becoming Hardys instead of Hardyes or le Hardys in the process, much as the fictional d'Urbervilles had declined to Durbeyfields, the historical Turbervilles to Troublefields, or the Phelipses to Phillipses.

Hardy gave much attention to the naming of his characters, and was particularly happy in the combination of the Norman-sounding d'Urberville, which also manages to suggest the urban origins of the *nouveau riche* family by whom the name has been appropriated, with the uncompromisingly rural and plebeian Durbeyfield, which none the less sounds like an authentic 'corruption'. The naming of Angel Clare was a particularly bold gesture on Hardy's part—who else, asks Dorothy Van Ghent, 'would have dared to give him the name Angel, and a harp too?'— and it may also have been a very personal one. It has generally been assumed that Hardy took Charles W. Moule as his model for

---

* The story that Kate once had an illegitimate child is unsubstantiated and seems to have originated in her own rambling death-bed references to a daughter whom 'they' took away from her.[6]

Angel, but he told an interviewer in 1892 that Angel was a 'subtle, poetical man' of 'fastidious temperament' whose 'great subtilty of mind' alone prevented him from following his brothers into the church.[8] These comments, taken together with Angel's musical gifts and his uneasy relationship with his parents, are more suggestive of Horace Moule than of Charles, while the episode of the books of which Angel's father disapproved was of course directly based upon the sequence of events by which the two volumes of Mantell's *Wonders of Geology* came into Hardy's possession (see above, p. 68). An identification of Angel with Horace Moule gives more significance to the perceptible links between Angel and the morally and sexually fastidious Henry Knight of *A Pair of Blue Eyes,* while the similarity between the names Angel and Alec opens up the further possibility that Hardy was deliberately dramatizing the two sides of Moule's fatally divided personality, its combination of extreme refinement with a capacity for sensual self-abandonment.

Tess herself was for a long time called Sue in Hardy's manuscript, and in July 1889 he was suggesting that the novel be called 'The Body and Soul of Sue'—only to change his mind within a week or two in favour of 'Too Late, Beloved!', a phrase familiar to him from Shelley's 'Epipsychidion'. But Hardy was obviously right to abandon, in its turn, a title which smacked so much of melodrama, especially since his eventual choice—itself a revision from 'A Daughter of the d'Urbervilles'[9]—so firmly establishes Tess's essential dignity and stresses from the first that she is, though born Durbeyfield, of d'Urberville descent, the inheritor (for good or ill) of distinctive family traits.

Tess of the d'Urbervilles is nevertheless a remarkably cool title for so passionate a book, and there is a sense in which those earlier titles were made unacceptable by the sheer undisguised directness with which they spoke to Hardy's central concerns. He was obsessed throughout his life by the struggle between soul and body: *Jude the Obscure* might very appropriately have been titled *The Body and Soul of Sue,* and in a comment on W. E. Henley's poem 'Invictus' Hardy once declared, 'No man is master of his soul; the flesh is master of it!'[10] He was no less haunted by the sheer irrevocability of moments of decision and choice—the opportunity lost, the word unuttered, the road not taken, the beloved recognized or reclaimed too late. It is upon such moments, explored in all their irony and despair, that so many of his novels and stories turn, and some of the most poignant of his personal poems. Almost always it is a woman who pays, who finds herself bereft or betrayed by some such trick of fate or failure of character, and what finally destroys poor Tess is not, of course, her sexual betrayal by Alec but the far more radical infidelity of the man in whom she has voluntarily invested all her trust and love. Whatever its specific sources, *Tess of the d'Urbervilles* was driven into being by the surging and almost uncontrollable movement of human compassion which is detectable throughout the work in the narrator's scarcely disguised advocacy of the heroine's case, and which finally emerges in that polemical sub-title which, at the very last moment, Hardy could not resist inserting: 'A Pure Woman, Faithfully presented'.[11]

Although Hardy was now well known in Dorchester and reasonably active in local affairs, he often felt isolated at Max Gate—most acutely, perhaps, towards the end of a winter of intensive labour such as he had devoted to his new novel. Writing to John Addington Symonds at Davos Platz on 14 April 1889, he found it possible to speak of himself as 'in a sense exiled. I was obliged to leave Town after a severe illness some years ago—& the spot on which I live here is very lonely. However I think that, though one does get a little rusty by living in remote places, one gains, on the other hand, freedom from those temporary currents of opinion by which town people are caught up & distracted out of their true courses.'[12] The end of April, however, found Hardy once again risking these currents and taking Emma up to London for a visit lasting to the end of July.* The summer followed a now familiar course of concerts, theatres, exhibitions, and hours in the British Museum Reading Room, of visits and entertainment received and returned. There was talk of Mary and Kate coming up for their Whitsun holiday in early June, but they wrote to Emma to say (apparently without intending a snub of any kind) that they had already arranged to spend the time at Bockhampton.[14]

Hardy, now nearing fifty, was becoming sensible of increasing age as well as of growing reputation, and London provided many occasions for him to be made sharply aware of the attractions of young women glimpsed in trains and buses or while walking about

* They were in a hotel at first, but later took 'two furnished floors' at 20 Monmouth Road, Bayswater—a street off Westbourne Grove, very close to the Newton Road house in which they lived for some months in 1875.[13]

the city. On 29 May, three days before his forty-ninth birthday, he remarks of a girl seen in an omnibus that she had 'one of those faces of marvellous beauty which are seen casually in the streets but never among one's friends. . . . Where do these women come from? Who marries them? Who knows them?' At the end of June he comments on the beauty of Lady Coleridge, wife of the Lord Chief Justice, encountered at dinner at Mrs Jeune's. On another occasion in July he found himself in the company of Amelie Rives, the American novelist, 'a fair, pink, golden-haired creature, but not quite ethereal enough, suggesting a flesh-surface too palpably. A girlish, almost childish laugh, showing beautiful young teeth.'[15]

Some time in late May or early June 1889 he met Arthur Graham Tomson, a landscape painter of some reputation, and his wife Rosamund, who at the age of twenty-nine had just published her first volume of verse, *The Bird-Bride,* under the pseudonym of Graham R. Tomson: it was on 7 June that she sent a copy of the book to Hardy, inscribed 'with the sincere admiration of G.R.T.' Mrs Tomson was described in 1890 as a 'tall, slight, brown-haired woman, with large grey eyes, that at times seemed to be a deep hazel, and a striking individuality pervading her carriage, manner, and dress, the artistic largely dominating the latter.' This combination of literary accomplishments and self-consciously projected charms for a time induced Hardy to see in Mrs Tomson his ideal of an emancipated woman —self-confident, even aggressive, yet evidently less threatening than the 'Faustina' he had met at Walter Pater's the previous summer and categorized as being 'of the class of interesting women one would be afraid to marry'. His earliest surviving letters to Mrs Tomson, in the autumn of 1889, show unusual warmth— they are signed 'Ever sincerely yours' and 'Always yours sincerely' —but also the kind of coy indirection which was to characterize his communications with his closest women friends over the next few years. In one he insists that wild horses would not drag out of him 'that estimate of a poetess's works which came to my ears— till I see her'. In another, he remarks that it is raining but that 'the lovers walk two-&-two just the same, under umbrellas—or rather under one umbrella (which makes all the difference)'.[16]

It was not long before Hardy broke off the relationship, having come to the painful realization that Mrs Tomson wanted merely to show him off as one of a long train of admirers.[17] For her the entire episode was evidently no more than an elaborate flirtation;

for Hardy its impact was considerable. It seems, in particular, to have marked a turning point in his relationship with Emma. From now onwards he was looking quite deliberately outside his marriage for emotional satisfaction, and potentially for sexual satisfaction. Like many men, Hardy perhaps enjoyed the public appearance of sexual privilege almost as much as its actual exercise, and although there is no evidence, and little likelihood, that his adventures went to the point, or even within the range, of adultery, he kept only the slackest of reins on his fantasy life at this time—as *The Well-Beloved* was to indicate—and made the most of his many opportunities to be in the company of handsome women and receive their attention and admiration. He was himself responsible for the seating arrangement at the dinner of the Incorporated Society of Authors on 3 July 1889 which gave him Mrs Tomson on his left hand, Mrs Mona Caird on his right, and Miss Mabel Robinson immediately opposite.[18]

At dinner at the Gosses' on 2 July 1889 Hardy sat next to Agatha, the wife of Gosse's sculptor friend, Hamo Thornycroft, who was himself in France. Mr Hardy, wrote Mrs Thornycroft to her husband the following day, was 'most attentive & nice, not shy, as he sometimes is, & quite talkative. He wanted to persuade me to go with the Gosses to the dinner of the Society of Authors to-night at the Criterion at which there are to be about 200 people, and at which Edmund [Gosse] makes a speech. He considered it was right I shd be gay while you were away; fearful morals with which to corrupt an inexperienced & innocent person!' The young face that Hardy was seeking to add to the galaxy which would already be surrounding him at the Authors' dinner belonged on this occasion to the woman (as he told Gosse some years later) whom he thought the most beautiful in England and who had provided him, all unconsciously, with the physical model for Tess Durbeyfield. Hardy's indebtedness is implicitly acknowledged in the pages of *Early Life*—where Mrs Thornycroft's mouth is praised in terms precisely echoing those used of Tess's mouth in the novel[19]—and its significance can be appreciated from surviving portraits of Mrs Thornycroft and the correspondences between these, the Herkomer illustration of Tess returning to the Durbeyfield cottage which Hardy so much admired, and photographs of Gertrude Bugler at the time she was acting Tess and other parts with the Hardy Players (see below, p. 534).

. . .

Hardy had apparently done some work on the novel now called
'Too Late, Beloved!' during his months in London, but he returned to Max Gate for the final weeks leading up to his September deadline. On 19 July 1889, some ten days before his departure,
he responded to the request of Jack T. Grein and Charles W.
Jarvis (soon to be associated in the Independent Theatre) for
permission to dramatize *The Woodlanders*. Although the novel
had been published only two years previously, Hardy now felt it
socially possible—or personally necessary—to face up to the full
implications of the situation he had created but left incompletely
explored. He therefore recommended that what had only been
hinted at in the final sentences of the novel—Grace's future unhappiness as the wife of a persistently unfaithful Fitzpiers—should
in the play be more explicitly brought out. The adapters' first
version of the ending was sent to Hardy that September:

FITZPIERS   You will come back to me?
GRACE   What else can I do? My father says so, he tells me, everybody tells me—to be unhappy.[20]

The dramatization was never produced, but Hardy at least had
the satisfaction of reading a version of *The Woodlanders* that
concluded in a manner directly expressive of his intentions.

Hardy's insistence on an 'honest' ending to *The Woodlanders*
is highly suggestive of his mood as he settled down at Max Gate
in early August to resume intensive work on his manuscript, at
a high pitch of creative and moral excitement, determined to say
his say without literary or social compromise. By early September
he was well advanced with the new novel and on the 9th he was
able to send off to Tillotson & Son a parcel of manuscript representing about a half of the whole.[21] It was at this point that
Mabel Robinson spent a 'delightful week' with the Hardys, both
of whom were as always '*very* kind':

Max Gate was then raw new & I never thought it shewed talent
in the designer, but it was pleasant[.] Hardy shewed me his beautiful manuscripts & after dinner Emma lit a bright fire in the
drawingroom and he read aloud bits from the novel he was
engaged on. He read very badly & was suddenly overwhelmed
with a sense of the inadequacy of his words 'No: No. Its not at
all what I thought!' much turning of pages 'Lets try here this
is—' etc etc, but neither was *that* what he expected, & he dipped
elsewhere in the vain hope of touching his own heart.[22]

At Tillotson's meanwhile the early sections of the manuscript had been passed, unread, to the printer and set up in type, ready for serialization to begin, to a point just prior to Tess's arrival at Talbothays. Hardy had not been asked to supply details of his story in advance—it was Tillotson's assumption that every author would naturally give of his best[23]—and it was only when the first proofs reached the firm's head reader that embarrassment set in. William Frederic Tillotson himself had died the previous February, but his strong Nonconformist beliefs and attitudes were still respected by his successors. There was consternation, therefore, at both the narrative content and the moral emphasis of Hardy's story, and when he declined to make the changes urged upon him Tillotson's refused outright to publish it, although they remained ready to make the payments to which they had engaged themselves in the original agreement. To this scrupulous if distressing gesture Hardy responded with the equally honourable suggestion that the contract simply be cancelled. Tillotson's agreed, and on 25 September 1889 they returned the manuscript along with such proofs as had been pulled—and demonstrated their undiminished good will by soliciting a short story for early syndication.[24]

Hardy next made an approach to Edward Arnold, the editor of *Murray's Magazine*. Despite obvious differences between them —Arnold arguing that young women should be protected from knowledge of the world's evil, Hardy insisting that his intention was to prevent those miseries which were the product of ignorance—Hardy persisted in the submission to *Murray's* of his still half-finished manuscript, taking advantage of the ensuing interval to complete the story, 'The Melancholy Hussar', requested by Tillotson's and attend to some damp stains that were showing up inside Max Gate. On 15 November Arnold replied. He had, he said, consulted Mr Murray, his publisher, in the matter, 'and we are agreed that the story, powerful though it be, is not, in our opinion, well adapted for publication in this Magazine.'[25] Hardy sent the manuscript straight off again to Mowbray Morris, the editor of *Macmillan's Magazine,* only to receive little more than a week later a rejection as firm as Arnold's and on essentially the same grounds of the story's moral unsuitability for the magazine's presumed readership:

You use the word *succulent* more than once to describe the general appearance & condition of the Frome Valley [the manuscript submitted had taken the story to a point corresponding to the early stages of Phase the Fourth]. Perhaps I might say that the general impression left on me by reading your story—so far as it has gone—is one of rather too much succulence. All this, I know, makes the story "entirely modern", & will therefore, I have no doubt, bring it plenty of praise. I must confess, however, to being rather too old-fashioned—as I suppose I must call it— to quite relish the entirely modern style of fiction.[26]

According to *Early Life,* Hardy now undertook an extensive revision of the novel, involving the removal of its most obviously offensive sections, before offering it to Arthur Locker, the editor of the *Graphic.* The sequence of events was, however, a good deal more complicated than that account suggests. Locker had asked Hardy for another novel-length serial as early as the autumn of 1887, less than eighteen months after the conclusion of the *Graphic* serialization of *The Mayor of Casterbridge,* but Hardy had repeatedly put him off, perhaps because he preferred to publish in monthly rather than weekly instalments, perhaps because he thought the *Graphic* would not pay enough. He may also have feared—with some justice, as events were to show—that pressures making for bowdlerization might be brought to bear. On 13 November 1889, however, when he was in the midst of his dealings with Arnold and Morris, Hardy confirmed with Locker the arrangements for a contribution to the Christmas 1890 Number of the *Graphic* and indicated that he was now in a position to contemplate a full-length serial, to begin in January 1891 or at the magazine's convenience. On 18 November, when he had heard from Arnold but not yet from Morris, Hardy accepted Locker's suggestion of July 1891 as a starting date for the new serial. Eleven days later, after Morris's letter had arrived, he told Locker that he now realized it might be difficult for him to submit copy by September 1890, as he had agreed, and made the request (subsequently approved by Locker) that he be allowed to submit just half of the manuscript by the end of September and the rest in instalments thereafter.[27]

These negotiations with Locker, though certainly prudential, do not seem to have been improper. Had either *Murray's* or *Macmillan's* accepted 'Too Late, Beloved!', Hardy would presumably have arranged for the *Graphic* to publish an entirely different work—probably *The Pursuit of the Well-Beloved,* a short novel which he had already 'sketched' some years before and which was in fact serialized in 1892. Locker had not asked for details of the story Hardy had in mind, and Hardy for his part was not anxious to court by premature submission a fourth rejection which might earn him the reputation among magazine editors of being no longer publishable. His only other obvious alternative, that of publishing the novel in book form without prior serialization, was attractive in principle but impracticable in economic terms.[28]

During the final weeks of 1889 Hardy occupied himself—quite deliberately, perhaps—with matters other than 'Too Late, Beloved!'. He was at Bockhampton as usual on Sunday, 1 December, hearing from his father about old Stinsford burial customs. In the middle of the month he shared with the Secretary of the Society for the Protection of Ancient Buildings his anxiety about the threatened destruction of Stratton Church, just to the north-west of Dorchester.[29] Later still Rosamund Tomson sent some photographs of herself, apparently in the wake of a call she had made at Max Gate, and Hardy responded with a decorous note of thanks on Emma's behalf as well as his own. That the photographs—or, rather, a second set received some five weeks later—were of some personal significance to him is suggested by some notes scribbled on the back of a letter the following July:

> Life in Little / Heartache
> Tale of Mrs Tomson's photo.[30]

Hardy evidently had a possible story or, more probably, a poem in mind. 'It sometimes occurs to me', he had written to Sir George Douglas at the end of 1888, 'that it is better to fail in poetry than to succeed in prose', and there are many indications of such poetic endeavour on Hardy's own part during 1889 and 1890. 'After Schiller', for example, and at least the central idea of 'Heredity' evidently date from 1889, a note of September 1889 shows him returning once more to the evolution of what was at this date called 'A Drama of Kings' and eventually became *The Dynasts,* while 'At Middle-Field Gate in February', a by-product of his writing about Tess Durbeyfield, belongs to the winter of 1889–90. It was perhaps the evocation in that poem of the 'bevy now underground',[31] the village beauties of his childhood, which prompted memories of another village beauty, his cousin Tryphena (Sparks) Gale, and of his romantic attachment to her in the late 1860s. In a note ascribed in *Early Life* to 5 March 1890—but self-evidently written at a later date—Hardy recalls how he wrote, in the London train, the first few lines of the poem now known as 'Thoughts of Phena', quite ignorant of the fact that Tryphena was even then close to death at her home in Devon.[32]

He spent the early months of 1890 at Max Gate, completing the six tales, lightly interconnected as 'A Group of Noble Dames', which he had undertaken to supply to the *Graphic* for its Christmas Number of 1890.[33] Though interrupted by minor illnesses and two brief trips to London, the writing went smoothly enough —perhaps because his best creative energies were by no means fully engaged—and when Sir George Douglas came down for the Easter weekend he had two of the tales read aloud to him. The two friends went together to William Barnes's grave and to the 'Isle' of Portland—very much in Hardy's mind at this period as the setting of *The Pursuit of the Well-Beloved*—and after dinner one evening Emma read out from a magazine a short story by Kipling, whose reputation was just becoming established. It must have been an exceptionally weak story, Douglas later recalled, 'for not one of us could find anything to commend in it. "What is he driving at?" was our unanimous verdict.'[34] Hardy soon learned to take Kipling seriously,* however, and at a time when there was much controversy over the respective merits of 'realism' and 'romance', and when American critics such as Howells were bearing down hard upon the narrative and stylistic extravagances of Dickens and Thackeray, Hardy no doubt found in Kipling's manner and material a reassuring sign that there were writers— and readers—who still shared his own view that story-tellers were essentially Ancient Mariners, justified in delaying the hurrying public only when possessed of 'something more unusual to relate than the ordinary experience of every average man and woman'. Critics such as Howells, he insisted, forgot 'that a story *must* be striking enough to be worth telling. Therein lies the problem— to reconcile the average with that uncommonness which alone makes it natural that a tale or experience would dwell in the memory and induce repetition.'[36]

'A Group of Noble Dames' was dispatched to the *Graphic* on

---

* On 10 May 1890 he wrote down in one of his notebooks summaries of what he considered the best stories in Kipling's *Plain Tales from the Hills*; four days later he was summarizing and quoting extracts from *Departmental Ditties* and especially from 'The Ballad of Fisher's Boarding House', which he described as 'excellent'. He met Kipling himself in London shortly afterwards.[35]

9 May 1890, two months ahead of the agreed delivery date, and with that task seemingly behind him Hardy set off once again with Emma for London and the pleasures and obligations of the 'season'. In early July Emma was called away to her father's death-bed, but Hardy stayed on in London until the end of the month.[37]* Mary Jeune, by now the closest of his London friends, asked him at short notice to write an Epilogue for a special performance of *The Taming of the Shrew* to be given on 23 July on behalf of her Holiday Fund for poor city children. He was not present to hear the verses delivered (by Ada Rehan, the actress who had played Katharina) but the occasion constituted his first appearance as a poet—apart from unattributed fragments in one or two of the novels—since the publication of 'The Fire at Tranter Sweatley's' in 1875 and he was much irritated by the *Globe*'s dismissal of his verses as 'poor stuff, poetically—Johnsonian in heaviness of thought, and sesquipedalian in verbal expression'. Stirred up by a direct request from Hardy, the editor of the *World* inserted in his own paper the following week a mild rebuke to the *Globe* for criticizing so severely what had been written for a charitable pur-pose and at short notice.[39] Though minor in itself, the episode indicated a new readiness on Hardy's part to defend himself and his work by whatever means, direct or indirect, he might have available to him.

Hardy perhaps felt that he was now old enough—and well enough established—not to have to suffer indignities in passive silence. On this particular occasion his annoyance may have been intensified by the distressing exchanges with the *Graphic* in which he was concurrently involved. The directors of the paper, and especially its founder, William Luson Thomas, had been offended by 'A Group of Noble Dames' when it came into their hands some time in June, presumably after type had been set up and proofs pulled. The editor, Arthur Locker, was apparently away, but the assistant editor, his son William Algernon Locker, wrote on 25 June in terms all too reminiscent of the communications Hardy had received from Edward Arnold and Mowbray Morris the previous autumn:

* Hardy and his brother are said to have cycled to Topsham, near Exeter, in July 1890 to visit their cousin Tryphena's grave and call on her bereaved family.[38] But the journey was probably made at a somewhat later date and could not, in any case, have been made by bicycle earlier than 1896, the year in which Hardy first learned to ride.

Many fathers are accustomed to read or have read to their family-circles the stories in the *Graphic*; and I cannot think that they would approve for this purpose a series of tales almost everyone of which turns upon questions of childbirth, and those relations between the sexes over which conventionality is accustomed (wisely or unwisely) to draw a veil. . . .

Now, what do you propose to do? Will you write us an entirely fresh story, or will you take the 'Noble Dames' and alter them to suit our taste; which means slightly chastening 1, 2, 3 & 4; and substituting others for 5 & 6?[40]

The four stories Locker wanted revised were (to give them their final titles) 'Barbara of the House of Grebe', 'The Marchioness of Stonehenge', 'Anna, Lady Baxby', and 'The Lady Icenway'; the two he rejected altogether were 'Squire Petrick's Lady' and 'Lady Mottisfont'.* Hardy made fairly extensive revisions, chiefly but by no means exclusively to 'Squire Petrick's Lady', and agreement upon the publication of all six stories was eventually reached with the returned Arthur Locker on 30 July.[42]

But if he had not had to yield all of the ground so peremptorily demanded of him, he had undergone an experience sufficiently painful and humilating for a man of his years and standing. The difficulties over *Tess* and 'A Group of Noble Dames', coming hard upon the heels of the milder disagreements over the moral tone of *The Woodlanders,* constituted a rude reminder of his dependence not just upon the judgement of critics and the response of the reading public but also upon the anticipatory censorship of editors and publishers. In fairness to those editors and publishers it must be said that Hardy, for all his attentiveness to the public reception of his work, was a poor judge of the impression any given narrative was likely to make upon the sensibilities of others. It seems extraordinary, scarcely credible, that he should not have known the trouble he was likely to provoke by allowing his stories to drift into waters well known to be dangerous. And yet he appears to have persisted in believing, and in persuading his editors, that each new novel would sustain an impeccable

---

* These two had seemed to Locker 'to be hopeless. Frankly, do you think it advisable to put into the hands of the Young Person stories, one of which turns upon the hysterical confession by a wife of an imaginary adultery, and the other upon the manner in which a husband foists upon his wife the offspring of a former illicit connection?'[41]

moral tone and give offence to no one. When proved wrong, as he so often was, he responded with superficial co-operativeness— readily accepting cuts and revisions to serial texts—but with fundamental resentment of the implicit challenge not just to his literary judgement but to his achieved status as an artist and pro-fessional. On this occasion, his anger at being dressed down by young Locker found expression only in the scornful references to 'the tyranny of Mrs. Grundy' which survive on the manuscript of the stories,[43] but the entire episode augured ill for the submission of the new serial.

By the beginning of August 1890 Hardy was back in Dorset still with work to do on that serial—which must now be called *Tess of the d'Urbervilles,* although the precise date at which Hardy opted for his final title is not known. In the middle of August, however, Alfred Parsons the painter and illustrator was again at Max Gate, and later that same month Hardy took his brother to Paris. The short holiday was tailored primarily to Henry's tastes and expectations—though these did not necessarily run contrary to Hardy's own. He pencilled in the back of his Baedeker for *Paris and Environs* an index to its descriptions of circuses, cafés chantants, and dance halls (including the Jardin Mabille, said to be 'frequented by the more fashionable "cocottes" '), and during a visit to the Moulin Rouge he was struck—characteristically and even, it is tempting to say, inevitably—by the juxtaposition of the cancan performers with the cemetery of Montmartre visible through windows above their heads. The brothers gave their days to fairly strenuous sightseeing, however, and took in a good many places with Revolutionary and Napoleonic associations. They were at the Place de la Bastille on 22 August and at the Arc de Triomphe on the 23rd; three days later, at the Invalides, Hardy wrote 'very fine' in his Baedeker against the description of the 'twelve colossal Victories' on the walls of Napoleon's tomb.[44]

About a fortnight after Hardy's return from France Edmund Gosse and his wife arrived at Max Gate for a five-day visit, during which Gosse took with his 'Kodak' the blurred and distorted snapshots that are nevertheless precious as constituting the earliest —and very nearly the only—informal photographs of Hardy and Emma to have survived. They show a Hardy still bearded, a Max Gate still open to the winds. The camera 'gave in', as Gosse put it, before he had 'secured for posterity' the form and features of the Hardys' cat, Kiddleywinkempoops (Trot for short), but he did get a snap or two of their dog, Moss.[45] Much to Hardy's and Emma's distress, Moss died just a few days later, after having been savagely beaten by a prowling tramp, and was buried in the garden. This was the beginning of the pets' cemetery at Max Gate, although it is singular that all the other interments until the death of 'the famous dog Wessex'[46] in 1927 seem to have been of cats—perhaps because, to this childless couple who increasingly and almost pathologically made children of their pets, the experience of losing Moss was too painful to bear repetition.

That autumn of 1890 saw the completion of *Tess of the d'Urbervilles.* Hardy missed by just over a week his deadline for submitting the first half of his manuscript to the *Graphic*: promised for the end of September, it did not go off until 8 October. On the other hand, he was able to supply the remainder before the end of the same month, somewhat earlier than expected. For all his revisions and deletions Hardy seems not entirely to have forestalled the anticipated Grundyan objections on the part of the *Graphic*'s editor and directors, who are said to have insisted on yet further changes—including Angel's being made to carry the milkmaids across the flooded lane not in his arms but in a wheelbarrow.[47] It is in any case obvious that the serial text as finally published—with the substitution of a mock marriage for the seduction or rape of the heroine and the subsequent birth and death of her child—achieves decorousness only at a considerable cost in terms of narrative coherence and verisimilitude.

The two major excisions from the serial were separately published, 'The Midnight Baptism' in Frank Harris's *Fortnightly Review* early in April 1891 (John Verschoyle, the assistant editor, had been quite prepared to publish it as 'The Bastard's Baptism'),[48] and 'Saturday Night in Arcady', roughly corresponding to Chapters 10 and 11 of the novel, in W. E. Henley's *National Observer* the following November. Emma wrote out a considerable portion of the manuscript that went to Henley,[49] and in January 1892, when most (though not all) of the 'Saturday Night in Arcady' material had been reincorporated into the text of the first edition, it was Emma who wrote to the editor of the *Spectator* to explain that the word 'whorage', as used by Tess in reference to Car Darch and her companions, had 'ceased in Somerset, Dorset, &c., to carry with it the coarse idea of its root-meaning, being spoken by the most modest to imply simply a company of slatternly, bickering, and generally unpleasant women'.*

Since 1880 Hardy had had three different London publishers: Smith, Elder for *The Trumpet-Major* in 1880 and again for *The Mayor of Casterbridge* in 1886, Sampson Low for *A Laodicean* and *Two on a Tower* in 1881 and 1882, and Macmillan for *The Woodlanders* and *Wessex Tales* in 1887 and 1888. Still, at fifty, curiously unsettled in his publishing arrangements, he now took *A Group of Noble Dames* and *Tess of the d'Urbervilles* to the new firm of Osgood, McIlvaine & Co., established in April 1890 as a semi-autonomous London subsidiary of the New York house of Harper & Brothers. In part this was a gesture of friendship towards James Ripley Osgood, who had formerly acted as London agent for Harper. But Hardy also had reason to be satisfied with Harper & Brothers as the publishers, in their various magazines, of the American serial versions of several of his works: they had, in particular, accepted the six 'Group of Noble Dames' tales without the bowdlerizations insisted upon by the *Graphic*.[51] When, therefore, Rudyard Kipling wrote to the *Athenaeum* in November 1890 to accuse Harper & Brothers of sharp practice, Hardy—prompted by Osgood—felt obliged to join with Walter Besant and William Black in sending to the *Athenaeum* a letter testifying to their personal experience of unfailing fairness and liberality on Harper's part. The letter was not intended as an attack upon Kipling himself, nor did Kipling regard it as such, but his poem 'The Rhyme of the Three Captains', first published in the *Athenaeum* on 6 December, certainly made lively fun of Hardy ('Lord of the Wessex coast and all the lands thereby') and his co-signatories for demonstrating

> 'How a man may be robbed in Christian port while Three
> Great Captains there
> Shall dip their flag to a pirate's rag—to show that his
> trade is fair!'[52]

At the time when Kipling's ballad appeared, Hardy was in London by himself, Emma having experienced a recurrence of the lameness caused by her 'jointless' knee. He called on Osgood soon after his arrival to learn more details of the unexpected

---

* As published in the *Spectator*, the letter is signed 'C. L. H.'; the 'C.' has, however, been corrected to an 'E.' on the cutting pasted into Hardy's 'Personal' scrapbook.[50]

passage of a Copyright Bill by the United States House of Representatives, and was assured that the Bill would pass the Senate
and become law in July 1891, the date at which the serialization
of *Tess* was scheduled to commence. As Hardy wrote to Emma
that afternoon, the long-term advantages to English authors could
not as yet be measured, but the immediate implication would
seem to be that the many delays in the publication of *Tess* were
to have the effect of bringing it within the scope of the new law:
'If all goes well how fortunate,' he exclaimed.[53]

16

THE PUBLICATION OF *TESS*

HARDY returned to Dorset from London on 11 December 1890. Encouraged by the financial prospects opened up by the American copyright law, he lay awake before dawn on Christmas Day, 'thinking of resuming "the viewless wings of poesy"' and finding, as he did so, that 'new horizons seemed to open, and worrying pettinesses to disappear'.[1] In the meantime the proofs—'miserably small-typed'—of the *Tess* serial had begun to arrive. Hardy suggested ways in which the story might be divided up into the requisite number of weekly instalments, but evidently saw the problem in purely practical terms. 'It is immaterial about dividing the parts at ends of Chapters,' he told the *Graphic*'s printing-office manager: 'Any change of scene will do, the next part beginning "Chapter so & so *continued*."'[2] During the early months of 1891 he attended to the *Tess* proofs as they came in, completed the short stories 'The Son's Veto' and 'On the Western Circuit', and prepared for Osgood, McIlvaine the first book edition of *A Group of Noble Dames*, in which four previously published stories were added to the six which had appeared in the *Graphic*. His stints of work were diversified by a number of visits to London—by himself in January, with Emma in March—and by an increasingly busy programme of social engagements in and near Dorchester itself.[3]

Hardy was again in London without Emma in mid-April. It was dull, he reported; he felt lethargic, perhaps because he had been drinking milk and water instead of tea; and work on the 'Midnight Baptism' sketch for the *Fortnightly* was going slowly. A visit to the current burlesque at the Gaiety Theatre did not greatly excite him (' "The bogie man" which I went to hear, is not much'), and he could not work up enthusiasm for other forms of amusement.[4] These letters to Emma of April 1891 are quite long and detailed, and perhaps sufficiently affectionate for a husband to write home to the wife to whom he has been married for sixteen years and with whom he expects to be reunited within a week or two at most. On the other hand, Hardy was still on friendly terms with Mrs Tomson at this time and it is of course conceivable that the very length and specificity of the letters, and their stress upon the dullness of London, were deliberately designed as a smokescreen for other activities it was better that Emma should not know about.

Sir George Douglas, who during this period saw the Hardys at Max Gate, at his own home, and in London, believed them to be 'as well assorted as most of the happily married couples that one comes across in life'. He especially remarked Hardy's 'unremitted deference and chivalrous consideration' where Emma was concerned, but felt that she, for her part, had little sense of the true quality of her husband's work and was too eager 'to know the people whose names are well known'. Emma, he added, 'belonged essentially to the class of women, gifted with spirit and the power of deciding for herself, which had attracted Hardy in his early manhood. She had the makings of a Bathsheba, with restricted opportunities.' Though enigmatically phrased, the comment is certainly suggestive of Emma's capacity for independence and impetuosity—the sources equally of her 'admirable courage' in challenging the mistreaters of animals and of her inconvenient (from Hardy's point of view) and even disloyal support of the man with three children in the dispute over seats on the Paris-bound train. Mabel Robinson, writing of this same period, recalled that Emma's 'thoughts hopped off like a bird on a bough, but never then nor at any other time did the idea cross my mind that her mind (such as it was) was unhinged. It may have been, but as I saw her she was a perfectly normal woman without much brain power but who wanted to be a poet or novelist—I forget which— and found it hard that no-one took her literary accomplishment seriously.' Certainly, she added, Emma 'had not the intellectual value nor the tact it would have needed to hold the heart of her husband against all the world, but she had loved him dearly and was a nice loveable inconsequent little lady of whom one grew very fond.'[5] Emma's discontinuities were part of her charm, the counterpart of those teasing changes of mood that had so contributed to Hardy's enslavement at St. Juliot. But they could be exasperating in the practical world of every day and became in the long run a major source of marital difficulty. It was not secretiveness or meanness but simple necessity which induced Hardy to keep all financial matters, both business and domestic, in his own hands, and when, in these years, he asked Emma to copy manuscripts and other documents it was often because he wanted to give her pleasurable (and perhaps pacifying) employment rather than because he urgently needed the job done.[6]

They lived, visited, and entertained together. They necessarily shared in the practical, day-to-day business of living, and whatever the nature of their sexual relationship—at this or indeed at any other period of their marriage—they seem to have remained into the early 1890s on terms of cordiality and even of affection. But it was one thing for Hardy to remain publicly and even domestically loyal to the woman he had married, quite another for him to admit her to any genuine intimacy of an intellectual or even an emotional kind. In any case, loyalty to Emma did not encompass any diminution of devotion to Jemima, and tension between husband and wife flowed inevitably from that long-standing division between Max Gate and Bockhampton which Hardy did not sufficiently try to heal. He may even have come to recognize certain advantages in keeping the two sides of his life—where he had come from and where he had arrived—so sharply distinct even while geographically contiguous. The consequences, however, were serious: on his own part, an early-developed habit of keeping a major segment of his life very much to himself; on Emma's, a bitter and constantly renewed experience of finding herself isolated in essentially hostile territory. It was not simply that the Hardys were against her, or that she could never learn to think of Dorset as home, but that in marrying Hardy she had expected to live in London and not in semi-rural isolation.[7]

The annual visits to London, whatever their professional and personal benefits to Hardy himself, were thus an essential element in the marriage, and Hardy's growing reputation brought Emma into contact with a gratifying number of 'the people whose names are well known'. It was precisely in London, however, that Emma's eccentricities and impetuosities were most glaringly obvious. Those pretensions to gentility which had so offended her husband's family were in London regarded as inept affectations. She had neither the poise nor the wit—not even the gift of silence—which might have made her acceptable in those circles in which Hardy moved by right of his talent. Worse still, she was entirely lacking in beauty or sense of style. Mabel Robinson recalled that Emma's 'masses of silken golden hair' had already 'faded drab' by the time she first met her during the Tooting years. The American novelist Gertrude Atherton, sitting with T. P. O'Connor at a social gathering in the 1890s, saw Hardy walk by in the company of 'an excessively plain, dowdy, high-stomached woman with her hair drawn back in a tight little knot, and a severe cast of countenance. "Mrs. Hardy," said T. P. "Now you may understand the pessimistic nature of the poor devil's work." ' O'Connor himself remembered Emma, evidently from somewhat later years, as providing 'as striking a contrast to her husband as if he in his dramatic mood had invented her. He was small, frail-looking, sombre; she was full-blown, with an ample figure, a large rubicund face, and a defiantly jolly expression—whether it was good nature or revolt it is difficult to say.'[8]

As late as December 1890 Hardy could describe Emma as appearing at a Dorset social occasion looking 'rather well-dressed'.[9] In London, however, her looks, manner, and conversation were becoming an increasing source of embarrassment. Whatever his own feelings about his wife, Hardy was too much of a novelist to remain long unaware of her failure to adapt herself to the circles into which he introduced her. He knew that she was perceived as plain, foolish, and overdressed, and that he himself was often scorned or pitied on her account. He also discovered that there were in London numerous women, handsome, intelligent, and well-dressed, who were ready and even eager to claim his attention and be seen in his company. His natural, if not especially admirable, response was to leave Emma behind, at Max Gate or in their London lodgings, whenever he decorously could. For a time Emma accepted this situation dutifully enough. It was only later —and particularly after Hardy had seemed in *Jude the Obscure* to be attacking not only the institution of marriage but, by implication, his own marriage—that she was roused to active, bitter, and permanent protest.

· · ·

At the end of April 1891 Emma went up to join Hardy at the flat they had taken at 12 Mandeville Place, just south-east of Manchester Square, leaving Max Gate in charge of Mary Antell and her daughter Polly.[10] While the Hardys were away a Parliamentary by-election was held in the South Dorset constituency and Hardy's friend Robert Pearce Edgcumbe stood as a Gladstonian Liberal. Although Hardy had sat on the platform with Edgcumbe and other dignitaries at a Liberal Party election meeting in Dorchester in 1885, he now declined to take any active part in his friend's campaign, explaining that 'the pursuit of what people are pleased to call Art so as to win unbiassed attention to it as such, absolutely forbids political action'. He indicated that he had, in any case, little enthusiasm for the position either of the major parties had taken on the Irish question, but would certainly give his personal support to Edgcumbe as a man of superior intellectual capacity—though it is not clear that he went so far as to make a special visit to Dorchester to cast his vote.[11] Edgcumbe lost narrowly after a bitter campaign. Kate, reporting the outcome in a letter of 15 May, went on to talk of the inspection which she and Mary had just undergone at their school, the death of the Bockhampton cat ('Mother wont hear of having another'), the satisfactory condition of things at Max Gate ('Aunt Mary and Polly are quite happy out at Max. Henry goes in and visits them occasionally, & I have been out a few times'), and possible arrangements for a visit to Mandeville Place which Mary might—and in fact did—make later that month. She ended, in her usual cheerful fashion, by sending love to Emma and affectionate wishes to Hardy himself.[12] Kate and Mary and Henry, it is clear, were still on tolerably good terms with Emma, even if their mother was not.

In late April 1891 Hardy was notified of his election to the Athenaeum as a person of 'distinguished merit' in the field of literature—the culmination of a process which Lord Carnarvon, at Hardy's own instigation, had set in motion nearly three years previously—and he often used the club thereafter as an impeccably respectable address for his correspondence when in London. He remained for several years, however, a member of the more relaxed Savile, to which such friends as Gosse and Greenhill belonged, and during this particular summer he met Kipling there on a number of occasions. He went, as usual, to galleries, among them the Royal Academy and the English Art Club, and to the theatre, including the first performance of Gosse's translation of

Hedda Gabler.[13] He was deeply moved by a visit to a large private lunatic asylum under the guidance of T. Clifford Allbutt, a doctor and Commissioner in Lunacy, whom he had recently met at Gosse's, and much touched by what he saw at two London training colleges for women teachers, including the one which his cousin Tryphena had attended more than twenty years previously. He found pathos in the spectacle presented by such a community of young women: 'Their belief in circumstances, in convention, in the rightness of things, which you know to be not only wrong but damnably wrong, makes the heart ache, even when they are waspish and hard.' How much nobler their aspirations were, he added, than those of the people he had recently been encountering at fashionable parties.[14]

Early in June 1891 he went by train to Aldeburgh on the Suffolk coast to spend the weekend with a new friend, Edward Clodd, a banker whose leisure was given to writing works of popular science and anthropology and to publicizing the cause of rationalism. It was Clodd's cheerful custom to gather small groups of congenial companions at his house on the Aldeburgh sea front from time to time—especially, but not necessarily, over the Whitsun weekend. On this particular occasion, the first of several at which Hardy was to be present over the years, the other guests were Walter Besant and J. M. Barrie. Besant was already a good friend, Barrie was fast becoming one, and the weekend provided, as Clodd recorded in his pocket diary, 'plenty of good talk "de omnibus rebus" '.[15] Hardy's exchanges with Clodd, always eager in the pursuit of new ideas, may have done something to influence the direction of his reading that summer, when he worked his way with some care, entering quotations and occasional comments in his notebooks, through Schopenhauer's *Studies in Pessimism,* John Addington Symonds's *Essays Speculative and Suggestive,* and (what would most have interested Clodd) at least the first volume of the two-volume first edition of Frazer's *The Golden Bough.* He was quick to notice correspondences between Dorset folklore and some of the exotic customs and beliefs recorded by Frazer, and at least one of his Schopenhauer notes points in the direction of *Jude the Obscure:* 'Tragedy. "Only when intellect rises to the point where the vanity of all effort is manifest, & the will proceeds to an act of self-annulment, is the drama tragic in the true sense." '[16]

A Group of Noble Dames had appeared in a handsome one-volume edition at the end of May 1891, to be received with a general lack of enthusiasm and some outright hostility. When a reviewer in the *Pall Mall Gazette* on 8 July especially deplored the horrific aspects of 'Barbara of the House of Grebe', Hardy retorted in a letter published two days later that the tale-within-a-tale structure of the book had been deliberately designed to protect the reader's sensitivities by throwing back the action 'into a second plane or middle distance, being described by a character to characters, and not point-blank by author to reader'. Besides, he added: 'A good horror has its place in art. Shall we, for instance, condemn "Alonzo the Brave"? For my part I would not give up a single worm of his skull.'[17] The trouble with this line of argument, as the reviewer's reply effectively pointed out, was that the technical nicety did little, in fact, to modify the impact of the narrative itself, and that what was acceptable in fantasy or in the literature of the remote past might prove altogether less palatable within the context of a realistic fiction. Neither for the first nor for the last time, Hardy's vigorous but somewhat ponderous reaction to adverse criticism demonstrated not so much deliberate disingenuousness as that curious incapacity to see his work as it might be seen by others, to appreciate its potential impact upon minds and imaginations not precisely attuned to his own. Later that same year he was to provide Tillotson's with a prospectus of *The Pursuit of the Well-Beloved* which concluded with the assurance—no doubt firmly grounded in his own conception of the story as a kind of fantasy-parable—that it contained 'not a word or scene' that could 'offend the most fastidious taste'.[18] Hardy's paper on 'Candour in English Fiction', published as part of a symposium in the *New Review* for January 1890, occasionally shows a sense more of persecution than of proportion, and he always insisted, in response to invitations to write reviews, introductions, and so forth, that his critical faculties were poorly developed. On the other hand, 'The Science of Fiction', his contribution to another *New Review* symposium of April 1891, contains a remarkably concise and coherent statement of the fundamental issues in the current debate over realism and naturalism.

Although he tended to refer to *A Group of Noble Dames* in somewhat deprecating terms, Hardy ventured none the less to send copies to several of his friends, including Gosse, Clodd, and Lord Lytton. Hutchins's *History and Antiquities of the County of Dorset* had been his chief source for the historical narratives of which the book is composed, but in writing to Lytton he spoke of having drawn upon 'some legendary notes I had taken down from the lips of aged people in a remote part of the country, where traditions of the local families linger on, & are remembered by the yeomen & peasantry long after they are forgotten by the families concerned'.[19] What he did not say was that one of the 'aged people' was his own mother, almost certainly a source for the tradition of the Ilchester family of Melbury House which was eventually worked up into 'The First Countess of Wessex'. The Earl of Ilchester of the day was distinctly annoyed by the public allusion to his family past, but there seems no basis for the story that publication of *A Group of Noble Dames* led to a general ostracism of the Hardys, first by the families concerned and then by all levels of local society.[20]

Before returning to Dorset from London at the end of July 1891 the Hardys spent a few days in Suffolk with one of Lady Portsmouth's daughters, Lady Camilla Gurdon, and her husband.[21] Back at Max Gate Hardy resumed the task—begun but by no means completed while he was in London—of preparing *Tess of the d'Urbervilles* for its long-delayed appearance in volume form. Although this was largely a matter of restoring omitted sections to their original places, by no means all of the changes made in adapting the manuscript for serialization were in fact reversed: one fragment, the description of the dance at Chaseborough which had formed a portion of 'Saturday Night in Arcady', was not reabsorbed into the text until the Wessex edition of 1912. While he was thus engaged Hardy received a visit from W. Robertson Nicoll, who was anxious to include an article on 'Wessex', together with a map of the fictional places, in the first number of a magazine called *The Bookman* which was about to appear under his editorship. Though Hardy declined to contribute a map himself, Nicoll found him most co-operative in supplying the information upon which an adequate map could be based: 'I have seen a good deal of Hardy lately,' Nicoll wrote to a friend later that same month, 'and am much taken by him. He is certainly the most winning literary man I have ever met—shy and silent in company, but in private remarkably communicative and interesting.'[22]

In September 1891 Hardy and Emma were in Scotland, staying with Sir George Douglas at Springwood Park near Kelso and visiting places associated with Scott. Hardy—who always valued Scott's verse above his fiction and was accustomed to speak of

Marmion as 'the most Homeric poem in the English language'—
was particularly anxious to see and climb Smailholme Tower, the
setting of 'The Eve of St. John', while Douglas later recalled as
peculiarly poignant the sight of Hardy bending silently above
Scott's death mask at Abbotsford. The Hardys, said Douglas, were
very accommodating guests, who

> threw themselves at once into the interests of our family life.
> A portrait of Mrs Opie by her husband hung in my drawing-
> room, suggesting to Hardy that I might read them one of her
> *Simple Tales* after dinner, which of course I was only too pleased
> to do. Then, next morning after breakfast, Mrs Hardy said at
> once, 'Let's go and visit the horses,' whereupon she and my sister
> provided themselves with lumps of sugar, and we trooped off to
> the stables, which thenceforth became a part of our routine.

Although Emma had been a horsewoman in her girlhood, Douglas
added, she seemed not to possess 'any special knowledge of
horses'.[23] * When Emma attempted one day to make a sketch of
Springwood Park there ensued what Douglas recalled as a 'delightful wrangle', though it would seem susceptible of other interpretations: ' "Now you'd better let me touch in the perspective," said
the quondam architect; or again, grasping the sketch-book, "Let
me put in the trees, and the gable and balustrades will come in
almost of themselves." But though Hardy was by much the better
draughtsman, and in fact wanted to do the whole picture himself,
his good lady had confidence in her own handiwork.'[25]

Hardy and Emma returned by stages down the eastern side of
England, visiting the cathedral towns of Durham, York, and
Peterborough, and were back at Max Gate by 20 September 1891.[26]
On 8 November, when he wrote to thank Douglas for some trees
he had sent for the garden at Max Gate, Hardy was correcting
proofs for the first edition of *Tess of the d'Urbervilles*, and it was
at this late moment that he sent off to the publisher, Osgood,
McIlvaine, a new title-page for the novel, insisting upon Tess's
status as 'a pure woman' and declaring a personal commitment to
her cause in terms of the added epigraph from *The Two Gentle-
men of Verona*: 'Poor wounded name! My bosom as a bed / Shall
lodge thee.' The sub-title, Hardy later declared, was inserted after

---

* Emma continued to ride on horseback—making some of her more
distant social calls by that means—at least until the autumn of 1893, despite
the statement in *Early Life* that she last rode in February 1891.[24]

his final reading of the proofs 'as being the estimate left in a candid mind of the heroine's character';[27] it was also a deliberate challenge, thrown out in mingled exasperation and assurance. The three volumes themselves appeared just over three weeks later, and Hardy sent off presentation copies to Douglas, Lady Jeune (as she had become that year as a consequence of her husband's knighthood), and William Morris (whom Hardy had not met, but who showed in his reply some familiarity with Hardy's earlier novels). Sending a copy also to Alfred Austin, Hardy added by way of delicate compliment a line and a half of verse from the volume Austin had sent him two years earlier—'Wrestlers born, / Who challenge iron Circumstance—and fail'—although it is not quite clear whether Hardy was applying the quotation to his characters or to himself, as one of the 'poets of contention' to whom, in context, the words refer.[28]

By the end of 1891 Hardy had received a number of encouraging letters about *Tess*. Frederic Harrison claimed the novel as 'a Positivist allegory or sermon'; Charles Kegan Paul called it a 'really great novel', although he was only the first of several people to point out that no parson would have dared to insist that Tess's baby be buried in unsanctified ground.[29] The first reviews were also enthusiastic—the *Speaker* on 26 December finding the novel painful but fine, the *Pall Mall Gazette* on 31 December speaking of it as the strongest English novel for many years—and Hardy was especially pleased by the sympathetic view of Tess's situation taken by the *Daily Chronicle* on 28 December: in a letter to the reviewer, H. W. Massingham, he congratulated him and his paper 'for frankly recognizing that the development of a more virile type of novel is not incompatible with sound morality'.[30] The note of almost unqualified praise was sustained early in the new year by the reviews in the *St. James's Gazette*, the *Athenaeum,* and *The Times*. In the *Saturday Review* of 16 January, however, the reviewer—Hardy later decided that it was George Saintsbury—declared that there was 'not one single touch of nature' in any of the characters, that Tess's sexual attractions were too much insisted upon, that the 'terrible dreariness' of the whole tale was relieved only by 'the few hours spent with cows', and that Hardy, in sum, had told 'an unpleasant story in a very unpleasant way'. The notice, Hardy told Walter Besant the next day, was an 'absolute misrepresentation' but also a personal embarrassment: how could he, after such an attack, re-enter the Savile Club, which was full of people who wrote for the *Saturday*? 'Unfortunately', he added, 'I have just paid my year's subscription, & have no other place so convenient for lunching when I am in Town.' It was also particularly annoying, as he complained in letters to Gosse and Clodd, that the reviewer should at one point have deliberately misquoted the text in such a way as to make a simple compositorial error look like authorial bad grammar; on the other hand, he told Gosse on 20 January, orders for the book had actually increased since the review's appearance, and it had in fact already become clear that Osgood, McIlvaine had a success on their hands.[31] Hardy was invited to make corrections for a second impression of the first edition, and on 18 January he had to write to Tillotson's to beg a little more time for the completion of *The Pursuit of the Well-Beloved*.[32]

The morality of *Tess* was attacked by R. H. Hutton in the *Spectator* for 23 January, and its theology—specifically the final invocation of 'the President of the Immortals'—by Andrew Lang in the February number of the *New Review*: 'If there be a God', Lang expostulated, 'who can seriously think of Him as a malicious fiend?'[33] But the weight of critical opinion continued to be heavily in *Tess*'s favour, and it was only with the publication of a review entitled 'Culture and Anarchy' in the April 1892 number of the *Quarterly Review* that Hardy was again moved beyond irritation to indignation. In addition to repeating some now familiar complaints—that there was an unnecessary emphasis upon the heroine's 'sensual qualifications' for her role, that Hardy displayed an uncertain grasp both of style and of grammar and had quite deliberately told 'a coarse and disagreeable story in a coarse and disagreeable manner'—the reviewer made scornful reference to the 'queer' and 'hole-and-corner' arrangement by which sections of the novel had been separately published in periodicals 'whose editors presumably take a more liberal view of their duties towards their neighbours, or whose readers are more habitually adult'. Hardy himself observed, with perhaps a touch of paranoia, that the *Quarterly* emanated from the same publishing house as *Murray's Magazine*, which had refused *Tess* and subsequently ceased publication. He does not seem to have discovered that the review itself was the work of Mowbray Morris, who had so officiously declined to accept the novel for *Macmillan's* and thus set Hardy upon the path to its dismemberment. Even in the absence of such endorsement of his senses of irony and persecution, Hardy's condemnation of the review's 'mendacity' was passionate and unforgiving. 'How strange', he noted immediately after reading it for the first time on Good Friday 1892, 'that one may write a book without knowing what one puts into it—or rather, the reader reads into it. Well, if this sort of thing continues no more novel-writing for me. A man must be a fool to deliberately stand up to be shot at.'[34]

Hardy's friends tried to dissuade him from taking the unfriendly reviews so much to heart. The *Saturday Review* notice of *Tess* was scandalous, Besant agreed, but there was nothing to be done about it—except to go to the Savile as usual and show that his withers were unwrung. The manifest bad faith of the review, said Gosse, undercut all of its force: in any case, the book was being so praised on all sides—by Besant, by Mrs Humphry Ward, by Henry James—that Hardy should not be concerned with what 'the "Saturday's" ape-leading and shrivelled spinster said or thought'.[35] Encountering Clodd and Lang together at the Savile after the publication of the latter's piece in the *New Review*, Hardy by some 'manoeuvre' induced Clodd to desert Lang's company for his own. Subsequently apprised of Hardy's displeasure, Lang wrote to tell him that he would not review any of his future works—adding, with deliberate malice, that he had begun by deleting from an introduction to *The Bride of Lammermoor* he was currently writing a comparison between Hardy's and Scott's methods of handling tragedy.[36]

But Hardy was in a combative mood, as his last-minute affirmation of his heroine's purity had already shown. When the first one-volume edition of *Tess* appeared later that same year he took the unusual step of commenting—in a new preface, dated July 1892—upon the critical reception of the novel thus far. Injudiciously, perhaps, he included a scarcely disguised allusion to Andrew Lang as a 'great critic' who had 'turned Christian for half-an-hour the better to express his grief that a disrespectful phrase about the Immortals should have been used'. Not surprisingly, Lang felt himself licensed by such comments to repeat and elaborate his earlier strictures. Whether or not it was he who (as Hardy suspected) originated the term 'Tessimism' as a synonym for pessimism, he certainly took Hardy to task in the November number of *Longman's* not only for that pessimism but also for his dubious morality and his defects of style and taste. Although Hardy kept public silence thereafter, his hostility towards Lang and Saintsbury never abated. After Hardy's death Saintsbury told his widow that he thought her husband had forgiven him for criticizing *Tess*: 'How little he knew!' she later exclaimed.[37]

. . .

Hardy's personal appearance at about the time of the publication of *Tess* was quite strikingly evoked by Rosamund Tomson, in an article published three years later:

> As to the outer man, Thomas Hardy presents a curious combination of force and fragility; he is slightly below the middle height, but strongly built, with rugged, aquiline features, pallid complexion, a crisp, closely trimmed brown beard, and mustache short enough to disclose an infrequent smile of remarkable sweetness; hair, neither light nor dark, thickly streaked with gray, and somewhat worn away from the temples; and, most noticeable feature, bright, deep-set eyes, keen as a hawk's, but, for all their watchfulness, full of a quiet *bonhomie*. Indeed, there is something not un-hawk-like about his whole physiognomy, with the predatory expression left out; in no other human face have I seen such a still intensity of observation.

It was a pity, she added, that the nervous strain of sitting for fashionable photographers brought to his usually mobile face 'an expression of almost harsh austerity which those who have the privilege of his intimate acquaintance feel to be a complete misrepresentation of the real man'.[38]

The 'crisp, closely trimmed brown beard' of this description also appears in the most recent of the set of photographs Hardy had himself supplied to the *Strand Magazine* for publication in its November 1891 issue, but by the time he was interviewed by Raymond Blathwayt in the early weeks of 1892 the beard was gone and only the moustache remained.* The second Mrs Hardy—evidently on the basis of what her husband had told her—linked the removal of the beard with the critical and commercial success of *Tess*.[40] As such, it was an outward sign of the many changes in Hardy's life which that success brought in its train. The prospect, both immediate and long-term, of substantial royalties on both sides of the Atlantic gave him for the first time the sense and reality of financial security, the possibility of accumulating funds over and above his day-to-day needs. His old dream of a literary life now began to seem realizable in terms quite other than those

---

* The beard is also absent from the portrait (by a Weymouth photographer) which Hardy sent off on 17 March 1892 for publication in an American magazine.[39]

he had originally projected: instead of being a country parson writing poems for his own satisfaction he might become a retired novelist living on the proceeds of his past work and writing poems, not in need or expectation of financial gain, but with some prospect, perhaps, of reaching an audience.

The sense of financial accumulation—and, implicitly, of an impending culmination of his novelistic career—emerges strongly throughout 1892. In January he asked Clodd, as a banker, about the merits of a particular stock he was thinking of buying. That spring he spoke of enlarging Max Gate, even while reaffirming his initial intention not to ruin himself by building a great house, as other literary men had done. In September he bought at auction, and as an investment, a house in the centre of Dorchester (51 High West Street) that he was to let to a series of tenants over the next several years.[41] It was consistent with the whole pattern of his life that one of his first concerns should be for the welfare of his still unmarried sisters, and that some of the shares mentioned to Clodd should have been bought in Kate's name.[42] It was, on the other hand, a combination of Emma's social ambitions with her husband's notions of what was due to his new situation that led to a gradual elevation and elaboration of the style of life kept up at Max Gate, especially when visitors were present.

Hardy, after all, was now a public figure in a way and to a degree that he had not previously experienced, the frequent subject of items of personal or literary gossip in places like the *Athenaeum* and the *Bookman*. Literary pilgrims began to descend on Dorchester in search of Casterbridge and a tangible Wessex and in the hope of catching a glimpse of its creator, the 'Author of *Tess*', as he was now so often called. John Lane began seeking information for a bibliography of Hardy's work, explanatory notes were requested for a Russian translation of *Tess,* and magazines on both sides of the Atlantic wrote to ask for photographs and biographical material.[43] Interviewers of varying degrees of competence and honesty found their way to Max Gate, some by prearrangement, others on a purely speculative basis, and over the succeeding years many so-called interviews were to be concocted out of previously published material by people who had never been near either Max Gate or its master.

The interview with Blathwayt was one of those solicited and arranged in advance, and one of the few to make reference to Emma. Blathwayt describes her—perhaps in deliberately ironic terms—as being 'so particularly bright, so thoroughly *au courant du jour,* so evidently a citizen of the wide world, that the, at first, unmistakable reminiscence that there is in her of Anglican ecclesiasticism is curiously puzzling and inexplicable to the stranger, until the information is vouchsafed that she is intimately and closely connected with what the late Lord Shaftesbury would term "the higher order of the clergy." ' Blathwayt had evidently been exposed, as were so many other visitors to Max Gate, to Emma's insistence upon her relationship to Archdeacon Gifford. But he had also registered that childlike yet almost febrile quality, at once attractive in its vitality and disturbing in its excess, which had been one of her charms when young but now increasingly struck observers as a mark of eccentricity. Hardy, meanwhile, was still making some effort to keep her in touch with his work and his rising literary fortunes: he told Blathwayt that the scene in which Tess wore the jewels was Emma's idea.[44] Another interviewer that same year noticed that Emma kept in a 'little book' a list of Hardy's Wessex place names and of the actual locations to which they more or less corresponded.[45]

But Emma's listing of Wessex names was a form of book-keeping that went back at least as far as their Tooting days, and probably earlier. More significant of the current state of their relationship were the secret diaries (begun in or about 1891 but undiscovered until after her death) to which she was now confiding her multifarious complaints against her husband's conduct, attitudes, and beliefs.[46] No obvious change in tone or content is discernible in Hardy's letters home from London that spring, when he stayed at Lady Jeune's on at least three separate occasions: they begin 'My dearest Em' and are signed 'Yours affectly'.[47] Emma was in poor health during these months, having never quite recovered from a severe attack of influenza the previous autumn. Even so, the fact that Hardy so often went to London alone may itself be significant, and the shaving off of his beard perhaps constituted a two-fold declaration of his independence, the signal of a determination to appear under his true colours in personal as well as in literary terms.

He certainly took advantage of Emma's absence from London, and no doubt of his own enhanced reputation, to expand his range of friendships with handsome and intelligent women. In March he called for the first time on Charles Kingsley's daughter, Mrs Mary St. Leger Harrison, who wrote novels under the pseudonym of 'Lucas Malet', and found her to be a 'striking woman: full, slightly voluptuous mouth, red lips, black hair and eyes; and most likeable'. He wrote her shortly afterwards a warm letter of thanks for the gift of her novel *The Wages of Sin,* and expressed sympathy with the particular difficulty faced by women writers in handling matters of which they were conventionally supposed to be ignorant. They met again in April, but the relationship seems not to have been long-lived, perhaps because Mrs Harrison did not appreciate Hardy's frankness in telling her that he found the wages of her novel's title—'that the young man falls over a cliff, & the young woman dies of consumption'—to be 'not very consequent'.[48] The names of other women also crop up during these months, including those of a 'Miss Norris (ballet dancer)' and Lady Hilda Brodrick ('charming in her girlish naïveté'), who claimed during a 'long and pleasant tête-à-tête' to have wept bitterly over *Tess.*[49]

On 22 May 1892 Hardy again went up to London by himself to attend the funeral of his friend and publisher, James Ripley Osgood. He stayed on at Lady Jeune's after the funeral and began searching, in somewhat desultory fashion, for lodgings in which he and Emma could spend the balance of the London season. Emma came up to join him at the end of the month, but before they could get properly settled they were summoned back to Dorchester by the news that Hardy's father had been taken seriously ill.[50] Thomas Hardy, Sen., had lived in seclusion as a semi-invalid for several years—'seen of nobody but ourselves', as his son told Sir George Douglas—and since he was eighty years old a fatal outcome to the illness seems to have been anticipated from the first.[51] He sank slowly, however, dying at last, without great suffering, on 20 July.* Hardy, who had not been present at the moment his father slipped away, took charge of the arrangements for the funeral and made on 23 July the first dated marking in his prayerbook for many years, against verse 10 of the 90th Psalm: 'and though men be so strong that they come to fourscore years: yet is their strength then but labour and sorrow; so soon passeth it away, and we are gone.' Verses 3 to 6 of the Tate and Brady metrical version of the same psalm, headed 'The grave-side hymn of this parish down to about 1840', were printed on the

---

* The death certificate gives the cause of death as atrophy of the liver and exhaustion and describes the deceased as having been 'of independent means'; since Hardy registered the death the last phrase was presumably his.

leaflet which Hardy designed for the memorial service to his father held at Stinsford Church on 31 July, the Sunday following the funeral; also included were the words *'In Memoriam Thomae Hardy olim in hac ecclesia viginti annos musici. Ob: Jul: Die XX. A.D. MDCCCXCII, Æ. suae LXXXI.'* The gesture, deeply felt as an act of filial piety, was significant also as a salutation to those vanished ways and days the father, in the son's eyes, had so ideally embodied: it was very important to Hardy that his father should have died in the house of his birth and asked at the last for a drink of fresh well water to assure himself that he was indeed 'at home'. In his 1855 copy of Horace's *Odes* Hardy wrote 'T.H. (sen.)' alongside the beginning of Carminum XXII (*'Integer vitae scelerisque purus'*), and he also applied to his father Hamlet's praise of Horatio as one that 'fortune's buffets and rewards / Hast ta'en with equal thanks'.[52]

The death of Thomas Hardy, Sen., seems to have removed an essential element of good-humoured kindliness that had served to temper latent hostilities and keep the Bockhampton and Max Gate households linked, however tenuously, together. Once he had gone there was no effective buffer between an always implacable Jemima and an Emma who was, in middle age, revealing her own capacity for wilful obstinacy. Just what occasioned the crucial breach between Emma and her husband's family is not known, but it seems to have occurred—if the second Mrs Hardy was at all accurate in saying that Mary and Kate had not been allowed inside Max Gate during the twenty years preceding Emma's death in November 1912—in or about 1892, perhaps as a consequence of Emma's jealous response to the demands Jemima made upon her eldest child in the first lonely days of her widowhood. Hardy's own loyalties remained, as always, divided: he did not assert himself to overcome his wife's prohibition, but neither did he break off his own relations with his brother and sisters or interrupt his weekly visits to his mother at Bockhampton. Immediately after his father's death, indeed, he walked in that direction even more frequently than usual, and it was on a Wednesday at the end of August that Jemima told him that she felt she had no real connection with the furniture around her: 'All those belonging to it, and the place, are gone, and it is left in her hands, a stranger.'[53] If Jemima could think of herself as a 'stranger' among the Hardys it is little wonder that Emma should have felt so excluded from the clan.

17

FLORENCE HENNIKER

I N THE summer of 1892 Rebekah Owen—an energetic, unmarried American woman of thirty-four—came on a purposeful
pilgrimage to Dorchester, dragging her elder sister in her train.[1]
She was armed with an introduction from one of the directors of
Sampson Low, Marston & Co. and was soon on friendly terms with
both Hardy and Emma, though the more romantic aspects of her
relationship with the former seem to have existed only in her own
imagination. He did find flattering and ingratiating, however, her
wide and enthusiastic knowledge of his work, and the Owen sisters
made several expeditions under his or Emma's guidance to Wool
Manor, Bindon Abbey, Weymouth, and other places drawn upon
in one or other of the novels. On 7 September they all four went
to Swanage, where Hardy attended a meeting of the Field Club
while Emma showed the Owen sisters around the town. At West
End Cottage the widowed Mrs Masters remembered the Hardys
from sixteen years earlier, but Emma declined to go inside, perhaps because she associated the place with a period of relative
poverty and obscurity; she also expressed a dislike of *The Hand
of Ethelberta,* so largely written there, on the grounds that it had
'too much about servants in it'.[2] Rebekah Owen has her tiny niche
in literary history as the chief of those 'good judges across the
Atlantic' who persuaded Hardy to restore to the text of *The Mayor*

of Casterbridge the episode of the starved goldfinch which had been included in American editions but omitted from English,[3] but the wearisome persistence of her visits and letters over the years exhausted Hardy's patience and it was soon left almost entirely to Emma and, later, to Florence Hardy to keep up the Max Gate end of a connection which Miss Owen would not let go and the Hardys did not quite know how to break.

Driving home from Dorchester one afternoon in September 1892, Hardy saw that Stinsford House was on fire, ran across the intervening meadows, and was in time to help carry out some of the books and furniture. The near-destruction of the house, following so closely upon the death of his father, brought a further 'bruising of tender memories'. Lady Susan Fox-Strangways had lived there after her romantic elopement with the actor William O'Brien; his own grandfather had built beneath Stinsford Church the vault which the bereaved and grieving Lady Susan had specified should be just big enough for her husband and herself; his father had sung in the house for Lady Susan in her old age and practised the violin there later on under the watchful eyes and ears of the Revd Edward Murray; it was there, too, that his mother had worked, and there or in the adjacent church that she had first seen her future husband. Mary Hardy—with almost symbolic appropriateness—was laying flowers on her father's grave when the fire broke out, and Hardy met her in the churchyard. He did not, on the other hand, encounter Emma, although she too had later made her way to the spectacle in the company of Bosworth Smith, with whose father they were engaged to dine at West Stafford that evening.[4]

At the end of September Hardy was in London, where he went over with Clarence McIlvaine the arrangements for the rights to his novels to be transferred to Osgood, McIlvaine & Co. Most of those rights had been held for some years by Sampson Low, Marston & Co., but Hardy had long been dissatisfied with the poor appearance of their much-reprinted editions and was enthusiastically co-operating in the plans, originally projected by James Osgood, for a handsomely produced collected edition.[5] He went on from London to Oxford and thence to Fawley, in the Berkshire countryside south of Wantage, where his grandmother Mary Head had been born one hundred and twenty years before: 'Though I am alive with the living', he wrote, 'I can only see the dead here, and am scarcely conscious of the happy children at play.'[6] That these scenes and associations were to be heavily drawn upon in the novel, eventually entitled *Jude the Obscure,* which he was now beginning to take seriously in hand is an indication in itself of the deliberateness with which he was moving towards a personal statement in what he seems clearly to have foreseen as his last major work of fiction.

The broad directions of such a statement were already being foreshadowed in the weekly parts of *The Pursuit of the Well-Beloved,* which ran as a serial in the *Illustrated London News* from 1 October to 17 December 1892 but appeared in volume form, as *The Well-Beloved,* only in 1897.* The novel had two main settings, the curiously isolated world of the 'Isle' of Portland, known to Hardy from childhood, and the crowded drawing rooms of London society. It is not clear to what extent he may have drawn upon personal reminiscence in presenting the Portland episodes, but he certainly seems to have felt free to make use of London occasions, personalities, and personal features which must have been recognizable at least to those most immediately concerned. Lady Portsmouth, her daughter Lady Gwendolen Wallop, and her niece Lady Winifred Burghclere (née Herbert) served as the 'originals' for Lady Channelcliffe and two of the ladies present at her fictional 'assembly'. A dinner at Lady Jeune's in January 1891 at which Ellen Terry was present provided the basis for the novel's description of a dinner at Lady Iris Speedwell's. Hardy's friend, the painter Alfred Parsons, who had chosen to live in London and let others do his thinking for him, is similar in several respects to Alfred Somers, the painter in the novel. Mrs Tomson supplied certain ingredients in the presentation of Mrs Nichola Pine-Avon, the handsome woman with intellectual aspirations whom the novel's hero rejects but Somers marries. Such dependence may indicate a severe shortage of what Hardy was accustomed to call 'novel padding'.[8] On the other hand, it may constitute a deliberate if indirect acknowledgement of an autobiographical element within the novel as a whole.

The story, Hardy said on various occasions, was 'a bygone, wildly romantic fancy', sketched long before the appearance of the serial, at a time when he was still 'comparatively a young man'. He jotted down early in 1889 the idea of 'a face which goes

---

* As early as January 1892 Hardy had specified to Harper & Brothers, who had purchased the American serial rights, that the story needed radical revision and would not be available for book publication until a later date.[7]

through three generations or more' and later insisted that the
'plot' had been suggested by a sculptor's account of how he 'had
often pursued a beautiful ear, nose, chin, &c, about London in
omnibuses and on foot!'⁹ He was also fascinated by Shelley's 'one
shape of many names'—the phrase from *The Revolt of Islam* subsequently used as the epigraph to the first edition of the novel—
and seems to have been deliberately harking back to *The Woodlanders,* in which Fitzpiers not only quotes Shelley at impressive
length but invokes, in cynical justification of his own infidelities,
the specific notion of an ideal quasi-Platonic beloved capable of
manifesting herself in a series of human avatars. In *The Pursuit
of the Well-Beloved*—which echoes Fitzpiers's name in that of
Jocelyn Pearston, its central figure, and gives the latter's London
address as Hintock Road—this aspect of *The Woodlanders* is
effectively inverted: Pearston's unresting pursuit of the well-
beloved, which renders him as susceptible to feminine beauty at
the age of sixty as he had been at forty or even twenty, is described
as being 'of the nature of tragedy', however much it might bear
'the aspect of comedy'.¹⁰

If Hardy had learned since the middle 1880s to perceive the
elusiveness of the well-beloved in terms of actual or potential
tragedy, that was perhaps because he had been forced to acknowledge to himself the implications of his own attitudes towards Mrs
Tomson and other women known socially or just casually glimpsed
––Mrs Thornycroft, Amelie Rives, the 'Cleopatra' in a French
railway carriage in the summer of 1890 who seemed 'a good-
natured amative creature by her voice, and her heavy moist lips'.
Hardy's responsiveness to such encounters was both intense and
long-lived: the prostitute in Piccadilly who for a moment in 1891
held a narcissus to his nose prompted years later the poem 'The
Woman I Met'; 'Thoughts of Phena' is only one among several
laments for lost 'prizes', for opportunities left ungrasped at the one
ripe moment and swept immediately into that realm of the unattainable where his imagination was always most at home—'O
could it but be', cries the speaker in 'Faintheart in a Railway
Train', 'That I had alighted there!' Hardy, 'a young man till he
was nearly fifty',¹¹ had now, in his fifties, been obliged to recognize a growing discrepancy between his increasing age and his
undiminished—or even reawakened—sexual susceptibility. But
what in his as in Pearston's youth had been pleasant fancies or, at
worst, transitory adolescent infatuations, had become in his as in

Pearston's middle age a source of permanent anguish, a regularly re-enacted tragi-comedy. For Hardy the situation was exacerbated, its ironies deepened, by the existence of a permanent, increasingly burdensome, yet unignorable domestic tie.

In the serial version of the novel Hardy permitted himself to treat this theme with almost brutal directness. Pearston and Marcia Bencomb marry in haste and become gradually disillusioned with each other over a period of years. She from the first believes that she has married somewhat beneath her; he feels that as a sculptor 'rising to fame by fairly rapid strides' he had in fact been no bad match 'for a woman who, beyond being the probable successor to a stone-merchant's considerable fortune, had no exceptional opportunities'. He nevertheless recognizes that family enmity would have driven even Romeo and Juliet apart after a month or two, Juliet going to live 'with her people, he with his'. As the narrator observes of the pair: 'In their ill-matched junction on the strength of a two or three days' passion they felt the full irksomeness of a formal tie which, as so many have discovered, did not become necessary till it was a cruelty to them.'[12] Much later in the serial Pearston, married to Avice III, granddaughter of the woman whom he had abandoned for Marcia's sake forty years earlier, realizes—much as Phillotson was to do in *Jude the Obscure* —that she loves someone else and that humanity if not legality would best be served by letting her go: 'to me', he declares, 'healthy natural instinct is true law, and not an Act of Parliament.'[13]

Emma's distress at these direct attacks on marriage can only have been intensified by the serial's final episode, in which Pearston, the successful sculptor cursed by the combination of an ageing body with a perpetually restless heart, is seized with hysterical laughter at finding himself permanently yoked to a Marcia grown shrivelled and old: ' "Oh—no, no! I—I—it is too, too droll—this ending to my would-be romantic history." ' The entire serial then closes with the exclamation 'Ho-ho-ho!'—outside quotation marks and hence presumably authorial. Hardy's last story, Henry J. Moule's daughter wrote to Rebekah Owen on the last day of 1892, 'ends pitifully. It reads to me like a disappointed home life, very thinly veiled, in the author's experience.'[14] If *The Pursuit of the Well-Beloved* was being perceived in such terms by people in Dorchester, it could scarcely fail to give offence to Emma herself. As a reflection of Hardy's dissatisfaction with his own marriage, its publication could only contribute to the further deterioration of that marriage. In so far as it may have constituted a conscious act of exorcism, a therapeutic course of self-flagellation, the exercise was to prove singularly inefficacious.

Almost immediately after his return from Oxford and Fawley in early October 1892 Hardy made a special trip to London to be present at Tennyson's funeral. The occasion could not but take on something of the character of a literary concourse—he spoke briefly with Meredith, James, and others, and after the service was taken off by Gosse to lunch with Austin Dobson, Theodore Watts-Dunton, and William Watson—but it was in other respects very much in tune with the profoundly melancholy mood in which he had remained, perhaps with a touch of self-indulgence, since his father's death: he had a very good place in the Abbey, he told Emma, and 'looked into the grave with the rest as we passed it on our way out'.[15] Blomfield (now Sir Arthur) was addressed in a letter of mid-October as one of the few people left by 'the ravages of time' for him to call 'very old friends'; a note of a week later not only registers the point of departure for a famous poem but sounds the note of mortality in terms at once deeply personal and immediately apposite to the serial then in progress: 'Hurt my tooth at breakfast-time. I look in the glass. Am conscious of the humiliating sorriness of my earthly tabernacle, and of the sad fact that the best of parents could do no better for me. . . . Why should a man's mind have been thrown into such close, sad, sensational, inexplicable relations with such a precarious object as his own body!'[16] There is a strong suggestion here of a recent rebuff from a younger woman—possibly Rosamund Tomson— and it was, in all the circumstances, an odd coincidence, if nothing more, that the illustrator of *The Pursuit of the Well-Beloved* should have drawn a Pearston who bore a quite striking physical resemblance to the author himself.

In late 1892 and early 1893 Hardy was occupied with the composition of one of his finest short stories, 'The Fiddler of the Reels', sent off on 13 January 1893 for publication in a special Chicago World's Fair number of *Scribner's Magazine*.[17] The negotiations with *Scribner's* had been conducted by A. P. Watt, a pioneer in the new profession of literary agent, and Hardy had several dealings during the early 1890s with another such agent, William Morris Colles, whose Authors' Syndicate was closely associated with the Incorporated Society of Authors. Although

Hardy usually found himself returning negative replies to Colles's requests for novels and stories, he did sell some properties through the Syndicate—notably 'An Imaginative Woman', which appeared in the newly founded *Pall Mall Magazine* in September 1893— and he sought the advice both of the Syndicate and of the Society of Authors during the summer of 1893, when he ran into difficulties with the house of Macmillan (as he had already done with Sampson Low) over the question of the transfer of rights to Osgood, McIlvaine.[18] Hardy always held agents at a distance, however, keeping control over his work very much in his own hands.

In the spring of 1893 Hardy asked the Authors' Syndicate, through Colles, to prepare typed copies of a one-act play, *The Three Wayfarers*, which he had just adapted from his short story 'The Three Strangers'.[19] The controversy over *Far from the Madding Crowd* and *The Squire* had soured Hardy's previous theatrical experience, and in the years immediately preceding 1893 he had more than once expressed, publicly as well as privately, a strong distaste for the contemporary stage, and especially for its excessive emphasis upon elaborate scenery and costumes. In a letter published in the *Weekly Comedy* in November 1889, for example, he advocated a form of arena stage, in which the spectators, 'sitting to a great extent round the actors, see the *play* as it was seen in old times, but as they do not see it now for its accessories'. The failure of Grein and Jarvis to get *The Woodlanders* produced, despite approaches to George Alexander, Henry Irving, and others, only served to increase Hardy's scepticism about the actor-manager system and its conservative adherence not only to stage spectacle but also to the moral 'formalities' of the day. Fiction, he believed, remained distinctly superior to the drama as a means of 'getting nearer to the heart and meaning of things'.[20]

Hardy was, on the other hand, by no means immune to the glamour of the theatre. From his earliest days in London he had been a frequent and enthusiastic theatre-goer; he still attended performances of every description—Lottie Collins's 'Ta-ra-ra-boom de-ay' number at the Gaiety, he told Douglas, was 'really a very unusual performance, & not altogether so silly as people say'[21] —and was early and enthusiastically aware of Ibsen's arrival on the English stage. Thanks largely to Lady Jeune, he was on friendly terms with Irving, Ellen Terry, George Alexander, Ada Rehan, and other leading theatrical figures of the day. Nor was he insensible of the financial rewards the theatre potentially offered.

The notion of adapting already-written material for the stage was attractive both in its promise and in its practicality, and Hardy acceded promptly to James Barrie's suggestion, of 19 April 1893, that he should make a play out of 'The Three Strangers' for inclusion in a programme of one-act plays to be given by Janet Achurch and her husband Charles Charrington. The idea had already occurred to him, Hardy replied, and he had even begun work on it: 'I do not know what became of my sketch. However the work wd not be difficult—& I am willing to attempt it again.'[22]* He was as good as his word, not only completing the play in time for the conclusion to be revised in line with Charrington's suggestions, but also supplying a sketch of the shepherd's cottage, inserting some old dance tunes and figures, and offering to give full details of the dances if required. The morning after the first performance on 3 June 1893 Lady Jeune wrote to scold him for 'running away as you did & leaving us, because everybody was most anxious to see you & they all called for you', but the production as a whole was coolly received and ran only until the end of the week.[24]

It was in the spring of 1893 that the Hardys for the first time took an entire house for the London season, bringing up their own servants from Max Gate. The house, 70 Hamilton Terrace, was in Maida Vale, not far from the church in Elgin Avenue where they had been married nearly nineteen years before. The success of *Tess* was apparent not only in their ampler style of London living but also in their expanded social activities. There were many encounters with the famous, the wealthy, and the well-born, and Hardy—famous now himself—moved in these elevated circles with an increased assurance: at dinner one evening he sat opposite Princess May of Teck, the prospective bride of the Duke of York (later King George V), and recorded in his notebook that she was 'not a bad-looking girl, and a man might marry a worse'.[25] He also found himself a centre of attention in more exclusively literary circles. Israel Zangwill, who had recently made a name

---

* On 21 April 1893, the day of his letter to Barrie, Hardy also sketched a scenario for a two-act play entitled *Birthwort*, very similar in its outlines to the poem 'A Sunday Morning Tragedy' and evidently based upon the same source material. In so far as it dealt with an attempted abortion, it would have been strong meat for the contemporary theatre: after Hardy had had difficulty getting the poem published fifteen years later, he told John Galsworthy that he had originally wanted to produce it 'as a tragic play', going so far as to 'shape the scenes, action, &c.', before realizing that the subject matter would prevent his ever finding a producer.[23]

for himself with his novel *Children of the Ghetto,* sought him out at an Authors' Club meeting in early May, finding him 'oldish' but warm and congenial, 'a nice simple old man'. A few days later Zangwill attended one of the Hardys' 'at homes' at 70 Hamilton Terrace. His hostess, 'pleasant, pretty and un peu invalide', chattered away with utter inconsequentiality, while Hardy himself spoke angrily of the delays and restrictions imposed by the conventions of serialization and declared that he now refused to accept commissions in advance, 'for fear of being tied'. He also expressed some resentment of things Henry James had said of his work in private conversation and some retaliatory distaste for James's recently published story 'The Real Thing': it was 'so futile', he said, and one simply didn't believe in the two aristocrats.[26]

On 18 May 1893 Hardy and Emma set off for Ireland, stopping overnight at Llandudno, the setting of that foreboding poem 'Alike and Unlike'. The next day they crossed over to Dublin, where they were to be the guests of the Lord-Lieutenant of Ireland, Lord Houghton, later the Marquess of Crewe. Hardy had been on friendly terms with Richard Monckton Milnes, the 1st Lord Houghton, during the years immediately preceding the latter's death in 1885, and had known his son, the present Lord Houghton, for some time; he seems not, however, to have met his host's sister, Florence Henniker, until she welcomed Emma and himself at the Viceregal Lodge. Mrs Henniker was then in her late thirties, the author of three moderately successful novels, and the wife, since 1882, of Arthur Henry Henniker-Major, professional soldier and younger son of the 4th Lord Henniker. Her father's literary reputation, her brother's political career, and her husband's military life had given her an unusually wide range of acquaintances and experiences, and she moved of right in those upper-class circles to which Hardy was admitted only on the basis of his hard-earned fame. She was, in short, a poised, intelligent, educated woman, well-qualified, according to Justin McCarthy, to become famous as 'the presiding genius of a *salon*'.[27] That she never quite attained such a position may be ascribed partly to her uncertain health, partly to the sharpness of her tongue, largely to her devotion to her soldier husband and the somewhat peripatetic life she consequently led. Though not a beauty, she was certainly both handsome and well dressed—in sharp contrast to Emma, who appeared in Dublin in an outfit of muslin and blue ribbons ludicrously inappropriate to her fifty-one years[28]—and Hardy was immediately and powerfully attracted to her.

He had of course been for some time engaged in an active search for someone to fall in love with, and there is no doubt that he 'chose' Mrs Henniker without much encouragement on her part—or even much realization of what was going on. 'A charming, *intuitive* woman apparently,' he wrote in his diary after that first meeting,[29] and while that *'intuitive'* hints at qualities in Mrs Henniker which were soon to be drawn upon for certain aspects of Sue Bridehead's personality, it also reveals a strong element of wishfulness in Hardy's early attitudes towards her, an assumption of a sexual as well as intellectual responsiveness which may simply not have existed. As a woman of intellectual ambitions and accomplishments, mixing freely and easily in many walks of society, as the childless wife, mature yet still attractive, of an often-absent soldier of philistine views, as (by no means least) the daughter of Monckton Milnes—in all these respects Mrs Henniker must have looked like the emancipated woman for whom Hardy had long been seeking, an ideal resting place for his personal vision of the well-beloved. It is not necessary to question the reality of his attraction, or the depth of his feelings, in order to recognize, in his early letters to her, the element of male predatoriness in his deliberate exploitation of whatever links—as substantial as literature or as tenuous as architectural history—might be established between them.

Those first letters, however, belong to early June 1893. While the Hardys were still in Ireland during the last two weeks of May they visited the sights of Dublin and shared in the activities and formalities of the Viceregal Lodge and its 'little Court', as Hardy rather sardonically called it[30]—among them a military display on the occasion of the Queen's birthday on 24 May, when he and Emma rode in one of the carriages in the procession through the city, a visit to the scene of the Phoenix Park murders, conversations with his old acquaintance John Morley, then Chief Secretary for Ireland, and various social occasions, including a dinner at which Mrs Henniker played the zithern. An apparently trivial notebook entry about the ale or dirty water splashed on to the ladies' clothes during a visit to the Guinness brewery on their final morning in Dublin perhaps served to memorialize for Hardy himself some unexpressed and inexpressible moment of real or imagined intimacy with Mrs Henniker. Later that same day, 25 May, the Hardys set off on a brief tour of the Killarney lakes, returning through

Max Gate, *c.* 1900

Hardy's study in 1900

Thomas Hardy, 1891, photographed by Barraud

Thomas Hardy, *c.* 1894, photographed by Elliott & Fry

Right Emma Hardy in late
middle age

Below Hardy in the garden at
Max Gate, *c.* 1900, photographed by Clive Holland

Dublin to Kingstown on 28 May, and by way of Holyhead to
London on the 29th. On the boat to Holyhead they were joined
by Mrs Henniker and by General Milman, Keeper of the Tower
of London, and his daughter Lena, a young woman of some linguistic and literary accomplishments whom Hardy was to engage
in mildly flirtatious, if somewhat desultory, correspondence over
the next several months.[31]

Back at Hamilton Terrace the Hardys resumed their active
social lives. Hardy met Mrs Craigie, the able and beautiful woman
who wrote under the pseudonym of 'John Oliver Hobbes', and
Gosse's friend the Dutch novelist 'Maarten Maartens', whose real
name was J. van der Poorten Schwartz. He visited the Tower of
London under General Milman's guidance and accompanied
Emma, Lena Milman, Maarten Maartens, and James Barrie to a
performance of the latter's successful play, *Walker, London*. Mrs
Henniker was briefly in London that same week, and Hardy went
with her, and with her brother-in-law and sister, Sir Gerald and
Lady Fitzgerald, to see Ibsen's *The Master Builder*—having
already seen *Hedda Gabler* and *Rosmersholm* a few days previously. At the theatre Hardy found an opportunity for some private
conversation with Mrs Henniker and even for a declaration of
affection, evidently received with distinct coolness: he was trying,
he wrote on 10 June, to 'redress by any possible means the one-
sidedness I spoke of, of which I am still keenly conscious', adding,
with awkward formality, 'I sincerely hope to number you all my
life among the most valued of my friends.'[32]

He had by this time sent Mrs Henniker a handbook on the
history of architecture, recommending that she familiarize herself
with certain sections, and arranged a meeting later in the month
when he would conduct her through Westminster Abbey and
other buildings nearby: 'Oral instruction in actual buildings', he
rather transparently observed, 'is, of course, a much more rapid
and effectual method than from books, and you must not think it
will be any trouble to me.' He suggested a rendezvous at Sloane
Square underground station, not far from Cadogan Gardens,
where Mrs Henniker was staying with her sister, and they seem to
have met there once or twice again in early July, during another
of Mrs Henniker's short trips up to town: her husband was at
that time stationed at Portsmouth and they had taken a house at
Southsea. The intervals between these meetings Hardy did his best
to fill with correspondence, and while Mrs Henniker's letters for
this period have all disappeared it is clear from those of Hardy's

that are still extant (some were destroyed by Mrs Henniker, others perhaps by Hardy after her death) that she was keeping him very much at arm's length, declining either deliberately or through simple unawareness to be drawn into exchanges of a romantic or potentially physical nature: 'Well—perhaps you are right [he wrote on 20 June] about the story of the two people spiritually united—as far as the man is concerned.' Hardy's grudging tone suggests that he was seeking something more concrete than spiritual affinity, and while later letters speak of his trying 'desperately' to dispel the intensity of his emotions by distractions and occupations of various kinds, the frequency and explicitness of such allusions, together with the confessions of 'poor results', reveal a lingering hope that his persistence will in the end be rewarded, that his correspondent will soften—at least to the extent of engaging in a sympathetic dialogue.[33]

Nor did Mrs Henniker remain entirely immune to such implicit appeals. Whatever her motives in giving Hardy, on 30 June, some of her verse translations from the French and Spanish, Hardy himself could scarcely have been blamed for interpreting as coquettish, or even cruelly teasing, the receipt of such lines as these:

> We were together,—her eyes were wet,
> But her pride was strong, & no tears would fall;
> And *I* would not tell her I loved her yet,
> And yearned to forgive her all!
>
> So, now that our lives are for ever apart,
> *She* thinks—"Oh! had I but wept that day!"
> And *I* ask in vain of my lonely heart—
> "Ah! why did I turn away?"[34]

And when, a little later, Hardy threatened, with ostensible playfulness, to give lessons in architecture to other attractive women of their acquaintance, she evidently responded with a gratifying (if mock-serious) display of jealousy: 'I will religiously obey orders about the architectural lessons,' Hardy wrote on 16 July. 'You shall hold the copyright in them. Is not that promise very handsome of me?' The remainder of that same letter, however, shows plainly enough that Hardy had already begun to realize that Mrs Henniker's views upon morality in general and marriage in particular were likely to prove too rigidly conventional to allow of any relationship that went beyond the strictly 'platonic'. Discover-

ing that they had both been reading Shelley's 'Epipsychidion'
Hardy expressed, with some sternness, his regret

> that one who is pre-eminently the child of the Shelleyean tradi-
> tion—whom one would have expected to be an ardent disciple
> of his school and views—should have allowed herself to be en-
> feebled to a belief in ritualistic ecclesiasticism. My impression
> is that you do not know your own views. You feel the need of
> emotional expression of some sort, and being surrounded by the
> conventional society form of such expression you have mechani-
> cally adopted it. Is this the daughter of the man who went from
> Cambridge to Oxford on the now historic errand! Depend upon
> it there are other values for feeling than the ordinances of
> Mother Church—my Mother Church no less than yours.

Hardy's allusion to her father's advocacy of Shelley suggests how
much his investment in Mrs Henniker had been of a theoretical
kind; so, equally, does a veiled reference, in the same letter, to
his earlier disappointment in Rosamund Tomson and his conclusion that he must, in future, 'trust to imagination only for an
enfranchised woman'.[35]

The Hardys left London for Dorchester in the first half of
July, but on the 19th Hardy went back alone to stay once more
with the Jeunes, taking a roundabout route in order to spend a
few hours with Mrs Henniker in Southsea.[36] On 5 August he
copied into a notebook some lines taken from Dante Gabriel
Rossetti's 'Spheral Change' in the copy of his *Poetical Works* just
given him by Mrs Henniker:

> O dearest, while we lived and died
> A living death in every day,
> Some hours we still were side by side
> When where I was you too might stay
> And rest and need not go away.
> O nearest, furthest! can there be
> At length some hard-earned heart-won home
> Where—exile changed to sanctuary—
> Our lot may fill indeed its sum,
> And you may wait, and I may come?[37]

The sentiment is in some respects strikingly similar to that of
Hardy's own poem 'At an Inn', based on the visit he and Mrs
Henniker paid together to Winchester on 8 August. They met at
Eastleigh, a railway junction just north of Southampton, and

Mrs Henniker seems immediately to have made it clear, once and for all, that things could not be as Hardy wished. As the poem 'The Month's Calendar' puts it: 'You let me see / There was good cause / Why you could not be / Aught ever to me!'[38] Arrived in Winchester, they lunched at the George Inn,* attended Evensong in the cathedral, and walked a little way out of the town to the spot from which, at the end of *Tess,* Angel and Liza-Lu watch the black flag rise above the prison in confirmation of Tess's execution. It was a pilgrimage sadly appropriate to Hardy's mood. As 'At an Inn' so painfully suggests, a meeting which had all the external appearance of a lovers' tryst proved in fact to be something very different: 'Yet never the love-light shone / Between us there! / But that which chilled the breath / Of afternoon, / And palsied unto death / The pane-fly's tune.' On 17 August, alluding to an indiscreet (and now vanished) letter he had sent her two weeks earlier, Hardy wrote: 'If I shd never write to you again as in that letter you must remember that it was written *before* you expressed your views—"morbid" indeed! *petty* rather—in the railway carriage when we met at Eastleigh.'[40]

Mrs Henniker's views did not, however, drive Hardy away. Another poem associated with her, 'In Death Divided', affirms 'The eternal tie which binds us twain in one', while 'The Division', reflecting the immediate aftermath of the Winchester meeting, implies an ideal relationship rendered unattainable only by 'that thwart thing betwixt us twain'—evidently to be identified with 'that which chilled the breath / Of afternoon' in 'At an Inn', where it is in turn associated with the barriers imposed by the 'laws of men'. Clearly, the sexual element in that relationship was not all-important to Hardy, and had perhaps not been dominant even at their first encounter: as 'A Thunderstorm in Town' suggests, and as Florence Hardy once confirmed, Hardy and Mrs Henniker never exchanged a single kiss, although Hardy, confiding in Clodd three years after the event, spoke of their clasping hands beside the high altar in Winchester Cathedral.[41] Since, indeed, it is not at all clear what conclusions Hardy had projected for his courtship, Mrs Henniker's unresponsiveness may even have been a source of unacknowledged relief. At the same time, the experience, in all its delusive excitement and ultimate disappointment, left a legacy of personal pain and of renewed hos-

* When Mrs Henniker wanted to wash her hands a servant, assuming that she and Hardy were married, showed them both into a bedroom.[39]

tility to those imprisoning aspects of marriage already cruelly portrayed in the pages of *The Pursuit of the Well-Beloved*. It also left a body of highly usable emotional material similar in kind to Hardy's regret for Louisa, Tryphena, and all the other lost prizes of earlier days, and of an intensity only to be exceeded by that grieving and guilty response to the death of Emma which produced the 'Poems of 1912–13'.

Most moving, perhaps, of all the poems associated with Mrs Henniker, and certainly eloquent of Hardy's longer view of the relationship, is the second stanza of 'A Broken Appointment':

> You love not me,
> And love alone can lend you loyalty;
> —I know and knew it. But, unto the store
> Of human deeds divine in all but name,
> Was it not worth a little hour or more
> To add yet this: Once you, a woman, came
> To soothe a time-torn man; even though it be
> You love not me?

The poem is fascinating in itself as an example of Hardy's capacity to evolve verse of almost classical elegance out of such essentially humdrum material—as an instance, too, of marvellously enriching revision, in that substitution of 'time-torn' for the earlier 'soul-sad'.[42] But it implicitly brings against Mrs Henniker a charge of hardness, of selfishness, of a lack of what the first stanza calls 'loving kindness' (always one of the most fundamental of Hardyan positives), and she does indeed seem—for all her charm and her passionate advocacy of humanitarian causes—to have been a little lacking in personal warmth: Florence Hardy, who was very fond of her, once said of Sir George Douglas that he appreciated Mrs Henniker, 'as few did'. She certainly showed some insensitivity—as Hardy did not hesitate to inform her—in reading out portions of some of his letters to her family and friends.[43] And yet she could scarcely have known, and probably never did know, the depth and complexity of Hardy's feelings for her, the extent to which he had so unreasonably focused upon her the accumulated dreams and desires of so many disappointed years.

In late August 1893 Hardy and Emma travelled to Shropshire to spend a few days with Catherine Milnes-Gaskell and her husband at Wenlock Abbey, where Hardy enjoyed Lady Catherine's attractive company, talked sexual politics on the basis of her confession that she had once engaged in a 'wanton' flirtation, and indulged his melancholia by discussing with her 'suicide, pessimism, whether life was worth living, and kindred dismal subjects'. Such topics were extremely germane to the new novel on which he would shortly begin working—having already visited Oxford in June to get the flavour of the Commemoration festivities.[44] Prior commitments, however, required that the first weeks after the return to Max Gate at the end of August should be devoted to work on short stories.

On 14 September he sent off to Colles the manuscript of 'An Imaginative Woman', the story of a romance-that-never-was between a publishing poet and an 'impressionable, palpitating' young married woman with literary ambitions of her own. The poet, Robert Trewe—given in the manuscript the maiden name, Crewe, of Mrs Henniker's mother—is strikingly similar to Hardy himself in his extreme sensitivity to unfair criticism ("lies that he's powerless to refute and stop from spreading") and in being 'a pessimist in so far as that character applies to a man who looks at the worst contingencies as well as the best in the human condition'. A reference to Trewe's 'mournful ballad on "Severed Lives" ' strongly suggests that 'The Division' and perhaps 'At an Inn' were already in existence, and while Ella Marchmill does not especially resemble Mrs Henniker—except in having eyes whose 'marvellously bright and liquid sparkle' is said to be characteristic of persons of an imaginative 'cast of soul'—a connection is unmistakably established by the militariness of her surname, by her husband's occupation of 'gunmaker', and by the use of Solentsea (i.e., Southsea) as a setting. That the story was in certain limited respects an ironic reworking of Hardy's recent emotional adventure seems clear enough; on the other hand, its affinities with *The Well-Beloved* suggest that *Later Years,* though wrong in dating Hardy's composition of the story, may be right in suggesting that its essential features had been sketched at an earlier date.[45]

Just over a week later another story, 'A Tryst at an Ancient Earthwork', which had earlier been published in America but not in England, was exhumed, refurbished, and sent off to the *English Illustrated Magazine* in response to the importunities of one of its editors, Hardy's recent and irrepressible acquaintance Clement Shorter.[46] Edward Cunnington, the 'original' of the archaeologist in the story, was still alive, but Hardy had in the meantime become much more prepared to 'publish and be damned', and it does not in fact appear that any repercussions followed the English publication, even though the Maiden Castle setting was specifically identified in accompanying photographs. In October, after a few pleasant days spent with the Jeunes at their country house near Newbury, Hardy gathered together the printed serial texts of the nine stories which were to make up a new volume entitled *Life's Little Ironies*. Telling Mrs Henniker on 22 October 1893 that the stories were ready to go off to the publisher, Hardy added that he was now free to 'turn to the "Desire" ', the story on which they were jointly engaged.[47] The idea of a literary collaboration, first mooted at least as early as July, had gained impetus following Hardy's realization that the relationship was destined to remain at an intellectual level. Mrs Henniker, for her part, seems always to have emphasized their shared literary interests, perhaps as a way of deflecting the unwelcome pressures Hardy was bringing to bear upon her, certainly because she felt his support and advice would be helpful to her own career. Her gift, in September 1893, of the silver inkstand which can still be seen on Hardy's desk in the Dorset County Museum was practical enough in itself—'Oddly enough I am badly off in inkstands,' Hardy gallantly declared[48]—but it also hinted at the direction she felt his interest and activity might best take.

The story itself was essentially Hardy's work—compromised not so much by Mrs Henniker's participation as by Hardy's attempts to give that participation a greater substance than the circumstances really allowed. He provided an initial outline and suggested a number of alternative directions which the narrative might take, especially at the very end. He also indicated to Mrs Henniker points within that outline which she might like to fill out with passages of description. When she had expressed her preference in the matter of the ending and supplied some 'pages of detail', Hardy wrote out the story in its entirety, adopting the ending she had chosen—though with further modifications of his own—and incorporating such of her material as seemed compatible with 'the proportion of the whole'. The completed manuscript, now entitled 'The Spectre of the Real: An end-of-the-age Narrative', was then sent away to be typed, with instructions that the completed typescript should be sent directly to Mrs Henniker. She, meanwhile, was asked, on 28 October, to read the story through from the beginning, so as to be able to judge the effect of the modified ending, and to pencil in any changes or additions she thought necessary—especially to the account of the heroine's wedding morning, where she might be able to supply details 'that would only be known to a woman'. Although the typescript survives, the faintness or subsequent erasure of many of the pencil markings make it difficult to determine just which of the ink revisions inscribed by Hardy had been suggested by his collaborator; it is of some interest, however, that much the largest alteration made at this stage was the restoration of Mrs Henniker's 'description of the pool, & the bird tracks', whose previous omission had been somewhat apologetically noted in the letter of 28 October. The changes were sufficiently extensive to make a fresh typescript desirable, and it was the carbon copy of this second typescript, still further revised, which was sent off to Jerome K. Jerome's magazine *To-Day*, accompanied by a firm instruction in Hardy's own hand: '*To the printer*: Insert all *accents* & hyphens, & punctuation precisely as in copy. T.H.'[49]

Hardy had conducted the negotiations for the sale of 'The Spectre of the Real' through A. P. Watt, chiefly to encourage him to be active in future in Mrs Henniker's behalf. But Watt, as Hardy acknowledged to his collaborator on 1 December, got them a 'very fair' price for so short a tale—and, he might have added, for so sour an exploration of social and sexual mismatching, full of tonal and structural uncertainties, and with an ending abrupt, violent, and insufficiently prepared for.[50] Familiar Hardyan formulae are invoked—including one of those deaths by drowning in water-meadows which may have had their origin in the tales Hardy had heard as a child of his namesake's fatal tumble into the Stour—and his obsession with the evils of marriage obtrudes itself throughout in ways that Emma, once again, can only have found offensive, although she perhaps did not read the story until its publication in November 1894.

18

THE MAKING
OF *JUDE*

AMIDST all the activity of that autumn of 1893—including the writing of 'The Spectre of the Real' and the reading and criticizing of Mrs Henniker's own work—Hardy found time for a temporary resumption of his old profession of architect. Between August 1893 and May 1894 the little church of St. Peter's, West Knighton, in the Frome valley, was extensively renovated— the chancel re-roofed, the gallery rebuilt, an old arch uncovered and restored, and alterations made to some of the windows. The contractor for the job was Hardy's brother Henry, the architect and supervisor Hardy himself. Hardy's treatment of the windows imitated old forms in a fashion quite contrary to the official doctrines of the Society for the Protection of Ancient Buildings; even so, the restoration as a whole was carried out with a discretion and moderation which rendered it acceptable in practice even if objectionable in theory.[1] Hardy had long been in the habit of giving occasional assistance to his brother in what he no doubt still regarded as the family business, and it was in the early 1890s* that he designed Talbothays, approximately two miles

---

* Talbothays Lodge first appears in the electoral register (as owned by Henry Hardy and occupied by the Revd Claude Homan, curate at West Stafford) in 1894 and was presumably built in 1893.

east of Max Gate, as a house for Henry to build and live in. It was apparently the breaking off of a projected marriage which resulted in Henry's letting the house for several years; he himself moved in only in 1911, in company with Mary, Kate, and Polly Antell.[2]

Whether by accident or design, Hardy's involvement in the West Knighton project closely coincided with the writing of *Jude the Obscure,* with its stonemason hero and its deeply personal roots. The poem, 'The Young Glass-Stainer', written in November 1893 on the basis of the West Knighton experience, also has obvious links with *Jude*:

> 'These Gothic windows, how they wear me out
> With cusp and foil, and nothing straight or square,
> Crude colours, leaden borders roundabout,
> And fitting in Peter here, and Matthew there!
>
> 'What a vocation! Here do I draw now
> The abnormal, loving the Hellenic norm;
> Martha I paint, and dream of Hera's brow.
> Mary, and think of Aphrodite's form.'[3]

The work at West Knighton corresponded in some respects to Hardy's journeys to Oxford and especially to Great Fawley to get the 'feel' of the actuality he was about to transpose into fiction —to render himself receptive to all those numinous influences he was capable of absorbing from places associated with past events and personages known to him through recorded history or family tradition. By taking up pencil and measure once more, exposing himself to the sight and sound of building tradesmen at work, the feel and smell of the materials they used, Hardy could more readily think himself back into that period of the 1860s in which his new novel was set and those practical details of church renovation which entered into much of its action.

Although so much of the emotional impetus of *Jude* was to be derived from Hardy's own experience, its narrative materials were drawn from many different sources and periods—among them, his grandmother's early years in Berkshire, the lives and personalities of John Antell and Horace Moule, the joys and agonies of his recent relationship with Mrs Henniker. It was in April 1888, at the time of a House of Commons debate on secondary education and 'the ladder from the primary schools to the university', that Hardy conceived the idea of a short story about a young man unable to go to Oxford and about his subsequent struggles, failure, and suicide. According to the Preface to the first edition of *Jude,* the scheme of the novel was 'jotted down in 1890, from notes made in 1887 and onwards, some of the circumstances being suggested by the death of a woman in the former year',[4] and the assumption has generally been made that the woman was Hardy's cousin Tryphena. But there are—apart from her college and teaching experiences—few significant similarities between Tryphena's life and Sue Bridehead's in the book, and Hardy perhaps had in mind the execution, on 23 December 1890, of twenty-four-year-old Mary Wheeler, also known as Mrs Pearcey, found guilty three weeks earlier of the murder of the wife and child of Frank Hogg, a man whom she had known for several years. The murder, carried out with considerable brutality, attracted much public interest, and Hardy, happening to arrive in London on the day of the verdict, mentioned in a letter to Emma that people everywhere were reading about it in the newspapers. A remarkable feature of the case, specifically commented upon by a leader writer in *The Times,* was the fact that Mary Wheeler's feelings for Frank Hogg seemed not to be of a sexual nature: the emphasis—as in Sue's relationships with the Christminster undergraduate and, later, with Jude himself—was all on 'friendship', on the maintenance of a kind of intimate comradeship. Given the centrality to *Jude* of the notion of an 'illicit' relationship not based on sexuality—given, too, the purely circumstantial nature of the evidence against Mary Wheeler, her youth and obvious intelligence, and the violence of her own death—it is tempting to think that Hardy was so deeply affected by what he read of the case that it became an integral part of the imaginative and emotional context of his most socially conscious novel. If so, the hereditary flaw in Jude's family may have had something to do with the newspaper story, later denied, that Mary Wheeler's father had himself been hanged for murder ten years previously.[5]

Although the death of Hardy's aunt Mary, the widow of John Antell, in November 1891,[6] cannot have been the occasion referred to in the *Jude* Preface, it nevertheless brought back for Hardy memories of the period in the late 1860s when he had spent a good deal of time in Puddletown, attracted there by the presence both of his cousin Tryphena and of the more darkly fascinating personality of his uncle by marriage, John Antell the shoemaker. An enigmatic and undated notebook entry—'Poem.

"The man who had no friend"—Auto. by John A–tell Sen. cf. "The Two Leaders." Swin.'[7]*—indicates that Hardy continued to think about his uncle and about the way in which he had been driven to drinking and violence, to isolation and self-disgust, and ultimately to an early grave, largely as a consequence of society's denial of any opportunity to develop his many and considerable talents.

That same Preface to *Jude* speaks of the final version of the novel as having been written 'from August 1893 onwards into the next year', but the crowding events of the latter half of 1893 effectively prevented Hardy from making much initial progress: 'What name shall I give to the heroine of my coming long story when I get at it?' he asked Mrs Henniker on 22 October. 'I don't quite know when that will be, though it must be this winter.' In mid-November, when he was tentatively negotiating with the *Graphic,* through Colles, and with the *Illustrated London News,* through Clement Shorter, he told the latter that the story was still in too chaotic a state for him to be able to estimate its eventual length. Writing to Mrs Henniker again on 1 December he confessed himself reluctant to get down to serious work on his manuscript, but added: 'However, as it is one I planned a couple of years ago I shall, I think, go on with it, & probably shall warm up.'[9] Early in that same month he came to terms with Harper & Brothers over the sale of all serial rights, an arrangement which avoided the necessity of supplying duplicate copy for a separate American printing and had the added convenience of allowing him to work through his English publishers, Osgood, McIlvaine, who acted as English agents for Harper and as publishers of the European edition of *Harper's New Monthly Magazine.*[10]

Intensive work on the manuscript now began—'I am burying myself alive here in hope of doing a little writing,' he wrote Lena Milman from Max Gate on 23 December—and by mid-January 1894 he could report to Mrs Henniker that he was 'creeping on a little' and getting interested in his heroine as she took on 'shape & reality', even though she remained 'very nebulous at present'.[11] Such progress brought its problems, however. He had assured Harper & Brothers that the novel would not offend 'the most fastidious maiden', but in early April he felt obliged to inform them that he was being carried 'into unexpected fields'

* Hardy presumably had in mind the line 'With all our hearts we praise you whom ye hate', one of those he particularly remembered on the day of Swinburne's funeral in 1909.[8]

and dared not predict 'its future trend'. He offered—'promptly and magnanimously', as J. Henry Harper later acknowledged—either to cancel their agreement or to allow the firm to make such changes in the serial as they felt to be necessary. Harper chose the latter alternative and Hardy agreed to do some rewriting, with the result that the serial version actually published between December 1894 and November 1895 was severely and, in some respects, ludicrously watered down. Episodes such as the pig-killing and Arabella's seduction of Jude were modified or omitted altogether; Jude and Sue were obliged to live not together but 'near'; and the one child (instead of two) murdered by Father Time was Sue's by adoption only. The criterion invoked was wearisomely familiar: the publishers, wrote H. M. Alden, the editor of *Harper's New Monthly Magazine,* on 29 August 1894, were 'pledged' to print 'nothing which could not be read aloud in any family circle'. 'You will see for yourself our difficulty', he went on, 'and we fully appreciate the annoyance you must feel at being called upon to modify work conscientiously done, and which is best as it left your hands, from an artist's point of view. I assure you that I felt properly ashamed for every word of protest I had to write to you. . . .'[12] Hardy had long learned the virtues of compromise in such situations, and as recently as January 1894 he had told the editor of the *Pall Mall Magazine* that he was quite willing to delete an offending passage from the text of 'An Imaginative Woman' and always gave editors a free hand in such matters, 'as I invariably reprint from the original copy for the book-form of my novels'.[13] Textually, the serial of *Jude* is of importance only in so far as Hardy did not in the end—despite his comment to the editor of the *Pall Mall Magazine*—restore all of its bowdlerizing changes. But it was a significant and painful episode in his personal history, and contributed its share of bitterness to his long-standing and still-accumulating dissatisfaction with the novel-writer's trade.

When the first instalment of the novel appeared in *Harper's* it was called 'The Simpletons', but someone pointed out that Charles Reade had already published (and in *Harper's*) a novel called *A Simpleton* in the early 1870s. Hardy then reverted to his earlier, discarded title 'Hearts Insurgent', and it was under that distressingly lurid heading that the remainder of the serial appeared—Hardy's third thought, 'The Recalcitrants', having reached New York only after the second instalment had gone to press.[14] The initial choice of 'Hearts Insurgent' as a title strongly suggests that the two central themes of the novel—education and marriage—were both in Hardy's mind from the first. The evidence of the surviving manuscript has been read as indicating, on the one hand, that the marriage theme was initially dominant, or, quite to the contrary, that the education theme had first place in Hardy's mind; it seems more likely that Hardy always conceived of his central characters as challenging conventional assumptions in both areas, and that his problem, as he tried to get the novel under way, was to establish plausible interconnections between the two. It was clear that Jude had to go to Christminster; it was also necessary that he fall in love with his cousin; the puzzle—only temporarily troublesome—was to justify Sue's presence in Christminster and allow a meeting to take place. If, as appears, Phillotson had originally no part in the opening pages of the manuscript, that was perhaps because there were other ways of setting Jude on the road to Christminster;[15] the subsequent introduction of the schoolmaster followed upon Hardy's realization of his potential usability *both* as a partner in the sexual quadrille and as a motivator of Jude's educational ambitions in the first chapter.

Jude seems, in the manuscript, to have been first called Jack, with a glance towards John Antell. But Hardy had on his shelves a copy of Charlotte M. Yonge's then standard *History of Christian Names*,[16] and in finally deciding to call his hero Jude he was well aware of the ill omen attaching to the name because of its similarity to Judas Iscariot. Indeed he drew deliberately upon that association, and perhaps upon the idea of the Wandering Jew, to establish from the first the sense of his hero as doomed to perpetual homelessness and pariah-hood. The surname was at one time Head, after Hardy's grandmother, at another Hopeson, a heavily allegorized version of her mother's maiden name of Hopson (or Hobson), and went through other variations before becoming fixed as Fawley, the name of the village from which Mary Head had come. The direct family reference thus removed from the name of the hero reappeared in the surname of the heroine, Sue Bridehead, and in the name, Marygreen, given to the village from which Jude sets out on his journey in search of knowledge and self-knowledge. Jude, as individual and as representative figure, was clearly present in Hardy's imagination from the first. He was the embodiment of, almost a scapegoat for, a long accumulation of personal and family distress—the poverty and violence suffered by Hardy's ancestors (including his mother and both his grandmothers), John Antell's anger against the world and its creator, and Hardy's own struggles for education, advancement, and sexual happiness. Hardy's troubled memories of Horace Moule's tragic alternations between intellectuality and sensuality may also have made a contribution, and Moule's alleged son in Australia is no doubt as plausible a candidate as the displaced child at Sturminster station (see above, p. 190) for the 'original' of Jude's son, Father Time.

But if Jude has obvious links with Hardy's biography, and even shadowy antecedents—the schoolmaster of 'An Indiscretion in the Life of an Heiress' and, beyond him, the hero of *The Poor Man and the Lady*—within Hardy's work, Sue's origins remain less clear. Although Hardy's heroines had often been exasperating creatures, given to flirtation and various forms of deliberate and innocent sexual teasing, they had rarely exhibited any fundamental uncertainty as to their suitability for, or willing acceptance of, the traditional female roles. The obvious exception had been Paula Power of *A Laodicean,* whose self-repressive austerity (befitting her name) and sexual 'Laodiceanism' strikingly anticipate elements in Sue Bridehead and hence offer an implicit commentary on Hardy's observation, 'Sue is a type of woman which has always had an attraction for me—but the difficulty of drawing the type has kept me from attempting it till now.' A version of the 'type' had evidently been in Hardy's mind at least as early as 1881, although his presentation of it in *A Laodicean* had, like the rest of the novel, been compromised by his illness. What sharply distinguishes Paula from Sue, however, is the depth of her emotional commitment to Charlotte De Stancy, her 'more than sister':[17] Sue, for all her fastidiousness in her relations with men, shows no such compensating preference for members of her own sex.

Hardy, in fact, pointedly eschewed an obvious opportunity for the exploration of Sue's relationships with women of her own age. Melchester Training College, which Sue attends, was directly based on the Salisbury training college which his two sisters had attended, and where Kate, in particular, had been bitterly unhappy: 'I dont mind if Tom publishes how badly we were used,' she had once declared. Mary's resentment seems to have been modified by memories of college friendships, and when she wrote to commiserate with her cousin, Nathaniel Sparks, on the death of his wife, she recalled how Annie Lanham (as she then was) had been one of her fellow pupils at Salisbury: 'I seem to see her now. She was rather delicate and fragile and so unassuming, yet so intelligent and sensible. Her bedroom was next to mine and we used to say "Good night" before going to bed,—dear, Sweet, gentle Annie!'[18] Hardy himself, visiting two London training colleges for women in 1891, had been moved by the thought of such friendships, and yet none appear in the novel as published. No significant relationship between Sue and any of the other girls is presented or mentioned, and the college thus becomes little more than a mildly repressive prison from which she escapes, a set of conventions against which she deliberately offends.

Probably the training college would not be in the novel at all if it were not for its association with Mary, and for the dependence of Hardy's presentation of the intimacy between Jude and Sue upon his own sense of Mary as his 'earliest playmate—a kind little sister, sharing with him, gladly, all she had, proud of him beyond words'. Given the isolation, both geographical and temperamental, within which Hardy and Mary grew up, that early sharing necessarily became a kind of defensive alliance against a largely uncomprehending world, approaching at its happiest moments the marriage of true minds which Jude and Sue achieve at the time of the Great Wessex Agricultural Show, when they seem 'almost the two parts of a single whole': in the poem 'Conjecture', indeed, Mary is spoken of in the same breath as Hardy's actual wives: 'If there were in my kalendar / No Emma, Florence, Mary, / What would be my existence now—.'[19]

Phillotson also speaks of Jude and Sue as resembling 'one person split in two', attributing the phenomenon partly to their cousinship. But cousinship in the novel was perhaps an available metaphor for confronting a still closer degree of consanguinity, and to think of Jude's early identification with Sue as deriving validity and force from Hardy's feelings for Mary does at least provide a context for the deletion from the manuscript of the passage in which Jude looks at the sleeping Sue and sees in her 'the rough material called himself done into another sex—idealized, softened, & purified'. It certainly lends point to Phillotson's comparison of Jude and Sue to Laon and Cythna, in Shelley's *The Revolt of Islam*. Shelley, after all, had first conceived of Laon and Cythna as brother and sister, and Hardy's habitual idealization of the relation between the sexes in Shelleyan terms seems to have depended heavily upon his own memories (themselves no doubt idealized) of the perfect understanding that had existed between Mary and himself in early childhood. It was perhaps of her that he was chiefly thinking when, in the copy of Shelley he carried with him during his days at Blomfield's, he marked with particular emphasis stanza 23 of the second Canto of *The Revolt of Islam*, in which Cythna is described as 'a shape of brightness' who 'did seem / Beside me, gathering beauty as she grew, / Like the bright shade of some immortal dream / Which walks, when tempest sleeps, the wave of life's dark stream'.[20]

In deliberately insisting, within the novel itself, upon Sue's full name, Susanna Florence Mary Bridehead, Hardy was thus incorporating an acknowledgement of his principal 'sources' for her characterization. He may have chosen the name Susanna for its meaning of 'lily' or (instructed once more by Charlotte M. Yonge) in allusion to the virgin martyrs who once bore it; on the other hand, Tess Durbeyfield was once to have been called Sue, and the name evidently had a special significance for Hardy, perhaps because of the romantic associations surrounding the local memory of Lady Susan O'Brien. The names Florence and Mary, however, point directly towards Florence Henniker and Mary Hardy, and what first took Hardy and the *Jude* manuscript into 'unexpected fields' was no doubt his growing awareness of the extent to which an initial Mary/Sue conception could be expanded and enriched by drawing upon his recent experiences with the unresponsive Mrs Henniker, and made, thus transformed, a central element in Jude's final tragedy rather than a mere elusive contrast to the destructive sexuality of Arabella.

Hardy's second title, 'The Simpletons', signalled a shift of emphasis to the idealistic folly of a young couple who attempt to share a private and independent life, isolated from the values and prejudices of the society which surrounds them; it also reflected wryly upon his doomed attempts to create an oasis of satisfaction within the desert his own marriage had increasingly become. 'Let us off and search, and find a place / Where yours and mine can be natural lives': so begins the poem, 'The Recalcitrants',[21] which preserves another of the abandoned titles for *Jude*. This is the grand motive of the life which Jude and Sue try to make together; that the attempt is doomed is implicit in its fictional premises— and in Hardy's personal recognition, painfully soon after meeting Mrs Henniker, that he would be wise to 'trust to imagination only for an enfranchised woman'. If, too, the book's implied judgement of Sue's character and conduct seems finally uncertain or inconsistent, that again can perhaps be related to the duality of Hardy's inspiration—what can be admired in a sister must sometimes be deplored in a mistress—and to that mixture of affection and resentment which marked his entire relationship with Mrs Henniker once she had clearly established the boundaries that must not be transgressed.

To these speculations may be added another, partly contradictory, partly supplementary: the possibility that Emma—with a sense of the deepest betrayal—may have recognized aspects of herself in the presentation both of Arabella and of Sue. If 'The Place on the Map' is indeed to be associated with Hardy and Emma, then the episode is in some degree echoed in Arabella's trick of the false pregnancy. If Emma, as Hardy once declared, was indeed free-thinking at the time he first met her, then Sue's decline from brilliant independence to bleak religiosity in some measure reflected Hardy's sense of such a progression in his own wife. There is a family tradition—and it makes for a plausible if unprovable hypothesis—that Hardy was sexually impotent, and that the difficulties of his marriage are largely attributable to that cause.[22]* But Hardy himself, in extreme old age, is said to have told Edmund Blunden that he had remained capable of sexual intercourse to the age of eighty-four, and it is at least worth considering the possibility that the failure was chiefly on Emma's part, that the sexual freedom shown during courtship was replaced after marriage by sexual 'nervousness', by real or affected fears and disabilities. Although Bridehead is a Dorset place-name, it seems within the novel to embody a deliberate play on 'maidenhead' and hence to hint at Sue's essential virginity even within marital or quasi-marital situations; if that was also Emma's case, it could have been of her that Hardy was thinking when he told Gosse that there was 'nothing perverted or depraved in Sue's nature. The abnormalism consists in disproportion: not in inversion, her sexual instinct being healthy so far as it goes, but unusually weak & fastidious; her sensibilities remain painfully alert notwithstanding, (as they do in nature with such women).'[24] If Mrs Henniker was the immediate 'model' for Sue, as Hardy once acknowledged in conversation with Edward Clodd, and her personality the key to that 'difficulty of drawing the type' which had deterred him from attempting it up to this time,[25] that was evi-

* It has also been speculated, on the basis of materials found among the papers of the late Harold Hoffman, that Hardy believed he had, or carried, some kind of hereditary disease.[23]

dently by virtue of her demonstration that the woman of fastidious sexual instincts might also be a woman of intellectual gifts—hence capable of articulating her situation in intellectual terms.

Whether or not Emma was privy to the composition of *Jude,* she was certainly aware of her husband's friendship with Mrs Henniker. He seems, indeed, to have made no secret of it, mentioning the meeting in Winchester to Rebekah Owen within a few weeks of its taking place. Some degree of publicity, after all, was needed to give validity to its status as a literary collaboration, and Mrs Henniker, who had neither desire nor motive for secrecy, put Hardy's name on the dedication page of her short-story volume, *Outlines,* published at the end of 1893. However much, or little, Emma knew or guessed about the deeper levels of Hardy's emotional engagement in the affair, she became disturbed and jealous, not least because of the slur which Hardy's collaboration with another woman seemed to cast upon her own literary pretensions. She had attempted to write before this time—'The Maid on the Shore', begun in the 1870s, seems to have been completed in the late 1880s—and early in 1894 she sought to place some of her work through the literary agent A. P. Watt, the very man whom Hardy had entrusted with the cultivation of Mrs Henniker's career.[26] Nothing seems to have come of that particular initiative —though she was to publish a few poems and articles later on— but it was significant of a growing tendency on Emma's part to assert her independence, to try to live a life separate from her husband's, and even in opposition to it.

The withdrawal into the Max Gate attic was still some way in the future—the attic itself had not yet been built—but the open criticism of her husband in conversation and letters began at this time, and she became increasingly taken up with a local social life in which Hardy himself took relatively little part, and with the prosecution of a variety of religious, humanitarian, and feminist causes. To her Evangelicalism, her instinctive compassion for the sufferings of animals, and her long-standing grievance against what she considered the socially demeaning aspects of her marriage* were now added a new enthusiasm for women's rights,

---

* 'A man who has humble relations', she told Clodd in 1895, 'shouldn't live in the place where he was brought up.' A few years later, talking to Desmond MacCarthy about her husband's family, she declared that the less one had to do with 'the peasant class' the better.[27]

based not so much upon theoretical principles (such as Sue Bridehead's reading of John Stuart Mill) as upon personal resentment against her husband and his governance. In taking up such causes she found not only outlets for her considerable energies but also convenient platforms for the harassment of her husband: 'His interest in the Suffrage Cause is nil, in spite of "Tess",' she wrote to Mary Haweis, probably in November 1894, '& his opinions on the woman question not in her favour—He understands only the women he *invents*—the others not at all—& he only writes for *Art,* though ethics show up.' Hardy's private protests against such outbursts only sharpened the growing estrangement, and led in their inevitable turn to an intensification of Emma's campaign: 'T.H. has always so much to say by voice, & pen', she rather touchingly protested to Rebekah Owen a few years later, 'that letter-writing is my only resource for having all the say to myself, & not hearing his eloquence dumbly.'[28]

Several times during the early years of their friendship Hardy and Mrs Henniker exchanged copies of books which interested them both, each making annotations for the other's benefit. A pocket edition of Browning, first given to Hardy by Mrs Henniker in July 1894, was one such volume, and it was presumably Hardy who drew the marginal line against the conclusion of 'Confessions': 'We loved, sir—used to meet: / How sad and bad and mad it was— / But then, how it was sweet!'[29] Another, earlier that same year, was *Keynotes,* a collection of short stories written by 'George Egerton', the pseudonym of Mrs Chavelita Clairmonte, who later married R. Golding Bright, Hardy's dramatic agent in the 1920s. The stories in *Keynotes* had created something of a sensation by the directness with which they treated of the relations between the sexes, and while Hardy's marginal annotations have to be read as contributions to the half-humorous debate being carried on with Mrs Henniker, they nevertheless indicate some hostility towards women in general or, at the least, a tendency to fall back upon the standard male attitudes of his time. Alongside a passage complaining of the common disregard of 'the eternal wildness, the untamed primitive savage temperament that lurks in the mildest, best woman', Hardy writes: 'This if fairly stated, is decidedly the *ugly* side of woman's nature.' And in a separate note on the word 'woman' in the same passage he adds: 'Hence her inferiority to man??' This conventional distinction between the grossness of sexuality and the delicacy of friendship recurs in his comment on the statement that men love women less when they speak the truth: 'This bears only on sensualism. It is untrue of man in his altruistic regard of woman as a fellow-creature; untrue of his *highest* affection for her.' His response to an observation on the unreality of men's imaginary conception of women more disturbingly reads: '*ergo*: *real* woman is abhorrent to man? hence the failure of matrimony??'[30]

Similar reservations about marriage as an institution, combined with the same assumption of male protectiveness towards women, appear in the contribution Hardy made in June 1894 to a *New Review* symposium on the desirability of informing young women of the facts of life prior to their necessary discovery of them in marriage. As practical measures, he recommended that 'a plain handbook on natural processes' and, subsequently, 'similar information on morbid contingencies' should be given to young people of both sexes: 'it has never struck me that the spider is invariably male and the fly invariably female.' He added, however, that this was to side-step 'the general question whether marriage, as we at present understand it, is such a desirable goal for all women as it is assumed to be; or whether civilisation can escape the humiliating indictment that, while it has been able to cover itself with glory in the arts, in literatures, in religions, and in the sciences, it has never succeeded in creating that homely thing, a satisfactory scheme for the conjunction of the sexes'.[31]

Despite the growing estrangement from Emma, the established patterns of Hardy's domestic life continued much as before. Throughout January and February 1894 he was at Max Gate, working on the *Jude* manuscript and playing his usual part in family and local affairs. In February, with Henry's assistance, he set up in Stinsford churchyard the tombstone he had designed for their father's grave. In April, as the result of an initiative taken by Robert Pearce Edgcumbe, he was elevated from his position as local magistrate to membership of the County bench and took his seat there for the first time.[32] He stayed at Lady Jeune's for a few March days (during which Emma, alone at Max Gate, was found by one friend to be in 'her *most* affable frame of mind') and met there and at Lady Londonderry's several of the leading politicians of the day, together with a sprinkling of journalists and soldiers. He took most pleasure, however, in a visit to the theatre with his hostess's daughters, Dorothy and Madeleine Stanley, by whom, as he told Emma, he was more amused than by the play itself:

' "I do hope it will be something very *risqué*" sd Dorothy. "So as to make our hair curl!"—the point of it being that they wd turn round & ask me *if it was risqué*—not knowing of their own judgment.'[33]

Life's Little Ironies was published by Osgood, McIlvaine in late February, to favourable reviews; shortly afterwards Hardy called on his publishers in order to negotiate a higher royalty (20 per cent on all copies sold instead of the 15 per cent he was getting for *Life's Little Ironies*) on the first edition of *Jude the Obscure*. There must also have been discussion of plans for the first collected edition of his novels, scheduled to appear following the expiration of the Sampson Low agreements that summer. He had in the meantime come to an amicable arrangement with the house of Macmillan by which they surrendered their (disputed) rights in *The Woodlanders* and *Wessex Tales* in return for the inclusion of all of Hardy's fiction (apart from the irrecoverable *Under the Greenwood Tree*) in their Colonial Edition. An agreement to this effect was signed by Hardy on 21 May 1894, after he had pointed out that the draft prepared by the publisher omitted *Desperate Remedies*—a book, he characteristically added, which always sold well.[34]

In mid-April 1894 Hardy and Emma moved into 16 Pelham Crescent, South Kensington, once again bringing with them their own servants from Max Gate. *Later Years* lists some of the many people of rank and fame Hardy encountered during the course of the season; it also mentions the frequency with which it was somehow deemed appropriate that he should, as the notorious author of *Tess,* be introduced to the reigning beauties of the day. He did not challenge that assumption, and Lady Jeune, well aware of his prejudice in favour of good-looking women, was careful when introducing him to the portrait-painter Winifred Thomson to insist that she was 'a *very* nice girl clever pleasant your sort but *not* pretty'.[35] Hardy did indeed find Miss Thomson congenial; he praised the portrait she painted the following spring and wrote to her over a number of years in that slightly arch, mildly flirtatious style he reserved for women whom he liked but did not deeply care for. In late May, and no doubt at other times, he was able to see something of Mrs Henniker, and on 25 April he reminded Clement Shorter, as editor, that her *Outlines* had not yet been reviewed in the *Sketch*—a piece of frank 'log-rolling' to which Shorter responded not only with the requested review but also with a full-page portrait of Mrs Henniker herself. Another portrait, in the *Illustrated London News,* was accompanied by an unsigned account of Mrs Henniker's career which was in fact Hardy's own work, praising in her writing qualities closely akin to that 'intuitiveness' he had first registered in her personality—'emotional imaginativeness, lightened by a quick sense of the odd, and by touches of observation lying midway between wit and humour'.[36]

Hardy made a number of short expeditions out of London during that spring of 1894. On 30 April he went with Clodd to dine with Meredith at Box Hill. In mid-May he joined Grant Allen the novelist and Edward Whymper the Alpinist in another weekend visit to Clodd's house at Aldeburgh, telling Clodd during a confidential talk of 'restrictions on his travelling about with a lady' and of his view that a woman should have the freedom to choose the father of her child, males being required to contribute to the support of all children.[37] In mid-June he went down to Dorchester for a few days to make arrangements for the extensions to Max Gate—a new kitchen and scullery, with a new study for himself above, and two small attics above that—which were to be carried out during the autumn. Emma, who had been unwell, took the opportunity to go off by herself to Hastings, to enjoy the sea air and put into practice her new programme of independence. Hardy, too, was beginning at fifty-four to feel some of the effects of increasing age. At dinner at Lady Jeune's one evening in May he talked until his throat was tired, a recurring problem which contributed largely to that quietness of speech noted by many people who met him, and when moving out of 16 Pelham Crescent at the end of July he hurt his back while dragging a heavy portmanteau downstairs.[38]

Work on 'The Simpletons', as it was still called, had continued intermittently in London during the spring and summer, much of it a matter of bowdlerizing copy already submitted. No more than a third of the novel had been written by the time he returned to Dorchester at the beginning of August; with serialization due to begin in December, completion of the remaining two-thirds began to take on a certain urgency. The mid-September 1894 date on a surviving drawing of 'Old Grove's Place', Shaftesbury, the house to which Phillotson takes Sue after their marriage, provides a possible clue to the stage of the narrative Hardy was then approaching, but the final pages, according to the date on the manuscript itself, were not written until March 1895[39]—largely because Hardy's ostensibly reclusive existence at Max Gate was subject in fact to a whole series of personal and professional distractions. He spent more than a week in London in October, sat on the bench at the County Petty Sessions on three occasions during the course of the autumn, and made his regular Sunday visits to Bockhampton, where his mother, now in her early eighties, was still capable of producing for her son's benefit an anecdote she had not previously told, or of singing the ballads she had heard and sung as a girl at Melbury Osmond and as a young woman at Stinsford.[40] A constant disturbance was the building in progress at Max Gate itself. On 13 November Emma complained that her husband's writing obliged them to stay in the house while work went forward. Twelve days later Hardy explained to H. Macbeth-Raeburn, the artist, that because of the alterations they were 'huddled into fewer rooms than usual' and thus unable to offer him a bed when he came down to discuss the pictorial frontis-pieces he had been commissioned to prepare for the forthcoming Osgood, McIlvaine collected edition.[41]

Especially demanding in time and energy was the textual work on that edition and on the various volumes in Macmillan's Colo-nial series. As the proofs of the latter arrived at Max Gate that autumn Hardy told Frederick Macmillan that he was inserting the corrections he had in mind for the forthcoming uniform edi-tion—an indication that well before the end of 1894 he had already completed, and inscribed in copies of the Sampson Low and other recent printings, the revisions later incorporated in the Osgood, McIlvaine edition of 1895–7. At the beginning of 1895, with *Jude* still unfinished, he had to turn his attention to the prefaces to the new edition—that to *Tess* is dated January 1895, three months before the book itself was published and the edition initiated.[42] Hardy's textual revisions were largely, though by no means exclusively, designed to make the topographical references in the different works more consistent one with another and thus to enhance that sense of imaginative and regional coherence he had sought to emphasize in the title, 'Wessex Novels', chosen for the Osgood, McIlvaine edition as a whole. The prefaces, written over a period of more than a year and a half, reflect Hardy's genial contemplation of the fictional world he had created over the previous quarter-century and was now about to leave permanently behind him.

The decision to work in terms not simply of an underlying

regional conception but of a distinct, internally coherent fictional entity—an imaginative construct grounded in geographical actuality—had been made at least as early as the serialization of *Far from the Madding Crowd*. As Hardy recalled when writing the Preface to that novel in February 1895: 'The series of novels I projected being mainly of the kind called local, they seemed to require a territorial definition of some sort to lend unity to their scene. Finding that the area of a single county did not afford a canvas large enough for this purpose, and that there were objections to an invented name, I disinterred the old one.'[43] Although Hardy was, strictly speaking, anticipated by William Barnes in his use of Wessex in a contemporary sense, he was certainly justified in claiming credit for the term's subsequent popularity, its acceptance 'as a practical provincial definition', and the transformation of a 'dream-country' into an actual, visitable place—a process that has gone still further in the twentieth century than it had done at the end of the nineteenth.[44] In 1895 the earliest Wessex maps had just begun to appear, and the first such map specifically authorized by Hardy was published in the Osgood, McIlvaine edition—the earliest volumes already displaying in their maps such locations as Marygreen and Alfredston, even though it was several months before *Jude* itself appeared, for the first time in book form, as the edition's eighth volume.

There had been a certain element of commercial shrewdness in Hardy's initial perception of the possible advantages of creating a separate fictional world: he was well aware of the precedents set by Scott, by Balzac, and especially by Trollope. But the invention and progressive elaboration of Wessex also answered magnificently to his needs as a novelist and his strategies as a regionalist, validating above all his adoption of an essentially pastoral approach—his mediation, with an almost Wordsworthian moral intent, between rural subject matter and urban audience, between a world still in touch with at least the memory of traditional values and ways of life and a society caught up in a succession of new excitements, inventions, and controversies. Wessex also provided a framework for the deliberately historical aspects of his writing, the endeavour to record as faithfully as possible the details of a vanishing way of life: 'At the dates represented in the various narrations things were like that in Wessex.'[45]

So, in 1894, he assured Edward Clodd that 'every superstition, custom, &c., described in my novels may be depended on as true records of the same (whatever merit in folklorists eyes they may

have as such)—& not inventions of mine'. The material immediately in question, the folk beliefs incorporated into 'The Superstitious Man's Story' from *Life's Little Ironies,* had been drawn,
like so much else, from that 'old woman' his mother's memories
of Melbury Osmond.[46] Jemima, again, was presumably the 'aged
friend' of the April 1896 preface to *Wessex Tales,* who had known
the original of Rhoda Brook of 'The Withered Arm' and told the
author he had weakened the story by describing Rhoda as throwing off the incubus at night instead of in broad daylight, as had
actually occurred. Hardy agreed that 'the occurrence of such a
vision in the daytime is more impressive than if it had happened
in a midnight dream', and added, in an astonishing acknowledgement of his own theoretical and practical obsession with fidelity
of representation: 'Readers are therefore asked to correct the mis-
relation, which affords an instance of how our imperfect memories
insensibly formalize the fresh originality of living fact—from
whose shape they slowly depart, as machine-made castings depart
by degrees from the sharp hand-work of the mould.'[47] For Hardy
'living fact' had an integrity to which fiction could offer, at best,
a poor approximation, an authenticity which the novelist ignored
at his peril. Hence those many pocket-books and notebooks, and
the anxiety that impelled the correction of topographical details
in works already published.

But while he insisted that the backgrounds of the Wessex
novels had been 'done from the real', Hardy did not specifically
accept, even though he did not deny, the identification of Dorchester with Casterbridge, of Sturminster Newton with Stour-
castle, Weymouth with Budmouth, and so on. The basic geography
of the fictional Wessex was made recognizable by the use of the
real names of such natural features as rivers and hills (Stour,
Frome, High Stoy, Vale of Blackmoor), but Hardy reserved to
himself the freedom to adapt the details of topography for his
own novelistic purposes: as he once said of the historical settings
of *The Dynasts,* it was 'sometimes necessary to see round corners,
down crooked streets, & to shift buildings nearer each other than
in reality (as Turner did in his landscapes)'.[48] So Lucetta's house
was moved for Casterbridge purposes to a location some distance
from its Dorchester location next to the home the Hardys had
occupied in Shire-hall Lane; so the mill in *The Trumpet-Major*
combined features of two or three separate mills at Sutton Poyntz,
Lewell, and Upwey; so the barn in *Far from the Madding Crowd*
drew upon actual barns at Abbotsbury and Cerne Abbas.

Hardy visited some of the scenes of his novels in March 1895 in company with Macbeth-Raeburn—who also went to Cornwall to sketch Boscastle Harbour for *A Pair of Blue Eyes* and to Oxford for the frontispiece to *Jude*. At Easter, during a stay with Emma at the Jeunes' country house just north of Newbury, Hardy was also able to return once more to some of the villages associated with Mary Head—and with Jude Fawley.[49] The novel itself was now finished, even though the final title had still not been decided upon: in talking to Macbeth-Raeburn in March, Hardy had referred to it as 'The Simpletons'; in a Memorandum of Agreement dated 4 April 1895 he granted to Osgood, McIlvaine & Co., for a period of seven years, the exclusive British publication rights to a work called 'Hearts Insurgent' or 'such other title' as he, the author, might select.[50]

In the early spring of 1895 Hardy was still assisting Mrs Henniker with her literary endeavours—to the extent of contributing the concluding episode to her 'A Page from a Vicar's History' and then recommending the story to Clement Shorter for the *English Illustrated Magazine*[51]—but most of the time he could spare from his work on the Osgood, McIlvaine edition was being given to a dramatization of *Tess of the d'Urbervilles*. The popular success of *Tess,* and its obvious dramatic (not to say melodramatic) qualities, had provoked much talk of its possible adaptation to the stage, and Hardy was besieged by a succession of well-known actresses— from Mrs Patrick Campbell and Elizabeth Robins to Bernhardt and Duse—who urged upon him by letter, in person, or through intermediaries their claims to create the part of Tess. As on subsequent occasions, Hardy seems to have found it difficult to reject such applications out of hand, and to have caused himself considerable embarrassment by allowing a number of more or less imperious women to believe that he had each of them definitively in mind for the part.

Hardy was at first enthusiastic about the play. Discussions with Forbes-Robertson and Mrs Campbell began in April 1895, and in early May, when arranging for Emma to come up from Max Gate to join him in the service flat he had taken at 90 Ashley Gardens, Hardy listed among the advantages of the location not only its proximity to Victoria Station, the Army & Navy Stores, and Westminster Abbey but also the fact that 'Mrs Patrick Campbell lives in an adjoining block—& if the play goes on that may be convenient for the work'. By July Mrs Pat was pressing him for a commitment as to her future representation of 'the dear woman Tess', and Hardy was assuring her that she *'must* be the Tess now we have got so far'.[52] At that time he was hoping to reach with Forbes-Robertson an early agreement for the play's production on the London stage, but there were infinite delays and complications and a corresponding hesitation on his own part as to the advisability of the whole enterprise.

No resolution had been arrived at by the time Hardy returned to Max Gate in late July 1895, and the matter was put aside while he recovered, in the early days of August, from an attack of what he called 'the English cholera'. His distress from that visitation was doubtless exacerbated by awareness of the divorce action brought (on 29 July 1895) by Arthur Tomson against his wife Rosamund. Mrs Tomson had caused Hardy some annoyance early in 1895 when, as Graham R. Tomson, she published in an article in an American journal the statement that it was only as a result of the personal intervention of the Prince of Wales that Hardy had been able to purchase the land for Max Gate. Agreeing with the Duchy of Cornwall official concerned that the story was quite inaccurate, Hardy added: 'A woman is at the bottom of it, of course! I have reason to know that the writer of the account is a London lady, pretty, & well known in society (The signature is not I believe her real name). Why she should have written it I cannot say—except that it was not to please me; for such gossip annoys me greatly even when true.' He may now have feared that his own name would be mentioned in some way or another in the divorce action—although it was in fact undefended.[53]*

In early September 1895, just before the *Jude* proofs began to flow in, Hardy and Emma spent a few days at Rushmore on the Dorset–Wiltshire border, the estate of General Augustus Lane Fox Pitt-Rivers, the archaeologist, whose wife Alicia was a niece of Mary Jeune's first husband, Constantine Stanley. Rushmore was remarkable not only for the archaeological 'digs' which Pitt-Rivers had carried out on the property but also for the Larmer

* Rosamund Tomson, after the divorce, married the co-respondent and became Rosamund Marriott Watson. Hardy owned a copy of her collected poems, published after her death in 1912; that she continued to haunt his memory is suggested by his own poem 'An Old Likeness (Recalling R.T.)', where she is associated with 'a far season / Of love and unreason', and by a note for another possible poem: 'A letter comes in the handwriting & postmark of a lady long since dead (e.g. the one I received like Graham Tomson's). He fears to open it, (delayed in P.O. say).'[54]

Tree Gardens, a combination of *ferme ornée,* amusement park, and handicrafts museum which he had built up over the years and opened, without charge, to the general public. The Hardys' visit had been timed to coincide with the festivities of 4 September, when the annual sports day for the local populace was followed after nightfall by dancing on the lawns. The light of the moon was supplemented by thousands of lamps strung amongst the trees, and for Hardy the romance of the scene was quickened by his leading off the country dancing in partnership with his host's youngest daughter.

Agnes Grove, wife of Walter (later Sir Walter) Grove, was in her early thirties at this date, beautiful, elegant, and intelligent, with ideas of her own on such matters as women's suffrage, and with literary ambitions which she had as yet scarcely ventured to pursue. Hardy found her attractive and sympathetic; she was no doubt flattered by the attentions of the 'author of *Tess*'. That first encounter was extremely brief—Mrs Grove leaving for the Continent with her husband the following morning—but she and Hardy were to meet and correspond with some frequency over the next few years, and she was to take Florence Henniker's vacated place as Hardy's literary 'pupil', accepting that role with rather more complaisance than her predecessor had generally displayed. The dance at Rushmore was, according to *Later Years,* the last occasion on which Hardy, 'passionately fond of dancing . . . from earliest childhood', ever 'trod a measure . . . on the greensward'. In the poem 'Concerning Agnes' which he wrote after Lady Grove's death in 1926 his retrospective vision was absorbed by the memory of that night 'when the wide-faced moon looked through / The boughs at the faery lamps of the Larmer Avenue'. Because of her death, he lamented,

> I could not, though I should wish, have over again
> That old romance,
> And sit apart in the shade as we sat then
> After the dance
> The while I held her hand, and, to the booms
> Of contrabassos, feet still pulsed from the distant rooms.[55]

Hardy was immediately aware of the parallels between his meeting with Agnes Grove and his meeting with Florence Henniker two years previously: writing to the latter on 11 September 1895, shortly after his return from Rushmore to Max Gate, he did not mention Mrs Grove herself but described the experience as a whole as 'the most romantic time I have had since I visited you at Dublin'.[56]

The weekend of 14–16 September 1895 there were two visitors to Max Gate itself, Clarence McIlvaine, Hardy's publisher, and George Gissing, a friend of long but still somewhat uncertain standing. Always warily appreciative of each other's work, Hardy and Gissing were distinctly uncomfortable in each other's company, and the correspondence begun in the middle 1880s had soon been allowed to lapse. In mid-July 1895, however, they met again, after an interval of nine years, at the dinner given for George Meredith at the Burford Bridge Hotel by the Omar Khayyám Club, then under the presidency of Edward Clodd. Both men made brief speeches at the dinner in praise of the guest of honour—Hardy recalling Meredith's encouraging reception of the 'very strange and wild' manuscript of *The Poor Man and the Lady*—and as the gathering broke up Hardy suggested that Gissing might write to him if he felt inclined to do so. In September Gissing acted upon that suggestion—more for the sake of writing, as he admitted, than because he had anything in particular to say —and Hardy responded with the invitation to Max Gate.[57]

The weekend was marred for Gissing, as he told his brother, by the obtrusive presence of Emma—'an extremely silly & discontented woman, to whom, no doubt, is attributable a strange restlessness & want of calm in Hardy himself'. It was to the influence of this 'paltry woman', as he called her in another letter, that he was also inclined to attribute Hardy's disturbing tendency to talk of 'fashionable society', of 'lords & dignitaries', and it is indeed sufficiently clear that Hardy was anxious to keep the conversation, so far as possible, on topics to which Emma might conceivably have something pertinent to contribute.[58] When Gissing complained that Hardy, 'good, gentle, and poetically minded' though he was, read little and did not even know the names of flowers, he was judging his host in terms of the 'high culture' of a Meredith and the technical knowledge of such a natural-history enthusiast as Grant Allen, not of that deeper and more instinctive relationship to local history, culture, and countryside upon which Hardy's distinctive strengths as a writer depended. It was later that same year that Hardy made to another friend his observation about the way in which the town-bred boy would, in his self-conscious appreciation of nature, 'rush to pick a flower which the country boy does not seem to notice. But it is part of the country boy's life. It grows in his soul—he does not want it in his button-hole.' Hardy, Gissing sadly concluded, 'is a very difficult man to understand, & I suspect that his own home is *not* the best place for getting to know him.'[59]

Later that month Edward Clodd and William Archer, the dramatist and critic, came to Max Gate for a few days and were taken for a 'romantic walk' on the heath after dark. Hamo Thornycroft and his wife arrived without notice one day and found Hardy and Emma together at tea, in which the visitors, tired from cycling over the hills near Maiden Castle, gladly joined. The Thornycrofts' advocacy of the virtues of bicycling seems to have been instrumental in arousing the Hardys' active interest in that new and increasingly fashionable form of amusement, exercise, and locomotion. Although they were now of course in their middle fifties, Emma, with the confidence of a horsewoman, quickly took to the saddle, and by the following January Hardy himself had begun to learn in order 'to keep her company'.[60]

Hardy had meanwhile been attending to the final stages of the publication of the book version of *Jude the Obscure*. In August he had completed the preparation of printer's copy—a process he described to Florence Henniker as one of 'restoring' the manu-script to its 'original state'—and the composition of a deliberately challenging Preface: 'For a novel addressed by a man to men and women of full age; which attempts to deal unaffectedly with the fret and fever, derision and disaster, that may press in the wake of the strongest passion known to humanity, and to point, without a mincing of words, the tragedy of unfulfilled aims, I am not aware that there is anything in the handling to which exception can be taken.'[61] In September the proofs arrived, and his corrections, though for the most part very minor, were numerous and occa-sionally significant: the introduction, for example, of the para-graph about Gibbon into the scene in which Jude hears the voices of Christminster's past; the change from Sepulchre to Biblioll as the name of the college whose Master sends Jude a dusty answer; a tendency to make the sexual references more explicit and to play down the cousinship of Jude and Sue in favour of their comrade-ship. Hardy, of course, was always a meticulous proofreader, but the closeness of his attention to the *Jude* proofs can at the very least be said to sustain the statement, in his 12 August letter to Mrs Henniker, that he was 'more interested in this Sue story than in any I have written'.[62]

19

THE
PUBLICATION
OF *JUDE*

Jude the Obscure was published by Osgood, McIlvaine on 1 November 1895. Sir George Douglas arrived at Max Gate that day for a short visit and later recalled that he was alone with Hardy in his study when the first copy of the novel was delivered: 'The auspices, I remember, were not flattering, the weather being gloomy, whilst Mrs Hardy was suffering from an accident sustained in learning to cycle.' Douglas believed, moreover, that Hardy was not 'lifted up by a sense of work well done' and 'as little expected conspicuous success for his new work as he did the resounding obloquy which was to be its portion'.[1] Still riding on the success and popularity of *Tess of the d'Urbervilles*, Hardy was indeed unprepared for the depth, extent, and directness of the hostility which marked many of the reviews of his new novel. Even those critics who praised *Jude* as a masterpiece were clearly dismayed by the unrelieved darkness and bleakness of the story, made uncomfortable by its blunt treatment of controversial issues, and irritated by its obvious purposefulness. Those who felt it was a disaster—above all in its startling departure from the manner and matter of the author's previous work—felt free to express themselves with open vituperation or savage irony.

The *Guardian* (the Church of England newspaper) called it on 13 November 'a shameful nightmare, which one only wishes to forget as quickly and as completely as possible'. The *Pall Mall Gazette* review of 12 November, headed 'Jude the Obscene', indulged in a blank trivialization of Hardy's passionate narrative:

> And so in due course an unblessed family appears; and soon early and later infants are attracting momentary attention by hanging each other with box-cord on little pegs all round the room. After this come inquests, and remorse, and a new consciousness of sin, ending up in the re-marriage of all the divorcees, making, to the best of our reckoning, a total of six marriages and two obscenities to the count of two couples and a half—a record performance, we should think. And they all lived unhappily ever after, except Jude, who spat blood and died; while Arabella curled her hair with an umbrella stay and looked archly at her old acquaintance the itinerant quack.[2]

On 13 November the London *World,* under the title 'Hardy the Degenerate', retracted its earlier protest against the bowdlerization of the serial version of the novel,* poked fun at such scenes as the pig-killing ('Perhaps, as the novel was primarily destined for an American audience, all this talk of chitterlings and "innerds" was meant as a delicate compliment to the inhabitants of Porkopolis, Ohio'), and then assumed a tone of high moral earnestness in order to accuse Hardy of creating, in Sue, an unfortunate model for 'not a few neurotic would-be heroines of real life' and of modelling himself upon 'the methods of Zola and Tolstoi—Zola of *La Terre,* and Tolstoi the decadent sociologist. . . . Humanity, as envisaged by Mr. Hardy, is largely compounded of hoggishness and hysteria.'[4]

Hardy's anguished response to such attacks emerges from the many letters he wrote that November. To such friends as Mrs Henniker, Lady Jeune, Douglas, Clodd, and Gosse he insisted again and again—often in almost identical words—that *Jude* was not at all intended as a purpose novel, least of all as a 'manifesto on the marriage question', that the pig-killing scene was at once a deliberately humanitarian gesture and a dramatization of Arabella's essentially animalistic nature, and that his only fear had been that the book would be perceived not as hostile to morality but as all too supportive of the Christian exhortation to mercy and as downright 'High-Churchy' in its emphasis upon Sue's final

---

* That earlier article, 'Pandering to Podsnap', in the issue of 16 October, had been written by William Archer, who now hastened to assure Hardy that he was not the author of 'Hardy the Degenerate'.[3]

return to orthodoxy.[5] Exaggerated as some of these claims may seem, they yet represented an attempt to meet, on their own terms, the still more grotesque distortions of the reviewers.

Especially revealing of Hardy's bewilderment and distress, and of his resentment at the unreliability of even the warmest of his literary friends, is the letter of 10 November acknowledging Gosse's review in the St. James's Gazette two days previously. The review was in many respects intelligent and sympathetic, but Gosse, like many another reader since, had found the bleakness of the story excessive and more than a little gratuitous, and hinted as much in his opening sentences:

> It is a very gloomy, it is even a grimy, story that Mr. Hardy has at last presented to his admirers. . . . The genius of this writer is too widely acknowledged to permit us to question his right to take us into what scenes he pleases; but, of course, we are at liberty to say whether we enjoy them or no. Plainly, we do not enjoy them. We think the fortunes, even of the poorest, are more variegated with pleasures, or at least with alleviations, than Mr. Hardy chooses to admit. Whether that be so or no, we have been accustomed to find him more sensible to beauty than he shows himself in 'Jude the Obscure'. . . . We rise from the perusal of it stunned with a sense of the hollowness of existence.

Hardy's letter acknowledged the perceptivity of some comments Gosse had made on the geometrical structure of the novel, and closed 'with sincere thanks for your review'. But he could not, in the end, contain his irritation at the tone and phrasing of the review's first paragraph and added a postscript eloquent of his dissatisfaction with his friend's lukewarmness and of his own profound commitment to the novel and its hero:

> One thing I did not answer. The "grimy" features of the story go to show the contrast between the ideal life a man wished to lead, & the squalid real life he was fated to lead. The throwing of the pizzle, at the supreme moment of his young dream, is to sharply initiate this contrast. But I must have lamentably failed, as I feel I have, if this requires explanation & is not self evident. The idea was meant to run all through the novel. It is, in fact to be discovered in every body's life—though it lies less on the surface perhaps than it does in my poor puppet's.[6]

When Gosse accepted, shortly afterwards, an invitation to review the novel for a new international magazine, Cosmopolis, Hardy sought to guide him towards a better informed and more consistently sympathetic reading. On the advice of his worried publishers, he seems also to have inspired the article, 'On Some Critics of *Jude the Obscure*', which Sir George Douglas contributed to the January 1896 number of the *Bookman*.[7] The later reviews in general—including those by William Dean Howells, H. G. Wells, and Havelock Ellis—were distinctly more favourable to the novel than the early ones had been; even so, Hardy had still to endure the opprobrium of Jeannette Gilder in the New York *World*, of Mrs Oliphant ('The Anti-Marriage League') in *Blackwood's*, of A. J. Butler ('Mr. Hardy as a Decadent') in the *National Review*, and of a good many others. It is possible to argue that there were, on balance, as many positive reviews as negative ones, and that Hardy ought, in any case, to have been thicker-skinned and certainly less surprised: 'My word, we should cultivate a little stoicism,' Andrew Lang had observed to Clodd on learning of Hardy's response to his criticism of *Tess*.[8] It would, however, be absurd to describe the reception of the novel in many quarters as other than exceptionally and unreasonably hostile, or to pretend that Hardy was unique among writers in failing to demonstrate a stoical superiority to attacks of such a nature. The thinness of his skin was inseparable from those personal qualities, and those aspects of his personal history, which made him an artist in the first place, and although Hardy at bay—seized by a blind, sullen, unforgiving, peasant anger—is not an attractive spectacle, it ought not to be a particularly puzzling one.

Hardy, like his Jude Fawley, was capable of being both 'Simpleton' and 'Recalcitrant'. Throughout his career he seems to have been repeatedly astonished at the responses made to his work first by editors and then by reviewers. He never quite realized the extent to which the simple directness of his treatment of the relationships between men and women, his disinclination to accept marriage as the necessary goal and conclusion of fictional action, was bound to cause uneasiness in many Victorian quarters: Mrs Oliphant, after all, was perfectly justified in discussing *Jude* within an 'anti-marriage' context. When challenged on such matters before serial publication, he was always prepared to execute a tactical withdrawal. Once, however, the book had appeared in volume form he was much less willing to give ground, even on minor points of a purely technical nature. When a reader objected that Angel Clare would in real life have been sentenced and jailed as an accessory to the murder of Alec, Hardy did not write back to tell him not to deal in foolish irrelevancies: instead, he disputed his correspondent's interpretation of the law and then declared that even if Angel had been sent to prison his sentence would have been sufficiently short to have made him a free man again in time to be present on the day of Tess's execution and, hence, on the novel's final pages.[9]

Unfairly or irrelevantly attacked, he did not consider long or deeply the justice or appropriateness of his own first self-defensive lunges. Nor, in his unwillingness or inability to separate attacks on the work from attacks on the author, did he ever forget or forgive those who had wounded him. At the most immediate level Hardy felt that hostile reviews reflected directly upon his professionalism: they were saying that he was *not,* as a matter of practical competence, a good hand at a serial, a novel, a short story, a poem—and in so saying they damaged his reputation and endangered his sales. Such criticism also tended, by extension, to cast a shadow over the position he had achieved as a result of his literary success, to expose him to personal ridicule, and bring to the fore those aspects of his life, often admirable in themselves, which the class conventions of the day had taught him to regard as sources of embarrassment—the humble background, the lack of a university education, the gulf between the Higher Bockhampton beginnings and the figure he now cut in literary and social circles.

Hardy's personal application of public references to him emerges with unusual sharpness from the incident of the burning of *Jude* by Bishop William Walsham How of Wakefield. In many respects this was a comic episode, and *Later Years* does observe that it is by no means easy to burn a good thick book like *Jude* and that since the Bishop chose the height of summer for his gesture he presumably had to stoke up a fire especially for the purpose. But Hardy was deeply disturbed by so symbolic an act on the part of a representative of 'that terrible, dogmatic ecclesiasticism—Christianity so called (but really Paulinism *plus* idolatry)' which he saw as persistently hostile to morality, to progress, and even—since it had so little in common with 'the real teaching of Christ'—to religion itself. He was also angered to discover, after How's death, that he had instigated the withdrawal of the novel from W. H. Smith's huge circulating library: 'Of this precious conspiracy Hardy knew nothing, or it might have moved a mind which the burning could not stir to say a word on literary garrotting.' The protest against literary garrotting, a term which splendidly combines the ideas of censorship and of economic

strangulation, rests solidly enough on objections of both a principled and a practical nature, but it is followed in *Later Years*
by a comment of quite another kind: 'The only sad feature in the
matter to Hardy was that if the bishop could have known him as
he was, he would have found a man whose personal conduct,
views of morality, and of the vital facts of religion, hardly differed
from his own.'[10] What is remarkable about this passage is not so
much that Hardy, surely no lover of the episcopate and least of
all of the 'miserable second class prelate'[11] in question, should
have imagined that he and the Bishop might have profited from
knowing each other, but that he should have felt the necessity,
in such a context, not merely of defending his work but of protesting his personal virtue and sense of morality.

If Hardy was capable of being hurt by attacks from people he
had never met, it is not surprising that attacks from people he
knew should have overwhelmed him with a sense of betrayal. His
distress at the thought that fellow members of the Savile Club
had written hostile reviews of *Tess* reflected his sense, ingrained
from childhood, that friendship was inseparable from loyalty, and
also his bitter realization that his years of investment in clubba-
bility and *bonhomie* were not, after all, standing him in good
professional stead. Of Mrs Oliphant, who not only criticized *Jude*
in *Blackwood's* but wrote to commend Bishop How for consigning
it to the flames, a note deleted from *Later Years* rather plaintively
complains that Hardy had gone out of his way to visit her in
Windsor during an illness. When he learned, years after the event,
that Henry James and Robert Louis Stevenson had exchanged
views on what they considered the abominable style and factitious
sexuality of *Tess of the d'Urbervilles*, Hardy called them the
Polonius and Osric of novelists and exclaimed: 'How indecent
of those two virtuous females to expose their mental nakedness
in such a manner.'[12] Nor was his old friend Edmund Gosse ever
quite forgiven for telling Hardy to his face that *Jude* was the
most indecent novel ever written.[13]

One might say, piously, that Hardy ought to have been capable of keeping his personal life distinct from his literary life. Yet
many writers more self-confident than Hardy would have found
difficulty in overlooking so brutal a remark from so close a friend,
and it is in any case quite clear that for Hardy the conventional
distinction between the professional and the personal, the world
of the imagination and the world of everyday, simply did not exist.
Far more than financial success or social reputation was ultimately

at stake in the reception of criticism by a man whose working life and personal life were so indistinguishably intertwined, virtually one and the same—who lived most intensely in, and almost exclusively for, those hours he spent in his study every day he was at home at Max Gate. To say that he worked consistently and even obsessively from the real, or to complain of his undue sensitivity to criticism even of a purely literary kind, is only to assert that indivisibility in other terms, to register the tense, suspicious, hard-won, and hard-clenched integrity with which Hardy strove to realize himself as an artist within the context not of the ideal life he had wished to lead but of 'the squalid real life' imposed upon him by the restrictions common to all mankind, by the quirks of his own personal fate, and by the harsh necessities of that system of commercial publishing through which alone he could win his way to a fuller self-expression. Hardy had cherished from the first an elevated conception of the artist's role. He had a great admiration for Shelley, a type of the artist as hero, and could praise Henry James, whom he disliked personally, for being a dedicated artist, 'a real man of letters'.[14] He was ruthless in the demands he made, as an artist, upon himself and upon an uncomprehending Emma. And when in defending his own work he twisted and turned, argued extravagantly or evasively, it was because he felt, with something close to panic, a threat not just to his fortunes as a tradesman of letters but to his innermost belief in himself as an artist, to the integrity of his artist self.

By the early 1890s Hardy's financial situation seemed sufficiently secure, in those noninflationary times, to warrant the long-contemplated return to poetry—a step from which he expected little in the way of royalties. He seems, therefore, to have determined from the first that he would in *Jude* say his say without hesitation or compromise—that he would denounce, once and for all, those denials of educational and sexual justice, of simple humanity, which he saw as actually and symbolically implicit in the British social structure and class system, and give expression at last to feelings which had been simmering in his memory and his imagination since before *The Poor Man and the Lady*. But while he had deliberately used the success of *Tess of the d'Urbervilles* as a springboard from which to launch the final comprehensive challenge of *Jude*, he remained quite unprepared for the violence of the critical response, for the psychological stresses consequent upon so extensive and painful a public exposure, or for the supervention of such stresses upon matrimonial crises, disappointments in relationships outside of marriage, depression over advancing age and the possibility of declining health, and disillusionment with what passed for comradeship and friendship in the literary world.

The darkness of the final weeks of 1895 was not entirely unrelieved. Hardy especially valued the letter in which Swinburne, acknowledging the gift of a copy of *Jude,* praised the novel for its beauty, terror, and truth, and there were other congratulatory messages from Mrs Craigie, Ellen Terry (who none the less found the novel's language unnecessarily coarse at times), and 'George Egerton', the author of *Keynotes,* who praised the characterization of Sue as a psychologically penetrating treatment of 'a temperament less rare than the ordinary male observer supposes'.[15] In London for a short visit at the beginning of December, Hardy and Emma saw Forbes-Robertson and Mrs Patrick Campbell in *Romeo and Juliet* and dined with them afterwards. He also saw Mrs Henniker and other friends and by the time of his return to Dorchester was able to assure Sir George Douglas that *Jude* was 'going very well' and that London society was 'not at all represented by the shocked critics'.[16]

Early in 1896 Mrs Campbell stayed in Dorchester, at the King's Arms, for several days and spent a good deal of time at Max Gate: on 12 January she reported to a friend that she had been dancing improvised steps to old tunes played by Hardy on his fiddle.[17] The possibility of a London production of the *Tess* play was again being actively discussed. Hardy called on Mrs Pat to discuss the matter when he was in London in early February, there were more negotiations with Forbes-Robertson and his partner, Frederick Harrison, and in mid-March—confessing that he was 'in a hopeless fog on the matter'—Hardy sought the advice of Henry Arthur Jones as to the terms he had been offered.[18] It was evidently with some relief that he was able that summer to arrange—through Harper & Brothers—for a New York production with Minnie Maddern Fiske in the title role. Though he urged that his own dramatization be used, he made no absolute stipulation to that effect, and the text was in fact heavily revised by Lorimer Stoddard before its first performance on 2 March 1897.[19] When Mrs Pat learned in August of 1896 that there was to be no London production she wrote a vehement letter of regret and begged once again to be allowed to create a character she had loved so much and for so long; Hardy gave no ground, however, and for many years thereafter consistently refused to contemplate a separate English production. He had nevertheless to go through the formality of a London copyright 'performance' to coincide with the American first night, and in 1900 was obliged to make a public disavowal of any participation in a 'pirated' version which played for a while in London until an injunction was successfully brought against it on behalf of Mrs Fiske.[20]

In February 1896 Emma suffered for the first time a severe attack of a kind which was to dog her for the rest of her life: she and Hardy called it eczema but it was perhaps, as Lady Jeune suggested, shingles.[21] While Emma was resting at home and, later, recuperating in Brighton Hardy went twice to London, where he accompanied Lady Jeune and her daughter Madeleine to a masked ball at Mrs Crackanthorpe's ('the most amusing experience I have lately had'), sat to Winifred Thomson while she completed the portrait begun the previous year, and called on Florence Henniker and her husband—whom he found, not for the first time, to be 'really a very good fellow'.[22] Although he was still taking a hand in Mrs Henniker's literary career from time to time, Hardy was by now much more actively engaged in encouraging and advising Mrs Grove, whose ambitions were polemical rather than purely literary in nature. He suggested possible topics of current interest, read and revised her drafts, and gave assistance, often of a very direct kind, in placing the finished work in magazines: he was deeply involved, for example, in the composition and publication of the essay, 'Our Children. What Children Should Be Told', published in the July 1896 issue of the *Free Review*, even the proofs passing through his hands on their way to the author herself.[23]

By the beginning of April, Emma's health had somewhat improved and they took up London residence in the usual way, in the same house at 16 Pelham Crescent as they had occupied in 1894. It was now Hardy's turn to be overcome by illness and depression—in a letter to Lady Jeune he mentions a chill, rheumatism (his father's particular scourge), and other unspecified discomforts—and after two or three weeks of confinement to the house he took the advice of the doctor Lady Jeune had recommended and went off with Emma to try for himself the virtues of Brighton air.[24] Mrs Grove was among those who took tea at Pelham Crescent on 21 May, shortly after the Hardys' return. There were other encounters with her during the course of the season—at a party given by Herbert and Margot Asquith, for instance, and at the wedding in July of Hardy's young favourite Dorothy Stanley to Henry Allhusen—and at one of the band concerts at the Imperial Institute which Hardy loved to attend he was in a sufficiently exuberant mood to lead Mrs Grove through a few turns of the 'Blue Danube' waltz.[25]

By the time of the return to Max Gate on 23 July 1896 Hardy had completely thrown off all traces of illness, and in early August he completed his work for the Osgood, McIlvaine 'Wessex Novels' edition by writing the Preface to *Under the Greenwood Tree*. This placing of *Under the Greenwood Tree*—though determined entirely by the publishing necessities consequent upon his having sold the copyright a quarter of a century earlier—provided Hardy with a happy opportunity to round out the sequence of prefaces with two and a half anecdotal pages describing the village choir of his father's and his grandfather's days. He concluded with a strong if quiet affirmation of loyalty to the customs and values of his Bockhampton childhood as symbolized by the old hand-written and hand-bound music books which had now passed into his own keeping: 'Some of these compositions which now lie before me, with their repetitions of lines, half-lines, and half-words, their fugues and their intermediate symphonies, are good singing still, though they would hardly be admitted into such hymn-books as are popular in the churches of fashionable society at the present time.'[26] A letter to Kate at the end of June, offering to send or bring from London any music she might want, testified to the persistence of music as an element in the life of the surviving Hardys, but when he went to see his mother at Bockhampton immediately upon his return from London he found her perceptibly shrivelled and realized that another link with the treasured past must soon be broken in its turn.[27]

In mid-August 1896 Hardy and Emma set off together on an eight-week holiday, spent partly in England and partly in Belgium. They went first to Malvern, Worcester, Warwick, and Kenilworth, stayed a week at Stratford-upon-Avon, and then travelled, somewhat circuitously, through Coventry and Reading—the Aldbrickham of *Jude* and a town, as *Later Years* observes, where Mary Head had lived for a time (see above, p. 18n.)—on their way to Dover and the Continent. At Dover, however, Emma suffered an accident while riding the bicycle (painted green and nick-named 'The Grasshopper') which she had chosen to take with her, and they were forced to remain on the English side of the Channel for almost two weeks while she recovered. During that period Hardy—with characteristic punctiliousness—reread *King Lear* and wrote the date, together with his own and Emma's initials, alongside 'Dover Beach' in a copy of Arnold's *Poetical Works* he had brought with him. Given the context of the extended holiday, it is tempting to think of the marking of 'Dover Beach' as reflecting an attempt to halt and reverse the erosion of their marriage, although such speculation is somewhat dampened by the placing of the annotation next to the title of the poem rather than to the famous exhortation, 'Ah, love, let us be true / To one another!'[28]

The Grasshopper accompanied the Hardys to Belgium in mid-September, underwent many adventures, became a burdensome nuisance, and arrived back safely with them at Max Gate in mid-October. The Belgian portion of their itinerary included Ostend, Bruges ('a bygone, melancholy interesting town'), Spa, and Dinant, where Hardy became much concerned for the fortunes and fate of the first really compulsive gambler he had ever encountered. At Brussels they stayed 'for association's sake' at the Hotel de la Poste, their lodging during their previous visit, but there is no evidence of any corresponding revival of old affections. Indeed, the hotel itself 'had altered for the worse since those bright days' of twenty years earlier, and the main consequence of the revisitation of old scenes seems to have been a sombre realization of time's passage and life's decay: 'It is 20 years since I was last in this part of Europe', wrote Hardy to Mrs Henniker from Liège, '& the reflection is rather saddening. I ask myself, why am I here again, & not underground!' He took pleasure none the less in visiting the galleries in Bruges and Brussels and in the renewed opportunity to walk (as he did, alone, on 2 October) over the field of Waterloo. On the whole, he told Mrs Henniker, in a letter written from Max Gate on 12 October, it had been 'an agreeable & instructive time—the English half of it perhaps more so than the foreign one'.[29]

The inclusion of 'The Spectre of the Real' in the short-story collection, *In Scarlet and Grey,* which Mrs Henniker published in the autumn of 1896 was the occasion of a brief renewal of the kind of attack which had so recently been made on *Jude the Obscure,* and Mrs Henniker was solemnly advised by the *Spectator* that 'Mr. Thomas Hardy, in his later phases, is hardly a judicious literary counsellor'.[30] Hardy told Agnes Grove in mid-November that he was himself 'basking in fields of innocence at present', with nothing forthcoming other than 'A Committee-Man of "The Terror" ' in the Christmas Number of the *Illustrated London News.* He had also, however, sold the *Saturday Review* another story, 'The Duke's Reappearance', based on a Swetman family tradition from the late seventeenth century, and was about to undertake a revision of *The Pursuit of the Well-Beloved,* as serialized four years previously, in order to make it publishable in volume form as *The Well-Beloved*: 'I fear I shall not be in London much, if at all, before Christmas,' he told Mrs Grove three weeks later, 'having rashly promised my publisher to have some copy ready by that date.'[31]

The Owen sisters reappeared in Dorchester in November 1896 and called as usual at Max Gate. Emma regretted, in a subsequent letter, that they had found the household somewhat disordered as a result of her long absence in the early autumn and complained that she was still experiencing domestic difficulties of various kinds. Hardy had moved his study once again, going 'bit by bit, & book by book, leaving a room unfit for use till the workmen have been!' The new maid, though 'sweet-tempered & sweet to look at', had 'the footfall of an earthquake! and daily crashes the china—*placidly!*' Meanwhile, 'The "boy" who says he has been a page, gapes at the visitors, & hardly gets them in, or out, of the house.'[32] Emma's habitual vehemence was engaging and even amusing at such moments, helping to make her a lively if alarmingly discontinuous letter-writer. It also bore a positive aspect in so far as it contributed to the urgency of her hopeful aspirations for mankind and her dedication to causes. A long letter of hers published in the *Daily Chronicle* had concluded with much rhetorical flourish its argument that human happiness not only could but should be taught to children, both at home and in the schools:

> Eliminate evil, stamp it out at its source. Eradicate selfishness, the rage for power and advancement, the accumulation of wealth by others' woes. Expenses will be moderated, violence utilised, punishment abolished; and through every necessary exercise of brain and body a world would be evolved progressing towards perfection from this present chaos. Lives would be prolonged blissfully, and in one or two generations nearly every person would in some way or other be a *maker of happiness.*[33]

One source of Emma's detestation of *Jude* was the cheerlessness of its presentation of the human condition, and by the mid-

1890s she was moving away from Hardy intellectually no less decisively than he was moving away from her emotionally. His increasingly outspoken criticism of established institutions and values ran directly counter to her own deepening religiosity, centred as it was in an old-fashioned Evangelicalism and directed outward chiefly in the form of hostility to Roman Catholicism and enthusiasm for a limited group of humanitarian causes. She was, for instance, like Mrs Henniker, an ardent anti-vivisectionist, but Hardy himself, though a passionate animal-lover, did not entirely share this potentially common ground, held back from total commitment by the possible contribution made by such experiments to the eventual alleviation of human suffering. Lamenting in February 1897 that Rebekah Owen was 'a Jude-*ite*', Emma declared that she herself abhorred the intellectual arrogance and 'blank materialism of Authors' and was increasingly interested as she grew older 'in ameliorations & schemes for banishing the thickening clouds of evil advancing'.[34]

Emma's nephew Gordon Gifford, who was attending school in Dorchester at this period and spending much of his time at Max Gate, always insisted that while husband and wife were certainly 'at odds' over *Jude,* the marriage itself could not be called unhappy. But there is ample evidence that the 'strange restlessness & want of calm' Gissing had observed in Hardy in 1895 was directly related to the state of unrest within his household. When Alfred Sutro, the dramatist, ventured to praise *Jude* during a visit to Max Gate shortly after its publication, Emma sharply responded that it was the first novel Hardy had published 'without first letting her read the manuscript; had she read it, she added firmly, it would *not* have been published, or at least, not without considerable emendation. The book had made a difference to them, she added, in the County. . . . Hardy said nothing, and did not lift his eyes from the plate.'[35] Hardy was to resort increasingly to such silences as time went on. When guests were present, it seemed the only way of covering his own embarrassment and avoiding public scenes of an even more distressing kind. Hardy had become accustomed over the years to Emma's childlike, sometimes charming, often exasperating inconsequentialities, and he long remained anxious to sustain the marriage as both a public and a private reality. But he knew of no response other than silent henpecked endurance to her open displays of antagonism, her public scoldings, her sudden, unannounced gestures of intellectual and personal independence. Ford Madox Ford's story of Emma imploring Richard Garnett to stop the publication of *Jude*[36] may well be apocryphal, but it sounds by no means atypical.

Henry Joseph Moule and his daughter, calling at Max Gate shortly before Christmas 1896, thought that both the Hardys were in good spirits and that Emma, in particular, was in an agreeable and even affectionate frame of mind.[37] Though extraordinarily consistent and persistent at the deepest levels of personality and of purpose, at more superficial levels Hardy was capable of rapid changes of mood. His frequent acknowledgement of the inconsistencies in the views expressed in his work ('a series of seemings' was the term he had used in the Preface to *Jude*)[38] was a direct reflection of his personal shifts in feeling and outlook. His darkest depressions were thus capable not only of coexisting with outward geniality but also of alternating with periods of actual cheerfulness. In so far, indeed, as the darker moods were conducive to creative activity they were actually productive of substantial satisfactions—of the kind of 'melancholy pleasure' which he found in designing a tombstone for a favourite cat whose death had plunged him into despair and rendered him capable of complaining that Providence had dealt him an 'entirely gratuitous & unlooked for blow'.[39] He was perfectly capable, if not of deliberately generating depression, at least of surrendering to it willingly and without resistance.

There is nothing in the least factitious about the bleakness which characterizes the finest verse of 1895–6. If *Jude the Obscure* is the story of a man who has touched bottom, then Hardy himself seems to have plunged nearly as low in such poems as 'Wessex Heights' and the three parts of 'In Tenebris'. Florence Hardy once said that it wrung her heart to re-read 'Wessex Heights' because she knew it was written in the aftermath of the reception of *Jude,* when Hardy was 'so cruelly treated'. Both it and 'In Tenebris', however, speak also to the more generalized despair of 'One who, past doubtings all, / Waits in unhope'—to an almost suicidal sense of isolation not only from human affection and trust ('friends can not turn cold . . . For him with none') but from the whole spirit of a grotesquely brash and optimistic age, a world in which 'nobody thinks as I'. If there is self-pity here it is, as always, balanced and corrected by a relentless honesty. The acknowledgement in 'Wessex Heights' of a certain falseness to 'my simple self that was'[40] reflects an acceptance of a degree of personal responsibility for what was happening to his life, a readiness both for a life of greater retirement and more even tenor and for the kind of reconciliatory gesture implicit in the long holiday with Emma and (as will shortly be seen) the toning down of *The Pursuit of the Well-Beloved*. Seized with such quietist ambitions, Hardy now learned to think of the return to poetry as promising not only the possibility of ultimate artistic fulfilment but also, more mundanely, a convenient mode of polemical indirection, a means of obtaining a hearing for ideas which, directly expressed, might well be howled down:

> Perhaps [he told himself in October 1896] I can express more fully in verse ideas and emotions which run counter to the inert crystallized opinion—hard as a rock—which the vast body of men have vested interests in supporting. To cry out in a passionate poem that (for instance) the Supreme Mover or Movers, the Prime Force or Forces, must be either limited in power, unknowing, or cruel—which is obvious enough, and has been for centuries—will cause them merely a shake of the head; but to put it in argumentative prose will make them sneer, or foam, and set all the literary contortionists jumping upon me, a harmless agnostic, as if I were a clamorous atheist, which in their crass illiteracy they seem to think is the same thing. . . . If Galileo had said in verse that the world moved, the Inquisition might have let him alone.[41]

Hardy himself was not to be left entirely in peace by the reviewers of *The Well-Beloved*, the last of his novels to appear in book form. When Osgood, McIlvaine published it on 16 March 1897—in a format matching that of *Jude* and of the remainder of their collected edition—the initial response was extremely favourable, if occasionally a little puzzled. That, indeed, was to prove the general pattern, but on 24 March the London *World* came out with a review, 'Thomas Hardy, Humorist', very much on the lines of its 'Hardy the Degenerate' attack of fifteen months previously. Expressing relief that Hardy had, in the new novel, 'resolutely abandoned all references to the pigstye', the anonymous reviewer condemned with heavy sarcasm the improbabilities and improprieties of the plot and declared: 'Of all forms of sex-mania in fiction we have no hesitation in pronouncing the most unpleasant to be the Wessex-mania of Mr. Thomas Hardy.' Scorning, with obvious reference to the controversy over *Jude*, the 'usual talk' of the author's 'whole-hearted devotion to the truth', the piece concluded with just the kind of *ad hominem* attack which had so distressed Hardy on that earlier occasion: 'Mr. Hardy has once more afforded a dismayed and disgusted public the depressing spectacle of genius on the down grade. Matthew Arnold once rudely referred to Burns as "a beast with splendid gleams," a description which was irresistibly recalled to the present writer by the perusal of *Jude the Obscure*. For in that book there were undoubtedly some splendid gleams. There are none in *The Well-Beloved*.'[42]

These are no longer—for better or for worse—the sort of terms in which literary disagreements are publicly aired, and it is necessary to catch the flavour of such reviews in order to understand the nature of Hardy's response. Refusing to allow himself to be cheered and reassured by the many positive reviews, or by the excellent sales, Hardy expressed repeatedly to friends and acquaintances his dismay at the open malice of the *World* reviewer and his astonishment that so innocent a story could be so perversely read. The 'horrid stab', he told Mrs Henniker, was the more astonishing in that one of his reasons for republishing the novel in book form was that 'it cd not by any possibility offend Mrs or Mr Grundy, or their Young Persons, even though it cd be called unreal & impossible for a man to have such an artistic craze for the Ideal in woman as the hero has'.[43] Hardy wisely declined the invitation of the editor of the *Academy* to reply to the *World* in kind, observing that abuse of so personal a nature best answered itself, but that did not deter him from writing privately to the editor of *The Times* to express the hope that their reviewer would not be influenced by what the *World* had said, nor from commenting, in a notebook entry, 'What foul cess-pits some men's minds must be, and what a Night-cart would be required to empty them!'[44]

Although the peculiar violence of the review makes comprehensible the violence of Hardy's own language, it remains remarkable that he should not have been more fully prepared—even in 1897, even after Ibsen—for adverse reactions to a story which so narrowly skirted so many sexual taboos and seemed, as a sympathetic reviewer put it, so comic 'in the abstract'.[45] Clearly, Hardy's anger and distress were exacerbated by his having deliberately sought to render the book version of the novel less outspoken and less overtly hostile to marriage than the 1892 serial had been—hence less offensive to Emma on the one hand and to the newspaper reviewers on the other. Such neutral pages as those dealing with fashionable London life were left essentially as they stood, with some pointing up of the social satire here and there: of the political discussions at Lady Channelcliffe's, for example, it was now said that 'No principles of wise government had place in any mind, a blunt and jolly personalism as to the Ins and Outs animating all'.[46] But several sections which treated directly of the relationships between Pierston (as his name was now spelled) and the various temporary incarnations of the well-beloved were radically rewritten or even entirely replaced, so that the novel in its revised form scarcely dealt with marriage at all, either thematically or as an element in the action, and became much more consistently a fable of the artistic temperament—'a fanciful, tragi-comic half allegorical tale of a poor Visionary pursing a Vision'. The savage 'Ho-ho-ho!' ending of the serial was replaced by the quietly ironic portrayal of Pierston as cured of his Shelleyan restlessness but only at the cost of the simultaneous disappearance of all his ambitions and capacities as an artist. Looking even older than his years, he enters into a marriage of amicable elderly nonsexual convenience, fosters a scheme for 'the closing of the old natural fountains' on the 'Isle', and pulls down, on account of their dampness, some 'old moss-grown, mullioned Elizabethan cottages', building in their place 'new ones with hollow walls, and full of ventilators'.[47]

On the face of it these are sad images of emasculation and surrender, pointing—if indeed they have any autobiographical significance—towards a resigned acceptance of age and of its familiar accompaniments, declining sexuality and diminished creativity. And Hardy did exclaim to Gosse, just after the novel's publication: 'I, too, am getting old like Pierston!'[48] But the ending of the book version of the novel is the product of a maturer vision than the ending of the serial. Like Ethelberta and Clym before him, Pierston becomes a half-sympathetically, half-ironically presented exemplar of the route not to be taken. Hardy indeed accepted what Pierston's career had demonstrated, the interdependence of romantic and creative aspiration, but he proposed in his own career to make that acceptance the occasion not for despair but precisely for an affirmation of the continued indivisibility of the two, on into the future. If the revision of *The Well-Beloved* constituted for Hardy a Prospero-like burning of his books, then it can only have been in the confident and even amused anticipation of an early Phoenix-like re-emergence of the poet from the ashes of the novelist. 'Poetry certainly has not had its day,' he had assured Sir George Douglas several years earlier. 'You must remember that the Muses have occasionally to "draw back for a spring"—or, as they themselves would probably express it, *reculer pour mieux sauter*: & they may have been doing so lately.'[49]

20

KEEPING
SEPARATE

HARDY had apparently determined the contents of *Wessex Poems* by February 1897, nearly two years ahead of its publication. He had certainly conceived by then the plan of illustrating the volume with his own sketches of the 'scenes' of some of the individual poems.[1] During the nearly thirty years in which he was necessarily preoccupied with the writing of fiction, Hardy's activity as a poet never entirely ceased. Quite apart from the long broodings on *The Dynasts,* he continued to accumulate in his notebooks a mass of material for use in the poems he hoped one day to have the opportunity to write—notes of natural phenomena, vignettes of human situations that struck him as especially poignant or ironic, ideas or outlines for entire poems, even fragmentary drafts. Few such notes survived the systematic destruction of his pocket-books (see below, p. 518n.), but there can be no doubt of the deliberateness with which Hardy kept his poetic ambitions alive. For obvious reasons, relatively few poems were brought to anything like final form in the period between *Far from the Madding Crowd* and *Tess of the d'Urbervilles,* and most of the poems in *Wessex Poems* itself date either from the 1860s or the 1890s. But many of the poems in the latter group had been conceived during those decades of apparent blankness, while many—perhaps all—of the poems with early dates had undergone fairly extensive revision before seeing print for the first time.

In the spring of 1897 the Hardys went up to London as usual, leaving Max Gate in the charge of one of the servants and Hardy's correspondence in the hands of Kate. Both the sisters had recently resigned from their teaching positions at the Bell Street girls' school, Mary on grounds of ill health, Kate for reasons of family obligation[2]—Jemima, now in her eighties, needing constant attention which Mary was not, by herself, strong enough to provide. In London the Hardys found nothing suitable to rent, chiefly because of the demand created by the forthcoming Diamond Jubilee celebrations, and after ten uncomfortable days they retreated to lodgings in Basingstoke, about an hour's train ride from Waterloo. During a series of one-day visits to town they managed to see friends, pictures, and plays (including two by Ibsen), and to attend once again the concerts at the Imperial Institute. In mid-June, about a week ahead of the official Jubilee ceremonies, they returned briefly to Max Gate before setting off for Switzerland and another continental holiday.[3]

Writing to Sir George Douglas from the Hotel Belle Vue, Berne, on 20 June 1897, Hardy spoke of moving on to Interlaken if the weather improved:

> But up to the present the statement that there are mountains in Switzerland seems a groundless tradition, & we appear to be in a fair way of accomplishing the unprecedented Alpine feat of journeying from one end of the country to the other without seeing a single sign of one. The clouds are so low as to touch the upper houses of the town, & the cathedral spire is the loftiest object really believed in by the few other English visitors besides ourselves.

Interlaken, reached two days later, happily provided finer weather and views of the mountains; on the following days they visited Grindelwald, took a steamer trip on Lake Thun, and went on to the Hotel Gibbon (now no more) in Lausanne. Hardy took pleasure in finding himself there on the 110th anniversary of the date on which Gibbon had completed the final page of *The Decline and Fall of the Roman Empire,* and his poem on the occasion, 'Lausanne: In Gibbon's Old Garden', not only embodied something of his personal sense of intellectual embattlement but did so in language suggested by a recent reading of Milton's *The Doctrine and Discipline of Divorce*:

'Still rule those minds on earth
At whom sage Milton's wormwood words were hurled:
"Truth like a bastard comes into the world
Never without ill-fame to him who gives her birth"?'[4]

By the end of the month the weather had turned uncomfortably hot. At Zermatt on the 29th Emma had a frightening ride on a mule to the Riffel-Alp Hotel and its view of the Matterhorn while Hardy laboured up on foot. Told that an Englishman* had disappeared a few days earlier while following that same route, Hardy, despite the heat, retraced his own steps, saw nothing suspicious—and reported as much in a letter to *The Times*. The price of this odd piece of officiousness was physical exhaustion and a few days in bed at a Geneva hotel while Emma, who had already made several independent expeditions, went exploring on her own and came upon the tomb of Sir Humphry Davy, the natural philosopher, whom she was able to claim as a distant relation. It was Emma, too, when they reached Paris a few days later, who set off for the suburbs to look for her nephew Gordon Gifford, who had been attending a school there in order to improve his French.[5]

In a letter written to Mrs Henniker just before his departure from Geneva, Hardy declared that he had given no thought to novels, his own or other people's, since correcting the proofs of *The Well-Beloved*. As soon as he got back to Max Gate, however, he found himself revising the story, 'The Grave by the Handpost', which he had promised for the Christmas Number of the *St. James's Budget,* and trying to sort out the confusion which had arisen over two rival French translations of *Tess*.[6] In mid-July he was briefly in London as Lady Jeune's guest at a Jubilee dinner held to celebrate the progress made by women during the reign of Victoria. Shortly thereafter, while some work was being done at Max Gate, he and Emma made a brief holiday excursion just beyond the boundaries of Dorset to Wells, Longleat, Frome, and finally Salisbury, where they stayed for several days. Writing from there on 7 August to ask Kate if she would like to 'run up' for a day, Hardy observed that the training college was closed for the holidays and that she would therefore be spared 'unpleasant reminders'. The same letter makes very plain his enjoyment of the beauty of the Cathedral, the peacefulness of the Close at night

---

* He was later identified as James Robert Cooper, father of the Edith Cooper who was one of the two authors known collectively as 'Michael Field'.

(as also reflected in the poem 'A Cathedral Façade at Midnight'), and the town's associations with Mary, Kate, and Horace Moule—and suggests, in so doing, that he was in reality (as distinct from poetry) entirely ready and even eager to confront in 'the tall-spired town' those 'forms now passed' which had loomed so portentously in 'Wessex Heights'.[7] Indeed, to juxtapose the Salisbury references of 'Wessex Heights' with those of 'In a Cathedral City' is immediately to suggest the danger of reading the verse, for all its deep autobiographical roots, as too literal a transcription from life, or of attributing permanence and definitiveness to the mood of any particular poem.

Hardy attended Evensong in the Cathedral with Emma two or three times during the Salisbury visit.* Much impressed by a reading from the sixth chapter of Jeremiah, he was struck by the applicability to himself, as an agnostic ostensibly engaged in worship, of the twentieth verse—'To what purpose cometh there to me incense from Sheba, and the sweet cane from a far country? your burnt offerings are not acceptable, nor your sacrifices sweet unto me'—and almost certainly had it in mind when writing his poem 'The Impercipient', with its moving testimony to the coexistence of the persistent yearning to believe with an unyielding incapacity to do so.[9]

Later that same month Hardy was back in Salisbury again for a brief meeting with Romain Rolland's sister, Madeleine Rolland, whose interests he had recently been trying to protect in the squabble over translation rights to *Tess*. He had already been impressed by the excellent English of Mlle Rolland's letters, and this first meeting was to lead to a long friendship maintained almost entirely by correspondence—in which Emma, too, took an active part, venturing now and then to write in French, a language in which she displayed much the same lively inaccuracy as she did in English.[10]

Although Hardy and Emma had travelled into Somerset and Wiltshire by train they were now seeing more and more of their local Dorset countryside by bicycle. Emma, whom neighbours later recalled as riding about in a green outfit of the kind

---

* He noted these occasions—in accordance with the old habit he had now intermittently resumed—not only in his Bible and prayerbook but also in the copy of *The Cathedral Psalter* he had recently purchased.[8]

advocated by Mrs Bloomer, was acknowledged to be the more skilful of the two, and she seems to have gone so far as to participate in a 'Bicycle Paper Chase' organized in Dorchester one Saturday afternoon in April 1897.[11] But her confidence betrayed her into the kind of impetuosity she so often displayed on paper and in conversation, and when out riding with her husband in early September she once again proved accident-prone and was incapacitated for some time by a badly bruised ankle. Hardy, however, continued to ride his cherished Rover 'Cob' throughout the autumn, either alone or with his brother, occasionally going as far afield as Sherborne in North Dorset, or even across the Somerset border to Wells and Glastonbury. A few days were spent accompanying Rudyard Kipling in his unsuccessful search for a house in the Weymouth area. The advantage of cycling for literary people, Hardy told Sir George Douglas on another occasion, was that 'you can go out a long distance without coming in contact with another mind,—not even a horse's—& dissipating any little mental energy that has arisen in the course of a morning's application'.[12]

Declining in late November 1897 an invitation to respond to the toast of 'Literature' at a forthcoming dinner of the Royal Institute of British Architects, Hardy pleaded 'physical reasons that always prevent my making a speech, & almost prevent my dining out'. He referred in the same letter, however, to a continuing sense of comradeship with his former profession, and indeed he had not only been engaged a few years before in restoring West Knighton Church and building Talbothays but had just recently written for the Society for the Protection of Ancient Buildings two technical reports on the dilapidated church at East Lulworth and on an old inn at Maiden Newton that was being threatened with destruction.[13] Some of the illustrations he was preparing for *Wessex Poems* were also architectural in character, and he may have taken advantage of his visit to East Lulworth to go further along the coast to Eliza Nicholls's former home at Kimmeridge and make the drawing of Clavel Tower to accompany 'She, to Him. I'. He clearly enjoyed these expeditions, whatever memories they brought back, and seems to have been made cheerful throughout the winter of 1897–8 by the way in which his discovery of the bicycle, his abandonment of fiction, and his return to poetry seemed to be combining in a single movement of liberation and renewal. 'As to a novel from me', he told William Archer,

I don't incline to one. There is no enlightened literary opinion
sufficiently audible to tempt an author, who knows that in the
nature of things he must always come short of real excellence. I
mean that the little sound & just opinion we get is swamped by
the flood of ignorant & venal opinion, & is as if it were not uttered
at all. And zest is quenched by the knowledge that by printing
a novel which attempts to deal honestly & artistically with the
facts of life one stands up to be abused by any scamp who thinks
he can advance the sale of his paper by lying about one.[14]

The sense of release from such internal and external pressures
emerges almost gaily from a letter to Kate written from 9
Wynnstay Gardens, Kensington, shortly after he and Emma had
moved into a flat there for the London season of 1898: 'The young
people seem to cycle about the streets here more than ever. I asked
an omnibus conductor if the young women (who ride recklessly
into the midst of the traffic) did not meet with accidents. He said
"Oh, nao; their sex pertects them. We dares not drive over them,
wotever they do; & they do jist wot they likes. 'Tis their sex, yer
see; & its wot I coll takin' a mean adventage. No man dares to go
where they go." ' He did some reading at the British Museum in
preparation for *The Dynasts* and resumed his faithful patronage
—even in inclement weather—of the concerts at the Imperial
Institute. His visits to London, so important for the access they
provided to theatres and art galleries, also gave him almost his
only opportunities to hear good music, which was of such deep
emotional importance to him throughout his life. His tastes were
not especially sophisticated, finding gratification in military band
performances as well as in orchestral and chamber concerts, but,
as he remarked to a friend, 'to be honest I am never tired of
music'.[15]

Emma's niece, Lilian Gifford, was at Max Gate that summer,
and Lilian's brother Gordon arrived in September; at the Hardys'
instigation, but with the ready acquiescence of the parents, both
visits were prolonged to the end of the year and probably beyond.[16]
This was only one of several extended periods which the two young
people spent with their aunt and uncle. Hardy was fond of both of
them, as he was of all children who were quiet and well-behaved,*
and their presence at Max Gate was one of several factors which

---

* Gosse's daughter Sylvia spoke of Hardy as understanding small children
and as never failing to come upstairs to say good night to her brother and
herself when he was visiting the house.[17]

helped to maintain an impression—even, to some degree, a reality
—of domestic regularity. For all their many differences, the
Hardys were at one in their love of children, animals, and plants.
They still dined together, entertained together, went to London
together, cycled together, and took holidays together. If Hardy
schooled himself to endure his wife's public scoldings, that was
perhaps because his superior strengths of intelligence and purpose
—his sheer obstinacy—enabled him to retain sufficient control
over their private life together.*

He did not, of course, read Emma's letters, nor did he know of
those diaries in which she regularly recorded her many grievances
against him. Matters were also considerably eased by Emma's
programme of greater independence and, hence, greater separateness. She was now quite prepared to go by herself to London,
where she had joined a women's club, the Alexandra, and to take
trips to the seaside at Hastings or Brighton when so prompted by
her health or her mood. Since the additions to the rear of Max
Gate Hardy had moved his study to the new east-facing room on
the first floor and Emma had claimed the two attic rooms on the
second floor, one of them over the new study, the other over the
previous study at what had been (before the extensions) the north-
west corner of the house. 'I sleep in an *Attic*—or *two!*' she exclaimed to Rebekah Owen. 'My boudoir is my sweet refuge &
solace—not a sound scarcely penetrates hither. I see the sun, & stars
& moon rise & the birds come to my bird table when a hurricane
has not sent it flying.'[19]

Emma spent much of her time sewing, reading, and painting
(in early 1899 she was attempting a portrait of Gordon Gifford,
'a lovely youth of the chestnut kind at present'), but she was also
writing both poetry and prose and trying to get the results
published. 'The Egyptian Pet', a brief, sometimes touching article
on cats ('Always give a cat free ingress and egress and attend to
his voice, remembering that he has no language but a cry'),
appeared in the *Animals' Friend* in 1898 and was later reprinted,

---

* Gordon Gifford, though devoted to Hardy, was less attached to his aunt,
and the two male members of the household seem often to have sat in
mutually sympathetic silence during Emma's tirades—a technique strikingly
reminiscent of that adopted by Hardy and his father for coping with Jemima's
outbursts at Higher Bockhampton. In later years Gordon Gifford, denying that
the Hardys' marriage had been an unhappy one, nevertheless acknowledged
that his aunt, as 'a very ardent Churchwoman and believer in the virtues and
qualities of women in general', strongly objected to *Jude the Obscure* and to
the views of some of its characters.[18]

so Emma's note on her own copy records, as a leaflet 'for circulation in Dublin etc.'. Otherwise she succeeded in publishing little beyond occasional letters to the newspapers—one on 'The Destruction of Larks' in *The Times*, for example, another on 'The Tormented Tiger' in the *Daily Chronicle*. The editor of the *Vegetarian* informed her in March 1898 that a story she had submitted had probably been destroyed (since she had enclosed no stamps to cover the cost of its return), and in early July a story called 'The Inspirers' was declined by the editor of *Temple Bar*—a journal to which Hardy had advised Agnes Grove to send a story.[20]

None of this deterred Emma from criticizing the publications of others. Her husband remained, of course, her most frequent target, but in March 1897 she wrote to Edward Clodd to attack the rationalist position he had adopted in his recent book, *Pioneers of Evolution*: 'The chapters I greatly object to, are those with which you seem to have taken so much pains to say—There is no God—There is no Christ.' Such writings, she persisted, caused despair to those of 'weak faith', though her own position was strong and clear: 'In spite of the theory of evolution, for my part I shall believe that man was always man.' She went on: 'I do not see why we should have doubts as to immortality, or that we should not be able to rise in *myriads* invisible to such eyes as ours. In the plan of creation there is no permanence of form, size, time, or quantity: all is limitless—'[21]

Hardy himself had been out of the public eye for some while prior to the publication of *Wessex Poems and Other Verses* at the end of 1898. Immediately after the volume appeared, he again became a controversial figure. For his first significant appearance as a poet he had drawn widely on the entire range of the verse he had written to that date, almost as if he were more concerned to expose the full compass of his work than to display it and himself in the most favourable light. The impression of idiosyncrasy given by the volume was heightened by the inclusion of the drawings, some hauntingly effective, others relatively crude in both conception and execution. The opening poem, 'The Temporary the All', immediately confronted readers with the kinds of problem that were to recur throughout the volume and are now recognizable as characteristically Hardyan—the dense stresses, the strict yet unfamiliar stanza form, the inverted syntax, the archaisms and odd coinages, the profoundly pessimistic mood, unromantically and unfashionably eloquent of nonprogression and unfulfilment:

> Mistress, friend, place, aims to be bettered straightway,
> Bettered not has Fate or my hand's achieving;
> Sole the showance those of my onward earth-track—
>   Never transcended![22]

The argumentative movement of the poem, from a hopeful past to a melancholy, backward-looking present, anticipates the structure of the volume as a whole, which follows a roughly (though by no means invariably) chronological sequence from such poems of the 1860s as 'Amabel', 'Hap', and 'Neutral Tones', through some of the rare poems of the 1870s and 1880s, most of them directly or indirectly related to the novels of the period, to those written within comparatively recent years, including 'Friends Beyond', 'Thoughts of Ph–a', 'At an Inn', and 'The Impercipient'. Oddly grouped, as 'Additions', at the very end of the book are the broadly comic 'The Fire at Tranter Sweatley's' (somewhat revised from its previous appearance), the sardonically moralistic 'Heiress and Architect' and 'The Two Men', the 'Lines' spoken by Ada Rehan on behalf of Mary Jeune's charity, and, finally, 'I Look Into My Glass', the finest and most obviously personal of the late poems, matched within the volume only by the equally bleak 'Neutral Tones':

> I look into my glass,
> And view my wasting skin,
> And say, 'Would God it came to pass
> My heart had shrunk as thin!'
>
> For then, I, undistrest
> By hearts grown cold to me,
> Could lonely wait my endless rest
> With equanimity.
>
> But Time, to make me grieve,
> Part steals, lets part abide;
> And shakes this fragile frame at eve
> With throbbings of noontide.[23]

Hardy felt little optimism about the likely response to his first appearance as a poet—and especially, or so he told Gosse, to his elevation of content above form at a time when poetry was generally regarded as 'the art of saying nothing with mellifluous preciosity'. The change of direction, so long contemplated in private, was totally unheralded in public, and several of his friends and admirers were not only surprised but dismayed—Meredith exclaimed, 'What induces Hardy to commit himself to verse!'[24] Some of the reviews were savagely dismissive: the *Saturday Review* spoke of 'this curious and wearisome volume, these many slovenly, slipshod, uncouth verses, stilted in sentiment, poorly conceived and worse wrought. . . . It is impossible to understand why the bulk of this volume was published at all—why he did not himself burn the verse, lest it should fall into the hands of an indiscreet literary executor, and mar his fame when he was dead.' But for the most part the reviewers were not so much hostile as puzzled and unsure. It was 'difficult to say the proper word', as E. K. Chambers confessed in the *Athenaeum,* and even a sympathetic critic such as Lionel Johnson, who had already written one of the earliest books on Hardy's fiction, qualified his praise of the 'arresting, strenuous, sometimes admirable' poems with regret at their almost uniform grimness and absence of humour. Suggesting that the entire volume might have been entitled 'The Temporary the All', Johnson observed that to call it *Wessex Poems* seemed 'somewhat cruel to Wessex, which is not an wholly Leopardian land'.[25] Hardy—who had in fact been reading Leopardi—acknowledged that there was some justification for Johnson's criticism of the title, and in general he neither had nor felt any great cause for dissatisfaction with the way the volume was received. His chief complaint was not that the critics had been unkind but that their comments had shown such depths of imperceptivity. What he chiefly valued, in any case, were the congratulatory letters received from such friends as Leslie Stephen, Swinburne, and Watts-Dunton, and he was sufficiently proud of Swinburne's letter to send Mrs Henniker a list of the poems that he had specifically praised.[26]

The most persistently adverse reaction to *Wessex Poems* seems to have come from Emma, who found the one poem addressed directly to her, 'Ditty (E.L.G.)', to be an inadequate compensation for what she took to be the implicit criticism of 'The Ivy-Wife' or for the various poems she knew, guessed, or suspected to refer to other women, among them Eliza Nicholls, Tryphena Sparks, and

Florence Henniker. She may also have been alert to some of the personal allusions Hardy had incorporated into the drawings. When, however, she confided her unhappiness to Alfred Pretor— a Dorset-born classicist and minor novelist, fellow of St. Catharine's College, Cambridge, with whom she had recently struck up a semi-literary friendship—she was told that her darker fears were quite unfounded: 'T. has said again & again to me', Pretor circumspectly wrote, 'little casual things that are absolute proofs that all his reminiscences are little fancies evoked from the days of his youth & absolutely without bearing on the real happiness of his life.' Emma persisted in the objection that Hardy's treatment of her, in the volume as in life, displayed monstrous ingratitude, and another letter from Pretor counselled her to be content with her lot as the helpmeet of genius and assured her that people did indeed believe that she copied and even composed passages in her husband's books: after all, he added, 'such an ideal union as the Brownings is (I venture to think) unique, at any rate between two such gifted people.'[27]

The Brownings figured largely in what was fast becoming Emma's standard rhetoric of complaint and self-pity. Believing that she was her husband's superior in birth, family connections, and education, and only slightly his inferior in literary gifts, she took great offence at the scant attention paid to her and her opinions by her husband's friends or, increasingly, by her husband himself. She objected to his taking the management of their lives and of the household itself more and more into his own hands (as it had become increasingly necessary for him to do), and his apparent habit—perhaps out of a sense of basic honesty—of keeping her aware of his meetings and correspondence with Florence Henniker, Mary Jeune, and Agnes Grove served rather to exacerbate her jealousy than to disarm it. Resentful of Hardy's encouragement of the literary ambitions of such women and of his apparent forgetfulness of those earlier times when he and she had worked together as a team, her role in the writing of the novels— which consisted, at most, of taking dictation (chiefly for *A Laodicean*), making clean copies of heavily corrected pages, or suggesting an occasional incident or detail—was greatly exaggerated for the benefit of neighbours and visitors,* and Henry

---

* It was apparently because of Emma's claims to have 'written' the novels that Hardy burned the manuscript of *A Laodicean*, so much of which was in her hand.[28]

Hardy's conveying to his brother a report of the resulting gossip seems to have marked a crucial stage in the estrangement between Emma and the people at Bockhampton.[29] Above all, by a relentless process of action and reaction, her religious and moralistic obsessions deepened as the irreligion and immorality of her husband's work became, in her eyes, more and more pronounced, and while in the 1890s she was still content to assure people that her husband didn't really mean what he said on such matters, before she died she had come to see him as a living embodiment of the evils to whose eradication she was so devoutly dedicated.

Emma made particular reference to Mrs Browning in a letter to Rebekah Owen of 14 February 1899, and two months later she expressed dislike for some of Hardy's own poems on the grounds that what passed for tenderness was really irony: 'He should be the last man to disparage marriage!' she continued. 'I have been a devoted wife for at least twenty years or more—but the last four or five alas! Fancy it is our silver wedding this year! The *thorn* is in my side still.' Later in the same long and typically rambling letter she burst out: 'I, too, keep state-apartments but am not permitted to ask anyone to occupy them: a woman's ruling of a house, & friends is far happier for *all*, than a man's, therefore *you* must needs be happy in new home—I often wonder if women's rule of the world would not have produced a better world than it is—'[30]

It was in August of this same year that she sent a long letter of marital advice to Winifred Thomson's sister Elspeth, who had evidently experienced difficulty and disillusionment in the early stages of her own somewhat middle-aged marriage to Kenneth Grahame, the author of *The Wind in the Willows*:

I can scarcely think that love proper, and enduring, is in the nature of men—as a rule—perhaps there is no woman 'whom custom will not stale.' There is ever a desire to give but little in return for our devotion, & affection—their's being akin to children's—a sort of easy affectionat*eness*—& at fifty, a man's feelings too often take a new course altogether Eastern ideas of matrimony secretly pervade his thoughts, & he wearies of the most perfect, & suitable, wife chosen in his earlier life. Of course he gets over it usually, somehow, or hides it, or is lucky!

Interference from others is greatly to be feared—members of either family too often are the cause of estrangement—A woman does not object to be ruled by her husband, so much as she does by a relative at his back,—man seldom cares to control such matters when in his power, & lets things glide, or throws his balance on the wrong side which is simply a terrible state of affairs, & may affect unfavourably himself in the end.

Keeping separate a good deal is a wise plan in crises—and being both free—& *expecting little* neither gratitude, nor attentions, love, nor *justice,* nor anything you may set your heart on—Love interest—adoration, & all that kind of thing is usually a failure complete—some one comes by & upsets your pail of milk in the end—If he belongs to the public in any way, years of devotion count for nothing.[31]

Emma's case against husbands in general was merely an elaboration of her case against her own husband, the phrase about 'a relative at his back' obviously alluding to Jemima, still very much alive at Bockhampton and still regularly visited there by her still devoted son. 'I have suffered much', she told Desmond MacCarthy's mother a little later on, '& greatly from the ignorant interference of others (of the peasant class).' She confessed that she was 'prejudiced against authors—living ones!—they too often wear out other's lives with their dyspeptic moanings if unsuccessful —and if they become eminent they throw their aider over their parapets to enemies below, & revenge themselves for any objections to this treatment by stabbings with their pen!' Those who married authors should therefore take care not to 'extinguish' their own lives but 'go on with former pursuits'.[32]

Bertha Newcombe, an artist friend of the Hardys, visited them at Max Gate in March 1900 and reported in a letter to Mrs Gosse that she had felt much sympathy and pity for the way in which Emma was 'struggling against her woes. She asserts herself as much as possible and is a great bore, but at the same time is so kind and goodhearted, and one cannot help realising what she must have been to her husband. She showed us a photograph of herself as a young girl, and it was very attractive.' Emma also gave Miss Newcombe, as she had given Mabel Robinson, her own version of how she had first met the 'ill-grown, under-sized young architect' in Cornwall, discovered his genius, and encouraged him to write. 'I don't wonder', Miss Newcombe continued, 'that she resents being slighted by every one, now that her ugly duckling has grown into such a charming swan. It is so silly of her though isn't it not to rejoice in the privilege of being wife to so great a man?'[33] Emma might have termed that very much the view of an outsider. If it was her privilege to marry a man of genius it was also her misfortune. Hardy's life—externally so conventional, yet internally of such intense creative preoccupation—was conducted with the necessary ruthlessness of an artist with work to do, and he had become over the years increasingly unable, or unwilling, to treat Emma with the patience she required or provide her with the audience she craved.

There is no doubt that Emma had some talent with both pencil and pen, that she was capable of a generous and even courageous compassion for creatures, human and animal, who were ill equipped to fend for themselves, and that she retained to her death something of that inner vitality, that quickness of sympathetic perception, which had been so important an element in Hardy's first attraction to her: 'She was so *living*, he used to say.'[34] But while it is proper to give Emma her due, to perceive her as, equally with Hardy, a victim of the situation created by the mismatching of families, temperaments, and emotional needs, it is impossible to ignore the almost universal contemporary impression of her as opinionated, inconsequential, vain, tiresome, and often downright disagreeable. Her uncle the Archdeacon, whose virtues she so often invoked ('Such a handsome and distinguished man,' she murmured, when showing his portrait to a visitor only a few months before her death), is said to have referred to her as the most horrible woman in the world. Even Rebekah Owen, ostensibly her friend for many years, left an unkind picture of her 'in virginal white muslin & blue ribbons, with fat feet in baby-slippers & open work stockings posing before her tea visitors'.[35] Those who knew her best—Mabel Robinson, George Douglas, Gordon Gifford, and later Florence Dugdale— saw her failings with equal clarity, but were also able to respond to the warm impulsiveness and instinctive kindliness of her nature, and Hardy himself remained sufficiently responsive to those same qualities to attempt to sustain the marriage even beyond the point at which Emma had surrendered to more or less continuous resentment. Impatient of distractions, contemptuous of domestic squabbles, concerned for the efficiency of his daily habits of life and work, Hardy was in the end obliged, in the interests of basic survival as man and as artist, to have recourse to that policy of maximum separateness which Emma had been the first to promulgate. But even if the Hardys met only at dinner each day, the evening had always been a time of shared relaxation, and the maintenance for many years of such customs as reading aloud prevented their life together from dissolving into a mere social charade.

The disappointments of Hardy's marriage—the absence of children, the early fading of Emma's physical charms, the persistence and even exaggeration of her various affectations, pretensions, and gaucheries—were a source of great sadness to a man whose imagination (as revealed in such works as *Far from the Madding Crowd*, *The Return of the Native*, and *Tess of the d'Urbervilles*) was deeply erotic, whose appreciation of women as emotional and intellectual beings was unusually sharp, whose need of social and sexual as well as creative reassurance was particularly great, and who was drawn by instinct and upbringing towards habits of rootedness and retirement, the values of the hearth and the continuities of family tradition. It was, however, a disappointment he bore, if not exactly with stoicism, nor without yearning glances elsewhere, yet without open complaint. Clodd was certainly the recipient of Hardy's confidences about Emma, as of Emma's about Hardy, but there is no criticism of Emma in any of Hardy's surviving correspondence, either before or after her death, and only the most occasional and unspecific references, in letters to friends who knew Emma, to those domestic embarrassments which, in the early years of the new century, made it increasingly difficult for him to invite people to stay at Max Gate.

On 2 June 1899, Hardy's fifty-ninth birthday, Emma gave him a Bible. That November, perhaps on the occasion of her own fifty-ninth birthday, she put her name into a copy of Mary Wollstonecraft's *A Vindication of the Rights of Women*.[36] Despite the private opposition thus marked out, their public lives went on as much as usual. In May they returned to Wynnstay Gardens (this time to No. 20 instead of No. 9, the flat they had rented the previous year), and at the end of the month Hardy went off to Aldeburgh to spend the Whitsun weekend with Clodd, the other guests on this occasion including Walter Besant and Flinders Petrie, the Egyptologist.[37] He visited Meredith again at Box Hill and spent a day or two with Dorothy Allhusen (formerly Dorothy Stanley) in her house at Stoke Poges, where he was much impressed by the Duchess of Manchester's faultless recitation, at Gray's graveside, of the whole of the 'Elegy in a Country Churchyard'— not only because the young and beautiful Duchess reminded him of a dairymaid who had mindlessly repeated biblical passages when he was conducting Sunday school at Stinsford as a youth, but also because the 'Elegy' had always been of peculiar importance to his sense of himself as the novelist and poet of isolated localities, so much so that on a later occasion he is said to have asserted that Stinsford, the Mellstock of *Under the Greenwood Tree, was* Stoke Poges.[38]

Back in Dorset in mid-July 1899 the cycle rides were resumed with much enthusiasm and energy, although a tour with Henry through the New Forest to Southampton proved too tiring on account of the heat and was cut short after two days. One Sunday in August Hardy and Emma rode to Turnworth to visit the rector, the Revd Thomas Perkins, who was congenial to both of them as, respectively, a campaigner on behalf of the Society for the Protection of Ancient Buildings and a crusading anti-vivisectionist. They stayed on to attend a harvest festival in the church which Hardy had been instrumental in restoring thirty years earlier and then cycled the seventeen or so hilly miles back to Max Gate in the moonlight.[39]

Hardy was in his cycling knickerbockers when James Milne of the *Daily Chronicle* suddenly descended upon him in late August to seek an interview on the subject of Stonehenge, which was about to be put on the market by the owner of the land on which it stood. Hardy agreed to be quoted on such a subject, although it was curious, as he told Mrs Henniker, that he should be approached as an authority on the strength of a single scene in *Tess of the d'Urbervilles* when someone like Lady Grove's father, General Pitt-Rivers, had 'devotedly crawled among the stones on his hands & knees inspecting rabbit-holes, &c.'[40] In the course of arguing that the monument should be purchased for the nation, Hardy in fact displayed an impressive knowledge of the ruins and of the problems involved in preserving them not only from wealthy Americans who threatened to carry them off across the Atlantic (where they would become meaningless, in Hardy's view, because of the loss of all association) but also from the elements. As he explained, it was a matter not just of normal erosion but of the way in which the stones were being 'gradually undermined by the trickling down of the rain they intercept, forming pools on the ground, so that the foundation sinks on the wettest side till the stone topples over'.* His interest in Stonehenge thus re-aroused, Hardy took advantage of an invitation to a house-party at the

---

* It was perhaps in order to ensure that these ideas were accurately conveyed that Hardy drafted the 'interview' himself, leaving Milne to cast it into a journalistic mould.[41]

'But Mr Hardy, Mr Hardy, if you only knew all the circumstances': cartoon by
Will Dyson (1880–1938)   From the original drawing

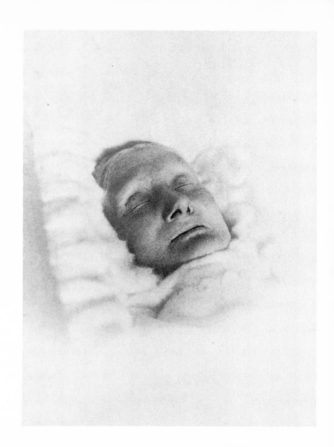

Right Jemima Hardy, photographed after death

Below The pets' cemetery, Max Gate

Portrait of Hardy by Jacques-Émile Blanche, 1906

A Singer Asleep

~~A South-Coast Nocturn~~

By Thomas Hardy.

(A . C . S . 1837 — 1909)

I.

In this ~~recess~~ ~~bright niche beside~~ fair niche above the ~~sleepless~~ unslumbering sea
That sentrys up & down all night, all day,
From cove to promontory, from ~~cape~~ ness to bay,
The Fates have fitly bidden that he should be
           Pillowed eternally .

II.

— It was as though a garland of red roses
Had fallen ~~upon~~ about the hood of some smug nun
When ~~in years faded~~ ~~my primness~~, dropped as from the sun
irresponsibly | In fulth of ~~canzons~~ numbers freaked with musical closes
Upon Victoria's formal middle time
           His leaves of rhythm & rhyme .

III.

O that far morning of a summer day,
When down a terraced street whose pavements lay
Glassing the sunshine into my bent eyes,
 I walked & read with a quick glad surprise
          New words, in classic guise ;

IV.

The ~~That~~ passionate ~~pages~~ ~~songs~~ of his earlier years,
Fraught with hot sighs, sad laughters, kisses, tears ! —
Fresh-fluted notes, yet ~~by~~ from a minstrel who
Blew them not naïvely, but as one who knew
          Full well why thus he blew.

V.

I still can hear the brabble & the roar
At those thy times, O still one, now passed through

Jeunes' the following month to arrange for his hosts to meet him at Stonehenge, explore the site with him, and then drive him back to Arlington Manor in their motor car.[42]

This was evidently Hardy's first experience of such a vehicle, but if he was struck by its juxtaposition with the antiquity of Stonehenge he was much more disturbed by the implications, both immediate and historical, of the prospect of hostilities in South Africa, which formed a principal topic of conversation among his fellow guests: 'It seems a justification of the extremest pessimism', he wrote to Mrs Henniker on his return home, 'that at the end of the 19th Centy we settle an argument by the Sword, just as they wd have done in the 19th centy B.C.' As the war became a reality, Hardy was torn—as he freely acknowledged—between a principled abhorrence of war and an irresistible responsiveness, now as in childhood, to the excitement generated by military activity: 'I constantly deplore the fact that "civilized" nations have not learnt some more excellent & apostolic way of settling disputes than the old & barbarous one, after all these centuries; but when I feel that it must be, few persons are more martial than I, or like better to write of war in prose & rhyme.'[43] Learning that Major Henniker was about to leave for South Africa with a contingent of the Coldstream Guards, Hardy wrote to wish him 'good fortune' and a 'speedy return', and took the letter with him to Southampton, where he stood at the dockside to watch the troops depart. He had hoped to meet Major Henniker there, but the Coldstreams, it transpired, were to leave the next day; the following morning, therefore, he roused up Gordon Gifford at an early hour, made him some fortifying cocoa, and sent him off on his bicycle to observe the scene and deliver the letter to Major Henniker by hand.[44]

Hardy's experiences, supplemented by his nephew's, became the basis of a poem entitled 'The Departure' (later 'Embarcation') which was published in the *Daily Chronicle* on 25 October. Much as he had been moved by the spectacle at Southampton, the poem remained critical of the failure of 'this late age of thought, and pact, and code' to settle disputes other than by 'the selfsame bloody mode' of ancient times. A few days later, the sight of an artillery battery moving out, at night and in pouring rain, from the Dorchester barracks on its way to South Africa prompted 'The Going of the Battery. Wives' Lament', a poem not overtly hostile to the war as such but unromantically and even pathetically insistent upon the bleakness of the particular scene and the deprivation and anxiety of those left behind. Not surprisingly, Hardy was distressed by the unqualified jingoism of Swinburne's sonnet 'The Transvaal', published in *The Times* in mid-October, and wrote to George Gissing specifically to congratulate him on an article in which he had criticized Swinburne's final exhortation, 'Strike, England, and strike home', for its irresponsible pandering to 'the old blood-thirst': it was, Hardy told him, 'the right word at the right moment'.[45]

Before the end of the year the first military engagements had been fought in South Africa and the first lists of casualties began to arrive back in England. Hardy again made a quick response in such poems as 'The Dead Drummer' (with its anticipation of the central idea of Rupert Brooke's 'The Soldier'), 'At the War Office After a Bloody Battle' (a scene, as he told Mrs Henniker, which he had not witnessed but could readily imagine),[46] and the magnificent 'The Souls of the Slain', whose prescience, its truth to the experience of subsequent wars, was of course grounded in its author's highly developed sense of history. It was significant of the profound change in Hardy's habits of thinking and writing that the verses should now come so swiftly and, on the whole, so richly, even while he found some difficulty, that November and December, in finishing the last two prose narratives he was ever to write, 'Enter a Dragoon' for *Harper's New Monthly Magazine* and 'A Changed Man' for Clement Shorter's *Sphere*.[47] No less significant was the readiness with which he devoted much of Christmas Day 1899 to the composition of a letter in defence of his recently published poem 'A Christmas Ghost-Story', criticized in that morning's *Daily Chronicle* on the grounds that its central figure, the 'puzzled' military ghost who asks when Christ's message of peace was 'ruled to be inept, and set aside', was scarcely heroic enough to be identified with 'one of the Dublin Fusiliers who cried amidst the storm of bullets at Tugela, "Let us make a name for ourselves!"' Arguing with point, erudition, and humour ('Hamlet's father, impliedly martial in life, was not particularly brave as a spectre'), Hardy suggested his portrayal had warrant both in logic and in literary precedent, and concluded: 'Thus I venture to think that the phantom of a slain soldier neither British nor Boer, but a composite, typical phantom, may consistently be made to regret on or about Christmas Eve (when even the beasts of the field kneel, according to a tradition of my childhood) the battles of his life and war in general, although he may have shouted in the admirable ardor and pride of his fleshtime, as he is said to have done: "Let us make a name for ourselves!" '[48]

The war against the Boers, a crisis of British imperialism which had certain similarities to the much later American experience in Vietnam, provoked in Hardy feelings compounded of fascination and revulsion. He followed the war news avidly and in early February 1900 visited the Dorchester barracks after learning that another local unit was about to leave for the war zone. At the same time, he was profoundly disturbed by doubts as to the validity of the cause itself and by awareness of the sufferings both of men and of horses, 'the mangled animals too, who must have terror superadded to their physical sufferings'. 'How horrible it all is,' he exclaimed, acknowledging that while he took 'a keen pleasure in war strategy & tactics, following it as if it were a game of chess', the moment he contemplated the conflict in human terms 'the romance looks somewhat tawdry, & worse'. He added that he had recently shocked one of the Moule brothers by suggesting that since Christianity had failed after almost two thousand years to teach countries how to keep the peace, there seemed no good reason not to abandon it in favour of some other religion, such as Buddhism.[49] Though implicitly consenting to the successful prosecution of the war once it had begun, Hardy had little sympathy with the resort to arms as an instrument of policy or with that imperial idea the policy was designed to uphold. As hostilities gradually diminished towards the end of 1900, and the first troops began to return home, Hardy wrote and published the most broadly acceptable, because least polemical, of his Boer war verses, 'Song of the Soldiers' Wives'. It was, he assured Mrs Henniker, the last of his 'war effusions, of which I am happy to say that not a single one is Jingo or Imperial—a fatal defect according to the judgment of the British majority at present, I dare say'.[50]

The sense of discrepancy between his own views and those of the country at large had exacerbated Hardy's sense of being at odds with his potential audience: 'I am puzzled what to do with some poems, written at various dates, a few lately, some long ago,' he wrote in October 1900. 'If I print them I know exactly what will be said about them: "You hold opinions which we don't hold: therefore shut up." '[51] His literary energies, nevertheless, were now entirely devoted to the writing of verse, and he concerned himself with his novels only retrospectively, as 'properties' to be managed and kept in the public eye. He had felt some anxiety about his financial position as a consequence of his abandonment of fiction and, more immediately, of the threatened bankruptcy, early in 1900, of Harper & Brothers, whose absorption of Osgood, McIlvaine & Co. had resulted in their becoming Hardy's principal publishers on both sides of the Atlantic. After yet another reorganization, however, Harper & Brothers not only emerged from their difficulties but sought to stimulate the sale of Hardy's fiction by publishing, at sixpence each, paper-covered editions of *Tess of the d'Urbervilles* and, a little later, *Far from the Madding Crowd*. Although Hardy's royalty on these was necessarily small, it was reassuring to be told that no less than a hundred thousand copies of the sixpenny *Tess* had been printed for sale in the United Kingdom alone.[52]

Hardy was still advising Lady Grove from time to time on the progress of her writing, the more willingly since she had now returned from a temporary excursion into fiction to lightly satirical essays on contemporary manners. Lady Grove paid two visits to Max Gate in March 1900 and it is possible that feelings of jealousy and emulation provoked by these encounters were instrumental in rekindling Emma's literary ambitions—especially since Lady Grove had seen fit to take issue with assertions about the irreligiousness of literature contained in some pamphlets which Emma had pressed upon her.[53] Stimulated—or perhaps irritated—by her husband's publication of poems in the pages of the *Westminster Gazette,* Emma submitted one of her own, only to receive from the editor a suggestion that it might be made 'a little simpler & more uniform in metre'.[54] She had more success with Clement Shorter, with whom she had recently begun to correspond, and in the 14 April 1900 number of the *Sphere* he included one of her poems in his own editorial section, the 'Literary Letter':

SPRING SONG.

Why does April weep?
 And why does April smile?
And why look we both sad and sweet
 A-wondering all the while?

If the winter's nights have flown,
And its dark days so lone,

And the summer's love's a-warm,
Coming like bees a-swarm—

Will not the sun's heart glow
To ours in a steady flow
Of joy and sure delight,
Of new deeds, and thought of might?

But none know what summer's days may bring.
That's why we weep and smile, come Spring.

Writing to Rebekah Owen shortly after the publication of her sonnet, as she called it, Emma remarked that two words—which she did not specify—would have been altered in the last verse had she been sent proofs. Shorter, it must be added, had somewhat undercut the gallantry of his gesture by explaining to his readers that he was publishing Emma's poem 'as one of the most enthusiastic admirers of her husband's books'.[55]*

A recurrence of an old ankle trouble of Emma's was one of several factors which deterred the Hardys from taking a house or flat in London in the spring of 1900. Emma felt 'pulled down very much', as she told Rebekah Owen, and did not in any case 'care greatly for the season & the extravagance, & attrition of society'.[57] They did, however, spend a few weeks in June at the West Central Hotel, Southampton Row. Hardy, who went up to London ahead of Emma and left again a week before she did, saw something of Lilian Gifford and especially of her brother, who had begun studying architecture in the offices of Sir Arthur Blomfield's old firm, now run by his two sons. Hardy had for some time been giving Gordon lessons in architectural theory and practice, taking him on visits to local churches and other buildings of architectural interest and going to some pains to encourage and develop his skills as a draughtsman. In January 1900 he had made arrangements with

---

* A year later the *Academy* printed on its literary gossip page another poem of hers, 'The Gardener's Ruse', with the comment: 'Mrs. Thomas Hardy tells us in the following interesting lines how rose trees are planted in Wessex.' The poem, descriptive of the dependence of the rose upon the onion which the gardener has dug in to feed its roots, might in fact be read as an ironic fable of Emma's perception of her relationship with her husband:

> Down far in the earth, hidden its worth,
>   The Onion, coarse and meek,
> Sought the roots of the roses, to give scent to its posies,
>   And brilliance in colour—a Freak![56]

Charles Blomfield for Gordon to receive more systematic training in London, pointing out that he had been able to teach his nephew in accordance with the firm's traditions. In London in the spring he checked on Gordon's progress and showed him how to use the library of art and architectural history at what is now the Victoria and Albert Museum. He also saw Mrs Henniker and spent another weekend at Stoke Poges with Dorothy Allhusen.[58]

By the end of June the Hardys had returned to Max Gate, where they received several groups of visitors over the next few weeks. Hamo and Agatha Thornycroft arrived, bringing their bicycles, in late July. A. E. Housman, Edward Clodd, and Arthur Symons—a somewhat surprising assortment—were there together the first weekend in August.[59] Gordon Gifford was invited down for a short visit; Lilian stayed for a longer period extending into the new year and joined Hardy and Emma, sometimes separately, often together, in cycle rides to Upwey, Cerne Abbas, Bulbarrow, and other places made attractive by their scenery or associations.[60]

In October news came of the serious illness of Helen Holder, the widow of the Revd Caddell Holder, and Emma left for the Hampshire seaside town of Lee-on-Solent to nurse her sister and try to set her financial affairs in order. As Helen Holder's condition worsened and Emma's absence from home was prolonged, Hardy became somewhat restive. Though Lilian was a pleasant enough companion for a cycle ride she was something of a nuisance to have around the house, especially as she had no real resources of her own and was not prepared to undertake any domestic tasks. In a letter of 6 November 1900 Hardy strongly hinted, although he did not specifically insist, that Emma should come home for a while and attend both to her niece and to household affairs in general. Emma did return briefly in mid-November, and for another day or two at the end of the month, but she otherwise remained at Lee-on-Solent until after Helen Holder's death and funeral in the first weeks of December. When Emma wrote to say that her sister had died, Hardy in his reply showed concern for her own physical well-being, and perhaps for her emotional state: 'I feel rather anxious lest you should have broken down under your exertions. There is now no need for continued effort, as, in settling up bills of a deceased person, Valuation for Probate, &c, the law allows a reasonable time for relatives to act in. So "take it stiddy" as they say here—the case now being no longer one in which a sick person is dependent on what you do.'[61]

Hardy's anxiety that Emma should return home in early

November may have been provoked in part by the return to Dorchester of Rebekah Owen, who remained throughout the next several weeks a sometimes amusing but often troublesome presence, constantly pressing for walks, cycle rides, visits to Max Gate, and inscriptions in her copies of Hardy's books. Miss Owen, who still liked to imagine that her relationship with Hardy had a strong romantic ingredient, thought of Lilian Gifford's presence on these occasions as that of a 'chaperon', and once gave a vivid, if exaggerated, description of her as being 'as fat as butter and the image of a China doll, with bushy frizzy dark hair, round red cheeks between which the tiny nose is scarcely visible'.[62] Emma herself, writing to Rebekah on 31 December 1900, spoke warmly of Lilian ('She is a bright little soul & we do not like to part with her to her parents') but gloomily of her own situation and of the world in general:

Do you read much of the new poetry—so involved, obscure, & so much of it? There is a mystical poem by Yeats—"The Shadowy Land" What does it mean? That no woman's love is worth offering to a man, who is as a god? I like *Ad Astra* by Chas Wentworth Wynne—a countryman of yours—Supposing women had always held the reins of this world would it not have been—by now, getting near the goal of happiness? This is a *man's world*— & in spite of their intellect shown most especially in science! it is in fact a terrible failure as to peace & joy—[63]

There is so much of Emma in this passage: her strenuous literary aspirations, often pathetic in their consequences but by no means contemptible in themselves; her earnest feminism, fed by raw resentment against her own husband but also by flashes of genuine insight; her belief, as urgent as it was confused, in not merely the possibility but the sheer necessity of a world better and happier than the one, full of war and cruelty and injustice, into which she had been born.

It seems an unkind coincidence that Hardy should have published, just two days before Emma's New Year's Eve letter to Rebekah Owen, some verses in which his own violently conflicting impulses had proved magnificently capable, if not of intellectual, at least of creative resolution. 'By the Century's Deathbed' was published by the *Graphic* as a reflection upon the moment of transition from the end of the nineteenth century to the beginning of the twentieth. Under its later title, 'The Darkling Thrush', it still eloquently testifies to the role of emotion in all of Hardy's thought, to the 'imaginativeness' of his reasoning—specifically, to his persistent hoping for the best even within the context of a profound conviction of the worst:

> So little cause for carolings
>   Of such ecstatic sound
> Was written on terrestrial things
>   Afar or nigh around,
> That I could think there trembled through
>   His happy good-night air
> Some blessed Hope, whereof he knew
>   And I was unaware.[64]

21

PESSIMISTIC
MELIORIST

REVIEWERS of *Wessex Poems,* like those of Hardy's later novels, had repeatedly invoked the term 'pessimism', as if in so doing they were simultaneously defining a distinctive philosophical position and making an adverse critical judgement. Hardy's exasperation at being so crudely categorized was exceeded only by his overwhelming sense of the inconceivability of 'optimism' in a world of such radical imperfection. Picking up a reference to Browning in an article on 'Form in Poetry' for which Gosse had taken *Wessex Poems* as his text, Hardy exclaimed: 'The longer I live the more does B.'s character seem *the* literary puzzle of the 19th century. How could smug Christian optimism worthy of a dissenting grocer find a place inside a man who was so vast a seer & feeler when on neutral ground?' In a much later note, prepared for inclusion in his own official 'Life' but not in fact used there, he drew a specific contrast between Browning's outlook and his own: 'Imagine you have to walk [a] chalk line drawn across an open down. Browning walked it, knowing no more. But a yard to the left of the same line the down is cut by a vertical cliff five hundred feet deep. I know it is there, but walk the line just the same.'[1]

Hardy's troubled musings upon the nature of existence and the problem of evil emerge with peculiar directness from the interview which William Archer conducted at Max Gate in February 1901. Having ventured the proposition that there might be 'a consciousness infinitely far off, at the other end of the chain of phenomena, always striving to express itself, and always baffled and blundering', Hardy accepted Archer's suggestion that this might be considered a new version of 'the good old Manichæan heresy, with Matter playing the part of the evil principle—Satan, Ahriman, whatever you choose to call it'. He insisted, however, that he did not necessarily believe that what Archer had called the 'evil principle' would ultimately prevail:

> For instance, people call me a pessimist; and if it is pessimism to think, with Sophocles, that 'not to have been born is best,' then I do not reject the designation. . . . But my pessimism, if pessimism it be, does not involve the assumption that the world is going to the dogs, and that Ahriman is winning all along the line. On the contrary, my practical philosophy is distinctly meliorist. What are my books but one plea against 'man's inhumanity to man'—to woman—and to the lower animals? . . . Whatever may be the inherent good or evil of life, it is certain that men make it much worse than it need be. When we have got rid of a thousand remediable ills, it will be time enough to determine whether the ill that is irremediable outweighs the good.

Challenged by Archer to say whether he really believed that mankind was ridding itself of such an evil as war, Hardy confidently declared:

> Oh yes, war is doomed. It is doomed by the gradual growth of the introspective faculty in mankind—of their power of putting themselves in another's place, and taking a point of view that is not their own. In another aspect, this may be called the growth of a sense of humour. Not to-day, not to-morrow, but in the fulness of time, war will come to an end, not for moral reasons, but because of its absurdity.[2]

Hardy's vision of the future was to become much darker during and after the First World War, but this unusually open exposition of his ideas at the very beginning of the century makes it possible to reconcile strands in his thought that might otherwise seem inconsistent. Fundamentally pessimistic about the human condition, in the sense that he believed birth and coming to consciousness to be a kind of original doom, Hardy could nevertheless respond with compassion to human (and animal) suffering and bring a reformist zeal to bear upon evils perceived as social and hence as potentially susceptible to amelioration or even eradication. He could also remain perpetually alert to the possibility, however faint, of some 'blessed hope' of which the most diligent search had thus far left him 'unaware'. Abstractly, theoretically, generally he could see only an incomprehensible and probably meaningless universe; concretely, practically, specifically he cared deeply about the human condition, perceived value in individual lives, supported humanitarian causes, and thought that things could and indeed did get better.

Where he differed from so many of his contemporaries was in the absoluteness, the literalness, with which he believed that not to be born was best, that consciousness was a curse, and that while death might be distressing to the bereaved the dead were not themselves to be pitied. *'Heu mihi, quia incolatus meus prolongatus est!'*; so wrote Hardy inside the back cover of his copy of *The Missal for the Use of the Laity*, marking also the passage and its translation ('Wo is me, that my sojourning is prolonged!') at the point at which they occurred within the volume. In February 1896 he insisted in conversation with Clodd that he wished he had never been born and, 'but for the effort of dying, would rather be dead than alive'; on Christmas Day 1890 he made a note for a poem: *'The amusement of the dead*—at our errors, or at our wanting to live on.' He told the grieving Rider Haggards that a child's death was 'never really to be regretted, when one reflects on what he has escaped', and when writing to Mrs Henniker about the fighting in South Africa, at a time when her husband was still on active service there, allowed himself to remark: 'It is sad, or not, as you look at it, to think that 40,000 will have found their rest there. Could we ask them if they wish to wake up again, would they say Yes, do you think?'[3] Ungracious as such opinions must have seemed to their recipients, they were for Hardy statements of the obvious, inherent in that bleak view of the human lot which gave him the courage—or perhaps the cruelty—to execute Tess and destroy Jude but also aligned him with some of the most austere of moralists and enabled him, agnostic though he was, to persist in the assertion of such traditional and officially Christian values as charity and what he himself called 'loving-kindness' at a time when those values were undergoing erosion and vulgarization, and when he himself was being vilified for their betrayal.

Whatever their formal austerity, Hardy's views did not teach him stoic detachment. That extraordinary capacity for imaginative identification which gave such strength to a novel like *Tess* was liable, at the level of everyday living, to take the form of an almost morbid sensitivity to the sufferings of others, and especially to the sufferings of animals. Lack of children no doubt had much to do with the extreme and indulgent fondness both Hardy and Emma displayed towards their pets, but it was at one level a protective tenderness entirely consistent with Hardy's larger vision of the scheme of things. When, in early April 1901, his favourite cat—'*my* cat—the first I have ever had "for my very own" '—was run over, like two other Max Gate cats before it, on the near-by railway line, Hardy exclaimed: 'The violent death of dumb creature[s] always makes me revile the contingencies of a world in which animals are in the best of cases pitiable for their limitations.' His distress at the involuntary and uncomprehending sufferings of horses and mules on the battlefields of the Boer War had already found expression in letters to Mrs Henniker, and when, in the summer of 1901, he was invited to share in the rejoicing at the demise of the Royal Buckhounds, he declared that such a development seemed a mere detail to one who believed, as he did, that it was in any circumstances 'immoral and unmanly to cultivate a pleasure in compassing the death of our weaker and simpler fellow-creatures by cunning, instead of learning to regard their destruction, if a necessity, as an odious task, akin to that, say, of the common hangman'.[4]

Despite the loss of the cat, the prolongation of the war in South Africa, and other sources of particular or general distress, Hardy felt somehow reinvigorated by the initiation of a new century and a new reign. Although he observed Queen Victoria's death in February 1901 with a poem of sober praise—written, so he claimed, during a bad headache, sent off immediately to *The Times,* and not revised before publication—he responded with instinctive cheerfulness to the 'general sense of the unknown lying round us, which in itself is a novelty. . . . [W]hat French editors call "Le God save" has to be sung somewhat differently by me when I feel musical, & my money all looks old-fashioned pending the new coinage.' Writing to Florence Henniker on 2 June, his sixty-first birthday, he spoke of the 'cheerful time' he had spent at Aldeburgh the previous weekend with Clodd and such fellow guests as Anthony Hope Hawkins, author of *The Prisoner of*

Zenda, and James Frazer of *The Golden Bough*; physically, he reported, he was still suffering from the effects of an earlier attack of influenza and had spent the day 'lying down, in sheer languor', but his mental condition was such that he could not recollect a year in which he had met his birthday 'with more equanimity'.[5]

The persistence of this lighter mood throughout most of 1901 perhaps reflected the establishment, at least temporarily, of some workable *modus vivendi* with Emma. She was in poor health and low spirits during the early part of the year and unwilling, for the second year running, to go to the trouble of taking a house or flat for the London season. They did, however, go up to town for a few weeks in May and June, staying in lodgings at 27 Oxford Terrace, on the south side of what is now Sussex Gardens. Hardy made his customary visit to the Private View of the Royal Academy, always a major social event of the season, and went with Emma to concerts by the violinists Ysaÿe and Kubelik—and almost certainly to other concerts as well. The music London could offer continued to rank high among his incentives for going there each year, and it was in April 1901 that he alluded to the recent deaths of Sir John Stainer and Sir Arthur Sullivan and confessed to a much deeper interest in the history of the concert hall than in the history of the theatre.[6]

Returning to Dorchester in the middle of June, the Hardys received shortly thereafter a visitation by the Whitefriars Club, a society of London journalists, some one hundred of whom came down to Dorset on 'A Pilgrimage to Wessex' and were entertained to tea in a marquee erected on the Max Gate lawn. The arrangements for the visit had been made chiefly by a journalist named Charles J. Hankinson ('Clive Holland'), whose persistent attentions and proliferating articles over the years irritated Hardy to the point of eventually refusing him admission to Max Gate, and the party was led by Clement Shorter, 'Prior' for the day, whom surviving photographs of the occasion show sitting in a position of honour on Hardy's left hand. He, too, was a man whom Hardy learned to distrust and dislike, although his multiple editorships made him useful as an occasional log-roller and printer of 'inspired' paragraphs. Soon after the Whitefriars visit, indeed, Hardy got Shorter to put into the *Sphere* a brief statement challenging a report in an American paper to the effect that some of the Whitefriars members had found the Wessex countryside somewhat dull: pointing out how little of Wessex they had in fact seen, Hardy tartly observed that 'The pilgrims were not absent from London much more than twelve hours altogether, returning there the same evening; and it is utterly impossible to see the recesses of this county in such a manner, not to mention those adjoining.'[7]

As the Whitefriars 'pilgrims' drove into Dorchester along the road from Puddletown, they did not realize that the old lady who waved a handkerchief to them from the roadside was Thomas Hardy's mother. Although she was in her late eighties, Jemima had insisted on making the gesture to those who were going to pay their respects to her now famous son, and Mary and Kate had little choice but to accompany her.* Always absolute in her opinions, Jemima had in old age become something of 'a character'— as Hardy himself was to call her at her death a few years later— strong-willed, sharp-tongued, very set in her ways and more than a little tyrannical. When in the summer of 1903 the Smith sisters of West Stafford visited the Bockhampton Hardys they found that 'the talk of the daughters who showed us their treasures, and the 90 year old Mrs. Hardy, in its salt and savour, made the ordinary party talk very insipid by contrast.' In a letter written to a relative in November 1903 Mary referred to her mother's having expressed herself 'with her old decisiveness': 'I hope', she added, 'her message will not offend but that you will only perceive she is as outspoken as ever.'[9] Though in full possession of her mental faculties, the old lady had become shrivelled in face, bent in body, and more and more confined to her bed; her health was a constant source of anxiety, her restlessness at her enforced inactivity a frequent cause of domestic friction. Since her daughters were no longer teaching they were able to devote themselves to her care, and although they retained the house in Dorchester they increasingly spent their time at Bockhampton: Kate in particular, assisted by her cousin Polly Antell (who had been taken into the household following her own mother's death), seems to have been occupied almost entirely with nursing and housework. Henry, having let his new house at Talbothays, was still living at the cottage with his mother, while Hardy himself continued as always to be a frequent visitor. It was entirely consistent with the dominance of Jemima's personality, and with that family loyalty she had so

* This anecdote was one of those introduced into *Later Years* at the suggestion of Sir James Barrie after Hardy's death (see below, p. 519 and n.). Though the story itself may be sufficiently authentic, it is questionable whether the accompanying allusion to Jemima's 'gay and youthful spirit even when approaching her ninetieth year' can be accepted entirely without qualification.[8]

persistently preached, that her children should have rallied so staunchly and unhesitatingly to her in her declining years.

Among the other relatives who came to Bockhampton during this period were James and Nathaniel Sparks, the sons of Jemima's nephew, Hardy's cousin, Nathaniel Sparks, who had gone to Bristol and become a maker and repairer of violins. In 1902 the two young men cycled over from Bristol along a scenic route which Hardy had mapped out for them and stayed for a time in Puddletown with Charles Meech Hardy, a distant but favourite cousin of Hardy's whom he sometimes employed to do building work on the house at 51 High West Street.[10]* During their call at Bockhampton, as Nathaniel later recalled, Jemima spoke of Emma, in a broad Dorset accent, as 'A thing of a 'ooman', insisting that 'She were wrong for I'—and, by implication, for her son. Both the Sparks brothers had unusual artistic gifts, James becoming an art teacher in Exeter, Nathaniel a distinguished engraver who exhibited regularly at the Royal Academy. Hardy recognized these qualities in his two young relatives, helped them from time to time in their careers, and kept in touch with them over the years—even though their one call at Max Gate in 1902 was marred by Emma's refusal to have anything to do with them. When Nathaniel Sparks, Sen., learned from his sons of Hardy's desire for a cello he found and sold him, at a very reasonable price, the one which now stands in the replica of Hardy's study in the Dorset County Museum: 'No doubt', said Hardy in his letter of thanks, 'the old viol has many a score time accompanied such tunes as "Lydia", or "Eaton".' And he added, with a reference to that Puddletown of a half-century earlier which both he and his cousin had known: 'the latter was the tune with which they used nearly to lift off the roof of Goddard's chapel of a Sunday evening.'[12]

The cheerfulness with which Hardy had greeted the new century had much to do with the sense of satisfaction with which he looked forward to the preparation and publication of his second volume of verse. Because of the visit of the Whitefriars Club on

---

* Hardy, however, is said to have opposed a contemplated marriage between Charles Hardy and Kate Hardy. The engagement between the couple drifted on desultorily over a period of many years and was formally terminated only by Charles's marriage to Elizabeth Veal in 1916—when he was fifty-seven and Kate sixty.[11]

29 June 1901, however, it was early July before he could give his full attention to the tasks of final selection and revision. Negotiations with Harper & Brothers had gone slowly and it was not until late May that agreement was reached upon the publication of an edition of 1,000 copies (half of them for England, the other half for the United States) of a book tentatively entitled 'Poems of Feeling, Dream, and Deed'. When it was eventually published, as *Poems of the Past and the Present,* in mid-November 1901, the collection enjoyed a generally favourable critical reception—though there were some reviewers who remained uncertain as to whether Hardy was writing poetry at all—and a second printing of 500 copies (again to be divided equally between the English and American markets) was ordered within two or three weeks.[13]

The poems on the war which Hardy had published in national newspapers had helped to make him better known as a poet, and it was perhaps for that reason that he placed them at the beginning of the volume, preceded only by the 'reverie' on the death of Queen Victoria. But *Poems of the Past and the Present* was, in any case, a distinct advance over its predecessor in almost every respect. Though still extremely heterogeneous, somewhat quirky in organization, and unequal in quality, it displayed those qualities less abrasively than *Wessex Poems* had done. More importantly, it contained a number of individual poems of great distinction and a sequence of thematically related texts, placed at the beginning of the section entitled 'Miscellaneous Poems', in which Hardy asserted and enforced—relentlessly, repetitiously, yet incrementally—the central tenets of his world view. 'The Mother Mourns', 'I Said to Love', 'At a Lunar Eclipse', 'The Lacking Sense', 'Doom and She', 'The Subalterns', 'God-Forgotten', 'The Bedridden Peasant', 'By the Earth's Corpse', 'To an Unborn Pauper Child'—in such poems, and in the three parts of 'In Tenebris' (placed separately from the other poems as reflecting a more directly personal grief), Hardy established, once and for all, the dominant mood and characteristic features of his philosophical verse. It is brooding, anguished, and discomforting. God is 'unknowing', Nature blind or asleep, controlling Doom indifferent to human suffering. In 'The Sleep-Worker' the complaint becomes first an appeal and then, in the sestet, a radical question:

> Should that morn come, and show thy opened eyes
> All that Life's palpitating tissues feel,
> How wilt thou bear thyself in thy surprise?—

> Wilt thou destroy, in one wild shock of shame,
> Thy whole high heaving firmamental frame,
> Or patiently adjust, amend, and heal?[14]

Sir George Douglas, in his *Bookman* review of January 1902, shrewdly observed that the poems grouped as 'Miscellaneous' were in fact those which had 'the most definite common characteristics' and were most strongly 'cumulative' in their effect. That effect, he continued, was 'one of a pessimism which leaves Leopardi's pessimism far behind, and makes that of James Thomson, of "The City of Dreadful Night," seem little more than posture-making.' Such beauty as the poems possessed lay, for Douglas, in their very austerity, and while he recognized the courage with which Hardy had given voice to his conclusions about the nature of the universe, he declined to share those conclusions or to accept the proposition that life was essentially and necessarily such a meaningless affair: 'The vast majority in this world are not unhappy.'[15] The kind of counter-arguments Hardy might have made to his friend, had it seemed worthwhile to take issue with such blank assertions, can be deduced from those he employed in May 1902 against a reviewer who had expressed admiration of Maeterlinck's view (in *The Buried Temple*) that while Nature appeared unjust she might in fact be behaving morally in ways mankind could not perceive:

> Pain has been, and pain is: no new sort of morals in Nature can remove pain from the past and make it pleasure for those who are its infallible estimators, the bearers thereof. And no injustice, however slight, can be atoned for by her future generosity, however ample, so long as we consider Nature to be, or to stand for, unlimited power. The exoneration of an omnipotent Mother by her retrospective justice becomes an absurdity when we ask, what made the foregone injustice necessary to Her Omnipotence?
>
> So you cannot, I fear, save her good name except by assuming one of two things: that she is blind, and not a judge of her actions, or that she is an automaton, and unable to control them; in either of which assumptions, though you have the chivalrous satisfaction of screening one of her sex, you only throw responsibility a stage further back.[16]

Although Hardy had no complaints about the way Harper & Brothers had handled *Poems of the Past and the Present* or, indeed, any of his previous books, he had for some time been

dissatisfied with the fact that their absorption of Osgood, Mc-
Ilvaine & Co. had resulted in his work being published in London
by 'a subordinate member of a New York house'. By February
1902, when Clarence McIlvaine wrote on behalf of Harper &
Brothers to remind him that it was time to renew the agreement
originally made with Osgood, McIlvaine & Co. for the 'Wessex
Novels' edition, Hardy had already decided to find another
English publisher, even while retaining Harper & Brothers as his
publishers in the United States. McIlvaine protested that Hardy's
defection would damage the firm's reputation, and Hardy, mindful of old loyalties, made a point of obtaining from G. Herbert
Thring and Anthony Hope Hawkins, both officers of the Incorporated Society of Authors, an assurance that, since the contract
had been signed for a limited term only, he was perfectly within
his professional and moral rights in allowing it to lapse. Anxious
to soften what McIlvaine so evidently regarded as a severe blow,
Hardy allowed an extra six months beyond the end of the original
contract during which Harper & Brothers could continue to act as
his sole publishers and sell off as much as they could of existing
stocks. He also undertook to try to persuade the new publishers,
whoever they might be, to enter into negotiations for the purchase
of plates and of any stock still on hand.[17]

Hardy did not approach the Macmillans until after his dealings
with McIlvaine had been concluded, but it is clear that he had
long had it in mind to move in their direction whenever the
opportunity offered itself. He had always been grateful for the
interest Alexander Macmillan had shown in his early work, and
though his subsequent dealings with the firm had not been uniformly happy he was well satisfied with their handling of the
colonial editions of his novels and had formed a high estimation of Frederick Macmillan, the current head, on both personal and professional grounds. The latter responded to Hardy's
initiative with understandable enthusiasm, guaranteeing that if
the move was indeed made Hardy would never have cause to
regret it. A comprehensive agreement was drawn up, giving Hardy
a royalty of one-fourth of the selling price on books sold at six
shillings and upwards, one-fifth on those sold at prices between
four and five shillings, and one-sixth on all cheaper volumes; the
existing arrangement for a royalty of fourpence a copy on all
Colonial Library volumes was reconfirmed. Once Hardy had
signed this agreement in April 1902, Macmillan suggested that
even though the change of publishers would not formally take

place until October, when the extended Harper contract ran out, there was no reason why the printing of titles in the new Macmillan format should not begin. Hardy agreed, stipulating only that he be allowed to make a number of minor revisions, including the incorporation of changes to the Preface of *Far from the Madding Crowd* which he had already made for the sixpenny edition recently published by Harper, and the toning down of the much-criticized pig's pizzle scene in *Jude the Obscure*.[18]

Emma, one of the most intransigent objectors to *Jude,* had also disapproved of *Poems of the Past and the Present,* at least of those particular poems she characterized to Rebekah Owen, with more vehemence than precision, as 'personal—moans, & fancies etc.— Written *"to please"* . . . others! or himself—but not <u>me</u>, far otherwise'. Her troubles with her husband, she insisted, would be less irksome if only 'his later writings were of a more faithful, truthful, & helpful kind'. Emma had another of her accidents on 2 June 1902, when Hardy's sixty-second birthday coincided with news of the much-delayed conclusion of the Boer War (an event deemed worthy of the flying of a celebratory flag at Max Gate), and it was largely because of her low spirits and lack of energy earlier that spring—abetted by their joint apprehension that London would be unusually crowded and expensive in a coronation year—that they did not go up to London during the entire season of 1902 but remained at home in Dorset.[19] In October, however, they made a brief holiday trip to Bath. On Sunday, 26 October, Hardy went with Emma to morning service at Bath Abbey and then rode to Bristol on the bicycle he had brought with him, attending Evensong at St. Mary Redcliffe before setting off on the return journey. Another expedition from Bath to Bristol—possibly to call on Nathaniel Sparks and his family—was the occasion of his falling off his bicycle, being 'rubbed down by a kindly coal-heaver with one of his sacks', and thus becoming such an object of pity that the woman from whose shop he sought to purchase an old copy of Hobbes's *Leviathan* had not the heart to ask him more than sixpence for it. He was much embarrassed to discover later that it was a first edition: as he confessed to Mrs Henniker, had he known that at the time he would 'hardly have had the conscience to take it'.[20]

Hardy and Emma had spent a week together at Bath during the period of their courtship, twenty-nine years previously, and in 1877 Hardy had gone there with his father—the occasion he had in mind when telling Florence Henniker that his October

1902 visit had been 'as pleasant as could be in a place last visited to see those who are now dead'. Bath was also full of other, more famous ghosts: 'I stayed [he told Douglas] close to where Pitt was living when he received the news of Austerlitz that is said to have killed him, & looking out of window in the small hours I could in fancy see his emaciated form.'[21] It is likely, indeed, that Hardy's visit to Bath was impelled less by marital or family sentiment than by the needs of the manuscript of *The Dynasts,* on which he was just beginning to work in earnest. Although a grand work on the Napoleonic period had been in contemplation from at least as far back as 1875, the final scheme for *The Dynasts* as published was apparently drawn up some time late in 1897. Hardy had always intended it to be in verse, and had gradually come to conceive of it as a verse drama, distantly modelled on Shakespeare's histories, with their differing levels of action and occasional use of 'chorus' figures. The choice of blank verse for the central historical sequences was, in the circumstances, almost automatic, but there was no ready solution to the basic difficulties involved in treating of such material in verse of any kind. Fortunately he was no longer under the pressures he had known as a writer of fiction and could work at his own pace, taking up and laying down the manuscript as mood and occasion suggested.

Hardy's mind dwelt much upon the past at this period, partly because of *The Dynasts,* partly because he was a frequent witness of the increasing frailty of his mother, partly because he was becoming more sharply aware of his own advancing years: in hot weather, he told Dorothy Allhusen, he was now much troubled by moisture exuding from one of his eyes, so that he had to keep wiping it.[22] During the course of the summer he had written three letters to the *Dorset County Chronicle* about Dorchester's associations with Edmund Kean, the actor, and in responding, in March, to Rider Haggard's request for some observations on the history of the Dorset argricultural labourer, he had welcomed recent economic improvements in the labourers' situation but regretted, as in his essay on 'The Dorsetshire Labourer', that their increased mobility had led to such a breakdown of the oral tradition: 'I can recall the time when the places of burial, even of the poor and tombless, were all remembered; the history of the squire's family for 150 years back was known; such and such ballads appertained to such and such localities; ghost tales were attached to particular sites;

and secret nooks wherein wild herbs grew for the cure of divers maladies were pointed out readily.'[23] He more and more saw his own published works as a repository of such vanishing information, and in one of his letters to Frederick Macmillan early in 1902 he had touched upon the possibility of an annotated edition, somewhat along the lines of Scott's *magnum opus* edition, which would give 'a really trustworthy account of real places, scenery, &c'.[24]

Wessex as a literary reality, however, he saw as very much his own property. In that same letter to Macmillan he expressed a sense of unfairness at the prospect 'that capital shd be made out of my materials to such an extent as promises to be done'. He objected, strongly and publicly, when he was accused of having caused confusion by popularizing an unhistorical identification of Wessex with Dorset—insisting that in both his writings and his maps he had always included five other counties as well—and was distressed by the omission of the words 'The Wessex Novels' from the proof of the half-title of *Tess of the d'Urbervilles,* published in October 1902 as the first volume under the new Macmillan imprint. As he told Frederick Macmillan: 'For commercial reasons, not to speak of literary ones, I fancy the words should be retained. Many people have heard of the Wessex novels who do not know their individual titles. This inclusive title is, moreover, copyright, & as several writers have used "Wessex" in their productions since I began it they may annex "Wessex Novels" if we let the name drop.'[25]

Hardy's sense of jealous proprietorship was exercised not just by the continuing flood of 'pilgrims' from London and other parts* (the marquee was re-erected on the Max Gate lawn in September 1905 for the visit of two hundred members of the Institute of Journalists), but by the proliferation of such topographical guides as Bertram Windle's *The Wessex of Thomas Hardy* (1902), Wilkinson Sherren's *The Wessex of Romance* (1902), Charles G. Harper's *The Hardy Country* (1904), Sir Frederick Treves's *Highways and Byways in Dorset* (1906), and Clive Holland's *Wessex* (1906).[27] At once amused and slightly appalled by the book-making he had provoked—he remarked of

---

* When, in 1906, Hardy apologized for being absent from home at the time when the members of the Society of Dorset Men in London would be touring Dorset, he suggested that he had in a sense already welcomed them to the neighbourhood—'in a rather lengthy speech of some twenty volumes, which I hope you will take as delivered on the occasion'.[26]

Harper's *The Hardy Country* that it was 'rather hard upon the landowners of this part of England that their property should be so called by these tourist-writers'—Hardy was shrewd enough to recognize that the circulation of such volumes could serve only to enhance the sale of his own books. Perhaps for that reason he co-operated with Windle and his illustrator, Edmund New, wrote a brief foreword to a guidebook to Dorchester, and took a lively interest in the paintings by Walter Tyndale which were used to illustrate the Clive Holland volume. He worked most closely, however, with Hermann Lea, an enthusiastic Dorset photographer, who produced a first, slim volume, *A Handbook to the Wessex Country of Thomas Hardy's Novels and Poems*, in 1905 and, in 1912, what amounts to the authorized version of Hardyan topography, the profusely (if not very vividly) illustrated *Thomas Hardy's Wessex*.[28]

None of this prevented him from being annoyed, from time to time, by the tourists and literary pilgrims who bought and used such books. He complained to Lea that he had been unknowingly 'Kodaked' while visiting the Bockhampton cottage, and he was anxious that neither the topographical details nor the photographs included by Lea should be so specific as actually to invite such intrusion upon his own privacy or that of other members of his family.[29] Passionate believer though he was in that dictum (misquoted from Southey) which he commended to the Wessex Society of Manchester in January 1902—'Whatever strengthens local attachments strengthens both individual & national Character'—Hardy had no intention of exposing unnecessarily to public gaze the precise nature and degree of his attachment to, and dependence upon, his own locality. He had at first declined to write an introduction to the new edition of the Dorchester town guide on the grounds that his doing so would tend to dissipate the feeling on the part of the Wessex pilgrims that they were 'penetrating a disguise which (as is quite true) I had no wish for them to penetrate', and suggested instead that he might draw the attention of the editor to appropriate quotations from *The Mayor of Casterbridge*.[30] Lea, however, had become a trusted friend who could be counted upon to keep a confidence, and in advising him on the completion of his *Handbook* Hardy practised a different kind of indirection, even to the point of supplying the actual wording of two passages which explained that the fictional Wessex corresponded not to Dorset alone but to 'the Wessex of history' and that the towns, villages, and houses given fictional names were only *'suggested* by such and such real places', even though they might in practice be quite readily identifiable.[31] It was another step in that adoption of authorial disguises which began with the placing of anonymous paragraphs in newspapers and magazines and ended, many years later, in the ghost-writing of his official biography.

In the first week of 1903 the Hardys went up to London for a day or two in order to attend the wedding of Madeleine Stanley, Lady Jeune's elder daughter, and St. John Brodrick (later Lord Midleton), who was then Secretary of State for War in the Conservative Government led by A. J. Balfour.[32] They otherwise spent the winter at Max Gate, where Hardy continued to work on the first part of *The Dynasts*. He had been put on a committee to oversee a proposed restoration of the ancient church of Fordington St. George, over which the Revd Henry Moule had so long presided, but he withdrew in February 1903 upon discovering that the proposed changes went beyond what he considered practically necessary, aesthetically desirable, or historically appropriate. A few weeks later he inspected a font in the church on behalf of the Society for the Protection of Ancient Buildings, and over the succeeding years he continued to make such protests as he could against the grandiose rebuilding which more than doubled the size of the church in the period between 1906 and 1927.[33]

Hardy was still acting as a local magistrate from time to time, though he had sat only on the county bench since being elevated to it in 1894, and in the early years of the new century he made a number of appearances as a grand juror at the thrice-yearly Dorset Assizes. Since it is the task of grand juries not to try cases but to decide whether there is a prima-facie case for trial, Hardy was not called upon to pronounce upon the guilt or innocence of the accused, nor, of course, was he involved or even necessarily present when sentences were handed down: in being called upon, for example, to 'find a true bill against two murderers', he was required to pass judgement solely upon the technical validity of the indictment itself.[34] Hardy's taste for the theatrical was gratified by the pomp and solemnity of the Assizes, and while he may also have enjoyed the local distinction his position conferred it would be equally true to say that he conferred distinction upon the proceedings by his presence: one of the Dorchester clergy spoke after Hardy's death of having seen 'more than one of His Majesty's judges look up sharply and curiously to identify the possessor of the quiet voice that answered "Here" to the name "Thomas Hardy" when the roll was called'.[35] Hardy had, in any case, the satisfactory sense of serving the community and performing an important and responsible legal function even while remaining comfortably insulated from ultimate issues of life and death. It was from within this context, in April 1903, that he responded with slightly troubled evasiveness to an American enquiry as to his views on capital punishment: 'As an acting [i.e., active] Magistrate I think Capital Punishment operates as a deterrent from deliberate crimes against life to an extent that no other form of punishment can rival. But the question of the moral right of a community to inflict that punishment is one I cannot enter into in a necessarily brief communication.'[36]

Emma was again in poor health in the spring of 1903 and hesitant about taking London lodgings for the season. Hardy went up to 'a couple of bachelor's rooms in St John's Wood' while she was regaining her strength and summoning up her courage, and at the very end of May he accepted an invitation from Clodd to spend the Whitsun weekend at Aldeburgh with Shorter, Flinders Petrie, Henry W. Nevinson, the essayist and journalist, Alfred Cort Haddon, the anthropologist, and Hugh Clifford, the colonial administrator, recently returned from service in Borneo. The talk one evening, Clodd recorded in his diary, was largely on the 'race question'; the following evening it was too various to summarize, prompting him to 'sigh for a phonograph to fix it'. In London a week or so later Clodd, Shorter, and Hardy went to Madame Tussaud's waxworks after hours, as the guests of the current proprietor, John Tussaud, who allowed them to handle the Napoleonic relics. Five years later, after reading the third and final volume of *The Dynasts,* Shorter was to recall to Clodd 'how, in the incubating period of that book, we three pranced about Tussauds' by night, Hardy wearing the Waterloo cocked hat!'[37]

To Nevinson, meeting him for the first time, Hardy seemed already, on the eve of his sixty-third birthday, an old man:

Face a peculiar grey-white like an invalid's or one soon to die; with many scattered red marks under the skin, and much wrinkled—sad wrinkles, thoughtful and pathetic, but none of power or rage or active courage. Eyes bluish grey and growing a little white with age, eyebrows and moustache half light brown, half grey. Head nearly bald on the top, but fringed with thin and soft light hair. The whole face giving a look of soft bonelessness, like an ageing woman's. Figure spare and straight; hands very white and soft and loose-skinned.

Though Nevinson's portrait was cruelly exaggerated—and was later resented by Hardy for that reason—photographs of this period do indicate a curious puffiness about the face and hands that had not been there when he was in his fifties and that increasing age was soon to refine away. Nevinson's description of Hardy's hands was to some extent endorsed by the French painter Jacques-Émile Blanche's first impression of Hardy a couple of years later: 'J'avais envie de baiser la main qu'il me tendait, une main blanche, un peu gonflée et inerte, de gouteux, aux doigts comme engourdis et inhabiles à l'exercice.' On the other hand, Nathaniel Sparks, himself an engraver, noticed at this same period the functional squareness of Hardy's fingertips, Florence Dugdale, just a few years later, was struck from the first by Hardy's 'capable' hands, and there is no evidence to suggest that those hands were ever gouty ('de gouteux') or arthritic—though in April 1898 he did injure the thumb and some fingers of his right hand by letting a sash-window fall on it.[38] Certainly the firmness and clarity of his beautiful handwriting remained undiminished to the day of his death.*

Emma did eventually come up to London at the beginning of June 1903—leaving Max Gate in the charge of Henry Joseph Moule, who was recuperating from a serious illness and valued the opportunity of direct daily access to the surrounding countryside—but she was soon driven home again by the bitter cold and continual rain: 'I have known about 30 London Junes', Hardy remarked, 'but never remember such an one as this.' The weather turned much warmer towards the end of the month and Hardy— though harassed by his having been recognized by the other people at his lodgings—stayed on long enough to escort Lilian Gifford to the Royal Academy soirée at the beginning of July: 'It was such a novelty & a delight to her', he told Emma the next day, 'that I was so glad I took the trouble; she never saw anything at all like it before, poor child, & though I felt past it all, I enjoyed

---

* Hardy's hand was drawn and analyzed by Eveline M. Forbes in 1894: 'The fingers of this hand are (with the exception of the first) square, and these square fingers tell of a desire to weigh and measure all arguments before coming to any decision; also of interest in moral science; while the pointed first finger declares imagination and love of literature.'[39]

it in an indirect way through her eyes.'[40] Back in Dorchester for the remainder of the summer, he discovered that the inconveniences of fame as experienced in terms of accidental London encounters could become still more acute when brought to his own doorstep: 'The usual rank & file of summer tourists have called here', he reported to Mrs Henniker, '& I have given mortal offence to some by not seeing them in the morning at any hour. I send down a message that they must come after 4 o'clock, & they seem to go off in dudgeon.' He turned the edge of the complaint by a humorous recollection of his own experience as a tourist being shown over Montacute House, Somerset, the previous week, when the residents had 'sat like statues, reading in their library, & without speaking a word, whilst I was inspecting it, as if they, too, were part of the architecture. They are a very ancient family, I admit.'[41]

Some of the visitors to Max Gate were more welcome—James Sparks, for example, came in early September to finish a bronze medallion of Hardy he had begun on a previous visit[42]—but Hardy was now working intensively, and even urgently, on the final stages of Part First of *The Dynasts*. Confessing to Clodd several months later that he had originally intended not to publish that part by itself but to wait until the entire work was ready, he explained: 'On my return here from London I had a sudden feeling that I should never carry the thing any further, so off it went.' On 28 September he dispatched the manuscript to Frederick Macmillan, pointing out that while it constituted the first part of an intended trilogy it was nevertheless complete in itself, and that the question of the completion of the two remaining parts might depend to some extent upon the fate of the first. The drama he had spoken of, he told Douglas, was 'at last about to see the light, but it has been an unconscionable time on the stocks, or rather on & off, for though I sketched it with fair completeness years ago I have only taken it up at odd moments till since my last volume of poems was published, never feeling sure that I was really going to finish it. This view I may hold yet, in one sense, for while the drama is sufficiently self-contained, it is but the first of a trilogy that I may not get to the end of except under favouring circumstances, one of which would be a welcome to this part that it may not get.'[43]

It was Hardy who suggested that the spine of the first volume should carry a single star rather than the words 'Part First', since the latter might 'suggest incompleteness too forcibly to the

would-be purchaser', and his comments to Frederick Macmillan
on the specimen page testify to the eye for typography and book
design which he had developed over the years:

> The size of the print-page I note, is 5¾ in. by 3⅜: therefore I
> gather that you propose to reset the book when, later on, it is
> brought into the 3/6 uniform edition, as it could not be cut down
> to that size without looking ugly. If it should be desirable to
> avoid resetting I suggest that the type-page be kept as in the old
> books 5¼ inches by 3 inches—the type being *small pica* old style
> for the main part, & *brevier* for the stage directions—so as to get
> the matter into the smaller compass.[44]

The proofs reached him for correction in mid-October 1903, but
hold-ups in the printing of the American edition and consequent
uncertainties over American copyright set back publication until
the following January. Short as the delay was by comparison with
the long years the work had already been in gestation, an anxious
Hardy found that it wore upon his nerves. Literary journalists
had pressed him for information about the title and subject of the
new book, he told Frederick Macmillan in November: 'Is there
any harm in letting them know a little?' And to Florence Henniker, just before Christmas, he exclaimed that whether 'the play'
would 'interest you at all, or anybody, I am in heathen ignorance,
never having attempted the kind of performance before'.[45]

22

THE DYNASTS

COMPOUNDING Hardy's uncertainty over his forthcoming public appearance in yet another new guise—as the author of a verse drama designed to be read rather than performed—were his private worries about Emma. Lilian Gifford had again been staying at Max Gate, and in mid-November 1903 Emma carried her off on a visit to Dover, whence they were tempted into crossing the Channel to Calais. Messages exchanged between Emma and Bessie Churchill, the Max Gate parlourmaid, were chiefly concerned with the health and comfort of the four household cats; learning that one of them had been brought home after an absence at the vet's, Emma counselled: 'Keep Marky away from Pixie—perhaps also from Snow-dove they will try to chase her off.'[1] Hardy, who wrote frequently, also mentioned the cats but included a good deal of other local and personal gossip—including news of his mother's health—apparently as a way of keeping Emma in touch with home and with reality. While he thought Emma was at Dover he could accept her absence with some equanimity, but once she and Lilian had gone to France he began to show signs of anxiety and to drop ever broader hints as to the desirability of an early return. Evidently fearing further unheralded movements, he warned her not to let herself run short of money, since it would take time to send funds from England, and urged: 'Mention the *town* when you give yr address as I am not sure sometimes. Also leave yr address when you come away, in case a late letter arrives, but the best plan is to stay to the day you say you are going to leave on. Wherever you go (if you go anywhere else) it will be best to keep near the sea, as you may get a cold inland, particularly at Paris.'[2]

Hardy ended this letter of 21 November by optimistically wishing Emma a pleasant Channel crossing, but more than a week later, after he had himself been up to London and caught his usual cold, she still showed no signs of returning—even though, as Hardy was careful to point out, her return ticket was valid only for a month. He now wrote with greater urgency, but still without peremptoriness, as if fearing to provoke her into a contrary response:

I think your wise course wd be not to stay there *much longer*: as winter weather may bring an illness, & from my experience Friday night & yesterday I know the misery of being unwell at an hotel—much more seriously ill, alone, with a foreign doctor. I should, of course, be delighted for Lilian to come on here, but my advice is that you do not stay there alone. Perhaps your plans may be influenced by the news Bessie tells me—that she is not going to be married after all, but will stay on here with us. This will enable us to go away anywhere after Christmas—not to London, but to some place where influenzas do not abound.[3]

Bessie Churchill wrote to Emma the same day to confirm her willingness to stay on and do the cooking, if Emma would pay her higher wages and employ a parlourmaid to perform the other household duties. Whether or not Emma had originally taken flight in the face of an impending servant crisis, she did now make a last sketch of Calais on 30 November and return to Max Gate in the first week of December. Although Hardy put a bold face on the whole episode when writing to Florence Henniker—'Em spent a month partly at Dover, partly at Calais, the air there having an invigorating effect upon her, but I did not go on to her as I had intended'—it is clear that he was disturbed by his wife's escapade and that the relative calmness of his letters to her had been hard-won.[4]

Part First of *The Dynasts,* finally published on 13 January 1904, met with a respectful but uncertain reception from the early reviewers. The sources of their difficulty were obvious enough.

Although its form was dramatic, it was not intended for stage presentation. Although written in verse, much of that verse was of an obviously and even deliberately prosaic quality. Although divided into acts, there were six such acts in this first volume, instead of the familiar and classical five, and a total of nineteen promised for the work in its three-volume entirety. Although the subject matter was historical, and most of the space devoted to the re-creation of great historical events, the reader was expected to supply sufficient knowledge and imaginative sympathy to flesh out the presented material with supplementary information and understanding:

> It may hardly be necessary to inform readers that in devising this chronicle-piece no attempt has been made to create that completely organic structure of action, and closely-webbed development of character and motive, which are demanded in a drama strictly self-contained. A panoramic show like the present is a series of historical 'ordinates' (to use a term in geometry): the subject is familiar to all; and foreknowledge is assumed to fill in the curves required to combine the whole gaunt framework into an artistic unity. The spectator, in thought, becomes a performer whenever called upon, and cheerfully makes himself the utility-man of the gaps.[5]

Hardy may have meant no more than that 'foreknowledge' of the subsequent pattern of historical events (e.g., that Nelson will die in his moment of triumph) could extort from the reader an intensely emotional response to scenes not especially dramatic or moving in themselves, but this apparent shifting of the burden of responsibility from the author's shoulders on to the reader's was to give offence to a number of reviewers. Others were offended, irritated, or simply puzzled by the curious machinery of the 'phantasmal Intelligences', whose function was to comment upon the unfolding action from their various points of view, and by the fundamental assumption of the entire work that the force ultimately controlling the universe was that blind, unconscious power invoked in the opening lines:

SHADE OF THE EARTH
What of the Immanent Will and Its designs?

SPIRIT OF THE YEARS
It works unconsciously, as heretofore,
Eternal artistries in Circumstance,
Whose patterns, wrought by rapt aesthetic rote,

Seem in themselves Its single listless aim,
And not their consequence.[6]

Two of the most acute among the early reviewers, Max Beer-bohm and A. B. Walkley, agreed in finding that the scale and mode of presentation had the effect of reducing the individual historical figures to the stature of marionettes. Walkley made mild fun with the proposition of presenting *The Dynasts* as a puppet play; Beerbohm, though his final judgement was more favourable than Walkley's, permitted himself some touches of broader humour:

> I confess that I, reading here the scene of the death of Nelson, was irresistibly reminded of the same scene as erst beheld by me, at Brighton, through the eyelet of a peep-show, whose proprietor strove to make it more realistic for me by saying in a confidential tone, ' 'Ardy, 'Ardy, I am wounded, 'Ardy.—Not mortially, I 'ope, my lord?—Mortially, I fear, 'Ardy.' The dialogue here is of a different and much worthier kind; yet the figures seem hardly less tiny and unreal. How could they be life-sized and alive, wedged into so small a compass between so remote and diverse scenes?

Beerbohm also concurred with Walkley in finding the Wessex peasants the only genuinely human figures, even to the extent of marring by their very vitality the over-all unity of effect.[7]

It was Walkley, however, with his considered rejection of 'closet-drama' as a form, who provoked Hardy to write to the *Times Literary Supplement* in defence of *The Dynasts* in particular and of 'unactable play-like poems'—including Shelley's *Prometheus Unbound* and Byron's *Cain*—in general. He argued not only that the artistic spirit was 'at bottom a spirit of caprice', so that an artist might quite legitimately 'borrow the methods of a neighbour art', but that Walkley was wrong in asserting that a work written in dramatic form did not lend itself to private reading:

> It surely ought to have occurred to him that this play-shape is essentially, if not quite literally, at one with the instinctive, primitive, narrative shape. In legends and old ballads, in the telling of 'an owre true tale' by country-folks on winter nights over a dying fire, the place and the time are briefly indicated at the beginning in almost all cases; and then the body of the story

follows as what he said and what she said, the action being often suggested by the speeches alone. . . . Of half-a-dozen people I have spoken to about reading plays, four say that they can imagine the enactment in a read play better than in a read novel or epic poem. It is a matter of idiosyncrasy.[8]

By thus insisting upon the narrative character of *The Dynasts* Hardy underlined its essential continuity with the world of his fiction, and, indeed, with the origin of that fiction in the tale-telling of his childhood—just as he had expressed the hope, before the first part appeared, that it would prove to be 'as readable as a novel, owing to certain arrangements in its construction'. A little later on he agreed with Arthur Quiller-Couch's suggestion that he had been impelled to find a new form by a growing sense of the inadequacy of the novel as a means of 'expressing how life strikes us', and he perhaps saw the multiple viewpoints of *The Dynasts,* its omnipresent commenting voices, as providing a solution to that problem of philosophical inconsistency which had troubled him in novels such as *Tess* and *Jude,* and the combination of the machinery of the spirits with the conventions of the dramatic soliloquy as offering methods of presenting those 'true realities of life, hitherto called abstractions' which had at once fascinated and eluded him in *The Woodlanders.*[9] In more recent years the resources of radio have made possible a fuller realization of the text than either private reading or the occasional attempts at public staging could supply in Hardy's own day. It has also become possible to argue that those bird's-eye views of battlefields and panoramic sweeps of entire continents which seemed so extraordinary in the first years of the twentieth century are potentially cinematic, and that Hardy in seeking for a narrative form more expansive and more flexible than the novel as he knew it was groping towards the methods of a 'neighbour art' which had not yet been fully born.*

When Walkley, in a subsequent comment, succeeded in demonstrating some of the flaws in the theoretical position Hardy had adopted, the latter retorted, in a second letter to the *Times Literary Supplement,* that the 'real offence' of *The Dynasts* in the eyes of the critics lay not in its form but in its philosophy, its unfashion-

---

* Hardy turned down proposals for a film version of *The Dynasts* which were made following the Granville-Barker stage production of 1914–15—perhaps because he had disapproved of that production and feared that the film would simply reproduce it.[10]

able world view.[11] The accusation was certainly inaccurate as far as Walkley himself was concerned, and only partly true of the reviewers in general, but it represented a strategy and a rationalization entirely consistent with Hardy's long-established habit of attributing hostile criticism to some specific cause which had little directly to do with the literary quality of the work under discussion—to the 'pure woman' issue in *Tess,* for example, or the 'marriage question' in *Jude.* He may genuinely have believed that the reviewers' 'appraisement of the work was in truth, while nominally literary, at the core narrowly Philistine, and even theosophic'. In private correspondence, however, he freely admitted that *The Dynasts* lacked 'finish'—he had been 'appalled', he told Gosse on 31 January, at some of the verbal infelicities he had found since the work was published—and it was, in fact, the quality of the verse, line by line and paragraph by paragraph, which was to provide the theme of much of the most serious, and most damaging, criticism both at the time of publication and over the succeeding years.[12]

Writing to his rationalist friend Edward Clodd in March 1904 Hardy was at pains to insist that there was nothing supernatural about his phantom observers and commentators: 'they are not supposed to be more than the best human intelligence of their time in a sort of quintessential form. I speak of the "Years". The "Pities" are, of course, merely Humanity, with all its weaknesses.' Shifting to the human level, he alluded to an illness of Meredith's and to the death of Leslie Stephen ('They are thinning out ahead of us') and spoke of the recent loss of an old Dorchester friend of forty-seven years, 'a man whose opinions differed almost entirely from my own on most subjects: & yet he was a good & sincere friend—the brother of the present Bp. of Durham, & like him in old fashioned views of the Evangelical school'. This was Henry Joseph Moule, the eldest of the Moule brothers and much the closest to Hardy in the twenty years since he had returned to Dorchester to live. Two days earlier Hardy had described the funeral to Arthur Moule, then pursuing his missionary labours in China, and added some observations of a deeply personal kind. That very afternoon, he reported, his mother had told him in her now feeble voice of her first sight of the Revd Henry Moule conducting a drumhead service at the Dorchester barracks as long ago as 1830. Henry Joseph Moule himself she had known for more than sixty years, and she had sent to his funeral a wreath made at Bockhampton from 'the old fashioned flowers up there (which he had often admired)'.[13]

Just two weeks later, on Easter Sunday (3 April) 1904, Jemima herself was dead. It was a moment for mingled regret and relief, as Hardy's 'After the Last Breath' finely brings out:

> There's no more to be done, or feared, or hoped;
> None now need watch, speak low, and list, and tire;
> No irksome crease outsmoothed, no pillow sloped
> Does she require.
>
> Blankly we gaze. We are free to go or stay;
> Our morrow's anxious plans have missed their aim;
> Whether we leave to-night or wait till day
> Counts as the same.
>
> The lettered vessels of medicaments
> Seem asking wherefore we have set them here;
> Each palliative its silly face presents
> As useless gear.
>
> And yet we feel that something savours well;
> We note a numb relief withheld before;
> Our well-beloved is prisoner in the cell
> Of Time no more.
>
> We see by littles now the deft achievement
> Whereby she has escaped the Wrongers all,
> In view of which our momentary bereavement
> Outshapes but small.[14]

In anticipation of Jemima's death Hardy had got Hermann Lea to make a photograph of Mary's oil painting of her mother in old age, and he now arranged for that photograph to be reproduced in a number of national papers, including the *Graphic* and the *Sphere.* Herbert von Herkomer, the illustrator of *Tess,* saw one of these reproductions, Hardy reported to Mary, and expressed regret that he had not had a chance to paint Jemima himself: ' "Such a profile as that we painters don't get every day".' Hardy seems also to have 'inspired' the brief obituaries of his mother which appeared in the local paper, the *Dorset County Chronicle,* and in *The Times,* and he was certainly the source, a few days later, of a note in the *Daily Chronicle* designed to correct some published statements which implied that Jemima had been neglected by her son in being allowed to live on in the relatively humble Bockhampton cottage—it was at her own insistence, as he pointed out, that she had remained in the 'original inconvenient' house.[15]

Because of her deafness and her inability, of recent years, to get about except in a Bath chair, Hardy's 'dear mother', as he referred to her in a letter to Mrs Henniker, had been 'for some time out of sight of the world, but to myself & my sisters she did not seem old'. Jemima's death, at the age of ninety, had long been expected, and her sufferings towards the end made her passing no occasion for rational regret. Yet, as Hardy confessed to Clodd, 'one does regret.'[16] It was not simply that Jemima was his mother. She had also been the single most important influence in his life, and the source, together with his father, of so much of that local and traditional material which formed the groundwork of his fiction and poetry alike. But even on 10 April, the day of her funeral, neither the background nor the foreground could remain entirely free of shadows: an annotation in Hardy's prayerbook shows that Mary, Henry, Katharine, and Polly Antell were all with him at the service, but it makes no mention of Emma, who —out of lingering resentment, or perhaps of simple tact—had evidently chosen to stay away.[17]*

His mother's death made Hardy acutely aware that the procession of the generations was about to falter and fail. He and Emma had no children; his brother and sisters had not married; Jemima had no grandchildren. Writing to Clodd of the gap created by her death Hardy observed: 'I suppose if one had a family of children one would be less sensible of it.' But these recognitions seem, at least in the short run, to have made not for increased bitterness between Hardy and Emma but for an easing of tensions, a greater kindliness, gestures towards normality —although at dinner at the Shorters' in June Clodd noted that Emma 'had her usual little digs' at her husband, who seemed for his part to have 'learned the virtues of silence & patience'.[18]

For the first time in several years they took a house in London —at 13 Abercorn Place, Maida Vale, close to the church in which

* She is not mentioned in the brief report of the funeral in the *Dorset County Chronicle*.

they had been married thirty years before—and remained there for rather more than two months.* Gosse entertained Hardy several times during that period, and for the first time in many years Emma's name appears alongside her husband's in the record which Gosse kept of his guests.[19] Max Gate was subject that summer of 1904 to the invasion of unpleasant odours from the sewage works in the Frome valley and Emma stayed on in London until she was assured that all was well.[20] Once she returned, Hardy lent her his unofficial assistance in the performance of her duties as a judge (with Lady Conan Doyle) of the *Tatler's* competition to determine, on the basis of photographs, the three prettiest babies in the United Kingdom. In January Hardy had observed to William Rothenstein's wife that they were much interested in babies at Max Gate, perhaps because they had none of their own. In September, when the results of the *Tatler* competition had been decided, Emma was able to report that at Max Gate they both felt the winner of the third prize was 'not a beauty exactly—he looks somewhat cross—but has fine limbs'.[21]

Hardy and Emma also remained at one in their devotion to their cats. One visitor at about this period reported that there were boards laid from one piece of furniture to the next, so that the cats could walk around the room without descending to the floor. Another, startled at Hardy's coming to the door in his stockinged feet, was told by Emma: 'I never let him wear his boots in the house until the kittens are three weeks old, in case they get hurt.' In October 1904, when Snowdove, like so many other Max Gate cats, was cut in two on the railway line, Emma relayed the sad news to friends while Hardy wrote to Hamo Thornycroft, the sculptor, to ask where he could get a chisel sturdy enough to keep its edge while he carved Snowdove's name on the piece of Portland stone to be placed over her grave in the pets' cemetery.[22]

Later that same month the death of Emma's brother Walter, the father of Gordon and Lilian Gifford, was an occasion for shared distress—and for concern as to what was to happen to Lilian and her mother, since Walter Gifford had left almost nothing and his pension from the Post Office (his former employer) ceased abruptly with his death.[23] Gordon Gifford's architectural

---

* Since the address was that of Emma's brother Walter, the arrangement was perhaps a way of contributing to the Gifford family income in the form of rent—or of obviating the usual search for lodgings.

training, to which Hardy had contributed, was to prove sufficient to ensure him a modest career in local government: by November 1902, in fact, he had already left the Blomfields for the security of the position in the Architect's Department of the London County Council in which he remained—quiet, cordial, but un-communicative—until his retirement forty years later.[24] But Lilian's combination of unstable personality, poor education, and social vanity made her virtually unemployable. She became a pathetic figure, drifting about from one cheap lodging to another, spending extended periods at Max Gate, a constant burden on her brother and a permanent (if irregular) object of Hardy's charity.

Although 1904 had brought more than its share of melancholy events,* Hardy was in good spirits during its closing months, largely because he was working on the second part of *The Dynasts*: 'I am doing the battle of Jena just now,' he told Mrs Henniker in late September, '—a massacre rather than a battle—in which the combatants were *close* together; so different from modern war, in which distance & cold precision destroy those features which made the old wars throb with enthusiasm & romance.'[26] Although the first part of *The Dynasts* had sold poorly, it had received a great deal of public notice and been recognized as a work, what-ever its faults, of philosophical seriousness, moral earnestness, and almost epic scope. It added, at the very least, a new dimension to the public perception of Hardy and had much to do—along with his advancing age and the corresponding recession into the past of the furores over *Tess* and *Jude*—with the honours which began to come his way during the Edwardian years.

The first of these, an honorary Doctorate of Laws from the

* In October Hardy received news from India of the suicide of Violet Nicolson, apparently prompted by the death the previous August of her husband General Malcolm Nicolson, many years her senior. Mrs Nicolson was the author of 'Pale hands I love' and other romantic love lyrics under the pseudonym of 'Laurence Hope', and although Hardy had met her only once he admired her as an 'impassioned & beautiful woman' and was much moved by contemplation of the devotion which had resulted in so desperate and romantic a gesture. As he said in the brief unsigned obituary which he wrote for the *Athenaeum*, 'The author was still in the early noon of her life, vigour, and beauty, and the tragic circumstances of her death seem but the impassioned closing notes of her impassioned effusions.'[25]

University of Aberdeen, was especially appreciated by its recipient as a gesture from that world of formal education which he had never known as a young man, and although the journey north was a long one—'almost as far as to the Pyrenees'—he determined to receive the degree in person. Arriving in Aberdeen in early April 1905 he was immediately charmed by the city and by the cordiality of his welcome at the University. Above all, he delighted in the ceremonials and accoutrements associated with the degree ceremony itself, and in sending Herbert Grierson, Professor of Rhetoric at Aberdeen, the personal measurements to be used in ordering a doctoral gown from a local outfitter, he demonstrated an appropriately pedantic precision, specifying his height as 5 feet 6¼ inches 'in shoes', his shoulders measurement ('over coat') as 45 inches, his chest measurement as 38 inches ('under arms & over coat'), and the distance round his head as 22½ inches.[27]

That same spring of 1905 the Hardys took a London flat (1 Hyde Park Mansions) for two months and pursued the kind of social round that had been so familiar to them in the 1880s and '90s but rather less so of recent years—concerts, plays, exchanges of visits, a conversazione at the Royal Society, a farewell dinner given by the Lord Mayor of London for the retiring American Ambassador, and so on. In June Hardy called on his old hero Swinburne at Putney, where he was living with Theodore Watts-Dunton, and found him looking boyish and even impish. They found no difficulty in agreeing that they had been the most abused of modern writers—for *Poems and Ballads* and *Jude the Obscure* —and Swinburne told of having been sent a paragraph from a Scottish paper which commented disapprovingly on Hardy's Aberdeen degree: 'Swinburne planteth, Hardy watereth, and Satan giveth the increase.' Swinburne himself had received no honours of any kind, but that same year Hardy lent his support to a proposal to nominate him for the Nobel Prize for Literature—something he had apparently not quite dared to do in January 1902 when the British Nobel Prize Committee, of which he was a member, had decided to support Herbert Spencer.[28] Before returning to Dorchester in early July of 1905 Hardy went down to Box Hill to call on George Meredith, another of the literary figures who had loomed so large for him in his beginning years. Meredith, though pleased to see his visitor, later confessed that he was 'afflicted by his twilight view of life' and had felt obliged to conceal his real opinion of *The Dynasts*—that Hardy could have 'made it more effective in prose—where he is more at home than in verse, though here and there he produces good stuff'. Hardy had 'no imagination', he told Clodd, and his verse could scarcely be called poetry at all.[29]

In mid-September 1905 Hardy went to Aldeburgh at Clodd's invitation to participate in the celebrations marking the 150th anniversary of the birth of George Crabbe. Emma, as usual, did not accompany her husband to Suffolk, explaining on this occasion that she and Hardy could never leave Max Gate at the same time 'until some sweet spirit acts as caretaker'. The French scholar René Huchon was present at Aldeburgh, also Clement Shorter and his wife Dora Sigerson, a pale but by no means unpublished poet. Shorter tried to draw Hardy out but, as one of the other guests recalled, Hardy 'remained unobtrusively himself, speaking in his gentle refined voice when he had something to say, but never for politeness' sake or for any other conventional reason'.[30] Though Hardy can scarcely be said to have been 'influenced' by Crabbe's realism, he was very much aware of his example, as is shown in a note of that same year upon the possible poetic uses of an aesthetic effect by which he had long been fascinated: 'The beauty in "Ugliness" or "Commonplace"—e.g. a dusty road. This, which has been recognized in prose, (I have exemplified it often), has not been much done in verse. Crabbe had the materials, but did not use them properly—i.e. make them beautiful.—In painting the English Art Club attempts it.'[31]

As this note suggests, Hardy the poet had by no means forgotten his past as a novelist. In July he sent F. W. Maitland his reminiscences of Leslie Stephen, especially as he had known him at the time of the writing of *Far from the Madding Crowd*. In October he commented with somewhat ponderous perceptivity upon a volume of stories and prose sketches sent him by Arthur Symons, raising the question whether it was proper to write inconclusive 'slice-of-life' sketches about fictional characters: since an author was in a godlike situation in respect to his own creations, had he the right to pretend to less than total knowledge of what existed, after all, solely in his own imagination? While it would be absurd to compare Symons's slight and slightly precious pieces with the massive 'documentary' novels of Zola, it is nevertheless possible to detect here some of the reasons for Hardy's distrust of 'realism', of the 'slice-of-life' school, on the grounds of that abandonment of total creative responsibility which he felt it involved. Zola, in particular, he persisted in finding 'no artist, & too material', although certainly remarkable as a social reformer.[32]

Hardy himself took a public stand on a number of issues during the course of the year, adding his name to a telegram to the Russian government in protest against the imprisonment of Maxim Gorky and to a letter in *The Times* calling for a better understanding between England and Germany. In November 1905 he wrote to Israel Zangwill, again for publication, a letter strongly supportive of the ultimate establishment of a Jewish state in Palestine. Acknowledging that if he were a Jew he would almost certainly be 'a rabid Zionist', Hardy expressed his profound interest—a legacy perhaps from the book his godfather had given him in childhood or from a much later reading of *Daniel Deronda* —in 'a people of such extraordinary history and character—who brought forth, moreover, a young reformer who, though only in the humblest walk of life, became the most famous personage the world has ever known'.[33] This was one matter on which Hardy and Emma thought alike, and when her husband's letter was published, with others, in the *Fortnightly Review* of April 1906 Emma wrote Zangwill a letter of her own, recalling a childhood interest in the Jews and offering such support (to the amount of seven shillings) as she felt she could:

> For weeks & months past I have had it in my mind to offer a mite, (I am poor personally on account of helping relatives) a small sum it is, but if you can imagine from what I have said, the feeling more than a sentiment, the burning desire with which I offer it, you will accept it in the spirit I wish, yes, a burning desire to be one in so grand a scheme. I have often found too, that I am fortunate for others and may I be so now! I have not liked to write before but I have decided to do so after reading your article & the letters yesterday but I am an atom beneath the clouds & upper regions you will probably think. Please treat this as *strictly confidential*.[34]

In acting more independently of each other the Hardys had in certain respects arrived at a closer intellectual affinity than they had known for some years, though that may be simply to say that by living more apart they had less opportunity to probe and inflame their differences. During the middle years of Edward VII's reign they seem—at least from the generally negative evidence available—to have maintained a reasonably stable relationship. Emma spent much of her time in her attic 'eerie', as she called it, writing, reading three newspapers a day, and keeping an alarmed eye on current political developments in England and in France

—'the country I love most after our own—& the one I shall want to fly to perhaps some day or other when fighting comes on here, or our beautiful free land changes its character.' But she came downstairs to at least the evening meal, she went with her husband to London in the old way, and she seems to have felt less necessity to make slighting references to his work. Hardy was not being wholly facetious or disingenuous, evidently, when he told Clement Shorter, at Christmas 1905, that he and Emma were 'having a nice dull time' at home at Max Gate.[35]

At the end of 1905 Hardy was awaiting publication, early in the new year, of the second part of *The Dynasts*, which dealt chiefly with the Peninsular War and brought the historical material to a point shortly before the beginning of Napoleon's fatal Russian campaign. The manuscript had been completed at the end of September and sent shortly afterwards to Macmillan, where it was somewhat gloomily received: Frederick Macmillan, writing to the firm's New York office, observed that it would have to be published, despite the 'disastrous' commercial failure of Part First, since they could not afford to 'disoblige an author of Mr. Hardy's standing'. Proofs were forthcoming in early November but, as with the first part, English publication was delayed by uncertainty as to the American publishing arrangements. Since sales were again expected to be low it was eventually decided not to print a separate American edition of Part Second but simply to send across the Atlantic some 250 unbound copies of the English edition.[36]

For Hardy, who had never anticipated substantial sales of any of his poetry, the completion of Part Second represented, as he told Mrs Henniker on 21 October 1905, the removal of 'a great weight' from his shoulders, since he was now two-thirds of the way through his task and no longer felt 'such a huge bulk of work' ahead of him. He went on to refer to that day's celebrations of the centenary of the battle of Trafalgar, in which Admiral Thomas Hardy of Portisham had played so prominent a role, and to assert that his brother and sisters at Bockhampton were 'the only people we can discover in this part of the county who are still living in the same house they occupied on the day of the battle 100 years ago (in the direct line of descent)'.[37] Such continuity of occupation was probably less unusual than Hardy suggests, but the observation is suggestive of the degree to which his contemplation of the past continued to be inextricably linked with thoughts of his own family and his own region. Although there were no Wessex scenes in Part Second of *The Dynasts,* it had sprung no less surely from that childhood fascination with Napoleon and Napoleonic times which had been stimulated by the talk of his elders, by the survival of visible relics in the local countryside, and by his sharing the name of Nelson's famous flag-captain on the *Victory.* It was a fascination which never left him. As late as 1923 T. E. Lawrence could write: 'Napoleon is a real man to him, and the country of Dorsetshire echoes that name everywhere in Hardy's ears. He lives in his period, and thinks of it as the great war.' Four years earlier, in 1919, Hardy had likened his personal sense of the past to 'a railway line covered with a blue haze': 'it goes uphill till 1900,' he added, 'and then it goes over the hill and disappears till about the middle of the century, and then it rises again up to about 1800, and then it disappears altogether.'[38]

Hardy well knew, however, that the elders from whom he had heard so many tales of the past had not shared his own obsession with that past. Their songs, their lore, their anecdotes, whether personal or inherited, were simply a part of all that they carried with them, naturally and unreflectingly, down that stream of time he had invoked in the opening pages of *The Trumpet-Major.* Hardy's consciousness of difference emerges sharply from a note of the period 1906–8 in which he records some thoughts he had had while walking from Bockhampton across the eweleaze he had so often traversed as a child: 'Thinking how at B. we are always looking back at those who have gone before, who did not look back in their time, but found the present all-sufficient.' A similar idea occurs in the poem 'Night in the Old Home', in which the speaker, having represented himself to the ghosts of his ancestors as a 'pale late plant of your once strong stock' and a 'thinker of crooked thoughts upon Life in the sere', is admonished to cultivate a wiser passivity:

'—O let be the Wherefore! We fevered our years not thus:
Take of Life what it grants, without question!' they answer me
     seemingly.
'Enjoy, suffer, wait: spread the table here freely like us,
And, satisfied, placid, unfretting, watch Time away beamingly!'[39]

Few men can have been less capable than Hardy of letting be 'the Wherefore'. For him, as for Arnold in 'The Scholar Gypsy', such 'unfretting' seemed as idyllic as it was unrealizable, and as he himself advanced in years his imagination became increasingly centred upon an increasingly idealized past crowded with increasingly faultless inhabitants. Though such conservatism—even resurrectionism—was to become a source of irritation and even grief to those around him, it was for Hardy an essential source of his continuing creativity on into old age. As those of the older generation themselves died off, so symbols and totems—such as the family graves at Stinsford—had to take their place, in order that the rituals of memory and celebration might still be sustained. Even the cello purchased from Nathaniel Sparks was destined not for use but for memorialization: it figures prominently in the sketch, entitled 'Silent Christmas Voices. The Study, Max Gate (Fiddle Corner)', which he drew on Christmas Eve 1905, in direct allusion to the playing of his father and grandfather, to his own childhood memories, and to the lost world-that-never-quite-was of the Mellstock Quire.[40]

23

AFTER
THE VISIT

O^N 2 January 1906 Hardy was writing to a young woman to thank her for the 'box of sweet flowers' she had sent him. They were, he said, 'at this moment in water on the table, & look little the worse for their journey'.[1] His correspondent was Florence Emily Dugdale, born on 12 January 1879, two months after the publication of *The Return of the Native.* The second of the five daughters of Edward Dugdale, an Enfield schoolmaster, and his wife Emma, a former governess, Florence Dugdale had from childhood been strongly drawn towards literature and towards modes of experience richer than those which surrounded her as she grew up. At the time she first met Hardy she was already seeking to lead some kind of literary life, to find a means of living by writing and so escaping from the teaching career to which the limited opportunities available to young women of her class had almost inevitably doomed her. Hardy had found himself in a somewhat similar situation in the 1860s, before the final choice between architecture and literature had been made, and it was perhaps sympathy for Miss Dugdale's aspirations and difficulties as much as responsiveness to her person and personality that first drew Hardy towards the woman who was to become his second wife.

Quiet, studious, and 'sweet-tempered' as a girl and young

woman, though always delicate in health, Florence Dugdale attended Upper Grade schools at Tottenham and Enfield and spent
four years as a pupil-teacher in the St. Andrew's Girls' School, a
Church of England infants school in Enfield. In 1897 she passed
the Queen's Scholarship Examination for entrance to training
college—achieving a first-class mark and a placing of 621= in the
country as a whole—only to be denied admission on medical
grounds. She thus had to seek certification as a teacher by obtaining an Acting Teacher's Certificate, a far more exacting and time-
consuming process requiring additional teaching—now in the St.
Andrew's Boys' School, of which her father was headmaster—and
part-time attendance at Cusack's Day Training College in central
London. Although often ill, especially with throat infections, and
often exhausted by the combined burden of teaching, studying,
and travelling to and fro between Enfield and the city, Florence
enjoyed the classes at Cusack's—as her elder sister later recalled,
she 'ever was a better, more willing student than a teacher'—and
eventually obtained the certification she sought. But that was not
until 1906, when she was already twenty-seven, and in the meantime the repeated bouts of laryngitis and pharyngitis had served
to confirm the judgement of the medical examiners for the training college that her health was not sufficiently robust to withstand
the rigours of elementary school teaching.[2]

She was also temperamentally unsuited to such work. Shy and
melancholy, even depressive, she preferred rather to withdraw
into the world of literature than to confront the realities of the
classroom. There were always books at home when she was a child
—her father had run a small bookshop in Enfield for a time and
been the local agent for the Society for the Propagation of Christian Knowledge—and an early love of reading gradually developed
into an ambition to be a writer, both for writing's sake and as an
alternative to teaching as a means of livelihood. Around the turn
of the century she began contributing occasional articles, stories,
and theatrical reviews to the local newspaper, the *Enfield Observer*, whose editor was a friend of the family. She also became
very friendly with a local writer named Alfred Hyatt, sympathizing deeply with his pathetic struggle against physical and financial
handicaps but also admiring his capacity, despite such handicaps,
to sustain himself as a working journalist and anthologist.[3] Although she did not yet abandon teaching, Florence began to seek
for ways of making herself financially independent by various
forms of journalism, and by the time she first met Hardy in 1905

she had embarked upon an active if not very remunerative career as a writer of children's stories.* She had also had a few items published in such London newspapers as the *Globe* and the *Daily Mail*.

Just how Hardy and Florence Dugdale first met is far from clear, especially since Florence herself seems to have given different accounts to different people. She told one of her sisters that she had been introduced to the Hardys by W.T. Stead, the crusading journalist, at a London garden party. She told another sister that while attending as a reporter an occasion at the Lyceum Club—founded in 1904 as a meeting place for women with literary and other intellectual interests—she had herself approached Emma, a member of the Club's original organizing committee, and asked if she might send flowers to Hardy on the occasion of his birthday.[4] What seems certain is that Florence had a long-standing admiration for Hardy's work—first stimulated by reading in a volume called *Gleanings from Favourite Authors* the cliff scene from *A Pair of Blue Eyes*—and that in August 1905, apparently while she was on holiday at Weymouth, she wrote to ask if she might call upon him at Max Gate. If Hardy had met her beforehand, it can only have been on a formal basis: addressing her as 'Dear Madam', he gave a version of what had by now become his standard reply to such requests—since she had undertaken not to publish anything about her visit he would be glad to see her.[5]

According to another of Florence's accounts of meeting Hardy for the first time, this visit was made in company with Mrs Henniker. As etiquette required, the two visiting ladies had arranged to call upon the lady of the house, but when they arrived at Max Gate a fly was waiting at the front door and it became quickly apparent that Emma had forgotten their appointment and was about to depart on some errand of her own. A page in buttons ushered them into the dining room, announced that Mrs Hardy was not at home, and sent off the fly empty—leaving Emma trapped somewhere upstairs. A few minutes later Hardy himself appeared, greeted Mrs Henniker warmly, and proceeded to make tea for them himself with his 'capable fingers'. Emma did not appear and Hardy chatted on with a freedom and ease that was

---

* These included *Old Time Tales, Cousin Christine,* and *Country Life,* all published by Collins between 1906 and 1908. Others, some of only pamphlet length, were written for the SPCK, among them *Tim's Sister, Jennie, Who Did Not Like Christmas, Little Lie-A-Bed; and Other Stories,* and *Jack Doane's Reward.*

quite unlike the silence he customarily maintained in Emma's voluble presence. He escorted them out of the house when the time came for their departure, and as they stood in the drive Florence drew his attention to the scent of privet when in flower, something he had never noticed for himself—'Until then the faint scent / Of the bordering flowers swam unheeded away', as he wrote in 'After the Visit', a poem which merges Hardy's immediate sense of attraction to Miss Dugdale with his later realization of the difficult paths into which that attraction had led them.[6]

Although the anecdote is made persuasive by its circumstantiality, it probably reflects a considerably later occasion—especially since it is doubtful whether Florence Dugdale and Florence Henniker had met as early as 1905. But a meeting between Hardy and Miss Dugdale had certainly taken place before the end of that year—'I do not think you stayed at all too long, & hope you will come again some other time,' he wrote in the letter of 2 January 1906—and Hardy felt drawn to her from the first by her quiet seriousness, her large solemn eyes, her literary ambitions, and, not least, her open admiration of him as a great author. The acquaintance deepened gradually during the summer of 1906—he gave her two signed photographs of himself that September[7]— and by the end of that year she was going to the Reading Room of the British Museum* on Saturdays and holidays in order to look up references and historical details that he needed in completing the third and final part of *The Dynasts*. She later acknowledged that he probably invented some of these tasks, 'knowing the pleasure I took in "helping" him'.[9]

Part Second of *The Dynasts* was generally well received upon its publication on 9 February 1906, and Hardy had, in any case, assured himself of some positive private responses by sending out presentation copies to a numerous group of friends and acquaintances, including Gosse, Clodd, Mrs Henniker, Arthur Symons, Henry Newbolt, and Sidney Lee, Leslie Stephen's successor as editor of the *Dictionary of National Biography*. Gosse in particular was warm and even gushing in his thanks, calling the volume a 'magnificent success', smoother-flowing than its predecessor, and

* Her application for a Reading Ticket, as it was then called, was dated 20 November 1906 and sponsored by John McEwan, J.P., a prominent tea merchant who lived in Enfield and was active in local education and politics.[8]

exhorting his friend: 'Slacken not in winding this glorious poem up to a noble and thrilling conclusion.'[10] When writing to friends Hardy tended to apologize for a certain hurriedness of execution, as he had done when Part First appeared, and sometimes went on to promise extensive revisions when the work was published in its entirety. But when Arthur Symons ventured to take issue with the basic principle of using verse for an historical subject, Hardy was firm in his own defence, arguing that 'unemotional writing which has no claim of itself to verse-form may properly be attracted into verse-form by its nearness to emotional verse in the same piece. Leave alone plays, some of our best lyrics are not lyrical every moment throughout, but the neutral lines are warmed by the remainder.'[11]

That spring and early summer of 1906—from mid-April to mid-July—the Hardys occupied the same flat in Hyde Park Mansions that they had rented the year before. Hardy went with Henry Arthur Jones to see Irving in *Othello*, was induced by Arthur Symons to attend a private performance of Wilde's *Salome*, and slipped in, alone, one afternoon to see a performance of Maxim Gorky's *The Bezsemenoffs*. Henry Nevinson, who happened to encounter him there, noted that he was 'in his usual mood, gentle, sensible, unpretentious', becoming 'a little alarmed' after the performance, however, at the prospect of going to a Lyons teashop, 'being used only to an A.B.C.' As they emerged again, Hardy was brought up short by a newspaper placard announcing 'Family Murdered with a Penknife': 'He couldn't get over that,' Nevinson recalled. 'The vision of the penknife seemed to fascinate him'[12]—perhaps because he associated it with the long-ago but never forgotten death of Horace Moule.

Hardy told Nevinson that he preferred concerts to plays, and he seems at that period to have taken a particular interest in Tchaikovsky, in whom he detected 'exactly the modern note of unrest', and in Wagner. He attended a series of Wagner concerts in the spring of 1906 and confessed his own preference, whatever the current taste might dictate, for late Wagner as for late Turner, 'the idiosyncracies of each master being more strongly shown in these strains'. He added, in terms that perhaps reflect his sense of his own endeavour in *The Dynasts*: 'When a man not contented with the grounds of his success goes on and on, and tries to achieve the impossible, then he gets profoundly interesting to me. To-day was early Wagner for the most part: fine music, but not so particularly his—no spectacle of the inside of a brain at work like the inside of a hive.' To the more specifically 'fashionable' aspects of the season he paid little heed: London, he told Mrs Henniker in June, was 'carrying on its old games of the season as usual, though I have nothing to do with them.'[13]

Though harassed by the heavy cold he seemed doomed to catch in London every spring, Hardy remained generally fit and well—despite the determination of Jacques-Émile Blanche to portray him as far more decrepit than he actually was. The sitting was in June 1906, and Blanche—evidently remembering the image he had created on the canvas rather than Hardy's actual appearance—later described how, in the excessive heat of the studio, 'La lumière froide du zénith, dans un ciel bleu dépouillé par la chaleur, teintait d'un vert cadavérique le crâne, les joues plates, la moustache tombante de mon nouveau grand ami.' Exhausted as perhaps Hardy was that day, and as he undeniably looks in both versions of the Blanche portrait, his own comment upon it remains the most appropriate. Told that Blanche had made him look ten years older than he was, he remarked: 'time will cure that fault.'[14] That August he was certainly fit enough to go with his brother Henry on a cycling tour of Lincoln, Ely, Cambridge, and Canterbury, and one day in September he cycled to Yeovil and back in company with his younger sister, probably to visit some distant cousins who lived there.[15]

Shortly after returning to Max Gate from London in mid-July 1906 Hardy told Gosse that he was 'trying to enter into' the third part of *The Dynasts*. He worked without particular urgency, permitting himself to break off for an occasional cycling expedition, but by the end of October he was already 'distractedly trying to give something like a clear picture of that maelstrom of confusion the Battle of Leipzig'.[16] Although Part Third was to be considerably longer than either of its predecessors, Hardy seems in fact to have moved quite easily through its densely crowded incidents—Borodino, the retreat from Moscow, Vittoria, Leipzig, Napoleon's exile and return, and finally Waterloo. The prospect of the culminating presentation of Waterloo was an incentive to progress, as was the thought of completing so massive an undertaking; it may also have been true, as Gosse had suggested, that Hardy's imagination was now flowing with greater freedom and confidence.

He was also more assured about his own philosophical position, as it was incorporated into the structure and argument of *The Dynasts* and as it might be independently formulated. In May he took the (for him) unusual initiative of writing to the philos-

opher J. McT. E. McTaggart to express his admiration of Mc-
Taggart's *Some Dogmas of Religion,* in which he had found
support for the view he had himself expressed in *The Dynasts*:
'The clearness, acuteness and vigour of the thinking throughout,
its entire freedom from sophisms and the indubitable moral good
to be derived from a perusal of it are cheering to others whose
minds have run more or less in the same groove but have rather
despaired of seeing harmful conventions shaken—in this country
at least—by lucid argument and, what is more, human emotions.'
What Hardy felt to be distinctive about the line he had taken in
The Dynasts was the idea that 'the Unconscious Will of the Universe' was 'growing aware of Itself' and might ultimately become
not merely conscious but sympathetic.[17] It was in this sense that
he was able to think of himself as a 'meliorist' and end the third
and final part of the drama on a note of modest optimism.

At the same time, it was not a kind of optimism that made for
short-term cheerfulness, as he pointed out in October to his old
Positivist friend, Frederic Harrison:

> I, too, call myself a "meliorist", but then, I find myself unable to
> be in such good spirits as you are at the prospect. In regard of
> Sport for instance, will ever the great body of human beings,
> of whom the commonplace & degenerate breed most, ever see its
> immorality? Worse than that, supposing they do, when will the
> still more numerous terrestrial animals—our kin, having the
> same ancestry—learn to be merciful? The fact is that when you
> get to the bottom of things you find no bed-rock of righteousness
> to rest on—nature is *un*moral—& our puny efforts are those of
> people who try to keep their leaky house dry by wiping off the
> waterdrops from the ceiling.[18]

From a late-twentieth-century standpoint Hardy's especial concern
with the sufferings of animals tends to seem mildly eccentric and
beside the main point. And yet Henry Nevinson, who had another
long conversation with Hardy in Dorchester in the autumn of
1906, was surely right to identify his feeling for animals as essentially a pushing to its logical limits of the wincing rawness of
Hardy's response to all forms of suffering. Recording Hardy's tales
of the slaughter of game birds and of the hangings, whippings,
burnings, and other brutal punishments in Dorchester's not-so-
very-distant past, Nevinson commented: 'These subjects have for
him a horrible fascination that comes of extreme sensitiveness to
other people's pain. I suppose that if we all had that intensity of

imagination we should never do harm to any human being or animal or bird, certainly not in cruelty.'[19]

Hardy worked on Part Third of *The Dynasts* throughout the early weeks and months of 1907, finishing the first complete draft on 29 March at 11:30 at night. From mid-April to mid-July he was in London with Emma, again at the Hyde Park Mansions flat, encountering, among others, George Bernard Shaw and his wife, the Blanches, the Maxim Gorkys, H. G. Wells, Joseph Conrad, and J. M. Barrie—the latter one of his closest friends from this period onwards. Hardy went with Emma to the Gosses' on 7 June and three days later lunched at the House of Lords, where Gosse was luxuriating in his privileges as Librarian, a post to which he had been appointed in 1904.[20] When, late in June 1907, the Hardys went to Windsor for a royal garden party they travelled down in the train with Blanche, who later reported that Emma ('au long voile vert victorien') had insisted that Hardy, despite the hot sun, should walk up the hill to the Castle instead of taking one of the seats in the waiting carriage. It is in fact only a short distance from the station to the Castle gates, but Blanche took Emma's bossiness to be typical of the Hardys' domestic life, and painted a cruel verbal portrait of her as a woman reft of all her former charm and freshness: 'decharnée, l'âge l'ayant comme rapetissée, elle plastronnait, gardait le sourir stéréotypé d'antan, comme si le photographe le lui avait fixé une fois pour toutes.'[21]

The process of completing the final stages of Part Third of *The Dynasts* began with Hardy's return from London to Max Gate in mid-July 1907. Early in August he was trying to cut the manuscript down, but when, on 10 October, he sent it off to Frederick Macmillan, he was forced to acknowledge that it was still substantially longer than its two predecessors. The proofs arrived in December and by the end of the year Hardy had almost finished correcting them, feeling, after his long involvement in Napoleonic events, 'like an old Campaigner—just as if I had been present at the Peninsular battles & Waterloo (as they say Geo. IV imagined of himself)'. Though he was glad to be almost finished with his massive task, Hardy confessed that he would 'miss the work', and it was this sense of residual emptiness and anticlimax which, towards the end of the year, he reported both to Mrs Henniker and to Gosse—though he insisted to the latter that he was not 'habitually gloomy, as you can testify'.[22] He was also depressed at the difficulty he found, even at this moment in time and in his own career, in placing a poem such as 'A Sunday Morning Tragedy'—rejected by the editor of the *Fortnightly* in October on the grounds that his magazine 'circulate[d] among families'—and perhaps by the news that the Nobel Prize for Literature had been awarded to Kipling, whose genius he admired but whose political views he deplored: as he observed to Florence Henniker, 'It is odd to associate him with "peace".'[23]

The Dynasts Part Third was published on 11 February 1908 to almost universal acclamation. Though particular reviewers were less than happy with particular aspects of the work—its verse, its historical accuracy, its philosophy—there was widespread agreement that it was a great and unique achievement. Later critics, however, have tended to see the grandeur of the over-all design as being seriously undercut by weaknesses of detail, by slack rhythms and inert language. Hardy found it all too easy to 'poeticize' his sources—or his own prose draft*—into a technically correct and minimally serviceable blank verse. And the absence of any obligation to rhyme removed what was probably the most fruitful—the most stimulative of happy invention and variation—of all the disciplining limitations to which he normally subjected himself as a poet. For much the same reason, the writing of *The Dynasts* had no visible effect upon the other verse he was concurrently producing, or upon any of his late work, with the possible and not especially happy exception of *The Queen of Cornwall*. Its long-term importance lay in his own increased confidence in his capacity to write effectively in a wide range of forms, and in the public perception of him henceforth as not merely a great writer but *the* great writer of his day, demonstrably superior to authors such as James and Conrad who expressed themselves only in prose, challenged only by the less approachable Meredith—who died the following year—and the somehow less respectable Kipling, whose Nobel Prize could not quite offset the lack of anything equivalent to Hardy's capacity for sheer grandeur of description, narration, and emotion.

---

* It was Hardy's frequent, though not invariable, practice in writing *The Dynasts* to begin by outlining his material in prose, sketching out particular scenes and speeches in some detail and even incorporating direct quotations from his sources. This first 'blocking-in' would be followed by a separate stage at which the prose was, so to speak, converted into lines of verse that followed quite closely the movement and phrasing of the original prose, either Hardy's or his source's.[24]

Writing to Florence Dugdale on 29 April 1907, shortly after his
arrival at Hyde Park Mansions, Hardy referred to a piece of work
she had done for him at the British Museum and suggested that
she might join him in 'hunting up something' at the South Kensington Museum the following Saturday afternoon, when she would
not be teaching: 'I will look for you in the architectural gallery
at 4—say by the Trajan column. But please do not come if it is
wet, as you have had such a bad cold this winter. I am, of course,
assuming that you have *quite* got over it, & can come out with
impunity in this cold atmosphere.' Hardy was distressed by the
strain which school teaching placed upon Miss Dugdale's rather
light voice and frail physique and by the way in which she was
being exploited as a writer of children's stories, advising her to
hold out for a substantially larger sum for her next undertaking
than the publisher had offered: 'the *lowest* you should agree to
is 21 guineas—a guinea a thousand words. It is poor pay at that.'[25]
Though their relationship remained somewhat formal—a copy
of the pocket volume containing both *Wessex Poems* and *Poems
of the Past and the Present* is inscribed 'To / Miss Florence Dugdale / with the Author's kind regards. / June 1907.'—a more romantic note was introduced by his gift in July of a copy of Fitz-
Gerald's *Rubáiyát of Omar Khayyám,* and during the course of
that summer Hardy began to exert himself on her behalf in
various practical ways—not only by giving her occasional employment himself, but by recommending her to his own publisher,
Macmillan, and to the editor of the *Daily Mail Books Supplement,*
to which she had already contributed a few items. Miss Dugdale,
he told Maurice Macmillan, was a certificated teacher but would
be better employed in doing the kind of literary work (such as
editing children's books and classroom texts) to which her tastes
and abilities impelled her.[26] He also helped her with her own
writing, most immediately with a story, 'The Apotheosis of the
Minx', which he successfully submitted to the *Cornhill* on her
behalf and which incorporated in its structure and themes a number of distinctively Hardyan elements.[27]

The developing relationship with Florence Dugdale reinforced
—or reawakened—Hardy's old susceptibility to feminine companionship and caused him to fret anew at the restrictions placed
upon him by his own marriage—legal restrictions chiefly, but also
moral ones, at least in the sense that he had married Emma in

deliberate opposition to the wishes of both their families, and that to break openly with her now would not only constitute disloyalty to her but also invalidate one of the decisive acts of his life. He must also have shrunk, at this time and later, from the hostile publicity that would inevitably accompany such a step. It is at the same time understandable that Hardy, now approaching seventy, should have indulged a little the vanity of knowing that other women—younger, handsomer, cleverer than Emma—still valued his friendship, and of believing that it was not altogether ridiculous to allow himself to be attracted to them: a letter to Mrs Kenneth Grahame of late August 1907 refers in passing to the young women 'in fluffy blouses' who distracted his attention when he rode on the tops of omnibuses.[28]

Lady Grove was a frequent visitor at Hyde Park Mansions during the 1907 season—Blanche speaks, no doubt with his usual extravagance, of her presiding over Emma's little parties—and in the autumn she sent Hardy the proofs of her book *The Social Fetich*, a lightweight and lighthearted commentary on contemporary manners. He read the proofs with great attentiveness and occasional sternness—correcting her grammar and usage ('If you italicize one French word you must another'), suggesting ways of avoiding repetitions of the same word, and commenting on the soundness or otherwise of her arguments and illustrations. Alongside a paragraph dealing with the ascending warmth of the endings of letters from 'Yours truly' all the way to 'Your very loving' and, finally, 'Your most loving', he wrote: 'This is delightful! Would that some charitable person would bestow some of the latter ones upon me!' Earlier, fussing over the precise form of the dedication of *The Social Fetich*—'To / Thomas Hardy / in grateful recognition of timely aid / and counsel, and in memory / of old and enduring / friendship'—he had permitted himself to become quite 'romantical', as he put it, over his memories of 'that dance on the green at the Larmer Tree by moonlight'. Although he had ended that letter by insisting that he was 'long past all such sentiments', it is clear that they were, on the contrary, always liable to overwhelm him—to shake his 'fragile frame at eve / With throbbings of noontide'.[29]

Emma's response to *The Social Fetich* once again sharply and painfully underlined for Hardy the contrast between what might have been and what actually was. Given Lady Grove's rather obtrusive presence at Hyde Park Mansions that spring, given the subject of her book, its title, its dedication, and the handsome photograph of its author which formed the frontispiece, it was perhaps inevitable that Emma should have been quick to find jealous fault with it. Her criticisms, advanced in a letter to Lady Grove herself, were both general—'the disturbing elements of life generally in this present century are of such immensity & *importance* that the use or abuse of words are after all not matters of like importance'—and particular:

Perhaps you have already discovered an inaccuracy to be corrected in a new edition on page 12. in the use of the word *inculcate* with *into* instead of 'with which' & past participle. There is an infelicity in the sentence following the word 'wit' which has a different sense from un*wit*tingly—By-the-bye 'witting' is a pretty word but seldom used—never perhaps, neither by you. You may think me hypercritical perhaps but I love words, & pounce upon sentences by early habit having to search for errors & misprints. In the daily papers how many occur! My father allowed us no *slang,* no obsolete words no *affectations* at all—'plain English'. He was a fine classical scholar & a courtly man at *home* & abroad! Good-breeding meant simple manners with much stateliness then—a combination never achieved now —all is changed—culture even abhorred by some of the self-educated ' "Deportment," what is that?' they say. There is so much elasticity every way—but the old times seem best to those who knew them. However, I must own to liking a 'Cosey' & the *hot tannin* produced under it which benefits me as St Raphael's wine does invalids—*its tannin* though being *cold.* Few people, I know do care for the ingredient, therefore *no* tea-cosey for visitors![30]

Though not unintelligent, the letter is entirely characteristic of that naïve, self-absorbed, unreflecting randomness of Emma's which had long been a source of such embarrassment and even difficulty for her husband.

In September 1907 Hardy took the trouble to comment in some detail on *Our Fatal Shadows,* Mrs Henniker's latest novel, his praise modified by a sense of what he would himself have done with the same material, and especially with the heroine:

Of course *I* should not have kept her respectable, & made a nice, decorous, dull woman of her at the end, but shd have let her go to the d—— for the man, my theory being that an exceptional career alone justifies a history (i.e. novel) being written about a person. But gentle F.H. naturally had not the heart to do that. The only thing I don't care much about is her marrying the

Duke's son—whom she did not love; an action quite as immoral, from my point of view, & more so even, than running off with a married man whom she did love would have been. But convention rules still in these things of course.[31]

Clearly his interest in fiction, though diminished, was still vital. In correcting the proofs of *The Social Fetich* he had ventured to substitute for Lady Grove's rather bleak account of an encounter with an uncooperative shop assistant a brief passage instinct with imaginative sympathy: 'What could have happened? It was never explained. Probably there had only overflowed on me, by chance, a pent-up, well-justified indignation for heaps of wrong done her by society, wealth, or general circumstances, though I personally had had nothing to do with them.'[32]

Meanwhile he found himself being drawn back once again into theatrical matters, this time on the local and amateur rather than the metropolitan and professional level. In the autumn of 1907 he took much interest in a programme of dramatized episodes from *Far from the Madding Crowd* staged by Harry Pouncy, a Dorchester journalist and lecturer. In the early months of 1908 a scene from *The Trumpet-Major* was presented in Dorchester Town Hall as an illustrative accompaniment to a lecture on 'Napoleon and the Invasion of England', and three Wessex scenes from *The Dynasts* were performed as part of the town's 'Maie Fayre' festivities.[33]* As a natural sequel to these experiments *The Trumpet-Major* was dramatized in its entirety by A. H. Evans—a Dorchester chemist whose son Maurice was to become famous as a Shakespearian actor—and produced that November by a group of local amateurs, the Dorchester Debating and Dramatic Society. This, the first of the so-called 'Hardy Plays', naturally attracted a certain amount of attention from the London critics, although, as Hardy observed to Harold Child of *The Times*, the production itself was unsophisticated and its chief interest lay in the fact that so many of the actors would, in effect, be re-enacting the lives of their own great-grandparents.[35]

As it turned out, Hardy had a severe cold at the time of the Dorchester performance of *The Trumpet-Major* and Emma had

---

* Emma caused her husband some embarrassment on this occasion by inserting into the local newspaper a statement to the effect that she had not given permission for her name to appear, alongside her husband's, as a patron of the 'Maie Fayre'.[34]

to go by herself.[36] Earlier in 1908 it was she who had been attacked by severe bronchitis and worried by failing sight, to such an extent that she had felt unable to go to the trouble of finding and taking a London flat for the season. Instead, Hardy went up by himself for a series of short visits, sleeping at the West Central Hotel and using the Athenaeum as his main base. When Emma spoke of joining him in late June or early July, Hardy arranged for them to have a room together at the same hotel but raised so many questions about her health, the London heat, the discomforts of the hotel, and so on, as to make it clear that he was not eager for her presence: 'though I should like to see you in London I feel, to tell the truth, rather anxious about your venturing up here. The hotel is so very noisy just now, & the heat so great, that I fear you will be prostrated. Don't you think you ought to wait till the question of being able to *see* is settled—I mean till you know how much good the spectacles are going to do.'[37] Hardy was presumably seeing Florence Dugdale during this period—he recommended stories of hers (or perhaps the same story)* to two different magazines in July and August 1908[38]—but there is no evidence to suggest that Emma had any sexual peccadilloes of her husband's in mind when she told Rebekah Owen, in May 1908: 'My Eminent partner will have a softening of brain if he goes on as he does & the rest of the world does.'[39]

Hardy's disinclination to have Emma with him in London may indeed have been grounded, at least in part, by a real concern for her physical condition, and although his letters to her at this point scarcely suggest any particular affection—they tend to begin 'Dear E.' and end 'Yrs T.'—it is clear that the extensive building work at Max Gate that autumn was chiefly undertaken in order to enlarge her attic room, give it a new dormer window, and so make it an altogether pleasanter place.† Emma went away when the

---

* It was probably 'The Scholar's Wife', eventually published in the *Pall Mall Magazine* for January 1909—a Hawthornesque narrative with a sixteenth-century Italian setting and a Hardyan conclusion.

† The building work undertaken at Max Gate is one of several indications—along with the success of the Macmillan pocket edition and references to dividend warrants in his letters to Emma—that Hardy had by this period arrived at a comfortable plateau of affluence. Nor is this impression contradicted by his sale of 51 High Street West, Dorchester, that same year. Now that other forms of investment had become practicable it no longer seemed necessary for him to involve himself in the tedious business of finding suitable tenants, negotiating leases with them, and maintaining the property to their satisfaction—which could not always be guaranteed by a simple assurance that the house was built, high and dry, upon the chalk.[40]

work began—apparently with some suddenness, since she cancelled a garden party she had arranged and forgot to inform two of the guests, who came all the way from north-west Dorset on the appointed day—and on 10 September she sent her husband a postcard from Calais, saying that she had just arrived there straight from London, having reached Dover and found the Channel ideally smooth for a crossing. She added that she had taken a room at the Hotel Famille, where she had stayed five years earlier. It is not clear whether Emma had originally planned to go to Calais or only as far as Dover, but Hardy seems in any case to have taken the news calmly enough. He wrote frequently and quite fully, sending news of the three cats, Marky, Kitsey, and Comfy, and of the progress of building operations, and added a cautionary note or two: 'You must mind not to be too friendly with strangers, as you don't know who's who in a town through which the worst (& no doubt best) of the earth pass on their way out of our country when it gets too hot for them.' The work at Max Gate went smoothly, but the rebuilding of the front porch (long contemplated by Hardy as a means of cutting down draughts) meant that everyone had to come to the side door, and the new plaster in Emma's room simply would not dry: perhaps, suggested Hardy on 19 October, she should stay away until the first of November. Just three days later, however, she suddenly and quite unexpectedly reappeared, hard on the heels of a warning telegram.[41]

Shortly after her return Emma wrote a lively but disorganized article, 'In Praise of Calais', which was published in the *Dorset County Chronicle* at the very end of December 1908. Though attracted by the colour and vivacity of the town, and especially the area around the harbour, she was sternly disapproving of some of its social defects:

> The drainage still is imperfect, and the running of slop-water from the houses into its gutters is the greatest defect, which may be a hindrance to its favour with English people, who, however, find it healthy. The East wind clears all. The defect is put up with by the natives, who are well accustomed to it; but it causes surprise that the Municipal Council does not see the disadvantage of allowing its continuance, as well as some other obsolete practices, such as allowing the cellar trap doors to be open, the unnecessary whipping of horses, the use of dogs as draft animals, the trams running close to the pavements in one of the principal streets instead of starting them at a further distance—

a bell, however, is constantly ringing a warning, and there being no provision for the winding up of the numerous clocks.[42]

Such complaints reflect familiar preoccupations of Emma's, as does a scathing reference to the Cathedral at Calais as 'not important: it holds the usual paraphernalia of a Continental Roman Catholic country'. Her religious prejudices, always strongly Protestant, were now beginning to take on the stature of obsessions, and it was with deep distress that she learned in June 1908 of Rebekah Owen's conversion to Catholicism—which she regarded, as she was quick to inform her American friend, as nothing less than 'a *travesty* of Christ's life, teaching & death!' Though she did not shrink from specifically theological arguments, her main emphasis was upon what she saw as the repressive aspects of Catholicism: 'Consider, would you bear to see a near relative persecuted as a "heretic" with cruelty & say it was your duty to God—The Bible to be taken from you, & traditions & ordinances, & prohibitions of men substituted—Not to read God's truth, not to be permitted to enter a Protestant Church to hear it—not to listen or to read this Ah if you read the Bible with a prayer The Spirit of Truth will reveal it to you & Satan's guile will be gone.'[43]

The evening of Emma's unexpected return to Dorchester Hardy had planned to attend a vestry meeting at Stinsford Church in order to contribute his architectural expertise to a discussion of the need for repairs to the church fabric. It is easy, in following the course of his extraordinarily productive literary career and of his relationships with notable members of the London literary and social worlds, to lose sight of Hardy's many local friendships —which often, precisely because based on frequent meetings, left little record in terms of correspondence—and his considerable involvement in the affairs of the local community.* His obligations

---

* Henry J. Moule, indeed, had been only the closest of a number of such friends with whom Hardy kept in frequent if casual touch to the time of his death, or of theirs: Hermann Lea was one of these, Alfred Pope another, brought closer to Hardy in their shared old age by a common interest in local history; others included Hardy's solicitor, Arthur Lock, the latter's son, H. O. Lock, Reginald Thornton, the banker, of Birkin House, near Dorchester, the Wood Homers of Bardolf Manor, and Albert Bankes, Horace Moule's former pupil, of Wolfeton House.

as Justice of the Peace were at least intermittently fulfilled during these early years of the century, and he later served (from 1909 to 1925) as a governor of the Dorchester Grammar School—always mindful of the role his namesake, the Elizabethan Thomas Hardye, had played in its foundation.[44] He lent his sympathy and active support to the local dramatizations of his work, especially when the proceeds were to be devoted to charitable purposes, and Stinsford Church was only one of several buildings which he inspected and reported upon in the interests of their preservation. His attempt in such instances was always to reconcile associative and aesthetic values with simple realism: his impression of St. Catherine's Chapel, Abbotsbury, he told the Secretary of the Society for the Protection of Ancient Buildings in September 1908, was that 'to prevent its falling, the alternatives are the Scylla & Charybdis of putting in new stones, or cementing over the old ones, exposure having crumbled them a good deal'.[45]

Throughout almost the whole of 1908 Hardy was engaged, off and on, in another gesture in which local sentiment mingled with and strengthened professional obligation. When, in January 1907, he was first invited to edit a selection of William Barnes's poems for the Clarendon Press, Hardy pleaded his need to complete *The Dynasts*. A year later, however, he agreed to undertake at least the selection of the poems. About a hundred, he thought, would be enough, perhaps more than enough, to cover Barnes's best work, and some of those need not be printed in their entirety, being marred by the presence of 'an unfortunate stanza or two of a prosy didactic nature'. Sections were omitted from several poems on this principle, and difficulties over copyright not only made the task much more tedious than Hardy had anticipated but obliged him to print early versions of poems which he felt had been greatly improved by Barnes's subsequent revisions.[46] It was only when the proofs of the text had been corrected that he agreed to supply a Preface to the volume, using the occasion to emphasize that his participation had been an act of local and personal piety, performed almost in the spirit of a translator of a dead language: 'I chance to be (I believe) one of the few living persons having a practical acquaintance with letters who knew familiarly the Dorset dialect when it was spoken as Barnes writes it, or, perhaps, who know it as it is spoken now.' Hence he had attempted to select judiciously, introduce warmly, gloss whenever necessary (it was he who insisted that this be done on the page rather than in a separate Glossary), and so make it possible for some of Barnes's quality and charm to convey itself to 'persons to whom the Wessex R and Z are uncouth misfortunes, and the dying words those of an unlamented language that need leave behind it no grammar of its secrets and no key to its tomb'.[47]

Within six months of the publication of the *Select Poems of William Barnes* on 24 November 1908 the deaths occurred of two other writers who, in their very different ways, had especially influenced Hardy's early literary ambitions and the shape of his subsequent career. The response of the press to the news of Swinburne's death in April 1909 roused Hardy to an anger reminiscent of his indignation at the reception of *Poems and Ballads* more than forty years earlier: 'The kindly cowardice of many papers is overwhelming him with such toleration, such theological judgements, hypocritical sympathy, and misdirected eulogy that, to use his own words again, "it makes one sick in a corner"—or as we say down here in Wessex, "it is enough to make every little dog run to mixen".'[48]

The following month, during one of several forays to London that spring—Emma having again declined to take a London lodging for the season—Hardy came suddenly upon a placard announcing the death of George Meredith. Although Hardy admired Swinburne as a writer far more than he did Meredith, the latter's departure from the literary scene was of greater practical significance for him in that it left him in a position of clear pre-eminence among living English authors. It was almost inevitable that he should be asked, early in June, to succeed Meredith as president of the Incorporated Society of Authors, although he put up some resistance before eventually accepting the position. Reluctant as always to thrust himself into prominence or incur obligations likely to make substantial intrusions upon his time and privacy, he represented very forcefully to Maurice Hewlett, who had conveyed the invitation, not only that it was time for the society to have an active president rather than a mere figurehead, as he would necessarily be, but that it would in any case be inadvisable to choose a man whose work had been so controversial: 'No recent English writer has been so roundly abused by the press as I have been in past times, with the single exception of Swinburne, & he is dead.' Nor, he added, could he 'undertake never to kick over the traces again, for on one point I am determined—to exhibit what I feel ought to be exhibited about life to show that what we call immorality, irreligion, &c, are often true morality, true religion, &c, quite freely to the end'.[49]

. . .

In early July 1909 Hardy was again in London, attending the rehearsals and first night at Covent Garden of Baron Frederick
d'Erlanger's opera *Tess*. The adaptation by d'Erlanger and Illica
(the co-librettist of *La Bohème* and *Tosca*) was of course in Italian,
and since it ended with Tess disappearing—apparently to commit
suicide—immediately following her confession to Angel it is not
surprising that Hardy should have been left with little sense of
its relationship to his own novel. Following the successful first
night the press critics gave particular praise to Emmy Destinn's
performance in the title role: Hardy agreed that her voice was
magnificent but found some difficulty in associating her portly
figure with the Tess of his imagination. He had evidently wanted
to take Florence Dugdale to *Tess,* but felt obliged to ask Emma
whether she thought it worthwhile to come up from Max Gate
for the occasion. The question was put in an uncharacteristically
rambling and repetitious letter whose very disconnectedness perhaps suggested to its recipient that it might be advisable for her
to put in an appearance. It was at this point that Clodd, under
direct or indirect prompting from Hardy, offered to escort Miss
Dugdale to the opera, Hardy promising to visit them in their
seats between the acts if it were possible for him to do so.[50]*

Hardy found Clodd's sceptical cast of mind extremely congenial, and had gradually become more intimate with him, especially during the hearty Aldeburgh weekends, than with any other
of his male companions, always excepting his brother Henry.
Gosse was a much older friend, but Hardy had long been wary
of Gosse's propensity for gossip and had not yet recognized Clodd's
own capacities for indiscretion. He had been at Aldeburgh over
the weekend of 2–5 July, and in the train back to London talked
to Clodd more frankly than he had ever done before about his
'strained relations' with Emma and told him, apparently for the
first time, something about his 'amanuensis', whom he might one
day bring to Aldeburgh with him. After meeting Florence on the
night of the opera Clodd made complimentary references to her in
a letter to Hardy and suggested that they both come to Aldeburgh
soon. Gratefully embracing the invitation, Hardy said that he

* It has been said that Clodd and Florence Dugdale left the theatre early
in order to avoid detection, but it seems clear from Clodd's diary, and from
Hardy's letter to him of 13 July 1907, that he was chiefly concerned not to
miss his last train home.[51]

had known his 'young friend & assistant' for several years, was concerned for her health and general welfare, and wanted to get her away to the seaside lest she should 'break down quite'. If she did come to Aldeburgh, he added, 'there will be such a clicking of the typewriter as never was in your house before (she is not really what is called "a typist", but as she learns anything she has learnt that, though as I told you she writes original things, is a splendid proofreader, & a fine critic, her taste in poetry being unerring—only doing my typewriting as a fancy).'[52]

Although Florence was too unwell to go to Aldeburgh at the beginning of August, as originally arranged, she and Hardy were there for a week in the middle of the month. While sailing in Clodd's boat one day they stuck in the mud and were left stranded by the falling tide; Clodd flew a flag of distress, Hardy energetically waved his handkerchief, and a punt eventually came to their rescue. But the local paper reported the incident, headlining it 'Eminent Authors on the mud', and Hardy became alarmed at the possibility of the story's being picked up by the national press— presumably because he did not want Florence's presence to become known to Emma.[53] But if Emma knew little of the increasingly important role Florence was playing in her husband's life, the relationship can scarcely be described as secret: various friends of Clodd's—including William Archer, Professor J. B. Bury, the historian, and the Revd Robert Frew—were also at Aldeburgh during the period of the August visit; Florence wrote to her family from Clodd's; and in October 1909 she and Hardy, after visiting Chichester Cathedral together, were joined by Henry Hardy in a trip to York, Durham, and Edinburgh.[54]

Florence's availability for a series of shared expeditions during the summer and autumn of 1909 suggests that she was not in continuous employment. It was apparently early in 1908 that she taught her last class at her father's school in Enfield, subsequently supporting herself by her writing, by the typing she did for Hardy, and possibly by acting for a time as companion to the mentally ill wife of Sir Thornley Stoker, a distinguished Dublin surgeon, brother of Bram Stoker, the author of *Dracula*. Florence probably met the Stokers through her friendship with the Irish writer Katharine Tynan Hinkson, who lived in Enfield for many years and knew Florence's literary friend Alfred Hyatt, as well as Clement Shorter and his wife, Dora Sigerson: a copy of Katharine Tynan's *New Poems* is inscribed 'To my dear Florence Dugdale from her loving K.T.H. October 1911'. Florence was devoted to both the Stokers—'my dear lost friends in Dublin', as she called them in later years—and her affection was evidently returned: they bought her a typewriter when she was first trying to break away from teaching and at Sir Thornley's death in 1912 she inherited the considerable sum of £2,000.[55] The arrangement by which she acted as companion to Lady Stoker was no doubt based on a friendly understanding rather than on regular payment, and it cannot in any case have been of long duration. Just when Florence began doing journalistic chores for Clement Shorter's *Sphere* is very much in doubt,* but during 1909–10 she worked for several months as a reporter for the London *Standard* newspaper, an experience she later alluded to as 'the most degrading work anybody could take up—typewriting is a lady's occupation by comparison'.[57]

Although the friendship between Hardy and Florence Dugdale was now deep and intimate, it is questionable whether it was, or became, actively sexual. Hardy would scarcely have been so eager to accompany Florence to Clodd's if he had been conducting the sort of liaison for which his solitary visits to London would have provided much readier opportunities. There was undoubtedly a strong sexual element in Hardy's attraction to Florence: when, during these years, she recited to him the last line of his poem 'The Revisitation', 'Love is lame at fifty years', he cried out that it wasn't true. But it seems doubtful whether she, with her strong ties to a warm and thoroughly conventional home background, was quite the liberated woman he had been searching for in the early 1890s, and it is perhaps significant that she confessed, many years later, to an inability to 'enter into' the lovemaking described in Marie Stopes's novel, *Love's Creation*: 'a lack of real feeling on my part I suppose.'[58] Nor would it have been easy for Hardy, at the age of sixty-nine, to have overcome the reticences of a lifetime.

But Hardy was not restrained, at this or any time, by any sense of emotional reticence, and the poems written about Florence Dugdale, like those about Florence Henniker fifteen years earlier, are full of the anguish of impermanence, of meetings in uncomfortably public places, or partings so accelerated that the happiness

---

* She seems not to have known Shorter earlier than August 1908, and there is no substantial evidence to indicate that she acted as the *Sphere's* fashion correspondent for the six months from June 1908 or, indeed, at any other time. She did, however, write book reviews for the magazine over a period of several years.[56]

Emma Hardy, *c.* 1905

Above Hardy receiving the
freedom of the Borough of
Dorchester, 1910

Right Henry and Kate Hardy
in front of Talbothays Lodge,
1914

Thomas and Florence Hardy at the time of their marriage, 1914

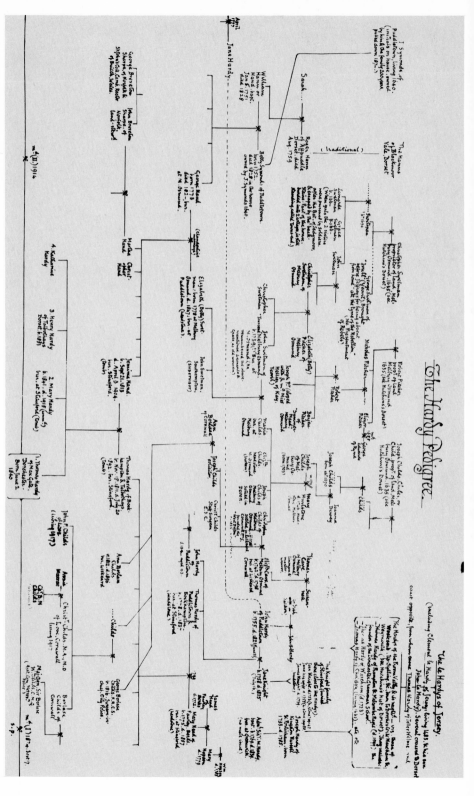

The Hardy Pedigree, written out by Hardy c. 1917; not shown are the Gifford and Dugdale pedigrees to the left and right.

of the moment had scarcely had time to be realized: 'On the Departure Platform', 'After the Visit', and the poignant 'To Meet, or Otherwise' ('By briefest meeting something sure is won; / It will have been'). But though they are as surely love poems as those to Mrs Henniker, addressed to the 'girl of my dreams', 'maiden dear', and 'she who was more than my life to me', their persistent theme is that of 'human tenderness', of the beloved's 'mute ministrations to one and to all / Beyond a man's saying sweet'.[59] What Hardy valued above all in Florence Dugdale was a gentleness, a peacefulness, a quietness even, such as he had scarcely ever known before in his relationships with women. She was admiring, anxious to serve and to please; because she had literary ambitions of her own she could be helped and encouraged, as Mrs Henniker and Lady Grove had been before her; unlike them she had neither the beauty, the personality, nor the consciousness of superior social class to make her resentful of such patronage and assertive of her own independence. Even when her relationship with Hardy deepened still further, so that they regarded themselves as emotionally 'betrothed', Florence seems to have accepted an uncomfortable and apparently irresolvable situation with a kind of temperamental and even self-indulgent melancholy that was very close to Hardy's own: 'After the Visit' concludes with an evocation of her 'large luminous living eyes', looking with mute enquiry

> As those of a soul that weighed,
> Scarce consciously,
> The eternal question of what Life was,
> And why we were there, and by whose strange laws
> That which mattered most could not be.[60]

Despite the opportunities he had had of seeing Florence in London, in Aldeburgh (where they spent a weekend at the end of October), and elsewhere during the second half of 1909, Hardy was deeply depressed, overwhelmed with a sense of what he had missed in the life he now felt to be slipping away from him: 'I am not in the brightest spirits, to tell the truth,' he told Florence Henniker in November. 'Still, who can expect to be at my age, with no children to be interested in.'[61] Precious as Florence Dugdale had become, it only accentuated his depression to be unable to see any way in which she could play a part in his everyday life: 'To Meet, or Otherwise' proclaims an almost desperate determination to make

The most I can
Of what remains to us amid this brake
    Cimmerian
Through which we grope, and from whose thorns we ache,
    While still we scan
Round our frail faltering progress for some path or plan.

Since it was above all her companionship that he craved, her quiet and soothing presence, he suffered all the more acutely from the simple fact of her absence over long periods. Max Gate, where he must necessarily spend so much of his time, was the one place where she could not come: 'Did my Heartmate but haunt here at times such as now', he wrote in 'The Difference', 'The song would be joyous and cheerful the moon; / But she will see never this gate, path, or bough, / Nor I find a joy in the scene or the tune.'[62]

Even the normally absorbing activity involved in the preparation and publication of a new collection of poems, *Time's Laughingstocks*, did little to relieve Hardy's gloom, perhaps because he had not published such a volume since 1901 and felt renewed uncertainty as to the likely critical response. One particular source of doubt was the inclusion not only of 'A Trampwoman's Tragedy' and 'A Sunday Morning Tragedy'—both rejected by magazine editors as likely to offend their readers on moral grounds—but also of 'Panthera', which seemed likely to give offence on religious grounds and which one or two of his friends had advised him to leave out. As Hardy told Sir Frederick Macmillan (as he became that year) in September 1909, scholars were thoroughly familiar with the legend he had drawn upon—that of the Roman centurion who believes the figure on the Cross to be the son he had unknowingly fathered some thirty years earlier—and he had even gone so far as to rewrite the poem in such a way as to throw doubt on the truth of the events narrated. Even so, he did not 'want to provoke acrimony among well-meaning but narrower minded people for the sake of one poem, good or bad', and would leave Macmillan to decide whether or not it ought to be left out.[63] Macmillan, with that decisiveness upon which Hardy had already learned to depend, took the view that the poem ought certainly to be published, and while 'Panthera' did indeed cause some distress among the reviewers when *Time's Laughingstocks* appeared in early December 1909 the general response to the volume was extremely favourable—even Hardy acknowledged that it had been received 'wonderfully well'—and sales were brisk enough to exhaust the first printing of 2,000 copies and necessitate a second printing early in the new year.[64]

In March 1910 Hardy went with Florence Dugdale to stand beside Swinburne's grave at Bonchurch on the Isle of Wight. Though much offended by the cross which had been placed over the tomb, Hardy made the visit the occasion of his tribute, in 'A Singer Asleep', to the poet whose early work had impinged so disturbingly 'Upon Victoria's formal middle time' and upon his own imagination, as he first 'read with a quick glad surprise / New words, in classic guise,—'. Shortly afterwards Hardy and Florence were at Aldeburgh, and when he came to London in late April they were again often together: in early June, in the interval of a performance at the Court Theatre, he introduced her to Lady Gregory as his 'young cousin'. Although Florence was no longer a regular contributor to the London *Standard* and *Evening Standard*, her former employers were glad to publish the article she wrote, with Hardy's active co-operation, on the occasion of his seventieth birthday, 2 June 1910, and this was followed up by a similar celebration of Clodd's seventieth birthday a month later.[65]

Emma was also nearing seventy, and had been in indifferent health for some years. In May 1906, while alone at Max Gate, she appears to have suffered a seizure of some kind: 'My heart seemed to stop; I fell, and after a while a servant came to me.'[66] Her description of this as her 'first strange fainting-fit' suggests that it was followed by others, but by 1910 there seems to have been a marked improvement in her general health. She resumed cycling in the summer of that year, after sufficiently rousing herself in the spring to take a place in London and to renew her private assault upon the world of letters. It was, as usual, Hardy who found the flat—at 4 Blomfield Terrace in Maida Vale, not far from such long-familiar locations as Westbourne Park Villas and Elgin Avenue. Emma came up from Dorchester in early May, bringing with her one of the Max Gate maids to answer the door and do the shopping.[67]

It was at just this moment that the death of Edward VII occurred. Hardy watched the funeral procession but felt no inclination to write anything on the occasion—although he was moved on his own birthday, two weeks later, by the reflection that he was, at seventy, a year older than the dead king.[68] The sense of having reached old age no doubt played a part in impelling

him to try and change the terms of his relationship with Florence
Dugdale and draw her more directly and permanently into the
basic patterns of his life. Since the relationship did not involve
him in technical 'infidelities' to Emma it seemed exasperating that
it should have to be conducted with such discretion. Since he
could make good use of Florence's secretarial skills and since she
—with feelings intricately compounded of personal affection,
literary idealism, and sheer dislike of journalism—was only too
eager to place them at his service, it seemed ridiculous that he
should not be able to avail himself of such assistance on a more
regular basis. It is possible that the meeting with Emma at the
Lyceum Club—when Florence, present in a journalistic capacity,
came forward to help Emma when she got into a muddle with
the pages of a speech she was supposed to be giving—took place
in the late spring of 1910 rather than in 1905. In early June 1910,
at all events, Florence received an invitation to one of Emma's 'at
homes' at Blomfield Terrace, and it seems to have been Hardy
himself who saw to it that Lady Grove and the novelist May
Sinclair were invited on the same day—perhaps on the principle
that the presence of women with whom he was already known to
be friendly might prevent Emma from divining the true nature
of his relationship with Miss Dugdale.[69]

Emma responded with eager impulsiveness to Florence's quiet
charm and ingratiating readiness to be of service. At the next
Thursday 'at home' but one Florence was given the honour of
pouring out the tea; in early July, when Emma had already left
for Max Gate, Florence reported to her that she had visited the
Blomfield Terrace flat as requested and found that all was well;
later in July she went down to Max Gate herself as Emma's guest
and assistant.[70] By this time she was on close and affectionate terms
with Emma, encouraging her literary ambitions and Protestant
prejudices, typing her manuscripts—religious writings in prose
and verse, the memories of her childhood later published as *Some
Recollections,* even her ageing Cornish romance, 'The Maid on
the Shore'—and doing her best to get them published. They
talked of collaborating in a novel, and Florence was sufficiently
anti-Catholic to be able to enter sympathetically into Emma's
'campaign' against the infiltration of the Church of England by
the forces of Rome.[71] Because Florence's surviving letters to Emma
during the latter half of 1910 contain praise of writings which she
must have known were of little value, and endorsement of
attitudes which she must have thought extreme and even obsessive,

it is easy to accuse her of hypocrisy and callous deception. But it is clear that she felt a genuine affection and sympathy for Emma, that she was charmed and amused by her lively if disconnected chatter, and that she believed it to be the course of kindness to indulge her in schemes and ambitions which might be wholly unrealistic but which did no one any harm; Emma, after all, was technically the patroness, Florence the protégée; she was also an elderly lady of seventy, forty years Florence's senior, and on neither ground would it have seemed appropriate to the latter to venture upon criticisms and contradictions.

Florence knew, of course, that the security of her relationship with Hardy depended largely upon her remaining on good terms with Emma. But she may never have permitted herself to think very deeply about what she was doing or where it might lead her. She can scarcely have indulged in any thoughts of marrying Hardy —especially since there was no reason to think that Emma would die first—and since she was not Hardy's mistress she had no reason to feel that she was doing anything wrong. It is in any case perfectly clear that as she got to know both Hardy and Emma better, and saw at first hand what conditions at Max Gate were like, her sympathies became for a time quite evenly balanced: as early as 23 June 1910, when she met Clodd to talk over the article she was writing about him, she had decided that Hardy was 'a great writer, but not a great man'.[72]

By the autumn of 1910 Florence had become accepted almost as a regular part of the Hardy household. Miss Dugdale, his 'handyman', had arrived with her typewriter the previous day, Hardy told Clodd on 15 November; on that same date he wrote to Henry Newbolt to say that a 'friend' who was staying at Max Gate had read some of Newbolt's poems to Emma and himself the previous evening.[73] Even before this visit, however, Florence had confided to Clodd—with an indiscretion that would have deeply shocked Hardy had he known of it—that she had learned to view the ' "Max Gate menage" ' in something of a comic and ironical light. Although Hardy had professed to be in despair over the death of Kitsey, his favourite cat, his letters had shown that he was none the less 'very pleasurably excited' over the forthcoming Dorchester production of *The Mellstock Choir*, a dramatization of *Under the Greenwood Tree*, and that he was taking 'a melancholy pleasure' in devising an inscription for Kitsey's headstone. When Florence accused him of ingratitude in daring to write of Kitsey, 'That little white cat was his only friend', Hardy only smiled and protested that he was not writing about himself exactly but about some 'imaginary man in a similar situation'— and, indeed, the poem eventually took the shape now known as 'The Roman Gravemounds'. Emma, she reported, remained 'good to me, beyond words', and grew more affectionate than ever: 'I am *intensely* sorry for her,' she added, 'sorry indeed for both.'[74]

Hardy managed to tie Florence more tightly to him in a number of ways during the course of her various visits to Max Gate that autumn. He took her to visit his sisters at Bockhampton; he had her sketched by William Strang when he came down in September to prepare a portrait of Hardy himself; and the date 25 September 1910 and the words 'Maiden Castle' attached to a tiny bunch of dried flowers evidently memorialize an occasion of special emotional significance.[75] None of this made life at Max Gate any easier for Florence. Precisely because of the sympathy she felt for both husband and wife it became increasingly painful for her to be a witness, and even an occasion, of an antagonism that always threatened to burst out into violent quarrels. During the November visit Emma not only suggested to Florence that they should go off to Boulogne together, because that would ' "have a good effect on T.H." ', but asked if she didn't think Hardy looked very like Crippen, adding that she quite expected to find herself dead in the cellar one morning. (On other occasions she is said to have reported Hardy to the police and to have so frightened him with threats to kill him that he went to Henry for protection.)[76] When Florence returned a month later to spend Christmas at Max Gate she had to endure, on Christmas Day itself, an appalling quarrel between Hardy, who wanted to take her with him to Bockhampton to visit his sisters, and Emma, who declared that the sisters would poison Florence's mind against her. Thenceforward, Florence seems to have avoided visiting Max Gate while Hardy and Emma were both present. She did not, however, break off her friendship with Emma, and although she dodged the threatened visit to Boulogne by suggesting, on her father's authority, that it would be too cold for a winter holiday, she did spend a week or so with Emma in Worthing the following July.[77]

It was during this period of private distress that Hardy received some of his most cherished public honours. In November 1908 the offer of a knighthood from H. H. Asquith (as Prime Minister) had been gently declined, but in June 1910 Hardy's name appeared

in the first Birthday Honours List of the new king, George V, as
a recipient of the Order of Merit—a greater and more appropriate
distinction, and less invidious in social terms.* Among the many
letters of congratulation he received, that from Evangeline Smith
sounded the happiest note: 'How pleased your dear Mother would
have been!'[78] Emma, who would dearly have liked to become Lady
Hardy, subsequently complained that it was characteristic of her
husband's selfishness that he would accept honours for himself
only. Hardy was nervous in advance of the investiture on 19 July,
and Florence Dugdale was asked, independently, by Hardy's
sisters and by Emma herself (who remained at Max Gate) to keep
an eye upon him that day and see he was properly dressed. All
went off well enough, although he felt he had 'failed in the
accustomed formalities' and was so flustered when he rejoined
Florence that he could not at first find the insignia of the Order,
which he had dropped, loose, into one of his pockets.[79]

Four months later, on 16 November 1910, Hardy received the
freedom of the Borough of Dorchester. Although the honour was
long overdue, and even now had perhaps been extracted from
doubtful councilmen only by the recent royal distinction of the
Order of Merit, it meant more to him, precisely because it was
local, than any national or international recognition could do.†
His satisfaction was reflected in the unusual length and eloquence
of his speech of thanks, which turned both on the need to preserve
the visible relics of the local past and on the sadness of the
realization that the 'human Dorchester' he had once known could
not be so preserved. He had now, he said, to go to the cemetery
to find 'the Dorchester that I knew best; there are names on white
stones one after the other, names that recall the voices, cheerful
and sad, anxious and indifferent, that are missing from the
dwellings and pavements'. The speech itself was a deeply felt
testimony to his sense of local identification, made all the more
poignant by its being immediately followed, that same evening,
by a performance of the dramatization of *Under the Greenwood*

---

* During the Parliament Bill crisis of 1913 Hardy was one of the Liberal
sympathizers selected by Asquith as potential recipients of peerages.

† Another form of local recognition earlier that same year had been the
announcement of a line of 'Thomas Hardy' pottery, made in Dorset and
distributed by a local firm. Hardy himself was said to have supplied the
pictorial designs painted on the vases and to have been the author of the
accompanying couplets—among them: 'No girl in Wessex rivalled Tess / In
beauty, charm, and tenderness' and 'Far from the madding crowd / Where
lovers' hearts beat loud'.[80]

Tree. The peculiar emotional significance of the occasion was further intensified by its being probably the only time in his life when Hardy was present in the same room not only with Emma (who sat beside him on the platform in elaborate evening dress) and with his brother and sisters but also with Florence Dugdale.[81]

24

A FUNERAL
AND A
MARRIAGE

ALTHOUGH Florence Dugdale no longer visited Max Gate when
Hardy was there she still saw him fairly often in London,
at Clodd's, and during visits she made to Weymouth—they spent
2 June 1911, Hardy's seventy-first birthday, together at Bockhampton with his family. She and her younger sister Constance
accompanied Hardy and his brother on a visit to Lichfield, Worcester, and Hereford cathedrals in April that year, and also on a
similar expedition in June when Hardy chose to explore Carlisle
and the Lakes rather than stay in London and participate in the
excitement and discomforts associated with the coronation of
George V: he had been officially invited to the coronation in
February but pleaded 'unavoidable circumstances' as his reason
for declining. Also of the Lakes party was Florence's father, who
had long been aware of the friendship between Florence and a
man considerably older than himself. Remarkably, Hardy seems
to have been engaged at this period in trying to bring about a
marriage between Constance Dugdale and his sixty-year-old bachelor brother, perhaps simply because it seemed a happy arrangement in itself, perhaps because he thought it would provide
occasion and excuse for Florence to spend more time in Dorset.[1]

In December 1911 there was yet another little tour, to Bath, Gloucester, and Bristol, and Hardy and Florence were on this occasion accompanied by one of Hardy's sisters—presumably Kate, since Mary's health had been declining for some time and beginning to give cause for anxiety. Shortly after the West Country excursion, Hardy sent Florence a card bearing, cryptically enough, a text from Galatians: 'Ye have been called unto liberty.' The message sounds significant and may indeed be so—the remainder of the same verse reads: 'only use not liberty for an occasion to the flesh, but by love serve one another'. On the other hand, it may simply have registered Hardy's sense of Florence's relief at being released from the constant companionship of Kate, whose ebullient temperament and country manners she had no doubt found a little oppressive. Florence on her return home reported to Clodd that Hardy seemed well and even light-hearted, and that she had concluded—since Mrs Henniker had also found him in excellent spirits recently—that his depressive moods ought not to be taken too seriously.[2]

Florence, whom Hardy was now addressing as 'My dearest F.', was still doing occasional typing for Emma, for Hardy himself, and especially for Mrs Henniker. But she was also continuing to write things of her own, and Hardy helped her very considerably with both the composition and the placing of the story 'Blue Jimmy the Horse-Stealer' in the February 1911 issue of the *Cornhill*.[3] Meanwhile, in the aftermath of *The Dynasts,* his own work was going well and he was becoming increasingly at ease with himself as a poet. For whatever reasons—his long apprenticeship in both verse and prose, the sheer creative tenacity which enabled him to worry at lines until he got them exactly right, the trenchant simplicity of his assumption that poetry was an entirely natural medium of human expression and, as such, entirely appropriate to almost any human situation—Hardy found that verse flowed, not freely perhaps but certainly frequently, from his pen. 'Tragic narrative poems, like the Trampwoman's Tragedy, seem to be liked most,' he remarked to Sir Frederick Macmillan in September 1910, '& I can do them with ease'[4]—although the years 1910–12 were in fact to be more remarkable for love poems such as 'To Meet, or Otherwise', for brooding philosophical excursions such as 'A Plaint to Man' and 'God's Funeral', and for demonstrations (notably in his *Titanic* poem, 'The Convergence of the Twain') of an extraordinary gift for the occasional poem that would have equipped him, had he been deemed sufficiently 'safe', to be an outstanding Poet Laureate.*

In the closing months of 1911 Hardy gave active support to the production by the Dorchester amateurs of a double bill consisting of his own play *The Three Wayfarers* and a dramatization of 'The Distracted Preacher' by A. H. Evans. He also became deeply involved in the preparation of an Anglo-American *édition de luxe* of all his works, verse as well as prose, which had recently been agreed upon. In welcoming the project, he had specified that the text of all volumes would be reset (making alterations possible), that he would himself correct the proofs, and that the spelling would not be American. When the arrangements with the American publisher collapsed, Sir Frederick Macmillan came forward at the beginning of 1912 with his own proposal for a 'definitive' edition with a first printing of 1,000 copies and a price of 7s. 6d. per volume, of which 1s. 6d. would go to the author. Hardy was again enthusiastic—despite his earlier expressions of gloom at the prospect of 're-reading old books of mine, written when my spirits were brisker than they are now, & full of artistic errors which cannot be altered'. For this Wessex Edition, as it was to be called, he gave all his texts a thorough revision, revised and updated his authorial prefaces, added a new 'General Preface', and divided the prose volumes into categories which would have the effect of separating the major from the lesser works and at the same time, as he told Macmillan, give reviewers something to write about.[6] He also supplied Macmillan with his own map of his fictional Wessex, suggesting that it could either be used as it stood or be professionally redrawn with the addition of ships, fishes, trees, and other decorative devices such as the old map-makers had affected; Macmillan chose the second of these alternatives and Hardy subsequently gave his warm approval to a proof of the map, with its whale- and dolphin-crowded seas. It was Hardy, too, who specified both the photographer (Hermann Lea) and the individual photographs to be used as frontispieces to the successive

---

* Since Hardy was not known as a poet in 1896, when Alfred Austin was appointed to the Laureateship, he could in fact have been considered for the position only at Austin's death in 1913, when the choice fell upon Robert Bridges. Hardy observed to Gosse at the time that his poem 'God's Funeral' would have been 'enough in itself to damn me for the Laureateship, . . . Fancy Nonconformity on the one hand, & Oxford on the other, pouring out their vials on poor Mr Asquith for such an enormity!' Gosse later told Rupert Brooke that Hardy had secretly hoped for the appointment.[5]

volumes, and while there is perhaps a hint here of a desire to emulate the photographic frontispieces to Henry James's New York Edition it is worth remembering that Hardy had for many years been in the habit of advising the illustrators of his books and even of providing them with sketches of specific episodes.[7]

The experience of reading through his own work was, on the whole, deeply satisfying. During the process of reading the proofs of *The Return of the Native,* he told Florence Dugdale on 22 April 1912, he 'got to like the character of Clym. . . . I think he is the nicest of all my heroes, and *not a bit* like me.' Reading *The Woodlanders* for the first time in many years, he found that he liked it *'as a story,* the best of all. Perhaps that is owing to the locality and scenery of the action, a part I am very fond of.' Though this scarcely amounts to the self-congratulatory pleasure which so charmingly exudes from the pages of James's Preface to *The Ambassadors,* it is an indication—among many others—that Hardy's tendency in later years to make deprecating remarks about his fiction was chiefly a strategy for insisting upon the superior excellence of his verse. In early September 1912 Edmund Gosse recorded a conversation with him about *Desperate Remedies*: ' "A melodrama, of course," he said; "but better as a story than one would think. Have you read it lately? Don't you think, just as a story, it is rather good? Of course, I put all that in just in obedience to George Meredith. He said there must be a story. I did not care." ' He spoke of the novel, as Gosse recalled, 'as if it was some book written a long time ago, by someone who was no longer of much importance'.[8] This was the same sort of modesty he had shown the previous year in allowing, and even encouraging, Sydney Cockerell, director of the Fitzwilliam Museum in Cambridge, to present his manuscripts to libraries on both sides of the Atlantic which would be interested in having them. Characteristically, he wanted negotiations to be carried through without publicity of any kind and the responsibility of the distribution to be clearly Cockerell's, since he felt it would 'not be becoming for a writer to send his own MSS to a museum on his own judgement'.[9]

Modesty did not, however, prevent him from taking pleasure in the further honours which came his way, especially those conferred by his literary colleagues. Indeed, his pleasure seems to have been enhanced by the very unexpectedness of such recognition, as if it had never ceased to amaze and puzzle him that he had somehow become a great man in the world's eyes without ever ceasing to be rather an insignificant figure in his own. When in 1912 the Royal Society of Literature decided to present him with its gold medal on the occasion of his seventy-second birthday, he asked that the occasion be private, and Henry Newbolt and W. B. Yeats went down to Max Gate on 2 June to make the presentation on the Society's behalf. Already made uncomfortable by the absence of other guests and by an awkward lunch at which Hardy talked exclusively with Newbolt about architecture while Emma discoursed to Yeats upon the lives and habits of the two cats who sat on the table beside her plate, the visitors were moved to protest at Hardy's insistence that his wife should be excluded from the ceremony which followed. Hardy stood firm, however, Emma quietly left the room, and the presentation went forward with all the formality that would have attended a public occasion. When the time came for his expression of thanks—which took the form of a warning against the increasing corruption of the English language—Hardy insisted on reading the speech aloud, explaining that he had already supplied copies to the London reporters, who would report that he had addressed the deputation, and that it would not be proper of him to turn them into liars.[10]

Hardy's behaviour on this occasion lends some colour to Emma's frequent complaint that her husband wanted all the glory for himself and would share none of it with her. Some years earlier she had warned Clement Shorter that he had better not publish a portrait of her in the pages of the *Sphere*: 'I think the photo: must be returned—as I fear that T.H: will not like it added to his affairs he has an *obsession* that I must be kept out of them lest the dimmest ray shoud alight upon me of his supreme story— *"This is to please his family,"* chiefly. He is like no other man— nor himself as *"was"*.'[11] On the other hand, Hardy perhaps had some justification for feeling that the award was indeed being made to him alone—despite the claims Emma had so often made of having written much of the fiction herself—and for fearing that the occasion might be marred by some embarrassing intervention on her part. By that summer of 1912 her mental instability —her shifts between paranoiac protest, childish playfulness, and aggressive religiosity—had become very marked, showing itself not only in her public and domestic behaviour but also in the writings, both verse and prose, to which she now devoted so much of her time.

At the very beginning of 1911 Emma had completed 'Some Recollections'—that charming evocation of her childhood and of her first meeting with Hardy—and incorporated in its final paragraph a declaration not only of religious faith but of an essentially cheerful, optimistic attitude towards life which could scarcely have been more at odds with her husband's world view: 'I have some philosophy and mysticism, and an ardent belief in Christianity and the life beyond this present one, all which makes any existence curiously interesting. As one watches *happenings* (and even if should occur *unhappy happenings*) outward circumstances are of less importance if Christ is our highest ideal. A strange unearthly brilliance shines around our path, penetrating and dispersing difficulties with its warmth and glow.' Against this happier aspect of Emma's faith must be set its darker, more obsessive side. Her violent hatred of Catholicism was reflected in her support for a wide range of Protestant organizations: her charitable contributions for the year 1909 included, in addition to a number of societies in aid of animals and children, the Salvation Army, the National Church League, the Protestant Alliance ('against all encroachments of Popery'), the Evangelical Alliance, the Children for Protestantism, Protestantism in Parliament, the Tower Hamlets Mission, and the Christian Colportage Association for England. She was a great believer in the efficacy of pamphlets and much given, in and out of season, to leaving them in the shops and houses she visited. As she told a young relative in October 1911: 'I have been scattering beautiful little booklets about—which may, I hope, help to make the clear atmosphere of pure Protestantism in the land to revive us again in the *truth*—as I believe it to be—so I send you some of them. Do read & *pass them* on.'[12]

At the end of 1911 she had privately printed (in Dorchester) a little volume entitled *Alleys* which contained fifteen of her poems, ranging from that cheerful little nature poem 'Spring Song' (see above, p. 404) to the ponderously patriotic 'God Save Our Emperor-King', structured as an 'antiphon' between India and Great Britain and bearing the very recent date of November 1911. 'Ten Moons', the most interesting of the small group of religious poems, was rendered unduly mysterious by printing errors, especially the one which rendered the 'world' of line 2 as 'whirled':

In misery whirled
   Is this One-Moon world,
      But there's no sorrow or darkness there
   In that mighty Planet where
There is no night.
   Ten moons ever revolving
All matter its long years resolving
   To sweetness and light.[13]

A fuller exposition—if that is the word—of her religious attitudes appears in the prose volume *Spaces,* dated from Max Gate in April 1912, in which a rhapsody on 'The High Delights of Heaven' is followed by a homily on the need to be an 'acceptor' rather than a 'non-acceptor' of God's salvation, a vision of the Day of Judgement, and a brief dramatic dialogue depicting Satan's ejection from Heaven. Emma's faith was undoubtedly sincere, the source of that curious serenity which enabled her to pursue her own preoccupations quite unaffected by—because oblivious to— the effect she was having on other people,* but the entire pamphlet is no less clearly the product of a mind at once obsessed, muddled, and naïve. Although 'Retrospect', her potted *Paradise Lost,* is perhaps the most vacuous of the four sections, there is more obvious mental disturbance, thrown into relief by the prevailing reasonableness of tone, in 'The New Element of Fire', the section dealing with the Day of Judgement:

> The Last Day must not be considered as literally a day of twenty-four hours more or less, but as any prolongation, neither must the sound of the Trumpet—that awful call—be supposed to be one sudden shout, for the Divine order is usually slow, lengthy, culminating from an almost unnoticeable beginning. So will the end of all here on earth follow that order—an earthly day is, as it were, a hundred years or more by heavenly reckoning. . . . And then will occur the general darkening of the sun, moon, and stars by blackest clouds, as at the Crucifixion, and the power of that awful Trumpet accelerated till the final blast, when suddenly a spot of light will appear in the East at 4 o'clock a.m. according to western time—and dark night of Eastern time or about that hour, varying at distances, the hot sunshine there gone completely, leaving however the weariness and dreariness of the afternoon heat of hot latitudes.[15]

* One of her relatives, Léonie Gifford, recalled that when she visited Emma in London in 1910 she was shown the elegant tea prepared for some distinguished visitor expected that day but offered nothing herself.[14]

Even the benign Charles Moule, now President of Corpus Christi College, Cambridge, had advised Emma against the publication of *Spaces*.[16]* Hardy's own embarrassment is easy to imagine, and Emma's derangement served to confirm him in the long-held views he summarized for Mrs Henniker in October 1911 in answer to her criticism of H. G. Wells's *The New Machiavelli*: '[Y]ou know what I have thought for many years: that marriage should not thwart nature, & that when it does thwart nature it is no real marriage, & the legal contract should therefore be as speedily cancelled as possible. Half the misery of human life would I think disappear if this were made easy.' He repeated these sentiments almost word for word in a contribution early the following year to a magazine symposium on 'How Shall We Solve the Divorce Problem?'[18]

Because Hardy saw no hope of ameliorating his situation in the world as it was, he determined to bear his lot with whatever stoicism he could muster, to avoid public exposure of his domestic difficulties, and to maintain Emma, economically and socially, in the manner she had a right to expect. There is, in all the circumstances, something very admirable about the resolution and dignity with which he maintained such a position. At the same time—as he himself later saw—it was a position based on principle rather than on sympathy, on obligation rather than loyalty or affection. Precisely because of his long-standing intellectual adherence to a particular view of marriage, Hardy was too apt to find confirmation for that view in his own experience, too rigid in his judgement of Emma, too quick to abandon hope (always an enticing prospect for one of his temperament) and settle comfortably into a self-justifying satisfaction at being so cruelly frustrated by fate and circumstance—by the treachery of the flesh, the elusiveness of the well-beloved, and the injustice of the prevailing social order. He had also learned all too well those techniques of passive resistance so long practised by his father in his dealings with Jemima. What Hardy was most to regret, most to blame himself for, in later years, was precisely the inflexibility of his behaviour towards Emma, his failure to see her as a fellow sufferer, and his betrayal of that moral and emotional touchstone of 'loving-kindness' he had so movingly embodied in his own finest work.

It is not necessary, however, to judge him more harshly than

---

* Emma told Clodd in 1904 that twelve Cambridge men had praised her writings. Moule must have been one of these twelve, Alfred Pretor another; the remaining ten have not been identified.[17]

he did himself. He had work to do, after all, a creative need and obligation to whose imperatives he had necessarily—and properly —to respond. Criticism of Hardy's conduct during these years seems sometimes to ignore the fact that he was an artist; it is as if he could be forgiven for grandly sinning in traditional artist fashion, like a Byron or an Augustus John, but not for the lack of enthusiasm with which he tried to live with his own great mistake. Nor is it necessary, in sympathizing with poor Emma, to underestimate the extent of her deterioration, nor the gravity of its public and private consequences. Emma's vanity, gaucherie, unpredictability, and exasperating foolishness emerge with painful vividness from the entry which A. C. Benson made in his diary immediately following a visit to Max Gate in company with Edmund Gosse in early September 1912. Benson's impression of Emma, whom he had not previously met, was of 'a small, pretty, rather mincing elderly lady with hair curiously puffed & padded rather fantastically dressed' whom Gosse took by both hands and addressed in 'a stream of exaggerated gallantry which was deeply appreciated'. Gosse, for his part, recorded of that same visit that Emma greeted them effusively, 'absurdly dressed, as a country lady without friends might dress herself on a vague recollection of some nymph in a picture by Botticelli'. After lunch—rather coarse fare, according to the fastidious Benson, in the 'rather slatternly' dining room, with streaks and stains showing on the purple distemper— Gosse mischievously insisted that Emma should smoke one of the cigarettes he had produced. Hardy did not, of course, smoke; Emma declared that she had never done so either, but nevertheless 'lit a cigarette & coughed cruelly at intervals, every now & then laying it down & saying "There that will be enough" but always resuming it, till I [Benson] feared disaster. Hardy looked at her so fiercely & scornfully that I made haste to say that I had persuaded my mother to smoke.' In conversation with Gosse that same afternoon Emma voiced her usual complaint that Hardy, full of self-conceit, was becoming more difficult to live with than ever, accepting only honours he could keep to himself, and refusing to let her have a motor car. She later showed Benson around the dining room, 'talking in a low hurried voice, as if she was thinking aloud & not regarding me at all', and then the garden, where she became so absorbed in pinching the pods of the *Noli me tangere* to make them eject their seeds that she went on doing it 'with little jumps & elfin shrieks of pleasure'.[19]

Benson also had some rather acid comments to make on Max

Gate itself as a house at once mean and pretentious, uncomfortable and shabby, sunk deep, dark, and airless in the midst of a jungle-like plantation—hopelessly overgrown as a consequence of Hardy's reluctance to 'injure' any growing thing even by pruning or cutting back. He found Hardy himself to be of unprepossessing appearance ('One would take him for a retired half-pay officer, from a not very smart regiment') and thought that his manner, while certainly kindly and courteous, was lacking in openness, showing something of the instinctive self-protectiveness of his peasant background. But at the end of the visit Benson was above all oppressed by a sense of 'something intolerable' in the thought of 'the old rhapsodist' having 'to live day & night with the absurd, inconsequent, puffy, rambling old lady'. It was true that Hardy did not behave very agreeably towards Emma either, but 'his patience must be incredibly tried. She is so queer, & yet has to be treated as rational, while she is full, I imagine, of suspicions & jealousies & affronts which must be half insane.'[20]

Benson did not care for women, and his distaste for Emma must be read in that context. But Emma had struck Gosse as odd and difficult ('she means to be very kind', he had told his wife) as long ago as 1883 (see above, p. 240), and almost everyone who encountered her came to similar conclusions. Even those who spoke of her as lovable and childlike often did so in terms suggestive of condescension or pity, and Hardy could certainly have treated her with more kindness and consideration. But it is common enough for irritation, anger, and despair to be provoked with peculiar vehemence by the deterioration, for whatever reason, of the object once beloved. During their early continental holidays Hardy had got angry whenever Emma felt too tired to keep up with him. So, in later years, he got angry when she acted gauchely, dressed inappropriately, talked foolishly—while her natural response to that anger, whether prompted by defiance or by sheer nervousness, was to intensify whatever in her behaviour was giving offence. And while the programme of keeping apart, suggested by Emma, embraced by Hardy, made for a reduction in day-to-day tensions, it also entrenched their basic differences to the point at which they finally stopped listening to each other.

Well before 1912 the situation had been pushed beyond hope of recovery by Emma's mental decline. Sir Clifford Allbutt, as a Commissioner in Lunacy, once gave it as his unofficial opinion that Emma was probably certifiable. Hardy's own poem, 'The Interloper'—with its epigraph, 'And I saw the figure and visage of Madness seeking for a home'—suggests not only that he shared this view but that he believed that the symptoms of Emma's condition ('that under which best lives corrode') were visible, had he been able to recognize them, from the time of their first meeting.[21] Emma would perhaps have been happier in her later years if Hardy had been more sympathetic, if he had not become emotionally absorbed in a relationship with Florence Dugdale, if he had not possessed such extraordinary dedication and longevity as an artist. But her personal tragedy, it is clear, would eventually have overtaken her whatever the pattern of her life had been.

At the time of the September 1912 visit Gosse found Hardy looking small, white, dried-up, and old, his eyes drawn with fatigue, his hair mostly gone, his moustache faded from its original yellowish red and thinned out, 'like the sparse whiskers of some ancient rodent, a worn-out squirrel for instance', his lips inclined to tremble, though less from age than from 'an excess of introspection'. Nevertheless he talked freely and easily—'with an exquisite simplicity, with no parade or self-assertion, without curiosity, of things at hand'—and seemed altogether 'brisk and well, without any species of malady or incommodity'. Though neither Gosse nor Benson commented specifically on Emma's health, it is clear from both accounts that she displayed no obvious disability but, on the contrary, a considerable and even excessive physical energy —in Benson's phrase, a 'flighty & peevish activity'.[22] She had certainly been busy in and around Dorchester during the first eight months of 1912. For the first time in many years she attended a Field Club meeting with her husband in February— rather pathetically exhibiting the coloured drawing of an ancient gold collar which she had made in Cornwall before her marriage —and one hot day in mid-July, dressed in her usual girlish outfit of white frock and blue sash, she held a garden party at Max Gate. Later in July she hired a two-horse brake to take the young members of the Fordington St. George Needlework Guild to the seaside, supplying the party with a picnic on the beach and with more refreshments back at Max Gate and presenting each of the children with a cup and saucer. Lilian Gifford was again invited to stay for much of the summer—until she quarrelled with Emma and was banished—and it was no doubt the need to entertain their bored and rather lethargic niece which prompted the Hardys to take her to Weymouth in August to see a performance of

Bunty Pulls the Strings, a popular comedy of the day which Hardy himself had already seen in London two months previously.[23]

Emma's health, however, had been poor—though not dramatically so—for some time. She now had a maid, fourteen-year-old Dolly Gale, to sleep in the attic bedroom next to her own, bring up her breakfast and lunch (she still went down to dinner), and perform such personal tasks as brushing her hair and scalp to relieve the eczema with which she was afflicted. Although Dolly was supposed to be on call day and night, her mistress was much too considerate to disturb the girl's sleep.[24] By the autumn of 1912 Emma was distinctly weaker. She suffered, sometimes severely, from angina attacks, and from gallstones—apparently the source of the back pains which the maid tried to alleviate by patting or rubbing—and although she seems not to have consulted a doctor she did have occasional resort to a standard pain-killer (sedative solution of opium, or *Liquor opii sedativus*) prepared largely from opium, sherry, and alcohol. On Sundays she would sometimes get the gardener to push her to church in a Bath chair, not because she had become entirely immobile but because the walk was too far for anyone in poor or indifferent health—and because Hardy had persisted in his refusal to set himself up with a car and chauffeur.

One day in mid-November 1912 Emma was taken out in an open motor car to visit her friends the Wood Homers, beyond Puddletown; that night she had a violent attack of what Hardy persuaded himself was dyspepsia. During the next few days she had severe back pains and felt too unwell to eat but still declined to see a doctor. On 22 November she was well enough to copy out, in a neat hand, a cheerful little poem called 'Winter!' ('Gaze, gaze at the Mosses! / Winter joys for flower losses') and to write down, less neatly (and more pathetically), six lines of verse beginning 'Oh! would I were a dancing child'.[25] On Monday, 25 November (the day after her seventy-second birthday), Emma kept to her room as usual until she was summoned to the tea table by the importunities of Rebekah and Catharine Owen, who had come to Dorchester to see the performance of *The Trumpet-Major,* a revised version of the 1908 dramatization, the following Wednesday. She came in very slowly, Rebekah Owen later recalled, wept a little, and was very obviously depressed, but she so resisted the idea of seeing a doctor—pleading her fear of operations—that they 'thought it as likely to be nerves and melancholia as anything'. When Dr Gowring did come the following day,

Emma is said to have refused to let him examine her; in any case, according to Hardy, he treated her only for the weakness from which she was suffering, largely as a result of lack of nourishment.[26]

When Dolly Gale looked in upon her mistress at about eight o'clock the next morning, 27 November, she was terrified by the change that had taken place, by Emma's distorted face and moans of pain. Told to summon Hardy, who was already working in his study, just at the foot of the attic stairs, she had (according to her own account) difficulty in persuading him of the seriousness of the situation: 'Your collar is crooked,' he said. When he did follow her back up the stairs—no doubt the first time he had climbed them in many months—he found Emma already too far gone to speak. Within a few minutes she was dead. The causes of death were subsequently certified as impacted gallstones and heart failure—or, as Dr Gowring put it to Hardy, heart failure 'from some internal perforation'. On her desk was a pencilled note directing one of the servants to fetch from the chemist's a supply of her usual pain-killer: 'Mrs Hardy finds that she must have Lib: Op: Sed:—which she knows to take.'[27]

The doctor's diagnosis, as Hardy recognized, clearly indicated that 'mischief had been working for some while', but there seems no reason to question the truth of his statements, in so many letters written at the time to people who knew Emma well and had seen her recently, that her death was 'absolutely unexpected', by the doctor as well as by himself, and that while she had certainly been in indifferent health for some time he had no suspicion that anything was radically wrong—that she was other than 'robust and sound and likely to live to quite old age'. Her family were shocked at the news of her death, since nothing in her recent letters to them had led them to suspect that she was ill.[28]

Emma was buried at Stinsford the following Saturday, 30 November, in the plot which Hardy had already marked out for her, and for himself, alongside the graves of his parents and grandparents. Although Emma had herself worshipped at churches in Fordington and Dorchester—and might in any case have chosen other company—Hardy can scarcely have considered an alternative location. His whole conduct towards Emma had been founded on the principle that she was his wife, whom he had chosen in the face of all the world, and it would have been unthinkable that she should lie apart from him in death. After all, to put Emma alongside Jemima was no more of an offence and affront to the memory of the former than to the memory of the latter. Mary Hardy, even so, did not attend the funeral, although among the wreaths placed on Emma's coffin was one inscribed with 'affectionate memories' from her Hardy relatives. There were other ironies. Neither Emma's cousin, Charles Gifford (who was suffering from a 'nervous breakdown'), nor her nephew, Gordon Gifford, was present at the funeral, while her niece Lilian arrived at the churchyard only after the service was over. Emma was thus isolated from her family in her death as she had been ever since her marriage; nor was she attended to her grave by any of those literary friends and London dignitaries who were to crowd to her husband's funeral fifteen years later. And yet the shape of her posthumous triumph was already foreshadowed in the wording of Hardy's wreath: 'From her Lonely Husband, with the Old Affection.'[29]

Immediately upon Emma's death one of Hardy's sisters—presumably Kate—moved into Max Gate to act as her brother's housekeeper. Hardy also summoned Florence Dugdale from Weymouth —like the Owen sisters, she had come down to be present at the performance of *The Trumpet-Major*—and upon her arrival they behaved with what Emma's loyal young maid, taught by Dorchester gossip to regard Florence as Hardy's 'mistress', viewed as unseemly levity. A death often provokes such responses among the living, of course, and it is likely enough that both Hardy and Florence were at first overwhelmed by the sense of the freedom and opportunity which Emma's departure had so unexpectedly created. But the moment for euphoria soon passed. Florence went back to Enfield for a few days, and when she returned to Max Gate in early December she found not only that Kate was still running things but that Lilian Gifford had moved in too. There were business matters to be attended to, letters to be written, malicious tongues to be challenged and, if possible, silenced: Hardy had been criticized for allowing the performance of *The Trumpet-Major* to go forward on the day of his wife's death and he felt obliged to send to *The Times* a supplementary obituary of Emma which incorporated the statement, in the third person, that he had decided not to interfere with the play simply out of consideration for those who had come a long way to see it.[30]

Within a very short period, too, there began that process of imaginative re-creation which was to make possible the 'Poems of

1912–13'. By 13 December Hardy was writing to Clodd about the way in which one tended, after a bereavement, to forget all recent differences and go back in memory to 'the early times when each was much to the other—in her case & mine intensely much'. Four days later he told Mrs Henniker that he was reproaching himself for not having paid more attention to Emma's health:

> In spite of the differences between us, which it would be affectation to deny, & certain painful delusions she suffered from at times, my life is intensely sad to me now without her. The saddest moments of all are when I go into the garden and to that long straight walk at the top that you know, where she used to walk every evening just before dusk, the cat trotting faithfully behind her; & at times when I almost expect to see her as usual coming in from the flower-beds with a little trowel in her hand.[31]

The note, and even some of the vocabulary, of Hardy's rhetoric of remorse is already audible in that letter, and at the end of 1912 and beginning of 1913, as he later recalled, he wrote more poems than he had ever done in a comparable space of time. All were about Emma, stimulated by a profound regret for what he now acknowledged as his neglect of her in recent years, and by a still more poignant sense of the bitter contrast between the magic of their first meeting and the desolation of their final years together. Both sets of emotions were sharpened and intensified by the discovery, when he began going through Emma's papers, not only of the naïvely charming 'Some Recollections', but also of the extensive diaries she had kept since their marriage and which, as he now discovered, had been largely devoted, during the last twenty years or so of her life, to harsh comments upon her husband's conduct, character, and genius.

Although precise datings are not always possible, the earliest poems seem to have been those of immediate loss and self-reproach —'Your Last Drive', 'Best Times', 'An Upbraiding', and 'Without Ceremony' ('It was your way, my dear, / To vanish without a word') and 'The Walk':

> You did not walk with me
> Of late to the hill-top tree
> > By the gated ways,
> > As in earlier days;
> > You were weak and lame,
> > So you never came,
> And I went alone, and I did not mind,
> Not thinking of you as left behind.[32]

The magnificent poems which harp back specifically to the earliest days of their romance were almost all of them products of a melancholy pilgrimage which Hardy made to St. Juliot in early March 1913—the forty-third anniversary of that first meeting at the rectory door. Hardy took Henry with him—an uncongenial companion, in one sense, given his bluff commonsensicality and hearty dislike of Emma, for such a sentimental expedition, but undoubtedly valuable as a reminder of present realities and hence as an antidote to the memories in which Hardy was now so deliberately immersing himself. Indeed, it is clear from the verbal and rhythmic control of these poems that Hardy remained very much in command of his emotions at this period, that he cherished his melancholy rather than surrendered to it.

So Florence Dugdale, writing to Clodd from Max Gate on 16 January 1913, could speak of Hardy as having regained, according to Kate, the happy laugh of his young manhood and, in the next sentence, go on to describe the depressing effect upon him of his nightly reading of what she later called those 'diabolical diaries' of Emma's: 'Nothing could be worse for him,' she understandably, but perhaps mistakenly, exclaimed. When Hardy went off to Cornwall she felt such luxuriating in misery could only do him harm: 'He says that he is going down for the sake of the girl he married, & who died more than twenty years ago. His family say *that* girl never existed, but she did exist to him, no doubt.' She comforted herself with the thought that, as Kate had observed, no great damage would be done so long as he didn't 'pick up another Gifford down there', and felt justified when Hardy himself confessed, in a letter from Boscastle, that the visit had been a very painful one and that he could not think what had possessed him to go there.[33]

But it is perfectly clear that, as on many previous occasions, what gave Hardy pain was precisely what provided the fuel for his art. It is no less clear that what, more than anything else, determined the power, the embodied passion, of the finished product, whether prose or verse, was the anguished intensity of the original creative impulse—the degree to which his imagination had been seized by some sense of compassionate identification with suffering guessed at or actually witnessed, with some place or person perceived as richly symbolic, with some personal experience revisited and intensified. 'Hereto I come to view a voiceless ghost', he wrote in the opening line of 'After a Journey', and the poem as a whole is nothing less than a deliberate invocation and

confrontation of the Emma he had met in 1870 and drifted away
from all too shortly thereafter:

> Yes: I have re-entered your olden haunts at last;
>   Through the years, through the dead scenes I have tracked you;
> What have you now found to say of our past—
>   Scanned across the dark space wherein I have lacked you?
> Summer gave us sweets, but autumn wrought division?
>   Things were not lastly as firstly well
>   With us twain, you tell?
> But all's closed now, despite Time's derision.[34]

Such intensification could, up to a point, be consciously pursued and achieved, induced almost as if by contemplative discipline. Thus there is a sense in which regret for Emma, like regret
for Kitsey ('the little white cat was his only friend'), flourished in
a condition of deep melancholy which was to some degree willed,
deliberately cultivated—a kind of enclosed mental garden in
which Hardy's creativity could uniquely flourish but which he
was none the less capable of entering or leaving almost at will.
There are, however, times when this trick of the imagination does
not quite come off, when that marvellous poetic tact—the held
balance between directness of thought, grainy naturalness of language, and elegance of form—is coarsened by a hint of morbidity,
of sheer self-flagellation. Among the poems in which the mood of
remorse seems to have been quite artificially stimulated and sustained can be numbered 'The Circular', 'Two Lips', 'A Leaving',
and some lines headed 'The Sound of Her',[35] about the sound of
Emma's coffin lid being screwed down, which Hardy was persuaded not to publish.

Before his return from Cornwall in March 1913 Hardy arranged
for a memorial to Emma, designed by himself, to be placed on the
walls of St. Juliot Church—where it was inspected by Gordon
Gifford the following August—and before the end of April he
had seen to the erection of her tombstone, again to his own design, in the churchyard at Stinsford.[36] For Florence Dugdale,
Hardy's obsession with his dead wife was both painful and bewildering. Painful because she knew from first-hand experience
what his later years with Emma had been like—she once said
that Hardy and Emma had been in the midst of a violent quarrel

in November 1912 and about to separate—and because in sancti-
fying Emma he seemed to be undervaluing her own devotion.
Bewildering because he seemed not to make, in his own mind,
any clear correlation between his feelings for Emma and his feelings for Florence. In the same letter in which he could dismiss
the abuse of him in Emma's diaries as 'sheer hallucination in her,
poor thing, & not wilfulness', he could go on to tell Florence that
once she returned to Max Gate he would keep her there till
spring: 'If I once get you here again won't I clutch you tight.'
While he was visiting Boscastle, deliberately pursuing his newly
found obsession, he could simultaneously insist upon his continuing need for Florence's presence: 'Looking back it has seemed
such a cruel thing altogether that events which began so auspi-
ciously should have turned out as they did. And now suppose
something shd happen to you, physically, as it did to her mentally!
I dare not think of it, & I am sure you will not run any risk if
you can help. I have told H[enry] I am charging you strictly to
stay indoors, & he ridicules the idea that you will listen to me for
a moment.'[37]

In April 1913 Hardy visited Mrs Henniker's house in Suffolk
when Florence was there in the role of secretary and companion.
He then went on by himself to Aldeburgh, where he talked to
Clodd at length about Emma and the way in which her delusions
about being followed and conspired against were consistent with
what he believed to be 'the mad strain in the family blood'.* He
spoke also of her belief that she was the author of the Wessex
novels and referred to a manuscript she had left about a wife who
inspired her husband's novels.[38]

Once she arrived back at Max Gate later that spring, Florence
seems to have remained there more or less continuously, despite
Hardy's (entirely justified) fears of what Dorchester gossip would
say if it discovered her presence, even if 'chaperoned' by Kate,
Mary, or Lilian Gifford. Hardy was apprehensive, too, of the
inquisitiveness of Clement Shorter—unaware that intimate details of his domestic life were being regularly conveyed by Florence
to Clodd, who was accustomed to pass on all such tidbits to
Shorter—and it was perhaps in an attempt to purchase Shorter's
discretion by a controlled indulgence of his curiosity that Hardy

---

* Though this notion has been attributed to Florence, it is evident that
it had been in Hardy's mind long before Emma's death and that Florence
was simply repeating what her husband had told her.

invited him down to Max Gate with Clodd for a long weekend in mid-July 1913. The two visitors were taken to Bockhampton, to Emma's grave, and to Talbothays, to which Henry Hardy and his sisters had recently moved. Clodd found Henry 'a well-set, sensible man' and the two sisters 'quite as Miss Dugdale told me— ladylike, refined, well-informed', and observed that it was a shame that Hardy had allowed 'his half mad wife' to forbid them and their mother access to Max Gate. It was also a shame, he thought, that Hardy had not let him 'know these good folk earlier. He should be proud of them.'[39] It would have been difficult for Hardy to make Clodd and Shorter understand that it was precisely be- cause he was so proud of his family, and so devoted to them, that he had previously sought to protect them from the public eye.

The slight shift in Hardy's attitudes towards his family was evidently related to the final departure of Mary, Kate, and Henry from that Bockhampton cottage which—as Hardy noted on 1 January 1913 when making out the cheque for the last quarterly rent—the Hardys had occupied for 112 years. The old lifehold lease had expired in 1892 upon the death of Hardy's father, but the owners of Kingston Maurward, although unwilling to sell the property, had allowed the family to go on living there at a very modest rent. The move was a sharp and in many respects a sad break with the past, but once Jemima had died her three un- married children—especially the cheerful, extroverted Kate and Henry—had almost inevitably succumbed to a desire for modern convenience. As Mary told their cousin Nathaniel Sparks, it was a wrench to leave Bockhampton, but the house there had got out of repair and it seemed a pity not to occupy Henry's 'comfortable new one'. By June 1913 they were well established at Talbothays and Mary was able to report to her elder brother that Henry's garden was growing well, its successive rows of carrots, onions, potatoes, broad beans and other vegetables already giving it the look of their father's garden 'in the olden time'.[40]

Florence meanwhile was helping Hardy with his voluminous correspondence—typing out letters he had drafted and sometimes sending them out over her own initials as 'Secretary'—and begin- ning to get the disorganized household into good order. The house itself, as Benson had remarked the previous year, was in a sadly run-down condition, and during the autumn of 1913 Hardy had it redecorated throughout and a small conservatory, leading out of the drawing room, added to the east side—projects, as Florence reported to Clodd, which amused him 'tremendously'. He was, indeed, as cheerful and affectionate as she had ever known him, and she, for her part, had accommodated herself, not gladly but perforce, to his poetic obsession with an idealized Emma—although when he suggested to Florence that she should wear half-mourning permanently as a sign of devotion to Emma's memory she was provoked to wonder whether there might not be 'something in the air of Max Gate that makes us all a little crazy'. What she could not endure was the continuing presence of Lilian Gifford. Lilian had learned long before to regard Max Gate as her second home, and she had evidently seen the death of her aunt (despite their recent quarrel) as an opportunity to reintroduce herself into Hardy's domestic life on a more permanent basis, as a substitute for the wife he had lost and the daughter he had never had: presenting him with a lamp on the first anniversary of Emma's death she called him 'Daddy-Uncle' and declared that she always thought of him in those terms. Lilian represented for Florence not so much a threat to her own position as a constant, irritating reminder of the woman whose lingering presence—more formidable now than ever in life—she was trying to exorcise. She complained to Clodd in December 1913 that while Lilian sought to ingratiate herself with Hardy by talking sentimentally of Emma and of St. Juliot, she refused to help in the house, gave herself superior airs, made contemptuous references to Florence's family background—and provoked, on the occasion of a visit by Florence's sister Constance, a scene described by Florence as equalled only by what she had seen when staying at Max Gate in Emma's time.[41]

Hardy was sympathetic towards Lilian precisely because her childlike speech and behaviour reminded him of Emma, but by the beginning of 1914 Florence had made it clear that if Lilian did not leave she could not herself remain, and that she would therefore be unable to go through with the marriage 'compact' into which she and Hardy had already entered. Although marriage would give Florence the position—and the respectability—she needed, it would be meaningless unless she had clear authority over the running of the household. Both Kate and Henry apparently supported her in this view—Henry saying that it was the only way to avoid a life of misery—and Lilian was sent away, having first been provided with at least a minimal financial security in the form of an annuity and some stocks.[42]

.   .   .

During this period of domestic upheaval, profound emotional disturbance, and extraordinary creativity Hardy led a public life even quieter than usual. In June 1913 he went to Cambridge to receive the honorary degree of Litt.D. He stayed with Sydney Cockerell, who had been largely instrumental in prompting the honour, and lunched with the Vice-Chancellor, S. A. Donaldson, at Magdalene. It was there that A. C. Benson found him, wearing a Doctor of Laws gown by mistake and looking 'very frail & nervous, but undeniably pleased'. Mary wrote to congratulate him, reminding him of his abandonment of his Cambridge ambitions in the 1860s: 'Now you have accomplished it all with greater honour than if you had gone along the road you then saw before you.' Florence's already wifely concern was for his health, and she began what was to prove a long and voluminous correspondence with Cockerell to warn him that Hardy was being much troubled by varicose veins and must rest his leg horizontally to prevent any clot of blood being carried to the heart or brain. That November he was again in Cambridge to be installed as an Honorary Fellow of Magdalene, taking pleasure in the company of Clifford Allbutt, A. E. Housman, and others, and especially in the splendour of his robes.[43]

At the beginning of 1913 Macmillan published the last two of the original twenty volumes of the Wessex Edition, which had begun to appear in April 1912. That same summer Hardy rather doubtfully put together a volume of previously uncollected stories, calling it *A Changed Man* after the story he thought, on the whole, to be the best of a rather poor bunch. Since he protested that he would never have revived the stories at all if they had not been so frequently reprinted in cheaper American editions—especially the novella-length 'Romantic Adventures of a Milkmaid'—he was gratified by the warm reception given the volume upon its appearance in late October. 'This book', wrote Gosse, 'is a cluster of asteroids, which take their proper place in your planetary system, and differ from your novels only in the matter of size. They are uniformly and wonderfully worthy of you, and are wholly precious.'[44] Not surprisingly Sir Frederick Macmillan raised the possibility of reprinting 'An Indiscretion in the Life of an Heiress', the one extensive prose work which remained uncollected: Hardy's remarkable reply was that the story was only a shadow of the larger work, *The Poor Man and the Lady*, from which it had been abstracted, and that he had thought of using it, together with a few surviving pages of the original manuscript, as the basis for an attempted reconstruction of *The Poor Man and the Lady* itself.[45]

This reawakened interest in his abortive first novel was per-haps stimulated by the visit Hardy received, some time in 1913, from Eliza Bright Nicholls, whose relationship with him in the 1860s had formed part of the emotional context of *The Poor Man and the Lady*. She had never married, never discarded Hardy's ring or portrait, and seems to have persuaded herself, upon hear-ing the news of Emma's death, that her long devotion might yet receive its due reward. Whether out of courtesy or curiosity—or out of a sense that she was another woman to whom he had be-haved less well than he might have done—Hardy agreed to see her at Max Gate, only to tell her, when she arrived, that he in-tended to marry Miss Dugdale.[46] Another figure from his early life, Louisa Harding, the subject of 'Louisa in the Lane', had died in September 1913 and been buried in Stinsford churchyard, while a more recent attachment, Rosamund Tomson, had also passed away—as Rosamund Marriott Watson—in December 1911. By a final little Hardyan irony, Florence Henniker had been widowed in February 1912, less than a year before the death of Emma. Hardy wrote a short poem to General Henniker's memory but seems not to have thought of proposing marriage to Mrs Henniker—partly, perhaps, because he felt that their moment had long passed (like that of the lovers in 'The Waiting Supper'), but chiefly because she had never returned his devotion at any stage of their relationship and because he was, in any case, too deeply, and happily, committed to Florence Dugdale. Florence, for her part, was perhaps the more ready to contemplate marriage to a man thirty-eight years her senior in that the only other men for whom she seems to have cared at all deeply had both died not long before, Alfred Hyatt in December 1911 and Sir Thornley Stoker in June 1912.

Hardy probably proposed marriage to Florence Dugdale as early as 16 April 1913—the date attached, together with the sim-ple inscription 'To F.E.D.', to another of those bunches of dried flowers which seem to have marked important stages in their rela-tionship. He had certainly done so, and been at least tentatively accepted, by the summer of 1913: Florence confided as much to Clodd during his visit to Max Gate in mid-July. The apparently hasty arrangements for the marriage itself, on 10 February 1914—a special licence was obtained on 6 February[47]—evidently reflected nothing more than a desire to keep the affair private. For the same reason no one outside the two families concerned* was told of the approaching event, and the ceremony at Enfield Parish Church was held at eight o'clock in the morning—in the presence only of Henry Hardy and of Florence's father and youngest sister.[49] The newly married couple left for Dorchester immediately, just ahead of a crowd of reporters who had somehow got wind of the event and arrived at Mr Dugdale's door an hour or so later.

Although Hardy insisted in a letter to Lady Grove that the occasion had not been without romance, he represented it to most of his friends in severely practical terms. 'We thought it the wisest thing to do,' he told Cockerell, 'seeing what a right hand Florence has become to me.' To Frederic Harrison he remarked that the step had been soberly taken in the hope that 'the union of two rather melancholy temperaments may result in cheerfulness, as the junction of two negatives forms a positive'.[50] To both Cockerell and Harrison he had spoken of the satisfying continuity provided by Florence's former friendship with Emma, and he developed the same point for Florence Henniker's benefit in a letter made ungainly by conflicting memories and emotions:

I am rather surprised that *you* were surprised at the step we have taken—such a course seeming an obvious one to me, being as I was so lonely & helpless. I think I told you in my last letter that I am very glad she knew Emma well, & was liked by her even during her latter years, when her mind was a little unhinged at times, & she showed unreasonable dislikes. I wonder if it will surprise you when I say that according to my own experience the second marriage does not, or need not, obliterate an old affection, though it is generally assumed that the first wife is entirely forgotten in such cases.

To the current rector of St. Juliot he declared that the romance of St. Juliot would abide none the less, even if he lived to be a hundred.[51]

---

* 'You are taking the right step under existing circumstances,' wrote Mary Hardy to her brother immediately before his departure for London, 'and I think you really will be happy this time. You are so young minded and if Florence is loyal, making you comfortable at all times, as we think she will, you are likely to live as long as Mother. She used to have an airy fancy, that on the deaths of their respective husbands Aunt Mary [Antell] & she might marry again and she would talk to me about the two men she had selected, much to my annoyance: I need not add it was only fun.'[48]

25

WAR YEARS

HAD the second Mrs Hardy been aware of the terms in which her husband was speaking of their marriage she might well have felt a degree of foreboding. Her situation was not, in any case, an easy one. She had married Hardy not just to escape the alternative prospect of becoming an old maid and eking out a meagre living by various forms of secretarial and literary drudgery, but out of profound admiration for his genius and a deep appreciation of his kindness towards her: his 'tender protective affection', she confided to a woman friend later that year, was like that of 'a father for a child'. It was, as she acknowledged, 'a feeling quite apart from passion', balanced, on her own part, by a similar nonsexual protectiveness and concern, as of a 'mother towards a child with whom things have somehow gone wrong—a child who needs comforting—to be treated gently & with all the love possible'. It is true that in a letter to Marie Stopes of September 1923 Florence spoke as though it might have been possible for her to have a child when she was first married, but she seems rather to have been resisting than offering confidences, and neither her remarks nor her husband's boasting of his sexual capacity in old age (see above, p. 354) can be taken as reliable evidence of their marital relations.[1]

But though Florence was capable of seeing the situation in

perspective, of recognizing that her role thenceforward was to serve that great man her husband as secretary, companion, housekeeper, and, when necessary, nurse, she was still (at thirty-five) a young woman. She was also, as Hardy had recognized, the possessor of a temperament scarcely less depressive than his own, and she was to prove capable of descents deep into melancholy, of impulsive confidences to people believed to be sympathetic, and of suspicions, jealousies, and resentments, sometimes justified, sometimes not, of those who seemed to threaten her position or her capacity to carry out efficiently the many different tasks which that position involved. Her husband's continuing tenderness towards Emma's memory and Emma's relatives was just one such irritant she could well have done without—much as Emma, in her time, had been exasperated by Hardy's refusal to place her feelings and interests above those of his own family. Florence responded with ill grace to the brief visits paid to Max Gate by both Gordon and Lilian Gifford within the first year of her marriage, and especially to Gordon's insistence that Emma had promised (on what authority is not clear, unless she had counted on being the survivor of the marriage) that Max Gate and its contents would be left to him.[2]

Returning to Max Gate immediately after the wedding ceremony, they were both kept busy for several days responding to the many letters and telegrams of congratulations which poured in. Later in that same month of February 1914 they spent a brief 'honeymoon' in Teignmouth, Dartmouth, and Torquay, and during the ensuing spring Florence was able to enjoy some of the public rewards of being the wife of so famous a man. They went to Cambridge together at the beginning of May, were entertained in London by Gosse and by Lady St. Helier*—who organized a large dinner party in their honour, with Mr and Mrs Winston Churchill prominent among the guests—and spent a weekend with Sir Henry and Lady Hoare at Stourhead, their magnificent estate just over the Wiltshire border.[3] Although Hardy was much less interested in having visitors at Max Gate than Florence would have liked, there were enough of them to present an occasional pleasant diversion: Ellen Glasgow, the American novelist, in June; Henry Dickens, Charles Dickens's last surviving son, in early July; Amy Lowell at the end of that same month. Hardy mean-

---

* The former Lady Jeune; her husband had been created Baron St. Helier shortly before his death in 1905.

while was working with happy intensity at the final revision of
the volume which was to contain 'Poems of 1912–13' and discussing with Sir Frederick Macmillan the plans for a limited *de
luxe* edition of his works—which must include the poems, he
insisted, even if they had to be printed in smaller type.[4]

At the beginning of August 1914, international crises succeeded swiftly upon one another, and the whole of Europe was
suddenly at war. Although he had written that spring what
seemed in retrospect the prophetic stanzas of 'Channel Firing',
Hardy declared that he had not the slightest anticipation of the
approaching conflict. All his philosophical assumptions, indeed,
as embodied in poems like 'The Sick Battle-God', and in *The
Dynasts* itself, had tended in the direction of an eventual improvement in the relationships between men and between nations, especially as the senselessness of modern warfare came to be more
generally appreciated. The outbreak of war on so vast a scale
seemed entirely to undercut all such views, and he was forced to
reconsider even the note of limited long-term optimism on which
he had concluded his treatment of the previous great European
conflagration. Hardy seemed to have been aged ten years by the
war, Florence told Sydney Cockerell on 15 August: 'I think he
feels the horror of it so keenly that he loses all interest in life.'
At the end of the month Hardy himself gloomily observed to
Cockerell that the enforced recognition of the brutality of the
age 'does not inspire one to write hopeful poetry, or even con-
jectural prose, but simply make[s] one sit still in an apathy, &
watch the clock spinning backwards, with a mild wonder if, when
it gets back to the Dark Ages, & the sack of Rome, it will ever
move forward again to a new Renascence, & a new literature.'[5]

As that autumn of 1914 drew on, Hardy's despondency over
the war news was matched by Florence's increasing dismay at the
nature and difficulty of the task she had voluntarily assumed.
Hardy's reluctance to change his ways, or anything around him,
greatly restricted her freedom of action in household matters. Just
as he could not bear to wound the Max Gate trees, even by prudential pruning, so he was soft-hearted towards servants whose
inefficiency seemed attributable to some handicap or misfortune
for which they were not to blame. When their parlourmaid persuaded them to hire her deaf-and-dumb but appealingly pretty
sister, who at first made little contribution to the work of the
house, it was Hardy who insisted that she be kept on. Florence,
relatively unaccustomed to servants, or to household management,

found such worries 'soul-destroying', and in mid-October, when the cook served up a 'simply uneatable' meal on the occasion of a visit by Granville-Barker, she was close to despair.[6]

Understandably, therefore, her response to the publication on 17 November of *Satires of Circumstance* was one of profound distress. It was in this volume that Hardy had brought together those 'Poems of 1912–13' which constituted the most poignant expression of his regret for the decay of his first marriage and probably the highest point of his achievement in verse:

> Woman much missed, how you call to me, call to me,
> Saying that now you are not as you were
> When you had changed from the one who was all to me,
> But as at first, when our day was fair.
>
> Can it be you that I hear? Let me view you, then,
> Standing as when I drew near to the town
> Where you would wait for me: yes, as I knew you then,
> Even to the original air-blue gown!
>
> Or is it only the breeze, in its listlessness
> Travelling across the wet mead to me here,
> You being ever dissolved to wan wistlessness,
> Heard no more again far or near?
>
> > Thus I; faltering forward,
> > Leaves around me falling,
> Wind oozing thin through the thorn from norward,
> > And the woman calling.

Florence was not deaf to the eloquence of such poems, and she was thoroughly accustomed to Hardy's way of adapting immediate emotions to other and larger purposes, and yet she could not prevent herself from reading the poems in the new volume as a series of directly personal statements of the most melancholy kind: 'It seems to me', she wrote to Lady Hoare, 'that I am an utter failure if my husband can publish such a *sad sad* book. He tells me that he has written *no* despondent poem for the last eighteen months, & yet I cannot get rid of the feeling that the man who wrote some of those poems is utterly weary of life—& cares for nothing in this world. If I had been a different sort of woman, & better fitted to be his wife—would he, I wonder, have published that volume?' When Lady Hoare very sensibly pointed out that many of the poems were essentially dramatic and that Hardy the man must not be held directly responsible for the utterances of Hardy the poet, Florence thanked her for restoring her sense of perspective.[7] Such reassurance did not, however, entirely remove her sense of grievance at the inclusion of so many poems to Emma, nor the more fundamental perception of the kind of life that now stretched before her.

Though she never lost her admiration and affection for her husband, nor her sense of being privileged to serve and cherish his genius, many of the day-to-day realities of her marriage were not of an enlivening kind. It was not simply that Max Gate was made gloomy by its trees, burdensome by its domestic worries, and lonely by its location, nor even that Hardy, for all his simplicity and sympathy, was showing with advancing age a perhaps inevitable tendency towards greater rigidity, obstinacy, and querulousness. It was also that she had, while still a comparatively young woman, to stand aside and watch the decay of what remained of her youth and her ambitions. Although Florence continued to write book reviews and stories, it was clear that Hardy would have preferred her not to;* although she liked to get away to pay brief visits to London and her family, Hardy so fretted while she was gone that she became increasingly reluctant to leave him, even for a single day; and although she seems to have accepted that her marriage would bring her no sexual satisfaction, the celebration of Emma in *Satires of Circumstance* now seemed to deprive it of its last shreds of romance. Writing in early December 1914 to sympathize with Rebekah Owen on the recent death of her sister, Florence allowed herself to exclaim, in an apparent reference to Alfred Hyatt, that she had herself lost, some three years before, the friend who had been more to her than all the rest of the world, 'the only person who ever loved me—for I am not loveable'.[9]

Florence Hardy's deeply personal reading of *Satires of Circumstance* as a wholly pessimistic volume was echoed, in impersonal terms, by most of the reviewers. Even Lytton Strachey, one of the more perceptive among them, spoke of its prevailing mood as one

---

* He must particularly have disliked the crudely patriotic tale, ' "Greater Love Hath No Man . . .": The Story of a Village Ne'er-Do-Weel', which she published, as Mrs Thomas Hardy, in the *Sunday Pictorial* for 13 June 1915, and immediately felt ashamed of.[8]

of melancholy—'the melancholy of regretful recollection, of bitter speculation, of immortal longings unsatisfied; it is the melancholy of one who has suffered, in Gibbon's poignant phrase, "the abridgment of hope".' The presence of the 'Satires of Circumstance', that group of bitterly ironic narratives which Hardy had hesitated to include, did much to distort the reception of the volume. Because the title made them seem self-evidently central, critics felt obliged to respond to them, and tended in so doing to repeat what had already become established commonplaces—Hardy's previous collection, after all, had been called *Time's Laughingstocks*. Even those, such as Laurence Binyon in the *Bookman,* who recognized the tenderness and poignancy of the 'Poems of 1912–13' did not fully confront them but quickly shifted their ground to the more accessible and discussible 'satires'; while those hostile to Hardy found it easy to ask, in the tone earlier adopted by some of the critics of *Jude,* whether one who dwelt so consistently on 'the seamy side of things' had any right to be called a poet at all.[10]*

It was, in all truth, a sufficiently depressing and distressing time. As the scope and violence of the war increased Hardy felt his whole framework of assumptions—both abstract and day-to-day—severely shaken. Though hostile to war and even, as the 1913 poem 'His Country' would suggest, to patriotism itself in any narrowly nationalistic sense—though deeply distrustful, too, of Britain's position in view of its past record of imperialist aggression—he became persuaded that his own country was 'innocent for once', that the fundamental source of conflict had been the will to power of the German rulers, and that Britain had had to fight because Germany had left her no alternative. Even in the early months of the war he had found no difficulty, on grounds of simple compassion, in joining in appeals on behalf of Belgian refugees, and he was to contribute another poem to that cause in the summer of 1915 in response to a request from Henry James, writing on behalf of Edith Wharton. He had even written, at the very beginning of the war, ' "Men Who March Away" ', designed specifically as a marching song and qualified in its patriotism only by the incorporated reference to the poet himself as the 'Friend with the musing eye' who watches the marchers 'With doubt and dolorous sigh'.[12] In early September 1914, in

---

* Hardy made his own, characteristically self-deprecating, comment on the volume in sending to Gosse a copy inscribed 'To / Edmund Gosse: / the mixture as before, of unstable / fancies, conjectures, & contradictions: / from / Thomas Hardy.'[11]

the hope of making some contribution to the national interest, Hardy participated along with Barrie, Galsworthy, Chesterton, Arnold Bennett, H. G. Wells, and many other writers in a meeting summoned by C. F. G. Masterman, Chancellor of the Duchy of Lancaster, to consider what role eminent authors might play in formulating and publicizing British principles and war aims.* In much the same spirit he gave permission for the presentation at the Kingsway Theatre of Granville-Barker's stage version of *The Dynasts*. He had not, of course, intended *The Dynasts* to be performed, and he objected strongly to several features of the production, but felt that, as a specifically patriotic gesture, it behoved him to give it his support, at least to the extent of writing a new Prologue designed to anticipate—and if possible dispel—the obvious objection that France was not now the national enemy but the national ally.[14]

Since England (right or wrong) was engaged in another life-and-death struggle, the author of *The Dynasts* (rightly or wrongly) could not but wish and work for her survival; nor did he have any sympathy with those who directly opposed the war on political or pacifist grounds. At the same time, the author of 'A Christmas Ghost-Story', 'The Souls of the Slain', and 'The Sick Battle-God'— and, more recently, of 'Channel Firing' and 'His Country'—could not readily surrender to the national war hysteria. His poem 'In Time of the "Breaking of Nations"', based on notes made at St. Juliot in 1870, was completed in 1915, and in the April 1915 number of the *Fortnightly Review* he published 'The Pity of It', with its poignant insistence upon the similarities between the German language and the dialect of Dorset:

> Then seemed a Heart crying: 'Whosoever they be
> At root and bottom of this, who flung this flame
> Between kin folk kin tongued even as are we,
>
> 'Sinister, ugly, lurid, be their fame;
> May their familiars grow to shun their name,
> And their brood perish everlastingly.'

As he put it to Florence Henniker when sending her a proof of the poem: 'I, too, like you, think the Germans happy & contented

---

* In the minutes of the meeting Hardy is recorded as suggesting that 'a list of German mis-statements' should be published, 'together with answers to them in succinct language'.[13]

as a people: but the group of oligarchs & munition-makers whose
interest is war, have stirred them up to their purposes—at least so
it seems.'[15] That final qualifying note of scepticism, audible too in
the poem itself, is only a distant echo, even so, of Hardy's Boer
War verses. But he was older and less flexible now, and believed
that the likelihood of defeat was greater, and its potential consequences far graver, than they had been at the beginning of the
century. He had, in the first months of the war, a lively fear of
German invasion and believed, early and late, that Germany was
unlikely to be beaten—a characteristic 'full look at the worst'
which enabled him, so Florence told a friend in 1916, to remain
relatively calm in the face of the military and other disasters which
had followed.[16]

Nor was the war by any means the only source of anxiety for
Hardy at this time. Florence, who had suffered painfully from
sciatica at the beginning of the year, had to go up to London in
late May 1915 to undergo an operation on her nose, intended to
cure her 'nasal catarrh'. After the operation, performed by Macleod Yearsley, she spent a week in a nursing home in Welbeck
Street which had been established by Hardy's distinguished Dorchester contemporary, Sir Frederick Treves, and then stayed a day
or two with Lady St. Helier before returning home. Since Florence
was in good hands throughout and receiving visits from her own
family—since, too, he had such a dread of doctors and hospitals
and was in any case still weak from the severe attack of diarrhoea
he had suffered on a recent visit to London—Hardy decided to
stay at Max Gate.[17]*

While Florence was having her operation in London, Hardy
was told by his sisters that he ought to make his will in favour of
someone who had been 'born a Hardy'—their preferred candidate
being Basil Augustus Hardy, a grandson of Hardy's cousin Augustus, the third son of his father's older brother James. Hardy seems
not to have been moved by the suggestion—especially since he
had never met the young man in question and had a low opinion
of his father, the Revd Henry Hardy, who became rector of a
parish in Suffolk in 1915—but the discussion prompted him to

---

* Concerned at the possibility that she would try to resume her normal
activities too quickly, he wrote to urge Florence to stay longer at the nursing
home, adding: 'I don't at all mind paying the extra days'—a remark which
perhaps qualifies, if it does not necessarily contradict, Florence's comment
to Rebekah Owen that she would be paying all the costs of the operation
herself.[18]

think seriously about the question of a possible inheritor of Max Gate. He finally fixed upon a distant cousin named Frank George, one of the Puddletown Hardys,* who had marked himself out from most of the other Hardys of his generation by his energy, ability, and consequent social mobility. After some years of working in banks in Dorchester and Bristol, he was called to the bar at Gray's Inn and—with occasional assistance from Hardy himself —seemed headed for a respectable legal career. At the beginning of the war, however, he had volunteered for the Army and been commissioned as a lieutenant in the Dorset Regiment. A recent visit by Frank George to Max Gate had confirmed Hardy's liking and respect for a young man who had worked his way determinedly upwards and was one of the very few Hardys who had shown any interest in, or aptitude for, education and the life of the mind.[19]

Gordon Gifford, who still cherished hopes of inheriting Max Gate, fell out of favour in the early summer of 1915 when he contracted a marriage of which Hardy did not approve. Florence, who took a somewhat malicious satisfaction in this turn of events, made the ironical suggestion that the young couple should be presented with 'the Gifford relics', including the portrait of the Archdeacon, but Hardy stiffly replied that he had bought them all from the Giffords at a good price, and proposed to hang on to them.[20] Talk of heirs reminded Florence of her own childlessness and made her more than usually sensitive to the way in which the local mothers showed her their babies 'with a sort of compassion'. For much the same reasons as Emma, abetted by Hardy, had spoiled her cats, Florence now cherished her wire-haired terrier Wessex, who had first entered the Max Gate household in December 1913, when he was four months old. Wessex was quarrelsome, snappish, and generally ill-behaved, a perpetual cause of trouble and anxiety, but Hardy treated him with a tenderness and indulgence even greater than Florence's.[21]

Although profoundly depressed by the worsening war news, Hardy was in excellent health that summer. He arranged to have Hermann Lea (at a rate of $4\frac{1}{2}d.$ per mile) take Florence and himself

* Frank George's father, a Bere Regis publican, had died some years before; his mother, Angelina, was the daughter of William Jenkins Hardy of Puddletown (a first cousin of Hardy's father) and the sister of Charles Meech Hardy, with whom Hardy always kept on friendly terms.

out for drives in his car—to the seaside with Kate or Henry, into Devon to call on Eden Phillpotts—and welcomed several callers at Max Gate. Nevertheless he seemed to Florence to be growing more and more of a recluse. His mind still dwelt upon the past— he was now corresponding with distant relatives of Emma's about the whereabouts of the Gifford family graves—and he refused either to go up to London or to invite people to stay.[22]

At the end of August 1915 these domestic worries and irritations were temporarily overlaid by the news that Frank George had been killed in action at Gallipoli.[23] Hardy was much shocked, and although there seems a touch of extravagance and even of factitiousness about his grief for someone he did not in fact know especially well, there is no doubt that he was deeply moved, both personally and, as it were, dynastically by the loss of the young man whom he had thought of as the probable inheritor of Max Gate and who was, as he told Mrs Henniker, 'about the only, if not the only, blood relative* of the next generation in whom I have taken any interest'.[25] He had, of course, taken some interest in the promising artistic careers of Nathaniel and James Sparks, who were somewhat more closely related to him, but he seems not only to have liked them less well but to have been at one with his sisters in placing far greater importance upon the descendants of the Hardy side of the family than upon those of the Hand side.

Hardy went to see Frank George's mother and sisters, offered them financial assistance, and in subsequent years made himself entirely accessible to any members of the family who came to call at Max Gate. He wrote a short obituary of Frank for *The Times,* and by the end of September he had composed the poem 'Before Marching and After (In Memoriam F.W.G.)' and sent it off for publication in the *Fortnightly Review*.[26] But he was soon to be overtaken by a much nearer and severer bereavement. Since September 1912 Mary and Kate had been gradually settling into Henry's house at Talbothays, emptying first the Bockhampton cottage and finally the house they had formerly occupied together in Wollaston Road. In June 1915 the last remnants of the Wollaston Road furniture were sold at auction and the sisters settled

---

* Hardy's use of 'blood relative' is of course intended to exclude from his generalization Emma's nephew and niece, Gordon and Lilian Gifford, in whom he had taken a great deal of interest; this is also the bearing of the much-misinterpreted reference in *Early Life* to Hardy's having 'no blood-nephew or niece'.[24]

down, with Henry and with Polly Antell, in an isolation which Mary at least found congenial and which was intruded upon only by close friends and members of the family—including, virtually every Sunday, the elder brother and his young wife, occasionally accompanied by one or other of Florence's sisters.[27]* At the beginning of November 1915, however, Mary, who had long been a semi-invalid, became severely and distressingly ill with emphysema, and on the 24th—three years almost to the day after Emma's death and within a month of her own seventy-fourth birthday—she died. Hardy wrote an obituary notice of his sister for the local newspaper, laying particular emphasis upon her talents in music and painting, and prompted Clement Shorter to publish in the *Sphere* a photograph of the self-portrait she had painted several years previously.[29]

Mary suffered a great deal during her last illness, but in death her face seemed to Kate more than happy, reminding her of how she used to look when they were living together at Denchworth. But there was little serenity at Talbothays in the next few days. Kate was at first 'utterly bewildered' at her sister's death, Henry quarrelled with his brother because the latter was unwilling to go back to Talbothays after the funeral, and Florence, unused to country ways, had already been appalled by the rituals of death as observed in the Hardy family, and especially by Kate's repeated insistence that she kiss the corpse. No less shocking to her, however, was the haggling and bickering over the quite considerable amount of money which Mary (thanks almost entirely to Hardy's generous care) had left—without making a will of any kind. Once Kate had been assured that the money would come to her (Hardy and Henry having apparently waived their rights in the matter) the strain was removed, although the serious illness of Henry during December—he had already suffered a slight stroke in the spring of 1914— brought up once again the whole question of who should eventually inherit the Hardy money when all those of the present, entirely childless, generation had passed away. The overwhelming concern was that the inheritor should be *'a Hardy born'* and while Florence appreciated to some extent the combination of peasant

---

* Margaret Soundy, the youngest of Florence's sisters, later recalled of one of her visits to Talbothays that Mary sat on an ottoman, saying nothing but gazing with admiration into Hardy's face. As early as 1906 Hardy had referred to Mary as 'almost a hermit', although she seems to have kept up to the last her custom of making a day trip to London each year in order to see the Summer Exhibition at the Royal Academy.[28]

instinct, family loyalty, and bitter experience which entered into such feelings, she for the first time gained from Kate's tenacity some sense of what Emma had been up against in her dealings with the Hardys.[30] Nor was the situation entirely different, for where the Hardys had scorned Emma for being 'poor gentry' they were no less suspicious of the lower-middle-class Dugdales and of the designs which Florence's relatives might have, singly and collectively, upon Hardy's prospective estate.

It was of course Kate who suffered most directly from the loss of Mary, with whom she had lived so long and intimately and who had stood in many respects in an almost maternal relation towards her. Hardy took Mary's death with apparent calm, seeming to be relieved that she had been spared further pain, but his deliberate avoidance of Talbothays is suggestive of severe inner distress, and by the middle of the month he had developed a heavy cold and taken to his room. Though the cold was real, its seriousness was exaggerated in order to justify a withdrawal that was primarily emotional, and Christmas was made miserable by his continuing refusal to see anyone other than Florence in her capacity as nurse—a role, she assured Rebekah Owen, in which she felt entirely happy. Kate, grieving over Mary and exhausted by her nursing of Henry, felt desolate and deserted, but it seems clear that Hardy, profoundly shocked by the death of the sister who had been so much to him in childhood and early manhood, did not feel ready to encounter the other sister who so acutely reminded him of Mary yet meant so much less to him. On 10 February 1916, the second anniversary of Hardy's wedding, Kate went up to Max Gate to offer her congratulations, only to find that he seemed not to want to see her. Writing to Nathaniel Sparks, Sen., she reported that her brother had changed utterly and aged considerably since Mary's death. Even at the beginning of April, when Hardy at last resumed his old habit of Sunday visits to Talbothays, the conversation struck Kate as flatter and duller than it had been when Mary was alive.[31]

Mary's death had made Hardy think once more about his own, and he arranged in February 1916 that Sydney Cockerell and Florence should become his literary executors—to be recompensed out of royalties for their services. He completed the design for Mary's stone in Stinsford churchyard and saw that it was properly executed and erected, exactly positioned in relation to the two accompanying tombs, one for Thomas and Jemima, the other for Emma—and eventually, so Hardy intended, for Florence and himself. When Florence's friend Ethel Inglis was taken on a visit to Stinsford in May 1916 Hardy produced a brush with which to clean up the family tombs and used a penknife to scrape away the moss on the stone of Robert Reason, the 'original' of Mr Penny in *Under the Greenwood Tree,* saying as he did so that he felt just like Old Mortality.[32] Nor had his obsession with Emma's memory yet faded. He kept in touch with Gordon and Lilian and required Florence, rather against her inclinations, to do the same. He also cultivated other Gifford relatives—even those who had never known Emma in her lifetime—and called upon some of them at Launceston while on a brief visit to St. Juliot with Florence in September. Melancholy as the purposes of the expedition were, Florence was at least able to regard it as a much-needed disruption of Hardy's increasingly reclusive habits. The actual visit to St. Juliot passed off pleasantly enough, with an inspection of the tablet to Emma's memory and tea at the rectory with the current incumbent and his sister, but when they visited Tintagel Church in order to see how much it had changed in the years since Emma had sketched it, Hardy was appalled to be told by the vicar, in peremptory tones, to get out of the way of the processional route of the choir. It was almost the only time, Florence later recalled, that she had seen him really angry. Writing to Cockerell from Tintagel, she expressed the hope that her husband had 'found the germ of an Iseult poem'—a hope that seven years later bore fruit in *The Famous Tragedy of the Queen of Cornwall.*[33]

Florence's feelings about Cockerell fluctuated greatly during the course of 1916. On the one hand he was immensely helpful to Hardy, almost like a son; on the other, he was so domineering as to be quite frightening. Hardy was sharply narrowing down his range of trusted friends at this time and became so sensitive about gossip, even on quite trivial matters, that he instructed Florence not to mention to his sister Kate the names of visitors to Max Gate. Clodd, their considerate host of Aldeburgh days, was now shut out of all confidence because of his habit of sharing secrets with Shorter, and there was a moment of sheer terror when news arrived that he was about to publish his reminiscences. Florence, at her husband's bidding, sent off a letter of stern warning, but Clodd's *Memories,* when they arrived, proved to be of the discreetest kind, containing nothing—as Florence assured their author —'that the most ultrasensitive person could object to'.[34] Shorter himself had long been beyond the pale—though Florence liked him and appreciated his having given her literary work before her marriage and kept her on ever since as a reviewer for the *Sphere*—and during the war years he caused further annoyance by issuing private printings of some of Hardy's poems. Finally exasperated in May 1916 by Shorter's request to be allowed to reprint in this fashion 'To Shakespeare after Three Hundred Years'—originally included in a volume honouring the tercentenary of Shakespeare's death—Hardy returned a negative reply, and encouraged Florence to publish the poem herself. Cockerell, who had recommended this course of action, oversaw the printing of the pamphlet at the Chiswick Press, where more than a dozen such pamphlets were to be printed over the next few years.[35] Their co-operation in these projects helped to bring Cockerell and Florence closer together—at least for the time being.

Apart from the brief visit to Cornwall, Hardy stayed at Max Gate throughout the whole of 1916. It was astonishing, he observed to Gosse in December, that he, who had once been half a Londoner, should not have been to London all year. His routine was now one of long hours of work in his study each day, interrupted only by meals and a modicum of exercise. He would descend from his room at teatime, especially if visitors were present, and break off finally for the day when he came down to dinner—after which Florence would read aloud to him until he went to bed at 10.30. When the work was going with especial smoothness, however, he hated to interrupt it—believing that when the wheels were going round it was a mistake to stop them, lest they prove impossible to re-start—and there were days when he would have all meals, including dinner, in his study and even give up his daily walk.[36]

Hardy continued to be very productive as a poet and became more than ever insistent upon the superiority of his verse over his prose. He was impatient with books and articles about him which made no reference to the poetry, and in June 1915—in a gesture that seems attributable either to supreme vanity or to the most modest practicality—he asked Cockerell to go to the British Museum to arrange for the addition of 'poet' to 'novelist' after his name in the main catalogue. Although no volume of new poems appeared during the year 1916, Hardy took much interest in the compilation and publication (on 3 October) of *Selected Poems of Thomas Hardy*, which did indeed contain a few poems not previously published but was chiefly designed to make his verse more immediately accessible to a wider public in terms both of its price (2s. 6d.) and its exclusion of poems he thought likely to give offence. Agreeing with Cockerell that it was a pity Hardy had omitted 'A Trampwoman's Tragedy', Florence explained that he had wanted to make the volume one which could be given 'to a school girl, or the most particular person'.[37]

During that autumn Hardy also completed the William Barnes section—consisting of a biographical survey, a critical preface, and a small group of poems—of the fifth and final volume of Thomas Humphry Ward's anthology, *The English Poets*. He did little more than extract material from his Clarendon Press edition of 1908, but his willingness to undertake the task at all reflects the persistence, in this as in so many other matters, of long-standing loyalties. That August he congratulated the Curator of the Dorset County Museum upon his acquisition of the manuscript of Barnes's *Rural Poems in Common English*, which he recalled as having been undervalued by the reviewers at the time of its publication,[38] and there was more than a hint of local loyalty in the putting together of a series of *Wessex Scenes from 'The Dynasts'*, first performed by the Dorchester amateurs in Weymouth in June 1916

Although these *Wessex Scenes* were based upon those which had been presented in Dorchester in 1908, Hardy undertook a good deal of revision and expansion in preparation for the new production. A little romance thread, for example, involving a young waiting-woman and her soldier husband, is initiated in the opening scene and tied up in the third and last, and it would appear that Hardy wrote in the part of the waiting-woman specifically for the young local actress named Gertrude Bugler who had made a striking Marty South in A. H. Evans's 1913 adaptation of *The Woodlanders*. Hardy was actively involved in the whole production, devoting to it much of the late spring of 1916, and he was present at most of the rehearsals of the original Weymouth performance, insisting, however, that the interest of the production lay 'not in the artistic effect of the play—which was really rather a patchwork affair, for the occasion—but in the humours of the characters whom we knew in private life as matter-of-fact shopkeepers & clerks'. It was remarkable that a man of his age— he was now seventy-six—should have been willing and able to devote so much energy to such a project, but Florence noticed that what had started out as a source of pleasurable excitement became in the end a source of constant worry, and she resolved to discourage his participation in any future productions: 'He is too old for the worry and responsibility,' she complained, 'for of course if it is a failure it will reflect on him. It *has* worried him so.'[39]

Because the proceeds of the performances went to the Red Cross, Hardy was able to regard his labours as a contribution to the war effort. The news of the war continued to be mostly bad, and the Dublin rising of Easter 1916 only confirmed Hardy's prejudice against all things Irish. On the other hand, he responded sympathetically to the plight of the many German prisoners-of-war housed in a camp not far from Dorchester. Although he had gone to the camp unwillingly, Florence reported to Cockerell, his 'kind heart melted at the sight of the wounded & he expressed his sympathy with them by eloquent gestures to which they responded in a most friendly manner—& also he wished many of the *well* prisoners "Good-day" to which they replied with alacrity, & now he is sending them some of his books in German—for their library.' Inevitably, Hardy was struck by the irony implicit in the location near by of a hospital in which a great many English wounded lay in an equivalent state of helplessness. There was talk of the Kaiser's head gardener, who was among the prisoners, coming to Max Gate to superintend the cutting down of some of the thickly grown trees, and a few prisoners did work there early in the following year, removing trees from the kitchen garden to make room for more potatoes. 'They are amiable young fellows', Hardy reported to Florence Henniker, '& it does fill one with indignation that thousands of such are led to slaughter by the ambitions of Courts & Dynasties. If only there were no monarchies in the world, what a chance for its amelioration!'[40]

In the early stages of the Russian revolution of 1917 Hardy was very much of two minds, for while he felt sympathetic to the revolution in the abstract, there was no doubt that Russia's slackening her effort against Germany was greatly adding to the burden on the Allies. Throughout this whole dark period of the war he tried to sustain a balanced view. In March 1917 he published, at government request and after immense labour, his poetically weak 'A Call to National Service', with its exhortation to all classes of men and women to come forward 'That scareless, scathless, England still may stand', but his belief in the necessity of his own country's survival and in the essential justice of its cause did not prevent him from repeating his old insistence that 'the sentiment of *Patriotism*' be extended until it covered 'the whole globe'. As he told John Galsworthy the following year, he found it difficult to write patriotic poems, since he saw the other side too clearly.[41]

In May 1917, in one of his earliest letters to Siegfried Sassoon, Hardy said that he did not know how he would stand 'the suspense of this evil time if it were not for the sustaining power of poetry' —by which he seems to have meant that concentration on his own verse kept him from brooding on external events. According to his wife, Hardy kept reasonably calm because he had faced the worst possibilities of the war at its very beginning, and the two statements can perhaps be reconciled in terms of some of the poems in the new volume, *Moments of Vision,* which Hardy was preparing for publication at the end of 1917—poems, he observed, which tended to 'mortify the human sense of self-importance by showing, or suggesting, that human beings are of no matter or appreciable value in this nonchalant universe'. As he struggled to see the present in an historical perspective his mind dwelt, as so often before, upon the long and bitter Napoleonic struggle. He noted the anniversaries of Quatre Bras and Waterloo as they occurred, and in excusing himself, on grounds of age, from an invitation to visit the French battlefields in company with Barrie and John Buchan he remarked that he would have to content himself with his study of the battles of the past.[42]

Although his reluctance to make such a trip at the age of seventy-seven had been entirely understandable, it seemed part and parcel of that more general unmovability which had been steadily coming over him of recent years and which Florence, for his sake and certainly for her own, was anxious to combat. They did, however, stay with Barrie in Adelphi Terrace for two nights at the end of July—an occasion oddly compounded for Hardy of old memories of his days with Blomfield and the novel experience of watching the searchlights sweeping the sky over south London in search of German aircraft—and Florence had earlier won a small victory when she was allowed not only to go to Enfield to be present at her sister Margaret's wedding to a young airman (Reginald Soundy), but also to bring the couple to spend their honeymoon at Max Gate: 'Bravo F!!!!!' exclaimed Kate Hardy, who had made her own first visit to London in many years in order to be present at the wedding.[43] In June Florence went up to London to see

Macleod Yearsley again and another specialist, a bacteriologist who prescribed a course of bacteriological inoculations as treatment for the chronic pharyngitis which had now been diagnosed. Once again she paid all the costs herself—as she would not have had to do, she complained to Rebekah Owen, if she had been a Gifford.[44]

Florence's expression of resentment seems, as on a good many other occasions, to have been in excess of what the situation really warranted. Hardy shared Kate's and Henry's dislike and distrust of the medical profession: 'If you send for a doctor I shall be ill' was his customary cry whenever Florence became anxious about his health. He evidently had no faith that the inoculations would have any effect—even Florence herself feared that the money would be wasted—and he may have suspected that Florence's recurrent medical problems were a ploy to win his sympathetic attention. At the same time, he felt it improper to prevent his wife from spending her own money as she saw fit. She presumably had a small private income derived from the investment of Sir Thornley Stoker's legacy, she certainly earned something from her journalism, and although no formal settlement was made at the time of her marriage, it seems to have been established early on that she would meet from her own resources such personal outlays as went beyond the allowances her husband made her for clothes, household expenses, and so on.[45] Hardy might even so have paid his wife's medical bills, but for the simple fact that he had achieved affluence too late to be fully at ease with it. In financial matters he fell back increasingly upon the careful habits of his own earlier years and upon that 'peasant' caution—strict budgeting in the present to permit saving for a potentially disastrous future—which he and his sisters had learned from their mother and from generations of past experience, from a kind of racial memory. Some allowance must also be made for the war situation, the decline in the value of investments, the constant sense of the need for austerity, especially at the height of the German submarine campaign, and Hardy's own apocalyptic fears of the state to which his household might conceivably be reduced: in April 1917 he was speculating (as Florence informed Cockerell) whether they could, if driven to it, feed Wessex and even themselves upon the cow-parsley which grew so profusely at Max Gate.[46]

Florence's persistence in writing complaining letters to Rebekah Owen and Sydney Cockerell involved her in acts of indiscretion which Hardy would never have countenanced, had he been aware of them, and in a kind of disloyalty that was disturbingly similar to Emma's—although Emma had obviously intended her complaints to get abroad while Florence at least requested her correspondents to keep her revelations to themselves: 'My dear Betty,' she implored Rebekah Owen, 'if anything should happen to me I *entreat* you to burn every scrap of my writing. I do write so carelessly & injudiciously that I fear there are letters of mine preserved that I should hate to have seen.' Such letters were no doubt an essential element in her psychological economy, as Emma's protests may also have been in hers, the outlet for a sense of grievance that was fed as much by the exasperations of housekeeping—and of dealing with Hardy's relatives—as by the behaviour of Hardy himself. Not many months of marriage had been needed to bring her to a sharper appreciation of how difficult it had been for Emma to confront, without friends, allies, or even local roots of her own, the solid phalanx of the Hardy clan. At bottom, however, there remains the fact that Florence's melancholy temperament, which she herself fully recognized, not only predisposed her to 'profuse grumbling', as she called it,[47] but plunged her into moods so profoundly depressive that she could scarcely control—and sometimes did not seek to control—the reckless extravagance of her complaints and accusations. Since the mood of exasperation or despair was often exhausted by the mere act of expressing it in writing, she was sometimes surprised by the response of her correspondents to letters she had dashed off and then promptly forgotten.

A three-day trip to Plymouth and Torquay with Hardy in October 1917 was marred by heavy rain and by Hardy's persistence in visiting the decaying houses and overgrown graves of departed Giffords. A still sterner trial was the publication, on 8 December, of *Moments of Vision*. Hardy had engrossed himself with great enthusiasm in the completion of the volume, and when he was correcting the proofs in early September Florence reported him as being extremely cheerful, as he always was when a piece of work had reached that stage. She felt, however, that the volume, like *Satires of Circumstance*, showed her in a poor light, suggesting by its continual memorialization of Emma that the author's second marriage was 'a most disastrous one & that his sole wish is to find refuge in the grave with her with whom alone he found happiness. Well—all things end somewhere.' Florence had been familiar with the contents of the volume long before its publication—she and Cockerell had joined forces in August to dissuade Hardy from including 'The Sound of Her' (see above, p. 489) and she ought, perhaps, to have been mollified by Hardy's inscription in her own copy ('From Thomas Hardy, this first copy of the first edition, to the first of women Florence Hardy. Nov: 1917'). She might also have recalled the wise advice about the danger of identifying the poet with the man which Lady Hoare had sent her at the time when *Satires of Circumstance* appeared. But she did none of these things, until—up in London for another round of visits to specialists—she broke down and wept at a matinée of *Dear Brutus,* that poignant play about the 'might-have-beens' of life, and submitted to being comforted afterwards by an 'old friend of my husband'—almost certainly the author of *Dear Brutus* himself, Sir James Barrie.[48]

The new volume—the largest collection of new poems Hardy had published—does indeed contain a great many poems devoted to Emma in the mood, if not always of the quality, of the 'Poems of 1912–13'. The scenes and occasions of these later poems, however, now extend beyond the St. Juliot days to other phases of the marriage, and the fading of romance is confronted for the first time in terms of Emma's mental deterioration—notably in 'The Interloper' but also, by implication, in 'Near Lanivet'. There are also numerous poems on autobiographical themes not related to Emma, and it is clear that many of them represent what, in an abandoned title for the volume, Hardy once called 'Moments from the Years'[49]—poems evolved upon the basis of vividly recollected moments from the past, brought to mind either spontaneously, by some memory-triggering accident of sight, sound, touch, or smell, or deliberately, by the kind of memory-stimulating exercises in which Hardy was quite consciously indulging when he looked from Max Gate out across the fields to Kingston Maurward, Stinsford Church and churchyard, and the woods and heaths surrounding Higher Bockhampton, when he walked among the graves at Stinsford or along the cliffs near St. Juliot, when he worked his way through old notebook entries and pondered upon the things he had seen, thought, sketched, or half-written in years long past. It was in just this kind of exercise that Hardy was engaged in September 1916 when he walked up on to the heath, stood on the old coach road, and 'had visions' of George III and his court, of Admiral Hardy, and of his mother as a child.[50] In October 1917 Hardy cited 'In Time of the "Breaking of Nations" '—recently written on the basis of that 'moment of vision' at St. Juliot in 1870—as an instance of his 'faculty . . . for burying an emotion in my heart or brain for forty years, and exhuming it at the end of that time as fresh as when interred', but it is clear that the same kind of intense autobiographical recovery is present in almost all his best work, in verse and prose alike. Much as Florence hated those melancholy visits to St. Juliot and Stinsford churchyard, they made a crucial contribution to the extraordinary poetic creativity of Hardy's old age —and to the exceptional happiness with which, as Florence proudly reported to Cockerell, Hardy approached the end of 1917.[51]

The persistence of a retrospective mood throughout 1917 was intimately related to the beginning of work on the biographical narrative that was eventually published, after Hardy's death, as *The Early Life of Thomas Hardy* and *The Later Years of Thomas Hardy*, the two-volume official biography attributed, on the title-pages, to Florence Emily Hardy. In fact, the 'Life', as it is generally called, was almost entirely Hardy's own work, and ever since the essential facts of its authorship first became known in 1940* it has been customary to speak of it as an autobiography. Early in 1918, however, Florence told Cockerell that they must never use the word 'autobiography' or Hardy would destroy all the 'notes' he had prepared: he had said he would never write an autobiography and was annoyed at the very idea of one.[52] And it is clear not only that Hardy himself fiercely rejected the term but that it is impossible, given the circumstances in which the 'Life' was conceived, composed, revised, and published, to speak of it, without question or qualification, as the direct, unmediated, autobiographical embodiment of the image of himself that Hardy wished to project to the world after his death.

There seems, to begin with, no reason to doubt the insistence of the Prefatory Note to *Early Life* that it was at Florence's 'strong request' that the project was first launched, although the original suggestion may have been Cockerell's. In September 1917 Florence wrote to Cockerell to say that Hardy was happily at work on the last batch of proofs for *Moments of Vision* and that as soon as he had finished the job he intended 'to go on giving me facts about his life. I have got as far as the time he started work in London,

* They were revealed by Richard L. Purdy during the course of a lecture at the Grolier Club on 25 April 1940 and reported in the *New York Times Book Review* of 12 May 1940.

but a lot can be filled in. He seems quite enthusiastic now about the idea, and of course I love doing it.'[53] Since Hardy disapproved of his wife's journalistic activities it is conceivable that he was persuaded to look upon the 'Life' as an alternative means of absorbing her literary energies and ultimately realizing her literary ambitions, and certainly the presence of so enthusiastic and competent a collaborator—an expert typist and an author and journalist in her own right—must have made the whole project, once mooted, seem entirely feasible and full of attractive possibilities.

It was not simply that Hardy was, as he had always been, an intensely private man who felt (as many another author has done) that the world should be concerned only with his writings, not with the life or personality of the writer himself. By 1917 Hardy was approaching eighty. He had been famous for many years, exposed to the importunities of literary pilgrims, the sensationalism of journalists, and the book-making of academics, and he realized that such assaults on his privacy would continue for the rest of his life, and on into the years after his death.* He must therefore have perceived that, if biographies there must be, the best counter-strategy was a pre-emptive strike in the shape of an official biography on the lines of those familiar Victorian 'Life and Letters' volumes in which the exercise of family piety by the widow or bereaved children of the deceased was often facilitated by the foresight of the subject himself in setting his papers in order before his death and destroying whatever he did not wish to survive him.

In embarking upon the actual composition of the 'Life', Hardy seems first to have written—or possibly dictated to Florence—an account of his childhood years. Stimulated by that initial exercise in retrospection, he then went through all his old notebooks—especially the little pocket-books of observations, plots, and occasional drawings which he had kept at least since the 1860s—and cut or copied out individual items for incorporation into the composite narrative he intended to build up. He also sorted through and largely destroyed the mass of incoming correspond-

* He had by no means forgotten the distressing experience of reading F. A. Hedgcock's *Thomas Hardy: penseur et artiste,* published in Paris in 1911. Though the book was primarily a critical study, it opened with a biographical chapter to which Hardy took violent exception: his copy bears numerous marginal annotations (e.g., 'All this is too personal, & in bad taste, even supposing it were true, which it is not. . . . It betrays the cloven foot of the "interviewer" '), and he effectively discouraged the publication of an English translation.[54]

ence which had accumulated over the years, and—since the need for secrecy made it impossible to ask friends to return the letters he had sent them—he looked out the drafts or copies he had retained of particularly important outgoing letters: in practice, these were often letters written for publication in newspapers and magazines. The term 'Materials' was used at Max Gate to designate the collection of items for potential inclusion in the 'Life', although Hardy did not in any sense regard them as sacrosanct 'documents' and was quite prepared to revise old notes and letters which no longer struck him as happily phrased, or to refurbish diary entries in the light of subsequent events. Such adjustments of the historical record were entirely in accordance with the 'Life and Letters' tradition—which allowed for the suppression of details which threatened to mar the broad picture being painted and the adjustment of chronology at least to the extent of, say, conflating two or more letters into one—and would have mattered less had not so many of the basic documents been subsequently destroyed.*

The procedure adopted for the actual composition of the 'Life' was chiefly designed to ensure the secrecy that was essential for Florence's eventual sake as well as for Hardy's own.[55] Hardy's manuscript—written in strictest privacy, the sheets slipped under the blotting paper whenever anyone came to the study—was typed up by Florence in three copies, a ribbon copy and two carbons. Hardy would revise and correct the third of these copies, and then pass it to his wife for her to transfer the changes into copy two and subsequently, when his final approval had been given to them, into the ribbon copy destined for the printer—which thus showed no visible trace of his participation. Well before the end of 1919 he had brought the narrative into completed form for the years up to 1918;[56] as the years went by he added to the 'Materials' notes, diary entries, copies of letters, and so on, which Florence would be able to draw upon in writing the final chapters. He specifically gave her the responsibility of making, after his death, whatever additions or deletions she thought proper, and while it is almost impossible to distinguish

---

* The destruction of the pocket-books seems to have been carried out by Cockerell immediately after Hardy's death. Writing to the *Times Literary Supplement* (14 March 1968) about the poetical notebooks of A. E. Housman, John Carter quoted Cockerell as saying, in a letter, that he had 'spent a whole morning burning (by his instructions) similar notebooks of Thomas Hardy'.

the cuts she made on her own initiative from those she made while her husband was still alive, she certainly removed or abbreviated, at the suggestion of Sir James Barrie, some of Hardy's diatribes against critics and reviewers and several of the numerous references to encounters with members of the aristocracy and London society. More significantly, perhaps, she inserted the early letters from Hardy to his sister Mary and added, again at Barrie's instigation, a number of anecdotes of Hardy's childhood and youth, including the important detail of his disliking to be touched.[57]

Told, so to speak, in cold blood, the circumstances in which the 'Life' was written and published can be, and have been, made to sound eccentric, fantastic, and vaguely discreditable. And, indeed, neither Hardy nor Florence can be wholly exonerated from the charge of disingenuousness, even though the title-page of *Early Life* came remarkably close to strict accuracy in its statement that the volume had been 'compiled' by Florence 'largely from contemporary notes, letters, diaries, and biographical memoranda, as well as from oral information in conversations extending over many years'. But for Hardy and Florence it was a perfectly sensible, down-to-earth undertaking, putting Florence essentially in the position of an authorized biographer blessed with unlimited access to an ideally co-operative subject and enabling Hardy to throw over what he wanted to say the aura of authenticity and impersonality implicit in the use of the third-person point of view. The confessional and revelatory impulses were entirely foreign to him, and he had in any case woven his richest autobiographical experiences into the very texture of his novels and poems. His concern as he approached the end of his life was simply to set straight the basic record of his career, to obtain a final hearing for his thoughts on the nature of existence, cruelty to animals, and other favourite topics, and to project into the future that protection he had so long and earnestly sought to extend to the deepest sources of his inspiration and the innermost recesses of his extraordinarily private self.

26

TEA AT
MAX GATE

Although most reviewers responded positively to *Moments of Vision,* a few expressed themselves puzzled and even repelled by its melancholy and its unconventionality. It was probably in response to the *Athenaeum* review of 12 January 1918, which accused him of writing 'with something of the gracelessness of a youth learning to skate', that Hardy jotted down some harsh comments about the imperceptiveness of reviewers, their incapacity to appreciate that art might be deliberately employed in the concealment of art. To Florence Henniker he complained that although his publishers had sent him some fifty reviews, all but five or six of them were 'deplorably inept, purblind, & of far less *value* than the opinion of one's grocer or draper, though they were friendly enough, I must say. I always fancy I could point out the best, & the worst, in a volume of poems, which none of these did. But perhaps that is my self-conceit, for I have had no experience as a reviewer.' He was also provoked by the persistence of the conventional romantic view of what 'true poets' must necessarily be like: 'They must all be impractical in the conduct of their affairs; nay, they must almost, like Shelley or Marlowe, be drowned or done to death, or like Keats, die of consumption.' What was so often forgotten was that some of the greatest writers of the ancient world—Homer, Aeschylus, Sophocles, and Euripides—had done their best work in old age.[1] Though Hardy's successful career as a novelist had provided him with the springboard from which to launch *Wessex Poems,* it had since been something of an impediment, allowing and even encouraging reviewers to comment upon the prosaic qualities of his verse and lament that he had ever abandoned prose at all. He believed that his being 'unpoetically' old in years and uninterestingly domestic in his habits further discouraged critics from taking him seriously as an artist, and made it more than ever necessary for him to insist upon the absoluteness of his dedication to what he had called in the General Preface to the Wessex Edition the 'more individual part of my literary fruitage'.[2]

This was the principal point upon which he insisted when supplying information for an article Edmund Gosse was writing for the April 1918 number of the *Edinburgh Review*: 'For the relief of my necessities, as the Prayer Book puts it, I began writing novels, & made a sort of trade of it; but last night I found that I had spent more years in verse-writing than at prose-writing! (prose 25½ yrs—verse 26 yrs) Yet my verses will always be considered a bye-product, I suppose, owing to this odd accident of the printing press.' Gosse duly pointed up this theme in his own opening paragraph and then proceeded to survey the whole of Hardy's poetic career from 1860 to *Moments of Vision,* stressing his friend's remarkable capacity for discerning and dramatizing the extraordinary and the ordinary, the tragic and the mundane: 'There is absolutely no observation too minute, no flutter of reminiscence too faint, for Mr. Hardy to adopt as the subject of a metaphysical lyric. . . . [H]e seems to make no selection, and his field is modest to humility and yet practically boundless.' Astonishingly, however, Gosse dismissed *Satires of Circumstance* as the most dispensable of Hardy's volumes—sufficient grounds in itself for Hardy's somewhat oblique reference, in thanking Gosse for the article, to his having read it 'as if it were concerning a writer altogether unknown to me'.[3]

The year 1918 was devoted almost entirely to the completion of the 'Life' and to the various clearing-out and tidying-up operations connected with it. By 11 June Florence had typed up the narrative as far as 1895. Later that same month, after Hardy had revised the work up to 1892, he insisted, much to Florence's distress, upon burning the holograph manuscript for the entire

1840–92 period. That autumn he spent much of his time going through the piles of reviews that had gathered over the years, eliminating almost everything of a 'belittling or invidious nature', and pasting the items he wished to preserve into the large scrap-books which still survive.[4] Since those scrapbooks contain a fair number of critically hostile reviews, it is clear that by 'belittling or invidious' Hardy did not so much mean critically disparaging as dealing offensively in personalities.

Hardy worked at these tasks with immense energy and eager-ness, insisting that they be done right even at the cost of the laborious revision and re-writing of what Florence had thought of as finished work. Though she sometimes remonstrated, she had already learned that Hardy would not go back on a decision once made: apologizing to Rebekah Owen in February 1918 for Hardy's refusal to autograph his new book for her, she explained that at his age there was naturally a certain 'fixity of purpose'. Yet he retained, as she remarked to Cockerell, a marvelous 'inner radi-ance' which made him 'a true sun-shine giver' and helped them both to withstand the continuing depression produced by the war news.[5] Although he reacted with horror to the suggestion that Florence's sister Margaret might have her baby at Max Gate, he was perfectly willing to allow Margaret to stay in the house throughout the spring of 1918, even though, as Florence confessed, he much preferred the two of them to be alone there together. He raised no objection to the child's being named Thomas in his honour, and he must have thought what Florence said—how much a baby would have been welcomed at Max Gate in years gone by. To Mrs Henniker, however, he commented a little sourly on the event, observing that if he were a woman he would 'think twice before entering into matrimony in these days of emancipation, when everything is open to the sex'.[6]

He remained well during most of the year—apart from a brief illness in October and a severe attack in March caused by eating a tart made of bottled plums—and physically active. When in April he and Florence cycled out to the Higher Bockhampton cottage (now occupied by Hermann Lea) on the afternoon the recently rediscovered manuscript of *Far from the Madding Crowd* was auctioned at a Red Cross sale in London, Hardy found the ride something of an effort. But it had been his first outing of the year, and he made many more such trips in the course of the spring and summer—most of them to Talbothays, where he and Florence were frequent visitors, some a little further afield.[7] He also remained remarkably active in local affairs. Although he had rarely served as a J.P. on the Dorchester bench since becoming a county magistrate in 1894, Hardy returned there on five occasions in the years 1917–19, chiefly in order to adjudicate in a number of food-profiteering cases. He seems to have seen it as another form of war work, but Florence, faced with the day-to-day difficulties of shopping in a time of severe food shortages, was exasperated by her husband's fining their own grocer £15 for selling ground rice at a halfpenny per pound too much. In January 1918 he had taken a lively interest as usual in the local revival of *The Mellstock Quire,* and at one of the last rehearsals of the dances incorporated into the production he picked up a fiddle and played one of the tunes: 'He did not dance', Florence told Cockerell, 'but he was *longing* to I could see, & would have footed it as bravely as any.'[8]

Cockerell made two visits to Max Gate in 1918, and had by this time established himself almost as a member of the household. There were visits, too, from actual members of the family, although Max Gate, largely because its owner was so jealous of his time, still remained on the fringes rather than at the centre of the Hardy family network. While Jemima was alive, the Bockhampton cottage had functioned as the clearing-house for family news and local gossip, as well as a focus for the preservation and recital of family memories and the legends and traditions of the countryside. That role had now passed, with some inevitable diminishment, to Talbothays, and especially to Kate—whose diary for these years makes frequent mention of calls from relatives and family friends. Hardy thus kept in touch, directly and indirectly, with many members of his own family—including the children and even the grandchildren* of his first and second cousins—as well as with Florence's parents and sisters and with several of Emma's relatives. He bought the house Charles Meech Hardy was living in at Puddletown in order to prevent his being turned out, and when, after his death, his widow left Puddletown, Hardy wrote to assist her admission to an almshouse. When Gordon Gifford made it known, early in 1923, that he was worried about losing his position as an architect with the London County Council, Hardy asked Lady St. Helier, as an alderman of the Council, to make enquiries of the head of Gordon's department, and was

---

* Some affectionate reminiscences of the Bockhampton Hardys, including Hardy himself, have been recorded by Lillie May Farris, granddaughter of his first cousin Christopher Hand.[9]

soon able to assure his nephew that his position was quite secure.[10] Hardy was also exercised about the future of Lily Whitby, a granddaughter of William Jenkins Hardy and first cousin of Frank George, although he did not feel comfortable with the suggestion that she should stay at Max Gate when Florence was away. He had been 'so kind and generous to distant relatives of his', Florence told Cockerell, 'even those he dislikes.' Though sharply conscious of his own childlessness, and that of his brother and sisters—'I am at the fag end of my family,' he wrote to one of Emma's cousins in 1919—Hardy held tenaciously to his belief in the family as a force for cohesion and a focus of loyalty, and told Sir George Douglas how much he regretted 'the way in which families scatter themselves with a light heart'.[11]

Hardy's omission of most of his uncles, aunts, and cousins from the family tree he drew up at about this time has frequently been regarded as a sign of deliberate obfuscation or of snobbishness, or of both. But 'The Hardy Pedigree', never intended for publication, sprang—like most such exercises—from Hardy's interest in his own ancestry, in the identity of his grandparents, great-grandparents and other forebears, and it thus took the form of an inverted pyramid, with his own name at the foot of the page, linked to left and right with the corresponding genealogies of his two wives, headed 'The Gifford Pedigree' and 'The Dugdale Pedigree'. Hardy was careful to indicate the number of children in his parents' families, but any attempt to record each name and the name of each spouse—let alone the names of all the children and all the children's children—would have resulted in a hopelessly confused and crowded page. He had nearly fifty first cousins, after all, in addition to a number of second cousins to whom he felt particularly close. Nor is it likely that he could, with the best will in the world, have compiled anything like a complete account of the ramifications of his Aunt Martha's family in Canada or the families of his cousins Emma and Martha Sparks in Australia—* or, for that matter, the crowd of Hand and Hardy cousins and their descendants who had scattered to London, Bristol, Windsor, and other parts of England. Hardy has also been accused of being concerned only with those family members and connections who belonged or attained to the middle class. That does not in fact

---

* There had been occasional correspondence, however, between Bockhampton and Martha Sharpe's descendants, and in 1902 one of Martha (Sparks) Duffield's grandsons was brought to England to be christened in Puddletown Church—and admired at Max Gate.[12]

appear to be a sustainable generalization, but even if it were, that would only be to say that he took an entirely natural interest in those few who had in some way departed from the otherwise monotonous pattern of employment and marriage within the inherited boundaries of place, caste, and occupation. If he gave particular attention to such remote relatives as the Childses, that was partly because they displayed some literary interests—otherwise undiscoverable in his background—but also because he was able to draw conveniently upon genealogical information volunteered by living members of that family.

At Max Gate the parade of teatime visitors continued: 'No-one to tea—blessed relief,' wrote Florence in her diary one day early in 1918. John Cowper Powys, arriving during the following summer, found Hardy ready to talk 'gaily and cheerfully' about 'all manner of little things', from a punctured bicycle tyre to 'a honeysuckle bush given him by his mother that had forced its way into the conservatory from outside' or 'the names in the cemetery near Portland Bill'; recounting the visit to his brother Llewelyn, Powys described Florence as looking like 'a grave ascetic art student or a Chelsea socialist, follower of William Morris', with 'her hair parted Madonna-wise and a very responsible air'. Clement Shorter, though dignified in Florence's eyes by the recent loss of his wife, Dora Sigerson (whose poems she had reviewed), confirmed himself in Hardy's low opinion by arriving uninvited at Max Gate on its owner's seventy-eighth birthday. When Arthur Compton Rickett came to tea, Hardy, suspecting his visitor of biographical designs, delayed coming downstairs for more than an hour.[13]

Among the newcomers to Max Gate none created so deep an impression as Siegfried Sassoon and Charlotte Mew. Hardy—'always longing to come across some great new poet', as Florence told an American correspondent early in 1918—had taken an early and eager interest in Sassoon's work; they exchanged letters for a time but did not meet until 6 November 1918, when Sassoon immediately became Hardy's '*adored* young friend' and, for Florence, 'one of the most brilliant, & handsome & likeable young men I know'. Miss Mew, first brought to their attention by Cockerell, proved to possess singularly little personal charm ('a plain shabby little thing'), and to be not Hardy's type of woman at all.[14] But her conversation and her poems were alike impressive, and Hardy became and remained deeply interested in her work and in her welfare.

Another welcome visitor was Elliott Felkin, a lieutenant stationed at the prisoner-of-war camp at Blandford, who quickly
established himself as a favourite at Max Gate, and found himself
the recipient of many Hardyan observations and reminiscences.
One day Hardy took Felkin on the standard tour of Stinsford
churchyard and showed him Emma's tomb:

> As he talked about it and her his voice became quavery, and
> there were tears in his eyes, and all the time we were round the
> spot he lost the thread of what he was saying. . . . He said if you
> ever want to put up a tomb that you think won't be much cared
> for, put one up like that, not a cross, which falls over and has
> bad lettering. That will last for hundreds of years. I thought of
> it like that because, you see, I have no descendants. He said he
> could not make up his mind about the inscription—'THIS FOR
> REMEMBRANCE'—which was partly from Shakespeare and partly
> from the Bible, and where to put it, at the head or the side. I
> felt at first embarrassed by all these private questions, but he
> went on talking quite simply about it, so that one could give
> frank answers.

Hardy had, Felkin noted, an extraordinary capacity 'of treating
young people not as if you were pretending to make yourself
young out of politeness, nor as if you were instructing or guiding
by the wisdom of experience, but as if you really felt that age and
youth had something to give each other. . . . I should like to be
like that when I am old.'[15]

At this period Hardy's memory of his early childhood was
still 'miraculous', as Florence told Cockerell, and he was still
in good health: at the same time, he was ageing very perceptibly and becoming very forgetful of recent events. 'When I
first met him', she added, 'he was so wonderful—he was writing
"The Dynasts" and his mind was luminous. Not but that he isn't
far beyond the average young man even now.' He was childishly
persistent in his indulgence of Wessex—he gave him an eider-
down to lie on in the study and fed him goose and plum pudding
at Christmas, making no offer to clear up the mess when he was,
predictably, sick—and pleaded poverty when Florence talked of
taking a holiday and of replacing the old kitchen range at Max
Gate with a new and more efficient one. Some months later,
however, the new range was installed, and Florence, in fact, seems
usually to have got her way in the end, at least so far as household
matters were concerned.[16]

. . .

The Armistice of November 1918 was greeted at Max Gate with
relief but not with much optimism: the event is not even mentioned in the pages of *Later Years*. But the return of peace, endorsed by the return of spring, did rouse Hardy at the beginning
of May 1919 to take Florence for a short visit to London, where
they stayed with Barrie at his Adelphi Terrace flat. Hardy went
with Barrie to the Royal Academy dinner; with Florence he attended the Royal Academy Private View, called on Maurice Macmillan and on the Gosses, dined at Lady St. Helier's, and lunched
with Sir Frederick and Lady Macmillan.[17] Although the Royal
Academy dinner had been the occasion for the trip, the need to
discuss several matters with Sir Frederick Macmillan had perhaps
been its principal motivation. A new volume of the Wessex Edition, containing *Satires of Circumstance* and *Moments of Vision*,
was shortly to appear (Hardy read proof later that same month);
a one-volume *Collected Poems*, incorporating all the volumes
thus far published, was also to be brought out that autumn, in a
format matching that of the one-volume edition of *The Dynasts*;
and Macmillan had recently set in motion arrangements for the
publication of the thirty-seven-volume Mellstock Edition, the
édition de luxe which had first been proposed before the outbreak
of the war.[18]

Although the year 1919 was free from the now familiar losses
of old friends—Mrs Sheridan, for example, had died the year
before—and the wartime deaths of the sons of other friends like
the Hoares, that August brought one especially poignant piece of
news. Lilian Gifford, whose mother had died in February, had
been diagnosed as a paranoiac and committed, as 'a person of
unsound mind', to the London County Council asylum at Claybury in Essex. Florence, distressed by thoughts of her own past
hostility to Lilian, went to Claybury to see her. She also saw
Gordon Gifford and his wife and seems to have arranged for
Lilian to be released from confinement a year or so later on the
basis of financial and other guarantees both from Max Gate and
from some of Lilian's relatives.[19] Although Lilian had been admitted to Claybury as a 'pauper', Hardy had in fact provided for
her more liberally than Florence had imagined: in addition to the
small but (for those days) by no means derisory annuity, which
was still intact, he had purchased in her name some gilt-edged
securities which Lilian, much to his annoyance, had traded for

more speculative stocks. Because of Lilian's relation to Emma and his own affectionate memories of her as a child and young woman, Hardy at first spoke of having her to live at Max Gate as soon as she was released, but Henry, Kate, and of course Florence were all opposed to the idea, and he himself—despite, as Florence observed to Cockerell, his habit of idealizing people as soon as they were out of reach—recognized that Lilian's unreasoning discontents were all too reminiscent of Emma's afflictions, and that it might be unwise to expose himself to the repetition of an experience which had already caused such anguish.[20]

That October Siegfried Sassoon came to Max Gate for the weekend, bringing with him the 'Poets' Tribute', a handsomely bound volume in which forty-three poets—from Bridges, Kipling, and Yeats to Graves, Sassoon, and D. H. Lawrence—had each inscribed in Hardy's honour a copy of one of his own poems. Hardy was much touched by the gesture and set himself the task of thanking personally, and distinctively, each of the poets involved.[21] He also took more trouble than might have been expected in composing the little speech he made—at the request of Mrs Hanbury, wife of the current owner of Kingston Maurward—on the occasion of the opening (on 2 December 1919) of the Bockhampton Reading-room and Club, erected as a local war memorial almost on the spot where Robert Reason's shoemaker's shop had once stood. Hardy's immersion in the past was now so habitual and so intense as to threaten almost to overwhelm the present, and it seems to have surprised neither Florence nor himself that he saw a ghost in Stinsford churchyard that Christmas Eve, just after putting a sprig of holly on the grave of the grandfather he had never known. A figure in eighteenth-century costume said, 'A green Christmas'; Hardy replied, 'I like a green Christmas'; but when he followed the strange figure into the church he found no one there.[22]

Looking back upon the world and his own career from the vantage-point of his eightieth year, Hardy found little cause for rejoicing. Although there had been an immense material advance in the years since his birth there had been no corresponding advance in 'real civilization'—in human kindness, in consideration for other people and for the lower animals. The war was over but the peace concluded at Versailles in June 1919 seemed to him disastrous (a view for which he found support in his reading of John Maynard Keynes's *The Economic Consequences of the Peace*) and there seemed little hope for a future which depended

Gertrude Bugler as Marty South in the dramatization
of *The Woodlanders*, 1913

Florence Hardy, *c.* 1927

Above Hardy on his way to lay the foundation stone of the Dorchester Grammar School, 1927

Left Hardy with Edmund Gosse in the porch of Max Gate, 1927

Thomas Hardy in old age, photographed by Wheeler of Weymouth

upon 'the young and feeble League of Nations'. To his old friend
Pearce Edgcumbe he speculated about 'our probable retrogres-
sion during the next 60 years to the point from which we started
(not to say further)—to turnpike-road travelling, high postage,
scarce newspapers (for lack of paper to print them on), oppression
of one class by another, etc., etc.' Art and poetry, he believed,
would be among the first casualties of the impending decline in
civilization, and the belief was sustained by the continuing incomprehension (as he somewhat extravagantly saw it) of his own
work.[23]

In July 1919 he wrote a stinging letter to Robert Lynd about
his failure, when reviewing *Moments of Vision,* to recognize the
onomatopaeic element in the poem 'On Sturminster Foot-Bridge'.
He was still more dismayed by the February 1920 issue of the
Fortnightly, in which Frederic Harrison attacked his pessimism
on personal as well as on literary and philosophical grounds:
'Byron, Shelley, Keats, were all exiles from home, decried, destined
to early death abroad. And yet their pessimism was occasional.
But Thomas Hardy has everything that man can wish—long and
easy life, perfect domestic happiness, warm friends, the highest
honour his Sovereign can give, the pride of a wide countryside.'
Clearly, then, Harrison concluded, the 'monotony of gloom' in
his verse 'is not human, not social, not true'. Hardy spent two
days drafting replies, but was eventually dissuaded by Florence
from sending any of them; his long friendship with Harrison,
however, he regarded as totally at an end.[24] When Alfred Noyes,
a far less intimate acquaintance, made a similar attack on Hardy's
'philosophy' later that same year, Hardy did respond, and at some
length, insisting that, like many other thinkers, he saw the power
behind the universe not as malign, as Noyes had argued, but
simply as without feeling, purpose, or morality of any kind whatsoever—and as, in any case, unknowable:

In my fancies, or poems of the imagination, I have of course
called this Power all sorts of names—never supposing they would
be taken for more than fancies. I have even in prefaces warned
readers to take them only as such—as mere impressions of the
moment, exclamations, in fact. But it has always been my misfortune to presuppose a too intelligent reading public, and no
doubt people will go on thinking that I really believe the Prime
Mover to be a malignant old gentleman, a sort of King of
Dahomey,—an idea which, so far from my holding it, is to me
irresistibly comic. "What an fool one must have been to write for

such a public!" is the inevitable reflection at the end of one's life.[25]

To many of Hardy's friends his insistence upon the unfairness of contemporary criticism seemed unreasonable and lacking in proportion. But Hardy did not undertake statistical surveys of favourable and unfavourable comments, nor had he lost with age the sensitivities of earlier years. The famous public figure of the 1920s was the same man who had been made wretched by the *Spectator* review of the anonymously published *Desperate Remedies* fifty years earlier. And while he had become accustomed to the trivialities and crudities of journalistic reviewing, he could still be brought close to despair by displays of incomprehension on the part of 'serious' critics, especially those who had enjoyed his friendship over many years. It was perhaps not surprising that he was deeply impressed by the calmness and repose of the cathedrals of Exeter and Wells when he visited them that spring, and felt that he would have preferred to be a cathedral organist to anything else in the world.[26]

On 2 June 1920, Hardy's eightieth birthday, Augustine Birrell, Anthony Hope Hawkins, and John Galsworthy arrived at Max Gate to present him with an address of congratulation from the Incorporated Society of Authors. Barrie—with whom Hardy had stayed in April when he attended the wedding of Harold Macmillan and Lady Dorothy Cavendish—was also at Max Gate that summer and was confirmed in his sense of Hardy's having 'something about him more attractive than I find in almost any other man—a simplicity that really merits the adjective *divine*—I could conceive some of the disciples having been thus.'[27] Charles Morgan, as manager of the Oxford University Dramatic Society, saw much of Hardy during the visit he made to Oxford in February 1920 to receive an honorary D.Litt. and to attend an OUDS production of scenes from *The Dynasts*. To Morgan's eyes there was something self-protective in Hardy's determination to be 'unspectacular', 'something deliberately "ordinary" in his demeanour which was a concealment of extraordinary fires'; at the same time, by neither pretending that he was young nor presuming upon his years, Hardy achieved without apparent effort or artifice the easy relationship with his juniors that Elliott Felkin had so admired. It was also in 1920 that Sydney Cockerell's friend Katharine Webb remarked how Hardy had changed in thirty years from 'a rather rough-looking man, dressed very unlike his fellows, with a very keen alert face and a decided accent of some kind', to 'a refined, fragile, gentle little old gentleman, with . . . a gentle and smooth voice and polished manners'.[28]

Mrs Webb thought Florence 'the most melancholy person' she had ever encountered, full of complaints about her inability to get away from Max Gate, especially during the grim winter months 'when the dead leaves stick on the window-pane and the wind moans and the sky is grey and you can't even see as far as the high road'. The trees at Max Gate were indeed thicker and higher than ever, making it increasingly difficult to grow flowers successfully, and Florence wondered whether Hardy's having been walled in by trees for so much of his life might not be one reason for the 'sombre hue' of his work. Meanwhile her own health was still fragile, the servant problem had again become acute, and the viciousness of Wessex—who not only bit postmen and terrorized servants but had once killed a stoat after a long and bloody battle—was prompting talk (neither for the first nor the last time) of having him put to sleep. Hardy's reluctance to take initiatives or spend money was also an obstacle. However, it was for Florence's convenience and pleasure that a telephone (Dorchester 43) was installed at Max Gate, not for Hardy's (who thoroughly distrusted it). In March 1920 she was blaming the repeated defection of servants on the primitiveness of the house, notably its lack of a bathroom and of hot water on tap upstairs, but by the beginning of May work had begun on the installation of an upstairs bathroom.[29] Though so set in his ways, so immovable in his likings and dislikings, Hardy was still capable of occasional flexibility and even of a little self-irony: 'We are reading Jane Austen,' reported Florence on 8 July 1920. 'We have read "Persuasion" and "Northanger Abbey", and are now in the midst of "Emma". T.H. is much amused at finding he has *many* characteristics in common with Mr. Woodhouse.'[30]

Reading aloud to her husband after dinner, often for an hour or more at a stretch, was only one of Florence's regular tasks—though a peculiarly trying one at times because of the persistent weakness of her throat. The publicity surrounding Hardy's eightieth birthday had finally confirmed his status as the universally acknowledged grand old man of English letters, and the practical implications of that status soon began to reveal themselves to the couple at Max Gate. The influx of letters and telegrams at the beginning of June was enormous, and the burden of answering them—and of sending back the copies of his works which Hardy refused to inscribe and the autograph books he declined to sign— fell largely upon Florence's shoulders. She also had the unpleasant responsibility of keeping away from Hardy the people he did not wish to see, and of ensuring that those who were admitted to Max Gate did not stay too long. Hardy was well, but increasingly frail and easily tired—especially since he was always anxious to be a genial host. When an Army officer with a reputation as a boxer called in 1920, Hardy took off his jacket and engaged in mock fisticuffs, and John Middleton Murry once spoke of the extraordinary act of kinetic memory by which the octogenarian Hardy, sitting with Murry's nine-month-old daughter on his knee, succeeded in accurately recollecting from childhood the way to make a handkerchief into the shape of a rabbit.[31]

What visitors did not realize, encountering the great man in lively and cheerful mood, was that he was exerting himself for their benefit after having already put in a full day's work in his study—described by one privileged visitor in 1921 as 'bare, simple, workmanlike and pleasantly shabby', its 'well-faded walls . . . distempered an unusual shade of coral-pink'.[32] There he sat each day, writing, reading proofs, answering letters, and keeping a close watch on the health and prosperity of his many publications. Nothing was allowed to interfere with his morning's labours, and at lunchtime he was always tired and unwilling to engage in conversation. After a rest, however, he was quite fresh again, and able, even eager, to greet teatime visitors. Florence regretted that this schedule meant, among other things, that they could never accept invitations to lunch, but she realized that it was only by resisting such temptations and distractions that her husband was able to remain actively at work so far into his old age. Hardy himself told a visitor that summer that, whatever his mood, he went to his study every day and wrote something, it scarcely mattered what: 'I never let a day go without using a pen. Just holding it sets me off; in fact I can't think without it. It's important not to wait for the right mood. If you do, it will come less and less.'[33]

One of Hardy's tasks during the spring and early summer of 1920 was the correction of proofs for the Mellstock Edition. He had taken the opportunity to change some of the topographical references in *A Pair of Blue Eyes* so as to connect the novel more directly with the St. Juliot area and, hence, with Emma; but the only alterations to the other prose volumes were of minor errors in the Wessex Edition which readers had drawn to his attention or which he had himself noticed from time to time: he undertook no systematic reconsideration of the texts and did not think of the new edition as in any sense challenging what he regarded as the 'definitive' status of the Wessex. In these circumstances he had thought it necessary to see the proofs only of the revised pages of *A Pair of Blue Eyes*. He did, however, read the proofs of the seven poetry volumes (including the three volumes of *The Dynasts*), lamenting that 'no human printer, or even one sent from Heaven direct, can be trusted with verse'.[34] Although he continued to rate his verse more highly than his fiction and sometimes referred to the latter in disparaging terms, he well knew that his novels remained his principal source of income—becoming much agitated when, in May 1920, Harper & Brothers announced that because of rising costs they proposed to reduce the author's royalty on one of the editions they had in print in the United States. The elaborate summary of his past dealings with the Harper firm which he then sent to Sir Frederick Macmillan is a remarkable instance of Hardy's careful record-keeping over the years and of the anxious zeal with which he watched over his publishing affairs.[35] To the end of his life he performed on his own behalf a great many troublesome tasks which an author later in the twentieth century would almost certainly have passed on to agents and accountants.*

Hardy seems genuinely to have regarded his novels as possessing, as works of literature, a purely antiquarian interest. When Florence Henniker, that summer of 1920, evinced an interest in *Two on a Tower*, Hardy sent her a copy. 'On looking into it it seems rather clever,' he remarked, with the same unselfconscious simplicity that enabled him to say, in response to Mrs Henniker's question about what happened after the end of the novel, that history did not record whether Swithin St. Cleeve married Tabitha: 'Perhaps when Lady C. was dead he grew passionately attached to her again, as people often do.' Expressing mild dissatisfaction with the rather abrupt conclusion of a novel by his

---

* Sir Frederick Macmillan and the other partners in the Macmillan house were always willing, however, to give advice on technical matters and, when so requested, to conduct negotiations with other publishers, with anthologists seeking reprint rights, with potential translators, and especially with the representatives of film companies, who had from an early stage regarded *Far from the Madding Crowd* and *Tess* as attractive 'properties'.

friend Eden Phillpotts, Hardy remarked that if he himself were
to write another novel—as he had no intention of doing—he
would surprise his readers by going back to the old-fashioned
style, practised 'in Fielding's time & onward', of telling the reader
what finally happened to all the characters.[36]

In poetry, on the contrary, he remained eager to catch the
sound of new and distinctive voices. The arrival of presentation
copies of Ezra Pound's *Hugh Selwyn Mauberley* and *Quia Pauper
Amavi* was at first greeted with polite discretion: 'I will not try
to express my appreciation of their contents, as I am a very slow
reader; & as, moreover, your muse asks for considerable delibera-
tion in estimating her.' But Hardy later grappled with the poems
and made what Pound called the 'impractical and infinitely in-
valuable suggestion' that 'Homage to Sextus Propertius' might be
made more accessible by being retitled something like 'Sextus
Propertius Soliloquizes'. When Robert Graves, introduced by
Siegfried Sassoon, spent a weekend at Max Gate with his wife
(Nancy Nicholson) in August 1920, Hardy was anxious to see
some of his recent poems and inquired about his working methods. Told that a particular poem was in its sixth draft and would
probably need two more before it was finished, Hardy said that
he had himself never made more than three, or at most four,
drafts of a poem for fear of its 'losing its freshness'. He showed
little sympathy for *vers libre* or other radical shifts in the technique of poetry, declaring that 'All we can do is to write on the
old themes in the old styles, but try to do a little better than
those who went before us'.[37]

At the time of the Graveses' visit Hardy had been happily busy-
ing himself with the restoration of the disused Norman font at
Stinsford—although he had himself been christened in the
eighteenth-century font presented to the church by Lorna Pitt.
He got out his old architectural notebook and took it with him
not only to Stinsford itself but to the church at Martinstown,
where he made a drawing of a similar font, and to the three
Dorchester churches, in each of which he measured the height of
the font above the floor and the height of the officiating step.[38]
He got a similar retrospective pleasure from the country dances
and the mummers' play of 'Saint George' which had been incorporated into the dramatization of *The Return of the Native*
with which the Dorchester amateurs were reviving the pre-war

'tradition' of the annual Hardy play. Hardy had little hand in the adaptation of his novel, but he had, by drawing on childhood memories, been responsible for the words of the mummers' play itself. That Christmas of 1920 the Hardy Players, as they now called themselves, appeared at Max Gate in mumming costume and performed the play in the drawing room before an audience consisting of Hardy, Florence, Kate, Henry, and the Max Gate servants. Carol-singers outside sang the old Bockhampton carols and the entire occasion, as Florence reported to Cockerell, gave Hardy 'intense joy'.[39]

An important ingredient of Hardy's pleasure was his responsiveness to the charms of the actress playing Eustacia Vye. Gertrude Bugler, said Florence in that same letter, looked 'prettier than ever in her mumming dress. T.H. has lost his heart to her entirely, but as she is soon getting married I don't let that cast me down *too* much.' But Hardy's feeling for Gertrude Bugler was something more complex than an old man's fondness. Although her father, prosaically enough, was a Dorchester confectioner who made his premises available to the Hardy Players for their rehearsals, her mother had been a dairymaid living in the old manor house at Kingston Maurward and one 'source' of the inspiration of *Tess*. Gertrude's own fresh beauty and slightly open-mouthed eagerness were extraordinarily reminiscent of Agatha Thornycroft and of the image of Tess Durbeyfield that Herkomer had captured in his drawings for the *Graphic*. She had, too, impersonated some of Hardy's most appealing female characters, and there is no doubt that she was impelled, both by genuine awe of Hardy and by her own natural desire for admiration and attention, to make herself as charming and agreeable to him as possible —especially since the publicity accorded *The Return of the Native* in the London papers had given her theatrical ambitions of a larger though as yet unformed kind. Hardy, still susceptible at eighty to feminine beauty and charm, found Miss Bugler quite captivating. To her, he seemed always a fatherly figure, and she was for him, in one respect, the incarnation of the ideal daughter he had never had. But in so far as she 'was' Tess Durbeyfield she also embodied the inextricable mesh of association and emotion that Hardy invested in perhaps the most personal of all his characters. Miss Bugler's marriage (at Stinsford Church) in September 1921 to a farmer cousin also surnamed Bugler did not remove her from the scene as completely as Florence could have wished. Her new home was at Beaminster in north-west Dorset and she was much preoccupied during the next two or three years with marriage and, eventually, motherhood; but she kept up her association with the Hardy Players, whose 'star' she was, and did not forget that Hardy, after the final performance of *The Return of the Native,* had suggested that she might one day play the part of Tess.[40]

Early in 1921 Florence was experiencing acute depression and some pain—though both seemed to disappear once she was away from Max Gate—and in April she went to London to have six of her teeth taken out, in accordance with the alarming orthodoxy of the time: 'I trust the extraction has been for the best,' wrote Hardy to her at Mrs Henniker's, 'though I don't quite see how the removal of a symptom cures a disease.' She was also worried about the future prospects of her sister Margaret Soundy, who stayed at Max Gate with her son Tom before leaving for Canada at the end of April: 'We are so occupied by the pranks of a two-and-a-half-year-old boy', Florence reported to Cockerell, 'that we haven't time to think of anything else.'[41] Hardy himself remained remarkably fit, still entirely capable of walking to Stinsford and cycling to Talbothays, occasionally afflicted by eye trouble but refusing to see an oculist and persisting in his loyalty to the pair of cheap spectacles he had himself picked out at the counter of the Civil Service Stores many years before. In late July 1921 he persuaded himself that he had heart trouble, but when the doctor was eventually summoned he reassuringly, if unromantically, diagnosed indigestion. Hardy then stopped talking about his heart but set Florence to work upon another revision and retyping of the 'Materials'.[42]

In April 1921 Hardy and Florence attended a special 'Warriors' Day' performance of scenes from *Far from the Madding Crowd,* in which Gertrude Bugler added Bathsheba to her repertoire of Hardyan heroines, and in June they drove with Cecil Hanbury, the current owner of Kingston Maurward (and hence of the cottage at Higher Bockhampton), to see the Hardy Players perform *The Return of the Native* in the castle ruins at Sturminster Newton. Hardy had tea with the cast at Riverside Villa, where he had lived with Emma in the 1870s, and insisted that Gertrude Bugler, who had been invited to come back and stay there, should sleep in the room in which he had written *The Return of the Native.* A day or two later Hardy drove over with Florence to the Granville-Barkers at Netherton Hall, and in July he opened a fête in Dorchester in aid of the county hospital, observing in his brief speech that he 'almost' remembered the original construction of the building and had known personally its architect, Benjamin Ferrey.[43]

These, however, were exceptional excursions. On most days Hardy was content to venture out into the immediate vicinity of Max Gate, just far enough to give Wessex and himself some exercise. But there was nothing truly reclusive about such an existence, at least during the warmer months of the year. Increasing use of the motor car contributed greatly to the rising incidence of visitors at Max Gate, making it seem 'almost suburban'.[44] The stream of teatime callers kept up steadily throughout the spring and summer and into the autumn: Barrie,* Sassoon, E. M. Forster, G. Lowes Dickinson, Cockerell, Middleton Murry, Galsworthy, and many others, known and unknown, old friends and strangers, neighbours and pilgrims from far distances. The conversations so doggedly recorded by Vere H. Collins took place at this period. Walter de la Mare came for the first time in 1921 and was an immediate favourite. Masefield arrived with the somewhat embarrassing gift of a model full-rigged ship he had made with his own hands: it was just what Hardy had always wanted when he was a boy, Florence confided to Forster, but he wasn't sure what to do with it now. A more obviously appropriate gift was a copy of the first edition of Keats's *Lamia, Isabella, the Eve of St. Agnes and Other Poems,* presented to Hardy by a group of his 'younger comrades in the craft of letters' on the occasion of his eighty-first birthday.[46]

'I am getting to know quite a lot of the Young Georgians,' Hardy remarked to Mrs Henniker in July 1921, '& have quite a paternal feeling, or grandpaternal, towards them.' The reminiscences of such visitors speak uniformly of Hardy's geniality and benignity, a radiating kindliness which seems to have expressed itself in terms of good manners and of flattering attentiveness rather than of articulated wisdom. 'Ah, yes, Hardy,' said E. M. Forster once. 'Such a nice man. He always wanted to know if you

---

* Barrie was accompanied on this visit by Lady Cynthia Asquith, who later told a lurid tale of the domination of the household by 'the most despotic dog' she had ever suffered under: 'Wessex very uninhibited throughout dinner, which he spent not under, but on, the table, walking about quite unchecked, and contesting with me every forkful of food on its way from plate to mouth. Undistracted by the snarling and scrunching of his dog, Hardy, who exerts himself much more as a host than as a guest, talked more than I had yet heard him. The only thing he seems to take the least pride in is his descent from the Trafalgar Hardy, and he much resents the attempt to convert Nelson's last words from "Kiss me, Hardy," into "Kismet, Hardy".'[45]

had had enough tea.' H. J. Massingham, who visited Max Gate with his father in 1921, could later recollect little of what was actually said but vividly retained the impression Hardy had made upon him:

> A man slow, deep-rooted, full of treasure within but hidden from the prying eye. A man who might have been mistaken for a country doctor, old-style, with humour in the mouth and tragedy in the eyes, but neither revealed except by that close scrutiny that awe and manners forbade. A kind host, a gentle manner of speaking, a low voice, an attentive listener with head slightly cocked of one side, like a bird's. No glitter whatever in the talk which (on his side) was reminiscent, as all true country things are.

That same year Hardy received two young men from the University of Birmingham with the utmost graciousness and talked fully and freely with them—which is not to suggest that he said anything he had not said many times before. His conversation in these later years became, indeed, more than a little repetitious, so that Cockerell, as a frequent visitor, once noted in his diary that there had been conversation 'as usual' about Shakespeare, Keats, and Shelley.[47]

Now that he was in his eighties, and famous, Hardy relaxed to some extent his concern for certain points of principle that had meant much to him in former years. A visitor of 1920 was much puzzled by his declaring, in response to a remark about his having pulled out 'all the stops' in *Jude*: 'Do you think so? My views on life are so extreme that I do not usually state them.' What he perhaps meant was that he had learnt since *Jude,* not to change his mind about the state of the world and of the universe, but to save some of the wear and tear consequent upon speaking that mind in public. At his age, and with so much work behind him, it no longer seemed necessary, profitable, or congenial to continue to testify in season and out: he had for some time taken the position that it was possible to be too vocal in a good cause. His sometimes discomforting facility for seeing all sides of a question had in any case obliged him to acknowledge that those who held radically different views might be perfectly sincere and honourable and, within their own terms of reference, perfectly justified. As early as 1912, after revising *Jude* for the Wessex Edition, Hardy had told Cockerell that when he read the new Preface and

Postscript, 'you will say to yourself (as I did to myself when I passed the proof for press) "How very natural, & even commendable, it is for old-fashioned cautious people to shy at a man who could write that!"' So, rereading in 1918 a sermon against *Tess*, he became convinced that the preacher was probably a good man.[48]

After 1920 there were fewer direct challenges, public or private, to critics and reviewers, and a less strenuous insistence upon the deliberate nonobservance of certain social and religious forms. He went to church from time to time, chiefly because he enjoyed the singing and the long-familiar rituals, but also because he remembered that the church had once been a centre of village life and felt that, in a period of immense social and political upheaval, it might still have a cohesive and 'disciplinary' role to play. 'I believe in going to church,' he told J. H. Morgan in 1922. 'It is a moral drill, and people must have something. If there is no church in a country village, there is nothing.' Asked by Mrs Hanbury of Kingston Maurward to stand as godfather to her daughter Caroline, Hardy not only agreed to do so but wrote a little poem ('To C.F.H. On her Christening-Day') for the occasion, inscribed it on parchment, and presented it in a silver box.[49]* When Robert Graves and Nancy Nicholson told him in 1921 that their children had not been baptized, he merely observed that 'his old mother had always said of baptism that at any rate there was no harm in it, and that she would not like her children to blame her in after-life for leaving any duty to them undone.' He added: ' "I have usually found that what my old mother said was right." '[51]

Florence found her husband's ancestor-worship extremely oppressive at times: she blamed the 'atmosphere of Mellstock Churchyard' for the melancholy tone of one of her letters to Cockerell. But those walks to Stinsford were still making their contribution

---

* Though charming in itself, the gesture was strikingly at odds with the position he had taken in 1907 when faced with an identical request from John Moule, second son of his old friend Henry J. Moule: 'I am honoured by your thinking of me as a god parent for your little boy, & I should have said yes in a moment if I had been a normal Churchman. But I have a conscientious objection to that & many other ceremonies, & though you may say the sponsorial rite means nothing I feel that I must maintain my objection in practice as well as in theory, although it happens to occur in relation to a family of whom I have known so many members & have such pleasant memories.'[50] John Moule had emigrated to Canada, however, and Hardy perhaps found it easier to refuse a request from such a distance than one from an energetic and influential neighbour.

to an extraordinary poetic flow that showed no sign of drying up; 'Voices from Things Growing in a Country Churchyard' was written in 1921, stimulated in part by the experience, in January of that year, of reading through some of the old Stinsford parish registers,[52] and in November 1921 Hardy told Sir Frederick Macmillan that he had enough poems for a new volume. His suggestion in the same letter that the sales of the one-volume editions of *The Collected Poems* and *The Dynasts* might be enhanced by the publication of thin-paper issues was characteristic of Hardy's unremitting attention to his own literary affairs; Macmillan's ready acceptance of the idea reflected not only an acknowledgement of its cogency, but also his eagerness to meet, so far as possible, the wishes of one of the firm's best- and certainly most consistently-selling authors.[53]

Hardy's royalties from Macmillan for the year 1920 amounted to something over £3,400, Florence reported to Cockerell (surely without Hardy's knowledge), and film and other such rights brought in £1,000 more. 'And yet I think [she added] that T.H. honestly believes that poverty & ruin stare him in the face. Argument does not convince him—merely irritates.' When visitors came to lunch or dinner, Hardy, mindful of the lavish hospitality he had received from wealthy friends in town and country, felt an obligation to entertain in some style, if not always with much grace. Appeals to his sympathy or his sense of family loyalty could often open his purse. But he otherwise lived with the utmost frugality, partly from long habit, partly in the belief that an author could only retain a sense of proportion and keep in touch with his essential material if he continued to live after his success in the same manner as he had lived before it.[54]

The standard generalization about Hardy's meanness is obviously in need of qualification, not only because it ignores the contradictory evidence of his generosity towards near and distant relatives, but also because it is based almost exclusively upon the prejudiced comments of Max Gate servants and the evidence of others—including Florence herself—who knew him only in old age, when many men become tight-fisted. Few of the servants felt any particular affection or admiration for their employer. He had never been accustomed to servants in his earlier years and had little sense of how to conduct himself towards them. He was inconveniently around the house all day long and sharply resentful of interruptions to his work. He was an object of perpetual suspicion, on the basis of local gossip about his irreligiousness and immorality, and gave offence to staff and tradesmen alike by his failure to appreciate that a tip which might have been minimally adequate in the 1880s was certainly not so in the 1920s. Everything in Hardy's experience had taught him to be cautious about money. He had imbibed from his mother a family history of poverty and a whole peasant tradition of thrift and prudentiality. He had been poor himself, and sharply and painfully aware of what it meant to be lacking in social and economic status. He had taken extraordinary financial risks in shifting in his early thirties from his first hard-won career in architecture to one which promised few chances of success and none of permanent security. His extreme sensitivity to hostile criticism was grounded in a permanent anxiety about the continuance of that popularity upon which his very livelihood depended, and when he abandoned fiction in the 1890s he was gambling that his novels would continue to sell in sufficient quantities to support his indulgence in yet another new career, as a poet, from which he anticipated financial loss rather than financial advantage.

It is true that Hardy's income in his last years was very substantial and that he could have well afforded to keep Florence better supplied with money for household and other expenses. But his habits had long been formed by that time, and they included a hatred of waste—he was not the only elderly Victorian to remove coals from a fire which had been heaped too high—and an imagination of disaster, fed by childhood memories, by the real difficulties and prospective perils of the First World War, and by the social and economic dangers which seemed to threaten England and Europe in the immediate post-war period. Finally, he had learned from his mother a keen and almost obsessive sense of family loyalty, of the need and obligation to look after one's 'own', and although he had no children he had had two unmarried sisters for whom he felt responsible and a great many impecunious and often envious relatives from whose importunities he naturally shrank but whose genuine distress he was always prepared to try to alleviate. Florence was the most vocal—because the most directly affected—of those who deplored the tight hold Hardy kept upon his purse; but she was also capable of criticizing her husband for his financial indulgence towards relatives—his 'little crowd of annuitants'—and freely acknowledged that while he was careful over shillings and pence he was often indifferent to larger sums and certainly not in the least interested in the accumulation of money for its own sake.[55]

In January 1922 Hardy was in bed with a severe chill accompanied by acute diarrhoea. He could eat little but found sustenance in an occasional half-bottle of champagne. Florence thought it was influenza, which she herself came down with shortly afterwards. He himself described it after the event as 'the old bladder complaint'. There had been a traumatic day or two, however, when their own doctor, seconded by a colleague, had diagnosed cancer and Florence had frantically summoned her sister Eva, a trained and experienced nurse.[56] Although this fear was soon dispelled, Hardy took several weeks to recover his full strength. By early February, however, he was out of bed and writing a preface to his forthcoming volume of poems. He had determined upon the preface and brooded upon its contents while he was ill, and later told Gosse that the illness had 'caused' the preface. Florence came upon him one day talking to himself about the iniquities of critics, until he suddenly burst out with: 'I wrote my poems for men like Siegfried Sassoon.' Once the preface, now called 'Apology', was completed he was anxious to assure himself that it was not too bitter—too 'cantankerous' as he put it—in its animadversions upon critics and reviewers. Florence thought the whole thing a mistake but hesitated to say so, and the decision was left to Cockerell, who urged publication with only minor revisions. Hardy accepted his advice, along with his offer to help in correcting the proofs of the volume, and the 'Apology' was duly included when *Late Lyrics and Earlier* was published on 23 May 1922.[57]

Although devoted in part to restating Hardy's gloomy view of the contemporary world, the 'Apology' chiefly reflected his long-standing resentment against those who insisted upon the ungainliness of his verse and the bleakness of his philosophy, and while it was in itself, as Florence recognized, a fine piece of argumentative prose, its tone and content naturally drew protests from that class of reviewers and critics against whom it was chiefly directed. Even Gosse claimed to have read it 'with surprise, and even with some pain', and pointed out that Hardy alone seemed to be unaware of the reverence with which he was now regarded. Hardy had taken the opportunity in the 'Apology' to express his particular annoyance at Harrison's *Fortnightly* article and at a more recent piece in the *London Mercury* by Joseph M. Hone:

It appears [wrote Gosse in the *Sunday Times*] that 'a Roman
Catholic young man' has reproved him for the 'dark gravity of
his ideas'. Let that young man be produced and exhibited in a
glass case, for he is a rare specimen. What in all the earth does
it matter what some young Catholic (or some old Protestant, if it
comes to that) has been silly enough to say? There is always
somebody willing to court attention by an imbecile paradox. . . .
It is part of Mr. Hardy's genius, no doubt, to be sensitive, but I
am vexed to find that he feels a pea under the seven mattresses
of our admiration.

Practically, logically, Gosse's expostulations were unanswerable.
But that extreme, delicate, ever-troubling sensitivity of Hardy's
could not be argued away, and it constituted a larger element in
his 'genius' than Gosse's qualification allowed for. As Hardy himself observed, what counted was not the strength of the blow itself
but the nature of the material on which the blow fell.[58]

Late Lyrics and Earlier was generally well received, however,
and Hardy persuaded himself that the 'Apology' had done much
to assure its success. It was in any case a remarkable collection for
a man in his eighty-second year to bring out, especially since about
half of the verses, so the 'Apology' claimed, had been written
'quite lately'. Dates appended to some of the other poems range
from the 1860s onwards, and although it is clear that Hardy had
gathered in, with or without revision, a number of works deemed
insufficiently strong or insufficiently 'finished' to be included in
earlier collections, the volume as a whole does not show any
significant falling off. It opens with the disarming cheerfulness
of 'Weathers', apparently one of the latest written of the poems,
and is generally less sombre in mood than either *Satires of Circumstances* or *Moments of Vision*—although Mrs Henniker,
even so, ventured to suggest that it was much sadder in tone than
Hardy was himself.[59] The several poems about Emma—including
'The West-of-Wessex Girl', 'A Man Was Drawing Near to Me'
(suggested by 'Some Recollections'), 'The Marble-streeted Town',
and 'A Duettist to Her Pianoforte'—are for the most part gently
nostalgic in feeling rather than fiercely remorseful. They are also
offset by poems commemorative of other women—Helen Paterson
('The Opportunity'), Louisa Harding ('The Passer-by'), the Miss
Marsh who sang at the Sturminster Newton concert in 1878 ('The
Maid of Keinton Mandeville'), and the Piccadilly prostitute who
once held a flower to Hardy's face as he passed by ('The Woman
I Met')—and Florence seems not to have felt, as she had done

when the two preceding volumes were published, that *Late Lyrics* cast doubt upon the validity and happiness of Hardy's second marriage by retrospectively celebrating his first. Florence and Cockerell had both hoped that the new volume would contain a poem about Wessex, but Hardy declared that he could write one only if the dog were dead—a consummation devoutly desired by a succession of servants and postmen but still some years away.[60]

The continuing alertness and suppleness of mind which everywhere displayed itself in the controlled and economical prose of the 'Apology' owed more than a little to that ever-rising stream of teatime visitors to Max Gate. Like Tennyson at Farringford in the previous century, Hardy was much annoyed by 'pilgrims' who lurked outside the gate to get a glimpse of him as he walked out to the letter-box which had been let into the street side of the garden wall, or who clung to the parapet of that wall in an attempt to peer over. Visitors who made a polite and more or less formal approach, usually by letter, were rarely turned away, whether they were famous or unknown, local or foreign. Hardy would generally settle into a smooth reminiscential rhythm on these occasions, and Florence was sometimes exasperated at his narrating to people whom she suspected of collecting material for biographical books or articles, details which had already been incorporated into 'my book'—itself now 'finished, so far as is possible', as she told Cockerell in August 1922, and 'put away'. But the appearance of such established friends as Sassoon, Cockerell, Barrie, and the Granville-Barkers gave pleasure to them both, and every now and then a newcomer would fill them with delight— Edmund Blunden, for example, who reminded Hardy of Keats, seemed to Florence every inch a poet, and reduced even Wessex to fawning adoration.[61]

Florence Henniker, now in her late sixties, stayed in Dorchester for a week that summer of 1922 and drove with the Hardys about the Vale of Blackmoor and other parts of the local countryside. Dorothy Allhusen came down with her daughter in November, and she too had to be asked to stay in the town rather than at Max Gate—an apparent ungraciousness which much disturbed Florence, mindful of the many hospitalities of Mrs Allhusen and her mother in the past, but which Hardy's age made unavoidable. Max Gate was not a large house, and he lacked the physical and nervous resilience to be exposed to visitors at all hours. Even his teatime performances gradually became something of a strain, and he would sometimes collapse into near-exhaustion after the last guest had left, giving Florence occasion for wry reflection upon the somewhat illusory image of health and vigour which he thus projected to a world which knew nothing of the care and attention he required during the remainder of the day.[62]

In early September 1922 Florence's elder sister, Ethel Richardson, was asked to stay at Max Gate for a few days while Florence went up to Enfield to see her parents. Mrs Richardson played to Hardy on the piano—everything from cathedral chants to modern dance tunes—and found him, despite the frailty of his appearance, to be in manner, bearing, and conversation 'like a man twenty years younger'. At breakfast one morning she was vouchsafed a glimpse of the puritanical absoluteness of Hardy's dedication as an artist. Responding to the news that Granville-Barker and his wife proposed to spend the winter in Italy, he declared that Barker had evidently given up all thought of writing: ' "For it is impossible," he said "to write, & have other interests. In writing, as in all work, there is only one way—*to stick to it.*" '[63]

That October Hardy walked to Talbothays and back one day, something Florence had not expected him ever to do again. He went with Florence to vote against Labour in the municipal elections at the beginning of November, though Florence at least 'felt mean in doing so', and took a lively pleasure in a new honour which came his way in the form of an honorary fellowship of Queen's College, Oxford.[64] As the winter drew on, however, he fell into one of the old depressive spirals from which he had for some years been almost entirely free. Emma's birthday on 24 November—consistently forgotten in her lifetime, as Florence wearily remarked—was now a major date on the Max Gate calendar, the more so since it precisely coincided with the day on which Mary had died; in 1922 it was followed almost immediately, on 27 November, by the tenth anniversary of Emma's death. 'E.'s death-day, 10 years ago,' reads his diary entry. 'Went with F. & tidied her tomb, & carried flowers for hers & the other two tombs.' In December a mild attack of the flu bereft him of what remained of his energy and spirits: 'He said', Florence told Cockerell on the 17th, 'he had never felt so despondent in his life. And he told me that if anything happened to me he would go out & drown himself, which, considered rightly is a compliment, isn't it.'[65]

In an article in the *Weekly Dispatch* (a London Sunday newspaper) of 27 August 1922 Florence had pronounced upon the great happiness women could find 'in willing self-surrender and devotion to others'. But the self-abnegatory role she had herself chosen did not always sit comfortably on her shoulders. That November, looking back over the years to the time of Emma's death, she believed that she could see 'a clear division' in her life, 'for on that day I seemed suddenly to leap from youth into dreary middle-age'. She acknowledged that she had not had serious responsibilities to carry before that time, but the despondent remark clearly reflected—as she moved through her early forties, faced sickness and surgery, coped with the increasing difficulties of life with her octogenarian husband, and anticipated with dread the miseries of yet another Max Gate winter—her familiar sense of all that, as a woman, she had never had. Nor was she much cheered, as she sat writing to Cockerell in mid-December, by the sound of her husband playing a Christmas hymn 'on that most pathetic old piano'.[66]

27

LAST THINGS

IN early January 1923 Mrs Henniker—stricken by the death of her maid and companion of many years—telegraphed to ask Florence to come up and keep her company for a while. Florence arranged for two of her sisters to come down, Constance to Max Gate, Eva to Talbothays, while she went up to Mrs Henniker, who had let her London house and was living in colder and damper conditions at Epsom. Already sadly broken down in both health and spirits at the time of Florence's visit, Mrs Henniker died of heart failure in early April, and there was an emotional moment at Max Gate when Hardy's letters to her, which had been bequeathed to Florence, were unsuspectingly opened by the latter in Hardy's presence. Although Hardy's only surviving note on Mrs Henniker's death is brief enough ('After a friendship of 30 years!'),[1] both he and Florence felt the loss severely, and the empty place she left in the ranks of Hardy's trusted friends and comfortable correspondents was never to be filled. There had been other occasions for mourning, individually less painful but cumulatively distressing, over the last few years. Charles W. Moule, the last of the 'seven brethren', died in 1921, Emma's cousin Charles Edwin Gifford in 1922, and Charles Meech Hardy in 1923. Later in 1923 the death occurred of Sir Frederic Treves, surgeon to the royal family, who had gone to the same Dorchester school as Mary

Hardy. 'So friends & acquaintances thin out,' Hardy had soberly observed to Mrs Henniker in March 1922, '& we who remain have to "close up".' He had long got beyond the point, however, of regarding death as a calamity, and had become so accustomed to contemplating the early prospect of his own departure—and so absorbed in the ritualization of his own especial griefs for Emma and Mary—that these more recent losses fell into place as little more than episodes, pauses for regret and salutation, in his own continuing pilgrimage. On 22 September 1921 he had written the day's date in his Spenser alongside the lines:

> Sleep after toyle, port after stormie seas,
> Ease after warre, death after life, does greatly please.[2]

Far more agitating were his expedition to Queen's College, Oxford, in June 1923, and the visit to Max Gate of the Prince of Wales in July. On the two-day visit to Queen's, the first and only time he went there as an Honorary Fellow, he and Florence went by car, passing through Salisbury and Wantage and turning aside for a brief visit to Fawley and a vain search for the graves of ancestors in the little churchyard. In Oxford they were somewhat over-entertained, but Hardy had made up his mind in advance that he wanted to see once again certain Oxford sights—the curve of the High Street, the Martyrs' Memorial, the Shelley Memorial —and he ensured their inclusion in his itinerary. The return journey was made by way of Winchester, another of those cathedral towns to which he was so devoted, and the New Forest, where they picnicked 'in the simple way that Hardy so much preferred'.[3]

There was nothing simple about the preparations for the Prince's visit on 20 July. Additional servants had to be brought in to see to the catering and Florence was much flustered because, as she told Cockerell, 'he will want to wash his hands—etc— here which is terrible. You know what our house is like.' But, she added, Hardy himself was pleased. When the anxiously awaited day came, everything went off smoothly enough, Florence being so determined to behave normally that Hardy subsequently scolded her for being a little too cool. The conversation could not in the nature of things have been very lively, however, and it was Sassoon who subsequently spread abroad the Prince's most notable utterance: 'My mother tells me you have written a book called *Tess of the d'Urbervilles*. I must try to read it some time.' Kate, Henry, and Polly Antell had been told that they might, if they wished, secrete themselves in one of the upstairs rooms at Max Gate while the royal visit was taking place, but Kate and Polly contented themselves with watching the Prince drive into town, Henry with running the Union Jack up the Talbothays flagpole. Hardy and Florence went to Talbothays the following day, but they were both, to Kate's eye, 'highly strung' and made off at the approach of some friends of Henry's.[4]

Florence had consulted Macleod Yearsley about the swelling on her neck during the spring of 1923. Hardy also wrote to Yearsley, in a letter eloquent both of his affectionate anxiety for Florence and of his unchanging dread of the surgeon's knife, and received the temporarily reassuring news that since the 'little gland' seemed not to be getting larger Florence had no immediate need to contemplate an operation.[5] She was, indeed, especially active that year, and although photographs of her sitting on the lawn at Max Gate between Hardy and the Prince of Wales suggest no lightening of her habitual melancholy, it is only fair to add that the Prince seems equally oppressed and Hardy only slightly less so. Florence managed—no doubt with the Prince's personal blessing—to obtain from the Duchy of Cornwall an extra paddock for her poultry adjoining the original Max Gate property, and counterbalanced this domestic gesture with one of a more frivolous kind when she persuaded T. E. Lawrence to give her a ride in the side-car of his motorcycle.[6]

Lawrence, then serving as Private Shaw at the Army camp near Wool, had himself sought out Hardy by writing to Robert Graves (who had in turn written to Florence) and made his first appearance at Hardy's tea table in April 1923. The liking and admiration on both sides was immediate and strong, and Lawrence returned to Max Gate whenever his duties would allow him to do so, trying (not always successfully) to avoid encounters with other visitors who might know and recognize him. Hardy, so Lawrence reported to Graves, was 'so pale, so quiet, so refined into an essence'. He was also 'so far-away. Napoleon is a real man to him, and the country of Dorsetshire echoes that name everywhere in Hardy's ears. He lives in his period, and thinks of it as the great war.' To return to the camp after a visit to Max Gate was like waking up from a restful sleep: 'There is an unbelievable dignity and ripeness about Hardy: he is waiting so tranquilly for death, without a desire or ambition left in his spirit, as far as I can feel it: and yet he entertains so many illusions, and hopes for the world, things which I, in my disillusioned middle-age, feel to be illusory. They used to call this man a pessimist. While really he is full of fancy expectations.'[7]

There were many other visitors to Max Gate that year. Bernard Shaw and his wife joined Lawrence at lunch one day. John Drinkwater arrived with his future wife, the violinist Daisy Kennedy, who played for them on Hardy's own fiddle. Lady St. Helier came for what was to prove the last time. Marie Stopes motored over from her lighthouse on Portland.[8] The reactions of these and other callers naturally varied. H. G. Wells and Rebbeca West, it is true, found Max Gate and its inhabitants infinitely dismal and depressing, but Romain Rolland, calling there with his sister, the translator of *Tess,* was struck both by Hardy's physical agility and his mental alertness ('sa mémoire est precise, son esprit ferme, clair, sans trace de vague ou de sentimentalisme') and described him as having 'l'air d'un vieux petit docteur suisse'. The American scholar Roger L. Loomis was there in June and recalled many years later that 'No one could have been more friendly to me a perfect stranger, more cheerful, more communicative'. As another visitor, one of the daughters of the Bankes family, drove off, Hardy remarked appreciatively that she was a fine figure of a woman.[9]

Loomis had been able to talk authoritatively about the Tristram legend, whose Cornish aspects were at that period very much in Hardy's mind. He had recently astonished Sir Frederick Macmillan, and almost everyone else, by producing the completed manuscript of *The Famous Tragedy of the Queen of Cornwall,* a poetic drama whose theme and setting obviously derived from the emotional and geographical circumstances of his long-ago meeting with Emma Gifford in Cornwall in 1870 and his return to those scenes in the company of his second wife in 1916—immediately after publication of the play on 15 November 1923 he spoke of it as '53 years in contemplation, 800 lines in result, alas!'[10]

The lack of any rich metaphorical or prosodic vitality in the verse of *The Queen of Cornwall* must be set against Hardy's specific presentation of it, on the title-page, as having been 'Arranged as a Play for Mummers'—as if it had pre-existed in a more poetic and literary form and was now to be presented somewhat in the mode he had described in the Preface to Part First of *The Dynasts*: 'a monotonic delivery of speeches, with dreamy conventional gestures, something in the manner traditionally maintained by the old Christmas mummers, the curiously hypnotizing impressiveness of whose automatic style—that of persons who spoke by no will of their own—may be remembered by all who ever experienced it.'[11] Hardy was necessarily conscious of drawing upon ancient legendary materials, and of rearranging those traditional elements into a new pattern. Even so, the reference to 'mummers', together with the insistence upon absolute simplicity of staging (the words 'Requiring no Theatre or Scenery' are actually part of the sub-title), seem designed both to emphasize the play's elemental qualities—its stark elements of love, jealousy, and death— and to disarm critics whose expectations might be pitched unrealistically high. The Tintagel setting and Hardy's references to Emma as 'an Iseult of my own' make it clear that the play carries a heavy autobiographical investment; at the same time it does not yield itself at all readily to an allegorical reading, perhaps because Hardy disinterred and completed it specifically for a performance by the Hardy Players and with Gertrude Bugler in mind for the role of Iseult—although she was prevented by pregnancy from taking part in the performance.[12]

Scarcely less remarkable than Hardy's composition of the play was the care and effort he put into its production. Before making the text available to the local group he sought the criticism and comments of Harley Granville-Barker,* who later sent a series of specific suggestions to Alderman A. H. Tilley, director of the

---

* It was to Barker's wife that Hardy sent an account of a dream he had had in the early hours of Sunday, 21 October 1923:

> I dreamt that I stood on a long ladder which was leaning against the edge of a loft. I was holding on by my right hand, & in my left I clutched an infant in blue & white, bound up in a bundle. My endeavour was to lift it over the edge of the loft to a place of safety. On the loft sat George Meredith, in his shirt sleeves, smoking; though his manner was rather that of Augustus John. The child was his, but he seemed indifferent to its fate, whether I should drop it or not. I said "It has got heavier since I lifted it last." He assented. By great exertion I got it above the edge, & deposited it on the floor of the loft: whereupon I awoke.

Although the dream has been persuasively interpreted in sexual terms, it is at least possible, given the fact that Meredith and John were fellow artists, that the baby somehow 'represented' the perceived burden of creative responsibility. On 15 December 1919 Hardy told Cockerell: 'My dreams are not so coherent as yours. They are more like cubist paintings & generally end by my falling down the turret stairs of an old church owing to steps being missing.'[13]

Dorchester production. Hardy concerned himself with the musical setting, heard the actors read through their parts, and sent Harold Child, who was to review the play for *The Times,* a long explanation of certain technical aspects of the play—including the preservation of the unities, the use of the English term 'Chanters' instead of the Greek 'Chorus', and the attempt to make the characters as timeless as possible. Although the critics were generous in their comments on the play, few of them spoke of what Hardy had seen as its most remarkable structural feature—'compactness and continuity without a moment's break in the action'.[14]

Hardy continued to be actively involved with *The Queen of Cornwall* well into 1924. Rutland Boughton, the composer, was in correspondence with him in January about a musical version of the play and asked if more songs could be introduced, as a way of relieving the tragic tone of the text as published. Hardy readily agreed—saying that he had 'always meant to revise it a little, to bring it roughly to the average length of Greek plays'—supplied some of the enlargements himself, and approved Boughton's suggestion for the incorporation of appropriate lyrics from Hardy's volumes of verse. His enthusiasm for the production was further enhanced by a meeting with Boughton, whom he immensely liked even while thoroughly disapproving of his communist sympathies.[15] Hardy determined to attend one of the performances of *The Queen of Cornwall* at that summer's Glastonbury Festival, but was thrown into great anxiety at the last minute by the prospect of making so long a journey by car. Florence, inured by now to such panic and indecision, observed to Cockerell that the only remedy was to remain quiet and allow him to calm down. Before she had finished her letter, indeed, she was able to report that Hardy had already forgotten about Glastonbury and was busily writing a poem: 'He asked me which was the better phrase "tender-eyed" or "meek-eyed". I pointed out that "tender-eyed" is used in the Bible (in reference to Leah) as meaning "sore-eyed"— which was why Jacob didn't want her. So a little biblical knowledge is handy at times: "tender-eyed" was promptly abandoned.'[16]

As this little episode suggests, Hardy's moods of anger or irritation tended to subside almost as suddenly as they erupted. He sat uncomplainingly to both R. G. Eves and Augustus John in 1923, and remarked upon seeing a photograph of the John painting, acquired by Cockerell for the Fitzwilliam Museum: 'Well, if I look like that the sooner I am under ground the better.' There was talk of a Sargent portrait late in the year, but while Hardy was attracted by the idea he would not consider going to London to pose. In any case, Florence told Cockerell, Hardy's patience was not inexhaustible, and the presence of the Russian sculptor Serge Youriévitch over a period of several days had so put him out that he would not speak at lunchtime while Youriévitch was there, but sat with his face permanently hidden behind *The Times.* 'And it seems rather late', she added, 'to have all these paintings & busts done.'[17]

In the spring of 1924 Hardy was 'nearly driven frantic' by Rutland Boughton's alarmed report of an unauthorized production of *The Queen of Cornwall* with musical settings which seemed to threaten both his position and his work. When, however, Florence suggested to her husband that he should hand over all such business matters to Cockerell, to one of the Macmillans, or even to a more recent friend, John Middleton Murry, he gradually calmed down—only to be thrown back into despair a day or two later by a revival of the public controversy begun earlier that year by the savage attack on his style and reputation in George Moore's *Conversations in Ebury Street.* Thanking Murry very warmly for coming to his defence in the pages of the *Adelphi,* Hardy confessed that he knew little of Moore's work, having mentally classed him among those writers who were negligible and therefore need not be read, and could not understand why the English press took him so seriously: 'Somebody once called him a putrid literary hermaphrodite, which I thought funny, but it may have been an exaggeration.'[18]*

On his eighty-fourth birthday, 2 June 1924, Hardy received more letters and telegrams than ever, and while Florence now enjoyed the occasional secretarial assistance of a young typist (and

---

* Moore's literary antagonism towards Hardy seems to have dated back at least as far as the publication of *Esther Waters,* just a year or two after that of *Tess,* and it is perhaps significant that much of the criticism in *Conversations* is directed at *Tess.* The more specifically personal enmity seems to have originated with Gosse telling Moore, some years previously, that Hardy had expressed a hope that he would not again encounter him at Gosse's house. On the present occasion Gosse was one of the many friends who, as Hardy bitterly observed, could have come to his defence but stayed safely silent instead.[19]

poet) named May O'Rourke,* she nevertheless remained responsible for the bulk of the correspondence, thoroughly earning the 'treat' of a day trip to London to meet Cockerell and go with him to *St. Joan*.[21] At the beginning of July Hardy took pleasure in a visit from the Balliol Players, a group of Oxford undergraduates who performed an English version of the *Oresteia*, entitled *The Curse of the House of Atreus*, on the Max Gate lawn to an audience consisting of Hardy, Florence, and Harley and Helen Granville-Barker. T. E. Lawrence had wanted to be present but could not get free from his military duties that afternoon. He had, however, entertained the Hardys and E. M. Forster to a sumptuous tea at his Cloud's Hill cottage ten days earlier, and continued to be a frequent and much valued visitor at Max Gate—Florence, in particular, admiring him as 'one of the few entirely satisfactory people in the world'.[22]

For Florence, and hence for Hardy, the early autumn of 1924 was a period of anxiety and even crisis. What had previously been diagnosed as a swollen gland on Florence's neck was now declared to be a potentially cancerous tumour, and she went once again to London to undergo, on 30 September, an operation for the removal of the tumour at the hands of James Sherren, the surgeon, who was the son of a Weymouth bookseller. Sherren reported to Hardy the next morning that the whole of the tumour had been successfully removed and that Florence's condition was quite satisfactory. Cockerell wrote twice to Hardy that same day and in general exerted himself both to keep Hardy reassured and to provide cheerful company for Florence at the Fitzroy Square nursing home. May O'Rourke, arriving at Max Gate the morning of the operation, was shocked by Hardy's physical appearance, and even after news of the operation's success had arrived he remained as if 'dazed'. He felt additional distress, and perhaps some guilt, at not being on hand in London himself, but Florence could only have been disturbed by his frail and fretful presence and Wessex would have 'broken his heart (literally) if we had both gone away'.[23] By 9 October Florence felt well enough to return home and Henry Hardy, with a local chauffeur to do most of the driving, went up to London to fetch her in the car he had purchased that

---

* Miss O'Rourke put on record, years later, her memories of a Max Gate full of activity, kindness, and good humour, a Hardy always pensive and sometimes stern but never morose, a Florence capable of youthful gaiety, and a Wessex moved to aberrant behaviour only by the nervous strain of an 'obvious determination to be as nearly human as possible'.[20]

summer—and which had made him, according to Florence, ten years younger. Elaborate plans were laid for the journey to and from town, Hardy supplied route maps for the driver and rugs for the patient, and Henry embraced the whole project with great enthusiasm: 'He is simply delighted over it I am sure,' wrote Kate to her elder brother, '& gets the hour of starting earlier & earlier, like father used to do in quite a merciless way. Do you remember?' All was safely accomplished, but it was after dark before the party reached Max Gate and Hardy (as he touchingly recorded in the poem 'Nobody Comes') spent an anxious hour or two standing at the house gate while car after car rushed by without stopping, having 'nothing to do with me'.[24]

While still weak from the operation, and still deeply worried about her future health,* Florence had to endure that autumn the excitement, anxiety, and occasional embarrassment of Hardy's involvement in the production by the Hardy Players of his own dramatization of *Tess of the d'Urbervilles*. First written in the 1890s, it had not been performed at the time, largely because of tedious practical difficulties (see above, p. 375). In 1924, according to Hardy, the Dorchester actors, led by Alderman T. H. Tilley, extracted the play from him against his better judgement—although there is some evidence that he had long wanted to produce it, with Gertrude Bugler as Tess, but had been deterred by the serious doubts expressed by Tilley and others as to its propriety and hence its suitability for the conservative Dorchester audience. Now that the production was finally determined upon, Hardy put even more of his heart into it than he had done into *The Queen of Cornwall* the year before. Tilley called at Max Gate while Florence was away—the only visitor Hardy would see during that period—and brought with him miniature models of the staging. In October there were discussions and rehearsals at Max Gate, and even a rehearsal in Wool Manor itself (the imagined scene of Tess and Angel's disastrous honeymoon) at which Gertrude Bugler as Tess, Dr E. W. Smerdon as a balding Angel, and Norman Atkins as a dark and villainous Alec went over the confession scene between Tess and Angel and Tess's subsequent re-encounter with Alec.[26]

* May O'Rourke, for one, believed that the persistent dread of cancer was largely responsible in subsequent years for what others sometimes perceived as Florence's 'bleak, difficult moods' and periods of 'inexplicable depression'.[25]

Hardy's interest in Gertrude Bugler was becoming more and more marked, and by the time of the first performance in Dorchester on 26 November it had given rise to a good deal of local gossip—much of it no doubt prompted by the jealousy of other members of the cast at the attention being paid to Mrs Bugler by visitors and journalists as well as by Hardy himself. They sat together at the tea given for the players between the matinée and evening performances, and Florence interpreted as intimate whispering what Mrs Bugler later blamed upon Hardy's saying quietly something about Augustus John which John, sitting on the other side of Hardy, was not to hear. At the Weymouth performance on 11 December Hardy, behind the scenes, pointed out that Mrs Bugler was wearing her wedding ring and offered to hold it for her; later, just before the scenes in which Tess was supposed to be married, Hardy gave her back the ring by putting it on her finger as in the marriage ceremony.[27]*

Florence had borne with her grievances and jealousies, real or imagined, on the assumption that the performances would soon come to an end and Mrs Bugler return permanently to Beaminster with her baby and her husband. But Mrs Bugler's Tess had been deeply moving in her beauty, her calm passivity, and her vulnerable innocence, and the enthusiastic response of some of the London critics who had travelled down to Dorchester to see the play had led to talk of its being produced in London with Mrs Bugler in the title role. Hardy told her that he did not quite like the idea of her going away to London: 'We are so proud of you down here that we wish to keep you for ourselves, so that you may be known as the Wessex actress who does not care to go away, & who makes Londoners come to her.' He recognized, however, that she had become seized with ambitions for a London acting career, felt that he had no right to stand in her way, and indeed did whatever he could to arrange for a series of matinée performances of the play to be put on at the Haymarket Theatre the following spring—although he made it clear to Frederick Harrison, the Haymarket manager, that he had also discussed with Lewis Casson the longer-term possibility of a London production with Sybil Thorndike as Tess.[29]

---

* When Mrs Bugler was recovering from the miscarriage which had prevented her from appearing in the 1922 production of *Desperate Remedies,* Hardy sent her a silver vase full of carnations, using one of the other Hardy players as an intermediary in order to avoid publicity.[28]

On 10 January 1925, when Cockerell arrived at Max Gate, he found a heavy cloud over the house as a consequence of Hardy's continuing and apparently increasing infatuation. Cockerell told Florence the next day that, given Hardy's age, she ought to be able to view the situation in a comic light: she replied that she had attempted to do so but that Hardy had spoken to her 'roughly' and shown that she was in the way. The next day was still worse. Florence told Cockerell that she had worried during the night until she thought she would go mad, and she complained bitterly that Hardy showed no consciousness that the date was 12 January, her birthday, but was entirely taken up with discussions with Frederick Harrison and Mrs Bugler about the proposed Haymarket matinées, now regarded as a settled thing.[30]

Rehearsals at the Haymarket were scheduled to begin in April 1925, but at the very beginning of February Florence suddenly appeared at Mrs Bugler's Beaminster home, saying that her husband didn't know she was there and begging Mrs Bugler, for Hardy's sake, to withdraw from the entire scheme. She argued that he would insist on going to London to see the performances, although he was not well enough to do so, that he would go to Mrs Bugler's dressing room, and that the resultant publicity would be bad both for his nerves and his reputation. In order to convey to the astonished Mrs Bugler some sense of the reality and depth of Hardy's infatuation, Florence told her that he had written poems to her, including one in which the two of them were imagined as going off together: 'But I destroyed it,' she added.[31] Shocked by such an assault, aware too that her husband and child would rather she did not go to London, Mrs Bugler wrote to Harrison to withdraw from the agreement she had entered into. Harrison, in his reply, regretted her choice but acknowledged that it was probably a wise one. She also wrote to Hardy, explaining that she could not bear to be parted from her daughter, that her husband was unenthusiastic about her going, and that she had no right to sacrifice their happiness. While he, too, accepted her decision—evidently in the belief that it had been quite freely taken—he also permitted himself a note of genuine regret: 'Although you fancy otherwise, I do not believe that any London actress will represent Tess so nearly as I imagined her as you did.'[32]

Gertrude Bugler never forgave Florence for denying her the chance of appearing in the West End in 1925. When, with Florence's active encouragement, she did at last play Tess in London after Hardy's death, she felt that she was already too old to embark upon a professional career as a romantic actress. Florence certainly emerges unhappily from this entire episode, the one occasion when her emotions ran beyond her control and drove her to interfere injudiciously and even cruelly in someone else's life and career. Clearly, Hardy had been behaving in ways she did not know how to cope with; she did indeed worry for his sake as well as for her own about the gossip which was already rife in Dorset and would have become a national scandal once it found its way into the London press. She may also genuinely have believed that there was more of natural charm than of developed skill in Mrs Bugler's acting, and that she was therefore dissuading her from a course all too likely to end in disappointment. Florence had surrendered to the melancholia induced by her operation, by her anxiety about her marriage, especially as it might be perceived by outsiders, and by the strain—earlier signalled by the onset of headaches and severe nervous disorders—of looking after Hardy when he was himself overwrought. She was also momentarily overwhelmed by a sense not just of her own advancing age but of her lack of precisely those things in which Gertrude Bugler, young and beautiful as she was, appeared so rich: 'Unlike you I have no child to promise future happiness,' she had written to Mrs Bugler in December 1924, 'no career before me—everything seems to lie behind.'[33]

Once Mrs Bugler had withdrawn, Hardy felt free to come to terms with Lewis Casson and Sybil Thorndike. But they wanted changes made which he felt unwilling to permit, and the project was finally taken in hand by a little-known manager, Philip Ridgeway, at the out-of-the-way Barnes Theatre. Hardy was grateful to Ridgeway for energetically attacking obstacles at which so many had faltered in the past, and was therefore prepared to deal generously with him in the matter of royalties and performing rights. Ridgeway, however, persisted in asking for American and colonial rights long before the opening night of the Barnes production, and Hardy was engaged both directly and through Florence in a bewildering correspondence as to just what he might and might not be allowed to have and do. When Ridgeway was searching for a suitable Tess, Hardy had recommended that he consider Gertrude Bugler if no London actress proved suitable. Barrie seems also to have mentioned her, and even after the choice had finally fallen upon Gwen Ffrangçon-Davies, Florence's reawakened fears prompted her to take steps to ensure that there would be no more Hardy plays in Dorchester in the future.[34]

Though Gwen Ffrangçon-Davies was not, as Gertrude Bugler had been, the physical approximation to Hardy's ideal image of Tess, she was a highly intelligent actress, deeply interested in the structure of the play as well as in its production and capable of making sensible suggestions for its improvement. She came down to Max Gate in August with Ridgeway and A. E. Filmer, the producer, to go over details of the play. Filmer, alarmed at the 'theatrical impossibility' of the script as it had been delivered to him, was much relieved when Hardy ('sweetness incarnate, his whole personality emanated gentleness') gave him a free hand to make whatever practical alterations he thought necessary.[35]* In December 1925, after the play had been successfully launched, the whole cast came down to Dorchester to put on a performance in the Max Gate drawing room, Hardy having followed both his doctor's orders and his own inclinations in refusing to go to London to see it—even after it transferred to the Garrick Theatre in the West End. 'That Ridgeway', as Florence now referred to him, persuaded Hardy to accept reduced royalties for a week in order to cover the cost of the Dorchester trip—even though, as she said, it had been undertaken to publicize the play rather than to give Hardy pleasure. Nevertheless, the occasion did please and interest him and even moved him to make another of his little speeches just as his visitors prepared to leave.[37]

Hardy's creative energies found their chief outlet at this period in the compilation, revision, and publication of yet another volume of verse, at first unpromisingly called 'Poems Imaginative & Incidental: with Songs and Trifles', later renamed *Human Shows Far Phantasies Songs and Trifles*—a less commonplace title, as Hardy remarked to Sir Frederick Macmillan, and easier to remember, since it would in practice simply be called *Human Shows*. The manuscript was sent to Macmillan at the end of July 1925, and when the proofs arrived in September Cockerell's assistance with the reading of them was again volunteered and accepted.

* These did not, apparently, involve changing or cutting the text to any significant extent: 'it was a matter of rebuilding (mainly to give each scene an effective curtain) and readjustment of speaking cues.'[36]

Florence had earlier worried that Hardy was no longer in the mood to accept advice as to whether or not a particular poem should be included—having decided that his own judgement about his work was always better than that of others—but he did adopt at least some of the suggestions for detailed changes which Cockerell wrote on the proofs themselves.[38]

Although most of the poems in the volume appeared to have been of recent composition, a substantial number were evidently derived from old notes or drafts which Hardy had come upon while sorting out his papers a few years earlier. The volume as a whole thus gives much the same effect of homogeneous miscellaneity (if one may use such a term) as *Late Lyrics* and indeed all the previous collections. Apart from 'The Absolute Explains' and ' "So, Time" ', there are relatively few poems of a formally 'philosophical' cast, but familiar Hardyan themes are everywhere rehearsed and even the little christening poem for Caroline Hanbury wonders 'what / You think of earth as a dwelling-spot, / And if you'd rather have come, or not?' The dangerous power of sexual attraction, a central element in so many of the novels, is dramatized on several occasions ('At Wynyard's Gap', 'The Turnip-Hoer'), and the cruel consequences of sexual mismatching are confronted with particular directness in 'A Hurried Meeting': ' "Love is a terrible thing: sweet for a space, / And then all mourning, mourning!" '[39] There are again several poems about Emma and St. Juliot, but while only one poem ('In the Street') seems to recall the early days of Hardy's relationship with his second wife, he does at least interrupt a sequence of Emma poems with one addressed to Louisa Harding ('Louie'). A poem later in the volume, 'Known Had I', returns to the 'lost prize' theme of 'Thoughts of Phena' but seems far more likely to pertain to Louisa Harding again, or even Eliza Bright Nicholls, than to Tryphena Sparks. There is even one poem about the death of Horace Moule ('Before My Friend Arrived'), although the over-all mood of this volume remains less persistently retrospective and elegiac than that of its posthumously published successor.

Sensitive to what had become the standard complaint about his sombreness of tone, and anticipating that the new volume would be similarly greeted, Hardy went through the list of contents, as set out in the page proofs, marking each poem with a 'T' (for tragedy), a 'C' (for comedy), an 'L' (for love song), or an 'O' (presumably for 'objective'), and jotted down the results of his calculation on the flyleaf:

Total: 152 poems.
              —of these there are, roughly,
    60—   poems of tragedy, sorrow or grimness
              ⎧ 65 of a reflective dispassionate kind
    92   ⎨ 11 of the nature of comedy
              ⎩ 16 love-songs & pieces, mostly for music
that is
              Tragedy or sadness ⅖ of the whole
              Reflection, love, or comedy ⅗ - - - -[40]

By this time the appearance in the United States of Ernest Brennecke's unauthorized and sometimes offensive biography* had served to turn Hardy's thoughts back once more to the 'Life'. He rejected Maurice Macmillan's proposal of April 1926 that the first part of the typescript be set up in type in anticipation of his death, fearing that knowledge of its existence and its contents would be leaked by the printers, but was prompted to take out that typescript once more and give it another careful revision. 'This may be wise, or the reverse,' Florence wrote to Macmillan. 'However he is greatly interested.'[42] Meanwhile, T. E. Lawrence, now stationed at Cranwell, had read one of the copies when Florence sent it to him in early 1926, and Sassoon had recently had to be admitted into the secret when Harper & Brothers approached him with the suggestion that he write 'the authorized biography'. Florence remained unsure even now as to Hardy's intentions regarding the 'Life', and recommended that one of the Macmillans should come to Max Gate to receive his instructions at first hand. When Daniel Macmillan duly arrived, Hardy made it clear that he was 'not disinclined' to eventual publication of the biography; that July, however, he was still so busy tinkering with the typescript, putting in new notes and then taking most of them out again, that Florence could see no early prospect of completion.[43]

On 31 December 1925 Hardy and Florence sat up late: 'Heard on the wireless various features of N.Y. Eve in London—dancing at Albert Hall, Big Ben striking twelve, singing Auld Lang Syne, G.S. the King, the Marseillaise, hurrahing.' A year later, on 31 December 1926, his notebook read simply: 'New Year's Eve. Did

* Brennecke, calling at Max Gate in November 1923, had been shown the marginal annotations in which Hardy had criticized the biographical 'impertinences' of Hedgcock's book of 1911;[41] if a warning was intended, it was one which Brennecke either mistook or ignored.

not sit up.'[44] While Hardy had certainly not made an invariable practice in earlier years of seeing in the new year, the difference between the beginning and end of 1926 seems significant of a more general decline. He resigned from the board of governors of the Dorchester Grammar School, the last public body in which he had continued to be at all active, in January 1926, and finally assumed his favourite role, as *Later Years* puts it, of the 'man with the watching eye'.*

In June 1926 he sent up to Macmillan some corrections to both the one-volume edition and the Wessex edition of *The Dynasts* with the intention of making them 'exactly alike, never to be touched again', while his eighty-sixth birthday, earlier that same month, was made the occasion of 'He Never Expected Much', a dispassionate retrospect upon a life he saw as having been un-dramatically composed of those 'neutral-tinted haps and such' his childhood had taught him to expect. In November he made what was to prove his last visit to the Bockhampton cottage to arrange for tidying up the garden and further 'secluding' the building itself from public view.[45] And at Christmas both he and Florence were plunged into grief by the death of Wessex, who was finally put to sleep on 27 December after having been ill for some time with a tumour. Wessex was Florence's dog. He had arrived at Max Gate just a few months before her marriage, and while it was Hardy who had spoiled him the most, it was always Florence who had taken responsibility for his misdeeds and protected him against the vengeance of those whom he had insulted or injured. 'Of course he was merely a dog,' she wrote to Cockerell, '& not a good dog always, but *thousands* (actually thousands) of afternoons & evenings I would have been alone but for him, & had always him to speak to. But I mustn't write about him, & I hope no one will ask me about him or mention his name.'[46]

Hardy was now showing his eighty-six years, but husbanding his energies so that he rarely got tired; a hernia was diagnosed in October 1926 but he refused to wear the light truss recommended by his doctor. Scarcely anyone other than Sir Frederick Macmillan now had any influence over her husband, Florence told Cockerell, although he did have confidence in the professional opinions of Dr Henry Head, the neurologist, a friend of some years who was now living near by.[47] Hardy was still busily writing verse—most

---

* The phrase may simply represent Florence's imperfect memory of the line 'Friend with the musing eye' from ' "Men Who March Away" '.

of it promptly burned—and still capable of turning off a little poem like 'The Aged Newspaper Soliloquizes' (in celebration of the 135th birthday of the *Observer*) within two or three days, and of making the revisions which contributed so distinctively to the final versions of 'He Never Expected Much' and other poems in the posthumously published *Winter Words*.[48] He continued to keep a watchful eye on the publication and reprinting of his work, both in prose and in verse, and on the fate of the various dramatizations then in production or contemplation.

He took much interest in the success of the touring version of *Tess,* with Christine Silver in the title role, and he and Florence found themselves further entangled in a proliferating correspondence with Ridgeway, Macmillan, Golding Bright (who was acting as Hardy's dramatic agent), and others about Ridgeway's importunately advanced and grandiosely conceived plans for producing stage versions of all Hardy's novels—Florence taking frequent opportunity to praise certain aspects of Gertrude Bugler's performance as Tess and to suggest that she ought to be considered for other parts. It was, as she said, disinterested advice, since she had no reason to like Mrs Bugler personally. In September 1926, at Hardy's suggestion, she went with Mrs Bugler to see the Barnes Theatre production of John Drinkwater's dramatization of *The Mayor of Casterbridge,* and Hardy was himself able to see it shortly afterwards at a special matinée put on at Weymouth largely for his benefit. The applause for him personally, both inside and outside the theatre, was warm and enthusiastic,[49] and gave him, perhaps for the first time, some tangible sense of how enormous his popular reputation had become—everywhere, that is to say, except in Dorchester itself, which had known him and his family too long to allow itself to be unduly impressed, or its suspicions of his irreligiousness and immorality entirely dispelled.

The Balliol Players came again to Max Gate in June 1926, performing on this occasion a translation of the *Hippolytus* of Euripides. In July Virginia Woolf called with her husband Leonard, subsequently entering in her diary perhaps the most vivid of all the many impressions of Hardy as he was in old age: 'a little puffy cheeked cheerful old man, with an atmosphere cheerful & businesslike in addressing us, rather like an old doctors or solicitors, saying "Well now—" or words like that as he shook hands.' Where so many friends and visitors had registered an extraordinary simplicity in Hardy, Mrs Woolf saw rather a complete assurance, a confident sense of a mind made up on all questions and of a life's work satisfactorily and in any case finally and irreversibly accomplished:

> What impressed me was his freedom, ease & vitality. He seemed very "Great Victorian" doing the whole thing with a sweep of his hand (they are ordinary smallish, curled up hands) & setting no great stock by literature; but immensely interested in facts; incidents; & somehow, one could imagine, naturally swept off into imagining & creating without a thought of its being difficult or remarkable; becoming obsessed; & living in imagination.[50]

Virginia Woolf's characterization of Florence, though a little ungenerous in tone, was no doubt accurate enough in substance: 'She has the large sad lack lustre eyes of a childless woman; great docility & readiness, as if she had learnt her part; not great alacrity, but resignation, in welcoming visitors; wears a sprigged voile dress, black shoes and a necklace.'[51] Florence had been depressed by Wessex's obvious decline and increasingly worried about some pains of her own she had mentioned to Cockerell earlier in the year. She was also becoming worn down by looking after a man who was at once frail and energetic, instinctively reclusive yet capable of being cheerfully gregarious for an hour or two each day. Thoroughly imbued with Hardy's own views of existence—they both, she had told a correspondent in March, felt that consciousness must be a disease which ought not to exist—she lacked his facility for sublimating those views into poetry and hence brooded upon them, and upon her own life, in ways that at once fostered and fed upon the intensity of her natural melancholy.[52]

Siegfried Sassoon, visiting Max Gate in January 1927, found no change in Hardy from a year earlier. Writing to Gosse from the King's Arms—' "the room which Mrs Henniker always used to have" (so T.H. says)'—Sassoon described their friend in 'what is, to me, his most characteristic attitude. Perched on the least *easy* chair, supporting his head with one hand, & gazing downward with a gentle & rather wistful expression. I noticed this evening, —when the half-lit room was dealing gently with his face—the great beauty of his expression.' There were some indications of an increasing weariness—'I think I've had enough of Napoleon!' he confessed to Sassoon on that same occasion—but no obvious slackening either of creative activity or of literary caretaking. In a letter to Sir Frederick Macmillan later that month Hardy spoke humorously of himself as a 'long-seller' rather than a 'best-seller', agreed to the republication of some poems in the pages of a popular magazine on the grounds that it would constitute 'a sort of advertisement', and hinted at the desirability of reprinting *Wessex Poems* complete with its illustrations.[53]

Three weeks later he wrote to propose the publication of a new edition of *Selected Poems* which would incorporate some of the verses published since its first appearance in 1916. By 18 September he had completed the pleasant if slightly worrying task of choosing the additional poems and was able to send off to Sir Frederick Macmillan the printer's copy for the enlarged selection. Although most of the new poems were from the most recent volumes—*Moments of Vision, Late Lyrics, Human Shows,* and *The Queen of Cornwall*—he had also included some songs from *The Dynasts* and gone back to *Wessex Poems* and *Time's Laughingstocks* to pick up 'Hap', 'The Fiddler', and, most strikingly, 'A Trampwoman's Tragedy', which in 1916 had still been judged unsuitable for a volume that might be used in schools. Concerned that Macmillan might think the revised text ran to too many pages, Hardy pointed out that the corresponding volume of Wordsworth contained an even greater number of poems, and that while there were fewer in the Byron volume some of them were 'rather long'. He was not at all anxious about the book's publication, he assured Macmillan, 'but felt it best to make sure you had the corrections in case anything should happen.'[54]

In March 1927 Hardy issued a brief public statement in support of the activities of the League for the Prohibition of Cruel Sports, and drew upon childhood memories in contributing to a pamphlet issued as an appeal for financial contributions to a Fund for the Preservation of Ancient Cottages. In July he made his last major public appearance on the occasion of the laying of the foundation stone of a new building for the Dorchester Grammar School, which was moving from the centre of the town to a new location on the outskirts. The site, not far from Max Gate, was open and windy, just as Max Gate itself had been when it was first built more than forty years before, and the weather on the actual day of the stone-laying proved to be blustery and unseasonably cold. But Hardy led the procession of dignitaries across the muddy field and delivered, in a firm and clearly audible voice, a speech chiefly—and characteristically—devoted to speculative ruminations about his Elizabethan namesake who had been the school's chief founder and benefactor: 'He was without doubt of the family of the Hardys who landed in this county from Jersey in the fifteenth century, acquired small estates along the river upwards towards its source, and whose descendants have mostly remained hereabouts ever since, the Christian name of Thomas having been especially affected by them.' No less characteristic was his endorsement of the choice of the site itself as being 'not so far from the centre of the borough as to be beyond the walking powers of the smallest boy', and as promising to be incomparably healthy, 'with its open surroundings, elevated and bracing situation, and dry subsoil, while it is near enough to the sea to get very distinct whiffs of marine air.'[55] Present here are those still-painful memories of his childhood trudges between Bockhampton and Dorchester, as well as the slightly suspect climatic reasons by which he had so long justified, to himself and to visitors, the otherwise somewhat inconvenient location of Max Gate.

Although Hardy was tired by the Grammar School stone-laying, Florence was able to report, just three days later, that he was working 'tremendously hard'—and that she had therefore had an opportunity to slip away and take her ailing mother, who had come down to Weymouth for a few days, on one or two drives into the Dorsetshire countryside. Outings by car now provided both Hardy and Florence with their principal source of recreation. In May they had been driven over to lunch with the Ilchesters at Melbury House and been offered a tiny puppy as a replacement for Wessex—a gift they decided they could not accept, partly because Hardy had already been presented with a blue Persian cat named Cobweb. On his eighty-seventh birthday they drove into Devonshire to spend the day with the Granville-Barkers at Netherton Hall—and thereby dodge the threatened attentions of an American journalist.[56] In early August the composer Gustav Holst was taken for a drive across the heath to Puddletown Church and there shown the wooden choir gallery in which Hardy's grandfather had sometimes performed,* and at the end of the month Hardy and Florence motored to Bath and back in the one day: Hardy was quite fresh when they got back, Florence told Cockerell, it was *she* who felt tired.[58] In June Hardy received what was to prove a last visit from Sir Edmund Gosse

---

* Just before this visit Hardy had accepted the dedication of Holst's tone poem *Egdon Heath*; he had, however, died by the time the work was published, and the dedication had to be rendered as 'Homage to Thomas Hardy'.[57]

(as he had been since 1925), a friend for more than fifty years; in July Sassoon came, and the Masefields, and the Balliol Players performed again on the Max Gate lawn; September saw a visit from John Galsworthy and his wife, an extended outing to Ilminster and Yeovil, and the acceptance of lunch invitations to Charborough Park and Lulworth Castle. At the end of the month Florence was able to speak of her husband as being 'very well indeed', although occasionally 'rather troubled by strange sensations about his heart'. She hoped these were merely the effects of indigestion, but Hardy—like Emma, she might have interjected —refused to be medically examined.[59]

That autumn Hardy continued active. On 25 October he attended a meeting at the Dorset County Museum summoned to take action to preserve a Roman mosaic pavement recently discovered in Fordington.[60] In November he corrected proofs of the enlarged edition of *Selected Poems,* made a few minor revisions to the text, and suggested that since some people foolishly confused 'Selected' with 'Collected' it might be sensible to change the title to *Chosen Poems of Thomas Hardy.* At the end of November he expressed particular delight at the arrival of copies of the handsome large-paper edition of *The Dynasts:* 'There was great excitement here when they came', he told Sir Frederick Macmillan, '& they are all that I expected. Leslie Stephen used to say that all modern books & newspapers would have perished in 100 years, but I fancy these volumes will hold out. I notice that you have embodied all the latest corrections, & I hope the booksellers will do well with their stock.' Hardy, indeed, retained to the last his old concern for the physical appearance, the textual correctness, and the financial viability of the volumes that bore his name: during the late summer he had even been rereading, and reconsidering, some of his short stories in preparation for a one-volume collected edition proposed by Macmillan, and a note indicating that he would have preferred a less conventionally comfortable ending to 'The Romantic Adventures of a Milkmaid' is dated as late as September 1927.[61]

Hardy had by now stopped making even the most minor additions to the 'Materials' upon which Florence was to draw for the final chapters of the 'Life', and she herself began to keep an intermittent diary, making particular note of those childhood reminiscences which flowed so freely and clearly into Hardy's mind at this period. On 4 November she recorded what were to be his final visits to the churchyard at Stinsford and to his brother and sister at Talbothays. A long entry for Armistice Day, 11 November, recounted how he came down from his study to listen to a broadcast service from Canterbury Cathedral and stood thinking of Frank George during the two minutes' silence. Later that same day, they took what Florence described as their usual 'melancholy little walk' alongside the railway line at the back of Max Gate and watched, as they had done so often before, a trainload of Portland stone being carried away. When they reached home Hardy—moved, perhaps, by some obscure impulse associated with the emotions of the morning—became concerned for the welfare of Florence's chickens and asked the gardener to build a shelter to protect them from the cold. Later still, his thoughts running on the blocks of building stone they had seen, he told Florence that 'if he had his life over again he would prefer to be a small architect in a country town, like Mr. Hicks at Dorchester, to whom he was articled'. A day or two later he had Henry Bastow, his fellow pupil at Hicks's, much upon his mind.[62]

A few days later still, his thoughts returning to the question of ambitions and their realization, he declared that 'he had done all that he meant to do, but he did not know whether it had been worth doing', adding that his one literary ambition had been to 'have some poem or poems in a good anthology like the Golden Treasury'. His mood, clearly, was that of 'He Resolves to Say No More', the poem which was to stand at the end of his final volume:

> Why load men's minds with more to bear
> That bear already ails to spare?
> From now alway
> Till my last day
> What I discern I will not say.

And yet Florence Hardy was to insist after her husband's death that the poem could not be regarded as his final statement, and that he had in fact experienced a great outburst of creativity late in 1927 and felt that he could have gone on writing almost indefinitely.[63]

The usual period of combined mourning for Mary and Emma at the end of November was marked—pathetically, as it seemed to Florence—by Hardy's wearing 'a very shabby little black felt hat' and carrying a black walking stick.[64] But he kept up his work on the revision of the poems to be included in *Winter Words,* the volume he was planning to publish on his ninetieth birthday. Although shorter than most of its predecessors, it was in every way comparable to them in its range of theme, subject matter, and technique. Whether or not Hardy had deliberately withheld until this moment such intensely personal poems as 'Standing by the Mantelpiece', specifically associated with Horace Moule, it is impossible to say, but it is certainly remarkable that so many phases of his life are reflected in this final volume—with its poems about Higher Bockhampton ('Childhood Among the Ferns', 'Yuletide in a Younger World'), Louisa Harding ('To Louisa in the Lane'), Eliza Bright Nicholls ('The Musing Maiden'), the winter he and Emma spent at Swanage ('The Lodging-House Fuchsias'), and an unidentified woman to whom he had briefly been attracted in the 1880s ('A Countenance'). His friendship with Lady Grove, who had died in 1926, is movingly commemorated in 'Concerning Agnes'; Wessex, already memorialized in stone in the pets' cemetery ('The / Famous Dog / Wessex / Aug. 1913–27 Dec. 1926. / Faithful, Unflinching.'),[65] receives a poetic tribute in 'Dead "Wessex" the Dog to the Household'; and there are other poems apparently based upon episodes from Hardy's own life and from his family's past history (notably 'A Mound' and 'Family Portraits') whose precise bearing seems irrecoverable. Though the poems he was gathering together originated in almost every stage of Hardy's poetic career from the 1860s onward, several of them were of recent date: it was at teatime on 27 November 1927, the anniversary of Emma's death, that he first showed Florence the manuscript of 'An Unkindly May',[66]* a poem expressive of that intense and even excessive compassion for all living things which had caused Hardy such anguish throughout his life and prompted his concern for the Max Gate chickens just two weeks before.

On 1 December Florence told Cockerell that she expected to be approached with the suggestion that H. M. Tomlinson be permitted to write a biography of her husband: 'Of course there is only one reply.' Hardy himself, she reported in the same letter, was 'very well, . . . exceedingly cheerful & busy. Not a cloud in the sky.' Five days later she reported that Hardy had felt tired and kept indoors all day, which was 'rather unusual with him'. He seemed well and cheerful nevertheless, had delighted in a visit

* Though the date '(1877)' in the manuscript suggests that the poem may have been revised from an earlier draft, or worked up from an earlier note.[67]

from Dorothy Allhusen two days previously ('She & T.H. were talking of old times, of the pranks she used to play when she was a child, & he stayed with her mother'), and was looking forward to a visit from Sassoon the following day. On 8 December Hardy was again not feeling quite himself, but he was alert enough to comment that Sassoon's friend Stephen Tennant was the only person he had ever known with a walk like Swinburne's, and Florence felt justified in assuring Cockerell that there was nothing seriously amiss.[68]

When Hardy went to his study the morning of 11 December, however, he found himself, for the first time in his life, quite unable to work; he took to his bed thereafter, spending just a few hours downstairs each day, and by the middle of the month Florence was obliged to tell Gosse that Hardy had tired himself by talking too long and energetically (to a representative of Harper & Brothers) on 10 December and that his heart had been affected in consequence, although the doctor expected that a day or two's rest would set all to rights. Four days later Hardy was still in bed and seemed very weak; he was said to have a chill, but his entire system was beginning to wear out and Florence found that he could no longer follow her when she read aloud—although she did subsequently read him some poems he asked to hear, among them de la Mare's 'The Listeners' and Browning's 'Rabbi Ben Ezra'.[69] There was a great panic to dispatch the text of his poem 'Christmas in the Elgin Room' in time for its publication in *The Times* on 24 December 1927, and when Gosse sent an immediate note of praise and appreciation Hardy roused himself sufficiently on Christmas Day itself to scribble a pencilled note of thanks and even to summon up a flash of that humour which had so consistently marked their correspondence over the years: 'I am in bed on my back, living on butter-broth & beef tea, the servants being much concerned over my not being able to eat any Christmas pudding, though I am rather relieved.'[70]

On 30 December Florence reported to Cockerell that Hardy was about the same. The doctor remained worried about his heart, but his having lunched that day on pheasant and champagne seemed an encouraging sign. She was doing all the nursing herself at present, she added, and it was perhaps a good thing that Henry and Kate had not offered to come. In the early days of 1928 Hardy's condition steadily worsened, and his exhaustion, both physical and mental, became so pronounced that the local practitioner, Dr E. W. Mann, summoned in Dr E. How White, a specialist from Bournemouth, for an urgent consultation. Dr White's opinion that Hardy's organs were all sound and his arteries those of a much younger man gave rise to temporary optimism, but the patient's strength did not return, the long period in a recumbent position produced fluid at the base of the lungs and the fear of hypostatic pneumonia, and by 8 January his condition had become critical.[71] On 9 January Florence, who had already enlisted her sister Eva's nursing expertise, summoned Cockerell by telegram to Max Gate, although neither he nor any-one other than Florence, Eva, Henry, and Kate was allowed into the sickroom. Cockerell arranged for a professional nurse to re-lieve Florence and Eva of some of their burden, but Hardy refused to have her in the room and Florence—remembering her husband's old fear of doctors and operations—said that it would kill him at once.[72]

On 10 January Sir James Barrie arrived, taking a room at a hotel in the town, and Hardy showed some signs of rallying, to the point of signing—in a hand of scarcely impaired firmness—a cheque for his annual subscription to the Pension Fund of the Incorporated Society of Authors, of which he was still president. On the 11th he took delight in the arrival of a huge bunch of grapes, a present from Newman Flower of Cassells, and asked for a rasher of bacon to be grilled for him in front of the open fire in his bedroom, as bacon had been cooked in his mother's time.[73] A touch of his mother also asserted itself that afternoon in the tough unforgivingness which impelled him to dictate brief bitter epitaphs on two men, George Moore and G. K. Chesterton, whose personal remarks about him had given lasting offence. 'Heap dustbins on him,' he wrote of Moore: 'They'll not meet / The apex of his self conceit.'[74]

When Kate called at Max Gate that day she found the pre-vailing mood of optimism difficult to share: 'I saw Tom,' she wrote in her diary, 'but I am afraid he is not going to be here long. He looks like father & altogether I cannot blind myself to what is coming.' At 8.15 that evening she telephoned from Tal-bothays to see how things stood and was again given an encourag-ing report. About that same time Dr Mann made one of his regular calls; Hardy chatted cheerfully about ways of celebrating his recovery and mentioned that he had been reading J. B. S. Haldane's recently published *Possible Worlds,* but found it too deep.[75] Shortly afterwards, however, his mind began to wander. Eva Dugdale heard him mutter some remarks about herself—'She is such a little person yet she has seen such big operations'—and speak the word 'blood'. Just before nine o'clock, as she was taking his pulse, he cried, 'Eva, what is this?'* As she held his hand to reassure and support him, his grip weakened and death came.[77]

* Eva Dugdale's memory of Hardy's last words is precisely confirmed by Nellie Titterington, the maid, who was sitting in the dressing room leading off from Hardy's bedroom. Just before the end, according to a passage deleted from the published text of *Later Years,* 'a few broken sentences, one of them heartrending in its poignancy, showed that his mind had reverted to a sorrow of the past';[76] Florence was apparently downstairs at the moment of death, however, and it is not clear that any such sentences were ever spoken.

28

AFTERWARDS

D R MANN rushed back to his patient,* but nothing could now
be done beyond certifying the cause of death as 'cardiac
syncope', contributed to by old age. A telephone call to Talbothays
received no reply, either because Kate and Henry did not hear the
bell or because, reassured by their 8.15 call, they saw no reason to
depart from their usual custom of not answering calls after they
had gone to bed. Eva washed the body and prepared it for burial
without the aid of an undertaker. She had also to remove a light
growth of beard, Hardy not having been shaved since he had
stopped shaving himself just a few days earlier. The following
morning, 12 January, Cockerell was at last admitted to the bedroom and assisted Eva in fitting Hardy's scarlet doctoral robe over
his white nightshirt.[2] Just before eight o'clock Nellie Titterington
arrived at Talbothays with the news. Henry and Kate went
straight to Max Gate and found their brother wearing 'the same
triumphant look on his face that all the others bore—but without
the smile'. Also admitted to the death chamber was an Irish
Catholic priest, Father James O'Rourke, who had visited Max

* According to Dr Mann's own account, he was still in the house when a
sudden shout called him back upstairs. Nellie Titterington's recollection is
that she herself summoned him by telephone, upon Eva Dugdale's instructions.[1]

Gate a few months earlier and now urged his request to see Hardy's body with such earnestness and gentleness that Florence felt she could not deny it.[3]

Once Hardy was dead Cockerell and Barrie began to assert their male authority over what Cockerell (in a letter to his wife) had already referred to as 'the housefull of women' and to advance what they represented—and doubtless believed—to be the claims of the world of letters and of the nation as a whole. Though Florence was consulted, she was too tired and distressed to be able to resist their arguments. Cockerell, who already knew that he had been named as literary executor, opened Hardy's will the night of his death and persuaded himself that the instructions relating to funeral arrangements did not absolutely direct that interment should take place in Stinsford churchyard, even though Hardy's parents and grandparents were buried there and his first wife was already lying beneath the tombstone he had designed to accommodate his own name as well.[4] Barrie, who had left Dorchester on the 10th, consulted with Cockerell by telephone, and by the time Henry and Kate arrived to view the body the decision to request interment in Westminster Abbey had already been made, and Barrie, in London, was busily marshalling the support of Stanley Baldwin, the Prime Minister, and Geoffrey Dawson, editor of *The Times,* in order to secure for Hardy a privilege that had been denied to Swinburne and Meredith and to other distinguished agnostics—in fact, no novelist had been buried there since Dickens in 1870, no poet since Tennyson in 1892. Henry and Kate, with their strong sense of local and family pieties, were stunned by the news, and they received two more shocks the following day when they learned not only that their brother would have to be cremated and his ashes placed in the Abbey but also that his heart would be removed before cremation and given a separate burial at Stinsford.[5]* A distressed Kate wrote in her diary that it was only by accident that she and Henry called at Max Gate on the 13th and saw Hardy's body for the second and last time.[7]

Formal permission for an Abbey burial had been received from the Dean of Westminster, Dr Foxley Norris, during the afternoon of the 12th, and that evening Dr Mann returned to Max Gate in company with his partner, Dr F. L. Nash-Wortham, in order to

* The idea of the heart burial seems to have originated with the vicar of Stinsford, the Revd H. G. B. Cowley, as a response to local disappointment at the news of the Abbey interment.[6]

remove Hardy's heart—the operation itself being performed by Nash-Wortham, who was a surgeon, and not by Mann himself. Once removed, the heart was wrapped in a small towel and placed in a biscuit tin. The tin was then carefully sealed and taken away by Dr Mann, to be brought back to Max Gate the next day (the 13th) and placed in the burial casket, which was itself immediately sealed.[8]*

At eight o'clock in the morning of the 13th (a Friday) Hardy's body was driven away from Max Gate on its way to the crematorium at Brookwood, near Woking. Barrie and Cockerell accompanied the coffin, oversaw the cremation, and subsequently delivered the urn containing the ashes to the Westminster Abbey authorities. Although the hour of departure was early, reporters and photographers from the national press were on hand outside Max Gate to record the occasion and make their contribution to the development of the week's major news story. The first word of Hardy's death had been greeted everywhere with editorials, obituaries, photographs, and feature articles, and the note sounded in the opening sentence of *The Times*'s two-column obituary on 12 January—that English literature had been deprived of 'its most eminent figure'—was echoed and enlarged upon not only in the British press but in newspapers around the world.[10]

The Westminster Abbey service on the Monday, 16 January, was a national event. Although no member of the royal family was present—both the King and the Prince of Wales having sent aides to represent them—the names of the pall-bearers were sufficiently eloquent of Hardy's standing. The list was headed by the Prime Minister and the leader of the opposition (Ramsay MacDonald); it included the heads of the two colleges (Magdalene, Cambridge, and Queen's, Oxford) of which Hardy was an Honorary Fellow; and it was completed by six of the most eminent literary figures of the day—Sir James Barrie, John Galsworthy, Sir Edmund Gosse, A. E. Housman, Rudyard Kipling, and George Bernard Shaw. The reserved seats in the Abbey were largely occupied by people with famous names, among them Arnold Bennett, John Masefield, Sir Arthur Pinero, Arthur Symons, John Burns, Jane Harrison, Gwen Ffrangçon-Davies, Walter de la Mare, Leonard and Virginia Woolf, and the members of the Macmillan

---

* Meanwhile a curious kind of authenticity had been bestowed upon these somewhat macabre proceedings by the arrival in the post of an article on medieval heart burials, off-printed from the current volume of the Field Club's published *Proceedings*.[9]

firm, which had been responsible for organizing the occasion. The seats available to the public were all filled long before the service began and outside in the pouring rain large crowds waited for the opportunity to file past the open grave in Poets' Corner.[11]

Florence and Kate, escorted by Cockerell, were the chief mourners at the Abbey service. Henry, who had been in poor health, was representing the family at the heart burial being held simultaneously at Stinsford, where the crowd was smaller, the formalities fewer, and the weather kinder. Kate, who felt numbed by the dismal trip to London and back and by the Abbey service itself, noted in her diary that at Stinsford, by contrast, 'the good sun shone & the birds sang & everything was done simply, affectionately & well.'[12]* A third event taking place at that same time was the memorial service at St. Peter's Church, Dorchester, at which Dorchester paid its own formal respects to the man who had made it famous. In accordance with the request of the Mayor, the local shops were closed that Monday afternoon for the one-hour duration of the three simultaneous services.[14]

'I regret Hardy's funeral service,' wrote T. E. Lawrence to William Rothenstein from Karachi. 'So little of it suited the old man's nature. He would have smiled, tolerantly, at it all: but I grow indignant for him, knowing that these sleek Deans and Canons were acting a lie behind his name. Hardy was too great to be suffered as an enemy of their faith: so he must be redeemed.' Edward Clodd found 'very repellent' the compromise that had resulted in the division of Hardy's remains.[15] At the same time, as commentators at the time perceived, and as Florence's friends repeatedly assured her, there was a certain appropriateness in the double or, more properly, divided funeral, in that it permitted her husband's heart to find its proper resting place in Wessex even while his ashes had been, as it were, claimed by the nation. A man like Hardy, Bernard Shaw told her, did not belong entirely to himself, nor would he have begrudged the people the performance at the Abbey any more than he had resented receiving American pilgrims at Max Gate. She herself wrote to Sir Owen Seaman, editor of *Punch,* to express her appreciation of the brief stanza of his own which he had put into the issue of 18 January 1928:

---

* Even the Stinsford service, however, was not without its ironies. Gertrude Bugler, who was there, was distressed by the presence of some people in hunting pink.[13]

The Nation's Temple claims her noblest Dead,
So to its care his ashes we confide,
But where his heart would choose a lowlier bed
There lay it, in his own loved countryside.[16]

She was none the less deeply and painfully aware that in yielding
to the pressures exerted by Barrie and Cockerell she had given
countenance to a situation whose proliferating grotesqueries re-
sembled one of Hardy's own most melancholic exercises in prose
and verse—a satire of circumstance indeed, one of time's laughingstocks, an outrageous instance of life's little ironies. As time
passed, she came to feel more and more strongly that the decision
had been a terrible mistake, but told herself that she had been
under such stress as to be scarcely responsible for her own actions.[17]

Florence was made a wealthy woman under the terms of
Hardy's will—which gave her possession of Max Gate and the income from all her husband's publications—and she was able to
enjoy a number of luxuries which had previously been denied
her, either by her husband or by simple circumstance. She bought
herself a car and hired a chauffeur, and sought to avoid the terrors
of winter at Max Gate by taking a London apartment—in Adelphi
Terrace, where her husband had worked for Blomfield in the
1860s and where Barrie now lived. But she had little opportunity
for personal happiness. Long haunted by ill health, she had probably foreseen the death from cancer which overtook her nine years
later. Burdened, too, by an overwhelming sense of obligation to
her husband's memory, she devoted much of her time to her duties
at literary executor—especially after a series of violent quarrels
with Cockerell had led to an almost complete break in communications between them—and to the defence, as she understood it, of
Hardy's reputation.

In 1928 she saw through the press with great and, one would
have thought, suspicious promptitude *The Early Life of Thomas
Hardy,* the first part of the official biography published under
her name. The second volume, which came out in 1930, required
much more work, especially since the last four chapters, covering
the period since 1918, had to be written from scratch on the basis
of the documents which Hardy had accumulated to just such an
end. Undertaken by Hardy chiefly as a means of deflecting the
unwelcome attentions of would-be biographers, the official 'Life'
became for Florence yet another worrying responsibility. Although
its publication can be said to have given her a somewhat spurious

literary reputation of her own, she always insisted upon the enormous assistance her husband had given her—even while loyalty
to Hardy's memory and to his passionate desire for secrecy made
it impossible for her to reveal the exact circumstances in which
the work was written.

Florence Hardy died in 1937, her last surviving sister in 1979.
Henry Hardy's death occurred within twelve months of his famous
brother's, leaving Kate to live on alone at Talbothays until her
own death in October 1940—long enough to share in the celebration of Hardy's centenary in the dark days of Dunkirk. With her
departure the line of the Bockhampton Hardys came abruptly to
an end. Only Hardy's own reputation, his unique standing as both
a major novelist and a major poet, has continued to strengthen
and develop, assuring into all foreseeable futures an affirmative
answer to the questions he himself so diffidently posed:

> When the Present has latched its postern behind my tremulous
>   stay,
>   And the May month flaps its glad green leaves like wings,
> Delicate-filmed as new-spun silk, will the neighbours say,
>   'He was a man who used to notice such things'?
>
> If it be in the dusk when, like an eyelid's soundless blink,
>   The dewfall-hawk comes crossing the shades to alight
> Upon the wind-warped upland thorn, a gazer may think,
>   'To him this must have been a familiar sight.'
>
> If I pass some nocturnal blackness, mothy and warm,
>   When the hedgehog travels furtively over the lawn,
> One may say, 'He strove that such innocent creatures should
>   come to no harm,
>   But he could do little for them; and now he is gone.'
>
> If, when hearing that I have been stilled at last, they stand at
>   the door,
>   Watching the full-starred heavens that winter sees,
> Will this thought rise on those who will meet my face no more,
>   'He was one who had an eye for such mysteries'?
>
> And will any say when my bell of quittance is heard in the gloom,
>   And a crossing breeze cuts a pause in its outrollings,
> Till they rise again, as they were a new bell's boom,
>   'He hears it not now, but used to notice such things'?[18]

ACKNOWLEDGEMENTS
FOR SOURCE MATERIALS

Thanks are due to the following institutions which have allowed me to see
and use Hardy letters and other materials, and to those members of their
staffs who have given me assistance and advice: Aberdeen University; Archi-
tectural Association; Albert A. and Henry W. Berg Collection, New York
Public Library; Berkshire Record Office; University of Birmingham; Bodleian
Library; Boston Public Library; Bowdoin College; University of British
Columbia; British Library; Brooks School; State University of New York at
Buffalo; University of California, Berkeley; University of California, Los
Angeles; University of California, Riverside; Cambridge University Library;
W. & R. Chambers, Ltd.; Claremont Colleges, Honnold Library; Claybury
Hospital; Colby College; Columbia University; Cornwall County Record
Office; Dorset County Library; Dorset County Museum; Dorset County Record
Office; Eton College, School Library; Fawcett Library; Fitzwilliam Museum;
Harvard University, Houghton Library; Hatfield House; Huntington Library;
King's College, Cambridge; King's College, London; University of Leeds,
Brotherton Library; Library of Congress; Magdalene College, Cambridge;
Manchester Public Libraries; Marlborough College; Miami University of
Ohio (the Hoffman papers); National Library of Scotland; New York Public
Library, Manuscripts and Archives Division; New York University, Fales
Library; University of Pennsylvania; Pierpont Morgan Library; Princeton
University Library; Public Record Office, London; Queen's College, Oxford;
Society for the Protection of Ancient Buildings; Signet Library, Edinburgh;
University of Texas at Austin, Humanities Research Center; University of
Toronto, Robarts Library; Victoria and Albert Museum; Westminster Public
Libraries; West Sussex Record Office; Wiltshire Record Office; Yale University,
Beinecke Library.

I am particularly grateful to the many collectors and private owners who
so kindly permitted me to see and use manuscript materials in their possession:
Mr Frederick B. Adams, Mr Seymour Adelman, Miss Gertrude S. Antell, Mr
John Antell, Mrs Celia Barclay, Dr C. J. P. Beatty, Mrs Gertrude Bugler, Mr
Alan Clodd, Mr Gregory Stevens Cox, Mr James Stevens Cox, Mr Robert S.
Darby, Mr David J. Dickinson, Dr James Gibson, Professor Henry Gifford,
Mr Peter Goodden, Mr R. E. Greenland, Major R. G. Gregory, Miss Vanessa
Hinton, Mr David Holmes, Mr Ian Kennedy, Miss Imogen Holst, Mrs H. O.
Lock, Mr Henry Lock, Mr Roger Lonsdale, Mrs Michael MacCarthy, Mrs
Elfrida Manning, the Revd G. R. K. Moule, Mr Richard L. Purdy, Miss F. F.
Quiller-Couch, Mr Gordon N. Ray, Miss Pamela Richardson, Mme Romain
Rolland, Mr Robert H. Taylor, and Mr Edwin Thorne.

ABBREVIATIONS

TH	Thomas Hardy	MH	Mary Hardy
ELH	Emma Lavinia Hardy (née Gifford)	KH	Katharine (Kate) Hardy
FEH	Florence Emily Hardy (née Dugdale)	SCC	Sydney Carlyle Cockerell

Principal sources of unpublished material:

Adams	Collection of Mr Frederick B. Adams
Barclay	Collection of Mrs Celia Barclay
Berg	Berg Collection, New York Public Library
BL	British Library
Colby	Colby College, Waterville, Maine
DCM	Dorset County Museum
DCRO	Dorset County Record Office
HP	Research materials gathered by the late Professor Harold Hoffman (Miami University of Ohio)
Lock	Collection of Mr Henry Lock (Dorset County Library)
NLS	National Library of Scotland
RLP	Richard Little Purdy, including private collection
Taylor	Collection of Mr Robert H. Taylor, Princeton, New Jersey
Texas	University of Texas at Austin, Humanities Research Center
WRO	Wiltshire Record Office
NS (Barclay)	Nathaniel Sparks, Jun.'s notes and biographical materials, now in the collection of Mrs Celia Barclay
RLP/FEH	Richard Little Purdy's notes on conversations with Florence Emily Hardy, 1929–36, now in his private collection
SCC/TH (RLP)	Sydney Carlyle Cockerell's notes on conversations with Hardy, now in the collection of Richard Little Purdy

Published sources frequently cited:

Bailey	J. O. Bailey, *The Poetry of Thomas Hardy: A Handbook and Commentary* (Chapel Hill, N.C., 1970)
Career	Michael Millgate, *Thomas Hardy: His Career as a Novelist* (London, 1971)
CL	*The Collected Letters of Thomas Hardy,* ed. Richard Little Purdy and Michael Millgate (Oxford, 1978–), vols. I and II

CP	*The Complete Poems of Thomas Hardy,* ed. James Gibson (London, 1976)
DCC	*Dorset County Chronicle*
EL	Florence Emily Hardy, *The Early Life of Thomas Hardy 1840–1891* (London, 1928)
Friends	*Friends of a Lifetime: Letters to Sydney Carlyle Cockerell,* ed. Viola Meynell (London, 1940)
LN	*The Literary Notes of Thomas Hardy,* ed. Lennart A. Björk, vol. I (Göteborg, 1974); original documents in DCM
LY	Florence Emily Hardy, *The Later Years of Thomas Hardy 1892–1928* (London, 1930)
ORFW	*One Rare Fair Woman: Thomas Hardy's Letters to Florence Henniker 1893–1922,* ed. Evelyn Hardy and F. B. Pinion (London, 1972); original letters in DCM
PN	*The Personal Notebooks of Thomas Hardy,* ed. Richard H. Taylor (London, 1978); original documents in DCM
Purdy	Richard Little Purdy, *Thomas Hardy: A Bibliographical Study* (London, 1954; repr. 1968, 1978)
PW	*Thomas Hardy's Personal Writings,* ed. Harold Orel (Lawrence, Kansas, 1969)
Weber, *Lady*	Carl J. Weber, *Hardy and the Lady from Madison Square* (1952; repr. Port Washington, N.Y., 1973)
Wessex edn.	Wessex Edition, 24 vols. (London, 1912–31)

Other sources referred to by short forms (e.g., Leeds) are listed in full in the Acknowledgements above. Unless otherwise indicated, all quotations of Hardy's verse are from *CP,* and all quotations of his fiction from the prose volumes of the Wessex Edition. Quotations from MSS follow the reading of the original document, even when a different reading appears in a printed text cited as a source. Interviews are by the author unless otherwise stated.

REFERENCES

1 HARDYS AND HANDS

[1] *EL*, 5–6; TH's copy of the 3rd edn. of Hutchins (4 vols., Westminster, 1861–73) is in DCM.
[2] SCC/TH, 3 July 1916 (RLP).
[3] TH to C. Kegan Paul, 18 April 1881 (*CL*, 1.89).
[4] NS (Barclay), citing a remark of KH's.
[5] TH to Lady Gregory, 24 July 1909 (Major Gregory); *EL*, 27; Gertrude Bugler (citing her mother), interview, 1974.
[6] 'Memoranda II' notebook (*PN*, 43–5); *EL*, 10.
[7] 'Memoranda I' notebook (*PN*, 8–9).
[8] Court Rolls of the Manor of Bockhampton (DCRO).
[9] *DCC*, 18 April 1833.
[10] Copy of lease, DCM; copy of will, Lock.
[11] *EL*, 15–16; accounts submitted to William Morton Pitt (Lock).
[12] *EL*, 16; Stinsford churchwardens' accounts (DCRO); NS (Barclay); will, DCM.
[13] TH to F. Henniker, 29 Nov 1896 (*CL*, II.139).
[14] TH to C. K. Shorter, 17 Jan 1910 (Taylor); cf. *EL*, 7.
[15] Hermann Lea, Hoffman interview, 1939 (HP); a printed genealogy of the Childs family is in DCM.
[16] Copy of entry in marriage register of St. James's Church, Poole, Dorset (Lock); *EL*, 8–9.
[17] RLP/FEH, 1936; Melbury Osmond records (DCRO and Melbury Osmond Church).
[18] *Tess*, 118–20; RLP/FEH, 1936.
[19] R. Gittings, *Young Thomas Hardy* (London, 1975), 8, cf. *EL*, 9; Betty Hand to Mary Hand, 17 Jan 1842 (Lock).
[20] 'Notes on Thomas Hardy's Life' (DCM).
[21] *EL*, 11, and *LY*, 12–13.
[22] *EL*, 10–15, 127.
[23] *EL*, 14; *Return of the Native*, 53–4; *The Reminiscences of Lady Dorothy Nevill*, ed. R. Nevill (London, 1906), 31.
[24] *EL*, 15, and E. Inglis to her sister, 30 May 1916 (DCM); Stinsford Vestry Minutes, 16 June 1843 (DCRO).
[25] *CP*, 252.
[26] NS (Barclay); *LY*, 10.
[27] NS (Barclay).
[28] 'Notes on TH's Life' (DCM).
[29] *EL*, 3.
[30] SCC, letter to *The Times*, 18 Oct 1932; SCC/TH, 23 Aug 1926 (RLP); TH to SCC, 29 Nov 1913 (Berg).
[31] *EL*, 18, inserted in red ink in 'Life' TS, fo. 17 (DCM), cf. *EL*, 20; *LY*, 73; FEH to SCC, 5 Oct 1925 (RLP).
[32] *CP*, 169; W. Blunt, *Cockerell* (London, 1964), 212; NS (Barclay).
[33] Betty Hand to Mary Hand, 17 Jan 1842 (Lock).

34 RLP/FEH, 1936; D. J. Winslow, 'A Call on Thomas Hardy's Sister', *Thomas Hardy Year Book 1970*, 95.
35 *EL*, 18; MH note, in Anon., *Cries of London* (DCM); SCC/TH, 3 July 1916 (RLP).
36 MH to J. Sparks, 13 Dec 1904 (Barclay); FEH to E. Clodd, Wednesday [24 Nov 1915] (Leeds).
37 K. M. Swatridge to H. Hoffman, 29 Oct 1939 (HP).
38 *CP*, 689, 490.
39 Cf. R. Gittings, *The Older Hardy* (London, 1978), 56–7; St. Mary's, Reading, parish records, and Chievely parish records (Berkshire Record Office).
40 *EL*, 14; and see J. Sparks, 'Piddletown Volunteer Broadside', *Somerset & Dorset Notes & Queries*, 1930, 58–60; *CP*, 4; *Two on a Tower*, 14.
41 *CP*, 275.
42 TH's copy of Hullah's *The Song Book* (London, 1866) is in DCM.
43 KH, Hoffman interview, 1939 (HP).
44 *EL*, 27, 16.
45 John Antell, interview, 1971; *Daily Chronicle*, 15 Nov 1911 7.
46 SCC/TH, 25 June 1920 (RLP); *EL*, 17.
47 *EL*, 27, and 'Life' TS, fo. 28 (DCM); RLP/FEH, 1936; NS (Barclay).
48 Mrs Belloc Lowndes, *The Merry Wives of Westminster* (London, 1946), 148.
49 *Tess*, 503; Desmond MacCarthy, Hoffman interview, 1939 (HP).
50 SCC note in copy of *The Return of the Native* (Adams), and RLP/FEH, 1936; *Return of the Native*, 44; *LY*, 258; A. L. Lloyd, *Folk Song in England* (London, 1967), 28.
51 TH to W. Blackwood, 29 Feb 1892 (*CL*, I.259); 'Memoranda I' notebook (*PN*, 6–7); *Jude*, 407.
52 RLP/FEH, 1933.
53 FEH to R. Owen, 30 Dec 1915 (Colby); *EL*, 26; FEH to SCC, 24 Oct 1917 (RLP).
54 *Jude*, 15; *EL*, 19–20.
55 SCC note in copy of *The Return*

of the Native (Adams); *CP*, 169; *Return of the Native*, 223.
56 *EL*, 42; cf. *LY*, 179.

2 BOCKHAMPTON

1 E. A. Last, *Thomas Hardy's Neighbours* (St. Peter Port, Guernsey, 1969), 189; TH note (DCM); TH drawing (DCM); note, D. Morrison, *Exhibition of Hardy's Drawings & Paintings* (Dorchester, 1968), 4; Purdy, 140.
2 Policy, DCM.
3 *EL*, 19.
4 Kingston Maurward estate papers (Berkshire Record Office).
5 FEH to R. Owen, 30 Dec 1915 (Colby).
6 Letter, *Journal of the English Folk Dance Society*, 1927, 53–4.
7 TH marginal annotation in F. A. Hedgcock, *Thomas Hardy: penseur et artiste* (Paris, 1911), quoted *Career*, 211; *CL*, I.2; NS (Barclay), cf. Gittings, *Older Hardy*, 16; TH to E. Gosse, 26 Oct 1888 (*CL*, I.181).
8 See, e.g., the poem 'Shortening Days at the Homestead'; *CP*, 810.
9 Letters, Lock.
10 KH's diary, 1915–30, Lock.
11 *CP*, 110; *Woodlanders*, 146.
12 *Jude*, 274–5.
13 Drawing, Lock.
14 *Career*, 342–4; Penley, RLP.
15 W. Archer, *Real Conversations* (London, 1904), 32.
16 Murray's *Handbook for Travellers in Wiltshire, Dorsetshire, and Somersetshire* (London, 1856), 84.
17 N. Flower, *Just As It Happened* (London, 1950), 92, cf. TH to W. Rothenstein, 11 Mar 1912 (Harvard). For the principal sources of this paragraph and the next see B. Kerr, *Bound to the Soil: A Social History of Dorset 1750–1918* (London, 1968), and *Career*, esp. 98–102, 206–20, and notes.
18 C. Kegan Paul, 'The Condition of the Agricultural Labourer', *Theological Review*, January 1868, 112.

19 H. Rider Haggard, *Rural England* (2 vols., London, 1902), I.282 (revised text in *LY*, 93); cf. TH to W. Rothenstein, 11 Mar 1912 (Harvard); *LY*, 194.

20 *Mayor of Casterbridge*, 293; Fordington census returns, 1841.

21 *LY*, 200; Betty Hand to Mary Hand, 17 Jan 1842 (Lock); NS (Barclay); John Antell, interview, 1972.

22 'Poetical Matter' notebook (photocopy, RLP).

23 *Greenwood Tree*, x.

24 TH to F. Harrison, 20 June 1918 (Taylor); Archer, *Real Conversations*, 33–6; *EL*, 27.

25 TH to W. H. Rideing, 13 Dec 1886 (*CL*, I.158); *CP*, 206.

26 RLP/FEH, 1933; *Tess*, 23; 'Memoranda I' notebook (*PN*, 12).

27 H. Child, 'Thomas Hardy', *Bookman*, June 1920, 102; SCC note in his copy of *The Return of the Native* (Adams); cf. J. McCabe, *Edward Clodd: A Memoir* (London, 1932), 109.

28 *EL*, 18–19; *LY*, 263 (cf. *EL*, 27: 'accordion'); *EL*, 28, 29–30; C. Lacey, *Memories of Thomas Hardy as a Schoolboy* (St. Peter Port, Guernsey, 1968), 105.

29 TH to SCC, 14 Apr 1923 (*Friends*, 292).

30 *Tess*, 24.

31 Archer, *Real Conversations*, 37.

32 TH to R. Garnett, 8 Sept 1901 (*CL*, II.298); *EL*, 19.

33 RLP/FEH, 1929.

34 RLP/FEH, 1933; D. Maxwell, *The Landscape of Thomas Hardy* (London, 1928), 17–18; *EL*, 32–3; G. H. Moule, *Stinsford Church and Parish* (Dorchester, 1940), 27–8; *LY*, 176.

35 *EL*, 17.

36 *Book Monthly*, May 1904, 524–6; F. B. Fisher, in C. M. Fisher, *Life in Thomas Hardy's Dorchester 1888–1908* (Beaminster, Dorset, 1965), 21.

37 See Chap. 3, 61, and n. 38; book, DCM; *EL*, 18.

38 TH note on anonymous MS, 'Thomas Hardy' (RLP); TH to Lord Lytton, 15 July 1891 (*CL*, I.240); G. Elton to TH, 13 Sept 1927 (DCM); TH to J. W. Mackail, 24 Dec 1924 (Yale).

39 John Antell, interview, 1976; both books in DCM.

40 Gifford's *History* RLP, *Companion* and *Psalter* Lock, remainder DCM.

41 T. Dilworth, *A New Guide to the English Tongue . . . and Select Fables* (London, n.d.), 110 (DCM).

42 *EL*, 21; *Paul and Virginia, and the Exiles of Siberia* (London, 1849), 94.

43 *EL*, 20, and Blunt, *Cockerell*, 213–14; *CP*, 511; P.O. Directory, 1848.

44 *CP*, 623; W. de la Mare, 'Meeting Thomas Hardy', *Listener*, 28 Apr 1955, 756; *LY*, 223; Stinsford registers (DCRO).

45 TH to SCC, 23 Mar 1919 (Taylor).

46 *EL*, 32; 'Life' TS, fo. 32 (DCM).

47 TH to SCC, 5 Dec 1915 (Victoria & Albert Museum).

48 R. Graves, *Good-Bye To All That* (London, 1929), 375.

49 TH to L. Stephen, [9 Jan 1874?] (*CL*, I.27).

50 MH to NS, 18 Oct 1908 (Barclay).

51 Child, 'TH', 102.

52 Mary Hand to Betty Hand, 11 Dec 1846 (DCM); M. Tomkins, 'Thomas Hardy at Hatfield', *Hertfordshire Countryside*, February 1976; report, Hatfield House.

53 'Notes on TH's Life' (DCM); *EL*, 21.

54 *EL*, 21; TH to F. Dugdale (FEH), [18 Nov 1909] (RLP).

55 J. B. Sharpe to Christopher Hand, 18 June 1841 (Lock); A. Winchcombe, 'Mr. Edward Sharpe from America', *Dorset*, Autumn 1971.

56 J. B. Sharpe to Lord Salisbury, [21 July 1851?], J. Bockett to Lord Salisbury, 22 July 1851 (both Hatfield House); *Ayr Observer*, 2 Sept 1859.

57 *EL*, 21; 'Notes on TH's Life' (DCM).

58 Tomkins, 'TH at Hatfield'.

59 *EL*, 22; S. M. Ellis, 'Thomas Hardy: Some Personal Recollections', *Fortnightly Review*, March 1928, 395; *EL*, 21–2; 'Notes on TH's Life' (DCM).

60 H. Lea, *Thomas Hardy Through the Camera's Eye* (Beaminster, Dorset, 1964), 38.
61 *Jude,* 20.
62 *EL,* 22.
63 *EL,* 22–3; *DCC,* 22 Aug 1844; Hutchins, *History . . . Dorset,* II.566.
64 *EL,* 23; J. A. Martin to TH, 21 Apr [1887?] (DCM).
65 *EL,* 20.
66 Copy book, DCM.
67 *EL,* 24; *CP,* 777; *LY,* 240; *EL,* 26.
68 Archer, *Real Conversations,* 32.
69 *EL,* 25.
70 Purdy, 198, based on conversation with FEH.
71 *EL,* 24, 53–4, 134.
72 'Life' TS, ff. 130–1 (*PN,* 220), not present in *EL.*

3   DORCHESTER

1 *EL,* 32; M. O'Rourke, *Thomas Hardy: His Secretary Remembers* (Beaminster, Dorset, 1965), 49; Lacey, *Memories,* 101–2.
2 NS (Barclay).
3 *EL,* 41.
4 *EL,* 27; *Career,* 242–3; *EL,* 27, and *PW,* 230–1.
5 RLP/FEH, 1931; cf. Lord Portman to TH, 10 Aug 1913 (DCM), and 471n. intra.
6 *EL,* 29–30.
7 TH to J. Murray, 9 July 1903 (Elisabeth Murray); *EL,* 30; book, Adams.
8 TH to E. Gosse, 22 Jan 1920 (Adams).
9 Lacey, *Memories,* 101.
10 'Notes on TH's Life' (DCM); book, DCM.
11 Receipt, Lock.
12 Eutropius, Colby; *Latin Grammar,* RLP (cf. *EL,* 29); *Manual,* Eton; *EL,* 32.
13 Both notebooks, DCM; cf. *EL,* 31.
14 *Scenes & Adventures,* DCM; Ellis, 'TH: Some Personal Recollections', 395–6; *EL,* 33, 31; *Novum Testamentum,* DCM; exercise book, Lock; *EL,* 32; *Popular Educator,* DCM.
15 *LY,* 236.
16 *TLS,* 23 Aug 1947, 432; see Purdy, 325.
17 *EL,* 43; see Purdy, 291–2.
18 *DCC,* 19 Oct 1854, 19 Feb 1857, 19 Mar 1857.
19 Receipt, DCM; 'Notes on TH's Life' (DCM).
20 RLP/FEH, 1933.
21 *EL,* 35–6; TH to J. G. Hicks, 12 June 1920 (draft, DCM).
22 Tracings, DCM.
23 Drawing, St. Peter's, Dorchester; *DCC,* 19 Jan 1928; *EL,* 43; see Purdy, 293. For TH's architectural career, see *The Architectural Notebook of Thomas Hardy,* ed. C. J. P. Beatty (Dorchester, 1966), and C. J. P. Beatty, 'The Part Played by Architecture in the Life and Work of Thomas Hardy' (Ph.D. thesis, Univ. of London, 1963).
24 *Cornhill Magazine,* August 1906, 194 (*PW,* 215).
25 'Poetical Matter' notebook (photocopy, RLP); *EL,* 33, 270, and Gittings, *Young TH,* 25–6.
26 *DCC,* 27 Nov 1902, 5.
27 *EL,* 32; for Louisa Harding, see *EL,* 33–4, O'Rourke, *TH: His Secretary Remembers,* 49–52, and M. Rabiger, 'The Hoffman Papers: An Assessment and Some Interpretations', forthcoming in *Thomas Hardy Year Book.*
28 *CP,* 665.
29 *EL,* 33–4; 'Life' TS, fo. 33a (DCM); J. M. Barrie to FEH, 26 Mar 1928 (DCM).
30 *EL,* 33; annotation in TH's Bible (DCM); SCC/TH, 29 Sept 1916 (RLP); Bailey, 578.
31 Rebecca Paine to Thomas and Emma Cary, 15 July 1876 (Ian Kennedy).
32 NS (Barclay).
33 Pamela Ganly (great-granddaughter), interview, 1971.
34 Receipt, Lock.
35 *EL,* 42; Lacey, *Memories,* 105.
36 'Literary Notes I' notebook (DCM), in *LN,* I.103.
37 Death certificate.
38 TH's letter has not survived but is

mentioned in Louisa Sharpe to
Jemima Hardy, 25 July 1870 (DCM);
G. B. Sharpe to TH, 21 Sept 1859
(DCM).
39 *EL*, 46.
40 FEH to SCC, 26 May 1926 (RLP).
41 *DCC*, 10 July 1856; cf. Weber,
Lady, 88.
42 *Southern Times*, 5 July 1856; cf.
TH to H. Lea, 1 Mar 1904 (DCM).
43 *Southern Times*, 15 Nov 1856.
44 *EL*, 37; *DCC*, 14 Aug 1856; TH to
Lady Pinney, 20 Jan 1926 (Bristol),
in Lady H. Pinney, *Thomas Hardy
and the Birdsmoorgate Murder 1856*
(Beaminster, Dorset, 1966), 2; E.
Felkin, 'Days with Thomas Hardy',
Encounter, April 1962, 29.
45 *EL*, 37.
46 *EL*, 36; W. R. Rutland, *Thomas
Hardy: A Study of His Writings and
Their Background* (1938; repr. New
York, 1962), 21–2; book, RLP; *Jude*,
40.
47 Photograph, John Antell; Bible
and hymn, DCM.
48 *EL*, 40, 37–9; book, RLP.
49 *EL*, 40, 39; 'Studies, Specimens
&c' notebook (RLP).
50 H. Bastow to TH, 13 Dec 1863, 17
Feb 1861, 23 May 1862 (DCM); TH's
letters to Bastow have not survived.
51 Bible, DCM.
52 H. C. G. Moule, *Memories of a
Vicarage* (London, 1913), 56; cf. *LY*,
212.
53 *EL*, 24; sketches, DCM; Morrison,
Exhibition, [1].
54 Drawing, Lock.
55 'H.J.M. Some Memories and
Letters', in H. J. Moule, *Dorchester
Antiquities* (Dorchester, 1906), 7
(*PW*, 66).
56 Book, DCM; *LY*, 212.
57 Book, DCM; Moule, *Memories of
a Vicarage*, 35.
58 Moule, *Memories of a Vicarage*, 35.
59 'Reprints—V', *London Mercury*,
October 1922, 631.
60 *Tempora Mutantur: A Memorial
of the Fordington Times Society*
(London, 1859), 80.
61 *EL*, 43.
62 RLP/FEH, 1931; book, RLP.

63 *DCC*, 18 Nov 1858.
64 Information and quotations from
the diary of Wynne Albert Bankes
(DCRO).
65 *Jude*, 156; TH to H. Newbolt, 21
June 1920, in Newbolt, *My World as
in My Time* (London, 1932), 286.
66 Diocesan records (WRO); cf. H.
Bastow to TH, 17 Feb 1861
(DCM).
67 TH's Bible, DCM; *LY*, 194.
68 *DCC*, 14 Feb 1861, 30 Jan 1862, 9
June 1864.
69 Cf. Rabiger, 'Hoffman Papers'.
70 *EL*, 42–3; *Times*, 7 Aug 1862, and
DCC, 14 Aug 1862.
71 *New York Times*, 4 Oct 1874, and
in TH, *Old Mrs Chundle and Other
Stories*, ed. F. B. Pinion (London,
1977), 23.
72 *DCC*, 16 Aug 1883; *EL*, 43–4; *DCC*,
16 Aug 1883.
73 *Marlburian*, 24 Nov 1866.
74 'A Chronological List of Thomas
Hardy's Works in verse & prose'
(DCM), cf. *Book Buyer* (New York),
May 1892, 152; H. Bastow to TH, 23
Dec 1863 (DCM).
75 *EL*, 40, 42; SCC/TH, 10 Apr 1926
(RLP).
76 Drawings, DCM; *DCC*, 29 Aug
1861.
77 Prayerbook, DCM.
78 C. M. Oliver, *Thomas Hardy
Proposes to Mary Waight*
(Beaminster, Dorset, 1964).
79 H. Bastow to TH, 17 Feb 1861
(DCM).
80 *DCC*, 6 Mar 1862.

4 LONDON

1 *EL*, 46, and TH's copy of Keble's
The Christian Year (DCM).
2 *Society of Dorset Men in London:
Year-book 1908–1909*, 3–4 (*PW*, 219).
3 *EL*, 46; SCC/TH, 22 Sept 1916
(RLP).
4 *EL*, 55–6; TH to MH, 17 Aug 1862
(*CL*, I.1).
5 *EL*, 48.
6 TH to the Revd H. R. L. Sheppard,

23 Apr 1923, in *St. Martin's Review*, February 1928.
[7] Minute Book 1857–1862 (Architectural Association); other information about TH and the Architectural Association from the relevant minute books in the Association's archives or from the annual 'Brown Books' published by the Association in the 1860s.
[8] SCC/TH, 10 Apr 1926 (RLP); *CL*, I.2; RLP/FEH, 1931.
[9] TH to MH, 3 Nov 1862 (*CL*, I.2).
[10] TH to MH, 19 Feb 1863 (*CL*, I.3).
[11] TH to H. Thornycroft, 8 Jan 1923 (DCM).
[12] *EL*, 69–70; *EL*, 54, E. Hardy, 'Hardy and the Phrenologist', *John O'London's Weekly*, 26 Feb 1954, and original report, DCM; *EL*, 67; *CL*, I.6; *EL*, 56.
[13] *EL*, 48.
[14] *CL*, I.1; John Antell, interview, 1973; *CL*, I.1; Purdy, 321.
[15] *DCC*, 16 Aug 1883 and *Times*, 7 Aug 1862.
[16] *CL*, I.1–2.
[17] *DCC*, 16 Aug 1883.
[18] *CL*, I.2.
[19] Diocesan Records (WRO); *CL*, I.4, 6; KH, Hoffman interview, 1939 (HP); Stinsford register (DCRO); notebook fragment, DCM.
[20] *LY*, 260; *CL*, I.2.
[21] *CL*, I.3.
[22] *RIBA Proceedings*, Report of the Council, 4 May 1863; information from Dr C. J. P. Beatty.
[23] Sidney Heath, 'Thomas Hardy', *Teacher's World*, 18 Jan 1928, 826.
[24] *CL*, I.4.
[25] Purdy, 159.
[26] *Architectural Notebook*, ed. Beatty, [159], 160; A.A. Brown Book, 1863–4.
[27] *EL*, 61–2; notebook and book, DCM.
[28] H. Bastow to TH, 23 Dec 1863 (DCM).
[29] H. Bastow to TH, 23 Dec 1863 (DCM); plans on deposit at Berkshire Record Office.
[30] R. Blomfield, *Memoirs of an Architect* (London, 1932), 35–6.
[31] RLP/FEH, 1935; *EL*, 49, 59.
[32] W. O. Milne to C. J. Blomfield, 23 May 1911 (Adams).
[33] Dated sketches, DCM and RLP.
[34] MH to TH, 28 Nov 1862 (DCM); TH to MH, 19 Feb 1863 (*CL*, I.4); KH, Hoffman interview, 1939 (HP); NS (Barclay); KH diary, 25 Nov 1915 (Lock).
[35] TH sketch of old church, Fawley (DCM); MH to TH, 19 May 1864 (DCM).
[36] Annotation in prayerbook (DCM); NS (Barclay).
[37] Information about Eliza Nicholls derived principally from her niece, Mrs Sarah Headley, interviewed by RLP in 1955 (RLP), and from letters written by Mrs Headley to RLP, 1955–7 (RLP).
[38] See I. Lees, comp., 'Findon and Findon Valley', TS (West Sussex Record Office).
[39] Photograph of *c.* 1862 given by TH to Eliza Nicholls (RLP); H. Bastow to TH, 20 May 1861 (DCM).
[40] Sketches, DCM.
[41] TH to J. W. Mackail, 13 Aug 1916 (Yale); Shakespeare, DCM; Neil, M'Culloch, RLP; Moule letter, DCM.
[42] Primers, DCM; TH to MH, 19 Dec 1863 (*CL*, I.5).
[43] H. M. Moule to TH, 21 Feb 1864 (DCM).
[44] Diary of Arthur Brett (DCRO).
[45] Book, RLP; the Revd G. H. Moule (citing FEH), Hoffman interview, 1939 (HP).
[46] W. & R. Chambers records; *Chambers's Journal*, 18 Mar 1865, 161–4; *Literary World* (Boston), 1 Aug 1878, 46; Purdy, 293.
[47] Books, DCM; notebook, RLP; *CL*, II.158.
[48] 'Studies, Specimens &c' notebook (RLP), Hardy's square brackets; E. Murray, *Caught in the Web of Words* (London and New Haven, Conn., 1977), 175.
[49] 'Studies, Specimens &c' notebook (RLP); RLP/FEH, 1937.
[50] 'Studies, Specimens &c' notebook (RLP); 'Poetical Matter' notebook (photocopy, RLP).

51 'Poetical Matter' notebook (photocopy, RLP), Hardy's square brackets.
52 Cf. Purdy, 242, and facing illustration.
53 Book, DCM.
54 *EL*, 65; TH to E. Barker, 19 June 1926 (King's College, London); Stièvenard, Adams; Mariette, Colby.
55 *LN*, 1.2–3; *LY*, 118–19, and *Times*, 11 July 1865; *EL*, 63–4, and *LN*, 1.4–6.
56 Books, RLP.
57 *EL*, 66.
58 TH to E. Gosse, 30 Aug 1887 (*CL*, 1.167); *Two on a Tower*, 255.
59 Felkin, 'Days with TH', 32.
60 *CP*, 8, 9.
61 *EL*, 63, 65; for Eliza Nicholls, see n. 37 above; *Architectural Notebook*, ed. Beatty, [22], original, DCM; annotation in *Christian Year* (DCM).
62 'Poetical Matter' notebook (photocopy, RLP).
63 *CP*, 903.
64 *CP*, 16.
65 *EL*, 72; notebook fragment, DCM (revised version of same note, *EL*, 73); *EL*, 72; sketch, DCM.
66 *EL*, 66; cf. *Career*, 37.
67 TH to MH, [1866] (*CL*, 1.7); *CP*, 299.
68 *EL*, 70; cf. *LY*, 183.
69 'Studies, Specimens &c' notebook (RLP).
70 TH to A. C. Swinburne, 1 Apr 1897 (*CL*, 11.158).
71 *EL*, 62, 64, and TH to SCC, 28 Feb 1922 (Adams); *LY*, 185.
72 *EL*, 59; *Bayswater Chronicle*, 23 June 1866; *EL*, 59.
73 *CP*, 610, 234.
74 *Bayswater Chronicle*, 10 March 1866, 18 July 1863, 26 March 1864, 2 Dec 1865; *EL*, 57.
75 H. M. Moule to TH, Monday [June 1867?] (DCM).
76 W. O. Milne to C. J. Blomfield, 23 May 1911 (Adams).
77 TH to J. W. Mackail, 13 Aug 1916 (Yale); Purdy, 143.
78 By Mr Henry Reed; see Purdy, 324.
79 *EL*, 71–2; *Times*, 27 Dec 1866, cf.

D. Hawkins, *Hardy: Novelist and Poet* (Newton Abbot, Devon, 1976), 14–15, and J. Ruskin, letter 5 in *Time and Tide by Weare and Tyne: Twenty-Five Letters to a Working Man of Sunderland on the Laws of Work* (London, 1867).
80 Palgrave, RLP; Wood, Dr James Gibson.
81 *CP*, 12.
82 *CP*, 806.
83 FEH to Lady Gosse, 6 Aug 1927 (Leeds); *EL*, 70; John Antell, interview, 1972.
84 *EL*, 70–1.

5   *The Poor Man and the Lady*

1 RLP/FEH, 1935.
2 *LY*, 262.
3 Drawing, DCM; J. Digby to MH, 27 May 1867 (Lock).
4 *EL*, 75.
5 Information from Miss Nancy Bastow and Mr Hedley James; also H. Bastow to TH, 28 May 1907 (DCM) and SCC/TH, 22 Sept 1916 (RLP).
6 School records, Puddletown; for Tryphena Sparks's personal history, see L. Deacon and T. Coleman, *Providence and Mr Hardy* (London, 1966).
7 I have surveyed the various stages of this controversy in *Victorian Fiction: A Second Guide to Research*, ed. G. Ford (New York, 1978), 313–14.
8 *CP*, 62.
9 Information from Mr Henry Reed, citing FEH; John Antell, interview, 1972; I. Cooper Willis, 'Thomas Hardy', *Colby Library Quarterly*, March 1971, 268; NS, note dated 7 Nov 1955 (Ian Kennedy).
10 Deacon and Coleman, *Providence and Mr Hardy*, 42; Charles Gale, interview, 1970.
11 Deacon and Coleman, *Providence and Mr Hardy*, 33.
12 Information about John Antell on pp. 107–8 supplied by John Antell (great-grandson); see *CL*, 1.92, and

Gittings, *Young TH,* fig. 14b; note, DCM.
[13] FEH to Lady Hoare, 30 July 1915 (WRO).
[14] TH to E. Gosse, 4 Feb 1918 (Adams); TH to Gosse, 18 Feb 1918 (BL); Purdy, 113, 242, 258; *EL,* 76.
[15] *EL,* 75.
[16] *Sunday Times,* 22 Jan 1928; Gosse's MS, dated 25 Apr 1915 (Leeds).
[17] G. B. Sharpe to TH, 21 Jan 1868 (Lock).
[18] *EL,* 76; *CL,* I.7.
[19] A. Macmillan to TH, 10 Aug 1868 (DCM).
[20] C. Morgan, *The House of Macmillan (1843–1943)* (London, 1943), 87–8.
[21] *EL,* 81.
[22] RLP/FEH, 1935.
[23] See *CL,* I.8; *EL,* 78.
[24] 'Poetical Matter' notebook (photocopy, RLP).
[25] See *EL,* 156.
[26] *CL,* I.8.
[27] Morgan, *House of Macmillan,* 92; *EL,* 78.
[28] Prayerbook, DCM.
[29] *EL,* 79; cf. TH to J. H. Morgan, 1 Dec 1924 (Berg).
[30] Chapman & Hall to TH, 8 Feb 1869 (DCM).
[31] *EL,* 79–80; *DCC,* 18 Feb 1869.
[32] Chapman & Hall to TH, 26 Feb and 3 Mar 1869 (DCM); TH, 'G.M.: A Reminiscence', *Nineteenth Century and After,* February 1928, 147 (*PW,* 153), cf. *EL,* 80; *CP,* 298; 'G.M.: A Reminiscence', 147.
[33] 'Memoranda I' notebook, DCM (*PN,* 4).
[34] *CL,* I.9–10; see Purdy, 276; TH to E. Clodd, 5 Dec 1910 (BL).
[35] *CL,* I.10.
[36] *EL,* 83–4; 'Life' TS, fo. 76, DCM (*PN,* 219); Beatty, thesis, 112–27; *EL,* 84.
[37] *CP,* 500; *EL,* 85.
[38] L. Patten, 'Tale of a Chimney Pot', *Society of Dorset Men in London: Year-book 1940–41,* 81; marriage certificate.
[39] See Hawkins, *Hardy, Novelist and Poet,* 29; also 1871 census returns.
[40] 'Poetical Matter' notebook (photocopy, RLP).
[41] F. B. Pinion, *Thomas Hardy: Art and Thought* (London, 1977), 2–6.
[42] *Desperate Remedies* (London, 1889), Prefatory Note.
[43] RLP/FEH, 1936.
[44] *Desperate Remedies* (London, 1871), I.43, 45–6; Wessex edn., 23, reads 'rather humble'.
[45] For Eliza Nicholls, see chap. 4, n. 37; *Desperate Remedies* (Wessex edn.), 278–9.
[46] *CP,* 15.
[47] Gosse MS, 'A Visit to Thomas Hardy in 1912' (Princeton).
[48] *Illustrated London News,* 1 Oct 1892, 425.
[49] *CP,* 718, 224.
[50] Findon parish registers (West Sussex Record Office).

6 St. Juliot

[1] *EL,* 85; information from Dr C. J. P. Beatty; G. R. Crickmay to TH, 11 Feb 1870 (DCM), and cf. *EL,* 85–6; *EL,* 86; *CP,* 312.
[2] *EL,* 98; Emma Hardy, *Some Recollections,* ed. E. Hardy and R. Gittings (London, 1961), 55 (original in DCM).
[3] *Some Recollections,* 53 (deleted passage).
[4] Marriage certificate.
[5] *Some Recollections,* 22, 16; FEH to R. Owen, 24 Oct 1915 (Colby); Mrs Hawes to Emma Gifford (ELH), 31 Oct 1872 (DCM).
[6] FEH to R. Owen, 24 Oct 1915 (Colby); *CP,* 457; D. Kay-Robinson, 'The Face at the Casement', *Thomas Hardy Year Book 1975,* 34–5.
[7] *EL,* 96, and *PN,* 219; M. Hawes to Emma Gifford (ELH), 'Wednesday' [1871?] (DCM); *Some Recollections,* 51; TH to the Revd J. H. Dickinson, 22 Aug 1913 (Berg).
[8] *EL,* 99.
[9] *Some Recollections,* 55; M. Hawes to Emma Gifford (ELH), 'Wednesday'

[1871?] (DCM); 'Maid on the Shore' TS (DCM).
10 *CP*, 342.
11 *CP*, 350, 354.
12 RLP/FEH, 1929; *EL*, 99; *CP*, 433.
13 St. Juliot plans, Texas; see C. J. P. Beatty, 'Thomas Hardy's St. Juliot Drawings', *Architectural Review*, February 1962, 139.
14 Copy of appeal, Cornwall County Record Office.
15 Letter, DCM; Morgan, *House of Macmillan*, 93–4.
16 W. Tinsley to TH, 7 Apr, 3 May, and 5 May 1870 (Taylor).
17 *EL*, 100; FEH MS, 'Places where T.H. has lived' (DCM); *EL*, 100–2; annotation in prayerbook (DCM); *Blue Eyes*, 141–2.
18 *Marlburian*, 20 Sept 1865, 7 June 1866, 24 June 1867, 3 Mar 1869, etc.; Marlborough College archives.
19 Rabiger, 'Hoffman Papers'; Bankes diary (DCRO).
20 *EL*, 104; J. B. Harford and F. C. Macdonald, *Handley Carr Glyn Moule, Bishop of Durham: A Biography* (London, 1922), 7.
21 *CP*, 18; 'Memoranda I' notebook (*PN*, 4).
22 *EL*, 103; *CP*, 346; *Some Recollections*, 57–8; annotation in prayerbook (DCM); *CP*, 457, and Purdy, 196; TH to the Revd J. H. Dickinson, 15 June 1920 (Berg).
23 *CP*, 441; *Blue Eyes*, 202.
24 *EL*, 104; book, RLP.
25 Sketches, DCM, and see *Some Recollections*, between 56 and 57; ELH sketch and note, Berg; TH sketch, DCM; 'Memoranda I' notebook (*PN*, 5–6).
26 *CP*, 321.
27 TH to F. Dugdale (FEH), 9 Mar 1913 (RLP).
28 I. Cooper Willis, pocket-book (DCM).
29 *EL*, 109.
30 Morgan, *House of Macmillan*, 93–4.
31 'Memoranda I' notebook (*PN*, 6); FEH to H. Bliss, 10 Jan 1931 (Princeton).
32 Bible, DCM; 'Memoranda I' notebook (*PN*, 6–7); book, DCM; *EL*, 109.
33 Book, DCM.
34 W. Tinsley to TH, 9 Dec and 19 Dec 1870 (Taylor); TH to Tinsley, 20 Dec 1870 (*CL*, I.10); Tinsley to TH, 21 Dec 1870 (Taylor); balance sheet repr. Purdy, opp. 5; *EL*, 110.
35 *Athenaeum*, 1 Apr 1871, 399; *Spectator*, 22 Apr 1871, 481, 482; *EL*, 111.
36 *EL*, 110; cf. *CL*, I.11.
37 'Memoranda I' notebook (*PN*, 10).
38 *Architectural Notebook*, ed. Beatty, [170–2]; information from Dr C. J. P. Beatty.
39 Detached notebook fragment, DCM.
40 *EL*, 111–12; Purdy, 5; *EL*, 111; W. Tinsley to TH, 5 Oct 1871 (Taylor).
41 *EL*, 112; drawings dated 'August 1871' (DCM).
42 *Cassell's Saturday Journal*, 25 June 1892, 944.
43 *Greenwood Tree*, x.
44 *EL*, 127; *Greenwood Tree*, 36; see M. R. Skilling, *Hardy's Mellstock on the Map* (Dorchester, 1968); *EL*, 122; *Greenwood Tree*, 210.
45 *CL*, I.11–12.
46 M. Macmillan to TH, 11 Sept 1871 (DCM); Morgan, *House of Macmillan*, 96–7; books, RLP.
47 G. R. Crickmay to TH, 6 Oct 1871 (DCM); *EL*, 105.
48 *CL*, I.13; Morgan, *House of Macmillan*, 99.
49 TH to W. Tinsley, 20 Oct 1871 (*CL*, I.13–14); Tinsley to TH, 23 Oct 1871 (Taylor).
50 *CP*, 479.
51 Bible, DCM.

7   *Far from the Madding Crowd*

1 *EL*, 114–15, 117; *CL*, I.15.
2 *CL*, I.16; annotation in prayerbook (DCM).
3 *CL*, I.15; W. Tinsley to TH, 22 Feb and 19 Mar 1872 (Taylor).
4 G. Moore, *Confessions of a Young Man* (London, 1937), 171.

[5] *EL*, 116; *CL*, 1.16; W. Tinsley to TH, 15 Apr and 22 Apr 1872 (Taylor).
[6] *CL*, 1.16; cf. *EL*, 116–17.
[7] *EL*, 115; H. M. Moule to TH, 17 Apr 1872 (DCM).
[8] *EL*, 117; Purdy, 8; *Athenaeum*, 15 June 1872; *Pall Mall Gazette*, 5 July 1872 (cf. *EL*, 117); *Saturday Review*, 28 Sept 1872, in *Thomas Hardy: The Critical Heritage*, ed. R.G. Cox (London, 1970), 13.
[9] *CP*, 717; W. Tinsley to TH, 8 July 1872 (Taylor); TH to Tinsley, 9 July and 27 July 1872 (*CL*, 1.17–18).
[10] *EL*, 118; book, DCM.
[11] *EL*, 119–20.
[12] MS of *A Pair of Blue Eyes*, fo. [1] (Berg).
[13] F. Dugdale (FEH) to E. Clodd, 7 Mar 1913, quoted Bailey, 350; V. H. Collins, *Talks with Thomas Hardy at Max Gate 1920–1922* (London, 1928), 26; *CP*, 517.
[14] *CL*, 1.18; *EL*, 120, and D. Kay-Robinson, *The First Mrs Thomas Hardy* (London, 1979), 70; *CP*, 436.
[15] *Blue Eyes* (London, 1873), 1.56–7 (passage not included in Wessex edn.).
[16] *Blue Eyes* MS (Berg); *Blue Eyes*, 57; *Blue Eyes* (London, 1873), 1.159–60.
[17] *Blue Eyes*, 78.
[18] *EL*, 98, and cf. *EL*, 119.
[19] See, e.g., *Blue Eyes* MS, fo. 34 (Berg); Benvill Lane references pointed out by Dr C. J. P. Beatty; *Blue Eyes*, 261 (1873 edn., 1.224), and see Gittings, *Young TH*, 166.
[20] *Blue Eyes*, 100.
[21] Information from Mr Henry Reed, citing FEH.
[22] R. Smith to TH, 10 Aug 1872 (DCM); TH to Lady Grove, 18 Apr 1910 (RLP).
[23] *EL*, 120; 'Memoranda I' notebook (*PN*, 10–11); *CL*, 1.18.
[24] Bible and prayerbook, DCM.
[25] 'Memoranda I' notebook (*PN*, 11); *CL*, 1.19; W. Tinsley to TH, 4 Oct 1872 (Taylor).
[26] F. Greenwood, 'The Genius of Thomas Hardy', *Illustrated London News*, 1 Oct 1892, 431.
[27] Stephen letter, DCM; *EL*, 125; L. Stephen to TH, 4 Dec 1872 (DCM).
[28] Holder letter, DCM; *EL*, 121; statement, Cornwall County Record Office.
[29] Statement, Cornwall County Record Office.
[30] *DCC*, 20 Feb 1873 (see *Career*, 99–100).
[31] *CL*, 1.20.
[32] L. Stephen to TH, 7 Apr 1873 (DCM); *EL*, 121; KH, Hoffman interview, 1939; E. Smith, Hoffman interview, 1939 (both HP).
[33] C. W. Moule to TH, 11 May 1873 (DCM).
[34] TH to Mrs Smith, 6 Jan 1874 (*CL*, 1.26).
[35] Information about James Pole and his daughter from HP and especially from Rabiger, 'Hoffman Papers'; other information from Mr Henry Reed, citing FEH.
[36] Rabiger, 'Hoffman Papers'.
[37] Purdy, 12; *Career*, 72–3.
[38] *Spectator*, 28 June 1873, 831; Hutton letter quoted in *Career*, 371.
[39] H. M. Moule to TH, 21 May 1873 (DCM); *EL*, 122–3.
[40] *EL*, 123, 120; *CL*, 1.22.
[41] H. Holt to TH, 29 May 1873 (DCM), and see S. Weiner, 'Thomas Hardy and His First American Publisher', *Princeton University Library Chronicle*, Spring 1978.
[42] *EL*, 125; *CL*, 1.17.
[43] *Madding Crowd*, 45; see R. C. Schweik, 'A First Draft Chapter of Hardy's *Far from the Madding Crowd*', *English Studies* (1972), 344–9.
[44] H. C. Minchin, letter (citing FEH), *TLS*, 9 Feb 1928, 96; RLP/FEH, 1929; FEH to SCC, 22 Apr 1918, in *Friends*, 298.
[45] TH to L. Stephen, [9 Jan 1874?] (*CL*, 1.27).
[46] Hullah, *The Song Book* (DCM); *EL*, 126.
[47] H. M. Moule to TH, Thursday [1870?] (DCM); 'The Story of Alcestis', *Fraser's*, November 1871;

'Achilles and Lancelot', *Macmillan's*, September 1871.
[48] *EL*, 123, 126; RLP/FEH, 1933; *CP*, 887.
[49] *Standard* (London), 23 Sept 1873, *DCC*, 25 Sept 1873, *Cambridge Chronicle*, 27 Sept 1873, *Cambridge Independent Press*, 27 Sept 1873; the actual record of the inquest appears to have been destroyed.
[50] Mary Blyth (great-niece), interview, 1973; also M. Blyth, letter, *TLS*, 13 Mar 1969, 272.
[51] *Standard*, 23 Sept 1873, 3.
[52] RLP/FEH, 1933.
[53] Date of poem, 'Chronological List' (DCM); M. Blyth, letter, *TLS*; E. Hardy, 'Thomas Hardy and Horace Moule', *TLS*, 21 Jan 1969, 89.
[54] M. Blythe, letter, *TLS*; M. Blythe, interview, 1973.
[55] Books, DCM; *London Mercury*, October 1922, 631.
[56] *CP*, 887.
[57] *EL*, 126; R. C. Schweik, 'The Early Development of Hardy's *Far from the Madding Crowd*', *Texas Studies in Literature and Language* (1967), 415–28.
[58] L. Stephen to TH, 6 Oct 1873 (DCM); *CL*, I.22–4.
[59] *EL*, 127; 'Memoranda I' notebook (*PN*, 14–15).
[60] F. W. Maitland, *The Life and Letters of Leslie Stephen* (London, 1906), 273–4.
[61] *EL*, 128.
[62] Dates of ELH's residence at St. Juliot from memorial tablet, St. Juliot Church; RLP/FEH, 1935; cf. *Some Recollections*, 46.
[63] TH to E. Gosse, 25 July 1906 (Adams); FEH to H. Bliss, 21 Apr 1936 (Adams); Maitland, *Stephen*, 255; E. McC. Fleming, *R. R. Bowker: Militant Liberal* (Norman, Okla., 1952), 150.
[64] Lady Ritchie to TH, 9 Nov 1916 (DCM); *Best of Friends: Further Letters to Sydney Carlyle Cockerell*, ed. V. Meynell (London, 1956), 81.
[65] E. Gosse, *Books on the Table* (London, 1921), 296.
[66] *CL*, I.30; *EL*, 132; A. Thackeray to

H. Paterson, Thursday [1874?] (Colby); TH to E. Gosse, 25 July 1906 (Adams); see D. Hawkins, 'A Strange Opportunity', *Contemporary Review*, April 1976, 179–81; *CP*, 621.
[67] *EL*, 131, 132.
[68] *Spectator*, 3 Jan 1874, 22; *Madding Crowd* MS, fo. 147 (Edwin Thorne); *Madding Crowd*, 117; L. Stephen to TH, 12 Mar and 13 Apr 1874 (Purdy, 338, 339); *Madding Crowd* MS, ff. 2–232 (Edwin Thorne).
[69] TH to L. Stephen, [18 Feb 1874?] (*CL*, I.28).
[70] Purdy, 294; TH to Smith, Elder, 4 Mar 1874 (*CL*, I.28).
[71] *EL*, 132; 'Memoranda I' notebook (*PN*, 17).
[72] Passport, DCM.
[73] *EL*, 132; 'Memoranda I' notebook (*PN*, 15–17).
[74] *Madding Crowd* MS, fo. 23v and fo. 45 (Edwin Thorne).

8   SURBITON TO SWANAGE

[1] *EL*, 132, and *CL*, I.30–1; L. Stephen to TH, 25 Aug 1874 (Purdy, 339).
[2] E. H. Gifford to TH, 4 and 12 Sept 1874 (DCM).
[3] ELH, *Some Recollections*, 60; *CL*, I.31.
[4] ELH, 1874–6 diary (DCM); *CL*, I.31; ELH, 1874–6 diary (DCM).
[5] TH's copy of F. Licquet, *Rouen: Its History, Monuments, and Environs* (Rouen, 1871), Yale; ELH, 1874–6 diary (DCM); Murray's *Handbook*, BL; *Ethelberta*, 330; ELH, 1874–6 diary (DCM).
[6] ELH, 1874–6 diary (DCM).
[7] ELH, 1874–6 diary (DCM).
[8] Information from Mrs Elsie Honeywell, 1980.
[9] Information largely from Dr Fran Chalfont.
[10] 'Memoranda I' notebook (*PN*, 18).
[11] *EL*, 133; Mrs Procter to TH, 4 Sept 1874 (DCM).
[12] Mrs Macquoid's letter has not survived; TH to K. S. Macquoid, 17 Nov 1874 (*CL*, I.33).

[13] *Nation* (New York), 24 Dec 1874; *Spectator*, 19 Dec 1874, in *TH: The Critical Heritage*, ed. Cox, 21; J. Hutton to TH, 23 Dec 1874 (DCM).
[14] L. Stephen to TH, 2 and 7 Dec 1874 (DCM).
[15] G. Smith to TH, 15 Jan 1875 (DCM); Purdy, 18–19; *CL*, I.34; W. Tinsley to TH, 5 Jan 1875 (Taylor); G. Smith to TH, 19 Jan 1875 (DCM).
[16] G. Smith to TH, 19 Jan 1875 (DCM); *CL*, I.35; Smith to TH, 9 Mar 1875 (DCM); L. S. Jennings to TH, 5 Mar 1875 (DCM).
[17] C. Patmore to TH, 29 Mar 1875 (DCM); letters from editors also DCM.
[18] *EL*, 137–8.
[19] Maitland, *Stephen*, 276; *EL*, 140.
[20] 'Poetical Matter' notebook (photocopy, RLP).
[21] *EL*, 138; *The Letters of Ezra Pound 1907–1941*, ed. D. D. Paige (New York, 1950), 294; Maitland, *Stephen*, 450.
[22] Maitland, *Stephen*, 263–4; the deed is formally recorded on Chancery roll 30 of 1875, sheet 35 (Public Record Office).
[23] TH to V. Woolf, 20 Jan 1915 (Berg); V. Woolf to TH, 17 Jan 1915, in *Letters of Virginia Woolf*, ed. N. Nicolson and J. Trautmann (London, 1975–80), II.58; *CP*, 322; *Letters of Virginia Woolf*, I.134.
[24] *EL*, 135.
[25] *Ethelberta*, 158.
[26] L. Stephen to TH, 13 and 20 May 1875 (DCM), and *EL*, 136–7; Maitland, *Stephen*, 276; TH to Stephen, 21 May 1875 (*CL*, I.37).
[27] *Times*, 11 May 1875; *EL*, 139.
[28] *CL*, I.37; programme, Yale; and see F. B. Pinion, 'A Hundred Years Ago: Hardy at Oxford', *Thomas Hardy Society Review*, 1975, 15–16.
[29] *EL*, 141.
[30] KH to ELH, [1875?; though dated '1881–3' by TH] (DCM).
[31] *CP*, 429; *Moments of Vision* MS, fo. 4 (Magdalene College, Cambridge).
[32] *Ethelberta*, 254, 255; see D. Lewer, 'Thomas Hardy's Winter Stay in Swanage', *Thomas Hardy Year Book 1970*, 45–9.
[33] Maitland, *Stephen*, 276.
[34] TH to Smith, Elder, 26 Jan 1876 (*CL*, I.42).
[35] Book, RLP.
[36] ELH, 1874–6 diary (DCM); sketches, Lock.
[37] ELH diary, 1874–6, and D'Arville letter (both DCM); Purdy, 22.
[38] R. Gowing to TH, 11 and 30 Sept 1875 (DCM); TH to H. Holt, 4 Nov 1875 (*CL*, I.40).
[39] TH to R. D. Blackmore, 4 Nov 1875 (*CL*, I.39–40).
[40] W. H. Dunn, *R. D. Blackmore: The Author of 'Lorna Doone'* (London, 1956), 164.
[41] TH to R. D. Blackmore, 8 June 1875 (*CL*, I.37–8); Blackmore to TH, 11 June 1875 (Berg).

9 STURMINSTER NEWTON

[1] L. Stephen to TH, 16 May 1876 (DCM), and Maitland, *Stephen*, 290–1.
[2] *CL*, I.43.
[3] C. B. Tauchnitz to TH, 22 May 1876 (DCM); TH to G. Smith, 5 Mar 1876 (*CL*, I.43); Smith, Elder to TH, 7 Mar 1876 (DCM); L. Boucher to TH, 24 Nov 1876 (DCM).
[4] *Westminster Review*, July 1876, 281; see W. J. Keith, 'Thomas Hardy and the Name "Wessex" ', *English Language Notes*, September 1968, 42–4.
[5] *Examiner*, 15 July 1876, 793; *Madding Crowd* (London, 1895), vii.
[6] *CL*, I.43–4.
[7] Information from Mr Norman Atkins.
[8] *CL*, I.43–4; Purdy, 23; *Spectator*, 22 May 1876, 532; *CL*, I.45; ELH, 1874–6 diary (DCM).
[9] ELH, 1874–6 diary (DCM).
[10] *EL*, 145; ELH, 1874–6 diary (DCM).
[11] ELH, 1874–6 diary (DCM).
[12] *EL*, 139–40; Baedeker (pub. 1875), BL; *EL*, 146.
[13] ELH, 1874–6 diary (quoted *Career*, 119).

14 *EL*, 142, 147.
15 Gertrude Bugler, interview, 1974; E. Stevens, *DCC*, 9 Sept 1926; *LY*, 222–3; photographs, Mrs Bugler and DCM; RLP/FEH, 1936; and see *Thomas Hardy Society Review*, 1980, 187–8.
16 *EL*, 147.
17 *EL*, 156; *CP*, 628.
18 *EL*, 150; R. Young ('Rabin Hill'), *Poems in the Dorset Dialect*, ed. the Revd J. C. M. Mansel-Pleydell (Dorchester, 1910); ELH, 1874–6 diary (DCM).
19 *EL*, 153, 150; 'Poetical Matter' notebook (photocopy, RLP).
20 ELH, 1874–6 diary (DCM); *EL*, 149.
21 John Antell, interview, 1972.
22 'Poetical Matter' notebook (photocopy, RLP); book, DCM.
23 *CL*, I.47; TH to J. Blackwood, 13 Feb 1877 (*CL*, I.47); *CL*, I.48.
24 *CL*, I.49; F. B. Pinion, 'The Composition of *The Return of the Native*', *TLS*, 21 Aug 1970, 931.
25 Maitland, *Stephen*, 276–7.
26 *CL*, I.50; Mrs Procter to E. Forrest, 5 Jan 1878 (Huntington).
27 TH's signed receipt for August 1878 instalment (Adams).
28 A. Trollope to TH, 27 Mar 1877, in *The Letters of Anthony Trollope*, ed. B. A. Booth (London, 1951), 650.
29 *CL*, I.50; *EL*, 154; SCC/TH, 22 Aug 1925 (RLP); TH to the Revd C. Bingham, 20 Sept 1877 (*CL*, I.51).
30 'Literary Notes I' notebook (*LN*, I. xx–xxi, 95–103).
31 *Jude*, 331–2; *Western Gazette*, 12 Jan and 9 Feb 1877; *Sherborne Journal*, 8 Feb 1877.
32 *Western Gazette*, 29 Nov 1877.
33 *Western Gazette*, 25 May 1877, 7; *EL*, 149–50; *Western Gazette*, 8 June 1877, and see H. C. and J. Brocklebank, *Marnhull: Records and Memories* (Gillingham, Dorset, 1940), 92–3; *DCC*, 5 July 1877; *EL*, 151.
34 ELH, 1874–6 diary (DCM); *EL*, 151–3.
35 Sturminster Newton parish records (DCRO); death certificate.
36 Sturminster Newton parish records (DCRO); *Tess*, 116–23; Hullah, DCM; Hutchins, III.355–8.
37 *Moments of Vision* MS, ff. 90–1 (Magdalene College, Cambridge).
38 *CP*, 482, 483, 629; *EL*, 153.
39 *EL*, 153; T. Hardy, Sen., to KH, Sunday [3 Nov 1878] (Lock).
40 *EL*, 155; 'Life' TS, fo. 152 (DCM).
41 *EL*, 156; RLP/FEH, 1936; I. Cooper Willis, note (Bailey, 383); RLP/FEH, 1933.
42 *EL*, 156; *DCC*, 7 Mar 1878; *Western Gazette*, 8 Mar 1878.
43 *EL*, 147, 156.

10   *The Return of the Native*

1 *EL*, 157; *CL*, I.58; Mrs Dashwood to ELH, 6 May 1878 (DCM).
2 C. B. Tauchnitz to TH, 8 Jan 1878 (DCM), Purdy, 63, 274–5.
3 Purdy, 25–6, and *CL*, I.52–5, 59; Hopkins's replies, DCM.
4 *CL*, I.56; MS (Bowdoin), cf. *Literary World* (Boston), 1 Aug 1878, 46 (the error, 'Queen's' for 'Queens' ', is in the MS).
5 *EL*, 159, 158–60, 168, 172–3.
6 '*Trumpet-Major*' notebook (*PN*, 120).
7 *CL*, I.52, 59; G. Smith to TH, 19 Sept 1878 (DCM).
8 *CL*, I.40; H. Holt to TH, 8 June 1878 (DCM); H. Holt, *Garrulities of an Octogenarian Editor* (Boston, 1923), 207; *CL*, I.58; C. B. Tauchnitz to TH, 8 Jan and 2 Nov 1878 (DCM).
9 TH to L. Stephen [18 Feb 1874?] (*CL*, I.28); J. Paterson, *The Making of 'The Return of the Native'* (Berkeley, Calif., 1963), and *Career*, 130–3.
10 Purdy, 27; *Athenaeum*, 23 Nov 1878, 654.
11 *Athenaeum*, 30 Nov 1878, 688 (*PW*, 91); *EL*, 162.
12 *Spectator*, 8 Feb 1879, 182; E. Gosse to F. A. Hedgcock, 28 July 1909 (Adams).
13 TH to Smith, Elder, 1 Oct 1878 (*CL*, I.61).

14 See Chap. 1, n. 50, above; Paterson, *Making of 'Return of the Native'*, 45–7.

15 'Life' TS, fo. 158 (*PN*, 222).

16 *EL*, 160; H. C. C. Moule (son of C. W. Moule), interview, 1973.

17 TH to Henry Hardy, 13 Sept 1878 (*CL*, 1.59–60).

18 *British Quarterly Review*, April 1881, 346; TH to C. Kegan Paul, 18 Apr 1881 (*CL*, 1.89).

19 For Kegan Paul, see *Career*, 117–18, 120–3; J. Panton, *Leaves from a Life* (London, 1908), 206.

20 TH to T. Woolner, 21 Apr 1880 (*CL*, 1.73); *Return of the Native*, 197.

21 *Return of the Native*, 203; Comte's influence on *Far from the Madding Crowd* pointed out by Professor L. A. Björk.

22 *EL*, 163; *CP*, 466.

23 'Poetical Matter' notebook (photocopy, RLP).

24 *EL*, 162–5; dated drawings (DCM).

25 L. Stephen to TH, 17 Feb 1879 (DCM) and in *EL*, 167.

26 G. A. Macmillan to TH, 20 May 1879 (DCM); TH to J. Blackwood, 9 June 1879 (*CL*, 1.65); D. Macleod to TH, 20 June 1879 (DCM); Purdy, 32–3.

27 *CL*, 1.66; *EL*, 168–9; 'Memoranda I' notebook (*PN*, 20); sketch, Miss Gertrude Antell; *CL*, 1.92; *EL*, 169–70.

28 See *Career*, 149–51; *CL*, 1.66–7, and Purdy, 34; J. Collier to TH, 20 Nov 1879 (DCM); '*Trumpet-Major*' notebook (*PN*, 177).

29 *New Quarterly Magazine*, October 1879, 472, 469.

30 *British Quarterly Review*, April 1881, 360.

31 W. Besant to TH, 7 Mar 1879 (DCM).

32 *CL*, 1.71, and *EL*, 168; *EL*, 166, 178–9, and Mrs Procter to TH, 7 Mar 1880 (DCM); *EL*, 177–8; list, DCM; *EL*, 179, and see L. Edel, *Henry James: The Conquest of London, 1870–1883* (Philadelphia and London, 1962), 354.

33 'Literary Notes I' notebook (*LN*, 1.130, 124, 130–1).

34 *EL*, 175; 'Literary Notes I' notebook (*LN*, 1.134).

35 TH to Harper & Brothers, 16 Apr 1880 (*CL*, 1.72); *CL*, 1.73–4; H. Allingham to TH, 5 June 1880 (DCM); *CL*, 1.74–5.

36 *CL*, 1.76–7; Fleming, *R. R. Bowker*, 146, 147.

37 *EL*, 181–2; *Laodicean*, 453; drawing (DCM), and see Purdy, 38.

38 *Good Words*, December 1880, 807; *The Trumpet-Major* (London, 1880), III.259.

39 Maitland, *Stephen*, 277.

40 *CL*, 1.92; *LY*, 190.

11 ILLNESS

1 *EL*, 182–3; *CL*, 1.73; *CP*, 623.

2 KH to ELH, 23 Sept 1881 and Thursday [1882?] (DCM).

3 Letter, DCM.

4 *CL*, 1.84; dated presentation copies of books by Handley Moule and Arthur Evans Moule (RLP); *EL*, 184; *CP*, 887.

5 *EL*, 187–8; *CL*, 1.88.

6 *CP*, 152; TH to E. Gosse, 14 Feb 1922 (BL); cf. TH to F. Henniker, 1 Mar 1922 (*ORFW*, 199); *EL*, 192.

7 C. Kegan Paul to TH, 24 Feb 1881 (DCM).

8 E. Gosse to TH, 16 Dec 1917 (DCM); information and suggestions from Mr Gordon Barclay, Dr Grant A. Farrow, Mrs Vera Jesty, and Mr Michael Rabiger.

9 Purdy, 39–40; TH to E. Gosse, 30 Dec 1917 (Leeds); Harper & Brothers to TH, 24 May 1880 (copy, NYPL); *CL*, 1.82.

10 W. Lyon Phelps, *Autobiography with Letters* (New York, 1939), 391, 394; TH to R. R. Bowker, 15 Nov 1880 (*CL*, 1.82); C. Kegan Paul to ELH, 14 Nov 1880 (DCM); G. Smith to ELH, 18 Nov 1880 (DCM); ELH to G. Smith, 19 Nov 1880 (draft, DCM).

11 MH to ELH, 28 Jan 1881 (DCM).

12 *Pall Mall Gazette*, 23 Nov 1880, 11.

13 *EL*, 192.

14 TH to R. R. Bowker, 15 Feb 1881 (*CL*, I.87); *CL*, I.88.

15 C. Kegan Paul to TH, 24 Feb and 7 Feb 1881 (DCM).

16 Jane S. Lock to ELH, 28 Apr 1881 (DCM); cf. Kay-Robinson, *First Mrs TH*, 232.

17 *EL*, 189, 192.

18 See *Career*, 174–82.

19 *EL*, 193; TH to J. Antell, 29 June 1881 (*CL*, I.92).

20 *CP*, 952.

21 Information from Mr Montague Harvey.

22 *EL*, 193; G. Douglas, *Gleanings in Prose and Verse*, ed. O. Hilson (Galashiels, n.d.), 28; Douglas, *A Love's Gamut and Other Poems* (London, 1880), 116.

23 *EL*, 195–6; *Blandford and Wimborne Telegram*, 6 Jan 1882.

24 *EL*, 197; information from Mr M. Harvey.

25 *Blandford and Wimborne Telegram*, 11 May 1883, 13 Apr 1883; *EL*, 195.

26 *EL*, 205; 'Memoranda I' notebook (*PN*, 21–4).

27 KH to TH and ELH, Wednesday [July 1881?] and Sunday [July 1881?] (DCM); KH to ELH, 23 Sept 1881 (DCM); M. E. Bath, 'Thomas Hardy and Evangeline F. Smith', *Thomas Hardy Year Book 1973–1974*, 40–1; *DCC*, 29 Sept 1881.

28 'H. J. M. Some Memories and Letters', in H. J. Moule, *Dorchester Antiquities*, 9 (*PW*, 68).

29 Douglas, *Gleanings*, 29.

30 *EL*, 188.

31 *EL*, 194–5; TH to R. R. Bowker, 13 Oct 1881 (*CL*, I.94).

32 T. B. Aldrich to TH, 28 Sept 1881 (DCM).

33 F. B. Pinion, *A Hardy Companion* (London, 1968), 39.

34 *Two on a Tower*, vii.

35 TH to the Royal Observatory, 27 Nov 1881 (*CL*, I.96), and *EL*, 195.

36 See *CL*, I.99–101, and Purdy, 28–30.

37 H. Tindal Atkinson to TH, 31 Dec 1881 (DCM); *Daily News*, 2 Jan 1882, 2; W. Black to TH, 2 Jan 1882 (DCM).

38 See *CL*, I.103–4, and C. J. Weber, *Hardy in America* (1946; repr. New York, 1966), 62–7.

39 Note copied by FEH from TH notebook subsequently destroyed (RLP).

40 Play MS, BL; *Era*, 4 Mar 1882; and see Purdy, 28–30, and J. F. Stottler, 'Hardy vs. Pinero: Two Stage Versions of *Far from the Madding Crowd*', *Theatre Survey*, November 1977.

41 *EL*, 198; J. Comyns Carr to TH, [1882] (DCM); *Mrs. J. Comyns Carr's Reminiscences*, ed. E. Adams (London, 1926), 78.

42 *CL*, I.104–5; Fleming, *R. R. Bowker*, 152.

43 *CL*, I.105; V. Liebert, '*Far from the Madding Crowd* on the American Stage', *Colophon*, September 1938.

44 *Mrs. J. Comyns Carr's Reminiscences*, ed. Adams, 77–8.

45 KH to ELH, Thursday [May 1882?] (DCM).

46 TH to W. Moy Thomas, 12 Aug 1882 (*CL*, I.108–9); F. B. Adams, Jr., 'Another Man's Roses', *New Colophon*, June 1949, 107–12.

47 TH to Houghton, Mifflin, 19 Sept 1882 (*CL*, I.109); *EL*, 199–201.

48 TH to E. Gosse, 21 Jan 1883 (*CL*, I.114).

49 C. Kegan Paul to TH, 12 Nov 1882 (DCM); *Saturday Review*, 18 Nov 1882, 675.

50 *CL*, I.109, and Purdy, 44.

51 *St. James's Gazette*, 16 Jan 1883, 14, and 19 Jan 1883, 14.

52 *Two on a Tower*, vii; cf. *Career*, 191–3.

53 W. H. Rideing, *Many Celebrities and a Few Others* (London, 1912), 286.

54 *CL*, I.110; E. Gosse to TH, 8 Dec 1882 and 18 Jan 1883 (Adams).

55 *Two on a Tower* (London, 1895), v; H. Holder to ELH, 28 Nov 1882 (DCM), and see *EL*, 201–3.

12 RETURN TO DORCHESTER

1 TH to E. Gosse, 10 Dec 1882 (*CL*, I.110).
2 Mr Montague Harvey (citing his mother), interview, 1975.
3 Mrs Dashwood to ELH, Friday [1883?] (DCM).
4 TH to E. Gosse, 12 June 1883 (David Holmes).
5 *EL*, 198, 199, 198.
6 *CL*, I.95; *CP*, 158.
7 *EL*, 199; *Blandford and Wimborne Telegram*, 9 Dec 1881.
8 Notebook fragment, DCM (quoted Bailey, 164).
9 Horace Seymour (for Mr Gladstone) to TH, 29 Oct 1883 (DCM); *CL*, I.118–19; *CL*, I.121, 123–4.
10 See *Career*, 214–20.
11 'The Dorsetshire Labourer', *Longman's Magazine*, July 1883, 255, 268.
12 *Westminster Review*, April 1883, 356.
13 *EL*, 205; MS, Pierpont Morgan Library.
14 *Westminster Review*, April 1883, 334; *CP*, 237.
15 TH to Perry Mason & Co., 5 Nov 1883 (*CL*, I.123); *Our Exploits at West Poley*, introd. R. L. Purdy (London, 1952), xii, 97.
16 *EL*, 207; RLP/FEH, 1933; *EL*, 208; signed menu card (Cambridge).
17 E. Gosse to H. Thornycroft, 23 July 1883, in E. Charteris, *The Life and Letters of Sir Edmund Gosse* (London, 1931), 156–7; Gosse to N. Gosse, 22 July 1883 (Cambridge).
18 E. Gosse to N. Gosse, 22 July 1883 (Cambridge).
19 L. Baxter, *The Life of William Barnes, Poet and Philologist* (London, 1887), 343; TH to W. Barnes, 13 July 1883 (*CL*, I.120); *EL*, 210; Charteris, *Gosse*, 157.
20 Death certificate; Daniel Defoe, *Rabinsán Krúso*, trans. into Persian by Sher Alí of Kabul, ed. in the Roman character by T. W. H. Tolbort (London, 1878); 'The Late Mr. T. W. H. Tolbort, B.C.S.', *DCC*, 16 Aug 1883, 10.
21 *LY*, 183; *Thomas Hardy Year Book 1973–1974*, 42; H. O. Lock, 'Max Gate', *Dorset Year Book, 1962–63*, 34.
22 *CL*, I.127; TH to ELH, 13 Mar 1885 (*CL*, I.131); *EL*, 221–2.
23 *EL*, 293.
24 *EL*, 222; *CL*, I.131; E. H. Gifford to ELH, 6 Apr 1885 (DCM).
25 G. Symonds to TH, 20 Aug 1884 (DCM), and see E. C. Sampson, 'Thomas Hardy—Justice of the Peace', *Colby Library Quarterly*, December 1977, esp. 264–5; see Anon., 'Mr. Thomas Hardy at Max Gate, Dorchester', *World*, 17 Feb 1886, 7; *Mayor of Casterbridge*, 231–2.
26 A. Everett to ELH, 14 Sept 1883 (DCM); *DCC*, 4 Oct 1883; TH to B. Harte, 18 Oct 1883 (*CL*, I.122).
27 DCM Minute Book, minutes of Annual General Meeting of 13 Jan 1886 (DCM).
28 H. J. Moule to TH, 31 Dec 1883 (DCM); [R. N. Peers], in J. Newman and N. Pevsner, *Dorset* (Harmondsworth, Middx., 1972), 485, and see 484; RLP/FEH, 1934.
29 'Some Romano-British Relics Found at Max Gate, Dorchester', *DCC*, 15 May 1883; Purdy, 61.
30 *CL*, I.135; Inland Revenue Valuation statement, 17 Sept 1910 (DCM); KH to ELH, [1882?] (DCM); estimate, DCM; *EL*, 226–7.
31 DCM Minute Book, minutes of meeting of 5 Dec 1885 (DCM).
32 TH to L. Milman, 17 July 1893 (*CL*, II.24–5).
33 'Literary Notes I' notebook (*LN*, I.122–3, 164–5); *EL*, 217, 281; M. Arnold, 'Wordsworth', *Macmillan's Magazine*, July 1879, 198 (cf. *LN*, I.122).
34 Books, RLP; and see W. F. Wright, *The Shaping of 'The Dynasts': A Study in Thomas Hardy* (Lincoln, Nebr., 1967), 38–53.
35 TH to F. Harrison, 17 June 1885 (*CL*, I.133–4); TH to J. Morley, 20 Nov 1885 (*CL*, I.136–7).
36 *EL*, 213; 'Poetical Matter' notebook (photocopy, RLP).

37 Notebooks, DCM.
38 *Career,* 237–43.
39 TH to E. Marston, [1888?] (*CL,* I.171).
40 'General Preface', *Tess,* ix, x (*PW,* 46).
41 *Mayor of Casterbridge,* 384, 385.
42 *EL,* 219, 221–3.
43 *EL,* 222.

13   MAX GATE

1 Drawings, DCM.
2 Fordington census returns, 1851.
3 TH to E. Gosse, 25 Sept 1890 (*CL,* I.217).
4 Kerr, *Bound to the Soil,* 241.
5 TH to A. Pope, 11 July 1904 (Hardy Society), and to the Mayor of Dorchester, 7 Aug 1905 (*DCC,* 10 Aug 1905, 12).
6 FEH to Mrs Belloc Lowndes, 29 Oct 1929 (Texas); *EL,* 226; NS (Barclay).
7 M. Holzmann to TH, 29 Sept 1886 (DCM).
8 G. Gissing to A. Gissing, 22 Sept 1895, in *Yale University Library Gazette,* January 1943, 52.
9 Envelope, DCM.
10 A. C. Benson, diary, 5 Sept 1912 (Magdalene College, Cambridge); Gissing letter, *Yale University Library Gazette,* 52.
11 *Architectural Notebook,* ed. Beatty, 108.
12 FEH to P. Lemperly, 7 Mar 1919 (Colby).
13 *World,* 17 Feb 1886, 6.
14 *World,* 17 Feb 1886, 6; *EL,* 227.
15 *World,* 17 Feb 1886, 6.
16 TH to H. Erichsen, 26 July 1884 (*CL,* I.128).
17 TH to A. A. Reade, 5 Dec 1882, in *Study and Stimulants,* ed. Reade (Manchester, 1883), 66, although the passage about tobacco is not present in *EL,* 204–5, or in the original letter (Washington Univ., St. Louis); DCM Minute Book (DCM).
18 *London and the Life of Literature in Late Victorian England: The Diary of George Gissing, Novelist,* ed. P. Coustillas (Hassocks, Sussex, 1978), 388.
19 TH to SCC, 3 June 1917, in *Friends,* 286.
20 TH to H. Newbolt, 16 Jan 1909 (Texas).
21 *EL,* 41; 'The Profitable Reading of Fiction', *Forum* (New York), March 1888, 57 (*PW,* 111).
22 See *CL,* I.69, 239–40.
23 *EL,* 223–4, 225.
24 TH to J. Alexander, 16 Sept 1880 (*CL,* I.152).
25 TH to C. Kegan Paul, 18 Apr 1881 (*CL,* I.89).
26 *EL,* 231.
27 TH to W. D. Howells, 9 Nov 1886 (*CL,* I.156); *Spectator,* 5 June 1886, in *TH: The Critical Heritage,* ed. Cox, 137; *Saturday Review,* 29 May 1886, in *Critical Heritage,* 135; *Pall Mall Gazette,* 9 July 1886, 5.
28 *Church of England Temperance Chronicle,* 23 Jan 1886, 38.
29 Purdy, 56–7; *EL,* 135, 230.
30 MS, DCM; see Purdy, 56, and D. Kramer, 'Revisions and Vision: Thomas Hardy's *The Woodlanders*', Pt. 1, *Bulletin of the New York Public Library,* April 1971, 203–4.
31 RLP/FEH, 1933.
32 *EL,* 229; F. Stevenson to S. Colvin, [early September 1885] (Yale).
33 SCC, letter, *TLS,* 4 Oct 1953, 2; RLP, notes on conversation with SCC, 1948.
34 F. Stevenson to D. Norton Williams, [Oct–Nov 1885] (Yale).
35 *EL,* 235, and see *CL,* I.146–7; *EL,* 237, and S. Colvin to TH, 12 June 1886 (DCM); E. Gosse to TH, 28 Aug 1887 (DCM).
36 *EL,* 232, and see *CL,* I.147–9; *EL,* 234.
37 *EL,* 233–4, 268.
38 FEH to R. Owen, 17 July 1915 (Colby), and see Kay-Robinson, *First Mrs TH,* 196–7; RLP, notes on conversation with D. Allhusen, 1931.
39 *EL,* 237, cf. *Career,* 353–8; *EL,* 236–7; G. Gissing to TH, 30 June 1886 (DCM), in P. Coustillas, 'Some Unpublished Letters from Gissing to

Hardy', *English Literature in Transition 1880–1920*, 1966, 198.

[40] *CL*, I.149, 147.

[41] F. Macmillan to TH, 29 Mar 1886; M. Morris to TH, 19 Sept 1886 (both DCM).

[42] Kramer, 'Revisions and Vision', 213.

[43] TH to J. T. Grein and C. W. Jarvis, 19 July 1889 (*CL*, I.195); 'Candour in English Fiction', *New Review*, January 1890, 19 (*PW*, 130).

[44] TH to E. Gosse, 18 Aug 1886 (*CL*, I.151); *Thomas Hardy Year Book 1973–1974*, 42.

[45] TH to E. Gosse, 8 Sept 1886 (*CL*, I.151); Gosse, *Critical Kit-Kats* (London, 1896), v–vi; Gosse to N. Gosse, Tuesday [31 Aug 1886] (Cambridge).

[46] *Athenaeum*, 16 Oct 1886, 501–2 (*PW*, 101, 104).

[47] See *CL*, I.159, 167; *CP*, 473.

14 *The Woodlanders*

[1] *Madding Crowd*, viii.

[2] R. R. Bowker, 'London as a Literary Centre. II', *Harper's New Monthly Magazine*, June 1888, 9.

[3] RLP/FEH, 1929.

[4] Drawing, DCM.

[5] *LY*, 151; *Woodlanders*, 247; *EL*, 127.

[6] *EL*, 243–4; *Times*, 3 Mar 1887; Purdy, 57.

[7] ELH, 1887/1897 diary (DCM); basic information for pp. 280–3 taken from this diary and from *EL*, 245–58; *CP*, 100.

[8] Book, BL.

[9] Quotations ELH, 1887/1897 diary (DCM).

[10] TH to E. Gosse, 31 Mar 1887 (*CL*, I.163); *EL*, 247–8; 'Literary Notes I' notebook (*LN*, I.131); *CL*, I.163.

[11] Quotations ELH, 1887/1897 diary (DCM); *EL*, 251.

[12] ELH, 1887/1897 diary (DCM); *EL*, 255.

[13] *EL*, 256–7; ELH, 1887/1897 diary (DCM).

[14] *Times*, 27 Apr 1887; *Saturday Review*, 2 Apr 1887, 485; E. Gosse to TH, 22 Mar 1887 (DCM); *John Bull*, 7 May 1887, 302; *St. James's Gazette*, 2 Apr 1887.

[15] *Dublin Evening Mail*, 30 Mar 1887.

[16] Lord Lytton to TH, 10 July 1887 (Univ. of California, Berkeley); TH to A. C. Swinburne, 9 May 1887 (*CL*, I.165).

[17] See Purdy, 340–1.

[18] Tillotson & Son to TH, 16 Mar 1887 (DCM); contract, Bodleian.

[19] *EL*, 242–3; 'Literary Notes I' notebook, ff. 206–10 (DCM); *EL*, 232, 283–4.

[20] G. Reynolds, *Painters of the Victorian Scene* (London, 1953), 77.

[21] *EL*, 276, 231–2.

[22] W. P. Frith, *My Autobiography and Reminiscences* (3 vols., London, 1887), III.432.

[23] *EL*, 261–4; *CL*, I.165.

[24] 'Life' TS, fo. 271 (*PN*, 228–9).

[25] See *Career*, 299–303; *EL*, 239, 262.

[26] E. Gosse to TH, 28 Aug 1887 (DCM); TH to Gosse, 30 Aug 1887 (*CL*, I.167); *EL*, 267.

[27] L. Stephen to TH, 19 Nov 1880 (DCM).

[28] *EL*, 265–6.

[29] C. J. Longman to TH, 27 Sept 1887; W. Blackwood to TH, 30 Dec 1887 (both DCM).

[30] L. Stephen to TH, 10 Jan 1888 (Maitland, *Stephen*, 393–4).

[31] TH to F. Macmillan, 29 Feb and 9 Mar 1888 (*CL*, I.174–5); F. Macmillan to TH, 6 Mar 1888 (DCM).

[32] *EL*, 267.

[33] *EL*, 270–3; 'Book of Gosse' (Cambridge).

[34] *EL*, 273–4.

[35] *EL*, 274–7.

[36] *CL*, I.177, 178; *EL*, 279; *CL*, I.179.

[37] *EL*, 281; see Weber, *Lady*, 239; contract, Bodleian.

15 THE WRITING OF *Tess*

[1] Notebook fragment (DCM); 'Poetical Matter' notebook (photocopy, RLP); *EL*, 270.

[2] *EL,* 281.

[3] 'Poetical Matter' notebook (photocopy, RLP); *Tess,* 299.

[4] RLP, notes on interview with Harold Child (citing TH).

[5] NS (Barclay).

[6] J. Stevens Cox (citing Harold Voss), interview, 1980; NS (Barclay).

[7] SCC/TH, 24 June 1920 (RLP).

[8] D. Van Ghent, *The English Novel: Form and Function* (New York, 1953), 201; R. Blathwayt, 'A Chat with the Author of *Tess*', *Black & White,* 27 Aug 1892, 240.

[9] *CL,* I.194, 196; F. B. Pinion, *A Hardy Companion* (London, 1968), 213; *Tess* MS, fo. 1 (BL); cf. Purdy, opp. 71. For the development of the MS, see J. T. Laird, *The Shaping of 'Tess of the d'Urbervilles'* (Oxford, 1975).

[10] RLP/FEH, 1933.

[11] *Tess,* xxi; cf. Purdy, opp. 71.

[12] *CL,* I.190.

[13] *EL,* 286.

[14] MH and KH to ELH, 8 June 1889 (DCM).

[15] *EL,* 288; 'Life' TS, ff. 299, 300 (*PN,* 230, 231).

[16] Maggs Bros. Catalogue 664 (1938), item 197; 'Max Eliot', 'Graham R. Tomson, the Poet', *Author* (Boston), 15 Sept 1890, 134; *EL,* 278; TH to R. Tomson, 5 Sept and 6 Oct 1889 (*CL,* I.199, 201).

[17] TH to F. Henniker, 16 July 1893 (*CL,* II.24).

[18] *CL,* I.193.

[19] A. Thornycroft to H. Thornycroft, 3 July 1889 (Mrs E. Manning); for TH's comment to Gosse, see *Career,* 401–2; *EL,* 288–9, and see *Tess,* 192.

[20] *CL,* I.195; C. W. Jarvis to TH, 16 Sept 1889 (DCM).

[21] *CL,* I.200.

[22] M. Robinson to I. Cooper Willis, 17 Dec 1937 (DCM).

[23] RLP, letter, *TLS,* 26 June 1943, 307.

[24] Purdy, 72–3; note of cancellation on agreement (Bodleian).

[25] E. Arnold to TH, 7 Oct 1889 (DCM); *CL,* I.201; E. Arnold to TH, 15 Nov 1889 (*Career,* 283–4).

[26] M. Morris to TH, 25 Nov 1889 (*Career,* 284).

[27] *EL,* 290–1; *CL,* I.170, 173–4, 201–4.

[28] Purdy, 94n.; *EL,* 290–1.

[29] *EL,* 291–2; *CL,* I.205.

[30] *CL,* I.206; note on verso of W. E. Henley to TH, 17 July 1890 (Texas).

[31] TH to G. Douglas, 21 Dec 1888 (*CL,* I.182); Purdy, 117; *EL,* 284, 290; Purdy, 199; *CP,* 480.

[32] *EL,* 293.

[33] Purdy, 65.

[34] *EL,* 294; Douglas, *Gleanings,* 30.

[35] 'Literary Notes II' notebook, ff. 12–14, 16–17 (DCM); *EL,* 295–6.

[36] *LY,* 16; *EL,* 314.

[37] *EL,* 294–5, 298–9.

[38] Deacon and Coleman, *Providence and Mr Hardy,* 64–5.

[39] *EL,* 299; *Globe,* 24 July 1890, 6; *CL,* I.214–15; *World,* 30 July 1890.

[40] W. A. Locker to TH, 25 June 1890 (DCM).

[41] W. A. Locker to TH, 25 June 1890 (DCM).

[42] *CL,* I.215–16.

[43] Purdy, 65.

[44] *EL,* 299–300; book, BL.

[45] E. Gosse to T. Gosse, 12 Sept 1890 (Cambridge); photographs, Cambridge and DCM; E. Gosse to TH, 14 Sept 1890 (DCM).

[46] *CL,* I.217; ELH to C. K. Shorter, 23 April [1908?] (RLP); *LY,* 251.

[47] Purdy, 70; *EL,* 315; but see J. T. Laird, 'New Light on the Evolution of *Tess of the d'Urbervilles*', *Review of English Studies,* November 1980, 414–35.

[48] J. Verschoyle to TH, 14 Apr 1891 (DCM).

[49] Purdy, 71; sections of MS in Berg, Taylor, and Texas.

[50] *Spectator,* 30 Jan 1892, 167; scrapbook, DCM.

[51] Purdy, 70.

[52] *CL,* I.218–19; *Athenaeum,* 22 Nov 1890, 701, and 6 Dec 1890, 776–7.

[53] *EL,* 301; *CL,* I.223; TH to ELH, 5 Dec 1890 (*CL,* I.222).

16   THE PUBLICATION OF *Tess*

[1] *EL*, 302.
[2] *CL*, I.230; TH to W. A. Fisher, 31 Dec 1890 (*CL*, I.226).
[3] Purdy, 85; *EL*, 304–6.
[4] TH to ELH, 11 Apr 1891 (*CL*, I.230–1).
[5] G. Douglas, 'Thomas Hardy. Some Recollections and Reflections', *Hibbert Journal*, April 1928, 289–91; M. Robinson to I. Cooper Willis, 17 Dec 1937 (DCM).
[6] FEH to H. Bliss, 3 Apr 1921 (Princeton).
[7] ELH to Lady Hoare, 24 Apr 1910 (WRO).
[8] M. Robinson to I. Cooper Willis, 17 Dec 1937 (DCM); G. Atherton, *Adventures of a Novelist* (New York, 1932), 263; T. P. O'Connor, 'Thomas Hardy as I Knew Him', *Living Age*, 1 Mar 1928, 456.
[9] 'Life' TS, fo. 317 (*PN*, 233).
[10] *CL*, I.232, 234.
[11] *DCC*, 5 Nov 1885; TH to R. Pearce Edgcumbe, 23 Apr 1891 (*CL*, I.234), and see *CL*, I.235, 236.
[12] KH to TH, 15 May 1891 (DCM).
[13] TH to Lord Carnarvon, 5 July 1888 (BL); *EL*, 298, 307; *CL*, I.236; *EL*, 307–8; *CL*, I.233.
[14] *EL*, 309–10, 308.
[15] E. Clodd, diary, 20 June 1891 (Alan Clodd).
[16] 'Literary Notes II' notebook, 37–43, 43–62, 63–4 (DCM), 39 (quoted Wright, *Shaping of 'The Dynasts'*, 41).
[17] *Pall Mall Gazette*, 10 July 1891, 2.
[18] Purdy, 95.
[19] Purdy, 67; TH to Lord Lytton, 15 July 1891 (*CL*, I.239–40).
[20] TH to F. Henniker, 21 Dec 1905 (*ORFW*, 124–5); S. Heath, 'How Thomas Hardy Offended the County Families of Dorset', unpub. TS (DCM).
[21] *EL*, 312–13.
[22] T. H. Darlow, *William Robertson Nicoll: Life and Letters* (London, 1925), 99.
[23] *EL*, 64, 313, and Douglas, *Gleanings*, 30; Douglas, 'TH: Some Recollections and Reflections', 386.
[24] *CL*, II.32; *EL*, 306.
[25] Douglas, 'TH: Some Recollections and Reflections', 389–90.
[26] *EL*, 314; *CL*, I.243.
[27] *CL*, I.246–7; MS, fo. 1 (BL); cf. Purdy, opp. 71; *Tess*, xxi.
[28] Purdy, 73; W. Morris to TH, 15 Dec 1891 (DCM); Purdy, 74; A. Austin, *Love's Widowhood and Other Poems* (London, 1889), 58.
[29] F. Harrison to TH, 29 Dec 1891 (DCM); C. Kegan Paul to TH, 25 Dec 1891 (DCM).
[30] TH to H. W. Massingham, 31 Dec 1891 (*CL*, I.250).
[31] *Saturday Review*, 16 Jan 1892, 73–4; TH to W. Besant, 17 Jan 1892, to E. Gosse, 18 Jan 1892, and to E. Clodd, 20 Jan 1892 (*CL*, I.252, 253, 254); *CL*, I.255.
[32] Purdy, 74–5; *CL*, I.253.
[33] *Tess*, 508; *New Review*, February 1892, 248.
[34] *Quarterly Review*, February 1892, 248; TH to J. Stanley Little, 17 May 1892 (*CL*, I.268); TH to R. Noel, 22 Apr 1892 (*CL*, I.265); *LY*, 7.
[35] W. Besant to TH, 18 Jan 1892 (Texas); E. Gosse to TH, 19 Jan 1892 (Adams).
[36] A. Lang to E. Clodd, 1 May 1892 (*Journal of the Rutgers University Library*, December 1949, 4); Lang to TH, 5 May 1892 (DCM).
[37] *Tess of the d'Urbervilles* (London, 1892), ix; *Daily News*, 11 Oct 1892, 4; cf. 'Life' TS, fo. 349 (*PN*, 238); RLP/FEH, 1933.
[38] R. Tomson, 'Thomas Hardy. I', *Independent* (New York), 22 Nov 1894, 2.
[39] *CL*, I.260, and see *Book Buyer* (New York), May 1892.
[40] FEH to SCC, 20 Apr 1928 (RLP).
[41] TH to E. Clodd, 20 Jan 1892 (*CL*, I.254); *Cassell's Saturday Journal*, 25 June 1892, 944; information about 51 High West Street from Mr Henry Lock.
[42] Receipt for shares in name of Katharine Hardy, 1 Mar 1892 (DCM).
[43] See *CL*, I.256, 281–3, and 260, 266.

⁴⁴ Blathwayt, 'Chat with the Author of *Tess*', 238, 239.
⁴⁵ *Cassell's Saturday Journal*, 25 June 1892, 945.
⁴⁶ F. Dugdale (FEH) to E. Clodd, 16 Jan 1913 (Leeds).
⁴⁷ *CL*, 1.269–70.
⁴⁸ 'Life' TS, fo. 338 (*PN*, 235); TH to Mrs Harrison, 18 Mar 1892, quoted in C. A. Wilson, *Thirteen Author Collections of the Nineteenth Century*, ed. J. C. S. Wilson and D. A. Randall (2 vols., New York, 1950), 1.74–5; TH to M. Fawcett, 14 Apr 1892 (*CL*, 1.264).
⁴⁹ TH to G. Douglas, 13 Apr 1892 (Eton); 'Life' TS, ff. 338a, 339 (*PN*, 235).
⁵⁰ *CL*, 1.268–9; 'Book of Gosse' (Cambridge); *LY*, 8–9, *CL*, 1.271.
⁵¹ TH to G. Douglas, 8 Oct 1892 (*CL*, 1.285).
⁵² *LY*, 10; prayerbook, DCM; TH's MS of leaflet (J. Stevens Cox); *LY*, 10; Horace, *Part I. Odes* (London, 1855), 17 (RLP); *LY*, 10.
⁵³ *LY*, 11.

17 FLORENCE HENNIKER

¹ For Rebekah and Catharine Owen see Weber, *Lady*.
² *DCC*, 15 Sept 1892; Weber, *Lady*, 67.
³ *Mayor of Casterbridge*, vii; Purdy, 53–4; Weber, *Lady*, 64–6, 86.
⁴ *LY*, 12; *EL*, 11–12, and *LY*, 12–13; *EL*, 12, and 'Notes on TH's Life' (DCM); *LY*, 12.
⁵ Purdy, 281.
⁶ Annotation in TH's copy of Alden's *Oxford Guide* (BL); *LY*, 13.
⁷ Harper Contract Book 6, 453 (Columbia).
⁸ *EL*, 305, 284, and see *Career*, 300–2; *EL*, 297.
⁹ TH to E. Gosse, 31 Mar 1897 (*CL*, II.157); TH, letter, *Academy*, 3 Apr 1897, 381 (cf. *LY*, 59); *EL*, 284; TH to F. Henniker, 3 [July] 1897 (*CL*, II.169).
¹⁰ 'The Pursuit of the Well-Beloved', *Illustrated London News*, 19 Nov 1892, 643.
¹¹ *EL*, 300, 308; *CP*, 566; *EL*, 42.
¹² All quotations, *Illustrated London News*, 15 Oct 1892, 481.
¹³ *Illustrated London News*, 17 Dec 1892, 774.
¹⁴ *Illustrated London News*, 17 Dec 1892, 775; Weber, *Lady*, 78.
¹⁵ *LY*, 13–14; TH to ELH, 12 Oct 1892 (*CL*, 1.287).
¹⁶ TH to A. Blomfield, 11 Oct 1892 (*CL*, 1.286); *LY*, 13–14.
¹⁷ *LY*, 15.
¹⁸ TH to W. M. Colles, 26 Mar and 10 June 1893 (*CL*, II.5–6, 13); Colles to TH, 26 June 1893 (copy, Berg).
¹⁹ W. M. Colles to TH, 5 May 1893 (copy, Berg).
²⁰ Letter, *Weekly Comedy*, 30 Nov 1889, 7; C. W. Jarvis to TH, 1 Apr 1891 (DCM); *EL*, 289; *Pall Mall Gazette*, 31 Aug 1892, 1 (*PW*, 139).
²¹ TH to G. Douglas, 13 Apr 1892 (Eton).
²² TH to J. M. Barrie, 21 Apr 1893 (*CL*, II.7).
²³ Scenario MS, DCM; TH to J. Galsworthy, 26 July 1909 (Purdy, 139–40).
²⁴ *CL*, II.9; Lady Jeune to TH, 4 June 1893 (DCM); Purdy, 79.
²⁵ 'Life' TS, fo. 352 (*PN*, 239).
²⁶ B. Winehouse, 'Thomas Hardy: Some Unpublished Material', *Notes and Queries*, October 1977, 433–4.
²⁷ *LY*, 18; for Mrs Henniker see Purdy, 342–8, and *ORFW*, *passim*; J. McCarthy, *Reminiscences* (New York, 1899), II.61.
²⁸ I. Cooper Willis (citing FEH), pocket-book (DCM).
²⁹ *LY*, 18.
³⁰ *LY*, 19.
³¹ *LY*, 18–20; 'Life' TS, fo. 356 (*PN*, 239).
³² *LY*, 20–1; TH to F. Henniker, 10 June 1893 (*CL*, II.13–14).
³³ TH to F. Henniker, 7 June, 20 June, and 2 July 1893 (*CL*, II.11, 17, 20).
³⁴ F. Henniker MS, 'From the Spanish of G. Bécquer', inserted in 'Literary Notes II' notebook (DCM);

cf. K. G. Wilson, 'Thomas Hardy and Florence Henniker: A Probable Source for Hardy's "Had You Wept",' *Thomas Hardy Yearbook 1977*.

35 TH to F. Henniker, 16 July 1893 (*CL*, II.23–4).

36 *CL*, II.25.

37 'Literary Notes II' notebook, 79 (DCM); book, Bertram Rota catalogue 58, item 416.

38 *CP*, 720.

39 Information from Mr Henry Reed, citing FEH.

40 Annotation in TH's prayerbook (DCM); Weber, *Lady*, 85; *CP*, 68; *CL*, II.28.

41 *CP*, 321, 221, 69; RLP/FEH, 1931; E. Clodd, diary, 18 July 1896 (Alan Clodd).

42 *CP*, 136; cf. *Poems of the Past and the Present*, MS, fo. 79 (Bodleian).

43 RLP/FEH, 1933; TH to F. Henniker, 16 Sept 1893 (*CL*, II.32).

44 *LY*, 24; 'Life' TS, ff. 360–1 (*PN*, 240–1); *LY*, 22.

45 *CL*, II.32; 'An Imaginative Woman', *Pall Mall Magazine*, April 1894, 952; MS, Aberdeen; 'Imaginative Woman', 964, 955, 959, 953, 952, 966; *LY*, 26.

46 *CL*, II.34.

47 *LY*, 25–6; *CL*, II.38.

48 TH to F. Henniker, 10 Sept 1893 (*CL*, II.30).

49 TH to F. Henniker, 28 Oct 1893 (*CL*, II.39–40); *CL*, II.39, 40; TS, fo. 24v (Adams); *CL*, II.40; carbon TS, fo. 1 (Adams).

50 *CL*, II.41, 43.

18 THE MAKING OF *Jude*

1 *Architectural Notebook*, ed. Beatty, Introduction, 30–4.

2 NS (Barclay); J. Stevens Cox (citing Harold Voss), interview, 1980.

3 *CP*, 532.

4 *Times*, 28 Apr 1888, 9; *EL*, 272; *Jude the Obscure* (London, 1896), v.

5 *CL*, I.222; *Times*, 4 Dec 1888, 9; *News of the World*, 7 Dec 1890.

6 Incorrectly dated in Gittings, *Older Hardy*, 66, 74.

7 'Poetical Matter' notebook (photocopy, RLP).

8 *LY*, 137.

9 *Jude the Obscure* (London, 1896), v; *CL*, II.38; W. M. Colles to TH, 10 and 13 Nov 1893 (copies, Berg); TH to C. Shorter, 15 Nov 1893 (*CL*, II.42); *CL*, II.43.

10 Purdy, 89, and note in Harper Memorandum Book 8 (Columbia).

11 *CL*, II.46; TH to F. Henniker, 15 Jan 1894 (*CL*, II.47).

12 Purdy, 89–90; J. Henry Harper, *The House of Harper* (New York, 1912), 530.

13 TH to Sir Douglas Straight, 20 Jan 1894 (*CL*, II.48).

14 Purdy, 87 and n.

15 *Jude* MS, Fitzwilliam; for the development of the MS see R. C. Slack, 'A Variorum Edition of Thomas Hardy's *Jude the Obscure*' (Ph.D. diss., Univ. of Pittsburgh, 1953), and P. Ingham, 'The Evolution of *Jude the Obscure*', *Review of English Studies*, February and May 1976.

16 Book, Univ. of British Columbia.

17 TH to E. Gosse, 20 Nov 1895 (*CL*, II.99); *Laodicean*, 476.

18 KH to ELH, Thursday [1883?] (DCM); MH to N. Sparks, Sen., 26 Nov 1907 (Barclay).

19 FEH to E. Clodd, Wednesday [24 Nov 1915] (Leeds, quoted Bailey, 27); *Jude*, 352; *CP*, 477, cf. Gittings, *Older Hardy*, 168–9.

20 *Jude*, 276; MS, fo. 149 (Fitzwilliam); book, Adams; see P. Bartlett, ' "Seraph of Heaven": A Shelleyan Dream in Hardy's Fiction', *PMLA*, September 1955, 627, 632–4.

21 *CP*, 389.

22 John Antell, interview, 1972; NS (Barclay).

23 Rabiger, 'Hoffman Papers'.

24 Information from Mr Henry Reed, citing Mr Michael Meyer; TH to E. Gosse, 20 Nov 1895 (*CL*, II.99).

25 E. Clodd, diary, 19 July 1896 (Alan Clodd); TH to E. Gosse, 20 Nov 1895 (*CL*, II.99).

26 Weber, *Lady,* 85; A. P. Watt to ELH, 10 Jan 1894 (DCM).

27 E. Clodd, diary, 1 Oct 1895 (Alan Clodd); D. MacCarthy, Hoffman interview (HP).

28 ELH to M. Haweis, 13 Nov [1894?] (Univ. of British Columbia); ELH to R. Owen, 14 Feb 1899 (Colby).

29 Book, DCM.

30 Quotations from copy of *Keynotes* annotated by both TH and Mrs Henniker (RLP).

31 *New Review,* June 1894, 681.

32 *LY,* 28; *CL,* ii.50.

33 *LY,* 28–9; Weber, *Lady,* 97; TH to ELH, 4 Mar 1894 (*CL,* ii.52).

34 Harper & Brothers Contract Book 6 (Columbia); TH to F. Macmillan, 19 and 22 May 1894 (*CL,* ii.57–9); contract, BL.

35 *LY,* 30–3; Lady Jeune to TH, [1894] (DCM).

36 *CL,* ii.55; *Sketch,* 30 May 1894, 219; *Illustrated London News,* 18 Aug 1894, 195.

37 *LY,* 30–1; E. Clodd, diary, 14 May 1894 (Alan Clodd).

38 *LY,* 32; 'Life' TS, fo. 369 (DCM); *LY,* 33–4.

39 Purdy, 90n.; drawing, DCM; *Jude* MS, Fitzwilliam.

40 *LY,* 34; Sampson, 'TH—Justice of the Peace', 273; *LY,* 34–5.

41 ELH to M. Haweis, 13 Nov [1894?] (Univ. of British Columbia); *CL,* ii.64.

42 *CL,* ii.63; Purdy, 279–81.

43 *Far from the Madding Crowd* (London, 1895), v.

44 *Career,* 127–8; *Far from the Madding Crowd* (London, 1895), vi.

45 *Tess,* ix.

46 TH to E. Clodd, 1 Apr 1894 (*CL,* ii.54).

47 *Wessex Tales* (London, 1896), v–vi.

48 *Tess,* x; TH to J. H. Morgan, 12 Oct 1922 (Berg)

49 *LY,* 35–6.

50 H. Macbeth-Raeburn's notes on verso of TH to Macbeth-Raeburn, March 1895 (Adams); agreement, Pierpont Morgan Library.

51 TH to C. Shorter, 7 and 14 Mar 1895 (*CL,* ii.71–2).

52 TH to ELH, 8 May 1895 (*CL,* ii.76); Mrs Campbell to TH, 10 July 1895 (DCM); TH to Mrs Campbell, 10 July 1895 (*CL,* ii.81).

53 TH to F. Henniker, 4 Aug 1895 (*CL,* ii.83); *Daily News,* 29 July 1895; *Independent* (New York), 22 Nov 1894; TH to G. Herriot, 10 Jan 1895 (*CL,* ii.66); certificate, Divorce Registry.

54 Book, DCM; *CP,* 670; 'Poetical Matter' notebook (photocopy, RLP).

55 *LY,* 37–8; *DCC,* 12 Sept 1895; for Agnes Grove see D. Hawkins, 'Concerning Agnes', *Encounter,* February 1977; *CP,* 878.

56 *CL,* ii.87.

57 W. Robertson Nicoll, *A Bookman's Letters* (London, 1913), 7; G. Gissing to TH, 3 Sept 1895 (DCM); *EL,* ii.86.

58 G. Gissing to A. Gissing, 22 Sept 1895, in *Yale University Library Gazette,* January 1943, 52; G. Gissing to E. Bertz, 22 Sept 1895, in *The Letters of George Gissing to Eduard Bertz 1887–1903,* ed. A. C. Young (London, 1961), 206.

59 *Letters of Gissing to Bertz,* 206; Archer, *Real Conversations,* 32; *Yale University Library Gazette,* January 1943, 52.

60 E. Clodd, diary, 29 Sept 1895 (Alan Clodd); Thornycroft visit, information from Dr C. J. P. Beatty; TH to G. Allen, 7 Jan 1896 (*CL,* ii.106).

61 TH to F. Henniker, 12 Aug 1895 (*CL,* ii.84); *Jude the Obscure* (London, 1896), vi.

62 *Jude the Obscure* (London, 1895), 97, 143, etc.; proofs, Signet Library, Edinburgh; *CL,* ii.84.

19   The Publication of *Jude*

1 Douglas, 'TH: Some Recollections and Reflections', 396.

2 *Guardian,* 13 Nov 1895, 1770; *Pall Mall Gazette,* 12 Nov 1895, 4.

3 TH to W. Archer, 17 Oct and 14 Nov 1895 (*CL,* ii.90, 96).

⁴ *World,* 13 Nov 1895, 15.
⁵ *CL,* II.92–9; quotations, 94, 99.
⁶ *St. James's Gazette,* 8 Nov 1895, 4; TH to E. Gosse, 10 Nov 1895 (*CL,* II.93).
⁷ *CL,* II.99, 105.
⁸ A. Lang to E. Clodd, 1 May 1892 (*Journal of Rutgers University Library,* December 1949, 4).
⁹ *CL,* I.290.
¹⁰ *LY,* 48; TH to E. Clodd, 17 Jan 1897 (*CL,* II.143); *LY,* 48, 49.
¹¹ TH to E. Clodd, 17 Jan 1897 (*CL,* II.143).
¹² 'Life' TS, ff. 388–9 (*PN,* 245); *LY,* 7, and 'Life' TS, fo. 340 (*PN,* 236).
¹³ TH to E. Gosse, 14 July 1909 (BL).
¹⁴ TH to F. Henniker, 17 Mar 1903 (DCM).
¹⁵ *LY,* 39–40; Pearl Craigie to TH, 19 Nov 1895, E. Terry to TH, 28 Nov 1895, 'George Egerton' to TH, 22 Nov 1895 (all DCM).
¹⁶ *LY,* 43–4; TH to G. Douglas, 9 Dec 1895 (*CL,* II.100).
¹⁷ Mrs Campbell to Mrs S. Coleridge, 12 Jan 1896 (DCM).
¹⁸ *CL,* II.109; J. Forbes-Robertson to TH, [January 1896] and 14 Feb 1896 (DCM); F. Harrison to TH, 4 Mar 1896 (DCM); TH to H. A. Jones, 15 Mar 1896 (*CL,* II.113–14).
¹⁹ TH to Harper & Brothers, 14 Feb 1896 (*CL,* II.111–12), and see *'Tess' in the Theatre,* ed. M. Roberts (Toronto, 1950), xxxiv–l.
²⁰ Mrs Campbell to TH, 4 Aug 1896 (DCM); TH to Mrs Campbell, 7 Aug 1896 (*CL,* II.128); *CL,* II.149; letter, *Times,* 21 Feb 1900.
²¹ *CL,* II.111, 112.
²² *LY,* 46; *CL,* II.112, 109, 108.
²³ *CL,* II.123.
²⁴ *CL,* II.116, 118.
²⁵ Hawkins, 'Concerning Agnes', 47; *LY,* 52–3.
²⁶ *Under the Greenwood Tree* (London, 1896), vi.
²⁷ *CL,* II.124; *LY,* 53.
²⁸ *LY,* 53–4; 'Life' TS, fo. 395 (*PN,* 246); *LY,* 54; book, DCM.
²⁹ *LY,* 54–7; TH to F. Henniker, 24 Sept 1896 (*CL,* II.130); *CL,* II.134.

³⁰ *Spectator,* 31 Oct 1896, 593.
³¹ TH to A. Grove, 15 Nov and 6 Dec 1896 (*CL,* II.137, 140).
³² ELH to R. Owen, 19 Feb 1897 (Colby).
³³ Cutting in DCM; the date, 'Sept 5. 1891', added in TH's hand, appears to be incorrect.
³⁴ ELH to R. Owen, 19 Feb 1897 (Colby).
³⁵ G. Gifford, letter, *TLS,* 1 Jan 1944, 7; A. Sutro, *Celebrities and Simple Souls* (London, 1933), 58.
³⁶ F. M. Ford, *Mightier Than the Sword* (London, 1938), 128–30; cf. Gittings, *Older Hardy,* 81, and Kay-Robinson, *First Mrs TH,* 153–6.
³⁷ Weber, *Lady,* 117.
³⁸ *Jude,* viii.
³⁹ F. Dugdale (FEH) to E. Clodd, 8 Nov 1910 (Leeds).
⁴⁰ FEH to Lady Grove, 9 Dec 1914 (WRO); *CP,* 167, 319.
⁴¹ *LY,* 57–8.
⁴² *World,* 24 Mar 1897, 13–14.
⁴³ TH to F. Henniker, 31 Mar 1897 (*CL,* II.157).
⁴⁴ TH to L. Hind, 27 Mar 1897 (*CL,* II.155); G. E. Buckle to TH, 10 Apr 1897 (DCM); 'Life' TS, fo. 401 (*PN,* 246–7).
⁴⁵ *Academy,* 25 Mar 1897, 345.
⁴⁶ *The Well-Beloved* (London, 1897), 88.
⁴⁷ TH to G. Douglas, 25 Mar 1897 (*CL,* II.154); *The Well-Beloved* (London, 1897), 338.
⁴⁸ TH to E. Gosse, 21 Mar 1897 (*CL,* II.153).
⁴⁹ TH to G. Douglas, 21 Dec 1888 (*CL,* I.182).

20 Keeping Separate

¹ *LY,* 58.
² *CL,* II.166, and cf. *CL,* II.192–3; *DCC,* 8 Apr 1897.
³ *LY,* 66; *CL,* II.165.
⁴ *CL,* II.166–7; *LY,* 67–8; ELH, 1887/1897 diary (DCM); *CP,* 106.
⁵ ELH, 1887/1897 diary (DCM); *LY,* 69–70; *Times,* 8 July 1897.
⁶ *CL,* II.169, 171, 170–2.

7 'Life' TS, fo. 411 (*PN, 248*); *LY, 71*; *CL*, II.172; *CP, 319*.
8 Bible and prayerbook, DCM; *Psalter*, RLP.
9 *LY, 72*, and see Purdy, 102.
10 *CL*, II.173–4; ELH letters, Mme Rolland.
11 C. M. Fisher, *Life in Thomas Hardy's Dorchester 1888–1908* (Beaminster, Dorset, 1965), 17; invitation card, DCM.
12 *CL*, II.174, 180; *LY, 72*; TH to G. Douglas, 3 Mar 1898 (*CL*, II.188).
13 TH to W. J. Locke, 27 Nov 1897 (*CL*, II.182); *CL*, II.176–7, 178–9.
14 TH to W. Archer, 24 Nov 1898 (*CL*, II.206).
15 TH to KH, 8 May 1898 (*CL*, II.193); *LY, 74*; TH to C. Shorter, [28 Apr 1901?] (*CL*, II.285).
16 W. Gifford to ELH, 7 Sept and 24 Oct 1898 (DCM).
17 K. Fisher, *Conversations with Sylvia: Sylvia Gosse, Painter, 1881–1968* (London, 1975), 27.
18 Mrs Ethel Skinner, interview, 1978; G. Gifford, letter, *TLS*, 1 Jan 1944, 7.
19 ELH to R. Owen, 24 Apr 1899 (Colby).
20 ELH to R. Owen, 24 Apr 1899 (Colby); *Animals' Friend*, March 1898, 108–9; ELH's copy of leaflet, DCM; *Times*, 26 Feb 1895; *Daily Chronicle*, 4 Sept 1899 (signed 'Protest'); E. H. Begbie to ELH, 8 Mar 1898 (DCM); Editor of *Temple Bar* to ELH, 8 July 1898 (DCM).
21 ELH to E. Clodd, 29 Mar 1897 (Leeds, quoted Kay-Robinson, *First Mrs TH*, 262–3).
22 *Wessex Poems* (London, 1898), 3.
23 *CP*, 81.
24 TH to E. Gosse, 27 Dec 1898 (*CL*, II.208); *Collected Letters of George Meredith*, ed. C. L. Cline (3 vols., Oxford, 1970), III.1338.
25 *Saturday Review*, 7 Jan 1899, 19; *Athenaeum*, 14 Jan 1899, 41; *Outlook*, 28 Jan 1899, 823.
26 'Literary Notes II' notebook, 73–4 (DCM); TH to L. Johnson, 9 Feb 1899 (*CL*, II.212–13); L. Stephen to TH, 3 Jan 1899, A. C. Swinburne to

TH, 26 Dec 1898, T. Watts-Dunton to TH, 23 Feb 1899 (all DCM); TH to F. Henniker, 1 Jan 1899 (*CL*, II.209).
27 A. Pretor to ELH, two undated letters [1899?] (DCM).
28 RLP/FEH, 1933.
29 RLP/FEH, 1933.
30 ELH to R. Owen, 24 Apr 1899 (Colby, partly quoted Bailey, 23).
31 ELH to E. Grahame, 20 Aug 1899 (Bodleian, quoted Kay-Robinson, *First Mrs TH*, 175).
32 ELH to Mrs MacCarthy, 3 Nov 1902 (Mrs Michael MacCarthy).
33 B. Newcombe to N. Gosse, 8 Mar [1900] (DCM).
34 *EL*, 96.
35 A. C. Benson, diary, 5 Sept 1912 (Magdalene College, Cambridge); FEH to R. Owen, 17 July 1915 (Colby); R. Owen, note on ELH to R. Owen, 26 Dec 1899 (Colby).
36 Bible, DCM; Wollstonecraft, RLP.
37 *CL*, II.222.
38 *LY*, 82–3; O'Rourke, *TH: His Secretary Remembers*, 7.
39 *CL*, II.226, 227.
40 TH to F. Henniker, 26 Aug 1899 (*CL*, II.228).
41 Purdy, 306; *Daily Chronicle*, 24 Aug 1899, 3.
42 *CL*, II.229.
43 TH to F. Henniker, 17 Sept and 11 Oct 1899 (*CL*, II.229, 232).
44 TH to A. Henniker, 19 Oct 1899 (*CL*, II.233, and n.); Mrs Ethel Skinner to RLP, 1 Jan 1973 (RLP), and interview, 1978.
45 *CP*, 86; *Times*, 11 Oct 1899; G. Gissing, 'Tyrtaeus', *Review of the Week*, 4 Nov 1899, in *Gissing Newsletter*, July 1974, 3; TH to Gissing, 5 Nov 1899 (*CL*, II.235).
46 TH to F. Henniker, 19 Dec 1899 (*CL*, II.241).
47 *CL*, II.238, 240.
48 *CP*, 90; *Daily Chronicle*, 25 Dec 1899, 4, and 28 Dec 1899 (*PW*, 202).
49 *CL*, II.247; TH to F. Henniker, 25 Feb 1900 (*CL*, II.248).
50 TH to F. Henniker, 24 Dec 1900 (*CL*, II.277).

51 TH to F. Henniker, 22 Oct 1900 (*CL*, II.269).

52 *CL*, II.265.

53 Lady Grove to ELH, 20 Mar 1900 (DCM).

54 Editor of *Westminster Gazette* to ELH, 27 Mar 1900 (DCM).

55 *Sphere*, 14 Apr 1900, 393; ELH to R. Owen, May 1900 (Colby); *Sphere*, 393.

56 *Academy*, 27 Apr 1901, 355.

57 ELH to R. Owen, May 1900 (Colby).

58 *LY*, 85; *CL*, II.257, 245, 257–8.

59 *LY*, 86; *CL*, II.263–4; A. E. Housman to TH, 11 July 1900 (DCM).

60 Lea, *TH Through the Camera's Eye*, 23.

61 *CL*, II.272; TH to ELH, 11 Dec 1900 (*CL*, II.276).

62 Weber, *Lady*, 136.

63 ELH to R. Owen, 31 Dec 1900 (Colby).

64 *CP*, 150.

21   PESSIMISTIC MELIORIST

1 E. Gosse, 'Form in Poetry', *Literature*, 4 Mar 1899; TH to Gosse, 6 Mar 1899 (*CL*, II.216–17); note, Adams.

2 Archer, *Real Conversations*, 45–7.

3 Book, RLP; E. Clodd, diary, 3 Feb 1896 (Alan Clodd); 'Poetical Matter' notebook (photocopy, RLP); TH to H. Rider Haggard [May 1891?] (*CL*, I.235); TH to F. Henniker, 22 Oct 1900 (*CL*, II.269).

4 TH to F. Henniker, 4 Apr 1901 and 22 Oct 1900 (*CL*, II.283, 269); *Humanity*, August 1901, 155–6.

5 TH to F. Henniker, 15 Feb and 2 June 1901 (*CL*, II.280, 288).

6 *CL*, II.282, 286, 287; *LY*, 88; TH to F. Harrison, 4 Apr 1901 (*CL*, II.283).

7 *LY*, 89; information from RLP, citing FEH; see T. O'Sullivan, *Thomas Hardy: An Illustrated Biography* (London, 1975), 143; *Sphere*, 7 Sept 1901, 288.

8 *LY*, 89.

9 *LY*, 89; Bath, 'TH and Evangeline F. Smith', 44; MH to N. Sparks, Sen., November 1903 (Barclay).

10 TH's diagram of route, Barclay; TH to C. M. Hardy, 22 Jan 1908 (Millgate).

11 NS (Barclay); KH, diary, 3, 4, 5, 9, 15 July 1916 (Lock).

12 NS (Barclay); TH to N. Sparks, Sen., 22 Nov 1902 (Barclay).

13 Purdy, 118–19.

14 *CP*, 122.

15 *Bookman*, January 1902, 131, 132.

16 Letter, *Academy*, 17 May 1902, 515.

17 TH to F. Macmillan, 18 Mar 1902 (BL); TH to C. McIlvaine, 28 Feb 1902, to G. H. Thring, 4 Mar 1902 (both DCM), and to McIlvaine, 10 Mar 1902 (Morgan Library).

18 TH to F. Macmillan, 18 Mar, 22 Mar, 31 Mar, and 9 July 1902 (all BL); for Macmillan's replies, see Morgan, *House of Macmillan*, 155–9. See also M. Millgate, 'The Making and Unmaking of Hardy's Wessex Edition', in *Editing Nineteenth-Century Fiction*, ed. J. Millgate (New York, 1978).

19 ELH to R. Owen, 4 Mar 1902 (Colby, partly quoted Bailey, 22); TH to E. Clodd, 2 June 1902 (Leeds).

20 Annotation in prayerbook (DCM); *LY*, 100; TH to F. Henniker, 28 Nov 1902 (*ORFW*, 107–8).

21 TH to F. Henniker, 28 Nov 1902 (*ORFW*, 107–8); TH to G. Douglas, 2 Dec 1902 (NLS).

22 TH to D. Allhusen, 5 Mar 1902 (Dr C. J. P. Beatty).

23 *LY*, 98–9, and Purdy, 308; Rider Haggard, *Rural England*, 1.283 (revised text in *LY*, 94).

24 TH to F. Macmillan, 31 Mar 1902 (BL).

25 TH to F. Macmillan, 31 Mar 1902 (BL); letter, *Guardian*, 16 Apr 1902; TH to F. Macmillan, 11 Oct 1902 (BL).

26 TH to W. Watkins, 11 June 1906 (*Society of Dorset Men in London: Year-Book 1906–7*, 45).

27 See W. J. Keith, 'Thomas Hardy and the Literary Pilgrims', *Nineteenth-Century Fiction*, June 1969.

28 TH to F. Henniker, 22 Dec 1904 (*ORFW*, 119–20); Henry W. Nevinson, *More Changes More Chances* (London, 1925), 165; *CL*, II.131–4; E. New to TH, 1 Apr 1900 (DCM); TH to W. Tyndale, 14 Sept 1905 (David Holmes); TH to H. Lea, 29 May 1905 and 5 July 1912 (DCM).

29 TH to H. Lea, 9 and 12 Nov 1904 (DCM).

30 TH to A. R. Andrews, 7 Jan 1902 (Yale), and to E. W. Kerr, 6 Apr 1902 (DCM).

31 TH to H. Lea, 1 June 1905 (DCM).

32 *ORFW*, 109.

33 TH to the Revd S. Boulter, 1 Feb 1903 (DCM); Beatty, 'Architecture in the Life and Work of TH', 71–84.

34 Sampson, 'TH—Justice of the Peace', 273; TH to E. Clodd, 2 June 1902 (Leeds).

35 *DCC*, 19 Jan 1928, 4.

36 TH to M. Shipley, [early April 1903] (DCM).

37 TH to G. Douglas, 27 May 1903 (NLS); E. Clodd, diary, 31 May and 9 June 1903 (Alan Clodd); C. Shorter to E. Clodd, 16 Feb 1908 (Leeds).

38 H. W. Nevinson, *Changes and Chances* (London, 1923), 307–8; FEH to E. Clodd, 27 Oct 1923 (Leeds); J.-É. Blanche, *Mes Modèles* (Paris, 1928), 82; NS (Barclay); RLP/FEH, 1935; *CL*, II.190.

39 E. M. Forbes, 'Some Noteworthy Hands', *New Review*, June 1894, 695.

40 TH, 'H.J.M.', 12–13 (*PW*, 71–2); TH to ELH, 20 June and 2 July 1903 (DCM).

41 TH to F. Henniker, 13 Sept 1903 (*ORFW*, 112–13).

42 TH to J. Sparks, 2 Sept 1903 (Barclay); medallion, Barclay.

43 TH to E. Clodd, 22 Mar 1904 (BL); TH to F. Macmillan, 28 Sept 1903 (BL); TH to G. Douglas, 31 Oct 1903 (NLS).

44 TH to F. Macmillan, 20 Nov 1903, and to Macmillan & Co., 4 Oct 1903 (both BL).

45 Purdy, 122–3; TH to F. Macmillan, 20 Nov 1903 (BL), to F. Henniker, 23 Dec 1903 (*ORFW*, 114–15).

22   *The Dynasts*

1 ELH to E. Churchill, 23 Nov 1903 (Millgate).

2 TH to ELH, 13, 16, and 21 Nov 1903 (DCM).

3 TH to ELH, 29 Nov 1903 (DCM).

4 E. Churchill to ELH, 29 Nov 1903 (DCM); ELH sketch, DCM; TH to F. Henniker, 23 Dec 1903 (*ORFW*, 114–15).

5 *The Dynasts*, Part First (London, 1904), ix.

6 *Dynasts*, Part First, viii, 1.

7 M. Beerbohm, 'Thomas Hardy as Panoramatist', *Saturday Review*, 30 Jan 1904, 137.

8 TH, letter, *TLS*, 5 Feb 1904, 37.

9 TH to B. Crackanthorpe, 3 Dec 1903 (Brigham Young Univ.); TH to A. Quiller-Couch, 15 Aug 1906 (Miss F. F. Quiller-Couch); *EL*, 232.

10 TH to A. E. Drinkwater, 6 Nov 1915 (copy, BL).

11 *TLS*, 19 Feb 1904, 53.

12 *LY*, 103; TH to E. Gosse, 31 Jan 1904 (Berg).

13 TH to E. Clodd, 22 Mar 1904 (BL); TH to A. E. Moule, 20 Mar 1904 (the Revd G. R. K. Moule).

14 *CP*, 270.

15 TH to H. Lea, 21 Mar and 5 Apr 1904 (DCM); TH to MH, 3 May 1904 (Barclay); Purdy, 309; *Daily Chronicle*, 9 Apr 1904, 4.

16 TH to F. Henniker, 18 Apr 1904 (*ORFW*, 117), to E. Clodd, 12 Apr 1904 (NYU).

17 Prayerbook, DCM.

18 TH to E. Clodd, 12 Apr 1904 (NYU); Clodd, diary, 22 June 1903 (Alan Clodd).

19 'Book of Gosse' (Cambridge).

20 TH to the Revd E. Filleul, 18 July 1904 (Colby).

21 *Tatler*, 25 May 1904; TH to A. Rothenstein, 16 Jan 1904 (Harvard); ELH to C. Shorter, 15 Sept 1904 (RLP).

22 H. C. C. Moule (citing his father, C. W. Moule), interview, 1975; D. Stickland, *Thomas Hardy at Cattistock* (St. Peter Port, Guernsey, 1968), 95; ELH to C. Shorter, 3

Oct 1904 (RLP); TH to H.
Thornycroft, 4 Oct 1904 (DCM).
23 Death certificate; TH to E. Gosse,
20 Oct 1904 (Leeds).
24 Information from Dr C. J. P.
Beatty, also from C. J. Norris and
F. Rampton (former colleagues of
G. Gifford).
25 TH to A. Symons, 23 Oct 1904
(David Holmes), to E. Gosse, 30 Oct
1904 (Leeds); *PN*, 290; *Athenaeum*,
29 Oct 1904, 591.
26 TH to F. Henniker, 25 Sept 1904
(*ORFW*, 117–18).
27 *LY*, 109; TH to H. Grierson, 12
Mar 1905 (transcript, RLP);
measurements, Adams.
28 *LY*, 110–12; G. H. Thring to TH,
November 1905 (DCM); A. C.
Benson, diary, 24 Jan 1902
(Magdalene College, Cambridge).
29 G. Meredith to E. Gosse, 2 July
1905 (*Collected Letters of George
Meredith*, III.1529); E. Clodd, diary,
28 Sept 1905 (Alan Clodd).
30 *LY*, 113–14; ELH to C. Shorter, 6
Sept 1905 (RLP); E. Sharp,
Unfinished Adventure (London,
1933), 96.
31 *LY*, 114; 'Poetical Matter'
notebook (photocopy, RLP).
32 F. W. Maitland to TH, 17 July
1905 (DCM); TH to A. Symons, 20
Oct 1905 (Texas); TH to F.
Henniker, 31 Mar 1897 (*CL*, II.157).
33 *Morning Leader*, 1 Feb 1905;
Times, 12 Jan 1906; *Fortnightly
Review*, April 1906, 638–9 (cf. *LY*,
115–16).
34 ELH to I. Zangwill, 30 Apr 1906
(Central Zionist Archives, and in
B. Winehouse, 'TH: Some
Unpublished Material', 435–6).
35 ELH to R. Owen, 26 Dec 1906
(Colby); TH to C. Shorter, 25 Dec
1905 (Leeds).
36 F. Macmillan to G. P. Brett, 12
Oct 1905 (NYPL); Purdy, 126, 128–9.
37 *ORFW*, 123.
38 T. E. Lawrence to R. Graves, 8
Nov 1923, in *The Letters of T. E.
Lawrence*, ed. D. Garnett (London,
1938), 429; Felkin, 'Days with TH',
30.

39 'Poetical Matter' notebook
(photocopy, RLP); *CP*, 270.
40 Sketch, DCM (Morrison,
Exhibition, 7).

23   AFTER THE VISIT

1 TH to F. Dugdale (FEH), 2 Jan
1906 (RLP).
2 Mrs Ethel Richardson, MS,
recollections of FEH (Pamela
Richardson); Education Department,
*Queen's Scholarship Examination,
December 1897*, 44; R. Gittings and
J. Manton, *The Second Mrs Hardy*
(London, 1979), 22.
3 E. Richardson, recollections of
FEH (Pamela Richardson); Gittings
and Manton, *Second Mrs Hardy*,
25–8.
4 E. Richardson, recollections of
FEH (Pamela Richardson); RLP,
citing Mrs Margaret Soundy.
5 RLP/FEH, 1935; TH to F.
Dugdale (FEH), 10 Aug 1905 (RLP).
6 RLP/FEH, 1935, 1931; *CP*, 309.
7 TH to F. Dugdale (FEH), 2 Jan
1906 (RLP); photographs, DCM.
8 British Library archives;
information from Mr David Pam.
9 FEH to Carroll A. Wilson, 20 Mar
1937 (copy, RLP); TH to F. Dugdale
(FEH), 21 Mar 1907 (RLP).
10 Purdy, 129; E. Gosse to TH, 26
Feb 1906, in Charteris, *Gosse*, 299.
11 TH to A. Symons, 2 Mar 1906
(Univ. of California, Berkeley).
12 *LY*, 117; TH to H. A. Jones, 4
June 1906 (NYU), to A. Symons,
2 June 1906 (Univ. of California,
Berkeley); Nevinson, *More Changes
More Chances*, 164–5.
13 Nevinson, *More Changes More
Chances*, 165; *LY*, 117; TH to F.
Henniker, 12 June 1906 (*ORFW*,
127–8).
14 Blanche, *Mes Modèles*, 82; TH to
D. Allhusen, 3 Aug 1907 (RLP).
15 *ORFW*, 130.
16 TH to E. Gosse, 25 July 1906
(Leeds) and 31 Oct 1906 (Adams).
17 TH to J. McT. E. McTaggart, 23
May 1906 (in G. Lowes Dickinson,

J. McT. E. McTaggart [Cambridge, 1931], 100–1), to E. Wright, 2 June 1907 (DCM).

[18] TH to F. Harrison, 17 Oct 1906 (Texas).

[19] Nevinson, *More Changes More Chances*, 181.

[20] *LY*, 123–4; 'Book of Gosse' (Cambridge); Charteris, *Gosse*, 292–3.

[21] Blanche, *Mes Modèles*, 85, 84.

[22] *ORFW*, 132–3, and TH to F. Macmillan, 10 Oct 1907 (BL); TH to F. Henniker, 31 Dec 1907 (*ORFW*, 135–6), to E. Gosse, 3 Nov 1907 (BL).

[23] W. J. Courtney to TH, 3 Oct 1907 (DCM); TH to F. Henniker, 31 Dec 1907 (*ORFW*, 135–6).

[24] See the draft page reproduced in Purdy, opp. 131.

[25] TH to F. Dugdale (FEH), 29 Apr and 21 Mar 1907 (RLP).

[26] *Poems*, Adams; *Rubáiyat*, RLP; TH to M. Macmillan, 8 July 1907 (BL), to A. Marshall, 9 July 1907 (Adams).

[27] TH to R. Smith, 26 Sept 1907 (NLS); F. Dugdale, 'The Apotheosis of the Minx', *Cornhill*, May 1908.

[28] TH to E. Grahame, 31 Aug 1907 (Bodleian).

[29] Blanche, *Mes Modèles*, 83–4; Lady Grove, *The Social Fetich* (London, 1907); *Social Fetich*, proofs (RLP); TH to Lady Grove, 16 Aug 1907 (RLP); *CP*, 81.

[30] ELH to Lady Grove, 9 Dec 1907 (RLP).

[31] TH to F. Henniker, 29 Sept 1907 (*ORFW*, 133–4).

[32] *Social Fetich*, proofs (RLP).

[33] TH to H. Pouncy, [21 Oct 1907] (Taylor); Purdy, 351; *DCC*, 7 May 1908.

[34] *DCC*, 7 May 1908.

[35] Purdy, 351; TH to H. Child, 16 Nov 1908 (Adams).

[36] *DCC*, 26 Nov 1908.

[37] *ORFW*, 136–7; TH to ELH, 6 July 1908 (DCM).

[38] TH to *Strand Magazine*, 31 July 1908 (present location unknown); TH to C. Shorter, 17 Aug 1908 (Univ. of California, Berkeley).

[39] ELH to R. Owen, 20 May 1908 (Colby).

[40] Information from Mr Henry Lock; cf. TH to E. Lane, 25 Feb 1905 (DCM).

[41] TH to ELH, 19 Sept 1908 (DCM); ELH to TH, 10 Sept 1908 (Eton); TH to ELH, 15 Sept 1908 (DCM); TH to ELH, [19 Oct 1908] (DCM), to the Revd C. Wix, 23 Oct 1908 (Taylor).

[42] *DCC*, 31 Dec 1908, 11.

[43] *DCC*, 31 Dec 1908, 11; ELH to R. Owen, 16 June 1908 (Colby).

[44] TH to the Revd C. Wix, 23 Oct 1908 (Taylor); Sampson, 'TH—Justice of the Peace', 273–4; *LY*, 134.

[45] TH to T. Turner, 27 Sept 1908 (SPAB).

[46] TH to W. Raleigh, 19 Jan 1907 and 29 Jan 1908 (Bodleian); for an excellent account, see W. J. Keith, 'Thomas Hardy's Edition of William Barnes', *Victorian Poetry*, Summer 1977.

[47] Preface, *Select Poems of William Barnes* (London, 1908), iii, xii (*PW*, 76, 82).

[48] TH to [F. Dugdale?], 12 Apr 1909 (*LY*, 136).

[49] *LY*, 137–8; TH to M. Hewlett, 11 June 1909 (draft, DCM).

[50] Luigi Illica, *Tess: A Drama in Four Acts* (London, 1909), 50, and see D. Hawkins, 'Tess in the Opera House,' *Contemporary Review*, July 1974; *LY*, 139; TH to ELH, 9 July 1909 (DCM); TH to E. Clodd, 13 July 1909 (BL).

[51] See Gittings and Manton, *Second Mrs Hardy*, 49; E. Clodd, diary, 14 July 1909 (Alan Clodd).

[52] E. Clodd, diary, 5 July 1909 (Alan Clodd); TH to Clodd, 22 July 1909 (BL).

[53] E. Clodd, diary, 16 Aug 1909 (Alan Clodd); Clodd to C. Shorter, 13 Aug 1909 (Leeds); *Aldeburgh, Leiston and Saxmundham Times*, 21 Aug 1909, 3.

[54] E. Clodd, diary, 14, 21, and 23 Aug 1909 (Alan Clodd); F. Dugdale (FEH) to E. Richardson, 18 Aug 1909 (Pamela Richardson); H. Hardy

to KH, 30 Sept 1909 (Millgate), and *LY*, 139.

55 Gittings and Manton, *Second Mrs Hardy*, 33, 39; K. Tynan, 'Dora Sigerson: A Tribute and Some Memories', *Observer* (London), 13 Jan 1918; K. Tynan Hinkson to F. Dugdale (FEH), 17 Dec 1911 (Berg); Maggs Bros. catalogue 664 (1938), item 207; FEH to R. Owen, 17 Dec 1915 and [15 Mar 1916?] (Colby); Gittings and Manton, *Second Mrs Hardy*, 66.

56 TH to C. Shorter, 17 Aug 1908 (Univ. of California, Berkeley); cf. Gittings and Manton, *Second Mrs Hardy*, 35–7.

57 'Mr. Thomas Hardy. Marriage with Ex-Member of "Standard" Staff', *Standard*, 11 Feb 1914; FEH to R. Owen [15 Mar 1916?] (Colby).

58 RLP/FEH, 1936; *CP*, 195; FEH to M. Stopes, 16 Sept 1928 (BL).

59 *CP*, 310, 310, 221, 310, 309.

60 *CP*, 311–12.

61 E. Clodd, diary, 30 Oct 1909 (Alan Clodd); TH to F. Henniker, 28 Nov 1909 (*ORFW*, 142).

62 *CP*, 310, 311.

63 TH to F. Macmillan, 18 Sept 1909 (BL).

64 TH to M. Rolland, 1 Feb 1910 (Mme Rolland); Purdy, 149–50.

65 *LY*, 141; FEH to SCC, 6 Dec 1918 (RLP); *CP*, 323; TH to Lady Gregory, 7 June 1910 (Major Gregory); *Standard*, 2 June 1910; TH to E. Clodd, 17 June 1910 (BL).

66 *LY*, 119.

67 *LY*, 142–3; TH to ELH, 3 May 1910 (DCM).

68 *LY*, 142.

69 TH to Lady Grove, [6 June 1910?] (RLP); TH to M. Sinclair, 4 June 1910 (Univ. of Pennsylvania).

70 F. Dugdale (FEH) to ELH, 18 June, early July, and 23 July 1910 (DCM).

71 F. Dugdale (FEH) to ELH, 27 Oct, 11 Nov, and 20 Nov 1910 (DCM).

72 E. Clodd, diary, 23 June 1910 (Alan Clodd).

73 TH to E. Clodd, 15 Nov 1910 (Leeds), to H. Newbolt, 15 Nov 1910 (Texas).

74 F. Dugdale (FEH) to E. Clodd, 11 Nov, 8 Nov, 19 Nov, 11 Nov 1910 (Leeds).

75 F. Dugdale (FEH) to KH, 20 Oct 1910 (Eton); Strang sketch, DCM (see *LY*, opp. 160); flowers, RLP.

76 F. Dugdale (FEH) to E. Clodd, 19 Nov 1910 (Leeds).

77 FEH to SCC, 25 Dec 1925 (RLP); F. Dugdale (FEH) to ELH, 20 Nov 1910 (DCM); 'Life' TS, fo. 504 (*PN*, 260).

78 TH to H. H. Asquith, 5 Nov 1908 (Bodleian); *LY*, 142–3; E. Smith to TH, 21 July 1910 (DCM).

79 A. C. Benson, diary, 5 Sept 1912 (Magdalene College, Cambridge); RLP/FEH, 1936; *LY*, 143.

80 *Times*, 17 June 1910, 8.

81 *LY*, 143; Purdy, 352; F. Dugdale (FEH) to E. Clodd, 19 Nov 1910 (Leeds).

24 A Funeral and a Marriage

1 F. Dugdale (FEH) to E. Clodd, 3 June 1911 (Leeds); *LY*, 148–9; E. Richardson, recollections of FEH (Pamela Richardson); TH to the Earl Marshal, 2 Mar 1911 (draft, DCM); H. Hardy to M. Antell, 19 June 1911 (Eton); RLP, notes on conversation with Constance Dugdale, 1948.

2 *LY*, 151; TH to F. Dugdale (FEH), December 1911 (RLP); F. Dugdale to E. Clodd, 11 Dec 1911 (Leeds).

3 TH to F. Dugdale (FEH), 11 Jan 1911 (RLP); Purdy, 314; TH to R. Smith, 12 Aug 1910 (NLS).

4 TH to F. Macmillan, 22 Sept 1910 (BL).

5 TH to E. Gosse, 18 July 1913 (Berg); C. Hassall, *Edward Marsh, Patron of the Arts: A Biography* (London, 1959), 226n.

6 *LY*, 150; TH to F. Macmillan, 12 Oct 1910 and 10 Jan 1912 (BL); TH to F. Henniker, 22 Aug 1911 (*ORFW*, 148); TH to F. Macmillan, 2 Apr 1911 (BL).

7 TH to Macmillan & Co., 25 Oct 1911, to D. Macmillan, 5 and 15 Feb 1912 (BL).

8 *LY*, 151–2; E. Gosse, MS, 'A Visit to Thomas Hardy in 1912' (Leeds).

9 *LY*, 149–50.

10 *The Later Life and Letters of Sir Henry Newbolt*, ed. M. Newbolt (London, 1942), 166–8.

11 ELH to C. Shorter, 23 Apr [1908] (RLP).

12 *Some Recollections,* ed. Hardy and Gittings, 61; list, DCM; ELH to L. Gifford, 18 Oct 1911, in H. Gifford, 'Thomas Hardy and Emma', *Essays & Studies of the English Association,* 1966, 113.

13 ELH, *Alleys* (Max Gate: privately printed, 1911), 2; ELH's copy, with corrections, Adams.

14 Professor C. H. Gifford, interview, 1975.

15 ELH, *Spaces* (Max Gate: privately printed, 1912), 25–6.

16 C. Moule to ELH, 3 Oct 1911 (DCM).

17 E. Clodd, diary, 22 June 1904 (Alan Clodd).

18 TH to F. Henniker, 3 Oct 1911 (*ORFW,* 149); *Nash's Magazine,* March 1912, 683.

19 A. C. Benson, diary, 5 Sept 1912 (Magdalene College, Cambridge); Gosse, 'Visit to TH in 1912' (Leeds).

20 A. C. Benson, diary, 5 Sept 1912 (Magdalene College, Cambridge).

21 Information from RLP, citing Margaret Soundy; *CP,* 488–9.

22 Gosse, 'Visit to TH in 1912' (Leeds); A. C. Benson, diary, 5 Sept 1912 (Magdalene College, Cambridge).

23 *Proceedings of Dorset Natural History and Antiquarian Field Club,* 1912, xi, xiii; *LY,* 153; Mrs C. F. Symes, Hoffman interview, 1939 (HP); Kay-Robinson, *First Mrs TH,* 225–6, and *Fordington Monthly Messenger,* August 1912; Alice Harvey (née Gale), interview, 1973; *LY,* 153, 152.

24 A. Harvey, 'I Was Emma Lavinia's Personal Maid', *Thomas Hardy Year Book 1973–1974,* 6–9;

Alice Harvey (née Gale), interview, 1973.

25 TH to Mrs Wood Homer, 21 Dec 1912 (Eton); TH to F. Henniker, 17 Dec 1912 (*ORFW,* 154); verse MSS, Berg.

26 Weber, *Lady,* 161–2; TH to Lady Grove, 21 Dec 1912 (RLP).

27 Harvey, 'I Was Emma Lavinia's Personal Maid', 9; death certificate; TH to Lady Grove, 21 Dec 1912 (RLP); ELH note, Berg.

28 TH to Lady Grove, 21 Dec 1912 (RLP); TH to F. Henniker, 17 Dec 1912 (*ORFW,* 154); C. Gifford to TH, 28 Nov 1912 (DCM).

29 Léonie Gifford to TH, 28 Oct 1912 (DCM); *DCC,* 5 Dec 1912.

30 TH to F. Henniker, 17 Dec 1912 (*ORFW,* 155); Harvey, 'I Was Emma Lavinia's Personal Maid', 9; *Times,* 30 Nov 1912, 9.

31 TH to E. Clodd, 13 Dec 1912 (BL); TH to F. Henniker, 17 Dec 1912 (*ORFW,* 154–5).

32 *CP,* 343, 340.

33 F. Dugdale (FEH) to E. Clodd, 16 Jan, 7 Mar, and 11 Mar 1913 (Leeds).

34 *CP,* 349.

35 TS, as sent by FEH to SCC (RLP).

36 *LY,* 156; TH to the Revd J. H. Dickinson, 22 Aug 1913 (Berg); TH to W. Hounsell, 29 Apr 1913 (Adams).

37 SCC/FEH, 24 Sept 1916 (RLP); TH to F. Dugdale (FEH), [29 Jan 1913], quoted in F. Dugdale to E. Clodd, 30 Jan 1913 (Leeds); TH to F. Dugdale, 9 Mar 1913 (RLP).

38 TH to E. Clodd, 14 Apr 1913 (Berg); E. Clodd, diary, 25 and 27 Apr 1913 (Alan Clodd).

39 E. Clodd, diary, 13 July 1913 (Alan Clodd).

40 Cheque-book counterfoil, DCM; MH to N. Sparks, Sen., 15 Feb 1913 (Barclay); MH to TH, 12 June 1913 (DCM).

41 F. Dugdale (FEH) to E. Clodd, 3 Dec 1913 (Adams); L. Gifford to TH, 27 Nov 1913 (DCM).

42 F. Dugdale (FEH) to E. Clodd, 1 Jan 1914 (Leeds).

43 *LY,* 156–7; A. C. Benson, diary, 10 June 1913 (Magdalene College, Cambridge); MH to TH, 12 June 1913 (quoted *CL,* I.7); F. Dugdale (FEH) to SCC, 9 June 1913 (RLP); *LY,* 158; A. C. Benson, diary, 1 Nov 1913 (Magdalene College, Cambridge).
44 TH to F. Macmillan, 19 Aug 1913 (BL); TH to G. Douglas, 27 Aug 1913 (NLS); E. Gosse to TH, 7 Nov 1913 (Cambridge).
45 TH to F. Macmillan, 4 Oct 1913 (BL).
46 Mrs Sarah Headley to RLP, 7 July 1956 (RLP).
47 Flowers, RLP; E. Clodd, diary, 13 July 1913 (Alan Clodd); licence, DCM.
48 MH to TH, 8 Feb 1914 (RLP).
49 TH to F. Henniker, 11 Feb 1914 (*ORFW,* 159); TH to Lady Hoare, 13 Feb 1914 (WRO).
50 TH to Lady Grove, 13 Feb 1914 (RLP); TH to SCC, 11 Feb 1914 (*Friends,* 277); TH to F. Harrison, 17 Feb 1913 (Texas).
51 TH to F. Henniker, 6 Mar 1914 (*ORFW,* 160); TH to the Revd J. H. Dickinson, 16 Feb 1914 (David J. Dickinson).

25 WAR YEARS

1 FEH to Lady Hoare, 9 Dec 1914 (WRO); FEH to M. Stopes, 14 Sept 1923 (BL).
2 FEH to R. Owen, 1 June 1914 (Colby).
3 *LY,* 159–60; 'Book of Gosse' (Cambridge); TH to F. Henniker, 17 July 1914 (*ORFW,* 163–4).
4 FEH to R. Owen, 1 June 1914 (Colby); FEH to Lady Hoare, 7 July 1914 (WRO); FEH to A. Lowell, 27 July 1914 (Harvard); TH to F. Macmillan, 15 July 1914 (BL).
5 *LY,* 161–2, 165; FEH to SCC, 15 Aug 1914 (RLP); TH to SCC, 28 Aug 1914, in *Friends,* 279.
6 FEH to Lady Hoare, 26 July 1914 (WRO); FEH to R. Owen, 14 and 17 Oct 1914 (Colby).
7 Purdy, 169; *CP,* 346; FEH to Lady Hoare, 6 and 9 Dec 1914 (WRO).
8 FEH to C. W. Saleeby, 8 July 1915 (Adams).
9 FEH to R. Owen, 1 Dec 1914 (Colby).
10 *New Statesman,* 19 Dec 1914, 271; *Bookman,* February 1915; *Academy,* 28 Nov 1914, 476.
11 Purdy, 172.
12 TH to F. Henniker, 23 Mar 1915 (*ORFW,* 166–7); Purdy, 191–2; *CP,* 538.
13 Minutes of Wellington House Conference, 2 Sept 1914 (copy, DCM).
14 *LY,* 163, 164–5; *CP,* 949–50.
15 *CP,* 542; TH to F. Henniker, 23 Mar 1915 (*ORFW,* 166).
16 FEH to R. Owen, 17 Oct 1914 (Colby); FEH to C. W. Saleeby, [23 Apr 1916] (Adams).
17 TH to F. Henniker, 23 Mar and 25 May 1915 (*ORFW,* 167, 168); TH to Lady St. Helier, 31 May 1915 (RLP); FEH to R. Owen, [6 June 1915?] (Colby); TH to M. Yearsley, 25 May 1915 (Roger Lonsdale).
18 TH to FEH, 31 May 1915 (RLP); FEH to R. Owen, [6 June 1915?] (Colby).
19 FEH to R. Owen, [1 Oct 1915?] and 1 Sept 1915 (Colby); F. George to TH, 19 May and 27 Oct 1913 (DCM); *DCC,* 9 Sept 1915; *LY,* 168.
20 FEH to R. Owen, 23 June 1915 (Colby).
21 FEH to C. W. Saleeby, 2 Oct 1915 (Adams); FEH to SCC, 3 Aug 1923 (RLP); FEH to R. Owen, 23 June 1915 (Colby).
22 FEH to R. Owen, 23 June 1915 (Colby); *LY,* 169; FEH to R. Owen, 17 July 1915 (Colby).
23 *LY,* 169.
24 *EL,* 18.
25 TH to F. Henniker, 2 Sept 1915 (*ORFW,* 170).
26 T. W. Jesty, interview, 1979; FEH to Lady Hoare, 30 Aug 1915 (WRO); FEH to R. Owen, 1 Sept 1915 (Colby); *Times,* 3 Sept 1915.
27 KH, diary, 4 Apr and 9 June 1915 (Lock).

[28] Information from RLP, citing Margaret Soundy; TH to F. Henniker, 11 Feb 1906 (*ORFW*, 126); V. Collins, *Talks with Thomas Hardy at Max Gate 1920–1922* (London, 1928), 58.

[29] *DCC*, 2 Dec 1915; *Sphere*, 25 Dec 1915.

[30] KH, diary, 25 Nov 1915 (Lock); KH to E. Clodd, 26 Nov 1915 (Leeds); FEH to R. Owen, 3 and 30 Dec 1915 (Colby).

[31] FEH to R. Owen, 3, 17, and 26 Dec 1915 (Colby); KH, diary, 31 Dec 1915, 10 and 18 Feb 1916 (Lock); KH to N. Sparks, Sen., 22 Feb 1916 (Barclay); KH, diary, 2 Apr 1915 (Lock).

[32] TH to SCC, 24 Feb 1916 (Victoria & Albert Museum); TH to W. Hounsell, 27 Sept 1916 (Adams); E. Inglis to her sister, 30 May 1916 (DCM).

[33] FEH to Lady Hoare, 5 Sept 1916 (WRO); *LY*, 172–3; RLP/FEH, 1935; FEH to SCC, 9 Sept 1916 (RLP).

[34] FEH to R. Owen, 15 Mar 1916 (Colby); FEH to SCC, 3 Mar 1916 (RLP); FEH to E. Clodd, 23 Sept 1916 (RLP).

[35] FEH to R. Owen, 15 Mar 1916 (Colby); Purdy, 349–50.

[36] TH to E. Gosse, 13 Dec 1916 (Adams); FEH to SCC, 12 Aug 1916 (RLP).

[37] SCC/TH, 30 June 1915 (RLP); Purdy, 187; FEH to SCC, 25 July 1916 (RLP).

[38] TH to J. Acland, 14 Aug 1916 (Manchester Public Libraries).

[39] *Wessex Scenes*, TS, Univ. of California, Riverside; *LY*, 171–2; TH to F. Henniker, 28 June 1916 (*ORFW*, 171–2); FEH to R. Owen, 5 June 1916 (Colby).

[40] FEH to SCC, 10 Nov 1916 (*Friends*, 294); *LY*, 173; FEH to SCC, 10 Nov 1916 (*Friends*, 294–5); TH to SCC, 23 Feb 1917 (SUNY, Buffalo); TH to F. Henniker, 4 Mar 1917 (*ORFW*, 176).

[41] TH to C. Shorter, 16 June 1917 (Univ. of British Columbia); *CP*, 546; *LY*, 174; TH to J. Galsworthy, 15 Aug 1918 (Birmingham).

[42] TH to S. Sassoon, 18 [May] 1917 (Eton); FEH to Lady Hoare, 20 May 1917 (WRO); FEH to C. W. Saleeby, 23 Apr 1916 (Adams); *LY*, 179; TH to J. Buchan, 20 June 1917 (Bodleian); *LY*, 177.

[43] *LY*, 177–8; KH, diary, 25 Mar 1917 (Lock).

[44] FEH to R. Owen, [29 July 1917?], [8 July 1917?] (Colby).

[45] RLP/FEH, 1933; FEH to R. Owen, 24 June 1917 and 30 Dec 1915 (Colby).

[46] FEH to SCC, 27 Apr 1917 (RLP).

[47] FEH to R. Owen, 13 Dec 1917 and [16 Feb 1916?] (Colby).

[48] FEH to SCC, 24 Oct 1917 (RLP); FEH to SCC, 8 Dec 1917 (*Friends*, 296); FEH to SCC, 19 and 22 Aug 1917 (RLP); Purdy, 207–8, book, Dr Marguerite Roberts; FEH to R. Owen, 13 Dec 1917 (Colby).

[49] Purdy, 207.

[50] FEH to SCC, 17 Sept 1916 (RLP).

[51] *LY*, 178; FEH to SCC, 25 Dec 1917 (RLP).

[52] FEH to SCC, 7 Feb 1918 (RLP).

[53] *EL*, vii; SCC to TH, 7 Dec 1915 (DCM), partly quoted in N. Page, *Thomas Hardy* (London, 1977), 141; FEH to SCC, 9 Sept 1917 (RLP).

[54] Annotation to Hedgcock book, 33 (DCM); FEH to V. H. Collins, 2 and 9 July 1922 (drafts, DCM).

[55] For details of the composition of the 'Life', see Purdy, 265–7, and *PN*, 189–202.

[56] FEH to F. Macmillan, 30 Nov 1919 (BL).

[57] *PN*, 288; J. M. Barrie to FEH, 3 Feb and 17 May 1928, in *Letters of J. M. Barrie*, ed. V. Meynell (London, 1942), 152, 154–5; Barrie to FEH, 26 Mar 1928 (DCM).

26 TEA AT MAX GATE

[1] *Athenaeum*, 12 Jan 1918, 33; *LY*, 184; TH to F. Henniker, 7 Feb 1918 (*ORFW*, 180); *LY*, 184.

2 *Tess,* ix (*PW,* 48).
3 TH to E. Gosse, 18 Feb 1918
(BL, quoted *Career,* 352); *TH: The
Critical Heritage,* ed. Cox, 459; TH
to Gosse, 16 Apr 1918 (Adams).
4 FEH to SCC, 11, 22, and 27 June
1918 (RLP); FEH to SCC, 15 Nov
1918 (RLP); scrapbooks, DCM.
5 FEH to SCC, 20 Jan 1918 (RLP);
FEH to R. Owen, 18 Feb 1918
(Colby); FEH to SCC, 24 Feb 1918
(*Friends,* 298).
6 FEH to L. Yearsley, 26 July and 25
May 1918 (Eton); FEH to Lady
Hoare, 22 Apr 1918 (WRO); TH to
F. Henniker, 27 Oct 1918 (*ORFW,*
182).
7 FEH to SCC, 22 Mar and 22 Apr
1918 (RLP); *LY,* 186; KH, diary, 9
and 19 July 1918, etc. (Lock).
8 Sampson, 'TH—Justice of the
Peace', 271; *LY,* 187; FEH to SCC,
19 Sept 1918 (RLP); FEH to SCC,
27 Jan 1918 (*Friends,* 297).
9 L. M. Farris, *Memories of the
Hardy and Hand Families* (St. Peter
Port, Guernsey, 1968).
10 FEH to L. Yearsley, 17 Sept 1922
(Eton); C. A. Baker to TH, 28 Aug
1923 (DCM); Lady St. Helier to TH,
7 Jan 1923 (DCM).
11 FEH to SCC, 26 Oct 1918 (RLP);
TH to C. Gifford, 3 Nov 1919
(Henry Gifford); TH to G. Douglas,
7 Dec 1915 (NLS).
12 KH to J. Sparks, 2 Dec 1902
(Barclay); Puddletown parish
records (DCRO).
13 *LY,* 187; FEH, diary fragment, 30
Jan 1918 (RLP); *Letters of John
Cowper Powys to His Brother
Llewelyn,* ed. M. Elwin (London,
1975), 258–9; FEH to SCC, 11 June
1918 (RLP); FEH, diary fragment,
28 Jan 1918 (RLP).
14 FEH to P. Lemperly, 10 Mar 1918
(Colby); FEH to L. Yearsley, 10 Nov
1918 (Eton); FEH, diary fragment,
4 Dec 1918 (RLP); FEH to SCC, 6
Dec 1918 (*Friends,* 298).
15 Felkin, 'Days with TH', 32, 30.
16 FEH to SCC, 18 Feb and 27 Dec
1919 (*Friends,* 302, 305); FEH to SCC,
2 Nov 1919 (RLP).

17 FEH to SCC, 1 and 9 May 1919
(RLP); *LY,* 190–1.
18 Purdy, 287, 288.
19 Claybury Asylum records,
admission order stamped 26 July
1919 (Claybury); FEH to SCC, 7 and
19 Aug 1919, and 18 Apr 1921
(RLP); FEH to Mrs Dicker, n.d.
(R. Greenland).
20 FEH to SCC, 7 and 19 Aug 1919
(RLP).
21 *LY,* 192–3; TH to SCC, 12 Oct
1919 (Adams); book, DCM.
22 *LY,* 198–200; FEH to SCC, 27 Dec
1919 (*Friends,* 305).
23 *LY,* 213; C. Hanbury to TH, 17
Jan 1920 (DCM); TH to R. Pearce
Edgcumbe, 14 June 1920 (Texas).
24 TH to R. Lynd, 30 July 1919 (*LY,*
193); F. Harrison, 'Novissima Verba',
Fortnightly, February 1920, 182;
FEH to SCC, 24 Feb 1920 (RLP);
RLP/FEH, 1933.
25 TH to A. Noyes, 20 Dec 1920
(quoted, dated 19 Dec 1920, in *LY,*
217).
26 *LY,* 211.
27 *LY,* 212; *LY,* 211; *Letters of J. M.
Barrie,* ed. Meynell, 175–6.
28 *LY,* 201–2; *LY,* 209, 205; *Best of
Friends,* ed. Meynell, 25.
29 *Best of Friends,* ed. Meynell, 25;
FEH to SCC, 27 Aug 1918 (RLP);
FEH to R. Owen, 23 July and 25
May 1920 (Colby); FEH to SCC, 24
Apr 1918 (RLP); FEH to R. Owen,
25 May 1920 (Colby); FEH to SCC,
17 Mar and 4 May 1920 (RLP).
30 FEH to SCC, 8 Aug 1920 (*Friends,*
306).
31 M. Lilly, 'The Mr Hardy I Knew',
Thomas Hardy Society Review, 1978,
101; BBC Home Service broadcast,
20 Feb 1955 (Henry Reed).
32 C. Asquith, *Portrait of Barrie*
(London, 1954), 110.
33 FEH to M. Yearsley, 16 May 1920
(Eton); Lilly, 'The Mr Hardy I
Knew', 103.
34 Purdy, 288; TH to F. Macmillan,
29 Jan 1920 (BL).
35 FEH to SCC, 14 Apr 1920 (RLP);
TH to F. Macmillan, 28 May 1920
(BL).

36 TH to F. Henniker, 5 Aug and 31 Oct 1920 (*ORFW*, 192, 193); TH to E. Phillpotts, 22 Dec 1920 (NYU).
37 TH to E. Pound, 3 Dec 1920 (Yale); E. Pound to F. E. Schelling, 8 July 1922, in *Letters of Ezra Pound*, ed. Paige, 178; TH to Pound, 18 Mar 1921 (Yale); Graves, *Good-bye to All That*, 376, 379.
38 *Architectural Notebook*, ed. Beatty, [115–17].
39 *LY*, 220; Purdy, 212–13; FEH to SCC, 26 Dec 1920 (*Friends*, 307).
40 FEH to SCC, 26 Dec 1920 (RLP, partly quoted in *Friends*, 307); Gertrude Bugler, interview, 1974, and see her *Personal Recollections of Thomas Hardy* (Dorchester, 1964).
41 FEH to SCC, 31 Jan 1921 (RLP); TH to FEH, 14 Apr 1921 (RLP); FEH to SCC, 18 Apr 1921 (RLP).
42 FEH to SCC, 28 July and 10 Aug 1921 (RLP).
43 *DCC*, 7 Apr 1921; *LY*, 222–3; Gertrude Bugler, interview, 1974; FEH to SCC, 12 June and 28 July 1921 (RLP); *DCC*, 21 July 1921, 5.
44 TH to F. Henniker, 2 July 1921 (*ORFW*, 197).
45 C. Asquith, *Portrait of Barrie*, 108.
46 Collins, *Talks with TH at Max Gate;* FEH to E. M. Forster, 17 June 1921 (King's College, Cambridge); *LY*, 224–5, 221–2.
47 TH to F. Henniker, 2 July 1921 (*ORFW*, 197); E. M. Forster, conversation, 1969; H. J. Massingham, *Remembrance: An Autobiography* (London, 1942), 45; E. Austin Hinton, unpublished interview with TH (Vanessa Hinton); SCC/TH, 12 Jan 1927 (RLP).
48 Lilly, 'The Mr Hardy I Knew', 102; TH to SCC, 15 May 1912 (*Friends*, 276); FEH, diary fragment, 23 Oct 1918 (RLP).
49 Graves, *Good-bye to All That*, 375; J. H. Morgan, letter, *Times*, 19 Jan 1928, 8; *LY*, 224.
50 TH to J. Moule, 21 Sept 1907 (RLP).
51 Graves, *Good-bye to All That*, 375.
52 FEH to SCC, 28 July 1921 (RLP); 'Memoranda II' notebook (*PN*, 43–4).

53 TH to F. Macmillan, 8 Nov 1921 (BL).
54 TH to H. Newbolt, 16 Jan 1909 (Texas).
55 FEH to J. Lane, 15 Oct 1922 (Taylor); RLP/FEH, 1934.
56 FEH to SCC, 11 Jan 1922 (RLP); 'Memoranda II' notebook (*PN*, 55); FEH to SCC, 4 Nov 1922 (RLP).
57 TH to E. Gosse, 28 May 1922 (Leeds); FEH to S. Sassoon, 9 Feb 1922 (Eton); TH to SCC, 15 Feb 1922 (Adams); FEH to SCC, 2 Apr 1922 (RLP); TH to SCC, 18 Feb 1922 (Adams); Purdy, 227.
58 FEH to SCC, 2 Apr 1922 (RLP); *Sunday Times*, 28 May 1922, 8 (which reads 'matrasses'); *LY*, 225.
59 FEH to SCC, 18 June 1922 (RLP); *Late Lyrics and Earlier* (London, 1922), v; F. Henniker to TH, 17 June 1922 (transcript, DCM).
60 FEH to SCC, 2 Apr 1922 (RLP).
61 FEH to SCC, 22 Oct and 25 Aug 1922 (RLP); FEH to S. Sassoon, 21 July 1922 (Eton).
62 TH to F. Henniker, 29 May 1922 (*ORFW*, 201–2); FEH to SCC, 18 June 1922 (RLP); FEH to R. Owen, 29 Oct 1922 (Colby); FEH to SCC, 21 June 1926 (RLP).
63 E. Richardson to her family, 5 Sept 1922 (Pamela Richardson).
64 FEH to SCC, 22 Oct and 4 Nov 1922 (RLP); *LY*, 229.
65 FEH to SCC, 26 Nov 1922 (RLP); 'Memoranda II' notebook (*PN*, 64), cf. *LY*, 229; FEH to SCC, 17 Dec 1922 (*Friends*, 308–9).
66 FEH, 'A Woman's Happiest Year', *Weekly Dispatch*, 27 Aug 1922, 8; FEH to SCC, 26 Nov and 17 Dec 1922 (*Friends*, 308, 309).

27 LAST THINGS

1 FEH to L. Yearsley, 6 Jan 1923 (Eton); FEH to SCC, 7 Jan and 13 May 1923 (RLP); *LY*, 230 (cf. *PN*, 69).
2 TH to F. Henniker, 1 Mar 1922 (*ORFW*, 200); book, DCM.
3 *LY*, 232–4.

[4] FEH to SCC, 30 June 1923 (RLP); RLP/FEH, 1933; TH to KH, 18 July 1923 (Mrs H. O. Lock); KH, diary, 20 and 21 July 1923 (Lock).

[5] TH to M. Yearsley, 7 June 1923 (Eton); Yearsley to TH, 14 June 1923 (DCM).

[6] FEH to L. Yearsley, 11 Oct 1923 (Eton); T. E. Lawrence to FEH, 14 and 20 Nov 1923 (Texas).

[7] R. Graves to FEH, [21 Mar 1923?] (DCM); T. E. Lawrence to FEH, 25 Mar and 4 Apr 1923 (Texas); Lawrence to Graves, 8 Sept 1923, in *Letters of T. E. Lawrence,* ed. Garnett, 429.

[8] *LY,* 236; 'Memoranda II' notebook (*PN,* 77, 74, 76); FEH to SCC, 4 Sept 1923 (RLP).

[9] G. N. Ray, *H. G. Wells and Rebecca West* (New Haven, Conn., 1974), 94–5; R. Rolland, MS journal, 5 May 1923 (Mme Rolland); R. Loomis to F. B. Adams, 8 June 1953 (Adams).

[10] Purdy, 228–9; TH to A. Noyes, 17 Nov 1923 (Texas).

[11] *The Dynasts,* Part First (London, 1904), xii.

[12] TH to SCC, 20 Sept 1916 (*Friends,* 284); FEH to SCC, 4 Sept 1923 (RLP).

[13] TH pencil note, DCM (cf. Gittings, *Young TH,* 29); TH to SCC, 15 Dec 1919 (*Friends,* 287).

[14] H. Granville-Barker to TH, 4 July 1923 (DCM); TH to H. Child, 11 Nov 1923 (*LY,* 235–6); TH to R. Boughton, 16 Jan 1924 (BL).

[15] TH to R. Boughton, 16 Jan 1924 (BL, quoted Purdy, 230); FEH to SCC, 21 June 1924 (RLP), and *LY,* 237–8.

[16] FEH to SCC, 18 Aug 1924 (*Friends,* 313).

[17] FEH to SCC, 7 Feb and 7 Sept 1924 (RLP); cf. *LY,* 243.

[18] FEH to SCC, 11 Apr 1924 (*Friends,* 310–11); J. M. Murry, 'Wrap Me up in My Aubusson Carpet', *Adelphi,* April 1924, 951–8; TH to Murry, 28 Mar 1924 (Berg).

[19] RLP/FEH, 1929; FEH to SCC, 11 Apr 1924 (RLP; incomplete text in *Friends,* 310–11); TH to J. M. Murry, 9 Apr 1924 (Berg).

[20] O'Rourke, *TH: His Secretary Remembers,* 41.

[21] O'Rourke, *TH: His Secretary Remembers,* 27.

[22] *LY,* 238–9; FEH to SCC, 24 June 1924 (RLP); FEH to SCC, 11 Apr 1924 (*Friends,* 311).

[23] FEH to SCC, 19 Sept 1924 (RLP); 'Memoranda II' notebook (*PN,* 84); J. Sherren to TH, 1 Oct 1924 (DCM); SCC to TH, 1 Oct 1924 (DCM); O'Rourke, *TH: His Secretary Remembers,* 32; TH to SCC, 3 Oct 1924 (transcript, RLP).

[24] 'Memoranda II' notebook (*PN,* 84); FEH to SCC, 7 July 1924 (RLP); TH to FEH, 6 Oct 1924 (RLP); KH to TH, 5 Oct 1924 (DCM); *CP,* 743.

[25] O'Rourke, *TH: His Secretary Remembers,* 33.

[26] *LY,* 240; Gertrude Bugler, interview, 1974; FEH to SCC, 25 Sept 1924 (RLP); TH to FEH, 6 Oct 1924 (RLP); N. J. Atkins, *Hardy, Tess and Myself* (Beaminster, Dorset, 1962), 11–16.

[27] Gertrude Bugler, interviews, 1974.

[28] Gertrude Bugler, interview, 1980.

[29] TH to G. Bugler, 16 Dec 1924 (Gertrude Bugler); TH to Frederick Harrison, 13 Dec 1924 (carbon copy, Gertrude Bugler).

[30] SCC, diary, in Blunt, *Cockerell,* 214–15.

[31] Blunt, *Cockerell,* 316; Bugler, *Personal Recollections,* 9–10; Gertrude Bugler, interview, 1974.

[32] Blunt, *Cockerell,* 216; Frederick Harrison to G. Bugler, 4 Feb 1925 (Gertrude Bugler); G. Bugler to TH, 4 Feb 1925 (DCM); TH to G. Bugler, 7 Feb 1925, in Bugler, *Personal Recollections,* 10.

[33] SCC note referring to FEH letter to SCC, 16 Jan 1925 (RLP; letter itself destroyed); FEH to G. Bugler, [22 Dec 1924?] (Gertrude Bugler).

[34] TH to P. Ridgeway, 3 Aug 1925 (Boston Public Library); FEH to SCC, 20 Aug 1925 (RLP).

[35] E. Blunden, *Thomas Hardy* (London, 1941), 170–1.

[36] Blunden, *TH*, 171.
[37] *LY*, 242–4; FEH to SCC, 22 Dec 1925 (RLP); *Daily Express*, 7 Dec 1925.
[38] TH to G. Macmillan, 29 July 1925, to F. Macmillan, 25 Aug 1925, to G. Macmillan, 29 July 1925 (all BL); TH to SCC, 12 Sept 1925 (Taylor); FEH to SCC, 17 July 1925 (RLP).
[39] *CP*, 811, 829.
[40] *Human Shows*, page proofs, DCM.
[41] E. Brennecke, Jr., *The Life of Thomas Hardy* (New York, 1925), 7–8.
[42] FEH to Paul Lemperly, 8 Apr 1915 (Colby); FEH to M. Macmillan, 18 Apr 1926 (BL).
[43] T. E. Lawrence to FEH, 13 Feb 1926 (Texas); FEH to M. Macmillan, 18 Apr 1926, to D. Macmillan, 14 July 1926 (both BL).
[44] 'Memorandum II' notebook (*PN*, 92, 96), cf. *LY*, 245, 252.
[45] *LY*, 246; TH to D. Macmillan, 24 June 1926 (BL); *CP*, 886; *LY*, 249.
[46] *LY*, 250–1; FEH to SCC, 29 Dec 1926 (*Friends*, 314, where it is misdated).
[47] FEH to SCC, 29 Aug, 27 Oct, and 7 Nov 1926 (RLP).
[48] FEH to E. Blunden, 31 Oct 1926 (Texas); J. L. Garvin to TH, 2 and 6 Mar 1926 (DCM); *Winter Words*, MS (Queen's College, Oxford).
[49] FEH to P. Ridgeway, 11 July and 12 Sept 1926 (Adams); *LY*, 248.
[50] *LY*, 247–8; *The Diary of Virginia Woolf, Volume III: 1925–1930*, ed. A. O. Bell (London, 1980), 96, 100.
[51] *Diary of V. Woolf*, III.96.
[52] FEH to SCC, 13 and 16 Apr 1926 (RLP); FEH to H. Bliss, 5 Mar 1926 (Princeton).
[53] S. Sassoon to E. Gosse, 15 Jan 1927 (BL); TH to F. Macmillan, 29 Jan 1927 (BL).
[54] TH to F. Macmillan, 18 Feb and 18 Sept 1927 (BL).
[55] *Times*, 5 Mar 1927; *The Preservation of Ancient Cottages* (London, 1927); *LY*, 255, 256.
[56] FEH to SCC, 24 July 1927 (Adams); FEH to SCC, 23 May 1927 (RLP); *LY*, 253–4; FEH to E. Gosse,

12 June 1927 (Leeds); RLP/FEH, 1929.
[57] G. Holst to TH, 4 Aug 1927 (DCM); TH to G. Holst, 6 Aug 1927 (Imogen Holst); M. Short, *Gustav Holst (1874–1934): A Centenary Documentation* (London, 1974), 36.
[58] *LY*, 256, 257; FEH to SCC, 31 Aug 1927 (RLP).
[59] FEH to E. Gosse, 18 June and 9 July 1927 (Leeds); *LY*, 254, 257–9; FEH to P. Lemperly, 29 Sept 1927 (Colby).
[60] Minute book, DCM; *DCC*, 27 Oct 1927.
[61] TH to F. Macmillan, 10 and 30 Nov 1927 (BL); TH's copy of *A Changed Man*, 399 (DCM), and see *Career*, 283.
[62] FEH, diary (DCM), partly quoted *PN*, 293; *LY*, 260–2.
[63] *LY*, 263; *CP*, 929; RLP/FEH, 1931.
[64] FEH, diary (*PN*, 294).
[65] Headstone, Max Gate (slightly mistranscribed, *LY*, 251).
[66] *LY*, 263.
[67] *Winter Words*, MS (Queen's College, Oxford).
[68] FEH to SCC, 1, 5, and 8 Dec 1927 (RLP).
[69] *LY*, 263–4; FEH to E. Gosse, 15 and 19 Dec 1927 (Leeds); FEH to SCC, 25 Dec 1927 (RLP, partly quoted *Friends*, 314–15); *LY*, 265.
[70] *LY*, 264; E. Gosse to TH, 24 Dec 1927 (DCM); TH to E. Gosse, 25 Dec 1927 (BL, quoted in *The Times*, 13 Jan 1928, 13).
[71] FEH to SCC, 30 Dec 1927 (RLP); *DCC*, 19 Jan 1928; FEH to S. Sassoon, 4 Jan 1928 (Eton); FEH to SCC, 8 Jan 1928 (RLP).
[72] Telegram, 9 Jan 1928 (RLP); E. Dugdale, diary fragment (RLP); SCC to Mrs Cockerell, 11 Jan 1928 (RLP).
[73] *LY*, 265; *Evening News*, 16 Jan 1928; *LY*, 265; E. E. T[itterington], *The Domestic Life of Thomas Hardy (1921–1928)* (Beaminster, Dorset, 1963), 16.
[74] *CP*, 954, 971; RLP/FEH, 1931.
[75] KH, diary, 11 Jan 1928 (Lock); KH to E. Clodd, 2 Feb 1928 (Leeds);

E. W. Mann, letter draft, 16 June
1963 (DCM).
[76] Titterington, *Domestic Life of TH*,
16; *PN*, 287.
[77] E. E. Titterington, *Afterthoughts
of Max Gate* (St. Peter Port,
Guernsey, 1969), 344; RLP, notes on
conversation with Eva Dugdale,
1953.

28   AFTERWARDS

[1] E. W. Mann, draft letter, 16 June
1963 (DCM); Titterington,
Domestic Life of TH, 16.
[2] Death certificate; KH, diary, 12 Jan
1928 (Lock); RLP, notes on
conversation with Eva Dugdale, 1953;
SCC to Mrs Cockerell, 12 Jan 1928
(RLP).
[3] Titterington, *Afterthoughts of Max
Gate*, 344; KH, diary, 12 Jan 1928
(Lock); May O'Rourke, interview,
1975; J. O'Rourke to TH, 28 Aug
1927 (DCM).
[4] SCC to Mrs Cockerell, 11 Jan 1928
(RLP); RLP/FEH, 1929.
[5] *Letters of J. M. Barrie*, 150;
J. M. Barrie to SCC, 12 Jan 1928

(*Friends*, 315–16); KH, diary, 12 and
13 Jan 1928 (Lock).
[6] *Daily Telegraph*, 14 Jan 1928.
[7] KH, diary, 13 Jan 1928 (Lock).
[8] *Daily Telegraph*, 14 Jan 1928;
J. M. Barrie to SCC, 12 Jan 1928
(*Friends*, 315–16); *LY*, 267; E. W.
Mann, draft letter, 16 June 1963
(DCM); E. Dugdale, diary fragment
(RLP).
[9] G. Dru Drury, *Heart Burials and
Some Purbeck Marble Heart-Shrines*
(Dorchester, 1927).
[10] SCC to Mrs Cockerell, 14 Jan 1928
(RLP); *DCC*, 19 Jan 1928; *Times*,
12 and 14 Jan 1928.
[11] *LY*, 267–8; *Times*, 17 Jan 1928;
DCC, 19 Jan 1928.
[12] KH, diary, 16 Jan 1928 (Lock).
[13] Gertrude Bugler, interview, 1974.
[14] *LY*, 268.
[15] T. E. Lawrence to W. Rothenstein,
14 Apr 1928 (*Letters of T. E.
Lawrence*, ed. Garnett, 582); E.
Clodd to J. M. Bulloch, 14 Jan 1928
(Texas).
[16] G. B. Shaw to FEH, 27 Jan 1928
(Berg); FEH to Sir O. Seaman, 1
Feb 1928 (DCM); *Punch*, 18 Jan
1928, 70.
[17] RLP/FEH, 1929.
[18] *CP*, 553.

INDEX

ABOUT THE AUTHOR

MICHAEL MILLGATE, born in England in 1929, was educated at St. Catharine's College, Cambridge, and at the universities of Michigan and Leeds. He taught at Leeds for six years before going to Canada in 1964 as chairman of the English Department at York University, Toronto; since 1967 he has been Professor of English at the University of Toronto. Professor Millgate has published widely on authors and topics in English and American litera-ture and is best known as the author of *The Achievement of William Faulkner* (1966) and *Thomas Hardy: His Career as a Novelist* (1971) and the co-editor (with Richard L. Purdy) of *The Collected Letters of Thomas Hardy,* of which the first volume (of an eventual seven) appeared in 1978 and the second in 1980.

Ch 1 – antecedents & unhisted stories, family incidents
    influence of mother // D.H. Lawrence.

ch 2 – Dorset setting, backwards wild; rural poverty &
    class distinctions; Hardy's awareness of old rural
    sights & customs, p. 35

ch 3 – ambitions, denounced by C. of E. clergyman

ch 4 – London, 1862–67; Dickensian; "Almacks"

ch 5 – Class hostility in first novel; read & rejected by
    Alex. Macmillan & J. Morley; then by George Meredith, p 144

ch 6 – St Juliot; need to alter mss. of Desperate Remedies –
    rejected by Macmillan & Morley; publ. by Tinsley; based
    on Poor Man, trapped into marriage, summer, 1870.
    Desperate Remedies published 1871; "coarse"; begun
    Under the Greenwood Tree

ch 7 Under published 1872, began serializing A Pair of Blue Eyes
    which also drew on Desperate Remedies and his courtship
    with Emma

ch 8 – less than perfect marriage + honeymoon; his heroines p. 165
    patronage of L. Stephen in London; financial dependence on
    readership, p. 173; sense of universal fate, p. 72

ch 9 – visit to Rhine Valley, Waterloo, obsession w. Napoleon (defence of fate?)
    "Jane Phillps" – inspiration for "Tess" 190–192 3 205
    no debt to Schopenhauer p 199   1877

ch 10 – Pessimism p 203
    Angel Clare prefigured 205

ch 11 – Publication of Trumpet-Major
    Winbourne & Shakespeare Reading Society

ch 12 – Dorchester; Mayor of Casterbridge; hope that Church will
    evolve into an Ethical Society. 240

ch 13 – Max Gate – H. sees mission as writer of rural stories for a
urban readership p 265
Fatalism, 269

ch 14 – Woodlanders – H's 'favorite story'

H.'s views that kings & autocrats were causes of war, p 511
concept of "Patriotism", p 512